THE EARTH AND ITS PEOPLES

A GLOBAL HISTORY

THE EARTH AND ITS PEOPLES

A GLOBAL HISTORY

BRIEF SECOND EDITION

VOLUME II

Since 1500

Richard W. Bulliet
Columbia University

Pamela Kyle Crossley
Dartmouth College

Daniel R. Headrick
Roosevelt University

Steven W. Hirsch
Tufts University

Lyman L. Johnson
University of North Carolina–Charlotte

David Northrup
Boston College

Houghton Mifflin Company   Boston   New York

Editor-in-chief: Jean L. Woy
Senior sponsoring editor: Nancy Blaine
Senior project editor: Carol Newman
Editorial assistant: Reba Frederics
Senior designer: Henry Rachlin
Senior production/design coordinator: Jill Haber
Manufacturing manager: Florence Cadran
Senior marketing manager: Sandra McGuire

Cover image: Detail from mural *The History of Medicine in Mexico: The People's Demand for Better Health*, 1953, *Hospital de la Raza, Mexico City, Mexico,* by Diego Rivera/Schalkwijk/ Art Resource, NY.

Printed in the U.S.A.

Library of Congress Catalog Card Number: 2001097075

ISBN: 0-618-21465-8

3 4 5 6 7 8 9-DC-06 05 04 03

BRIEF CONTENTS

Introduction: The World
Before 1500   xxix

15 The Maritime Revolution,
to 1550   342

PART FIVE

**THE GLOBE ENCOMPASSED,
1500–1800**   361

16 The Transformation of Europe,
1500–1750   364

17 The Americas, the Atlantic, and
Africa, 1530–1770   382

18 Southwest Asia and the Indian
Ocean, 1500–1750   405

19 Eastern Eurasia, 1500–1800   424

PART SIX

**REVOLUTIONS RESHAPE THE WORLD,
1750–1870**   441

20 Revolutionary Changes in the
Atlantic World, 1750–1850   444

21 The Early Industrial Revolution,
1760–1851   463

22 Africa, India, and China,
1750–1870   481

PART SEVEN

**GLOBAL DOMINANCE AND DIVERSITY,
1850–1949**   501

23 The New Power Balance,
1850–1900   504

24 The New Imperialism,
1869–1914   523

25 The Crisis of the Imperial Order,
1900–1929   541

26 The Collapse of the Old Order,
1929–1949   563

27 Striving for Independence: Africa,
India, and Latin America,
1900–1949   584

PART EIGHT

**THE PERILS AND PROMISES OF A
GLOBAL COMMUNITY, 1945–2001**   601

28 The Cold War and Decolonization,
1945–1975   604

29 Crisis, Realignment, and the Dawn
of the Post–Cold War World,
1975–1991   623

30 The End of a Global Century,
1991–2001   645

CONTENTS

MAPS   xvii
ENVIRONMENT AND TECHNOLOGY FEATURES   xviii
SOCIETY AND CULTURE FEATURES   xviii
PREFACE   xix
ABOUT THE AUTHORS   xxv
NOTE ON SPELLING AND USAGE   xxvii

INTRODUCTION: THE WORLD BEFORE 1550   xxix

15 THE MARITIME REVOLUTION, TO 1550   342

Global Maritime Expansion Before 1450   343
The Pacific Ocean   343   The Indian Ocean   343   The Atlantic Ocean   344

Iberian Expansion, 1400–1550   346
Background to European Expansion   346
Portuguese Voyages   347   Spanish Voyages   349

Encounters with Europe, 1450–1550   352
Western Africa   352   Eastern Africa   353   Indian Ocean States   354
The Americas   355   Patterns of Dominance   359

Conclusion   359

Key Terms   359

Suggested Reading   360

Notes   360

Society and Culture: European Male Sexual Dominance Overseas   357

PART FIVE

THE GLOBE ENCOMPASSED, 1500–1800
361

16 THE TRANSFORMATION OF EUROPE, 1500–1750   364

Religious and Political Innovations   365
Religious Reformation   365   The Failure of Empire   366

Building State Power   366
Royal Centralization, 1500–1750   367
Absolutism and Constitutionalism   371
War and Diplomacy   371
Politics and the Economy   373

Urban Society and Commercial Technology   374
Urban Social Classes   375   Commercial Techniques and Technology   375

Rural Society and the Environment   376
The Struggle for Food and Fuel   376
Peasantry and Gentry   376

The Realm of Ideas   376
Traditional Thinking   378
The Scientific Revolution   378
The Early Enlightenment   379

Conclusion   380

Key Terms   381

Suggested Reading   381

Environment and Technology: Mapping the World   377

17 THE AMERICAS, THE ATLANTIC, AND AFRICA, 1530–1770   382

Spanish America and Brazil   383
State and Church   383   Colonial Economies   384   Society in Colonial Latin America   386

English and French Colonies in North America   388
The South   389   New England   389
Middle Atlantic Region   390   French America   390

Plantations in the West Indies   391
Sugar and Slaves   391   Technology and Environment   394

Creating the Atlantic Economy   396
Capitalism and Mercantilism   397
The Great Circuit and Middle Passage   398

Africa and the Atlantic   399
The Gold Coast and the Slave Coast   399
The Bight of Biafra and Angola   400

The Columbian Exchange   401
Transfers to the Americas   401
Transfers from the Americas   402

Conclusion   403

Key Terms   403

Suggested Reading   404

Notes   404

Society and Culture: Colonial Wealth and the Exploitation of Indigenous Peoples   387

18 SOUTHWEST ASIA AND THE INDIAN OCEAN, 1500–1750   405

The Ottoman Empire   406
Expansion and Frontiers   406   Central Institutions   409   Crisis of the Military State, 1585–1650   410   Economic Change and Growing Weakness   412

The Safavid Empire   413
Safavid Society and Religion   413
Isfahan and Istanbul   414   Economic Crisis and Political Collapse   415

The Mughal Empire   416
Political Foundations   416   Hindus and Muslims   417   Central Decay and Regional Challenges   418

Trade Empires in the Indian Ocean, 1600–1729   418
Muslims in the East Indies   419
Muslims in East Africa   419
The Coming of the Dutch   421

Conclusion   422

Key Terms   423

Suggested Reading   423

Note   423

Environment and Technology: Metal Currency and Inflation   411

19 EASTERN EURASIA, 1500–1800   424

New Relations in Eurasia   425
The Land-Based Empires of Eurasia   425
New Global Influences   426

The Russian Empire   427
The Rise of Romanov Power   427
Russians and Turks   430   Peter the Great   430   The Russian Drive Eastward   431

The Later Ming and Early Qing Empires,   431
The End of the Ming   431   Power and Trade in the Early Qing   433   Emperor Kangxi   434   Tea and Diplomacy   434   Population and Social Stress   436

Tokugawa Japan, to 1800   437
Shogunate and Economy   437   The "Closing" of Japan   437   Elite Decline and Social Crisis   438

Conclusion   439

Key Terms 439

Suggested Reading 439

Note 440

■ Society and Culture: Style and Conversion: Christian Rivalries in Beijing 435

PART SIX

REVOLUTIONS RESHAPE THE WORLD, 1750–1870

441

20 REVOLUTIONARY CHANGES IN THE ATLANTIC WORLD, 1750–1850 444

Prelude to Revolution: War and the Enlightenment 445

The American Revolution 446
Frontiers and Taxes 446   The Course of Revolution 446   New Republican Institutions 449

The French Revolution 450
French Society and Fiscal Crisis 450
Protest Turns to Revolution 451
Reaction and Dictatorship 453
Retrenchment, Reform, and Revolution 454

Revolution in Haiti and Latin America 456
The Haitian Revolution 456   Latin American Revolutions 457
Mexico 458

Economic and Social Liberation Movements 458
The Abolition of Slavery 460   Equal Rights for Women and Blacks 461

Conclusion 462

Key Terms 462

Suggested Reading 462

■ Environment and Technology: The Pencil 448

21 THE EARLY INDUSTRIAL REVOLUTION, 1760–1851 463

Causes of the Industrial Revolution 464
Preconditions for Industrialization 464
Britain's Advantages 465

The Technological Revolution 466
Mass Production and Mechanization 466
Iron and Steam 469
Communication over Wires 471

The Impact of the Industrial Revolution 471
The New Industrial Cities 471   Rural Environments 472   Working Conditions 473   Changes in Society 474

Responses to Industrialization 474
Laissez Faire 475   Positivism and Utopian Socialism 475   Protests and Reforms 475   Emigration 476

The Effects of Industrialization in Russia and the Ottoman Empire 476
Russia 477   The Ottoman Empire 477   The Crimean War, 1853–1856 478

Conclusion 479

Key Terms 480

Suggested Reading 480

Note 480

■ Society and Culture: Charles Babbage, Ada Lovelace, and the "Analytical Engine" 468

22 AFRICA, INDIA, AND CHINA, 1750–1870 481

Changes and Exchanges in Africa 482
New African States 482
Modernization in Egypt and Ethiopia 485
European Penetration 485
Secondary Empires in Eastern Africa 487

India Under British Rule 488
Company Men 488 Raj and
Rebellion, 1818–1857 490 Political
Reform and Industrial Impact 491
Rising Indian Nationalism 492
Colonies and Commerce 492

The Qing Empire 495
Economic and Social Disorder 495
The Opium War, 1839–1842 495
The Taiping Rebellion, 1850–1864 497
Decentralization at the End of the Qing
Empire 499

Conclusion 499

Key Terms 500

Suggested Reading 500

Notes 500
▦ Environment and Technology: Whaling 494

PART SEVEN

GLOBAL DOMINANCE AND DIVERSITY, 1850–1949

501

23 THE NEW POWER BALANCE, 1850–1900 504

**New Technologies and the World
Economy** 505
The Steel and Chemical Industries 505
Electricity 505 Shipping and
Telegraph Cables 506 Railroads
506 World Trade and Finance 506

Social Transformations 506
Population and Migrations 507
Urbanization and Social Structures 507
Labor Movements and Socialist Politics
509 Working-Class Women and Men
509 The Victorian Age and Women's
"Separate Sphere" 510

**Nationalism and the Unification of
Germany** 510
National Identity Before 1871 512
The Unification of Germany 512
Nationalism After 1871 512

**The Great Powers of Europe,
1871–1900** 513
Germany at the Center of Europe 513
The Liberal Powers: France and Great
Britain 513 The Conservative Powers:
Russia and Austria-Hungary 514

**New Great Powers: The United States and
Japan** 515
The United States, 1865–1900 515
The Rise of Japan, 1850–1900 518

Conclusion 521

Key Terms 521

Suggested Reading 521
▦ Society and Culture: Demonstrating for
Women's Rights 511

24 THE NEW IMPERIALISM, 1869–1914 523

**The New Imperialism: Motives and
Methods** 526
Political and Economic Motives 526
Cultural Motives 526 The Tools of
the Imperialists 527 Colonial Agents
and Administration 527

The Scramble for Africa 528
Egypt 528 Western and Equatorial
Africa 528 Southern Africa 530
Political and Social Responses 531

Asia and Western Dominance 531
Central Asia 531 Southeast Asia and
Indonesia 533 Hawaii and the
Philippines, 1878–1902 533

Imperialism in Latin America 535
Railroads and the Imperialism of Free
Trade 535 American Expansionism
and the Spanish-American War 536

American Intervention in the Caribbean and Central America   537

The World Economy and the Global Environment   537
Expansion of the World Economy   538
Transformation of the Global Environment   538

Conclusion   539

Key Terms   539

Suggested Reading   539

Notes   540

  Environment and Technology: Imperialism and Tropical Ecology   534

25 THE CRISIS OF THE IMPERIAL ORDER, 1900–1929   541

The Crisis in Europe and the Middle East   542

The Ottoman Empire and the Balkans   542
Nationalism, Alliances, and Military Strategy   542

The "Great War" and the Russian Revolutions   545
Stalemate, 1914–1917   545   The Home Front and the War Economy   546
The Ottoman Empire at War   548
Double Revolution in Russia, 1917   548
The End of the War in Western Europe, 1917–1918   549

Peace and Dislocation in Europe   549
The Impact of the War   550   The Peace Treaties   552   Russian Civil War and the New Economic Policy   552
An Ephemeral Peace   552

China and Japan: Contrasting Destinies   553
Revolution in China   553   Japan and World War I   554   China in the 1920s   555

The New Middle East   556
The Rise of Modern Turkey   556   Arab Lands and the Question of Palestine   556

Science and Technology in the Industrialized World   558
Revolution in the Sciences   558   The New Technologies of Modernity   559
Technology and the Environment   560

Conclusion   561

Key Terms   562

Suggested Reading   562

  Society and Culture: The Experience of Battle   547

26 THE COLLAPSE OF THE OLD ORDER, 1929–1949   563

Stalin's Revolution   564
Five-Year Plans   564   Collectivization of Agriculture   564   Terror and Opportunities   566

The Depression   566
Economic Crisis   566   Depression in Industrial Nations   567   Depression in Nonindustrial Regions   567

The Rise of Fascism   567
Mussolini's Italy   568   Hitler's Germany   568   The Road to War, 1933–1939   569

East Asia, 1931–1945   570
The Manchurian Incident of 1931   570
The Chinese Communists and the Long March   571   The Sino-Japanese War, 1937–1945   572

The Second World War   573
The War of Movement   573   War in Europe and North Africa   574   War in Asia and the Pacific   574   The End of the War   576   Chinese Civil War and Communist Victory   576

The Character of Warfare   578
The War of Science   578   Bombing
Raids   579   The Holocaust   579
The Home Front   581   War and the
Environment   581

Conclusion   581

Key Terms   582

Suggested Reading   582
▪ Environment and Technology: Biomedical
Technologies   580

27 STRIVING FOR INDEPENDENCE:
AFRICA, INDIA, AND LATIN AMERICA,
1900–1949   584

Sub-Saharan Africa, 1900–1945   585
Colonial Africa: Economic and Social
Changes   585   Religious and Political
Changes   587

**The Indian Independence Movement,
1905–1947**   588
The Land and the People   588   British
Rule and Indian Nationalism   589
Mahatma Gandhi and Militant
Nonviolence   592   India Moves
Toward Independence   593   Partition
and Independence   593

Latin America, 1900–1949   594
The Mexican Revolution, 1910–1920   594
The Mexican Revolution Institutionalized,
1920–1940   595   The Transformation
of Argentina   597   Brazil and
Argentina, to 1929   597   Depression
and the Vargas Regime in Brazil   598
Argentina After 1930   599

Conclusion   599

Key Terms   600

Suggested Reading   600
▪ Society and Culture: Self-Government in
Africa   589

PART EIGHT

**THE PERILS AND PROMISES
OF A GLOBAL COMMUNITY,
1945–2001**
601

28 THE COLD WAR AND
DECOLONIZATION, 1945–1975   604

Decolonization and Nation Building   605
New Nations in South and Southeast
Asia   605   The Struggle for
Independence in Africa   608   The
Quest for Economic Freedom in Latin
America   609

The Cold War   610
The United Nations   611   Capitalism
and Communism   611   West Versus
East in Europe and Korea   613
U.S. Defeat in Vietnam   614   The Race
for Nuclear Supremacy   616

Beyond a Bipolar World   617
The Third World   617   Japan and
China   618   The Middle East   619
The Emergence of Environmental
Concerns   620

Conclusion   621

Key Terms   621

Suggested Reading   621
▪ Environment and Technology: The Green
Revolution   612

29 CRISIS, REALIGNMENT, AND THE
DAWN OF THE POST–COLD WAR
WORLD, 1975–1991   623

**Postcolonial Crises and Asian Economic
Expansion, 1975–1989**   624
Revolution, Repression, and Democratic
Reform in Latin America   624   Islamic

Revolutions in Iran and Afghanistan   626
Asian Transformation   628

**The End of the Bipolar World,
1989–1991**   631
Crisis in the Soviet Union   631   The
Collapse of the Socialist Bloc   631
The Persian Gulf War, 1990–1991   633

The Challenge of Population Growth   633
Demographic Transition   634   The
Industrialized Nations   636
The Developing Nations   637

**Unequal Development and the
Movement of Peoples**   637
The Problem of Growing Inequality   638
Internal Migration: The Growth of Cities
639   Global Migration   640

**Technological and Environmental
Change**   640
New Technologies and the World
Economy   641   Conserving and
Sharing Resources   641   Responding
to Environmental Threats   642

Conclusion   642

Key Terms   643

Suggested Reading   643

Notes   644
■ Society and Culture: China's
Family-Planning Needs   638

30 THE END OF A GLOBAL CENTURY,
1991–2001   645

A Fragmented World   646
Challenges to the Nation-State   646
Problems of the Global Economy   647
Old Threats, New Dangers   649
Human Rights   652   Women's
Rights   654

Elements of a Global Culture   654
The Medium and the Message   655
The Spread of Popular Culture   656
Global Connections and Elite Culture   657
The Endurance of Cultural Diversity   658

Conclusion   659

Key Terms   660

Suggested Reading   661

Notes   661
■ Society and Culture: Nelson Mandela   653

GLOSSARY   G-1
INDEX   I-1

MAPS

15.1 Exploration and Settlement in the Indian and Pacific Oceans Before 1500   346

15.2 European Exploration, 1420–1542   350

16.1 Religious Reformation in Europe   368

16.2 The European Empire of Charles V   369

17.1 The Atlantic World   392

18.1 Muslim Empires in the Sixteenth and Seventeenth Centuries   408

18.2 European Colonization in the Indian Ocean to 1750   420

19.1 The Expansion of Russia, 1500–1800   429

19.2 The Qing Empire, 1644–1783   433

20.1 The American Revolutionary War   449

20.2 Napoleon's Europe, 1810   455

20.3 Latin America by 1830   459

21.1 The Industrial Revolution in Britain, ca. 1850   466

21.2 Disintegration of the Ottoman Empire, 1829–1914   479

22.1 Africa in the Nineteenth Century   484

22.2 India, 1707–1805   489

22.3 Conflicts in the Qing Empire, 1839–1870   496

23.1 The United States, 1850–1920   517

23.2 Expansion and Modernization of Japan, 1868–1918   519

24.1 Africa in 1878 and 1914   529

24.2 Asia in 1914   532

25.1 The First World War in Europe   544

25.2 Territorial Changes in Europe After World War I   551

25.3 Territorial Changes in the Middle East After World War I   557

26.1 World War II in Europe and North Africa   575

26.2 World War II in Asia and the Pacific   577

27.1 The Partition of India, 1947   590

27.2 The Mexican Revolution   596

28.1 Decolonization, 1947–1990   606

28.2 Cold War Confrontation   615

29.1 The End of Soviet Domination in Eastern Europe   632

29.2 The End of the Soviet Union   635

30.1 World Religions   648

30.2 Estimated GNP per Capita, 1990s   650

ENVIRONMENT AND TECHNOLOGY

Mapping the World   377
Metal Currency and Inflation   411
The Pencil   448

Whaling   494
Imperialism and Tropical Ecology   534
Biomedical Technologies   580
The Green Revolution   612

SOCIETY AND CULTURE

Blaming the Black Death on the Jews,
   Strasbourg, 1349   332
European Male Sexual Dominance Overseas   357
Colonial Wealth and the Exploitation of
   Indigenous Peoples   387
Style and Conversion: Christian Rivalries in
   Beijing   435

Charles Babbage, Ada Lovelace, and the
   "Analytical Engine"   468
Demonstrating for Women's Rights   511
The Experience of Battle   547
Self-Government in Africa 589
China's Family-Planning Needs   638
Nelson Mandela   653

PREFACE

When we, the authors of *The Earth and Its Peoples,* received our first copies of its first edition in 1997, we breathed a collective sigh of deep relief. Merging six perspectives on world history into a single integrated global history had not been easy, nor had it been painless. But we had accomplished it.

Fortunately, none of us then realized how much we would have to rethink and reengineer to produce a second edition. As classroom teachers around the country used our book, they spotted many opportunities, both great and small, for improvement. These responses became our mandate for preparing a second edition, and our relief on accomplishing that task was no less heartfelt than it had been four years earlier.

But what of the Brief Edition that had succeeded and been based on our first edition? No one believed that minor amendments here and there would suffice. Thus we decided that nothing short of a completely new abridgement would do. And our heightened awareness of the needs of instructors and students steeled our determination to put full authorial effort into the job.

The Brief Edition is designed for a range of instructor choices. For those instructors who choose to assign a large amount of supplementary reading, the briefer narrative will provide the backbone of the story. The shorter narrative accommodates the needs of a quarter semester world history survey. It is also perfect for those instructors who prefer to assign less reading to students in general. The Brief Edition is produced in two formats: A complete edition covers the entire chronology from prehistory to the present, and a two-volume edition can be used for the two-semester survey. Volume I covers the period from prehistory to 1550 and Volume II covers 1500 to the present. There is a brief introduction to Volume II that orients students to the general political and social climate of the world at 1500.

Our overall goal, however, remains unchanged: to produce a textbook that not only speaks for the past, but speaks to today's student and today's teacher. Students and instructors alike should take away from this text a broad vision of human societies beginning as sparse and disconnected communities reacting creatively to local circumstances; experiencing ever more intensive stages of contact, interpenetration, and cultural expansion and amalgamation; and arriving at a twenty-first century world situation in which people increasingly visualize a single global community.

Process, not progress, is the keynote of this book: a steady process of change over time, at first differently experienced in various regions, but eventually interconnecting peoples and traditions from all parts of the globe. Students should come away from this book with a sense that the problems and promises of their world are rooted in a past in which people of every sort, in every part of the world, confronted problems of a similar character and coped with them as best they could. We believe our efforts will help students see where their world has come from and learn thereby something useful for their own lives.

CENTRAL THEMES

We have subtitled *The Earth and Its Peoples* "A Global History" because the book explores the common challenges and experiences that unite the human past. Although the dispersal of early humans to every liveable environment resulted in a myriad different economic, social, political, and cultural systems, all societies displayed analogous patterns in meeting their needs and exploiting their environments. Our challenge was to select the particular data and episodes that would best illuminate these global patterns of human experience.

To meet this challenge, we adopted two themes to serve as the spinal cord of our history: "technology and the environment," and "authority and diversity." The former represents the commonplace material bases of all human societies at all times. It grants no special favor to any cultural group even as it embraces subjects of the broadest topical, chronological, and geographical range. The latter expresses the reality that every human society has constructed or inherited structures of authority, whether political, religious, or cultural, but simultaneously recognizes that alternative lifestyles and visions of societal organization continually manifest themselves both within and in dialogue with every structure of authority.

With respect to "technology and the environment," it is vital for students to understand that technology, in the broad sense of experience-based knowledge of the physical world, underlies all human activity. Writing is a technology, but so is oral transmission from generation to generation of lore about medicinal or poisonous plants. The magnetic compass is a navigational technology, but so is a Polynesian mariner's hard-won knowledge of winds, currents, and tides that made possible the settlement of the Pacific islands.

All technological development, moreover, has come about in interaction with environments, both physical and human, and has, in turn, affected those environments. The story of how humanity has changed the face of the globe is an integral part of this central theme.

Yet technology and the environment do not by themselves explain or underlie all important episodes of human change and experience. In keeping with the theme of "authority and diversity," discussions of politics, culture, and society interweave with our presentation of the material base of human society to reveal additional historical patterns. Thus when narrating the histories of empires, we describe a range of human experiences within and beyond the imperial frontiers without assuming that the imperial institutions are a more fit topic for discussion than the economic and social organization of pastoral nomads or the life patterns of peasant women. And when religious and cultural traditions occupy our narrative, our primary concern is to complement descriptive presentation with commentary on cultural alternatives within the societies in question.

CHANGES IN THE SECOND EDITION

While an entirely fresh abridgment, based on the second edition of the comprehensive version of *The Earth and Its Peoples,* is the hallmark of this second edition, the adoption of a full color format not only brightens the page but makes maps clearer and more effective. The opening pages of each part have similarly been reconceived to give students an instant geographic and chronological overview of what is to come. The timelines and world maps that now accompany the part-opening essay unify content while focusing student attention on broad themes and historical benchmarks. Consolidated timelines within each chapter enable students to see at a glance the sorts of comparisons being made in the text.

Guides to pronunciation of uncommon words and foreign terms, previously at the back of the book, have been moved to the bottom of each page. In the area of study aids, the key terms bold-faced in the text and listed at the end of each chapter are now defined in the glossary at the end of the book. In addition, two-to-four focus questions have been placed at the end of the vignette opening each chapter to draw student attention to the main themes of the chapter.

We believe that these unobtrusive changes will improve student understanding of the main narratives and make it easier to grasp the main points of each chapter, as well as to review for examinations.

ORGANIZATION

The Earth and Its Peoples, Brief Edition uses eight broad chronological divisions to define its conceptual scheme of global historical development. In **Part I: The Emergence of Human Communities, to 1500 B.C.E.,** we examine important patterns of human communal organization. Small, dispersed human communities living by foraging spread to most parts of the world over tens of thousands of years. They responded to enormously diverse environmental conditions, at different times and in different ways discovering how to cultivate plants and utilize the products of domestic animals. On the basis of these new modes of sustenance, population grows, permanent towns appear, and political and religious authority, based on collection and control of agricultural surpluses, spreads over extensive areas.

Part II: The Formation of New Cultural Communities, 1000 B.C.E.–550 C.E., introduces the concept of a "cultural community," in the sense of a coherent pattern of activities and symbols pertaining to a specific human community. While all human communities develop distinctive cultures, including those discussed in Part I, historical development in this stage of global history prolonged and magnified the impact of some cultures more than others. In the geographically contiguous African-Eurasian land mass, the cultures that proved to have the most enduring influence traced their roots to the second and first millennia B.C.E.

Part III: Growth and Interaction of Cultural Communities, 300 B.C.E.–1500 C.E., deals with early episodes of technological, social, and cultural exchange and interaction on a continental scale both within and beyond the framework of imperial expansion. These are so different from earlier interactions arising from more limited conquests or extensions of political boundaries that they constitute a distinct era in world history, an era that set the world on the path of increasing global interaction and interdependence that it has been following ever since.

In **Part IV: Interregional Patterns of Culture and Contact, 1200–1550,** we take a look at the world during three centuries that saw both intensified cultural and commercial contact and increasingly confident self-definition of cultural communities in Europe, Asia, and Africa. The Mongol conquest of a vast empire extending from the Pacific Ocean to eastern Europe greatly stimulated trade and interaction. In the West, strengthened European kingdoms began maritime expansion in the Atlantic, forging direct ties with sub-Saharan Africa and laying the base for expanded global contacts after 1500.

Part V: The Globe Encompassed, 1500–1800, treats a period dominated by the global effects of European expansion and continued economic growth. European ships took over, expanded, and extended the maritime trade of the Indian Ocean, coastal Africa, and the Asian rim of the Pacific Ocean. This maritime commercial enterprise had its counterpart in European colonial empires in the Americas and a new Atlantic trading system. The contrasting capacities and fortunes of traditional land empires and new maritime empires, along with the exchange of domestic plants and animals between the hemispheres, underline the technological and environmental dimensions of this first era of complete global interaction.

In **Part VI: Revolutions Reshape the World, 1750–1870,** the word revolution is used in several senses: in the political sense of governmental overthrow, as in France and the Americas; in the metaphorical sense of radical transformative change, as in the Industrial Revolution; and in the broadest sense of a perception of a profound change in circumstances and worldview. Technology and environment lie at the core of these developments. With the rapid ascendancy of the Western belief that science and technology could overcome all challenges, environmental or otherwise, technology became not only an instrument of transformation but also an instrument of domination, to the point of threatening the integrity and autonomy of cultural traditions in nonindustrial lands.

Part VII: Global Dominance and Diversity, 1850–1949, examines the development of a world arena in which people conceived of events on a global scale. Imperialism, world war, international economic connections, and world-encompassing ideological tendencies, like nationalism and socialism, present the picture of a globe becoming increasingly interconnected. European dominance took on a worldwide dimension, seeming at times to threaten the diversity of human cultural experience with permanent subordination to European values and philosophies, while at other times triggering strong political or cultural resistance. The accelerating pace of technological change deepened other sorts of cleavages as well.

For **Part VIII: The Perils and Promises of a Global Community, 1945–2001,** we decided to divide the last half of the twentieth century into three time periods: 1945–1975, 1975–1991, and 1991–2001. Nevertheless, there is a good deal of continuity from chapter to chapter. The challenges of the Cold War and post-colonial nation building dominate the period and involve global economic, technological, and political forces that become increasingly important factors in all aspects of human life. Technology plays a central role in this part both because of its integral role in the growth of a global community and because its many benefits in improving the quality of life seem clouded by real and potential negative impacts on the environment.

SUPPLEMENTS

We have assembled an array of on-line supplements to aid students in learning and instructors in teaching. The web site, which features an *Instructor's Resource Manual*, web activities, and the ACE self-testing quiz program, in addition to our *Computerized Test Bank*, provides a tightly integrated program for teaching and learning.

New to the book-specific web site is the *Instructor's Resource Manual*, thoroughly revised by John Reisbord (Ph.D. Northwestern University), which provides useful teaching strategies for the global history course and tips for getting the most out of the text. Each chapter contains instructional objectives, a detailed chapter outline, discussion questions, in-depth learning projects, and audiovisual resources.

Students visiting our web site can access our ACE practice quizzes, which feature 10–20 multiple-choice questions per chapter. In addition to reinforcing important chapter material, the program provides useful feedback for every option so that students can note what material they need to review further. New to our student site are web activities, also created by John Reisbord, which are designed to encourage further critical thinking. Students can explore themes and issues covered in the text in more depth by using information on select sites to answer questions posed in the exercises.

Our *Computerized Test Bank*, prepared by Jane Scimeca of Brookdale Community College, offers 14 to 16 key-term identifications, 4 to 6 essay questions with answer guidelines, 24–26 multiple-choice questions, and 2 to 3 history and geography exercises.

The GeoQuest World CD-ROM, features thirty interactive maps that demonstrate for students the connection between history and geography from ancient times to the present. Each map is accompanied by exercises with answers and essay questions. Four different types of interactivity allow students to move at their own pace through each section.

ACKNOWLEDGMENTS

We have benefited from the critical readings of many colleagues. Our sincere thanks go in particular to the following instructors: Henry Abramson, Florida Atlantic University; Paul V. Adams, Shippensburg University/University of San Carlos; Maria S. Arbelaez, University of Nebraska at Omaha; William J. Astore, United States Air Force Academy; Fritz Blackwell, Washington State University; Corinne Blake, Rowan University; Thomas Borstelmann, Cornell University; Byron Cannon, University of Utah; David A. Chappell, University of Hawaii; Nancy Clark, California Polytechnic State University at San Luis Obispo; Aaron Cohen, California State University, Sacramento; Lee Congdon, James Madison University; James Coolsen, Shippensburg University; Bruce Cruikshank, Hastings College; Linda T. Darling, University of Arizona; Susan Deans-Smith, University of Texas at Austin; Gregory C. Ference, Salisbury State University; Alan Fisher, Michigan State University; Donald M. Fisher, Niagara County Community College; Cathy A. Frierson, University of New Hampshire; Rosanna Gatens, Belmont University; Lorne E. Glaim, Pacific Union College; Matthew S. Gordon, Miami University; Steve Gosch, University of Wisconsin at Eau Claire; Kolleen M. Guy, University of Texas at San Antonio; James R. Hansen, Auburn University; Randolph C. Head, University of California at Riverside; David Hertzel, Southwestern Oklahoma State University; Richard J. Hoffman, San Francisco State University; Catherine M. Jones, North Georgia College and State University; Joy Kammerling, Eastern Illinois University; Carol A. Keller, San Antonio College; Jonathan Lee, San Antonio College; Miriam R. Levin, Case Western Reserve University; Richard Lewis, St. Cloud State University; James E. Lindsay, Colorado State University; Charles W. McClellan, Radford University; Andrea McElderry, University of Louisville; Stephen L. McFarland, Auburn University; Gregory McMahon, University of New Hampshire; Mark McLeod, University of Delaware; Stephen S. Michot, Mississippi County Community College; Shawn W. Miller, Brigham Young University; Stephen Morillo, Wabash College; Kalala Joseph Ngalamulume, Central Washington University; Patricia O'Neill, Central Oregon Community College; Chandrika Paul, Shippensburg University; John R. Pavia, Ithaca College; Thomas Earl Porter, North Carolina A&T State University; Jean H. Quataert, SUNY at Binghamton; William Reddy, Duke University; Thomas Reeves, Roxbury

Community College; Dennis Reinhartz, University of Texas at Arlington; Richard Rice, University of Tennessee at Chattanooga; Jane Scimeca, Brookdale Community College; William Schell, Murray State University; Alyssa Goldstein Sepinwall, California State University at San Marcos; Deborah Shackleton, United States Air Force Academy; Anita Shelton, Eastern Illinois University; Jeffrey M. Shumway, Brigham Young University; David R. Smith, California State Polytechnic University at Pomona; Linda Smith, Samford University; Mary Frances Smith, Ohio University; George E. Snow, Shippensburg University; Charlotte D. Staelin, Washington College; Paul D. Steeves, Stetson University; Robert Shannon Sumner, State University of West Georgia; Yi Sun, University of San Diego; Willard Sunderland, University of Cincinnati; Thaddeus Sunseri, Colorado State University; Sara W. Tucker, Washburn University; John M. VanderLippe, SUNY at New Paltz; Mary A. Watrous-Schlesinger, Washington State University; James A. Wood, North Carolina A&T State University; Eric Van Young, University of California at San Diego; and Alex Zukas, National University, San Diego.

We also want to extend our collective thanks to Lynda Schaffer for her early conceptual contributions as well as to the history departments of Shippensburg University, the United States Air Force Academy, and the State University of New York at New Paltz for arranging reviewer conferences that provided crucial feedback for our revision of the book. Individually, Richard W. Bulliet thanks Jack Garraty and Isser Woloch for first involving him in world history; Pamela Kyle Crossley wishes to thank Gene Garthwaite, Charles Wood, and David Morgan; Steven W. Hirsch extends his gratitude to Dennis Trout and Peter L. D. Reid; Lyman L. Johnson extends his to Kenneth J. Andrien, Richard Boyer, Grant D. Hones, William M. Ringle, Hendrik Kraay, Daniel Dupre, and Steven W. Usselman; and David Northrup thanks Allen Howard and Prasanan Parthasarathi. Lyman Johnson also thanks the members of the Department of History of North Carolina A&T University for their many helpful and pertinent suggestions.

The three people who kept us on course in preparing the second edition deserve our special thanks: Jean L. Woy, Editor-in-Chief for History, Political Science, and Economics; Nancy Blaine, Senior Sponsoring Editor; and Annette Fantasia, Editorial Assistant. We also had the pleasure of working again with several people who helped so much with the first and second editions, including Carol Newman, Senior Project Editor; Reba Frederics, Editorial Assistant, Charlotte Miller, Art Editor; Carole Frolich, Photo Researcher; Jill Haber, Senior Production/Design Coordinator; and Florence Cadran, Manufacturing Manager.

We thank also the many students whose questions and concerns, expressed directly or through their instructors, shaped much of this revision. We continue to welcome all our readers' suggestions, queries, and criticisms. Please contact us at our respective institutions or at this e-mail address: history@hmco.com.

ABOUT THE AUTHORS

Richard W. Bulliet Professor of Middle Eastern History at Columbia University, Richard W. Bulliet received his Ph.D. from Harvard University. He has written scholarly works on a number of topics: the social history of medieval Iran (*The Patricians of Nishapur*), the historical competition between pack camels and wheeled transport (*The Camel and the Wheel*), the process of conversion to Islam (*Conversion to Islam in the Medieval Period*), and the overall course of Islamic social history (*Islam: The View from the Edge*). He is the editor of the *Columbia History of the Twentieth Century*. He has published four novels, co-edited *The Encyclopedia of the Modern Middle East*, and hosted an educational television series on the Middle East. He was awarded a fellowship by the John Simon Guggenheim Memorial Foundation.

Pamela Kyle Crossley Pamela Kyle Crossley received her Ph.D. in Modern Chinese History from Yale University. She is Professor of History, Rosenwald Research Professor in the Arts and Sciences, and Chair of Asian and Middle Eastern Studies at Dartmouth College. Her books include *A Translucent Mirror: History and Identity in Qing Imperial Ideology, The Manchus,* and *Orphan Warriors: Three Manchu Generations and the End of the Qing World.* Her research, which concentrates on the cultural history of China, Inner Asia, and Central Asia, has most recently been supported by the John Simon Guggenheim Memorial Foundation and the National Endowment for the Humanities.

Daniel R. Headrick Daniel R. Headrick received his Ph.D. in History from Princeton University. Professor of History and Social Science at Roosevelt University in Chicago, he is the author of several books on the history of technology, imperialism, and international relations, including *The Tools of Empire: Technology and European Imperialism in the Nineteenth Century, The Tentacles of Progress: Technology Transfer in the Age of Imperialism, The Invisible Weapon: Telecommunications and International Politics,* and *When Information Came of Age: Technologies of Knowledge in the Age of Reason and Revolution, 1700–1850.* His articles have appeared in the *Journal of World History* and the *Journal of Modern History,* and he has been awarded fellowships by the National Endowment for the Humanities, the John Simon Guggenheim Memorial Foundation, and the Alfred P. Sloan Foundation.

Steven W. Hirsch Steven W. Hirsch holds a Ph.D. in Classics from Stanford University and is currently Associate Professor of Classics and History at Tufts University. He has received grants from the National Endowment for the Humanities and the Massachusetts Foundation for Humanities and Public Policy. His research and publications include *The Friendship of the Barbarians: Xenophon and the Persian Empire,* as well as articles and reviews in the *Classical Journal,* the *American Journal of Philology,* and the *Journal of Interdisciplinary History.*

Lyman L. Johnson Professor of History at the University of North Carolina at Charlotte, Lyman L. Johnson earned his Ph.D. in Latin American History from the University of Connecticut. A two-time Senior Fulbright-Hays Lecturer, he also has received fellowships from the Tinker Foundation, the Social Science Research Council, the National Endowment for the Humanities, and the American Philosophical Society. His recent books include *The Faces of Honor* (with Sonya Lipsett-Rivera), *The Problem of Order in Changing Societies, Essays on the Price History of Eighteenth-Century Latin America* (with Enrique Tandeter), and *Colonial Latin America* (with Mark A. Burkholder). He also has published in journals, including the *Hispanic American Historical Review,* the *Journal of Latin American Studies,* the *International Review of Social History, Social History,* and *Desarrollo Económico.* He recently served as president of the Conference on Latin American History.

David Northrup Professor of History at Boston College, David Northrup earned his Ph.D. in African and European History from the University of California at Los Angeles. He has published scholarly volumes on precolonial Nigeria, on precolonial and colonial Congo, on the Atlantic slave trade, and on Asian, African, and Pacific Islander indentured labor in the nineteenth century. His recent work appeared in the *Oxford History of the British Empire, Revue française d'histoire d'outre-mer, Slavery and Abolition,* and the *Journal of World History.* He is vice president of the World History Association and has received research support from the Fulbright-Hays Commission, the National Endowment for the Humanities, and the Social Science Research Council.

Note on Spelling and Usage

Where necessary for clarity, dates are followed by the letters C.E. or B.C.E. The abbreviation C.E. stands for "Common Era" and is equivalent to A.D. (*anno Domini,* Latin for "in the year of the Lord"). The abbreviation B.C.E stands for "before the Common Era" and means the same as B.C. ("before Christ"). In keeping with our goal of approaching world history without special concentration on one culture or another, we chose these neutral abbreviations as appropriate to our enterprise. Because many readers will be more familiar with English than with metric measurements, however, units of measure are generally given in the English system, with metric equivalents following in parentheses.

In general, Chinese has been romanized according to the *pinyin* method. Exceptions include proper names well established in English (e.g., Canton, Chiang Kai-shek) and a few English words borrowed from Chinese (e.g., kowtow). Spellings of Arabic, Ottoman Turkish, Persian, Mongolian, Manchu, Japanese, and Korean names and terms avoid special diacritical marks for letters that are pronounced only slightly differently in English. An apostrophe is used to indicate when two Chinese syllables are pronounced separately (e.g., Chang'an).

For words transliterated from languages that use the Arabic script—Arabic, Ottoman Turkish, Perisan, Urdu—the apostrophe indicating separately pronounced syllables may represent either of two special consonants, the *hamza* or the *ain.* Because most English-speakers do not hear the distinction between these two, they have not been distinguished in transliteration and are not indicated when they occur at the beginning or end of a word. As with Chinese, some words and commonly used place-names from these languages are given familiar English spellings (e.g., Quran instead of Qur'an, Cairo instead of al-Qahira). Arabic romanization has normally been used for terms relating to Islam, even where the context justifies slightly different Turkish or Persian forms, again for ease of comprehension.

There is an ongoing debate about how best to render Amerindian words in English. It has been common for authors writing in English to follow Mexican usage for Nahuatl and Yucatec Maya words and place-names. In this style, for example, the capital of the Aztec state is spelled Tenochtitlán, and the important late Maya city-state is spelled Chichén Itzá. Although these forms are still common even in the specialist literature, we have chosen to follow the scholarship that sees these accents as unnecessary. The exceptions are modern place-names, such as Mérida and Yucatán, which are accented. A similar problem exists for the spelling of Quechua and Aymara words from the Andean region of South America. Although there is significant disagreement among scholars, we follow the emerging consensus and use the spellings khipu (not quipu), Tiwanaku (not Tiahuanaco), and Wari (not Huari). However, we keep Inca (not Inka) and Cuzco (not Cusco), since these spellings are expected by most of our potential readers and we hope to avoid confusion.

INTRODUCTION
THE WORLD BEFORE 1500

—*f*—

**Antiquity: Humans, Cultures, and Conquests, to 400 C.E. •
Growth and Interaction, 400–1200 • Interregional Conquests
and Exchanges, 1200–1500**

istory occurs in a continuous stream. Because new events are the products of their past, each historical period is intimately linked to what preceded it. As a Roman historian put it, "History doesn't make leaps." Nevertheless, modern historians find it useful to divide the past into eras or ages to make sense of the sweep of history. The longest historical eras are antiquity, the Middle Ages, and modern times. Volume II of *The Earth and Its Peoples* is devoted to the third of these—modern world history, the five centuries since about 1500.

In order to explain how the modern era came into being, the first chapter of Volume II of *The Earth and Its Peoples* (Chapter 15) begins in about 1450. To help the reader understand the broader sweep of history, this Introduction provides an overview of earlier eras. The Introduction reviews three periods of decreasing temporal length. The first is the very long period from human origins until the end of ancient history in about 400 C.E. Next comes the early medieval period down to about 1200; and, finally, the three hundred years immediately preceding 1500. Because the centuries after 1200 were most important for shaping the transition to the modern era, they receive the most detailed treatment.

ANTIQUITY: HUMANS, CULTURES, AND CONQUESTS, TO 400 C.E.

All historical periods were shaped by natural environment and human technology (whether simple tools, techniques, or complex machines). The paramount role played by environmental forces is apparent when historians seek to explain how human beings—and thus history—began. Like all other living creatures, early humans were products of biological adjustments to changing environments. Over millions of years, our ancestors in eastern and southern Africa evolved biologically to enhance their chances for survival. The evolution of an upright posture enabled early people to walk and run on two legs, thereby freeing their hands for tool making. The evolution of larger brains gave them the capacity to learn and understand all sorts of new things and devise techniques for putting them to use. Finally, evolutionary changes in the throat gave humans the capacity for speech, which, as language developed, had the dual effect of making complex social relations easier and fostering the development of intellectual culture.

With these physical traits in place, humans were able to develop in a direction taken by no other creature. Instead of relying on the glacially slow process of biological evolution to adapt their bodies to new environments, our ancestors used their minds to devise technologies for transforming nature to suit their needs. By the standards of today, these early technologies may seem crude—stone tools for cutting and chopping, clothing made from plants and animal skins, shelters in caves and huts—but they were sufficient to enable humans to survive environmental changes in their homelands. They also enabled bands of humans to migrate to new environments in every part of the world. Through trial and error Stone Age people learned what could safely be eaten in new environments. Other primates acted primarily by instinct; humans acted according to the dictates of culture. The capacity to create and change material and in-

tellectual culture marked the beginning of human history.

Agricultural Civilizations

Beginning about 10,000 years ago, the transition from food gathering to food production marked a major turning point in history. Human communities in many different parts of the world learned to alter the natural food supply. Some people promoted the growth of foods they liked by scattering seeds on good soils and restricting the growth of competing plants. In time some people became full-time farmers. Other communities tamed wild animals whose meat, milk, fur, and hides they desired, and they controlled their breeding to produce animals with the most desired characteristics. Promoted by a warmer world climate, these agricultural revolutions slowly spread from the Middle East around the Mediterranean. People in South and East Asia, Africa, and the Americas domesticated other wild plants and animals for their use. Just as humans had ceased to rely on evolution to enable them to adjust to new surroundings, so too they had bypassed evolution in bringing new species of plants and animals into existence.

The agricultural revolutions greatly enhanced people's chances for survival in two ways. One was a rapid increase in population fostered by the ability to grow and store more food. A second change was taking place in the composition of human communities. The earliest communities consisted of small bands of biologically related people and their spouses from other bands. However, more complex societies made their first appearances as more and more unrelated people concentrated in lush river valleys, whose soils, temperatures, and rainfall suited them for farming.

In the Fertile Crescent of the Middle East, Egypt, India, and China the existence of a regular food surplus enabled a few people to develop highly specialized talents and tools that were not tied to food production. Some specialized in fighting—to defend crops from raiders and to expand their lands. Some talented warriors became rulers of large areas and headed government with specialized administrators. Specialists constructed elaborate irrigation systems, monumental palaces, and temples. Others made special metal tools and weapons, first of bronze, then of iron. Because of the value of their talents these specialists acquired privileges. It was grandest to be a king, queen, or head priest. For the average person, life was harder in complex societies than in parts of the world where such specialization had not yet occurred.

rise to recorded literature and records that might be sent unchanged over long distances or even lost for millennia only to be discovered and deciphered in recent times, giving future generations specific records of what went before. Thoughtful people recorded the myths and legends passed down orally from earlier days, systematizing them and often adapting them to new social conditions.

Culture and Civilization

Complex and populous agricultural societies developed specialists who dealt with abstract and unseen forces. This development was not entirely new. For tens of thousands of years before the first settled societies, humans had used their minds to think about the meaning of life. The remains of elaborate burials and sites of worship suggest that some early societies had clear beliefs in an afterlife and in spiritual forces that controlled their lives. Many cultures believed the sun, moon, and nature had supernatural powers.

Another form of intellectual activity was the collection of technical knowledge about the environment. Cultural communities learned what plants were best for food, clothing, or building materials and passed this knowledge along to later generations. Most specialized was the knowledge of how to make medicines and poisons. Assigning names for all these facilitated the transmission of this knowledge. In the absence of written records, very little specific information about these early treasuries of knowledge exists, but the elaborate and beautiful paintings in caves dating to tens of thousands of years before the emergence of early agricultural societies provide the clearest evidence of the cultural sophistication of early humans.

Cultural change surged as settled agricultural communities became more specialized. Temple priests devised elaborate rituals and texts for state religions and studied the heavens for signs of the progress of the seasons or for more mystical meanings. In Mesopotamia, Egypt, and elsewhere a new class of scribes wrote down laws, bodies of knowledge, and records in special codes. Writing gave

Empires and Regional Cultures

In time governments weakened or fell victim to conquest. Egypt, for example, fell to the Assyrians from Mesopotamia, then to Nubians from up the Nile. Some conquerors created vast new empires. Late in the fourth century B.C.E., Alexander the Great brought everything from the eastern Mediterranean to India and Egypt under his sway, spreading Greek culture and language. After the collapse of Alexander's empire in the third century B.C.E., the first of a series of Indian empires arose. In the second and first centuries B.C.E., Latin-speakers spread their rule, language, and culture throughout the Roman Empire, which encompassed the Mediterranean and reached across the Alps into Gaul (France) and Britain. At much the same time, the Han consolidated control over the densely populated lands of China, and successive rulers extended the sway of imperial China over much of East Asia. In the isolated continents of the Americas, advanced agricultural societies were also building larger states in late antiquity.

Essential to empire formation was the significant enhancement of old technologies and the development of new ones. In many parts of the world iron replaced bronze as the preferred metal for tools and weapons. In the Middle East and China soldiers on horseback played important military roles. In most places there were advances in the fighting techniques and in defensive strategies and fortifications.

Empires encouraged the growth of cities to serve as administrative, economic, and cultural centers. Temples, palaces, monuments, markets, and public amenities advertised the glory of these imperial centers. Large states regularly mobilized large pools of labor for massive construction projects. By late antiquity, a few cities had populations in the hundreds of thousands—Alexandria in Egypt, Rome in Italy, Chang'an in China, Palaliputra in India—though such large numbers strained cities' capacities to supply food and water and dispose of waste. Such architectural monuments established "classical" styles that affected wide areas even after the empires were gone.

Other imperial building projects were more practical. The Roman and Chinese governments built thousands of miles of paved roads for moving troops and communication; long barrier walls and strings of forts defended frontier areas from invasion. Trade often flourished on these political frontiers, and good roads further encouraged trade. Improvements in shipping also encouraged the movement of goods over long distances. Much long-distance trade in antiquity was in luxury goods for the privileged classes in urban civilizations. The search for exotic items tied remote parts of the world together and gave rise to new specialists both within the urban civilizations and in less stratified parts of the world. Gold, animal pelts, and exotic feathers from inner Africa reached Egypt. Phoenician mariners marketed lumber, papyrus (for paper), wine, and fish around the Mediterranean Sea. Other merchants carried silk from China across arid Central Asia to the Middle East and lands to the west. The advent of coinage in the first millennium B.C.E. stimulated local and regional economies.

The routes that carried goods also helped spread religions, inventions, and ideas. The Zoroastrian religion of the Persians became one of the great ethical creeds of antiquity. The diaspora of Jews from Palestine after their northern kingdom was destroyed by the Assyrian Empire in the eighth century B.C.E. and the activities of Jewish traders also helped spread monotheistic beliefs. The beliefs and culture of the Greeks and Romans spread throughout their empires. Similarly, Indian traders introduced Hinduism to Southeast Asia.

GROWTH AND INTERACTION, 400–1200

During the Early Middle Ages expanding political and commercial links drew regions closer together. In addition, the growth of interregional trade and the spread of new world religions helped unite and redefine the boundaries of cultural regions, though divisions within religions undercut some of this cultural unity. All of these factors were interrelated, but let's begin with the one that left the most enduring impression on the course of history: the spread of world religions.

World Religions

The first religious tradition to experience widespread growth in this period was Buddhism, which spread from the Indian homeland where it had arisen around 500 B.C.E. One direction of growth was eastward into Southeast Asia. By 400 C.E. there were particular strongholds of the faith on the large islands of Ceylon and Java, whose kings supported the growth of schools and monasteries and constructed temple complexes. Traders also carried Buddhism to China and from there to Korea, Japan, and Tibet. In some places Buddhism's growing strength led to political reactions. In China the Tang emperors reduced the influence of the monasteries in 840 by taking away their tax exemption and by promoting traditional Confucian values. A similar effort by the Tibetan royal family to curtail Buddhism failed, and Buddhist monks established their political dominance in mountainous Tibet. In India, however, Buddhism gradually lost support during this period and by 1200 had practically disappeared from the land of its origin.

Meanwhile, people in western Eurasia were embracing two newer religious systems. In the fourth century, Christianity became the official religion of the Roman Empire, adding new followers all around the Mediterranean to this once persecuted faith. But when the western half of the empire collapsed under the onslaught of "barbarian" invasions in the late fifth century, the Latin Church had to shoulder alone the tasks of converting these peoples to Christianity and preserving the intellectual, political, and cultural heritage of Roman antiquity. In its religious mission the Latin Church was quite successful. One by one Frankish, German, English, Irish, Hungarian, and other leaders were converted, and their subjects gradually followed suit. Preserving other Roman achievements was more difficult. The church continued to use the Latin language and Roman law, and Christian monasteries preserved manuscripts of many ancient works. But the trading economy and urban life that had been the heart blood of ancient Rome became only a memory in most of the Latin West.

In the eastern Mediterranean, Byzantine Roman emperors continued to rule, and the Greek-speaking Christian church continued to enjoy political protection. Greek monks were also active Christian missionaries among the Slavic peoples of eastern Europe. The conversion of the Russian rulers in the tenth century was a notable achievement. However, by the middle of the next century, cultural, linguistic, and theological differences led to a deep rift between Greek and Russian Christians in the east and Latin Christians in the west.

Meanwhile, prophetic religion founded by Muhammad in the seventh century was spreading like a whirlwind out of its Arabian homeland. With great fervor Arab armies introduced Islam and an accompanying state system into the Middle East, across North Africa, and into the Iberian Peninsula. Over time most Middle Eastern and African Christians and members of other religions chose to adopt the new faith. Muslim merchants helped spread the faith along trade routes into sub-Saharan Africa and across southern Asia. Like Christianity, Islam eventually split along cultural, theological, and political lines as it expanded. Beginning in 1095, Latin Christians launched military Crusades against Muslim dominance of Christian holy places in Palestine. In later Crusades, political and commercial ends became more important than religious goals, and the boundaries between Christianity and Islam changed little.

Commercial and Political Contacts

In many other parts of the world empires played a fundamental role in defining and unifying cultural areas. Under the Tang and Song dynasties (618–1279) China continued to have stability and exhibited periods of remarkable economic growth and technological creativity. Ghana, the first notable empire in sub-Saharan Africa, emerged to control one end of the trans-Saharan trade. In the isolated continents of the Americas a series of cultural complexes formed in the Andes, among the Maya of the Yucatán, along the Mississippi, and in the arid North American southwest. But despite efforts by Christian northern Europeans to create a loosely centralized "Holy Roman Empire," a very decentralized political system prevailed in most of western Europe. In Japan development was moving in a similar direction.

Political and religious expansion helped stimulate regional and long-distance trade. The challenge of moving growing quantities of goods over long distances produced some important innovations in land and sea travel. Two of the most important land-based, long-distance routes in this period depended on pack animals, especially the camel. One was the Silk Road, a caravan route across Central Asia. On the other trade route, between sub-Saharan Africa and North Africa, camels carried goods across the Sahara, the world's largest desert.

The Silk Road took its name from the silk textiles that were carried from eastern China to the Mediterranean Sea. In return, the Chinese received horses and other goods from the West. In existence since about 250 B.C.E., this series of roads nearly 6,000 miles (9,000 kilometers) in length passed through arid lands whose pastoral populations provided guides, food, and fresh camels (specially bred for caravan work).

After 900 C.E. the Silk Road declined for a time. By coincidence, the trans-Saharan caravan routes were growing more important during the period from 700 to 1200. Here, too, horses were an important trade purchased by African rulers to the south in return for gold, slaves, and other goods. The pastoralists who controlled the Saharan oases became essential guides for the camel caravans.

Since ancient times sea travel had been important in moving goods over relatively short distances, usually within sight of land, as around the Mediterranean Sea, the Red Sea, the Persian Gulf, and among the islands of the East Indies. During this period the water links around and through the Indian Ocean were increasing enough to make it an alternative to moving goods from China to the Middle East. Shipments went from port to port and were exchanged many times. Special ships known as dhows made use of the seasonal shifts in the winds across the Indian Ocean to plan their voyages in each direction. These centuries also saw remarkable maritime voyages in the Pacific (see Chapter 15).

INTERREGIONAL CONQUESTS AND EXCHANGES, 1200–1500

Between 1200 and 1500, cultural and commercial contacts grew rapidly across wide expanses of Eurasia, Africa, the Americas, and the Indian Ocean. In part, the increased contacts were the product of an unprecedented era of empire building around the world. The Mongols conquered a vast empire spanning Eurasia from the Pacific to eastern Europe. Muslim peoples created new empires in India, the Middle East, and sub-Saharan Africa. Amerindian empires united extensive regions of the Americas. Most of Europe continued to lack political unity, but unusually powerful European kingdoms were expanding their frontiers.

Empires stimulated commercial exchanges. The Mongol conquests revived the Silk Road across Central Asia, while a complex maritime network centered on the Indian Ocean stretched around southern Eurasia from the South China Sea to the North Atlantic, with overland connections in all directions. Trade in the Americas and Africa also expanded. In the fifteenth century, Portuguese and Spanish explorers began an expansion southward along the Atlantic coast of Africa that by 1500 had opened a new all-water route to the riches of the Indian Ocean and set the stage for transoceanic routes that for the first time were to span the globe.

Mongol, Muslim, and European expansion promoted the spread of technologies. Printing, compasses, crossbows, gunpowder, and firearms—all East Asian inventions—found broader applications and new uses in western Eurasia. Both the Ottomans and the kingdoms of western Europe made extensive use of gunpowder technologies. However, the highly competitive and increasingly literate peoples of the Latin West surpassed all others of this period in their use of technologies that they borrowed from elsewhere or devised themselves. Europeans mined and refined more metals, produced more books, built more kinds of ships, and made more weapons than did people in any other comparable place on earth.

Why was so much change taking place all at once? Historians attribute many of the changes in South and Central Asia directly or indirectly to the empire building of the Mongols. But other changes took place far from that area. The role of simple coincidence, of course, should never be overlooked in history. And some historians believe that larger environmental factors were also at work—changes in climate that promoted population growth, trade, and empire building.

Mongols and Turks

The earliest and largest of the new empires was the work of the Mongols of northeastern Asia. Using their extraordinary command of horses and refinements in traditional forms of military and social organization, Mongols and allied groups united under Genghis Khan overran northern China in the early thirteenth century and spread their control westward across Central Asia to eastern Europe. By the later part of the century, the Mongol Empire stretched from Korea to Poland. It was ruled initially in four separate khanates: one in Russia, one in Iran, one in Central Asia, and one in China.

By ensuring traders protection from robbers and excessive tolls, the Mongol Empire revitalized the Silk Road. Never before had there been such a volume of commercial exchanges between eastern and western Eurasia. Easier travel also helped Islam and Buddhism spread to new parts of Central Asia.

The strains of holding such vast territories together caused the Mongol Empire to disintegrate over the course of the fourteenth and early fifteenth centuries. The Ming rulers of China overthrew Mongol rule in 1368 and began an expansionist foreign policy to reestablish China's predominance and prestige. Their armies repeatedly invaded Mongolia, reestablished dominion over Korea, and occupied northern Vietnam (Annam). One by one the other khanates collapsed.

The Mongols left a formidable legacy, but it was not Mongolian. Instead, Mongol rulers tended to adopt and promote the political systems, agricultural practices, and local customs of the peoples they ruled. Their encouragement of local languages helped later literary movements to flower. The political influence of the administrations the Mongols established in China, Iran, and Russia lingered even after locals had overthrown their rule, creating the basis for new national regimes.

At about the same time as the early Mongol expansion, Turkic war leaders from what is now Afghanistan were surging through the Khyber Pass and established a Muslim empire centered at Delhi. In short order, they overwhelmed the several Hindu states of north and central India and established a large empire ruled from the city of Delhi. The subsequent migration of large numbers of Muslims into India and the prestige and power of the Muslim ruling class brought India into the Islamic world. After their conquests in the Middle East, Mongols had recruited other Turkic-speaking Muslims from Central Asia to serve as their agents. In the decades after 1250, a large Turkic community in Anatolia (now Turkey) known as Ottomans took advantage of the weakness of the Byzantine Empire to extend their base in Anatolia. They then crossed into the Balkan Peninsula of southeastern Europe.

In the late 1300s, the Central Asian conqueror Timur (Tamerlane) shattered the Delhi Sultanate and stopped the expansion of the Ottoman Empire. The conquest and pillage of Timur's armies left the Delhi Sultanate a shadow of its former self, but the Ottoman Turks were able to reconstitute their empire in the fifteenth century. Ottoman conquerors swept deep into southeastern Europe (taking Constantinople, the last surviving remnant of the Byzantine Empire, in 1453) and southward into the Middle East, establishing a stable presence that was to endure into the twentieth century.

Indian Ocean Exchanges

In the wake of the Mongol Empire's collapse, the Indian Ocean assumed greater importance in the movement of goods across Eurasia. Alliances among Muslim merchants of many nationalities made these routes the world's richest trading area. Merchant dhows sailed among the trading ports, carrying cotton textiles, leather goods, grains, pepper, jewelry, carpets, horses, ivory, and many other goods. Chinese silk and porcelain and Indonesian spices entered from the east, meeting Middle Eastern and European goods from the west. It is important to note that Muslim merchant networks were almost completely independent of the giant Muslim land empires.

As a consequence of the Islamic world's political and commercial expansion, the number of adherents to the Muslim faith also grew. By 1500 Islam had replaced Buddhism as the second most important faith in India and was on its way to displacing Hinduism and Buddhism in Southeast Asia. The faith was also spreading in the Balkans. Meanwhile, raids by Arab pastoralists undermined ancient Christian states along Africa's upper Nile, leaving Ethiopia as the only Christian-ruled state in Africa. In the trading cities below the Sahara and along the Indian Ocean coast where Islam had established itself well before 1200, the strength and sophistication of Islamic religious practice was growing.

Mediterranean Exchanges

The Mediterranean Sea, which since antiquity had been a focus of commerce and cultural exchange for the peoples of Europe, the Middle East, and Africa, saw increased activity in the later Middle Ages. Part of the Mediterranean's importance derived from its trading links to the Indian Ocean by land and water routes. Another area that contributed to expanded trade was northern Africa. Camel caravans brought great quantities of gold and large numbers of slaves to the Mediterranean from the lands below the Sahara. This trade facilitated the growth of the powerful empire of Mali, which controlled some of the main gold-producing regions of West Africa. The rulers of Mali became rich and Muslim. Their wars and those of other states produced the captives that were sold north. In the fourteenth century the disruption of supplies of slaves from the eastern Mediterranean led to more slaves being purchased in southern Europe.

Another part of the expansion of Mediterranean trade was tied to the revival of western Europe. In 1204 the Italian city-state of Venice had shown its determination to be a dominant player in the eastern Mediterranean by attacking the Greek city of Constantinople and ensuring access to the Black Sea. Trade routes from the Mediterranean spread northward to the Netherlands and connected by sea to the British Isles, the Baltic Sea, and the Atlantic. The growth of trade in Europe accompanied a revival of urban life and culture. Both the cities and the countryside saw increased use of energy, minerals, and technologies from printing to gunpowder. Despite a high level of warfare among European states and devastating population losses in the fourteenth century, much of Europe was exhibiting cultural and economic vitality that was to have great consequences for the entire world in the centuries that followed.

The Aztecs and Inca

In the continents of the Western Hemisphere, American peoples were also creating important empires in the period from 1200 to 1500, although they had more limited resources with which to do so. For thousands of years their cultures had developed in isolation from the rest of humanity and thus had been unable to borrow any plants, animals, or technologies. Amerindian conquests were made without the aid of riding animals like the Mongols' horses, without the iron weapons all Old World empire builders had been using for many centuries, and without the new gunpowder weaponry that some Eurasians were employing in their conquests in this period.

In the wake of the collapse of the Toltec Empire, a martial people known as the Aztecs pushed southward into the rich agricultural lands of central Mexico. At first the Aztecs placed themselves at the service of strong indigenous residents, but after 1300 they began to build their own empire. Relying on their military skills, members of the Aztec warrior elite were able to conquer territories and reduce peasants to their service. The growth of a servile class at the bottom of society was paralleled by the growth of a powerful ruling class housed in well-constructed two-story dwellings in the Aztec capital cities. The servile laborers supplied the food needs of the growing cities and were impressed into building elaborate canals and land reclamation projects. Underpinning the power of the Aztec rulers were religious rituals that emphasized human sacrifice, mostly captives of the armies. By 1500 the Aztecs ruled a densely populated empire of subject and allied peoples.

Meanwhile, in the Andean highlands of western South America another powerful Amerindian empire was forming. Like central Mexico this region already had a rich agricultural base and a dense population when, in the fifteenth century, the Inca began using military skills to expand from a chiefdom into an empire. The Inca rulers, like the Aztecs, built impressive cities, promoted irrigation projects, and relied on religious rituals to bolster their authority. Tribute in goods and labor from their subject peoples supported their projects, and a network of mountain roads tied together the pieces of an empire that stretched for more than 3,000 miles (nearly 5,000 kilometers) north to south.

Both empires were cultural and commercial centers as well as political ones. In the Aztec Empire, well-armed private merchants controlled a long-distance trade in luxuries for the elites, including gold, jewels, feathered garments, and animal skins. There was also a network of local markets, large and small, that supplied the needs of more ordinary folks. State direction featured more prominently in Inca-ruled areas and promoted a vast exchange of specialized goods and a huge variety of foodstuffs grown at different altitudes.

THE MARITIME REVOLUTION,

TO 1550

**Global Maritime Expansion Before 1450 • Iberian Expansion,
1400–1550 • Encounters with Europe, 1450–1550**
SOCIETY AND CULTURE: **European Male Sexual Dominance Overseas**

n 1511, the young Ferdinand Magellan sailed from Europe around the southern tip of Africa and eastward across the Indian Ocean as a member of the first Portuguese expedition to explore the East Indies (maritime Southeast Asia). Eight years later, in the service of Spain, he headed an expedition that sought to reach the East Indies by sailing westward from Europe. By the middle of 1521, Magellan's expedition had sailed across the Atlantic, rounded the southern tip of South America, and crossed the Pacific Ocean—but at a high price.

One of the five ships wrecked on a reef; the captain of another deserted and sailed back to Spain. The passage across the Pacific took much longer than anticipated. Dozens of sailors died of starvation and disease. In the Philippines, Magellan himself was killed on April 27, 1521, while aiding a local king who had promised to become a Christian. Magellan's successor met the same fate a few days later.

The expedition's survivors consolidated their resources by burning the least seaworthy of their remaining three ships and transferring the men and supplies to the smaller *Victoria*, which continued westward across the Indian Ocean, around Africa, and back to Europe. Magellan's flagship, the *Trinidad*, tried unsuccessfully to re-cross the Pacific to Central America. The *Victoria*'s return to Spain on September 8, 1522, confirmed Europe's ability and determination to master the oceans. The Portuguese crown had backed a century of daring and dangerous voyages to open routes to Africa, Brazil, and the Indian Ocean. Since 1492, Spain had opened contacts with the American continents. Now the broad Pacific Ocean had been crossed.

Before 1500, powerful states and the rich trading networks of Asia had led the way in overland and maritime expansion. The Iberians set out on their voyages of exploration to reach Eastern markets, and their success began a new era in which the West gradually became the world's center of power, wealth, and innovation.

As you read this chapter, ask yourself the following questions:

- Why did Portugal and Spain undertake voyages of exploration?
- Why do the voyages of Magellan and other Iberians mark a turning point in world history?
- What were the consequences for the different peoples of the world of the contacts resulting from these voyages?

C

GLOBAL MARITIME EXPANSION BEFORE 1450

By 1450, mariners had discovered and settled most of the islands of the Pacific, the Atlantic, and the Indian Oceans, and a great trading system united the peoples around the Indian Ocean. But we know of no individual crossing the Pacific in either direction. Even the narrower Atlantic formed a barrier that kept the peoples of the Americas, Europe, and Africa in ignorance of each other's existence. The inhabitants of Australia were also completely cut off from contact with the rest of humanity. All this was about to change.

The Pacific Ocean

The vast distances that Polynesian peoples voyaged out of sight of land across the Pacific Ocean are one of the most impressive feats in maritime history before 1450 (see Map 15.1 on page 346). Though they left no written records, over several thousand years mariners from the Malay° Peninsula of Southeast Asia explored and settled the island chains of the East Indies and continued on to New Guinea and the smaller islands of Melanesia°. Beginning some time before the Common Era (C.E.), a wave of expansion from the area of Fiji brought the first humans to the islands of the central Pacific known as Polynesia. Their sailing canoes reached the easternmost Marquesas° Islands about 400 C.E.; Easter Island, 2,200 miles (3,540 kilometers) off the coast of South America, a century later; and the Hawaiian Islands by 500 C.E. Settlement in New Zealand began about 1200. Between 1100 and 1300, new voyages northward from Tahiti brought more Polynesian settlers to Hawaii.

Historians have puzzled over how the Polynesians reached the eastern Pacific islands without compasses to plot their way, particularly in view of the difficulties Magellan's flagship encountered sailing eastward across the Pacific. In 1947, explorer Thor Heyerdahl° argued that Easter Island and Hawaii were settled from the Americas and sought to prove his theory by sailing his balsawood raft *Kon Tiki* westward from Peru.

Although some Amerindian voyagers did use ocean currents to travel northward from Peru to Mexico between 300 and 900 C.E., there is now considerable evidence that planned expansion by Polynesian mariners accomplished the settlement of the islands of the eastern Pacific. The languages of the islanders relate closely to the languages of the western Pacific and ultimately to those of Malaya. In addition, accidental voyages could not have brought sufficient numbers of men and women for founding a new colony along with all the plants and domesticated animals common to other Polynesian islands.

In 1976, a Polynesian crew led by anthropologist Ben Finney used traditional navigational methods to sail the *Hokulea,* a 62-foot-long (19-meter-long) double canoe, from Hawaii south to Tahiti. Some old oceangoing canoes, using inverted triangular sails and steered by paddles (not by a rudder) measured 120 feet (37 meters) long. The Hokulea's crew navigated using only their observation of the currents, stars, and evidence of land.

The Indian Ocean

While Polynesian mariners settled the Pacific islands, other Malayo-Indonesians sailed westward across the Indian Ocean and colonized the large island of Madagascar off the southeastern coast of Africa. These voyages continued through the fifteenth century.

Malay (May-LAY)   **Melanesia** (mel-uh-NEE-zhuh)

Marquesas (mar-KAY-suhs)   **Heyerdahl** (HIGH-uhr-dahl)

To this day, the inhabitants of Madagascar speak Malayo-Polynesian languages. However, part of the island's population is descended from Africans who crossed the 600 miles (1,000 kilometers) from the mainland to Madagascar, most likely in the centuries just before 1500.

The rise of Islam gave Indian Ocean trade an important boost. The great Muslim cities of the Middle East provided a demand for valuable commodities, and networks of Muslim traders tied the region together (see Chapter 13). The Indian Ocean traders operated largely independent of the empires and states that they served, but in East Asia, China's early Ming emperors took an active interest in these wealthy ports of trade, sending Admiral **Zheng He**° on a series of expeditions (see Chapter 12).

The first Ming fleet in 1405 consisted of sixty-two specially built "treasure ships," large Chinese junks each about 300 feet long by 150 feet wide (90 by 45 meters). Most of the one hundred smaller accompanying vessels exceeded in size the flagship in which Columbus later sailed across the Atlantic. Each treasure ship had nine masts, twelve sails, many decks, and a carrying capacity of 3,000 tons (six times the capacity of Columbus's entire fleet). One expedition carried over 27,000 individuals, including infantry and cavalry troops. Although the ships carried small cannon, highly accurate crossbows dominated most Chinese sea battles.

One Chinese-Arabic interpreter kept a journal recording the customs, dress, and beliefs of the people visited, along with the trade, towns, and animals of their countries. Among his observations were these: exotic animals such as the black panther of Malaya and the tapir of Sumatra; beliefs in legendary "corpse-headed barbarians" whose heads left their bodies at night and caused infants to die; the division of coastal Indians into five classes, which correspond to the four Hindu varnas and a separate Muslim class; and the fact that traders in the Indian port of Calicut° could perform error-free calculations by counting on their fingers and toes rather than using the Chinese abacus. After his return, the interpreter went on tour in China, telling of these exotic places and "how far the majestic virtue of [China's] imperial dynasty extended."[1]

Interest in new contacts was not confined to the Chinese side. In 1415–1416, at least three trading cities on the Swahili° Coast of East Africa sent delegations to China. Although no record of African and Chinese reactions to one another survives, China's lavish gifts to local rulers stimulated the Swahili market for silk and porcelain.

The Atlantic Ocean

The Vikings, northern European raiders and pirates, used their small, open ships to attack coastal European settlements for several centuries. They also discovered and settled one island after another in the North Atlantic. Like the Polynesians, the Vikings had neither maps nor navigational devices. They found their way using their knowledge of the heavens and the seas.

The Vikings first settled Iceland in 770. From there, some moved on to Greenland in 982, and one group sighted North America in 986. Fifteen years later, Leif Ericsson established a short-lived Viking settlement on the island of Newfoundland, which he called Vinland. When the climate turned colder after 1200, the northern settlements in Greenland went into decline. Vinland became a mysterious place mentioned in Norse sagas.

Some southern Europeans also explored the Atlantic. In 1291, two Vivaldo brothers from Genoa set out to sail around Africa to India. They were never heard of again. Other Genoese and Portuguese expeditions into the Atlantic in the fourteenth century discovered (and settled) the islands of Madeira°, the Azores°, and the Canaries.

Mention also occurs of African voyages of exploration in the Atlantic. The Syrian geographer al-Umari (1301–1349) relates that when Mansa Kankan Musa°, the ruler of the West African empire of Mali, passed through Egypt on his lavish pilgrimage to Mecca in 1324, he told of voyages to cross the Atlantic undertaken by his predecessor, Mansa Muhammad. Muhammad had sent out four hundred vessels with men and supplies, telling them, "Do not return until you have reached the

---

Zheng He (jung huh)   **Calicut** (KAL-ih-kut)

Swahili (swah-HEE-lee)   **Madeira** (muh-DEER-uh)
Azores (A-zorz)
Mansa Kankan Musa (MAHN-suh KAHN-kahn MOO-suh)

CHRONOLOGY

	Pacific Ocean	Atlantic Ocean	Indian Ocean
Pre-1400	**400–1300** Polynesian settlement of Pacific islands	**770–1200** Viking voyages **1300s** Settlement of Madeira, Azores, Canaries **Early 1300s** Mali voyages	
1400 to 1500		**1418–1460** Voyages of Henry the Navigator **1440s** Slaves from West Africa **1482** Portuguese at Gold Coast and Kongo **1486** Portuguese at Benin **1488** Bartolomeu Dias reaches Indian Ocean **1492** Columbus reaches Caribbean **1493** Columbus returns to Caribbean (second voyage) **1498** Columbus reaches mainland of South America (third voyage) **1492–1500** Spanish conquer Hispaniola	**1405–1433** Voyages of Zheng He **1498** Vasco da Gama reaches India
1500 to 1550		**1500** Cabral reaches Brazil **1513** Ponce de León explores Florida **1519–1520** Cortés conquers Aztec Empire **1531–1533** Pizarro conquers Inca Empire	**1505** Portuguese bombard Swahili Coast cities **1510** Portuguese take Goa **1511** Portuguese take Malacca **1515** Portuguese take Hormuz **1535** Portuguese take Diu **1538** Portuguese defeat Ottoman fleet **1539** Portuguese aid Ethiopia
	1519–1522 Magellan expedition		

other side of the ocean or if you have exhausted your food or water." After a long time, one canoe returned, reporting the others had been swept away by a "violent current in the middle of the sea." Muhammad himself then set out at the head of a second, even larger, expedition, from which no one returned.

On the other side of the Atlantic, Amerindian voyagers from South America colonized the West Indies. By the year 1000, Amerindians known as the **Arawak°** had moved from the small islands of the Lesser Antilles (Barbados, Martinique,

Arawak (AR-uh-wahk)

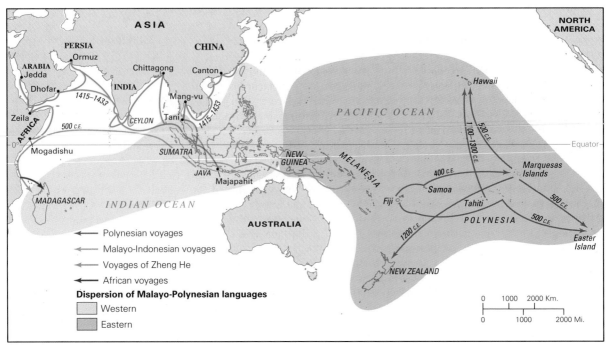

Map 15.1   Exploration and Settlement in the Indian and Pacific Oceans Before 1500   Over many centuries, mariners originating in Southeast Asia gradually colonized the islands of the Pacific and Indian Oceans. The Chinese voyages led by Zheng He in the fifteenth century were lavish official expeditions.

Guadaloupe) into the Greater Antilles (Cuba, Hispaniola, Jamaica, and Puerto Rico), as well as into the Bahamas. Another people, the Carib, followed their route. By the late fifteenth century, they had overrun most Arawak settlements in the Lesser Antilles and were raiding parts of the Greater Antilles. From the West Indies, Arawak and Carib also undertook voyages to the North American mainland.

IBERIAN EXPANSION, 1400–1550

The preceding survey shows that maritime exploration occurred in many parts of the world before 1450. The sea voyages sponsored by the Iberian kingdoms of Portugal and Spain attract special interest because they began a maritime revolution that profoundly altered the course of world history. The Portuguese and Spanish expeditions ended the isolation of the Americas and increased global interaction. The influence in world affairs of the Iberians and other Europeans who followed them overseas rose steadily after 1500.

Iberian overseas expansion arose from two related phenomena. First, Iberian rulers had strong economic, religious, and political motives to expand their contacts and increase their dominance. Second, improvements in maritime and military technologies gave them the means to master treacherous and unfamiliar ocean environments, seize control of existing maritime trade routes, and conquer new lands.

Background to Iberian Expansion

In many ways, these voyages continued four trends evident in the Latin West from about the year 1000:

Polynesian Canoes
Sailing canoes such as these, shown in an eighteenth-century painting, made long voyages of exploration and settlement. A large platform connects two canoes at the left, providing more room for the expedition. A sail supplements the paddlers. ("Tereoboo, King of Owyhee, bringing presents to Captain Cook," D. L. Ref. p. xx 2f. 35. Courtesy, The Dixon Library, State Library of New South Wales)

(1) the revival of urban life and trade, (2) a struggle with Islamic powers for dominance of the Mediterranean that mixed religious motives with the desire for trade with distant lands, (3) growing intellectual curiosity about the outside world, and (4) a peculiarly European alliance between merchants and rulers.

The city-states of northern Italy took the lead in all of these developments. By 1450, they had well-established trade links to northern Europe, the Indian Ocean, and the Black Sea, and their merchant princes had sponsored an intellectual and artistic Renaissance. But the Italian states did not take the lead in exploring the Atlantic, even after the expansion of the Ottoman Empire in the fourteenth and fifteenth centuries disrupted their trade to the East (see Chapter 19), because Venice and Genoa preferred to continue the lucrative alliances with Muslims that had given their merchants privileged positions and because Mediterranean ships were ill suited to the more violent weather of the Atlantic. However, many individual Italians played leading roles in Atlantic exploration.

By contrast, the Iberian kingdoms had engaged in anti-Muslim warfare since the eighth century, when Muslim forces overran most of the peninsula. By about 1250, the Iberian kingdoms of Portugal, Castile, and Aragon had conquered all the Muslim lands in Iberia except the southern kingdom of Granada, which finally fell to the united kingdom of Castile and Aragon in 1492 (see Chapter 14). These territories gradually amalgamated to form Spain, sixteenth-century Europe's most powerful state.

Christian militancy continued to drive Portugal and Spain in their overseas ventures. But the Iberian rulers and their adventurous subjects also sought material returns. Their small share of the Mediterranean trade made them more willing than the Italians to take risks to find new routes to Africa and Asia through the Atlantic. Moreover, both kingdoms participated in the shipbuilding changes and the gunpowder revolution under way in Atlantic Europe. Though not centers of Renaissance learning, both states had exceptional rulers who appreciated new geographical knowledge.

Portuguese Voyages

When the Muslim government of Morocco in northwestern Africa weakened in the fifteenth century, the Portuguese went on the attack, beginning with the city of Ceuta° in 1415. This assault combined aspects of a religious crusade, a plundering expedition, and a military tournament in which young Portuguese knights displayed their bravery. Despite the capture of several more ports along Morocco's Atlantic coast, the Portuguese could not

Ceuta (say-OO-tuh)

Chinese Junk This modern drawing compares one of Zheng He's ships with one of Vasco da Gama's. Watertight interior bulkheads made junks the most seaworthy large ships of the fifteenth century. Sails were made of pleated bamboo matting. A stern rudder provided steering. European ships had greater speed and maneuverability. (Dugald Stermer)

push inland and gain access to the gold trade they learned about, so they sought more direct contact with the gold producers by sailing down the African coast.

Young Prince Henry (1394–1460), third son of the king of Portugal, led the attack on Ceuta. Because he devoted the rest of his life to promoting exploration, he is known as **Henry the Navigator.** His official biographer emphasized his desire to convert Africans to Christianity, make contact with Christian rulers believed to exist in Africa, and launch joint crusades with them against the Ottomans. Profit also figured in his dreams. His initial explorations focused on Africa. His ships established permanent contact with the islands of Madeira in 1418 and the Azores in 1439. Only later did reaching India become a goal.

"The Navigator" himself never ventured farther from home than North Africa. Instead, he founded a sort of research institute at Sagres° for studying navigation and collecting information about new lands. His staff drew on the pioneering efforts of Italian merchants, especially the

Genoese, who had learned some of the secrets of the trans-Saharan trade, and of fourteenth-century Jewish cartographers who used information from Arab and European sources to produce remarkably accurate sea charts and maps of distant places. They also studied and improved navigational instruments that had come into Europe from China and the Islamic world: the magnetic compass, first developed in China, and the astrolabe, an instrument of Arab or Greek invention that enabled mariners to determine their latitude by measuring the position of the sun or the stars.

The Portuguese developed a new type of long-distance sailing vessel, the **caravel°.** The many-oared galleys of the Mediterranean could not carry enough food and water for long ocean voyages. The three-masted ships of the North Atlantic, powered by square sails, could not sail at much of an angle against the wind. The caravel, which was only one-fifth the size of the largest European ships and the large Chinese junks, could enter shallow coastal waters and explore upriver, yet it had the strength to weather ocean storms. When equipped with la-

Sagres (SAH-gresh)

caravel (KAR-uh-vel)

teen sails, caravels had great maneuverability and could sail deeply into the wind; when sporting square Atlantic sails, they had great speed. The addition of small cannon made them good fighting ships as well. The caravels' economy, speed, agility, and power justified a contemporary's claim that they were "the best ships that sailed the seas."[2]

Pioneering captains had to overcome crews' fears that the South Atlantic waters were boiling hot and contained ocean currents that would prevent their ever returning home. It took Prince Henry from 1420 to 1434 to coax an expedition to venture beyond southern Morocco in northwest Africa (see Map 15.2). The next stretch of coast, 800 miles (1,300 kilometers) of desert, offered little of interest to the explorers. Finally in 1444, the mariners reached the Senegal River and the populous, well-watered lands below the Sahara beginning at what they named Cape Verde (Green Cape) because of its vegetation.

In the years that followed, Henry's explorers learned how to return speedily to Portugal. Instead of battling the prevailing northeast trade winds and currents back up the coast, they discovered that by sailing northwest into the Atlantic to the latitude of the Azores, ships could pick up prevailing westerly winds that would blow them back to Portugal. The knowledge that ocean winds tend to form large circular patterns helped explorers discover many other ocean routes.

To pay for the research, ships, and expeditions, Prince Henry drew partly on the income of the Order of Christ, a military religious order of which he was the governor. The Order of Christ had been founded to inherit the Portuguese properties and the crusading tradition of the Order of Knights Templar (see Chapter 7), which had disbanded in 1314. The Order of Christ received the exclusive right to promote Christianity in all the lands that were discovered, and the Portuguese emblazoned their ships' sails with the crusaders' red cross.

The first financial returns came from selling into slavery Africans captured in raids on the northwest coast of Africa and the Canary Islands during the 1440s. The Portuguese had captured or purchased eighty thousand Africans by the end of the century. However, gold quickly became more important than slavery. By 1457, enough African gold was coming back to Portugal for the kingdom

to issue a new gold coin called the cruzado (crusade), another reminder of how deeply the Portuguese entwined religious and secular motives.

By the time Prince Henry died in 1460, his explorers had established a base of operations in the uninhabited Cape Verde Islands and explored 600 miles (950 kilometers) of coast beyond Cape Verde, as far as what they named Sierra Leone° (Lion Mountain). From there, they knew the coast of Africa curved sharply toward the east. After spending four decades covering the 1,500 miles (2,400 kilometers) from Lisbon to Sierra Leone, Portuguese explorers traveled the remaining 4,000 miles (6,400 kilometers) to the continent's southern tip in only three decades.

Royal sponsorship continued, but private commercial participation sped the progress. In 1469, a Lisbon merchant named Fernão Gomes purchased from the Crown the privilege of exploring 350 miles (550 kilometers) of new coast a year for five years and a monopoly on any resulting trade. Gomes discovered the uninhabited island of São Tomé° on the equator; in the next century, it became a major source of sugar produced with African slave labor. He also explored what later Europeans called the **Gold Coast,** which became the headquarters of Portugal's West African trade.

The expectation of finding a passage around Africa to the Indian Ocean spurred the final thrust down the African coast. **Bartolomeu Dias** rounded the southern tip of Africa (in 1488) and entered the Indian Ocean. In 1497–1498, **Vasco da Gama** led a Portuguese expedition around Africa to India. In 1500, ships in an expedition under Pedro Alvares Cabral°, while swinging wide to the west in the South Atlantic to catch the winds that would sweep them around southern Africa and on to India, came on the eastern coast of South America, laying the basis for Portugal's later claim to Brazil.

Spanish Voyages

Spain's early discoveries owed more to haste and blind luck than to careful planning. Only in the last decade of the fifteenth century did the Spanish monarchs turn their

---

Sierra Leone (see-ER-uh lee-OWN)
São Tomé (sow toh-MAY)   Cabral (kah-BRAHL)

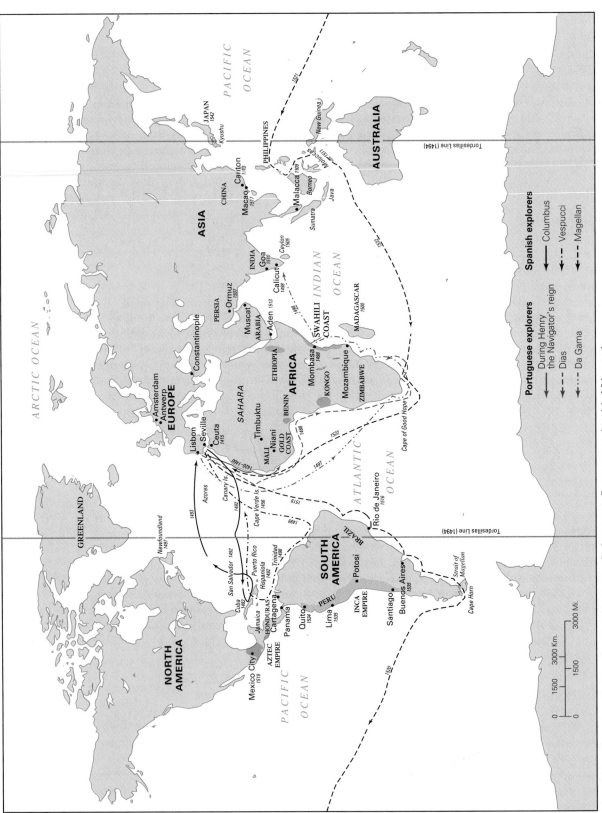

Map 15.2 European Exploration, 1420–1542 Before 1540, European trade with Africa and Asia exceeded that with the Americas. After the conquest of the Aztec and Inca Empires, transatlantic trade increased. Notice the Tordesillas line that theoretically separated Spanish and Portuguese spheres of activity.

Portuguese explorers
During Henry the Navigator's reign
Dias
Da Gama

Spanish explorers
Columbus
Vespucci
Magellan

ARCTIC OCEAN

PACIFIC OCEAN

JAPAN *1542*
Kyushu

CHINA
Canton *1513*
Macao *1517*

ASIA

PHILIPPINES

New Guinea

AUSTRALIA

Molucca *1511*

Malacca *1511*
Borneo
Java
Sumatra

INDIA
Goa *1510*
Ceylon *1505*
Calicut *1498*

PERSIA
Ormuz *1507*
Muscat
ARABIA
Aden *1513*

ETHIOPIA

SWAHILI COAST
INDIAN OCEAN

Mombasa *1498*
KONGO
Mozambique
ZIMBABWE

MADAGASCAR *1500*

Cape of Good Hope

Tordesillas Line (1494)

EUROPE
Amsterdam
Antwerp
Constantinople
Lisbon
Seville
Ceuta *1415*

SAHARA
Timbuktu
MALI
Niani
GOLD COAST
BENIN
AFRICA

1420–1460
1497
1522
1488

ATLANTIC OCEAN

Azores
Canary Is. *1492*
Cape Verde Is. *1456*

1493
1499
1519

GREENLAND

Newfoundland *1497*

San Salvador *1492*
Cuba
Puerto Rico
Hispaniola *1492*
Trinidad
Jamaica
HONDURAS
Cartagena
Panama

NORTH AMERICA

Mexico City *1519*
AZTEC EMPIRE

PACIFIC OCEAN

Quito *1534*
Lima *1535*
PERU
INCA EMPIRE
Potosí
Santiago
Buenos Aires *1535*

BRAZIL
Rio de Janeiro *1516*

SOUTH AMERICA

Strait of Magellan
Cape Horn

Tordesillas Line (1494)

1520
1522

0   1500   3000 Km.
0   1500   3000 Mi.

attention from reconquest and organization of previously Muslim territories to overseas exploration. By this time, the Portuguese had already found their route to the Indian Ocean.

The leader of their overseas mission would be **Christopher Columbus** (1451–1506), a Genoese mariner. His three voyages between 1492 and 1498 would reveal the existence of vast and unexpected lands across the Atlantic. But this momentous discovery fell disappointingly short of Columbus's intention of finding a new route to the Indian Ocean even shorter than that of the Portuguese.

As a younger man, Columbus had gained considerable experience while participating in Portuguese explorations along the African coast, but he dreamed of a shorter way to the riches of the East. By his reckoning (based on a serious misreading of a ninth-century Arab authority), a mere 2,400 nautical miles (4,450 kilometers) separated the Canary Islands from Japan. The actual distance was five times greater.

Portuguese authorities twice rejected his plan to reach the East by sailing west, first in 1485 following a careful study and again in 1488 after Dias had established the feasibility of the African route. Columbus received more sympathy, but initially no support, from Queen Isabella of Castile. A Castilian commission appointed by Isabella studied the proposal for four years and concluded that a westward sea route to the Indies rested on questionable geographical assumptions. Nevertheless, Columbus's persistence finally won over the queen and her husband, King Ferdinand of Aragon. In 1492, elated perhaps by finally expelling the Muslims from Granada, they agreed to fund a modest expedition.

Columbus recorded in his log that the *Santa María*, the *Santa Clara* (nicknamed the *Niña*), and a vessel now known only by its nickname, the *Pinta,* with a mostly Spanish crew of ninety men "departed Friday the third day of August of the year 1492," toward "the regions of India." Their mission, the royal contract stated, was "to discover and acquire certain islands and mainland in the Ocean Sea." Columbus carried letters of introduction from the Spanish sovereigns to Eastern rulers, including one to the "Grand Khan" (meaning the Chinese emperor). An Arabic-speaking Jewish convert to Christianity had the job of communicating with the peoples of eastern Asia.

Unfavorable headwinds had discouraged other attempts to explore the Atlantic west of the Azores. But on earlier voyages along the African coast, Columbus had learned about winds blowing westward at the latitude of the Canaries. After reaching the Canaries, he replaced the *Niña*'s lateen sails with square sails, for he knew that from then on, speed would be more important than maneuverability since his supplies would last for only a fixed number of days.

In October, the expedition encountered the islands of the Caribbean. Columbus called the inhabitants "Indians" because he believed he had reached the East Indies. A second voyage in 1493 did nothing to change his mind. On a third voyage in 1498, two months after Vasco da Gama reached India, Columbus sighted the mainland of South America, which he insisted was part of Asia. But by then, other Europeans had become convinced that his discoveries were of lands previously unknown to the Old World (Europe, Asia, and Africa). Amerigo Vespucci's explorations, first on behalf of Spain and then for Portugal, led mapmakers to name the new continents "America," after him.

To prevent disputes about exploiting these new lands and spreading Christianity among their peoples, Spain and Portugal agreed to split the world between them. The Treaty of Tordesillas°, negotiated by the pope in 1494, drew an imaginary north-south line down the middle of the Atlantic Ocean. Lands east of the line in Africa and southern Asia could be claimed by Portugal; lands to the west in the Americas belonged to Spain. Cabral's discovery of Brazil, however, gave Portugal a valid claim to the part of South America that bulged east of the line.

But if the Tordesillas line were extended around the earth, where would Spain's and Portugal's spheres of influence divide in the East? Given European ignorance of the earth's true size in 1494, no one knew whether the Moluccas°, the source of the valuable spices of the East Indies, belonged to Portugal or Spain. The missing information concerned

---

Tordesillas (tor-duh-SEE-yuhs)
Moluccas (muh-LOO-kuhz)

the size of the Pacific Ocean, which a Spanish adventurer named Vasco Núñez de Balboa° had spotted in 1513 when he crossed the isthmus (a narrow neck of land) of Panama from the east. The 1519 expedition of **Ferdinand Magellan** (ca. 1480–1521) sought to complete Columbus's interrupted westward voyage by sailing around the Americas and across the Pacific. The Moluccas turned out to lie well within Portugal's sphere, as Spain formally acknowledged in 1529.

Magellan's voyage laid the basis for Spanish colonization of the Philippine Islands after 1564. It also gave Magellan credit, despite his death, for being the first person to encircle the globe, for a decade earlier, he had sailed from Europe to the East Indies on an expedition sponsored by his native Portugal.

Columbus and those who followed in his path laid the basis for the colonial empires of Spain and other European nations. In turn, these empires promoted, among the four Atlantic continents, a new trading network whose importance rivaled and eventually surpassed that of the Indian Ocean. Of more immediate importance, Portugal's entry into the Indian Ocean led quickly to a major European presence and profit. Both the eastward and the westward voyages of exploration marked a tremendous expansion of Europe's role in world history.

ENCOUNTERS WITH EUROPE, 1450–1550

The ways in which Africans, Asians, and Amerindians perceived their European visitors and interacted with them influenced their future relations. Some welcomed the Europeans as potential allies; others viewed them as rivals or enemies. In general, Africans and Asians readily recognized the benefits and dangers of European contact. However, the long isolation of the Amerindians added to the strangeness of their encounter with the Spanish and made them more

vulnerable to the unfamiliar diseases they inadvertently introduced.

Western Africa

Many Africans welcomed trade with the Portuguese, which gave them new markets for their exports and access to imports cheaper than those coming by caravan across the Sahara. Miners in the hinterland of the Gold Coast, which the Portuguese first visited in 1471, had long sold their gold to merchants from trading cities along the southern edge of the Sahara for transshipment to North Africa. Recognizing the possibility of more favorable trading terms, coastal Africans negotiated with the royal representative of Portugal, who arrived in 1482 seeking permission to erect a trading fort.

The Portuguese noble in charge and his officers (likely including the young Christopher Columbus, who had entered Portuguese service in 1476) strove to make a proper impression. They dressed in their best clothes, erected a fancy reception platform, celebrated a Catholic Mass, and signaled the start of negotiations with trumpets, tambourines, and drums. The African king, Caramansa, staged his entrance with equal ceremony, arriving with a large retinue of attendants and musicians. Through an African interpreter, the two leaders exchanged flowery speeches pledging goodwill and mutual benefit. Caramansa then gave permission for a small trading fort, assured, he said, by the appearance of these royal delegates that they were honorable persons, unlike the "few, foul, and vile" Portuguese visitors of the previous decade.

Neither side made a show of force, but Caramansa warned that if the Portuguese failed to be peaceful and honest traders, he and his people would move away and deprive their post of food and trade. Trade at the post of Saint George of the Mine (later called Elmina) enriched both sides. The Portuguese crown was soon purchasing gold amounting to one-tenth of the world's production at the time. In return, Africans received shiploads of goods brought by the Portuguese from Asia, Europe, and other parts of Africa.

Early contacts involved a mixture of commercial, military, and religious interests. Some African rulers quickly saw the value of European firearms.

Balboa (bal-BOH-uh)

Afro-Portuguese Ivory   An ivory carver from the kingdom of Benin probably made this saltcellar. Intended for a European market, it depicts a Portuguese ship on the cover and Portuguese nobles around the base.   (Courtesy of the Trustees of the British Museum)

Coastal rulers also proved willing to test the value of Christian practices, which the Portuguese eagerly promoted. The rulers of Benin and Kongo, the largest coastal kingdoms, invited Portuguese missionaries and soldiers to accompany them into battle to test the Christians' religion along with their muskets.

The kingdom of Benin in the Niger Delta, near the peak of its power after a century of aggressive expansion, had a large capital city, also known as Benin. Its *oba* (king) responded to a Portuguese visit in 1486 by sending an ambassador to Portugal to learn more about their homeland. Then he established a royal monopoly on Portuguese trade, selling pepper and ivory tusks (to be taken back to Portugal) as well as stone beads, textiles, and prisoners of war (to be resold at Elmina). In return, Portuguese merchants provided Benin with copper and brass, fine textiles, glass beads, and a horse for the king's royal procession. In the early six-

teenth century, as the demand for slaves for the Portuguese sugar plantations on the nearby island of São Tomé grew, the oba first raised the price of slaves and then imposed restrictions on their sale.

Efforts to spread Catholicism ultimately failed. Early kings showed some interest, but after 1538, the rulers declined to receive further missionaries. They also closed the market in male slaves for the rest of the sixteenth century. Both steps illustrate their power to control how much interaction they wanted.

Farther south, on the lower Congo River, the *manikongo*° (king) of Kongo also sent delegates to Portugal, established a royal monopoly on trade, and expressed interest in missionary teachings. But here the royal family made Catholicism the kingdom's official faith. Lacking ivory and pepper, Kongo sold more and more slaves to acquire the goods brought by the Portuguese and pay missionary expenses.

Soon the royal trade monopoly broke down. In 1526, the Christian manikongo, Afonso I (r. 1506–ca. 1540), wrote to his royal "brother," the king of Portugal, begging for his help in stopping the slave trade because unauthorized Kongolese were kidnapping and selling people, even members of good families. Afonso's appeal that contacts be limited to "some priests and a few people to teach in the schools, and no other goods except wine and flour for the holy sacrament" received no reply. After 1540, the major part of the slave trade from this part of Africa moved farther south.

Eastern Africa

As Vasco da Gama sailed up the eastern coast of Africa in 1498, most rulers of the coastal trading states received him coolly. Visitors who painted crusader crosses on their sails raised their suspicions. The ruler of Malindi, however, saw in the Portuguese an ally who could help him expand Malindi's trade, and he provided da Gama with a pilot to guide him to India. The suspicions of most rulers came to fruition seven years later when a Portuguese war fleet bombarded and looted most of the coastal cities in the name of Christ and commerce. It spared Malindi.

manikongo (mah-NEE-KONG-goh)

Christian Ethiopia also saw benefits in allying with the Portuguese. In the fourteenth and fifteenth centuries, Ethiopian conflicts with Muslim states along the Red Sea increased. After the Ottoman Turks conquered Egypt and launched a fleet in the Indian Ocean to counter the Portuguese in 1517, the warlord of the Muslim state of Adal attacked Ethiopia. A decisive victory in 1529 put the Christian kingdom in jeopardy, making Portuguese support a crucial matter.

For decades, delegations from Portugal and Ethiopia had talked of a Christian alliance. Queen Helena of Ethiopia, who acted as regent for her young sons after her husband's death in 1478, sent a letter in 1509 to "our very dear and well-beloved brother," the king of Portugal, along with a gift of two tiny crucifixes said to be made of wood from the cross Christ was crucified on. She proposed to combine her land army and Portugal's fleet against the Turks. At her death in 1522, no alliance had come into being, but the worsening situation brought renewed Ethiopian appeals.

Finally, a small Portuguese force commanded by Vasco da Gama's son Christopher reached Ethiopia in 1539. With Portuguese help, another queen rallied the desperate Ethiopians. Muslim foes captured Christopher da Gama and tortured him to death but lost heart when their leader fell in battle. Portuguese aid helped save the Ethiopian kingdom from extinction, but Ethiopia's refusal to transfer their Christian affiliation from the patriarch of Alexandria to the pope prevented a permanent alliance.

As these examples illustrate, African encounters with the Portuguese before 1550 varied considerably. Africans and Portuguese might become royal brothers, bitter opponents, or partners in a mutually profitable trade, but Europeans were still a minor presence in most of Africa in 1550. The Indian Ocean trade by then was occupying most of their attention.

Indian Ocean States

Vasco da Gama's arrival on the Malabar Coast of India in May 1498 did not impress the citizens of Calicut. The Chinese fleets of gigantic junks that had called at Calicut sixty-five years earlier dwarfed his four small ships, which were no larger than many of the dhows° already filling the harbor. The *samorin* (ruler) of Calicut and his Muslim officials showed mild interest, but the gifts da Gama brought evoked derisive laughter: twelve pieces of striped cloth, four scarlet hoods, six hats, and six wash basins. When da Gama defended his gifts as those of an explorer, not a merchant, the samorin cut him short, asking whether he had come to discover men or stones: "If he had come to discover men, as he said, why had he brought nothing?"

Coastal rulers soon discovered that the Portuguese had no intention of remaining poor competitors in the Indian Ocean trade. Upon da Gama's return to Portugal in 1499, the jubilant King Manuel styled himself "Lord of the Conquest, Navigation, and Commerce of Ethiopia, Arabia, Persia, and India." Previously, the Indian Ocean had been an open sea, used by merchants (and pirates) of all the surrounding coasts. Now the Portuguese crown intended to make it Portugal's sea, which others might use only on Portuguese terms.

Portugal's hope of controlling the Indian Ocean stemmed from the superiority of its ships and weapons over the smaller and lightly armed merchant dhows. In 1505, the Portuguese fleet of 81 ships and some 7,000 men bombarded Swahili Coast cities. Goa, on the west coast of India, fell to a well-armed fleet in 1510, becoming the base from which the Portuguese menaced the trading cities of Gujarat° to the north and Calicut and other Malabar Coast cities to the south. The port of Hormuz, controlling the entry to the Persian Gulf, fell in 1515. Aden, at the entrance to the Red Sea, preserved its independence, but the capture of the Gujarati port of Diu in 1535 consolidated Portuguese dominance of the western Indian Ocean.

Farther east, the independent city of Malacca° on the strait separating the Malay Peninsula and Sumatra became the focus of their attention. During the fifteenth century, Malacca had become the main entrepôt° (a place where goods are stored or deposited and from which they are distributed) for the trade from China, Japan, India, the Southeast Asian mainland, and the Moluccas. The city's

---

dhow (dow)   **Gujarat** (goo-juh-RAHT)
Malacca (muh-LAH-kuh)   **entrepôt** (ON-truh-poh)

100,000 residents spoke eighty-four different languages, according to a Portuguese source, and included merchants from Cairo, Ethiopia, and the Swahili Coast. Many non-Muslim residents supported letting the Portuguese join this cosmopolitan trading community, perhaps to offset the growing solidarity of Muslim traders. In 1511, however, the Portuguese seized Malacca with a force of a thousand fighting men, including three hundred recruited in southern India.

On the China coast, local officials and merchants persuaded the imperial government to allow the Portuguese to establish a trading post at Macao° in 1557. Subsequently, Portuguese ships nearly monopolized trade between China and Japan.

Control of the major port cities enabled the Portuguese to enforce their demands that all spices be carried in Portuguese ships, as well as all goods on the major ocean routes such as between Goa and Macao. The Portuguese also tried to control and tax other Indian Ocean trade. Merchant ships entering and leaving their ports had to carry a Portuguese passport and pay customs duties. Portuguese patrols seized vessels that did not comply, confiscated their cargoes, and either killed the captain and crew or sentenced them to forced labor.

Reactions to this power grab varied. Like the emperors of China, the Mughal° emperors of India largely ignored Portugal's maritime intrusions (see Chapters 12 and 19). The Ottomans confronted the Christian intruders more aggressively. They supported Egypt's defensive efforts from 1501 to 1509 and then sent their own fleet into the Indian Ocean in 1538. However, Ottoman galleys proved no match for the faster, better-armed Portuguese vessels in the open ocean. They retained their advantage only in the Red Sea and Persian Gulf, where they controlled many ports.

Smaller trading states could not challenge the Portuguese. Mutual rivalry kept them from forming a common front. Some cooperated with the Portuguese to safeguard their prosperity and security. Others engaged in evasion and resistance.

When the merchants of Calicut put up sustained resistance, the Portuguese embargoed all trade with Aden, Calicut's principal trading partner, and centered their trade on the port of Cochin,

Macao (muh-COW) Mughal (MOO-gahl)

which had once been a dependency of Calicut. Some Calicut merchants evaded their patrols, but Calicut's importance shrank as Cochin gradually became the major pepper-exporting port on the Malabar Coast.

Farther north, Gujarat initially resisted Portuguese attempts at monopoly and in 1509 joined Egypt's futile effort to sweep the Portuguese from the Arabian Sea. But in 1535, with his state weakened by Mughal attacks, the ruler allowed the Portuguese to build a fort at Diu in return for their support. Once established, the Portuguese gradually extended their control. By midcentury, they were licensing and taxing all Gujarati ships. Even after the Mughals took control of Gujarat in 1572, the Mughal emperor, Akbar, permitted the Portuguese to continue their maritime monopoly in return for allowing one pilgrim ship a year to sail to Mecca without paying a fee.

The Portuguese never gained complete control of the Indian Ocean trade, but their domination of key ports and trade routes brought them considerable profit in the form of spices and other luxury goods. The Portuguese broke the trading monopoly of Venice and Genoa by selling pepper for less than what they charged for shipments obtained through Egyptian middlemen.

The Americas

In the Americas, the Spanish established a vast territorial empire, in contrast to the trading empire of the Portuguese. The Spanish kingdoms drew on somewhat greater resources, but the Spanish and Portuguese monarchies had similar motives for expansion and used identical ships and weapons. The isolation of the Amerindian peoples provided a key difference. The first European settlers in the Caribbean resorted to conquest and plunder rather than trade. They later extended this practice to the more powerful Amerindian kingdoms on the American mainland. After 1518, deadly epidemics among the Amerindians weakened their ability to resist.

The Arawak whom Columbus first encountered on Hispaniola (modern Haiti and the Dominican Republic) in the Greater Antilles and the Bahamas to the north cultivated maize (corn), cassava (a tuber), sweet potatoes, and hot peppers, as well as cotton

Arawak Women Making Tortillas   This sixteenth-century woodcut depicts techniques of food preparation in the West Indies. The woman at the left grinds cornmeal on a metate. The woman in the center pats cornmeal dough flat and fries the tortillas. The third woman serves tortillas with a bowl of stew.   (Courtesy of the John Carter Brown Library at Brown University)

and tobacco. They mined and worked gold, but they did not trade gold, nor did they have iron. They extended a cautious welcome to Columbus but told him exaggerated stories about gold in other places to persuade him to move on.

Columbus brought with him several hundred settlers from southern Iberia, as well as missionaries, on his second trip to Hispaniola in 1493. The settlers stole gold ornaments, confiscated food, and raped women (see Society and Culture: European Male Sexual Dominance Overseas), provoking the Hispaniola Arawak to war in 1495. With the advantage of horses and body armor, the Spaniards slaughtered tens of thousands of Arawak and forced the survivors to pay a heavy tax in gold, spun cotton, and food. Whoever failed to meet the quotas faced forced labor. Meanwhile, the cattle, pigs, and goats introduced by the settlers devoured the Arawak's food crops, causing deaths from famine and disease. A governor appointed by the Spanish crown in 1502 forced the Arawak on Hispaniola to become laborers under the control of Spanish settlers.

The actions of the Spanish in the Antilles reflected Spanish behavior during the wars against the Muslims in the previous centuries. They sought to serve God by defeating, controlling, and converting nonbelievers and to become rich in the process. Individual **conquistadors**° (conquerors) extended that pattern around the Caribbean. Some raided the Bahamas for gold and labor as both grew scarce on Hispaniola. Arawak from the Bahamas served as slaves on Hispaniola. Juan Ponce de León (1460–1521), a veteran of the conquest of Muslim Spain and the seizure of Hispaniola, conquered the island of Borinquen (Puerto Rico) in 1508 and in 1513 explored southeastern Florida.

An ambitious and ruthless nobleman, **Hernán Cortés**° (1485–1547), led the most audacious expedition to the mainland. Cortés left Cuba in 1519 with six hundred fighting men and most of the island's weapons to assault the Mexican mainland in search of slaves and trade. Learning of the rich Aztec Empire in central Mexico, Cortés expanded on the American mainland the exploitation and conquest carried out in the Greater Antilles.

Many of the Amerindians whom the Aztecs had subjugated during the previous century resented the tribute, forced labor, and the large-scale human sacrifices to Aztec gods their rulers imposed on them (see Chapter 10). Some gave the Spanish their support as allies against the Aztecs. Like the Caribbean people, the mainland Amerindians had no precedent by which to judge these strangers. Later accounts suggest that some believed Cortés to be the legendary ruler Quetzalcoatl°, whose return to earth had been prophesied, and treated him with great deference.

Another consequence of millennia of isolation proved even more fatal: the lack of acquired immunity to Old World diseases. Smallpox, the most deadly of the early epidemics, appeared for the first time on the island of Hispaniola late in 1518. An infected member of the Cortés expedition then transmitted smallpox to Mexico in 1519, where it spread with deadly efficiency.

---

conquistador (kon-KEY-stuh-dor)   **Cortés** (kor-TEZ)
Quetzalcoatl (ket-zahl-COH-ah-tal)

European Male Sexual Dominance Overseas

European expansion and colonization involved mainly men. Missionaries chose celibacy; other men did not, as these two letters make clear. The first, dated 1495, is from Michele de Cuneo, an officer on Columbus's second voyage.

While I was in the boat I captured a very beautiful Carib woman, whom the said Lord Admiral [Columbus] gave to me, and with whom, having taken her into my cabin, she being naked according to their custom, I conceived desire to take pleasure. I wanted to put my desire into execution but she did not want it and treated me with her finger nails in such a manner that I wished I had never begun. But seeing that, (to tell you the end of it all), I took a rope and thrashed her well, for which she raised such unheard of screams that you would not have believed your ears. Finally we came to an agreement in such manner that I can tell you that she seemed to have been brought up in a school of harlots.

The second letter, dated 1550, is from an Italian Jesuit missionary in India to Ignatius Loyola, the founder of the Society of Jesus (the Jesuits), in Rome.

Your reverence must know that the sin of licentiousness is so widespread in these regions [India] that no check is placed upon it, which leads to great inconveniences, and to great disrespect of the sacraments. I say this of the Portuguese, who have adopted the vices and customs of the land without reserve, including the evil custom of buying droves of slaves, male and female, just as if they were sheep, large and small. There are countless men who buy droves of girls and sleep with all of them, and subsequently sell them. There are innumerable married settlers who have four, eight, or ten female slaves and sleep with them, as is common knowledge. This is carried to such excess that there was one man in Malacca who had twenty-four women of various races, all of whom were his slaves, and all of whom he enjoyed. I quote this city because it is a thing that everybody knows. Most men, as soon as they can afford to buy a female slave, almost invariably use her as a girl-friend (*amiga*), besides many other dishonesties, in my poor understanding.

What circumstances gave European men such power over indigenous women? How do the writers attribute some responsibility for these encounters to the sexual license of the women involved? Are such attributions credible?

Source: The first letter is reprinted from Samuel Eliot Morison, trans. and ed., *Journals and Other Documents in the Life and Voyages of Christopher Columbus* (New York: Heritage Press, 1963), 212. The second letter is from C. R. Boxer, *The Portuguese Seaborne Empire, 1415–1825* (New York: Knopf, 1969). Copyright © 1969 by C. R. Boxer. Reprinted by permission of Alfred A. Knopf, Inc.

The Aztec emperor **Moctezuma**° II (r. 1502–1520) sent messengers to greet Cortés and determine whether he was god or man, friend or foe. Cortés advanced steadily toward the capital, Tenochtitlan°, overcoming Aztec opposition with cavalry charges and steel swords and gaining the support of discontented tributary peoples. When the Spaniards drew near, the emperor went out in a great procession, dressed in all his finery, to welcome Cortés with gifts and flower garlands.

Despite Cortés's initial promise of friendship, Moctezuma quickly found himself a prisoner in his own palace. The Spaniards looted his treasury, melting down its gold. Soon full-scale battle broke out. The Aztecs and their supporters briefly gained the upper hand. They destroyed half the Spanish force and 4,000 of their Amerindian allies, sacrificing fifty-three Spanish prisoners and four horses to their gods and displaying their severed heads in

---

Moctezuma (mock-teh-ZOO-ma)
Tenochtitlan (teh-noch-TIT-lan)

Coronation of Emperor Moctezuma   In this painting by an unnamed Aztec artist, Moctezuma, his nose pierced by a bone, receives the crown from a prince in the palace at Tenochtitlan.   (Oronoz)

rows on pikes. Reinforcements from Cuba enabled Cortés to regain the advantage. Smallpox, which weakened and killed more of the city's defenders than died in the fighting, also assisted his capture of Tenochtitlan in 1520. One source remembered that the disease "spread over the people as a great destruction."

After the capital fell, the conquistadores took over other parts of Mexico. Then some Spaniards began eyeing the Inca Empire, stretching nearly 3,000 miles (5,000 kilometers) south from the equator and containing half of the population in South America. The Inca had conquered the inhabitants of the Andes Mountains and the Pacific coast of South America during the previous century, and their rule was not fully accepted by the subjugated peoples (see Chapter 10).

The Inca rulers administered a well-organized empire with highly productive agriculture, exquisite stone cities (such as the capital, Cuzco), and rich gold and silver mines. The power of the Inca emperor rested on the belief that he was descended from the Sun God and on an efficient system of roads and messengers that kept him informed about major events. Yet at the end of the 1520s, before the Spanish had even been heard of, smallpox claimed countless lives, perhaps including the Inca emperor in 1530.

An even more devastating threat loomed: **Francisco Pizarro°** (ca. 1478–1541) and his motley band of 180 men, 37 horses, and 2 cannon. With limited education and some military experience, Pizarro had come to the Americas in 1502 at the age of twenty-five to seek his fortune. He had participated in the conquest of Hispaniola and in Balboa's expedition across the isthmus of Panama. By 1520 a wealthy landowner and official in Panama, he nevertheless gambled his fortune on exploring the Pacific coast to a point south of the equator, where he learned of the riches of the Inca. With a license from the king of Spain, he set out from Panama in 1531 to conquer them.

In November 1532, Pizarro arranged to meet the new Inca emperor, **Atahualpa°** (r. 1531–1533), near the Andean city of Cajamarca°. With supreme boldness and brutality, Pizarro's small band grabbed Atahualpa from a rich litter borne by eighty nobles as it passed through an enclosed courtyard. Though surrounded by an Inca army of at least 40,000, the Spaniards used their cannon to create confusion while their swords sliced the emperor's lightly armed retainers and servants to pieces.

Noting the glee with which the Spaniards seized gold, silver, and emeralds, the captive Atahualpa offered them what he thought would satisfy even the greediest among them in exchange for his freedom: a roomful of gold and silver. But after receiving 13,400 pounds (6,000 kilograms) of gold and 26,000 pounds (12,000 kilograms) of silver, the Spaniards gave Atahualpa a choice: being burned at the stake as a heathen or being strangled after a Christian baptism. He chose the latter. His death and the Spanish occupation broke the unity of the Inca Empire.

In 1533, the Spaniards took Cuzco and from there set out to conquer and loot the rest of the empire. The defeat of a final rebellion in 1536 spelled the end of Inca rule. Five years later, Pizarro himself met a violent death at the hands of Spanish rivals, but the conquest of the mainland continued. Incited by the fabulous wealth of the Aztecs and Inca, conquistadores extended Spanish conquest and exploration in South and North America, dreaming of new treasuries to loot.

Pizarro (pih-ZAHR-oh)   **Atahualpa** (ah-tuh-WAHL-puh)
Cajamarca (kah-hah-MAHR-kah)

Patterns of Dominance

Within fifty years of Columbus's first landing, the Spanish had located and occupied the major population centers of the Americas and penetrated many of the more thinly populated areas. Why did the peoples of the Americas suffer a fate so different from that of peoples in Africa and Asia? Why were the Spanish able to erect a vast land empire in the Americas so quickly?

First, unfamiliar illnesses devastated the Caribbean islands and then the mainland. Contemporaries estimated that between 25 and 50 percent of those infected with smallpox died. Repeated epidemics inhibited the Amerindians' ability to regain control. Estimates of the size of the population before Columbus's arrival, based on sparse evidence, vary widely. Yet historians agree that the Amerindian population fell sharply during the sixteenth century. The Americas became a "widowed land," open to resettlement from across the Atlantic.

A second factor was Spain's superior military technology. Steel swords, protective armor, and horses gave the Spaniards an advantage over their Amerindian opponents. Though few in number, muskets and cannon provided a psychological edge. However, the Spanish conquests depended heavily on large numbers of Amerindian allies armed with indigenous weapons. The most decisive military advantage may have been the no-holds-barred fighting techniques the Spaniards had developed during their wars at home.

The third factor in Spain's conquest was the precedent established by the reconquest of Granada in 1492: forced labor, forced conversion, and the incorporation of conquered lands into a new empire.

The same three factors help explain the different outcomes elsewhere. Centuries of contacts before 1500 meant that Europeans, Africans, and Asians shared the same Old World diseases. Only very isolated peoples in Africa and Asia suffered a demographic calamity. The Iberians enjoyed a military advantage at sea, but on land they had no decisive advantage against more numerous indigenous armies. Everywhere, Iberian religious zeal went hand in hand with a desire for riches. In Iberia and America, conquest itself brought wealth. But in Africa and Asia, existing trading networks made wealth dependent on commercial domination rather than conquest.

CONCLUSION

Historians consider the century between 1450 and 1550 a turning point in world history. Some assign names: the "Vasco da Gama epoch," the "Columbian era," the "age of Magellan," or simply the "modern period." During those years, European explorers opened new long-distance trade routes across the world's oceans, for the first time establishing regular contact among all the continents. By 1550, those who followed them had broadened trading contacts with sub-Saharan Africa, gained mastery of the Indian Ocean trade routes, and conquered a land empire in the Americas.

What gave this maritime revolution unprecedented importance had more to do with what happened after 1550 than with what happened earlier. European overseas empires would endure longer than the Mongols' and would continue to expand for three and a half centuries. Unlike the Chinese, the Europeans did not turn their backs on the world after an initial burst of exploration. Not content dominating the Indian Ocean, Europeans opened in the Atlantic a maritime network of comparable wealth. They also established regular trade across the Pacific. The maritime expansion begun between 1450 and 1550 marked the beginning of an age of growing global interaction.

■ Key Terms

Zheng He	Christopher Columbus
Arawak	Ferdinand Magellan
Henry the Navigator	conquistadors
caravel	Hernán Cortés
Gold Goast	Moctezuma
Bartolomeu Dias	Francisco Pizarro
Vasco da Gama	Atahualpa

■ Suggested Reading

The selections edited by Joseph R. Levenson, *European Expansion and the Counter Example of Asia, 1300–1600* (1967), describe Chinese expansion and Western impressions of China. Janet Abu-Lughod, *Before European Hegemony: The World System, A.D. 1250–1350* (1989), affords a speculative reassessment of the Mongols and the Indian Ocean trade in creating the modern world system; she summarizes her thesis in the American Historical Association (AHA) booklet *The World System in the Thirteenth Century: Dead-End or Precursor?* (1993).

The Chinese account of Zheng He's voyages is Ma Huan, *Ying-yai Sheng-lan: "The Overall Survey of the Ocean's Shores"* [1433], edited and translated by J. V. G. Mills (1970). On Polynesian expansion, see Jesse D. Jennings, ed., *The Prehistory of Polynesia* (1979). In it, the chapter "Voyaging," by Ben R. Finney, encapsulates his *Voyage of Rediscovery: A Cultural Odyssey Through Polynesia* (1994). Felipe Fernandez-Armesto, *Before Columbus: Exploration and Colonization from the Mediterranean to the Atlantic, 1229–1492* (1987), summarizes the medieval background to European intercontinental voyages.

For the technologies of European expansion, see Carlo M. Cipolla, *Guns, Sails, and Empires: Technological Innovation and the Early Phases of European Expansion, 1400–1700* (1965; reprint, 1985), or the more advanced study by Roger C. Smith, *Vanguard of Empire: Ships of Exploration in the Age of Columbus* (1993).

Surveys of European explorations based on contemporary records include Boies Penrose, *Travel and Discovery in the Age of the Renaissance, 1420–1620* (1952); J. H. Parry, *The Age of Reconnaissance: Discovery, Exploration, and Settlement, 1450–1650* (1963); and G. V. Scammell, *The World Encompassed: The First European Maritime Empires, c. 800–1650* (1981).

C. R. Boxer, *The Portuguese Seaborne Empire, 1415–1825* (1969), gives a general account, with more detail to be found in Bailey W. Diffie and George D. Winius, *Foundations of the Portuguese Empire, 1415–1580* (1977); A. J. R. Russell-Wood, *The Portuguese Empire: A World on the Move* (1998); and Luc Cuyvers, *Into the Rising Sun: The Journey of Vasco da Gama and the Discovery of the Modern World* (1998). John William Blake, ed., *Europeans in West Africa, 1450–1560* (1942), excerpts contemporary Portuguese, Castilian, and English sources. Elaine Sanceau, *The Life of Prester John: A Chronicle of Portuguese Exploration* (1941), covers Portuguese relations with Ethiopia. *The Summa Oriental of Tomé Pires: An Account of the East, from the Red Sea to Japan, Written in Malacca and India in 1512–1515*, translated by Armando Cortesão (1944), provides a firsthand account of the Portuguese in the Indian Ocean.

For Spanish expansion, see J. H. Parry, *The Spanish Seaborne Empire* (1967). Samuel Eliot Morison's excellent *Admiral of the Ocean Sea: A Life of Christopher Columbus* (1942) is available in an abridged version as *Christopher Columbus, Mariner* (1955). Tzvetan Todorov, *The Conquest of America*, translated by Richard Howard (1985), focuses on Spanish shortcomings. Marvin Lunenfeld, ed., *1492: Discovery, Invasion, Encounter* (1991), critically examines contemporary sources and interpretations. William D. Phillips and Carla Rhan Phillips, *The Worlds of Christopher Columbus* (1992), looks at the subject in terms of modern concerns. Peggy K. Liss, *Isabel the Queen: Life and Times* (1992), affords a sympathetic account. James Lockhart's *Men of Cajamarca: A Social and Biographical Study of the First Conquerors of Peru* (1972) contains biographies of Pizarro's men. A firsthand account of Magellan's expedition is *Antonio Pigafetta, Magellan's Voyage: A Narrative Account of the First Circumnavigation*, available in a two-volume edition (1969) that includes a facsimile reprint of the manuscript.

J. H. Elliott, *The Old World and the New, 1492–1650* (1970), describes the transatlantic encounters of Europe and the Americas. Alfred W. Crosby, *The Columbian Voyages, the Columbian Exchange, and Their Historians* (1987), available as an AHA booklet, surveys the first encounters and their long-term consequences. Mark A. Burkholder and Lyman L. Johnson, *Colonial Latin America*, 2d ed. (1994), give a balanced account of the Spanish conquest.

John Thornton, *Africa and Africans in the Making of the Atlantic World, 1400–1800*, 2d ed. (1998), examines encounters with Europeans, Africa in the Atlantic economy, and African impact in the New World. *The Broken Spears: The Aztec Account of the Conquest of Mexico*, edited by Miguel Leon-Portilla (1962), presents Amerindian chronicles, as does Nathan Wachtel, *The Vision of the Vanquished: The Spanish Conquest of Peru Through Indian Eyes* (1977). Anthony Reid, *Southeast Asia in the Age of Commerce, 1450–1680*, 2 vols. (1988, 1993), deals with that region.

■ Notes

1. Ma Huan, *Ying-yai Sheng-lan: "The Overall Survey of the Ocean's Shores,"* ed. Feng Ch'eng-Chün, trans. J. V. G. Mills (Cambridge, England: Cambridge University Press, 1970), 180.
2. Alvise da Cadamosto in *The Voyages of Cadamosto and Other Documents*, ed. and trans. G. R. Crone (London: Hakluyt Society, 1937), 2.

PART FIVE

THE GLOBE ENCOMPASSED, 1500–1800

CHAPTER 16
THE TRANSFORMATION OF EUROPE, 1500–1750
CHAPTER 17
THE AMERICAS, THE ATLANTIC, AND AFRICA, 1530–1770
CHAPTER 18
SOUTHWEST ASIA AND THE INDIAN OCEAN, 1500–1750
CHAPTER 19
EASTERN EURASIA, 1500–1800

European voyages of exploration greatly expanded global commercial, cultural, and biological exchanges between 1500 and 1750. Europeans built new commercial empires that grew stronger with each passing century. The Portuguese had begun the mastery of the seas by opening trade with sub-Saharan Africa and seizing control of maritime trading networks in the Indian Ocean. Then European colonization in the Americas stimulated the growth of a new Atlantic economy. From its colonial base in Mexico, Spain also pioneered new trade routes across the Pacific to the Philippines and China. In time, the Dutch, French, and English expanded these profitable maritime trading networks.

Commerce and colonization led to new interregional demographic and cultural exchanges. The introduction of unfamiliar diseases caused severe population losses in the Americas. To meet the resulting acute labor shortage, Europeans introduced enslaved Africans in ever-growing numbers. Europeans and Africans brought new languages, religious practices, music, and forms of personal adornment to the New World. Some Europeans who spent time overseas adopted new ways and developed new tastes that they later brought back with them when they returned to Europe.

In Asia and Africa, most important changes continued to come from internal causes rather than European expansion. The Islamic world

362

saw the growth of regional empires in the Middle East, South Asia, and West Africa and continued its expansion into sub-Saharan Africa, southeastern Europe, and southern Asia. Secure from external penetration, China experienced military expansion and population growth, and the expansion of educational institutions reinforced traditional values among China's upper classes. In Japan, a strong new national government promoted economic development and stemmed foreign influence, and the development of an indigenous merchant class widened the gap between popular and elite cultures.

Some of the farthest-reaching cultural changes in this period occurred in Europe. Reformers challenged established religious and political institutions, and new scientific discoveries and humanist concerns raised questions about traditional Western values and beliefs.

Important ecological changes occurred in areas of rising population and economic activity. The spread of new plants and animals around the world enhanced food supplies and altered landscapes. Forests were cut down to meet the increasing need for farmland, lumber, and fuel. But the most significant environmental changes resulted from the growing mastery of the winds and currents that propelled European ships across the world's oceans. Europeans' leadership in navigational technology went hand in hand with their emerging dominance in military technology. Lacking an expanding economic base, the great Islamic empires and China fell behind the smaller European nations in military strength. After 1750, the consequences of this widening technological and economic gap were to become momentous.

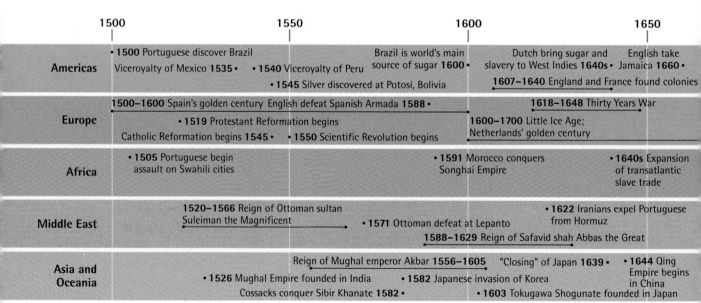

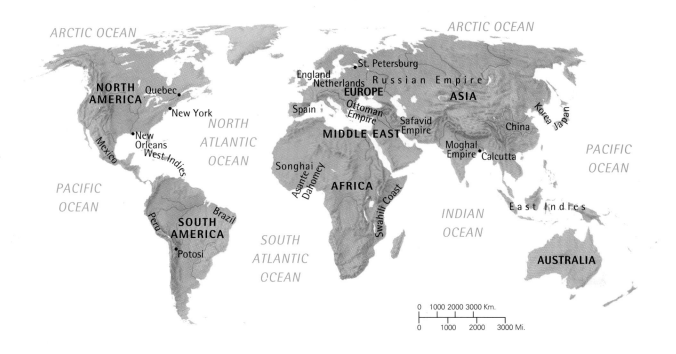

ARCTIC OCEAN

ARCTIC OCEAN

NORTH AMERICA

• Quebec

• New York

NORTH ATLANTIC OCEAN

• New Orleans

Mexico

West Indies

PACIFIC OCEAN

SOUTH AMERICA

Peru

Brazil

• Potosí

SOUTH ATLANTIC OCEAN

England

Netherlands

EUROPE

St. Petersburg

Russian Empire

Spain

Ottoman Empire

MIDDLE EAST

Safavid Empire

ASIA

Korea Japan

China

Moghal Empire

• Calcutta

PACIFIC OCEAN

Songhai

Asante

Dahomey

AFRICA

Swahili Coast

INDIAN OCEAN

East Indies

AUSTRALIA

0   1000 2000 3000 Km.

0   1000   2000   3000 Mi.

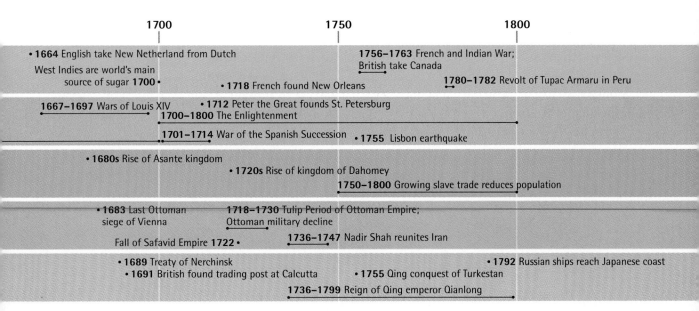

1700

1750

1800

• **1664** English take New Netherland from Dutch

West Indies are world's main source of sugar **1700** •

• **1718** French found New Orleans

1756–1763 French and Indian War; British take Canada

1780–1782 Revolt of Tupac Armaru in Peru

1667–1697 Wars of Louis XIV

• **1712** Peter the Great founds St. Petersburg

1700–1800 The Enlightenment

1701–1714 War of the Spanish Succession

• **1755** Lisbon earthquake

• **1680s** Rise of Asante kingdom

• **1720s** Rise of kingdom of Dahomey

1750–1800 Growing slave trade reduces population

• **1683** Last Ottoman siege of Vienna

1718–1730 Tulip Period of Ottoman Empire; Ottoman military decline

Fall of Safavid Empire **1722** •

1736–1747 Nadir Shah reunites Iran

• **1689** Treaty of Nerchinsk

• **1691** British found trading post at Calcutta

• **1792** Russian ships reach Japanese coast

• **1755** Qing conquest of Turkestan

1736–1799 Reign of Qing emperor Qianlong

THE TRANSFORMATION OF EUROPE,

1500–1750

**Religious and Political Innovations • Building State Power •
Urban Society and Commercial Technology • Rural Society and
the Environment • The Realm of Ideas**
ENVIRONMENT AND TECHNOLOGY: Mapping the World

n the winter of 1697–1698, Tsar° Peter I, the young ruler of Russia, traveled in disguise through the Netherlands and England, eager to discover how western European societies were becoming so powerful and wealthy. A practical man, Peter paid special attention to ships and weapons. With great insight, he perceived that western European success owed as much to trade and toleration as to technology. Trade generated the money to spend on weapons, while toleration attracted talented persons fleeing persecution.

Upon his return to Russia, Peter resolved to "open a window onto Europe," to reform features of his vast empire that he believed were backward. He ended the servile status of women and personally trimmed his noblemen's long beards to conform to Western styles. Peter also put the skilled technical advisers he brought back with him to work on modernizing Russia's industry and military forces. He then turned to redesigning Russia's government on a German model and copied French rituals of absolute royal power.

As Peter's actions imply, by the end of the seventeenth century, western European achievements in state administration, warfare, business, and ideas were setting standards that others wished to imitate. Along with maritime expansion (examined in Chapter 15), these internal transformations promoted Western global ascendancy. Yet such achievements did not come smoothly. Warfare, poverty, persecution, and environmental degradation were also widespread in Europe between 1500 and 1750.

As you read this chapter, ask yourself the following questions:

---

tsar (zahr)

- Was Tsar Peter right in thinking that military, economic, and political changes were moving western Europe ahead of other parts of the world?

- What were the immediate and long-term consequences of those changes and others in European religious and scientific ideas?

- How did the many conflicts and rapid changes of this period affect ordinary men and women in Europe?

RELIGIOUS AND POLITICAL INNOVATIONS

Two bitter struggles in the early sixteenth century marked the end of Europe's medieval era and the beginning of the early modern period. One was the Reformation, a movement that introduced many religious reforms but shattered the ideal of Latin Christian unity. The other was an unsuccessful attempt to unite Christian Europe politically in order to block the inroads of the Muslim armies of the Ottoman Empire. Instead of achieving unity, early modern Europe was plagued by division and persistent warfare, yet such conflict promoted innovations that propelled western Europe forward.

Martin Luther   This detail of a painting by Lucas Cranach (1547) shows the Reformer preaching in his hometown church at Wittenberg.   (Church of St. Marien, Wittenberg, Germany/The Bridgeman Art Library, New York and London)

Religious Reformation

In 1500, the **papacy,** the central government of Latin Christianity, was simultaneously gaining stature and suffering from corruption and dissent. Economic prosperity produced larger donations and tax receipts, allowing popes to fund ambitious construction projects in Rome, their capital city. During the sixteenth century, Rome's new churches and other buildings showcased the artistic **Renaissance** then under way. However, the church's wealth and power also attracted some ambitious men whose personal lives became the source of scandal.

The personal life of Pope Leo X (r. 1513–1521) was free from scandal, but he was more a man of action than a spiritual leader. One technique that he used to raise funds for the church's building projects was to authorize an **indulgence**—a forgiveness of the punishment due for past sins, granted as a reward for a pious act such as making a pilgrimage, saying a particular prayer, or making a donation to a religious cause. In one German state, a young professor of sacred scripture, a monk named Martin Luther (1483–1546) was very upset by the indulgence preachers, who he thought emphasized the act of giving money more than the faith behind the act.

This theological dispute quickly escalated into a test of wills. When the papacy condemned Luther in 1519, the German monk burned the papal bull (document) of condemnation, rejected Pope Leo's authority, and began the movement known as the **Protestant Reformation.** Luther insisted that the only way to salvation was through faith in Jesus Christ, not "good works." He declared that Christian belief must be based on the word of God in the Bible and on Christian tradition, not on the authority of the pope. Eventually his conclusions led him to abandon his monastic vows and marry a former nun.

Inspired by Luther, others raised their voices to denounce the ostentation and corruption of church leaders. John Calvin (1509–1564), a Frenchman, became a highly influential Protestant leader. Calvin's teaching differed from that of Roman Catholics and Lutherans in two respects. First, while agreeing with Luther's emphasis on faith over works, Calvin denied that even human faith could merit salvation. Salvation, said Calvin, was God's free gift to those God "predestined" for it. Second, Calvin went further than Luther in curtailing the power of ordained clergymen and simplifying religious rituals.

The Reformers appealed to religious sentiments, but political and social agendas also inspired many who joined them. Lutheranism appealed to many Germans for nationalistic reasons. Peasants and urban laborers sometimes defied their masters by adopting a different faith. Neither tradition had a special attraction for women, since both Protestants and Roman Catholics believed in male dominance in the church and the family. Most Protestants, however, rejected the medieval tradition of celibate priests and nuns and advocated Christian marriage for all adults.

Shaken by the intensity of the Protestant Reformers' appeal, the Catholic Church undertook its own reforms. The Council of Trent issued decrees in 1563 reforming the education, discipline, and practices of the Roman Catholic clergy, reaffirmed the supremacy of the pope, and clarified Catholic beliefs (including those concerning indulgences) in light of Protestant challenges. Also important to this **Catholic Reformation** were the activities of a new religious order, the Society of Jesus. Well-educated Jesuits helped stem the Protestant tide and win back some adherents by their teaching and preaching (see Map 16.1).

Given the complexity of the issues and the intensity of the emotions that the Protestant Reforma-

tion stirred, it is not surprising that violence often flared up. Both sides persecuted and sometimes executed those of differing views. Bitter wars of religion, fought over a mixture of religious and secular issues, continued in parts of western Europe until 1648.

The Failure of Empire

Meanwhile, another great medieval institution, the **Holy Roman Empire,** was also in trouble (see Map 16.2). The threat that the Ottoman Turks posed to Europe stirred interest in a pan-European coalition to stop Muslim advances. A Latin Christian coalition led by Holy Roman Emperor Charles V eventually halted the Ottomans at the gates of Vienna in 1529, but Charles failed in his efforts to forge his several realms into Europe's strongest state. In the imperial Diet (assembly) many German princes, swayed partly by Luther's appeals to German nationalism, opposed Charles, a French-speaking emperor who defended the papacy. Some Lutheran princes enriched themselves by seizing the church's lands within their states in the name of reform.

After decades of bitter squabbles, Charles V gave up his efforts at unification. By the Peace of Augsburg (1555), he recognized the princes' right to choose whether Catholicism or Lutheranism would prevail in their particular states, and he allowed them to keep church lands they had seized before 1552.

Thus, two institutions that had symbolized Western unity during the Middle Ages, the papacy and the Holy Roman Empire, were seriously weakened by the mid-sixteenth century. Both continued to exist, but national kingdoms assumed much of the religious and political leadership in western Europe.

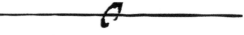

BUILDING STATE POWER

Talented rulers and their able ministers guided the rise of these European kingdoms. They worked to enhance royal authority by limiting the

CHRONOLOGY

	Politics and Culture	Environment and Technology	Warfare
1500	**1500s** Spain's golden century **1519** Protestant Reformation begins **1540s** Scientific Revolution begins **1545** Catholic Reformation begins		
		Mid-1500s Improved windmills and increasing land drainage in Holland	**1526–1571** Ottoman wars **1546–1555** German Wars of Religion **1562–1598** French Wars of Religion **1566–1648** Netherlands Revolt
	Late 1500s Witchhunts increase	**1590s** Little Ice Age begins	
1600	**1600s** Holland's golden century	**1600s** Depletion of forests growing **1609** Galileo's astronomical telescope	**1618–1648** Thirty Years War **1642–1648** English Civil War **1652–1678** Anglo-Dutch Wars **1667–1697** Wars of Louis XIV **1683–1697** Ottoman wars
		1682 Canal du Midi completed	
1700	**1700s** The Enlightenment begins		**1700–1721** Great Northern War **1701–1714** War of the Spanish Succession
		1755 Lisbon earthquake	

autonomy of the church and the nobility, while building the state's armed forces and economy.

Royal Centralization, 1500–1750

When the system of monarchical succession worked best, it brought to the throne a creative, energetic young person who gained experience and won loyalty over many decades. By good fortune, the leading states produced many such talented, hard-working, and long-lived rulers. Spain had only six rulers in the two centuries from 1556 to 1759, and France had but five between 1574 and 1774 (see Table 16.1). The long reigns of the Tudor monarchs Henry VIII and his Protestant daughter, Elizabeth I, helped stabilize sixteenth-century England, but their Stuart successors were twice overthrown by revolution during the next century.

Successful monarchs depended heavily on their chief advisers, who also eased the transition between rulers. Before 1650, advisers tended to be members of the clergy, but thereafter kings began to draw on the talents of successful businessmen. The prevalence of clerical advisers does not mean

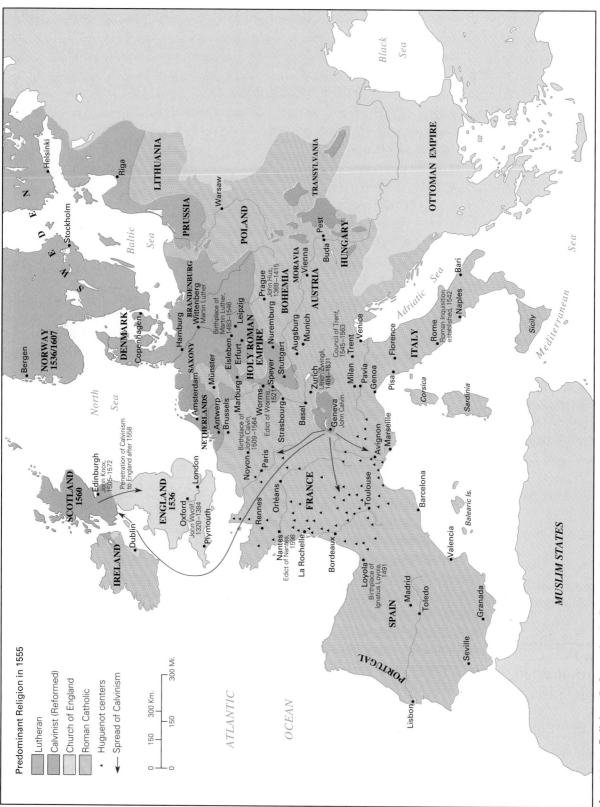

Map. 16.1 Religious Reformation in Europe The Reformation brought greater religious freedom but also led to religious conflict and persecution. In many places, the Reformation accelerated the trend toward state control of religion and added religious differences to the motives for wars among Europeans.

Predominant Religion in 1555

Lutheran
Calvinist (Reformed)
Church of England
Roman Catholic
▲ Huguenot centers
→ Spread of Calvinism

0   150   300 Km.
0   150   300 Mi.

ATLANTIC
OCEAN

North
Sea

Baltic
Sea

Black
Sea

Adriatic
Sea

Mediterranean
Sea

NORWAY
1536/1607

SWEDEN

DENMARK

SCOTLAND
1560

IRELAND

ENGLAND
1536

FRANCE

SPAIN

PORTUGAL

ITALY

HOLY ROMAN
EMPIRE

SAXONY

BRANDENBURG

PRUSSIA

POLAND

LITHUANIA

BOHEMIA

MORAVIA

AUSTRIA

HUNGARY

TRANSYLVANIA

OTTOMAN EMPIRE

MUSLIM STATES

NETHERLANDS

Corsica

Sardinia

Sicily

Balearic Is.

Helsinki
Riga
Warsaw
Stockholm
Bergen
Copenhagen
Hamburg
Wittenberg
Birthplace of
Martin Luther
Eisleben,
Birthplace of Martin Luther,
1483-1546
Leipzig
Erfurt
Prague
John Hus,
1369-1415
Nuremburg
Vienna
Buda
Pest
Münster
Amsterdam
Antwerp
Brussels
Marburg
Birthplace of
John Calvin,
1509-1564
Worms
Edict of Worms,
1521
Speyer
Strasbourg
Augsburg
Munich
Stuttgart
Basel
Zurich
Ulrich Zwingli,
1484-1531
Geneva
John Calvin
Council of Trent,
1545-1563
Trent
Milan
Venice
Pavia
Genoa
Pisa
Florence
Rome
Roman Inquisition
established, 1542
Naples
Bari
Avignon
Marseille
Toulouse
Bordeaux
La Rochelle
Nantes
Edict of Nantes,
1598
Rennes
Orleans
Paris
Noyon
Birthplace of
John Calvin,
1509-1564
Edinburgh
John Knox,
1505-1572
Penetration of Calvinism
to England after 1558
London
Oxford
John Wyclif,
1320-1384
Plymouth
Dublin
Loyola
Birthplace of
Ignatius Loyola,
1491
Madrid
Toledo
Granada
Seville
Lisbon
Valencia
Barcelona

Map. 16.2   The European Empire of Charles V   Charles was Europe's most powerful ruler from 1519 to 1556, but he failed to unify the Christian West. In addition to being the elected head of the Holy Roman Empire, he was the hereditary ruler of the Spanish realms of Castile and Aragon and the possessions of the Austrian Habsburgs in Central Europe. The map does not show his extensive holdings in the Americas and Asia.

Table 16.1   **Rulers in Early Modern Western Europe**

Spain	France	England/Great Britain
Habsburg Dynasty	**Valois Dynasty**	**Tudor Dynasty**
Charles I (1516–1556) (Holy Roman-Emperor Charles V)	Francis I (1515–1547)	Henry VIII (1509–1547)
	Henry II (1547–1559)	Edward VI (1547–1553)
Philip II (1556–1598)	Francis II (1559–1560)	Mary I (1553–1558)
	Charles IX (1560–1574)	Elizabeth I (1558–1603)
	Henry III (1574–1589)	
	Bourbon Dynasty	**Stuart Dynasty**
Philip III (1598–1621)	Henry IV (1589–1610)[a]	James I (1603–1625)
Philip IV (1621–1665)	Louis XIII (1610–1643)	Charles I (1625–1649)[a, b]
Charles II (1665–1700)	Louis XIV (1643–1715)	(Puritan Republic, 1649–1660)
		Charles II (1660–1685)
		James II (1685–1688)[b]
		William III (1689–1702)
		and Mary II (1689–1694)
Bourbon Dynasty		Anne (1702–1714)
Philip V (1700–1746)		
		Hanoverian Dynasty
	Louis XV (1715–1774)	George I (1714–1727)
Ferdinand VI (1746–1759)		George II (1727–1760)

[a]Died a violent death.   [b]Was overthrown.

the clergy controlled the throne; rather, the opposite was the case. Well before the Reformation, rulers in Spain, Portugal, and France had gained control over church appointments and had used church revenues to enhance royal power.

This co-opting of the church by the state made religious uniformity a hot political issue. Following the pattern used by his predecessors to suppress Jewish and Muslim practices, King Philip II of Spain used an ecclesiastical court, the Spanish Inquisition, to bring into line those who resisted his authority. In France, Prince Henry of Navarre switched his faith from Calvinist to Catholic after gaining the military advantage in the French Wars of Religion (1562–1598), so that, as King Henry IV (the first of the Bourbon kings), he would share the faith of the majority of his subjects.

Elsewhere, the Protestant Reformation made it easier for monarchs to increase their control of the church. In England, the church lost its remaining autonomy after the pope turned down King Henry

VIII's petition for an annulment of his marriage to Katharine of Aragon, and Henry ordered the English archbishop of Canterbury to annul the marriage. The breach with Rome was sealed in 1534 when Parliament made the English monarch head of the Church of England. Henry used his authority to disband monasteries and convents, giving some of their lands to his powerful allies and selling others to pay for his new navy. In other respects, religion changed little under Henry and his successors, despite growing pressures from English Calvinists known as Puritans to "purify" the Anglican church of Catholic practices and beliefs.

In addition to gaining control of the church, western European kings and queens enhanced their powers by promoting national institutions. In Spain, the Castilian dialect gained currency. In France, people increasingly imitated the speech of Paris. By 1750, uniform laws and administration were the pattern. Rulers also promoted common national languages. The Protestant emphasis on reading the Bible in vernacular languages (instead of in Latin) hastened the standardization of German and English.

Absolutism and Constitutionalism

The absence of any constitutional check on a ruler's power is called **absolutism.** Many seventeenth- and eighteenth-century European monarchs admired absolutism, but needed the approval of their representative assemblies to make war or levy new taxes.

In France, the strong Bourbon kings of the seventeenth and eighteenth centuries governed without summoning the Estates General that represented the clergy, the nobility, and the towns. By promoting economic development, collecting taxes more efficiently, and selling high offices, Louis XIV's astute ministers were able to bypass the Estates General's power to authorize new taxes, while permitting the king to wage a series of expensive wars and build a gigantic new palace at Versailles°. The palace was a sort of theme park of royal absolutism, where French nobles were diverted from the real politics of the kingdom through elaborate banquets and ceremonies centered on the king.

In England, King Charles I ruled for eleven years without summoning Parliament, his kingdom's representative body, by coercing "loans" from wealthy subjects and twisting tax laws to new uses. Then in 1640, a rebellion in Scotland forced him to summon the members of Parliament to approve new taxes to pay for an army. Before authorizing new taxes, Parliament insisted on strict guarantees that the king would never again ignore its traditional rights. King Charles refused to agree and in 1642 plunged the kingdom into civil war. When Charles refused to compromise even after being defeated on the battlefield, Parliament ordered him executed in 1649 and replaced the monarchy with a Puritan Republic under the Puritan general Oliver Cromwell.

The monarchy was restored in 1660, but when King James II refused to respect Parliament's rights,

Parliament forced him into exile in the bloodless Glorious Revolution of 1688. The Bill of Rights of 1689 specified that Parliament had to be called "frequently" and had to consent to changes in laws and to the raising of an army in peacetime. By these steps, Parliament checked royal power and established **constitutionalism,** a system of government that subjects the ruler's power to limits specified by law and custom.

War and Diplomacy

Early modern European rulers, whether absolutist or constitutional, developed some of the world's most powerful armed forces. Warfare was almost constant (see the Chronology at the beginning of the chapter). Their struggles for dominance first produced a dramatic change in the size, skill, and weapons of armed forces and then an advance in diplomacy.

The number of men in arms increased steadily throughout the early modern period. French forces, for example, grew to 400,000 by the early eighteenth century. Only England did not maintain a standing army in peacetime because the Royal Navy could protect the island nation from invasion.

Large armies required better command structures. New signaling techniques improved control of battlefield maneuvers, and frequent marching drills instilled better discipline in the troops. To defend against these forces, cities built new fortifications able to withstand cannon bombardments. Battles between evenly matched armies often ended in stalemates, as in the Thirty Years War (1618–1648). Victory in war increasingly depended on naval superiority.

The rapid changes in naval warfare are evident in two fleets used by Philip II of Spain. In 1571, a combined Spanish and Italian fleet of 200 ships met an even larger Ottoman force off Lepanto on the Greek coast. Both fleets consisted principally of oar-powered galleys, which had only light armaments. To attack, one galley rammed another so that armed men could climb aboard for hand-to-hand combat. Four hours after the battle began, the remains of 200 Ottoman galleys littered the

Versailles (vuhr-SIGH)

Versailles, 1722   This painting by P.-D. Martin shows the east expanse of buildings and courtyards that make up the palace complex built by King Louis XIV.   (Giraudon/Art Resource, NY)

sea's surface, and the waters were red with the blood of 30,000 slain men.

A very different Spanish fleet, the Catholic Armada, sailed from Lisbon in 1588 hoping to repeat the Lepanto success over the Protestant enemies of the north. The complex mission of these 130 heavily armed ships was to replace the Protestant ruler of England, Queen Elizabeth, with a Roman Catholic, then put down the rebellion in the Netherlands, and finally intervene on the Catholic side in the French Wars of Religion. But history did not repeat itself. The English could fire more rapidly because of their new cannon carriages, and their smaller, quicker ships successfully evaded the ram-and-board technique, which the Spanish retained from their Mediterranean victory. Moreover, a chance storm,

celebrated by the English as a providential "Protestant wind," scattered and sank many Spanish ships that had survived the sea battles, thus dooming Philip's other plans for the armada.

The armada's defeat signaled the end of Spain's military dominance in Europe. By the early 1600s, France had recovered from its Wars of Religion to become Europe's most powerful state. With twice the population of Spain at their command, France's forceful kings of the Bourbon dynasty deployed Europe's largest armies to squelch domestic unrest, extend France's boundaries, and intervene in the affairs of neighboring states.

After emerging from its own civil conflicts in 1689, England became France's major rival. By then, England ruled a North American empire as well as Ireland, and in 1707 England merged with Scotland to become Great Britain. England's rise as a sea power had begun in the time of King Henry VIII, who spent heavily on ships and promoted a domestic iron-smelting industry to supply cannon. Queen Elizabeth's victorious fleet of 1588 was considerably improved by the copying of innovative ship designs from the Dutch in the second half of the seventeenth century. The Royal Navy grew in numbers, surpassing the French fleet by the early eighteenth century.

In a series of eighteenth-century wars, beginning with the War of the Spanish Succession (1701–1714), the combination of Britain's naval strength and the land armies of its Austrian and Prussian allies was able to block French expansionist efforts and prevent the Bourbons from uniting the thrones of France and Spain. This defeat of the French monarchy's empire-building efforts illustrated the principle of **balance of power** in international relations: the European powers formed temporary alliances to prevent any one state from becoming too powerful.

Nearly constant warfare had the unintended effect of enhancing diplomacy. During the next two centuries, though adhering to four different branches of Christianity, the great powers of Europe—Catholic France, Anglican Britain, Catholic Austria, Lutheran Prussia, and Orthodox Russia—maintained an effective balance of power in Europe by shifting their alliances for geopolitical rather than religious reasons.

Politics and the Economy

To pay for the heavy costs of their wars, European rulers had to increase their revenues. Dutch governments pioneered mutually beneficial alliances with rising commercial interests. Rulers in France and Britain were quick to follow. Both parties understood that trade thrived where government taxation and regulation were not excessive, where courts enforced contracts and collected debts, and where military power stood ready to protect overseas expansion by force when necessary.

Spain illustrates how the failure to promote economic development led sixteenth-century Europe's mightiest state into decline. For a time, vast imports of silver and gold bullion from the American colonies filled Spain's treasury and financed ambitious wars against the Ottomans, northern European Protestants, and rebellious Dutch subjects. But the treasury often ran dry, and loans raised on the promise of future treasure fleets could not always be paid. As a Spanish saying put it, American silver was like rain on the roof—it poured down and washed away. The bullion flowed out to pay creditors, purchase manufactured goods, and even buy food in the seventeenth century. Spanish rulers had not only failed to develop the economy; their intolerant religious policies had driven out of the kingdom commercially talented Jews and Protestants and exiled tens of thousands of skilled farmers and artisans because of their Muslim ancestry.

The rise of the Netherlands as an economic power teaches the opposite lesson. The Spanish crown had acquired these resource-poor but commercially successful provinces as part of Charles V's inheritance. But when King Philip II imposed Spain's ruinously heavy sales tax and enforced Catholic orthodoxy, he drove the Dutch to revolt. High taxes and intolerance would have discouraged business and driven away the Calvinists, Jews, and others who were essential to Dutch prosperity. The Dutch fought with skill and ingenuity, raising and training an army and a navy that were among the most effective in Europe. By 1609, Spain was forced to agree to a truce that recognized the autonomy of the northern part of the Netherlands. In 1648, the independence of these seven United Provinces of the Free Netherlands (to give their full name) became final.

Rather than being ruined by the long war, the United Netherlands emerged in the seventeenth century as the dominant commercial power in Europe and the world's greatest trading nation. During this golden century, the wealth of the Netherlands multiplied. Holland's many towns and cities were filled with skilled craftsmen. Factories and workshops turned out goods of exceptional quality at a moderate price and on a vast scale. The textile industry concentrated on the highly profitable finishing and printing of cloth, transforming the cloth spun and woven by low-paid workers into fine textiles. Other factories refined West Indian sugar, brewed beer from Baltic grain, cut Virginia

Port of Amsterdam Ships, barges and boats of all types are visible in this busy seventeenth-century scene. The large building in the center is the Admiralty House, which housed the headquarters of the Dutch East India Company. (Mansell Collection/Time Inc.)

tobacco, and made imitations of Chinese ceramics. Printers published books in many languages, free from the censorship imposed by political and religious authorities in neighboring countries. For a small province barely above sea level, lacking timber and other natural resources, this was a remarkable achievement.

Amsterdam, Holland's major city, was seventeenth-century Europe's financial center and major port. From there, Dutch ships dominated the sea trade of Europe, carrying over 80 percent of the trade to Spain from northern Europe, even while Spain and the Netherlands were at war. The Dutch dominance of Atlantic and Indian Ocean trade was such that by one estimate, they conducted more than half of all the oceangoing commercial shipping in the world (see Chapters 17 and 18).

URBAN SOCIETY AND COMMERCIAL TECHNOLOGY

Just as palaces were early modern Europe's centers of political power, cities were its economic power centers. The urban growth under way since the eleventh century was accelerating and spreading. In 1500, Paris was the only northern European city with over 100,000 inhabitants. By 1700, both Paris and London had populations over 500,000, Amsterdam had burgeoned from a fishing village to a metropolis of some 200,000, and twenty other European cities contained over 60,000 people apiece.

Urban Social Classes

The cities' growth depended primarily on the prosperous merchants who managed the great expansion of regional and overseas commerce, but wealth was unevenly distributed and social tension often ran high. The French called the well-off who dominated the cities **bourgeoisie**° (town dwellers).

Some bourgeoisie grew rich supplying the growing urban populations with grain, wine, and beer. Others imported exotic luxuries from the far corners of the earth: Caribbean and Brazilian sugar and rum, Mexican chocolate, Virginian tobacco, North American furs, East Indian cotton textiles and spices, and Chinese tea. The rise of the bourgeoisie was aided by mutually beneficial alliances with monarchs who saw economic growth as the best means of increasing state revenues. Unlike the old nobility, who shunned productive labor, members of the bourgeoisie devoted long hours to their businesses and poured their profits into new business ventures or other investments rather than spending them. Even so, they still had enough money to live comfortably in large houses with many servants.

Europe's cities were also home to craftworkers and many poor people. From 10 to 20 percent of the permanent city dwellers were so poor they were exempt from taxation. Cities also contained large numbers of temporary immigrants from impoverished rural areas, itinerant peddlers, beggars, and gangs of criminals.

In contrast to the arranged marriages common in much of the rest of the world, young men and women in early modern Europe generally chose their own spouses and after marriage set up their own households instead of living with their parents. The age of marriage was also later in Europe than elsewhere, so that young people could complete their education or apprenticeship to learn a trade and save enough money to live on their own. The late age of marriage in early modern Europe held down the birthrate and thus limited family size. Even so, about one-tenth of the births in a city were to unmarried women, often servants, who generally left their infants on the doorsteps of churches, convents, or rich families. Delayed marriage also had links to public brothels, where men satisfied their lust in cheap and impersonal encounters with unfortunate young women, often newly arrived from impoverished rural villages.

Commercial Techniques and Technology

The expansion of trade in early modern Europe prompted the development of new techniques to manage far-flung business enterprises and invest the profits they produced. As elsewhere in the world, most businesses ran on family funds or borrowed money. But a key change in Europe was the rise of large financial institutions to serve the interests of big business and big government. In the seventeenth century, private Dutch banks developed such a reputation for security that wealthy individuals and governments from all over western Europe entrusted them with their money. The banks invested these funds in real estate, local industries, loans to governments, and overseas trade.

Another commercial innovation was the **joint-stock company,** which sold shares to individuals. Often backed by a government charter, such companies offered a way to raise large sums for overseas enterprises while spreading the risks (and profits) among many investors (the operation of chartered joint-stock companies in the overseas trade is examined in Chapter 17). Investors could buy and sell shares in specialized financial markets called **stock exchanges.** The greatest stock market in the seventeenth and eighteenth centuries was the Amsterdam Exchange, founded in 1530.

Changes in technology also facilitated economic growth. Improvements in water transport expanded Europe's superb natural network of seas and navigable rivers for moving bulk items such as grain, wine, and timber. Governments financed the constructions of shipping canals with elaborate systems of locks to cross hills. The Canal du Midi in France, built between 1661 and 1682, linked the Atlantic and the Mediterranean.

The expansion of maritime trade led to new designs for merchant ships. Dutch ports built vast

---

bourgeoisie (boor-zwah-ZEE)

fleets of large-capacity cargo ships, including the heavily armed "East Indiaman" that helped the Dutch establish their supremacy in the Indian Ocean. The Dutch also excelled at mapmaking (see Environment and Technology: Mapping the World).

RURAL SOCIETY AND THE ENVIRONMENT

For all its new political, military, and commercial strengths, early modern Europe rested on a fragile agrarian base. Bad years brought famine; good ones provided only small surpluses. The circumstances of most rural Europeans probably worsened between 1500 and 1750.

The Struggle for Food and Fuel

Besides the devastation of warfare and other human-engineered calamities, rural Europeans also felt the adverse effects of a century of relatively cool climate. During this **Little Ice Age,** average temperatures fell only a few degrees, but the effects were startling. Rivers and canals important to commerce froze solid from bank to bank. Crops ripened more slowly during cooler summers and were often damaged by frosts that came unexpectedly late in spring or early in fall. When one cold year followed another, deaths due to malnutrition and cold increased sharply. The cold spell of 1694–1695 carried off between a quarter and a third of the population of Finland.

By 1700, new crops from the Americas were helping the rural poor avoid starvation. At first eaten only in desperate times, potatoes and maize (corn) became staples for the rural poor in the eighteenth century because they yielded more abundant food from small garden plots. Potatoes sustained life in northeastern and Central Europe and in Ireland. Peasants along the Mediterranean who could not afford to eat the wheat they raised for urban markets grew maize for their own consumption.

Another threat to rural life came from **deforestation,** which emerged as a serious issue in the seventeenth and eighteenth centuries. Early modern Europeans cut down their great hardwood forests to provide timbers for ships; lumber for buildings, wagons, and barrels; fuel for heating and cooking; and charcoal for smelting ores and other industrial processes. Dependent on woodlands for abundant supplies of wild nuts and berries, free firewood and building materials, and wild game, the rural poor felt the depletion of the forests most strongly. Some flocked to the cities in hopes of finding better jobs, but most were disappointed.

Peasantry and Gentry

The bright side of rural life in western Europe was the remarkable personal freedom of the peasantry in comparison with people of similar status in many other parts of the world. Serfdom, which bound men and women to land owned by a local lord, declined sharply after the great plague of the mid-fourteenth century. Most remaining serfs in western Europe gained their freedom by 1600. By that date, slavery had also come to an end.

Legal freedom in western Europe did little to make the peasants' lives safe and secure, however. Rising debts caused many to lose their land to large landowners who loaned them money. The desire of many successful members of the bourgeoisie to buy country estates and thus join the ranks of the gentry accelerated the transformation of rural ownership. These new owners of rural estates affected the lifestyle of the old aristocracy and sometimes received the aristocracy's exemption from taxation, but they did not have titles of nobility. The exemption of the wealthy from taxation was a complaint frequently mentioned during the many rebellions that rural misery provoked in early modern Europe.

THE REALM OF IDEAS

New ideas and old beliefs pulled early modern Europeans in several different directions, even after the Reformation controversies subsided. The hold of biblical and traditional folk beliefs on the

Mapping the World

In 1602, the Jesuit missionary Matteo Ricci in China printed an elaborate map of the world. Working from maps produced in Europe and incorporating the latest knowledge gathered by European maritime explorers, Ricci introduced two changes to make the map more appealing to his Chinese hosts. He labeled it in Chinese characters, and he split his map down the middle of the Atlantic so that China lay in the center. This version pleased Chinese elites, who considered China the "Middle Kingdom" surrounded by lesser states. A copy of Ricci's map in six large panels adorned the emperor's Beijing palace.

The stunningly beautiful maps and globes of sixteenth-century Europe were the most complete, detailed, and useful representations of the earth that any society had ever produced. The best mapmaker of the century was Gerhard Kremer, who is remembered as Mercator (the merchant) because his maps were so useful to European ocean traders. By incorporating the latest discoveries and scientific measurements, Mercator could depict the outlines of the major continents in painstaking detail, even if their interiors were still largely unknown to outsiders.

To represent the spherical globe on a flat map, Mercator drew the lines of longitude as parallel lines. Because such lines actually meet at the poles, Mercator's projection greatly exaggerated the size of every landmass and body of water distant from the equator. However, Mercator's rendering offered a practical advantage: sailors could plot their course by drawing a straight line between their point of departure and their destination. Because of this useful feature, the Mercator projection of the world remained in common use until quite recently. To some extent, its popularity came from the exaggerated size this projection gave to Europe. Like the Chinese, Europeans liked to think of themselves as at the center of things. Europeans also understood their true geographical position better than people in any other part of the world.

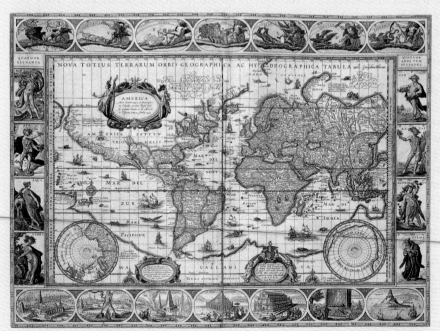

Dutch World Map, 1641
It is easy to see why the Chinese would not have liked to see their empire at the far right edge of this widely printed map. Besides the distortions caused by the Mercator projection, geographical ignorance exaggerates the size of North America and Antarctica.
(Courtesy of the Trustees British Museum)

thinking of most people showed itself in widespread new fears about witches and the power of the devil. In education, writings from Greco-Roman antiquity popularized in the Renaissance remained most influential, but a few thinkers broke new scientific ground in deciphering the motion of the planets and constructing mathematical models of the force of gravitation. In time, the new laws of science encouraged some to reevaluate traditional social and political systems, with important implications for the future.

Traditional Thinking

In the minds of most Europeans, pre-Christian ideas of magic and folk spirits mixed with Christian teachings about miracles, saints, and devils. If crops failed or domestic animals died unexpectedly, many people blamed unseen spirits. When an earthquake destroyed much of Lisbon, Portugal's capital city, in November 1755, both educated and uneducated saw the event as a punishment sent by God to punish the city's residents for their sins.

Nowhere was the belief in unseen forces more evident than in the **witch-hunts** that swept across northern Europe in the late sixteenth and seventeenth centuries. It is estimated that secular and church authorities tried over 100,000 people— some three-fourths of them women—for practicing witchcraft. Some were acquitted, some recanted, but over half were executed. The trial records make it clear that both the accusers and the accused believed that evil magic and the power of the devil could cause people and domestic animals to sicken and die or crops to wither in the fields.

Modern historians believe that the fact that many accused of witchcraft were older women, especially widows, may reflect fears that women not directly under the control of fathers or husbands were likely to turn to evil. The Reformation had focused attention on the devil and may have helped revive older fears of witchcraft. Self-confessed "witches" may even have found release from the guilt they felt for wishing evil on their neighbors. No single reason can explain the rise in witchcraft accusations and fears in early modern Europe, but for both the accusers and the accused, there are

plausible connections between the witch-hunts and rising social tensions, rural poverty, and environmental strains.

The Scientific Revolution

Among intellectuals, prevailing ideas about the natural world were based on the physics of Aristotle, the ancient Greek philosopher who taught that all matter was reducible to four elements. He held that the earth was composed of two heavy elements, earth and water, while the heavens were made of air and fire, which floated above the ground.

The prevailing conception of the universe was also influenced by the calculations of the ancient Greek mathematician Pythagoras, who proved the validity of the famous theorem that still bears his name: In a right triangle, the square of the hypotenuse is equal to the sum of the squares of the other two sides ($a^2 + b^2 = c^2$). Pythagoreans attributed to mystical properties the ability of simple mathematical equations to describe physical objects. They attached special significance to the simplest (to them perfect) geometrical shapes: the circle (a point rotated around another point) and the sphere (a circle rotated on its axis). They believed that celestial objects were perfect spheres orbiting the earth in perfectly circular orbits.

In the sixteenth century, however, the careful observations and mathematical calculations of some daring and imaginative European investigators began to challenge these prevailing conceptions of the physical world. These pioneers of the **Scientific Revolution** demonstrated that the workings of the universe could be explained by natural causes.

The first was a Polish monk and mathematician named Nicholas Copernicus (1473–1543). Copernicus did not challenge the idea that the sun, moon, and planets were light, perfect spheres, but his placement of the sun, not the earth, at the center of things began a revolution in understanding about the structure of the heavens and the central place of humans in the universe. To escape controversy, Copernicus delayed the publication of his heliocentric (sun-centered) theory until after his death.

Galileus Galileus   Florentinus

Superio
16

licentia
24.

Eques Octauius Leoe   Roman° pictor fecit

Galileo in 1624   This engraving by Ottavio Leone shows the Italian scientist in full vigor at age sixty, before he was hounded by the Roman Inquisition.   (British Museum)

The most brilliant of those who improved on Copernicus's model was the Italian Galileo Galilei° (1564–1642). In 1609, Galileo built a telescope through which he saw that the moon had mountains and valleys, the sun had spots, and other planets had their own moons. In other words, the earth was not alone in being heavy and changeable.

At first, the Copernican universe found more critics than supporters. How, demanded Aristotle's defenders, could the heavy earth move without producing vibrations that would shake the planet apart? Is the Bible wrong, asked the theologians, when it says that, by God's command, "the sun stood still . . . a whole day" to give the ancient Israelites victory in their conquest of Palestine? Galileo's enemies had his ideas condemned by the Roman Inquisition in 1616.

Galileo Galilei (gal-uh-LAY-oh gal-uh-LAY-ee)

Despite official opposition, printed books spread the new scientific ideas among scholars across Europe. In England, members of the Royal Society were enthusiastic missionaries of mechanical science. One of them, Isaac Newton (1642–1727), formulated a set of mathematical laws demonstrating that the heavens and earth share a common physics. It was the force of gravity, not angels, that governed the elliptical orbits of heavenly bodies and caused cannonballs to fall back to earth. As president of the Royal Society from 1703 until his death, Newton used his prestige to promote the new science of physics that bears his name.

The Early Enlightenment

Advances in scientific thought had few practical applications until long after 1750, but they inspired governments and private groups in many countries to reexamine the reasonableness of everything from agricultural methods to laws, religion, and social hierarchies. The belief that human reason could discover the laws that governed social behavior and were just as scientific as the laws that governed physics energized a movement known as the **Enlightenment.** Like the Scientific Revolution, this movement was the work of a few individuals who often faced bitter opposition from the political, intellectual, and religious establishment. Leading Enlightenment thinkers became accustomed to having their books burned or banned, and many spent long periods in exile to escape being imprisoned for their ideas.

Influences besides the Scientific Revolution affected the Enlightenment. The partisan bickering and bloodshed of the Reformation era led some to doubt the superiority of any theological position and recommend toleration of all religions. The killing of suspected witches also shocked many thoughtful people. The leading French thinker Voltaire declared, "No opinion is worth burning your neighbor for."

Accounts of cultures in other parts of the world also led some European thinkers to question assumptions about the superiority of European political institutions, moral standards, and religious beliefs. Reports of Amerindian life, though romanticized, led some to conclude that those whom they had called savages were in many ways nobler than European Christians. Jesuit missionaries contrasted the lack of territorial ambition of the Chinese with the constant warfare in the West and attributed the difference to the fact that China was wisely ruled by educated men.

Another influence on the "enlightened" thinkers of the eighteenth century was the English political philosopher John Locke (1632–1704), who disputed the prevailing idea that government was sacred and kings ruled by divine right. He argued that absolute monarchy was incompatible with civil society and wrote that monarchs, like everyone else, were subject to the law that laid the basis for the compact that brought civil society into existence. If monarchs overstepped the law, Locke argued, citizens had not only the right but the duty to rebel. The consequences of this idea are considered in Chapter 20.

The Enlightenment was more a frame of mind than a coherent movement. Individuals who embraced it drew inspiration from different sources and promoted different agendas. By 1750, its proponents were clearer about what they disliked than about what new institutions should be created. Some "enlightened" thinkers thought society could be made to function with the mechanical orderliness of planets spinning in their orbits. Nearly all were optimistic that at least in the long run, human beliefs and institutions could be improved. This belief in progress would help foster political and social revolutions after 1750.

Despite the enthusiasm the Enlightenment aroused in some circles, Europe in 1750 was neither enlightened nor tolerant. Nevertheless, its political and religious divisions, growing literacy, and the printing press made possible the survival of the new ideas that would profoundly change life in future centuries.

CONCLUSION

Historians use the word *revolution* to describe many different changes that took place in Europe between 1500 and 1750. The inflation of the sixteenth century has been called a price revolution, the expansion of trade a commercial revolution, the reform of state spending a financial revolution, the changes in weapons and warfare a military revolution. We have also encountered a scientific revolution and the religious revolution of the Reformation.

These important changes in early modern European government, economy, society, and thought were parts of a dynamic process that began in the later Middle Ages and led to even bigger industrial and political revolutions before the eighteenth century was over. Yet the years from 1500 to 1750 were not simply—perhaps not even primarily—an age of progress for Europe. The conflicts of royal armies, religious beliefs, and contending ideas exacted a terrible price in death, destruction, and misery. The expanding economy benefited members of the emerging merchant elite and their political allies, but most Europeans became worse off as prices rose faster than wages. New scientific and enlightened ideas ignited new controversies long before they yielded any tangible benefits.

The historical significance of this period of European history is clearest when viewed in a global context. What stands out is the growing power and efficiency of European armies, economies, and governments. From a global perspective, the balance of political and economic power shifted slowly but inexorably in the Europeans' favor from 1500 to 1750. In 1500, the Ottomans threatened Europe. By 1750, as the remaining chapters of Part Five detail, Europeans had brought the world's seas and a growing part of its land and people under their control. No single group of Europeans accomplished this. The Dutch eclipsed the pioneering Portuguese and Spanish; then the English and French bested the Dutch. Competition, too, was a factor in the European success.

Other changes in Europe during this period had no great overseas significance yet. The full effects of the Scientific Revolution and the Enlightenment lay in the period after 1750.

■ Key Terms

papacy	bourgeoisie
Renaissance (Europe)	joint-stock company
indulgence	stock exchanges
Protestant Reformation	Little Ice Age
Catholic Reformation	deforestation
Holy Roman Empire	witch-hunt
absolutism	Scientific Revolution
constitutionalism	Enlightenment
balance of power	

■ Suggested Reading

Overviews of this period include Euan Cameron, *Early Modern Europe* (1999), and H. G. Koenigsberger, *Early Modern Europe: Fifteen Hundred to Seventeen Eighty-Nine* (1987). Global perspectives can be found in Fernand Braudel, *Civilization and Capitalism, 15th–18th Century,* trans. Siân Reynolds, 3 vols. (1979), and Immanuel Wallerstein, *The Modern World-System,* vol. 2, *Mercantilism and the Consolidation of the European World-Economy, 1600–1750* (1980).

Technological and environmental changes are the focus of Geoffrey Parker, *Military Revolution: Military Innovation and the Rise of the West, 1500–1800,* 2d ed. (1996); William H. McNeill, *The Pursuit of Power: Technology, Armed Force, and Society Since A.D. 1000* (1982); Robert Greenhalgh Albion, *Forests and Sea Power: The Timber Problem of the Royal Navy, 1652–1862* (1965); and Jean M. Grove, *The Little Ice Age* (1988).

Steven Stapin, *The Scientific Revolution* (1998), and Hugh Kearney, *Science and Change, 1500–1700* (1971), are accessible introductions. An excellent place to begin examining the complex subject of witchcraft is Brian Levack, *The Witch-Hunt in Early Modern Europe,* 2d ed. (1995).

Good single-country surveys are J. A. Sharpe, *Early Modern England: A Social History,* 2d ed. (1997); Emmanuel Le Roy Ladurie, *The Royal French State, 1460–1610* (1994) and *The Ancien Régime: A History of France, 1610–1774* (1998); Jonathan Israel, *The Dutch Republic: Its Rise, Greatness and Fall, 1477–1806* (1995); and James Casey, *Early Modern Spain: A Social History* (1999).

THE AMERICAS, THE ATLANTIC, AND AFRICA,

1530–1770

Spanish America and Brazil • English and French Colonies in North America • Colonial Expansion and Conflict • Plantations in the West Indies • Creating the Atlantic Economy • Africa and the Atlantic • The Columbian Exchange
SOCIETY AND CULTURE: Colonial Wealth and the Exploitation of Indigenous Peoples

ecause of their long isolation from other continents, the peoples of the New World lacked immunity to diseases introduced from the Old World. Smallpox arrived in the Caribbean in 1518, killing most of the native peoples there. In short order, smallpox killed 50 percent or more of the Amerindian population of Mexico and Central America. The disease then spread to North and South America with equally devastating effects. Other diseases added to the toll: measles in the 1530s, followed by diphtheria, typhus, influenza, and perhaps pulmonary plague. Between 1520 and 1521, influenza in combination with other ailments attacked the Cakchiquel of Guatemala. Their chronicle recalls:

> Great was the stench of the dead. After our fathers and grandfathers succumbed, half the people fled to the fields. The dogs and vultures devoured the bodies. . . . So it was that we became orphans, oh my sons! . . . We were born to die![1]

By the mid-seventeenth century, malaria and yellow fever were also present in tropical regions.

The development of English and French colonies in North America in the seventeenth century led to similar patterns of contagion and mortality. In 1616 and 1617, epidemics nearly exterminated many of New England's indigenous groups. French fur traders transmitted measles, smallpox, and other diseases as far as Hudson Bay and the Great Lakes.

Although there is very little evidence that Europeans consciously used disease as a tool of empire, the deadly results of contact clearly undermined the ability of native peoples to resist European settlement. Europeans and their African slaves occupied these depopulated lands. The

Americas were transformed biologically and culturally. They were subjected to Europeans' political and economic demands.

The colonies of the Americas were crucial pieces of a new **Atlantic system.** This network of trading links moved people and cultures as well as goods and wealth around the Atlantic. The Atlantic system also affected Africa, but less severely than the Americas. Despite the loss of millions of people to the slave trade, Africa did not suffer such severe population loss as the Americas. Most important, Africans remained in control of their lands.

Amerindians, Europeans, and Africans all contributed to the creation of new cultures in the Americas. The societies that arose reflected each colony's mix of native peoples, its connections to the slave trade, and the policies of its European rulers.

As you read this chapter, ask yourself the following questions:

- How different and how similar were the colonial societies and economies of the Americas?

- Why did forced labor and slavery become so important in many New World colonies?

- How did participation in the Atlantic system affect Europe, Africa, and the Americas?

Spanish America and Brazil

The frontiers of conquest and settlement expanded rapidly. Within one hundred years of Columbus's first voyage to the Western Hemisphere, the Spanish Empire in America included most of the islands of the Caribbean, Mexico, the American southwest, Central America, the Caribbean and Pacific coasts of South America, the Andean highlands, and the vast plains of the Río de la Plata region (a region that includes the modern nations of Argentina, Uruguay, and Paraguay). Portuguese settlement in the New World developed more slowly. But before the end of the sixteenth century, Portugal occupied most of the Brazilian coast.

Early settlers from Spain and Portugal sought to create colonial societies based on the institutions and customs of their homelands. They viewed society as a vertical arrangement of estates (classes of society), as uniformly Catholic, and as an arrangement of patriarchal extended-family networks. Despite the imposition of foreign institutions and the massive loss of life caused by epidemics, indigenous peoples still exercised a powerful influence on the development of colonial societies. Aztec and Inca elite families sought to protect their traditional privileges and rights through marriage or less formal alliances with the Spanish settlers. They also often used colonial courts to defend their claims to land. Nearly everywhere, Amerindian religious beliefs and practices survived beneath the surface of an imposed Christianity. Amerindian languages, cuisine, medical practices, and agricultural techniques also survived the conquest and influenced the development of Latin American culture.

The African slave trade added a third cultural stream to colonial Latin American society. By the end of the colonial era, Africans and their descendants were living throughout Latin America, enriching colonial societies with their traditional agricultural practices, music, religious beliefs, cuisine, and social customs.

State and Church

The Spanish crown moved quickly to curb the independent power of the conquistadors and establish royal authority over both the defeated native populations and the rising tide of European settlers. Created in 1524, the **Council of the Indies** in Spain supervised all government, ecclesiastical, and commercial activity in the Spanish colonies. Political and economic power was concentrated in Mexico City, capital of the Viceroyalty of New Spain, and in Lima, capital of the Viceroyalty of Peru. Each viceroyalty was divided into a number of judicial and administrative districts. Until the seventeenth century, almost all of the officials appointed to high positions in Spain's colonial bureaucracy were born in Spain. Later, local-born members of the colonial elite gained many offices.

In the sixteenth century, Portugal concentrated its resources and energies on Asia and Africa, because early settlers found neither mineral wealth nor rich native empires in Brazil. Finally, the king appointed a governor-general in 1549 and designated Salvador, in the northern province of Bahia, Brazil's capital. In 1720, the first viceroy of Brazil was named.

Just as these colonial bureaucracies imposed Iberian economic and political institutions, the Catholic Church became the primary agent for the introduction and transmission of Christian belief and European culture in South America. Spain and Portugal justified their American conquests by assuming an obligation to convert native populations to Christianity. In Mexico alone, hundreds of thousands of conversions and baptisms were achieved within a few years of the conquest.

The Catholic clergy sought to win over the Amerindians by first converting native elites. But these efforts were abandoned when church authorities discovered that many converts were secretly observing old beliefs and rituals. In the 1560s, Spanish clergy resorted to torture, executions, and the destruction of native manuscripts to eradicate traditional beliefs and rituals among the Maya. Repelled by these events, the church hierarchy ended both the violent repression of native religious practice and efforts to recruit an Amerindian clergy.

Despite its failures, the Catholic clergy did provide native peoples with some protections against the abuse and exploitation of Spanish settlers. The priest **Bartolomé de Las Casas** (1474–1566), who served as the most important advocate for native peoples, wrote a number of books that detailed their mistreatment by the Spanish. His most important achievement was the enactment of the New Laws of 1542, which outlawed the enslavement of Amerindians and limited other forms of forced labor.

Despite the disapproval of most European clergy and settlers, Amerindians blended Catholic Christian beliefs with important elements of traditional native cosmology and ritual. Most commonly, indigenous beliefs and rituals came to be embedded in the celebration of saints' days or Catholic rituals associated with the Virgin Mary. Instead, it was one component of the process of cultural borrowing and innovation that contributed to a distinct and original Latin American culture.

After 1600, the Catholic Church redirected most of its resources from the countryside to growing colonial cities and towns with large European populations. One important outcome of this altered mission was the founding of universities and secondary schools, which stimulated urban intellectual life.

Colonial Economies

The silver mines of Peru and Mexico and the sugar plantations of Brazil dominated the colonial economy and fueled the early development of European capitalism. Profits produced in these economic centers also promoted the growth of colonial cities, concentrated scarce investment capital and labor resources, and stimulated the development of livestock raising and agriculture in neighboring rural areas. Dependence on mineral and agricultural exports was an enduring theme in Latin America.

Although millions of pesos of gold were mined in Latin America, silver mines generated more wealth and exercised greater economic influence. In 1545, the single richest silver deposit in the Americas was discovered at **Potosí°,** in what is now Bolivia, and until 1680 the silver production of Bolivia and Peru dominated the Spanish colonial economy.

Silver mining also greatly altered the environment. Within a short time, wasteful use of forest resources for fuel destroyed forests near the mining centers. Faced with rising fuel costs, miners developed an efficient method of chemical extraction that relied on mixing mercury with the silver ore. But mercury is a poison, and its use contaminated

---

Potosí (poh-toh-SEE)

CHRONOLOGY

	Latin America	North America	West Indies	Atlantic
1500	**1518** Smallpox arrives in Caribbean	**1524–1554** French explore Newfoundland and Gulf of St. Lawrence	**ca. 1500** Spanish settlers introduce sugar cane cultivation	**1530** Amsterdam Exchange opens
	1535 Creation of Viceroyalty of New Spain			
	1540s Creation of Viceroyalty of Peru			
	1542 New Laws outlaw Amerindian enslavement			
	1545 Silver discovered at Potosí, Bolivia			
1600		**1607** Jamestown founded		
		1608 Quebec founded		
	By 1620 African slaves the majority of Brazilian plantation workers	**1620** Plymouth founded	**1620s and 1630s** English and French colonies in Caribbean	**1621** Dutch West India Company chartered
	1625 Population of Potosí reaches 120,000			
			1640s Dutch bring sugar plantation system from Brazil	**1638** Dutch take Elmina
			1655 English take Jamaica	
		1660 Slavery in Virginia begins to grow rapidly		**1660s** English Navigation Acts
		1664 English take New York from Dutch		
			1670s French occupy western half of Hispaniola	**1672** Royal African Company chartered
				1698 French *Exclusif*
1700		**1699** Louisiana founded	**1700** West Indies surpass Brazil in sugar production	**1700–1830** Slave trade at its peak
		1756–1763 French and Indian War		

the environment and sickened the Amerindian work force.

From the time of Columbus, indigenous populations had been compelled to provide labor for European settlers in the Americas. Until the 1540s in Spanish colonies, Amerindian peoples were divided among the settlers and were forced to provide them with labor or with textiles, food, or other goods. This form of forced labor was called the **encomienda°**. The discovery of silver in Peru led to a new form of compulsory labor called the mita°. Under this system, one-seventh of the adult male Amerindians were compelled to work for six months each year in mines or on farms or in textile factories. The most dangerous working conditions existed in the silver mines.

In the Spanish mita, few Amerindian workers could survive on their wages. Wives and children were commonly forced to join the work force to help meet expenses (see Society and Culture: Colonial Wealth and the Exploitation of Indigenous Peoples). Even those who remained behind in the village were forced to send food and cash to support mita workers.

The Portuguese, who had developed sugar plantations that depended on slave labor on the Atlantic islands of Madeira, the Azores, the Cape Verdes, and São Tomé, transferred this profitable form of agriculture to Brazil. By the seventeenth century, sugar dominated the Brazilian economy. At first, the Portuguese enslaved Amerindian men as field hands, but sugar planters eventually came to rely more on African slaves, who were more resistant to disease. Imports of African slaves rose from an average of 2,000 per year in the late sixteenth century to approximately 7,000 per year a century later, far outstripping the immigration of free Portuguese settlers.

The mining centers of Latin America exercised global economic influence. American silver increased the European money supply, promoting commercial expansion. Large amounts of silver also flowed across the Pacific, where it was exchanged for Asian spices, silks, and pottery. In the Americas, the rich mines stimulated urban population growth, as well as commercial links with agricultural and textile producers.

The sugar plantations of Brazil played a similar role in integrating the economy of the south Atlantic region. At the end of the seventeenth century, the discovery of gold in Brazil helped overcome this large region's currency shortage and promoted further economic integration.

Both Spain and Portugal attempted to control the trade of their American colonies, but the combination of monopoly commerce and convoy shipping slowed the flow of European goods to the colonies and kept prices high. Frustrated by these restraints, colonial populations established illegal commercial relations with the English, French, and Dutch. By the middle of the seventeenth century, a majority of European imports were arriving in Latin America illegally.

Society in Colonial Latin America

With the exception of a few early viceroys, few members of Spain's great noble families came to the New World. *Hidalgos°*—lesser nobles—were well represented, as were Spanish merchants, artisans, miners, priests, and lawyers. Small numbers of criminals, beggars, and prostitutes also found their way to the colonies. Spanish settlers, however, were always a tiny minority in a colonial society numerically dominated by Amerindians and rapidly growing populations of Africans, **creoles** (whites born in America to European parents), and people of mixed ancestry.

Conquistadors and early settlers who received from the Crown grants of labor and tribute goods (encomienda) from Amerindian communities as rewards for service to Spain dominated colonial society in early Spanish America. These *encomenderos* sought to create a hereditary social and political class comparable to the nobles of Europe. But their systematic abuse of Amerindian communities and the catastrophic loss of Amerindian life during the epidemics of the sixteenth century undermined their position, as did the growing power of colonial viceroys, judges, and bishops appointed by the king.

By the end of the sixteenth century, the elite of Spanish America included both European immigrants and creoles. Europeans dominated the

---

encomienda (in-co-mee-EN-dah)   **mita** (MEE-tah)

hidalgos (ee-DAHL-goes)

Colonial Wealth and the Exploitation of Indigenous Peoples

The conditions imposed on indigenous peoples in the Spanish colonies generated contentious debates from the early sixteenth century to the end of the colonial period. Two Spanish naval officers who accompanied a French scientific expedition to South America in the mid-eighteenth century wrote the following description.

Without having to assume anything that cannot be proved absolutely or exaggerating to stretch the truth, we can agree indisputably that all the wealth produced in the Indies [Spain's American colonies], even what is consumed there, stems from the toil of the Indians. From close observation one sees that Indians work the silver and gold mines, cultivate the fields, and raise the livestock. In a word, there is no heavy labor that the Indians do not perform. They are so badly recompensed for their work that if one wanted to find out what the Spaniards paid them, he would discover it to be nothing except consistently cruel punishment, worse than that meted out in the galleys. . . . The gold and silver which the Spaniards acquire at the expense of the natives' sweat and toil never falls into the hands of the Indians. [T]hose who contribute most are the ones who enjoy its fruits least and are the most poorly paid for the most arduous tasks. . . .

There are two ways to remedy the abuse perpetrated on the free and mita Indians [the mita was a forced labor system]. The most reasonable and just method would be to eliminate the mita entirely and have free labor work the haciendas, mines, obrajes [textile mills] and everything else. . . .

In the second place it would be fitting to prohibit completely all physical punishment of the Indians in the haciendas and obrajes under severe penalties.

How important were Amerindians to the economy of the Spanish Empire? How did these two visitors judge the treatment of Amerindian peoples? What remedies did these authors suggest?

Source: Jorge Juan and Antonio de Ulloa, *Discourse and Political Reflections on the Kingdom of Peru,* ed. John J. Tepaske and Besse A. Clement (Norman: University of Oklahoma Press, 1978), 126–148.

---

highest levels of the church and government, as well as commerce. Creoles commonly controlled colonial agriculture and mining. Although tensions between Spaniards and creoles were inevitable, most elite families had members from both groups.

Before the Europeans arrived in the Americas, the native peoples were members of a large number of distinct cultural and linguistic groups. Cultural diversity and class distinctions were present even in the highly centralized Aztec and Inca empires. The loss of life provoked by the European conquest undermined this rich social and cultural complexity, and the imposition of Catholic Christianity further eroded ethnic boundaries among native peoples. Colonial administrators and settlers broadly applied the racial label "Indian," which facilitated the imposition of special taxes and labor obligations while erasing long-standing class and ethnic differences.

Indigenous Amerindian elites survived only briefly in the Spanish colonies and Brazil. Some of the conquistadors and early settlers married or established less formal relations with elite Amerindian women, but fewer of these alliances occurred after European women began to arrive. Some

Painting of Castas   This is an example of a common genre of colonial Spanish American painting. In the eighteenth century, there was increased interest in ethnic mixing, and wealthy colonials, as well as some Europeans, commissioned sets of paintings that showed mixed families. Commonly, the paintings also indicated what the artist believed was an appropriate class setting. In this painting, a richly dressed Spaniard is depicted with his Amerindian wife dressed in European clothing. Notice that the painter has the mestiza daughter look to her European father for guidance. (Private Collection. Photographer: Camilo Garza/Fotocam, Monterrey, Mexico)

descendants of the powerful Amerindian families prospered in the colonial period as ranchers, muleteers, and merchants; many others lived in the same materially deprived conditions as Amerindian commoners.

Thousands of blacks participated in the conquest and settlement of Spanish America, and the opening of a direct slave trade with Africa added millions more. Settlers' views of African slaves' cultural differences as signs of inferiority ultimately served as a justification for slavery. By 1600, any-

one with black ancestry was barred from positions in church, government, and many skilled crafts. Even so, African languages, religious beliefs, and marriage customs mixed with European (and in some cases Amerindian) languages and beliefs to forge distinct local cultures. The rapid growth of an American-born slave population accelerated this process of cultural change.

African slaves became skilled artisans, musicians, servants, artists, cowboys, and even soldiers. However, the vast majority worked in agriculture. To escape harsh discipline, brutal punishments, and backbreaking labor, many slaves rebelled or ran away. Communities of runaways (called *quilombos°* in Brazil and *palenques°* in Spanish colonies) were common. The largest quilombo was Palmares, where thousands of slaves defended themselves against Brazilian authorities for sixty years until they were finally overrun in 1694.

ENGLISH AND FRENCH COLONIES IN NORTH AMERICA

The North American colonial empires of England and France and the colonies of Spain and Portugal had many characteristics in common. The governments of England and France hoped to find easily extracted forms of wealth or great indigenous empires like those of the Aztecs or Inca. Like the Spanish and Portuguese, English and French settlers responded to native peoples with a mixture of diplomacy and violence. African slaves proved crucial to the development of all four colonial economies.

There were also important differences. The English and French colonies were founded nearly a century after Cortés's conquest of Mexico and initial Portuguese settlement in Brazil. Distracted by ventures elsewhere, neither England nor France imitated the large and expensive colonial bureaucra-

---

quilombos (ley-LOM-bos)   *palenques* (pah-LEN-kays)

cies that Spain and Portugal established. Instead, private companies and individual proprietors pioneered the development of English and French colonies. This practice led to greater regional variety in economic activity, political institutions and culture, and social structure than was evident in Latin American colonies.

The South

London investors, organized as the privately funded Virginia Company, got off to a rocky start. Nearly 80 percent of the settlers at Jamestown in 1607 and 1608 soon died of disease or Amerindian attacks. After the English crown dissolved the Virginia Company in 1624 because of its mismanagement, colonists pushed deeper into the interior, developing a sustainable economy based on furs, timber, and, increasingly, tobacco. The profits from tobacco soon attracted new immigrants and new capital. Along the shoreline of Chesapeake Bay and the rivers that fed it, settlers spread out, developing plantations and farms.

Indentured servants eventually accounted for approximately 80 percent of all English immigrants to the Chesapeake Bay region. Young men and women unable to pay for their transportation to the New World accepted indentures (contracts) that bound them to a term ranging from four to seven years of labor in return for passage, a small parcel of land, and some tools and clothes. During the seventeenth century, approximately fifteen hundred indentured servants, mostly male, arrived each year. As life expectancy in the colony improved, planters began to purchase more slaves. They calculated that greater profits could be secured by paying the higher initial cost of slaves owned for life than by purchasing the contracts of indentured servants bound for short periods of time. As a result, Virginia's slave population grew rapidly from 950 in 1660 to 120,000 by 1756.

Ironically, this dramatic increase in the colony's slave population occurred along with the expansion in colonial liberties and political rights. At first, colonial government had been administered by a Crown-appointed governor and his council, as well as by representatives of towns meeting together as the **House of Burgesses.** When these representatives began to meet alone as a deliberative body, they initiated a form of democratic representation that distinguished the English colonies of North America from the colonies of other European powers. The intertwined evolution of freedom and slavery gave England's southern colonies a unique and conflicted political character.

Colonial South Carolina was the most hierarchical society in British North America. Planters controlled the economy and political life. The richest maintained households in both the countryside and Charleston, the largest city in the southern colonies. Small farmers, cattlemen, artisans, merchants, and fur traders held an intermediate but clearly subordinate social position. African slaves were present from the founding of Charleston. They were instrumental in introducing irrigated rice agriculture and in developing indigo (a plant that produced a blue dye) plantations. Native peoples remained influential participants in colonial society through commercial contacts and alliances, but they were increasingly marginalized.

New England

New England was colonized by two separate groups of Protestant dissenters. The **Pilgrims** established the colony of Plymouth on the coast of present-day Massachusetts in 1620. Although nearly half of the settlers died during the first winter, the colony survived. In 1691, Plymouth was absorbed into the larger Massachusetts Bay Colony of the **Puritans.** The Puritan leaders had received a royal charter to finance the Massachusetts Bay Colony. By 1643, more than 20,000 Puritans had settled in the Bay Colony.

Unlike the southern colonies, most newcomers to Massachusetts arrived with their families. A normal gender balance and a healthy climate resulted in a rapid natural increase in population. Massachusetts also was more homogeneous and less hierarchical than the southern colonies.

Political institutions evolved out of the terms of the royal charter. A governor was elected, along with a council of magistrates drawn from the board of directors of the Massachusetts Bay Company. Disagreements between this council and elected representatives of the towns led, by 1650, to the creation of a lower legislative house that selected its own speaker and began to develop procedures and rules similar to those of the House of Commons in England.

Economically, Massachusetts differed dramatically from the southern colonies. Agriculture met basic needs, but poor soils and harsh climate offered no opportunity to develop cash crops like tobacco or rice. To pay for imported tools, textiles, and other essentials, the colonists began to provide commercial and shipping services to the southern colonies, the smaller Caribbean islands, Africa, and Europe.

In contrast to Latin America's heavily capitalized monopolies, New England merchants' success rested on market intelligence, flexibility, and streamlined organization. With 16,000 inhabitants in 1740, Boston was the largest city in British North America.

Middle Atlantic Region

The rapid economic development and remarkable cultural diversity of the Middle Atlantic colonies added to the success of English-speaking North America. The **Iroquois Confederacy,** an alliance of several native peoples, established treaties and trading relationships with the Dutch. When confronted by an English military expedition in 1664, the Dutch surrendered their colony of New Netherland without a fight. Renamed New York, the colony's success was guaranteed in large measure by the development of New York City as a commercial and shipping center. Located at the mouth of the Hudson River, the city played an essential role in connecting the region's grain farmers to the booming markets of the Caribbean and southern Europe. By the early eighteenth century, New York Colony had a diverse population that included (in addition to English colonists) Dutch, German, and Swedish settlers, as well as a large slave community.

Pennsylvania began as a proprietary colony in 1682 and as a refuge for Quakers, a persecuted religious minority. The founder, William Penn, quickly lost control of the colony's political life, but the colony enjoyed remarkable success. By 1700, Pennsylvania had a population of more than

21,000, and Philadelphia, its capital, soon passed Boston to become the largest city in the British colonies. Healthy climate, excellent land, and relatively peaceful relations with native peoples attracted free workers, including a large number of German families. As a result, Pennsylvania's economic expansion in the late seventeenth century occurred without reproducing South Carolina's hierarchical and repressive social order. By the early eighteenth century, however, the prosperous city of Philadelphia included a large population of black slaves, servants, and skilled tradesmen.

French America

French settlement patterns more closely resembled those of Spain and Portugal than of England. The French were committed to missionary activity among Amerindian peoples and emphasized extracting resources—in this case, furs.

Coming to Canada after spending years in the West Indies, Samuel de Champlain founded the colony of **New France** at Quebec°, on the banks of the St. Lawrence River, in 1608. The European market for fur, especially beaver, fueled French settlement. Young Frenchmen were sent to live among native peoples to master their languages and customs. These men and their children by native women organized the fur trade and led French expansion to the west and south. Amerindians actively participated in this trade because they came to depend on the goods they received in exchange for furs: firearms, metal tools and utensils, textiles, and alcohol.

The Iroquois Confederacy responded to the increased military strength of France's Algonkian allies by forging commercial and military links with Dutch and later English settlements in the Hudson River Valley. Well armed by the Dutch and English, the Iroquois Confederacy nearly eradicated the Huron in 1649 and inflicted a series of humiliating defeats on the French. At the high point of their power in the early 1680s, Iroquois

---

Quebec (kwuh-BEC)

hunters and military forces gained control of much of the Great Lakes region and the Ohio River Valley. A large French military expedition and a relentless attack focused on Iroquois villages and agriculture finally checked Iroquois power in 1701.

Use of firearms in hunting and warfare moved west and south, reaching indigenous plains cultures that previously had adopted the horse introduced by the Spanish. This intersection of horse and gun frontiers in the early eighteenth century dramatically increased the military power and hunting efficiency of the Sioux, Comanche, Cheyenne, and other indigenous peoples and slowed the pace of European settlement in North America.

In French Canada, the Jesuits led the effort to convert native peoples to Christianity. Building on earlier evangelical efforts in Brazil and Paraguay, French Catholic missionaries mastered native languages, created boarding schools for young boys and girls, and set up model agricultural communities for converted Amerindians. The Jesuits' greatest successes coincided with a destructive wave of epidemics and renewed warfare among native peoples in the 1630s. Nevertheless, local cultures persisted.

Although the fur trade flourished, settlers were few. Founded at about the same time, Virginia had twenty times as many European residents as Canada by 1627. Canada's small settler population and the Amerindians' profitable fur trade allowed then to retain greater independence and more control over their encounters with new religious, technological, and market realities.

The French aggressively expanded. Louisiana, founded in 1699, depended on the fur trade with Amerindians. France's North American colonies were threatened by a series of wars with England and the neighboring English colonies. The "French and Indian War" (also known as the Seven Years War, 1756–1763) proved to be the final contest for North American empire (see Map 17.1). England committed a larger military force to the struggle and, despite early defeats, took the French capital of Quebec in 1759. The peace agreement forced France to yield Canada to the English and cede Louisiana to Spain. The French then concentrated their efforts on their sugar-producing colonies in the Caribbean.

PLANTATIONS IN THE WEST INDIES

The West Indies was the first place in the Americas that Columbus reached and the first part of the Americas where native populations collapsed. It took a long time to repopulate these islands from abroad and forge new economic links between them and other parts of the Atlantic. But after 1650, sugar plantations, African slaves, and European capital made these islands a major center of the Atlantic economy.

Spanish settlers had introduced sugar cane cultivation into the West Indies shortly after 1500, but these colonies soon fell into neglect as attention shifted to colonizing the American mainland. After 1600, the West Indies revived as a focus of colonization, this time by northern Europeans interested in growing tobacco and other crops. The islands' value mushroomed after the Dutch reintroduced sugar cultivation from Brazil in the 1640s and supplied the African slaves and European capital necessary to create a new economy.

Sugar and Slaves

The English colony of Barbados illustrates the dramatic transformation that sugar brought to the seventeenth-century Caribbean. In 1640, Barbados's economy depended largely on tobacco, mostly grown by European settlers, both free and indentured. By the 1680s, sugar had become the colony's principal crop, and enslaved Africans were three times as numerous as Europeans. Exporting up to 15,000 tons of sugar a year, Barbados had become the wealthiest and most populous of England's American colonies. By 1700, the West Indies had surpassed Brazil as the world's principal source of sugar.

The expansion of sugar plantations in the West Indies required a sharp increase in the volume of the slave trade from Africa. During the first half of the seventeenth century, about 10,000 slaves a year had arrived from Africa, most destined for Brazil

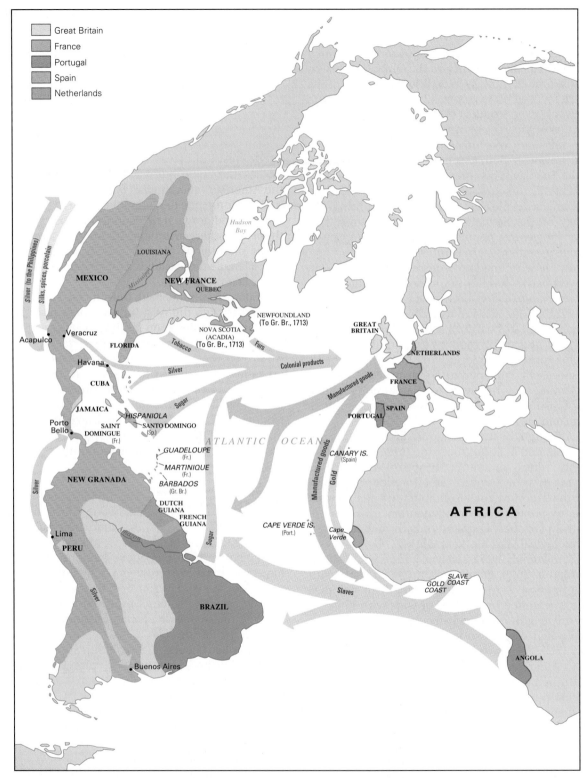

Map 17.1   The Atlantic World   European colonization of the Americas and the opening up of trade to coastal Africa created a vast flow of goods and people that by 1750 rivaled the Indian Ocean basin in importance. A silver trade to East Asia gave birth to a Pacific Ocean economy.

and the mainland Spanish colonies. In the second half of the century, the trade averaged 20,000 slaves a year. More than half were intended for the English, French, and Dutch West Indies and most of the rest for Brazil. A century later, the volume of the Atlantic slave trade was three times larger.

What produced this shift in favor of African slaves? Recent scholarship has cast doubt on the once-common assertion that Africans were more suited than Europeans to field labor; in fact, both died in large numbers in the American tropics. The West Indian historian Eric Williams has also refuted the idea that the rise of African slave labor was primarily motivated by prejudice. Citing the West Indian colonies' prior use of enslaved Amerindians and indentured Europeans, along with European convicts and prisoners of war, he argued, "Slavery was not born of racism: rather, racism was the consequence of slavery."[2] Williams suggested the shift was due to the lower cost of African labor.

Yet slaves were far from cheap. Cash-short tobacco planters in the seventeenth century preferred indentured Europeans because they cost half as much as African slaves. Poor European men and women were willing to work for little in order to get to the Americas, where they could acquire their own land cheaply at the end of their term of service. However, as the cultivation of sugar spread after 1750, rich speculators drove the price of land in the West Indies up so high that end-of-term indentured servants could not afford to buy it. As a result, poor Europeans chose to indenture themselves in the mainland North American colonies, where cheap land was still available. Rather than raise wages to attract European laborers, Caribbean sugar planters switched to slaves.

Rising sugar prices helped the West Indian sugar planters afford the higher cost of African slaves. The planters could rely on the Dutch and other traders to supply them with enough new

Market in Rio de Janeiro   In many cities of colonial Latin America, female slaves and black free women dominated retail markets. In this scene from late colonial Brazil, Afro-Brazilian women sell a variety of foods and crafts.   (Sir Henry Chamberlain, *Views and Costumes of the City and Neighborhoods of Rio de Janeiro*, London, 1822)

slaves to meet the demands of the expanding plantations. Rising demand drove slave prices up steadily during the eighteenth century. These high labor costs were one more factor favoring large plantations over smaller operations.

To find more land for sugar plantations, France and England founded new Caribbean colonies. In 1655, the English had wrested the island of Jamaica from the Spanish (see Map 16.1). The French seized the western half of the large Spanish island of Hispaniola in the 1670s. During the eighteenth century, this new French colony of Saint Domingue° (present-day Haiti) became the greatest producer of sugar in the Atlantic world, while Jamaica surpassed Barbados as England's most important sugar colony.

Technology and Environment

What made the sugar plantation a complex investment was that it had to be a factory as well as a farm. Freshly cut canes needed to be crushed within a few hours to extract the sugary sap. Thus, for maximum efficiency, each plantation needed its own expensive crushing and processing equipment.

At the heart of the sugar works was the mill where canes were crushed between sets of heavy rollers. From the mill, lead-lined wooden troughs carried the cane juice to a series of large copper kettles in the boiling shed, where the excess water boiled off, leaving a thick syrup. Workers poured the syrup into conical molds in the drying shed. The sugar crystals that formed in the molds were packed in wooden barrels for shipment to Europe.

To make their operation more efficient and profitable, investors gradually increased the size of the typical West Indian plantation from around 100 acres (40 hectares) in the seventeenth century to at least twice that size in the eighteenth century. A plantation became a huge investment. One source estimated that a planter had to invest nearly £20,000 ($100,000) to acquire a Jamaican plantation of 600 acres (240 hectares) in 1774: a third for

land, a quarter for equipment, and £8,000 for 200 slaves. Jamaica specialized so heavily in sugar production that the island had to import most of its food. Saint Domingue was more diverse in its economy.

In some ways, the mature sugar plantation was environmentally responsible. The crushing mill was powered by water, wind, or animal power, not fossil fuels. The boilers were largely fueled by burning the crushed canes, and the fields were fertilized by cattle manure. In two respects, however, the plantation was very damaging to the environment: soil exhaustion and deforestation.

Instead of rotating sugar with other crops in order to restore the nutrients naturally, planters found it more profitable to clear new lands when yields declined too much in the old fields. When land close to the sea was exhausted, planters moved on to new islands. Many of the English who first settled Jamaica were from Barbados, and the pioneer planters on Saint Domingue came from older French sugar colonies. In the second half of the eighteenth century, Jamaican sugar production began to fall behind that of Saint Domingue, which still had access to virgin land. Thus, the plantations of this period were not a stable form of agriculture but one that gradually laid waste to the landscape.

Deforestation, the second form of environmental damage, continued a trend begun in the sixteenth century. By the end of the eighteenth century, only land in the interior of the islands retained dense forests.

The most tragic and dramatic transformation in the West Indies occurred in the human population. During the eighteenth century, West Indian plantation colonies were the world's most polarized societies. On most islands, 90 percent or more of the inhabitants became slaves. A small number of very rich men owned most of the slaves and most of the land as well. Between the slaves and the masters might be found only a few others: a few estate managers and government officials and, in the French islands, some small farmers, both white and black. The profitability of a Caribbean plantation depended on extracting as much work as possible from the slaves through the use of force and the threat of force.

Saint Domingue (san doh-MANGH)

Caribbean Sugar Mill   The windmill crushes sugar cane whose juice is boiled down in the smoking building next door.   (From William Clark, *Ten Views in the Islands of Antigua, 1823.* British Library)

On a typical Jamaican plantation, about 80 percent of the slaves actively engaged in productive tasks; the only exceptions were infants, the seriously ill, and the very old. The table also illustrates how slave labor was organized by age, sex, and ability. About 70 percent of the able-bodied slaves worked in the fields, generally in one of three labor gangs. Women formed the majority of the field laborers, even in the great gang. As the table shows, a little over half of the adult males were employed in nongang work, tending the livestock or serving as blacksmiths and carpenters. The most important artisan slave was the head boiler, who oversaw the delicate process of reducing the cane sap to crystallized sugar and molasses.

Skilled slaves received rewards of food and clothing or time off for good work, but the most common reason for working hard was to escape punishment. A slave gang was headed by a privileged male slave, appropriately called the **driver,** whose job was to ensure that the gang completed its work. Production quotas were high, and slaves toiled in the fields from sunup to sunset, except for meal breaks. Those who fell behind due to fatigue or illness soon felt the sting of the whip. Openly rebellious slaves who refused to work, disobeyed orders, or tried to escape were punished with flogging, confinement in irons, or mutilation.

The harsh conditions of plantation life played a major role in shortening slaves' lives, but the greatest killer was disease. The very young were carried off by dysentery caused by contaminated food and water. Slaves newly arrived from Africa went through a period of adjustment to the new environment known as **seasoning,** during which one-third on average died of unfamiliar diseases. Slaves also suffered from diseases they brought with them, including malaria. On one plantation, for example, more than half of the slaves incapacitated by illness had yaws, a painful and debilitating skin disease common in Africa.

Such high mortality greatly added to the volume of the Atlantic slave trade, since plantations had to purchase new slaves every year or two to re-

Punishment for Slaves   In addition to whipping and other cruel punishment, slave owners devised other ways to shame and intimidate slaves into obedience. This metal face mask prevented the wearer from eating or drinking.   (By permission of the Syndics of Cambridge University Library)

place those who had died. The additional imports of slaves to permit the expansion of the sugar plantations meant that the majority of slaves were Africans born on most West Indian plantations. As a result, African religious beliefs, patterns of speech, styles of dress and adornment, and music were prominent parts of West Indian life.

Given the harsh conditions of their lives, it is not surprising that slaves in the West Indies often sought to regain the freedom into which most had been born. Individual slaves often ran away, hoping to elude the men and dogs who would track them. Sometimes large groups of plantation slaves rose in rebellion against their bondage and abuse. For example, a large rebellion in Jamaica in 1760 was led by a slave named Tacky, who had been a chief on the Gold Coast of Africa. One night, his followers broke into a fort and armed themselves. Joined by slaves from nearby plantations, they stormed several plantations, setting them on fire and killing the planter families. Tacky died in the fighting that followed, and three other rebel lead-

ers stoically endured cruel deaths by torture that were meant to deter others from rebellion.

Because they believed rebellions were usually led by slaves with the strongest African heritage, European planters tried to curtail African cultural traditions. They required slaves to learn the colonial language and discouraged the use of African languages by deliberately mixing slaves from different parts of Africa. In French and Portuguese colonies, slaves were encouraged to adopt Catholic religious practices, though African deities and beliefs also survived. In the British West Indies, where only Quaker slave owners encouraged Christianity among their slaves before 1800, African herbal medicine remained strong, as did African beliefs concerning nature spirits and witchcraft.

As in Latin America, slavery provoked rebellion and flight. In the Caribbean, runaways were known as **maroons.** Maroon communities were especially numerous in the mountainous interiors of Jamaica and Hispaniola, as well as in the island parts of the Guianas°. The Jamaican maroons, after withstanding several attacks by the colony's militia, signed a treaty in 1739 that recognized their independence in return for their cooperation in stopping new runaways and suppressing slave revolts. Similar treaties with the large maroon population in the Dutch colony of Surinam (Dutch Guiana) recognized their possession of large inland regions.

CREATING THE ATLANTIC ECONOMY

The West Indian plantation colonies were at once archaic in their cruel system of slavery and oddly modern in their specialization in a single product. Besides the plantation system itself, three other elements went into the creation of the new Atlantic economy: new economic institutions, new partnerships between private investors and

---

Guianas (guy-AHN-uhs)

governments in Europe, and new working relationships between European and African merchants. The new trading system is a prime example of how European capitalist relationships were reshaping the world.

Capitalism and Mercantilism

The Spanish and Portuguese voyages of exploration in the fifteenth and sixteenth centuries were government ventures, and both countries tried to keep their overseas trade and colonies royal monopolies. Monopoly control, however, proved both expensive and inefficient. The success of the Atlantic economy in the seventeenth and eighteenth centuries owed much to private enterprise, which made trading venues more efficient and profitable.

Two European innovations, capitalism and mercantilism, enabled private investors to fund the rapid growth of the Atlantic economy. **Capitalism** was a system of large financial institutions—banks, stock exchanges, and chartered trading companies—that enabled wealthy investors to reduce risks and increase profits. Early capitalism was buttressed by **mercantilism,** policies adopted by European states to promote their citizens' overseas trade and defend it, by armed force when necessary.

Chartered companies were one of the first examples of mercantilist capitalism. A charter issued by the government of the Netherlands in 1602 gave the Dutch East India Company a legal monopoly over all Dutch trade in the Indian Ocean. This privilege encouraged private investors to buy shares in the company. They were amply rewarded when the Dutch East India Company captured control of the long-distance trade routes in the Indian Ocean from the Portuguese (see Chapter 18). A sister firm, the **Dutch West India Company,** was chartered in 1621 to engage in the Atlantic trade and to seize sugar-producing areas in Brazil and African slaving ports from the Portuguese.

Such successes inspired other governments to set up their own chartered companies. In 1672, a royal charter placed all English trade with West Africa in the hands of the new **Royal African Company,** which established its headquarters at Cape

Coast Castle, just east of Elmina on the Gold Coast. The French government chartered East India and West India companies to reduce French colonies' dependence on Dutch and English traders.

French and English governments also used military force in pursuit of commercial dominance, especially to break the trading advantage of the Dutch in the Americas. Restrictions on Dutch access to French and English colonies provoked a series of wars with the Netherlands between 1652 and 1678, during which the larger English and French navies defeated the Dutch and drove the Dutch West India Company into bankruptcy.

With Dutch competition in the Atlantic reduced, the French and English governments moved to revoke the monopoly privileges of their chartered companies. England opened trade in Africa to any English subject in 1698 on the grounds that ending monopolies would be "highly beneficial and advantageous to this kingdom." It was hoped that such competition would also cut the cost of slaves to West Indian planters, though the demand for slaves soon drove the prices up again.

Such new mercantilist policies fostered competition among a nation's own citizens, while using high tariffs and restrictions to exclude foreigners. In the 1660s, England had passed a series of Navigation Acts that confined trade with its colonies to English ships and cargoes. The French called their mercantilist legislation, first codified in 1698, the *Exclusif°*, highlighting its exclusionary intentions. Other mercantilist laws defended manufacturing and processing interests in Europe against competition from colonies, imposing prohibitively high taxes on any manufactured goods and refined sugar imported from the colonies.

As a result of such mercantilist measures, the Atlantic became Britain, France, and Portugal's most important overseas trading area in the eighteenth century. Britain's imports from its West Indian colonies in this period accounted for over one-fifth of the value of total British imports. The French West Indian colonies played an even larger role in France's overseas trade. Only the Dutch, closed out of much of the American trade, found Asian trade of greater value. Profits from the Atlantic

Exclusif (ek-skloo-SEEF)

economy, in turn, promoted further economic expansion and increased the revenues of European governments.

The Great Circuit and the Middle Passage

At the heart of the Atlantic system was a great clockwise network of trade routes known as the **Great Circuit.** It began in Europe, ran south to Africa, turned west across the Atlantic Ocean to the Americas, and then swept back to Europe. Like Asian sailors in the Indian Ocean, Atlantic mariners depended on the prevailing winds and currents to propel their ships. What drove the ships as much as the winds and currents was the desire for the profits that each leg of the circuit was expected to produce.

The first leg, from Europe to Africa, carried European manufactures—notably metal bars, hardware, and guns—as well as great quantities of cotton textiles brought from India. Some of these goods were traded for West African gold, timber, and other products, which were taken back to Europe. More goods went to purchase slaves, who were transported across the Atlantic to the plantation colonies in the part of the Great Circuit known as the **Middle Passage.** On the third leg, plantation goods from the colonies returned to Europe. Each leg of the circuit carried goods from where they were abundant and relatively cheap to where they were scarce and therefore more valuable. Thus, in theory, each leg of the Great Circuit could earn much more than its costs, and a ship that completed all three legs could return a handsome profit to its owners. In practice, shipwrecks, deaths, piracy, and other risks could turn profit into loss.

The three-sided Great Circuit is only the simplest model of Atlantic trade. Many other trading voyages supplemented the basic circuit. Cargo ships made long voyages from Europe to the Indian Ocean, passed southward through the Atlantic with quantities of African gold and American silver, and returned with the cotton textiles necessary to the African trade. Other sea routes brought to the West Indies manufactured goods from Europe or foodstuffs and lumber from New England.

European interests dominated the Atlantic system. The manufacturers who supplied the trade goods and the investors who provided the capital were all based in Europe, as were the principal consumers of the plantation products. Before the seventeenth century, sugar had been rare and fairly expensive in western Europe. By 1700, annual consumption of sugar in England had risen to about 4 pounds (nearly 2 kilograms) per person. Rising western European prosperity and declining sugar prices promoted additional consumption, starting with the upper classes and working its way down the social ladder. People spooned sugar into popular new beverages imported from overseas—tea, coffee, and chocolate—to overcome the beverages' natural bitterness. By 1750, annual sugar consumption in Britain had doubled, and it doubled again to about 18 pounds (8 kilograms) per person by the early nineteenth century.

The flow of sugar to Europe depended on another key component of the Atlantic trading system: the flow of slaves from Africa. The rising volume of the Middle Passage also measures the Atlantic system's expansion. During the first 150 years after the European discovery of the Americas, some 800,000 Africans had begun the journey across the Atlantic. During the boom in sugar production between 1650 and 1800, the slave trade amounted to nearly 7.5 million. Of the survivors, over half landed in the West Indies and nearly a third in Brazil. Plantations in North America imported another 5 percent, and the rest went to other parts of Spanish America.

In these peak decades, the transportation of slaves from Africa was a highly specialized trade. Most slaves were carried in ships that had been specially built or modified for the slave trade by the construction between the ships' decks of additional platforms on which the human cargo was packed as tightly as possible.

Seventeenth-century mercantilist policies placed much of the Atlantic slave trade in the hands of chartered companies. During their existence, the Dutch West India Company and the English Royal African Company each carried about 100,000 slaves across the Atlantic. In the eighteenth century, private English traders from Liverpool and Bristol controlled about 40 percent of the slave trade. The French, operating out of Nantes and Bordeaux, handled about half as much, and the Dutch hung on to only 6 percent. The Portuguese, supplying

Brazil and other places, had nearly 30 percent of the Atlantic slave trade, in contrast to the 3 percent carried in North American ships.

To make a profit, European slave traders had to buy slaves in Africa for less than the cost of the goods they traded in return. Then they had to deliver as many healthy slaves as possible across the Atlantic for resale in the plantation colonies. The treacherous voyage to the Americas lasted from six to ten weeks. Some ships completed it with all of their slaves alive, but large, even catastrophic losses of life were common. On average between 1650 and 1800, about one slave in every six perished during the Middle Passage.

Some deaths resulted from the efforts of the captives to escape. To inhibit such attempts, African men were confined below deck during most of the voyage, and special netting was installed around the outside of the ship. Some slaves fell into deep psychological depression, known to contemporaries as "fixed melancholy," from which many perished. Others refused to eat, so forced feeding was used to keep slaves alive. When opportunities presented themselves (nearness to land, illness among the crew), some cargoes of enslaved Africans tried to overpower their captors. Such "mutinies" were rarely successful and were put down with brutality that occasioned further losses of life.

Other deaths during the Middle Passage were due to the ill treatment slaves received. Although it was in the interests of the captain and crew to deliver their slave cargo in good condition, whippings, beatings, and even executions were used to maintain order and force the captives to take nourishment. Moreover, the dangers and brutalities of the slave trade were so notorious that many ordinary seamen shunned such work. As a consequence, cruel and brutal characters abounded among the officers and crews on slave ships.

Although examples of unspeakable cruelties are common in the records, most deaths in the Middle Passage were the result of disease rather than abuse, just as on plantations. Dysentery spread by contaminated food and water caused many deaths. Others died of contagious diseases such as smallpox, carried by persons whose infections were not detected during the medical examinations of slaves prior to boarding. Such maladies spread quickly in the crowded and unsanitary con-

fines of the ships, claiming the lives of many slaves already physically weakened and mentally traumatized by their ordeals.

Crew members who were in close contact with the slaves were equally exposed to the epidemics and regularly suffered heavy losses. Moreover, sailors often fell victim to tropical diseases, such as malaria, to which Africans had acquired resistance. It is a measure of the callousness of the age, as well as the cheapness of European labor, that over the course of a Great Circuit voyage the proportion of crew deaths could be as high as the slave deaths on the Middle Passage.

AFRICA AND THE ATLANTIC

The Atlantic system took a terrible toll in African lives both during the Middle Passage and under the harsh conditions of plantation slavery. Many other Africans died while being marched to African coastal ports for sale overseas. The overall effects on Africa of these losses and of other aspects of the slave trade have been the subject of considerable historical debate. It is clear that the trade's impact depended on the intensity and terms of different African regions' involvement.

Any assessment of the Atlantic system's effects in Africa must also take into consideration the fact that some Africans profited from the trade by capturing and selling slaves. They chained the slaves together or bound them to forked sticks for the march to the coast, then bartered them to the European slavers for trade goods. The effects on the enslaver were different from the effects on the enslaved.

The Gold Coast and the Slave Coast

The transition to slave trading was not sudden. Even as slaves were becoming Atlantic Africa's most valuable export, non-slave goods remained a significant part of the total trade. For example, during its eight decades of operation from 1672 to 1752, the English Royal African Company made 40 percent of its profits from dealings in gold, ivory, and forest products. In some parts of West Africa, such nonslave exports remained predominant even at the peak of the trade.

African merchants were very discriminating about what merchandise they received in return for slaves or other goods. A European ship that arrived with goods of low quality or unsuited to local tastes found it hard to purchase a cargo at a profitable price. Africans' greatest demands were for textiles, hardware, and guns. Of the goods the Royal African Company traded in West Africa in the 1680s, over 60 percent were Indian and European textiles and 30 percent hardware and weaponry. Beads and other jewelry formed 3 percent. The rest consisted of cowrie shells that were used as money. In the eighteenth century, tobacco and rum from the Americas became welcome imports.

Both Europeans and Africans naturally attempted to drive the best bargain for themselves and sometimes engaged in deceitful practices. The strength of the African bargaining position, however, may be inferred from the fact that as the demand for slaves rose, so too did their price in Africa. In the course of the eighteenth century, the goods needed to purchase a slave on the Gold Coast doubled and in some places tripled or quadrupled.

African governments on the Gold and Slave Coasts made Europeans observe African trading customs and prevented them from taking control of African territory. Rivalry among European nations, each of which established its own trading "castles" along the Gold Coast, also reduced Europeans' bargaining strength.

How did African kings and merchants obtain slaves for sale? Most accounts agree that prisoners taken in war were the greatest source of slaves for the Atlantic trade, but it is difficult to say how often capturing slaves for export was the main cause of warfare. An early-nineteenth-century king of Asante stated, "I cannot make war to catch slaves in the bush, like a thief. My ancestors never did so. But if I fight a king, and kill him when he is insolent, then certainly I must have his gold, and his slaves, and his people are mine too. Do not the white kings act like this?"[3] English rulers

had indeed sentenced seventeenth-century Scottish and Irish prisoners to forced labor in the West Indies.

The Bight of Biafra and Angola

In the eighteenth century, the slave trade expanded eastward to the Bight (bay) of Biafra. In contrast to the Gold and Slave Coasts, where strong kingdoms predominated, the densely populated interior of the Bight of Biafra contained no large states. Even so, the powerful merchant princes of the coastal ports still made European traders give them rich presents. Because of the absence of sizable states, there were no large-scale wars and consequently few prisoners of war. Instead, kidnapping was the major source of slaves.

As the volume of the Atlantic trade along the Bight of Biafra expanded in the late eighteenth century, some inland markets evolved into giant fairs, with different sections specializing in slaves and imported goods. An English ship's doctor reported that in the 1780s, slaves were "bought by the black traders at fairs, which are held for that purpose, at a distance of upwards of two hundred miles from the sea coast." He reported seeing from twelve hundred to fifteen hundred enslaved men and women arriving at the coast from a single fair.[4]

Angola, south of the Congo estuary, was the greatest source of slaves for the Atlantic trade. This was also the one place along the Atlantic coast where a single European nation, Portugal, controlled a significant amount of territory. Portuguese residents of the main coastal ports served as middlemen between caravans that arrived from the far interior and ships from Brazil.

Many of the slaves sold at Angolan markets were prisoners of war captured by expanding African states. As elsewhere in Africa, such prisoners seem to have been a by-product of African wars rather than the purpose for which the wars were fought.

Recent research has linked other enslavement with environmental crises in the hinterland of Angola. During the eighteenth century, these southern grasslands periodically suffered severe droughts, which drove famished refugees to areas with more plentiful water. In return for food and water, powerful African leaders gained control of many refugees and sold into the Atlantic trade the men, who were more likely than the women and children to escape or challenge the ruler's authority. The most successful of these inland Angolan leaders became heads of powerful new states that stabilized areas devastated by war and drought and repopulated them with the refugees and prisoners they retained. The slave frontier then moved farther inland. This cruel system worked to the benefit of a few African rulers and merchants at the expense of the many thousands of Africans who were sent to death or perpetual bondage in the Americas.

It is impossible to assess with precision the complex effects of the goods received in sub-Saharan Africa from these trades. Africans were very particular about what they received, so it is unlikely that they could have been consistently cheated. Some researchers have suggested that imports of textiles and metals undermined African weavers and metalworkers, but most economic historians calculate that on a per capita basis, the volume of these imports was too small to have idled many African artisans. Imports supplemented rather than replaced local production. The goods received in sub-Saharan Africa were intended for consumption and thus did not serve to develop the economy. Likewise, the sugar, tea, and chocolate Europeans consumed did little to promote economic development in Europe. However, both African and European merchants profited from trading these consumer goods. Because they directed the whole Atlantic system, Europeans gained far more wealth than Africans did.

Historians disagree in their assessment of how deeply European capitalism dominated Africa before 1800, but Europeans clearly had much less political and economic impact in Africa than in the West Indies or in other parts of the Americas. Still, it is significant that Western capitalism was expanding rapidly in the seventeenth century, while the Ottoman Empire, the dominant state of the Middle East, was entering a period of economic and political decline (see Chapter 21). The tide of influence in Africa was thus running in the Europeans' direction.

THE COLUMBIAN EXCHANGE

The term **Columbian Exchange** refers to the transfer of peoples, animals, plants, diseases, and technology between the New and Old Worlds that European trade in the Atlantic opened up. We have already seen how Old World diseases devastated Amerindian peoples and led to the resettlement of the Americas by Europeans and Africans. In addition, the domesticated livestock and major agricultural crops of the Old World had spread over much of the Americas, and Amerindians' staple crops had enriched the agricultures of Europe and Africa. This vast exchange of plants and animals radically altered diets and lifestyles around the Atlantic.

Transfers to the Americas

Within a century of Columbus's first voyage, new settlers in the Americas were growing all the staples of southern European agriculture—wheat, olives, grapes, and garden vegetables—along with African and Asian crops—rice, bananas, coconuts, breadfruit, and sugar cane. Native peoples remained loyal to their traditional staples but added many Old World plants to their diet. Citrus fruits, melons, figs, and sugar, as well as onions, radishes, and salad greens, all found a place in Amerindian cuisine.

By the eighteenth century, nearly all of the domesticated animals and cultivated plants in the Caribbean were ones that Europeans had introduced. The Spanish had brought cattle, pigs, and horses, all of which multiplied rapidly. They had also introduced new plants. Of these, bananas and plantain from the Canary Islands were a valuable addition to the food supply, and sugar and rice formed the basis of plantation agriculture, along with native tobacco. Other food crops arrived with the slaves from Africa, including okra, black-eyed peas, yams, grains such as millet and sorghum, and mangoes. Many of these new animals and plants were useful additions to the islands, but they crowded out indigenous species. The central importance of sugar cane in transforming Brazil and the Caribbean has already been noted.

The introduction of European livestock to the mainland had a dramatic impact. Faced with few natural predators, cattle, pigs, horses, and sheep, as well as pests like rats and rabbits, multiplied rapidly in the open spaces of the Americas. On the vast plains of present-day southern Brazil, Uruguay, and Argentina, herds of wild cattle and horses exceeded 50 million by 1700. Large herds of both animals also appeared in northern Mexico and what became the southwest of the United States.

Where Old World livestock spread most rapidly, environmental changes were most dramatic. Marauding livestock often had a destructive impact on Amerindian agriculturists. But on the plains of South America, northern Mexico, and Texas, cattle provided indigenous peoples with abundant supplies of meat and hides. In the present-day southwestern United States, the Navajo became sheepherders and expert weavers of woolen cloth. Individual Amerindians became muleteers, cowboys, and sheepherders.

No animal had a more striking effect on the cultures of native peoples than the horse, which increased the efficiency of hunters and the military capacity of warriors on the plains. The horse permitted the Apache, Sioux, Blackfoot, Comanche, Assiniboine, and others to hunt the vast herds of buffalo in North America more efficiently.

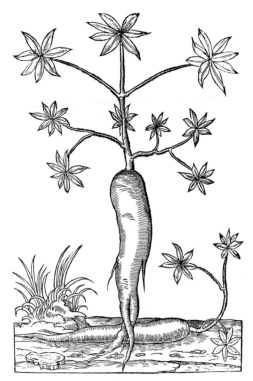

Cassava plant   Both the leaves and the starchy root of the cassava plant could be eaten.   (Engraving from André Thevet, *Les Singularitez de la Franc Antarctique.* Paris: Maurice de la Porte, 1557. Courtesy of the James Bell Library, University of Minnesota)

Transfers from the Americas

In return, the Americas offered the Old World an abundance of useful plants. The New World staples of maize and potatoes revolutionized agriculture and diet in parts of Europe, because they provided more calories per acre than any of the Old World staples except rice. Beans, squash, tomatoes, sweet potatoes, peanuts, chilis, and chocolate also gained widespread acceptance in Europe and other parts of the Old World. The New World also provided the Old with plants that provided dyes, medicines, and tobacco.

Maize and cassava (a Brazilian plant cultivated for its edible roots) moved across the Atlantic to Africa. The varieties of maize that spread to Africa were not modern high-bred sweet corn but starchier types found in white and yellow cornmeal. Cassava became the most important New World food in Africa. Truly a marvel, cassava had the highest yield of calories per acre of any staple food and thrived even in poor soils and during droughts. Both the leaves and the root could be eaten. Ground into meal, the root could be made into a bread that would keep for up to six months, or it could be fermented into a beverage.

Cassava and maize were probably introduced accidentally into Africa by Portuguese ships from Brazil that discarded leftover supplies after reaching Angola. It did not take long for local Africans to recognize the food value of these new crops, especially in drought-prone areas. By the eighteenth century, Central African rulers hundreds of miles from the Angolan coast were actively promoting the cultivation of maize and cassava on their royal estates in order to provide a more secure food supply. Some historians believe that in the inland areas, these Amerindian food crops provided the nutritional base for a population increase that partially offset losses due to the Atlantic slave trade.

CONCLUSION

The New World colonial empires of Spain, Portugal, France, and England had many characteristics in common. All subjugated Amerindian peoples and introduced large numbers of enslaved Africans. Within all four empires, forests were cut down, virgin soils were turned with the plow, and Old World animals and plants were introduced. Colonists in all four applied the technologies of the Old World to the resources of the New, producing wealth and exploiting the commercial possibilities of the emerging Atlantic market. Yet each of the New World empires also reflected the distinctive cultural and institutional heritages of its colonizing power.

Mineral wealth allowed Spain to develop the most centralized empire. Political and economic power was concentrated in the great capital cities of Mexico City and Lima. Portugal and France pursued similar objectives in their colonies. However, neither Brazil's agricultural economy nor France's Canadian fur trade produced the financial resources that made possible the centralized control achieved by Spain. Nevertheless, all three of these Catholic powers were able to impose and enforce significant levels of religious and cultural uniformity.

Greater cultural and religious diversity characterized British North America. Thus, colonists there were better able to respond to changing economic and political circumstances. Most important, the British colonies attracted many more European immigrants than did the other New World colonies. The new Atlantic trading system had great importance and momentous implications for world history. In the first phase of their expansion, Europeans had conquered and colonized the Americas and captured major Indian Ocean trade routes. The development of the Atlantic system showed Europeans' ability to move beyond the conquest and capture of existing systems to create a major new trading system that could transform a region almost beyond recognition.

The West Indies felt the transforming power of capitalism more profoundly than did any other place outside Europe in this period. The establishment of sugar plantation societies was not just a matter of replacing native vegetation with alien plants and native peoples with Europeans and Africans. More fundamentally, it made these once-isolated islands part of a dynamic trading system controlled from Europe. To be sure, the Caribbean was not the only place affected. Parts of northern Brazil were touched as deeply by the sugar revolution, and other parts of the Americas were yielding to the power of European colonization and capitalism.

Historians have seen the Atlantic system as a model of the kind of highly interactive economy that became global in later centuries. For that reason, the Atlantic system was a milestone in a much larger historical process, but not a monument to be admired. Its transformations were destructive as well as creative, producing victims as well as victors. Yet one cannot ignore that the system's awesome power came from its ability to create wealth. As the next chapter describes, southern Asia and the Indian Ocean basin were also beginning to feel the effects of Europeans' rising power.

■ Key Terms

Atlantic system	driver
Council of the Indies	seasoning
Bartolomé de Las Casas	maroons
Potosí	capitalism
encomienda	mercantilism
creoles	chartered companies
indentured servants	Dutch West India Company
House of Burgesses	Royal African Company
Pilgrims	Great Circuit
Puritans	Middle Passage
Iroquois Confederacy	Columbian Exchange
New France	

■ Suggested Reading

Alfred W. Crosby, Jr., is justifiably the best-known student of the Columbian Exchange. See his *The Columbian Exchange: Biological and Cultural Consequences of 1492* (1972) and *Ecological Imperialism* (1986). William H. McNeill, *Plagues and People* (1976), puts the discussion of the American exchange in a world history context. Elinor G. K. Melville, *A Plague of Sheep: Environmental Consequences of the Spanish Conquest of Mexico* (1994), is the most important recent contribution to this field.

Colonial Latin America, 2d ed. (1994), by Mark A. Burkholder and Lyman L. Johnson, provides a good introduction to colonial Latin American history. *Early Latin America* (1983) by James Lockhart and Stuart B. Schwartz and *Spain and Portugal in the New World, 1492–1700* (1984) by Lyle N. McAlister are both useful introductions as well.

Among the useful general studies of the British colonies are Charles M. Andrews, *The Colonial Period of American History: The Settlements*, 3 vols. (1934–1937); David Hackett Fischer, *Albion's Seed: Four British Folkways in America* (1989); and Gary B. Nash, *Red, White, and Black:*

The Peoples of Early America, 2d ed. (1982). For slavery, see David Brion Davis, *The Problem of Slavery in Western Culture* (1966).

On French North America, William J. Eccles, *France in America*, rev. ed. (1990), is an excellent overview; see also his *The Canadian Frontier, 1534–1760* (1969).

The global context of early modern capitalism is examined by Immanuel Wallerstein, *The Modern World-System*, 3 vols. (1974–1989), and by Fernand Braudel, *Civilization and Capitalism, 15th–18th Century*, 3 vols. (1982–1984). The best general introductions to the Atlantic system are Philip D. Curtin, *The Rise and Fall of the Plantation Complex* (1990), Herbert S. Klein, *The Atlantic Slave Trade* (1999), and David Ellis, *The Rise of African Slavery in the Americas* (2000). A useful collection of primary and secondary sources is David Northrup, ed., *The Atlantic Slave Trade*, 2d ed. (2001).

The cultural connections among African communities on both sides of the Atlantic are explored by John Thornton, *Africa and Africans in the Making of the Atlantic World, 1400–1800*, 2d ed. (1998). Herbert S. Klein's *African Slavery in Latin America and the Caribbean* (1986) is an exceptionally fine synthesis of research on New World slavery, including North American slave systems. For recent research on slavery and the African, Atlantic, and Muslim slave trades with Africa, see Paul Lovejoy, *Transformations in Slavery: A History of Slavery in Africa*, 2d ed. (2000).

■ Notes

1. Quoted in Alfred W. Crosby, Jr., *The Columbian Exchange: Biological and Cultural Consequences of 1492* (Westport, CT: Greenwood, 1972), 58.
2. Eric Williams, *Capitalism and Slavery* (Charlotte: University of North Carolina Press, 1944), 7.
3. King Osei Bonsu, quoted in David Northrup, ed., *The Atlantic Slave Trade*, 2d ed. (Boston: Houghton Mifflin, 2001), 176.
4. Alexander Falconbridge, *Account of the Slave Trade on the Coast of Africa* (London: J. Phillips, 1788), 12.

Southwest Asia and the Indian Ocean, 1500–1750

The Ottoman Empire • The Safavid Empire • The Mughal Empire •
Trade Empires in the Indian Ocean
ENVIRONMENT AND TECHNOLOGY: Metal Currency and Inflation

A nthony Jenkinson, merchant-adventurer for the Muscovy Company, founded in 1555 to develop trade with Russia, was the first Englishman to set foot in Iran. Eight years after the first English ship dropped anchor at Archangel on the White Sea in Russia's frigid north, Jenkinson made his way through Russia, down the Volga River, and across the Caspian Sea. The local ruler he met when he disembarked in 1561 in northwestern Iran was an object of wonder, "richly apparelled with long garments of silk, and cloth of gold, embroidered with pearls of stone; upon his head was a *tolipane* [headdress shaped like a tulip] with a sharp end pointing upwards half a yard long, of rich cloth of gold, wrapped about with a piece of India silk of twenty yards long, wrought in gold richly enameled, and set with precious stones; his earrings had pendants of gold a handful long, with two rubies of great value, set in the ends thereof."

Moving on to Qazvin°, Iran's capital, Jenkinson met the shah. After presenting a letter from Queen Elizabeth in Latin, English, Hebrew, and Italian but finding no one capable of reading it, he managed nevertheless to propose trade between England and Iran. The shah rejected the idea, since diverting Iranian silk from the markets of the Ottoman sultans, with whom he was negotiating a truce after a half-century of intermittent war, would have been undiplomatic.

Though Central Asia's bazaars were only meagerly supplied with goods, as Jenkinson and later merchants discovered, the idea of bypassing the Ottomans in the eastern Mediterranean and trading directly with Iran through Russia remained tempting. By the same token, the Ottomans were tempted by the idea of outflanking Safavid Iran. In 1569, an Ottoman army tried unsuccessfully to dig a 40-mile (64-kilometer)

Qazvin (kaz-VEEN)

canal between the Don River, which opened into the Black Sea, and the Volga, which flowed into the Caspian. Their objective was to enable Ottoman ships to reach the Caspian and attack Iran from the north.

The Ottomans' foe was Russia, then ruled by Tsar Ivan IV (r. 1533–1584), known as Ivan the Terrible or Awesome. Ivan transformed his principality from a second-rate power into the sultan's primary competitor in Central Asia. In the river-crossed steppe, where Turkic nomads had long enjoyed uncontested sway, Slavic Christian Cossacks from the region of the Don and Dnieper Rivers used armed wagon trains and river craft fitted with small cannon to push southward and establish a Russian presence.

A contest for trade with or control of Central Asia was natural after the centrality conferred on the region by three centuries of Mongol and Turkic conquest, highlighted by the campaigns of Genghis Khan and Timur. But as we shall see, changes in the organization of trade were sapping the vitality of the Silk Road. Wealth and power were shifting to European seaborne empires linking the Atlantic with the Indian Ocean. Though the Ottomans were a formidable naval power in the Mediterranean, neither they nor the Safavid shahs in Iran nor the Mughal emperors of India deployed more than a token navy in the southern seas.

As you read this chapter, ask yourself the following questions:

- What were the advantages and disadvantages of a land as opposed to a maritime empire?
- What role did religion play in political alliances and rivalries and in the formation of states?
- How did trading patterns change between 1500 and 1750?

THE OTTOMAN EMPIRE

The most long-lived of the post-Mongol Muslim empires was the **Ottoman Empire,** founded around 1300 (see Map 18.1). By extending Islamic conquests into eastern Europe, starting in the late fourteenth century, and by taking Syria and Egypt from the Mamluk rulers in the early sixteenth, the Ottomans seemed to recreate the might of the original Islamic caliphate, the empire established by the Muslim Arab conquests in the seventh century. However, the empire was actually more like the new centralized monarchs of France and Spain (see Chapter 17) than any medieval model.

Enduring more than five centuries, until 1922, the Ottoman Empire survived several periods of wrenching change, some caused by internal problems, others by the growing power of European adversaries. These periods of change reveal the problems faced by huge land-based empires around the world.

Expansion and Frontiers

Established around 1300, the Ottoman Empire grew from a tiny state in northwestern Anatolia because of three factors: (1) the shrewdness of its founder, Osman (from which the name "Ottoman" comes), and his descendants, (2) control of a strategic link between Europe and Asia on the Dardanelles strait, and (3) the creation of an army that took advantage of the traditional skills of the Turkish cavalryman and the new military possibilities presented by gunpowder.

At first, Ottoman armies concentrated on Christian enemies in Greece and the Balkans, in 1389 conquering a strong Serbian kingdom at the Battle of Kosovo°. Much of southeastern Europe and Anatolia was under the control of the sultans by 1402. In 1453, Sultan Mehmed II, "the Conqueror," laid siege to Constantinople. His forces used enormous cannon to bash in the city's walls,

---

Kosovo (KO-so-vo)

CHRONOLOGY

	Ottoman Empire	Safavid Empire	Mughal Empire
1500		**1502–1524** Shah Ismail establishes Safavid rule in Iran	
	1514 Selim I conquers Egypt and Syria (1516–1517)	**1514** Defeat by Ottomans at Chaldiran limits Safavid growth	
	1520–1566 Reign of Suleiman the Magnificent; peak of Ottoman Empire **1529** First Ottoman siege of Vienna		**1526** Babur defeats last sultan of Delhi at Panipat **1556–1605** Akbar rules in Agra; peak of Mughal Empire
	1571 Ottoman naval defeat at Lepanto	**1587–1629** Reign of Shah Abbas the Great; peak of Safavid Empire	
1600	**1610** End of Anatolian revolts		
			1658–1707 Aurangzeb imposes conservative Islamic regime
1700	**1718–1730** Military decline apparent to Austria and Russia	**1722** Afghan invaders topple last Safavid shah **1736–1747** Nadir Shah temporarily reunites Iran; invades India (1739)	**1739** Iranians under Nadir Shah sack Delhi

dragged warships over a high hill from the Bosporus strait to the city's inner harbor to get around its sea defenses, and finally penetrated the city's land walls through a series of direct infantry assaults. The fall of Constantinople—henceforth commonly known as Istanbul—brought to an end over eleven hundred years of Byzantine rule and made the Ottomans seem invincible.

Selim° I, "the Inexorable," conquered Egypt and Syria in 1516 and 1517, making the Red Sea the Ottomans' southern frontier. His son, **Suleiman° the Magnificent** (r. 1520–1566), presided over the greatest Ottoman assault on Christian Europe.

Suleiman seemed unstoppable as he conquered Belgrade in 1521, expelled the Knights of the Hospital of St. John from the island of Rhodes the following year, and laid siege to Vienna in 1529. Vienna was saved by the need to retreat before the onset of winter more than by military action. In later centuries, Ottoman historians looked back on the reign of Suleiman as the period when the imperial system worked to perfection and spoke of it as the golden age of Ottoman greatness.

While Ottoman armies pressed deeper and deeper into eastern Europe, the sultans also sought to control the Mediterranean. Between 1453 and 1502, the Ottomans fought the opening rounds of a two-century war with Venice, the most powerful of

Selim (seh-LEEM)   Suleiman (SOO-lay-man)

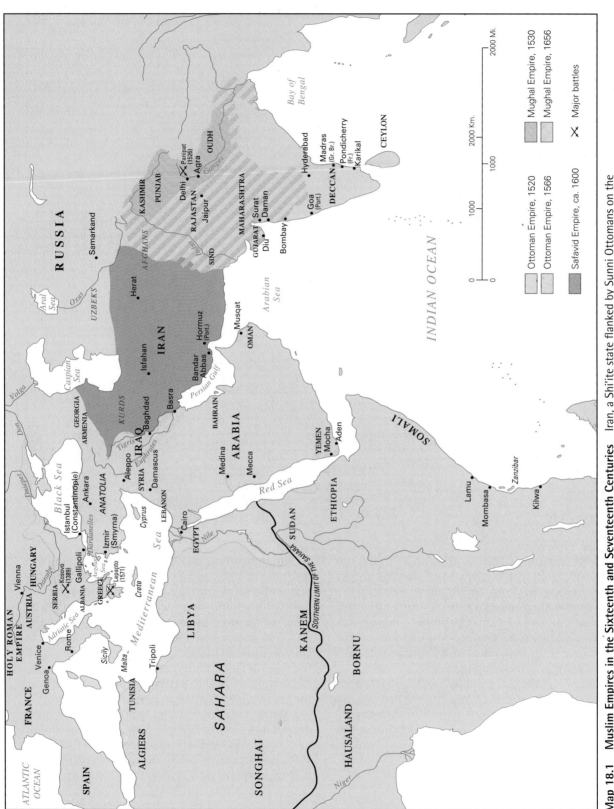

Map 18.1 Muslim Empires in the Sixteenth and Seventeenth Centuries Iran, a Shi'ite state flanked by Sunni Ottomans on the west and Sunni Mughals on the east, had the least exposure to European influences. Ottoman expansion across the southern Mediterranean Sea intensified European fears of Islam. The areas of strongest Mughal control dictated that Islam's spread into southeast Asia would be heavily influenced by merchants and religious figures from Gujarat instead of from eastern India.

Italy's commercial city-states. The initial fighting left Venice in control of its lucrative islands for another century. But it also left Venice a reduced military power compelled to pay tribute to the Ottomans.

It never occurred to the Ottomans that a sea empire held together by flimsy ships could truly rival a great land empire fielding an army of a hundred thousand men. In the early sixteenth century, merchants from southern India and Sumatra sent emissaries to Istanbul requesting naval support against the Portuguese. The Ottomans responded vigorously to Portuguese threats close to their territories, such as at Aden at the southern entrance to the Red Sea, but their efforts farther afield were insufficient to stifle growing Portuguese domination.

Eastern luxury products still flowed to Ottoman markets. Portuguese power was territorially limited to fortified coastal points, such as Hormuz at the entrance to the Persian Gulf, Goa in western India, and Malacca in Malaya. Why commit major resources to subduing an enemy whose main threat was a demand that merchant vessels, mostly belonging to non-Ottoman Muslims, buy protection from Portuguese attack? The Ottomans did send a small naval force to Indonesia, but they never formulated a consistent or aggressive policy with regard to political and economic developments in the Indian Ocean.

Central Institutions

By the 1520s, the Ottoman Empire was the most powerful and best-organized state in either Europe or the Islamic world. Its military was balanced between cavalry archers, primarily Turks, and **Janissaries°,** Christian prisoners of war induced to serve as military slaves.

Slave soldiery had a long history in Islamic lands, but the conquest of Christian territories in the Balkans in the late fourteenth century gave the Ottomans access to a new military resource. Converted to Islam, these "new troops," called *yeni cheri* in Turkish and *Janissary* in English, gave the

Janissaries (JAN-nih-say-rees)

Ottoman Glassmakers on Parade   Celebrations of the circumcisions of the sultan's sons featured parades organized by the craft guilds of Istanbul. This float features glassmaking, a common craft in Islamic realms. The most elaborate glasswork included oil lamps for mosques and colored glass for the small stained-glass windows below mosque domes.   (Topkapi Saray Museum)

Ottomans unusual military flexibility. Since horseback riding and bowmanship were not part of their cultural backgrounds, they readily accepted the idea of fighting on foot and learning to use guns, which at that time were still too heavy and awkward for a horseman to load and fire. The Janissaries lived in barracks and trained all year round.

The process of selection for Janissary training changed early in the fifteenth century. The new system imposed a regular levy of male children on Christian villages in the Balkans and occasionally elsewhere. Recruited children were placed with Turkish families to learn their language and then were sent to the sultan's palace in Istanbul for an education that included instruction in Islam, military training, and, for the most talented, what we might call liberal arts. This regime, sophisticated for its time, produced not only the Janissary soldiers but also, from among the chosen few who received special training, senior military commanders and heads of government departments up to the rank of grand vizier.

The cavalrymen were supported by land grants and administered most rural areas in Anatolia and the Balkans. They maintained order, collected taxes, and reported for each summer's campaign with their horses, retainers, and supplies, all paid for from the taxes they collected. When not campaigning, they stayed at home.

A galley-equipped navy was manned by Greek, Turkish, Algerian, and Tunisian sailors, usually under the command of an admiral from one of the North African ports. The balance of the Ottoman land forces brought success to Ottoman arms in recurrent wars with the Safavids, who were much slower to adopt firearms, and in the inexorable conquest of the Balkans. Expansion by sea was less dramatic. A major expedition against Malta in the western Mediterranean failed in 1565. Combined Christian forces also achieved a massive naval victory at the Battle of Lepanto, off Greece, in 1571. But the Ottomans' resources were so extensive that in a year's time, they had replaced all of the galleys sunk in that battle.

The Ottoman Empire became cosmopolitan in character. The sophisticated court language, Osmanli° (the Turkish form of *Ottoman*), shared basic grammar and vocabulary with Turkish, but Arabic and Persian elements made it distinct from the language spoken by Anatolia's nomads and villagers. Everyone who served in the military or the bureaucracy and conversed in Osmanli was considered to belong to the *askeri*°, or "military," class. Members of this class were exempt from taxes and owed their well-being to the sultan.

The Ottomans saw the sultan as providing justice for his "flock of sheep" (*raya*°) and the military protecting them. In return, the raya paid the taxes that supported both the sultan and the military. In reality, the sultan's government remained comparatively isolated from the lives of most subjects. As Islam gradually became the majority religion in Balkan regions, Islamic law (the Shari'a°) conditioned urban institutions and social life. Local customs prevailed among non-Muslims and in many rural areas; and non-Muslims looked to their own religious leaders for guidance in family and spiritual matters.

Crisis of the Military State, 1585–1650

As military technology evolved, cannon and lighter-weight firearms played an ever-larger role on the battlefield. Accordingly, the size of the Janissary corps—and its cost to the government—grew steadily, and the role of the Turkish cavalry diminished. To pay the Janissaries, the sultan started reducing the number of landholding cavalrymen. Revenues previously spent on their living expenses and military equipment went directly into the imperial treasury. Inflation caused by a flood of cheap silver from the New World (see Environment and Technology: Metal Currency and Inflation) bankrupted many of the remaining landholders restricted by law to collecting a fixed amount of taxes. Their land was returned to the state. Displaced cavalrymen, armed and unhappy, became a restive element in rural Anatolia.

This complicated situation resulted in revolts that devastated Anatolia between 1590 and 1610. Former landholding cavalrymen, short-term soldiers released at the end of the campaign season, peasants overburdened by emergency taxes, and even impoverished students of religion formed bands of marauders. Anatolia experienced the worst of the rebellions and suffered greatly from emigration and the loss of agricultural production. But an increase in banditry, made worse by the government's inability to stem the spread of muskets among the general public, beset other parts of the empire as well.

In the meantime, the Janissaries took advantage of their growing influence to gain relief from prohibitions on their marrying and engaging in business. Janissaries who involved themselves in commerce lessened the burden on the state budget, and married Janissaries who enrolled sons or relatives in the corps made it possible in the seventeenth century for the government to save state funds by abolishing forced recruitment. These savings, however, were more than offset by the increase in the total number of Janissaries and in

---

Osmanli (os-MAHN-lee) *askeri* (AS-keh-ree)
raya (RAH-yah) Shari'a (sha-REE-ah)

Metal Currency and Inflation

Inflation occurs when the quantity of goods and services available for purchase remains stable while the quantity of money in circulation increases. With more money in their pockets, people are willing to pay more to get what they want. Prices go up, and what people think of as the value of money goes down.

Today, with paper money and electronic banking, governments try to control inflation by regulating the printing of money or by other means. Prior to the nineteenth century, money consisted of silver and gold coins, and governments did not keep track of how much money was in circulation. As long as the annual production of gold and silver mines was quite small, inflation was not a worry. In the sixteenth and seventeenth centuries, however, precious metal poured into Spain from silver and gold mines in the New World, but there was no increase in the availability of goods and services. The resulting inflation triggered a "price revolution" in Europe—a general tripling of prices between 1500 and 1650. In Paris in 1650, the price of wheat and hay was fifteen times higher than the price had been in 1500.

This wave of inflation worked its way east, contributing to social disorder in the Ottoman Empire. European traders had more money available than Ottoman merchants and could outbid them for scarce commodities. Lacking silver and gold mines, the Ottoman government reduced the amount of precious metal in Ottoman coins. This made the problem worse. Hit hardest were people who had fixed incomes. Cavalrymen holding land grants worth a set amount each year were unable to equip themselves for military campaigns. Students living on fixed scholarships went begging.

Safavid Iran needed silver and gold to pay for imports from Mughal India, which imported few Iranian goods. Iranians sold silk to the Ottoman Empire for silver and gold, worsening the Ottoman situation, and then passed the precious metal on to India. Everyday life in Iran depended on barter or locally minted copper coinage, both more resistant to inflation. Copper for coins was sometimes imported from China.

Though no one then grasped the connection between silver production in Mexico and the trade balance between Iran and India, the world of the sixteenth and seventeenth centuries was becoming more closely linked economically than it had ever been before.

Set of Coin Dies   The lower die, called the anvil die, was set in a piece of wood. A blank disk of gold, silver, or copper was placed on top of it. The hammer die was placed on top of the blank and struck with a hammer to force the coin's image onto it.   (Courtesy, Israel Museum, Jerusalem)

their steady deterioration as a military force, which necessitated the hiring of more and more supplemental troops.

Economic Change and Growing Weakness

A very different Ottoman Empire emerged from this crisis. The sultan once had led armies. Now he mostly resided in his palace and had little experience of the real world, and the affairs of government were overseen more and more by the chief administrators—the grand viziers.

The Janissaries took advantage of their increased power to make membership in their corps hereditary. Their involvement in crafts and trading took a toll on their military skills, but they continued to be a powerful faction in urban politics. Land grants in return for military service also disappeared. Tax farming arose in their place. Tax farmers paid specific taxes, such as customs duties, in advance in return for the privilege of collecting a greater amount from the actual taxpayers.

Rural administration, already disrupted by the rebellions, suffered from the transition to tax farms. The former military landholders had kept order on their lands in order to maintain their incomes. Tax farmers were less likely to live on the land. The imperial government therefore faced greater administrative burdens and came to rely heavily on powerful provincial governors or on wealthy men who purchased lifelong tax collection rights and behaved more or less like private landowners.

Rural disorder and decline in administrative control sometimes opened the way for new economic opportunities. The Aegean port of Izmir° (ancient Smyrna) was able to transform itself between 1580 and 1650 from a small Muslim Turkish town into a multiethnic, multireligious, multilinguistic entrepôt because of the Ottoman government's inability to control trade and the slowly growing dominance of European traders in the Indian Ocean. Local farmers who previously had grown grain for subsistence shifted their plantings more and more to cotton and other cash crops sought by European

traders at Izmir. After its introduction in the 1590s, tobacco quickly became popular in the Ottoman Empire despite government prohibitions. In this way, the agricultural economy of western Anatolia, the Balkans, and the Mediterranean coast—the Ottoman lands most accessible to Europe—became enmeshed in the seventeenth century in a growing European commercial network.

The Ottoman Empire lacked both the wealth and the inclination to match European economic advances. Overland trade from the east dwindled as political disorder in Safavid Iran cut deeply into Iranian silk production. Coffee, an Arabian product that rose from obscurity in the fifteenth century to become the rage first in the Ottoman Empire and then in Europe, was grown in the highlands of Yemen and exported by way of Egypt. By 1770, however, Muslim merchants trading in the Yemeni port of Mocha° (literally "the coffee place") were charged 15 percent in duties and fees. But European traders, benefiting from long-standing trade agreements with the Ottoman Empire, paid little more than 3 percent. Such trade agreements led to European domination of Ottoman import and export trade by sea.

To most people, the downward course of imperial power was not evident, much less the reasons behind it. Far from seeing Europe as the enemy that eventually would dismantle the weakening Ottoman Empire, the Istanbul elite experimented with European clothing and furniture styles and purchased printed books from the empire's first (and short-lived) press.

In 1730, however, a conservative Janissary revolt with strong religious overtones toppled Sultan Ahmed III. The rebellion confirmed the perceptions of a few that the Ottoman Empire was facing severe difficulties. But decay at the center spelled benefit elsewhere. In the provinces, ambitious and competent governors, wealthy landholders, urban notables, and nomad chieftains were well placed to take advantage of the central government's weakness.

By the middle of the eighteenth century, groups of Mamluks had regained a dominant position in Egypt, and Janissary commanders had become vir-

Izmir (IZ-meer)

Mocha (MOH-kuh)

tually independent rulers in Baghdad. Although no region declared full independence, the sultan's power was slipping away to the advantage of a broad array of lower officials and upstart chieftains in all parts of the empire, and the Ottoman economy was reorienting itself toward Europe.

THE SAFAVID EMPIRE

The **Safavid Empire** of Iran (see Map 18.1) resembled its long-time Ottoman foe in many ways: it initially relied militarily on cavalry paid through land grants; its population spoke several different languages; and it was oriented inward away from the sea. It also had distinct qualities that to this day set Iran off from its neighbors: it derived part of its legitimacy from the pre-Islamic dynasties of ancient Iran, and it adopted the Shi'ite form of Islam.

Safavid Society and Religion

The ultimate victor in a complicated struggle for power among Turkish chieftains west of the Ottoman Empire was Ismail°, a boy of Kurdish, Iranian, and Greek ancestry. In 1502, at the age of sixteen, Ismail proclaimed himself shah of Iran and declared that from that time forward, his realm would be devoted to **Shi'ite** Islam, which revered the family of Muhammad's son-in-law Ali. Although Ismail's reasons for compelling Iran's conversion to Shi'ism are unknown, the effect of this radical act was to create a deep chasm between Iran and its neighbors, all of which were Sunni. Iran became a truly separate country for the first time since its incorporation into the Islamic caliphate in the seventh century.

The imposition of Shi'ite belief made the split permanent, but differences between Iran and its neighbors had long been in the making. Persian, written in the Arabic script from the tenth century onward, had emerged as the second language of Is-

Ismail (IS-ma-eel)

lam. Iranian scholars and writers normally read Arabic as well as Persian and sprinkled their writings with Arabic phrases, but their Arab counterparts were much less inclined to learn Persian. After the Mongols destroyed Baghdad, the capital of the Islamic caliphate, in 1258, Iran developed largely on its own, having more extensive contacts with India—where Muslim rulers favored the Persian language—than with the Arabs.

In the post-Mongol period, artistic styles in the East also went their own way. Painted and molded tiles and tile mosaics, often in vivid turquoise blue, became the standard exterior decoration of mosques in Iran but never were used in Syria and Egypt. Persian poets raised verse to peaks of perfection that had no reflection in Arabic poetry, generally considered to be in a state of decline.

To be sure, Islam itself provided a tradition of belief, learning, and law that crossed ethnic and linguistic borders, but Shah Ismail's imposition of Shi'ism set Iran significantly apart. Shi'ite doctrine says that all temporal rulers, regardless of title, are temporary stand-ins for the **"Hidden Imam":** the twelfth descendant of Ali, the prophet Muhammad's cousin and son-in-law who disappeared as a child in the ninth century. Some Shi'ite scholars concluded that the faithful should calmly accept the world as it was and wait quietly for the Hidden Imam's return. Others maintained that they themselves should play a stronger role in political affairs because they were best qualified to know the Hidden Imam's wishes. These two positions, which still play a role in Iranian Shi'ism, tended to enhance the self-image of religious scholars as independent of imperial authority and stood in the way of their becoming subordinate government functionaries, as happened in the Ottoman Empire.

Shi'ism also affected the psychological life of the people. Annual commemoration of the martyrdom of Imam Husayn (d. 680), Ali's son and the third Imam, regularized an emotional outpouring with no parallel in Sunni lands. Day after day for two weeks, preachers recited the woeful tale to crowds of weeping believers, and elaborate street processions, often organized by craft guilds, parade chanting and self-flagellating men past crowds of reverent onlookers. Of course, Shi'ites elsewhere observed rites of mourning for Imam

Safavid Shah with Attendants and Musicians This painting by Ali-Quli Jubbadar, a European convert working for the Safavid armory, reflects Western influences. Notice the use of light and shadow to model faces and the costume of the attendant to the shah's right. The shah's waterpipe indicates the spread of tobacco, a New World crop, to the Middle East. (Courtesy of Oriental Institute, Academy of Sciences, Leningrad. Reproduced from *Album of Persian and Indian Miniatures* [Moscow, 1962], ill. no. 98)

Husayn, but the impact of these rites was especially great in Iran, where 90 percent of the population was Shi'ite. Over time, the subjects of the Safavid shahs came to feel more than ever a people apart.

Isfahan and Istanbul

Outwardly, the Ottoman capital of Istanbul looked quite different from Isfahan°, which became Iran's capital in 1598 by decree of **Shah Abbas I** (r. 1587–1629). Built on seven hills on the south side of the narrow Golden Horn inlet, Istanbul boasted a skyline punctuated by the gray stone domes and thin, pointed minarets of the great imperial mosques. The mosques surrounding the royal plaza in Isfahan, in contrast, had unobtrusive minarets and brightly tiled domes that rose to gentle peaks. High walls surrounded the sultan's palace in Istanbul. Shah Abbas in Isfahan focused his capital on the giant royal plaza, which was large enough for his army to play polo, and he used an airy palace overlooking the plaza to receive dignitaries and review his troops.

The harbor of Istanbul, the primary Ottoman seaport, teemed with sailing ships and smaller craft, many of them belonging to a colony of European merchants perched on a hilltop on the north side of the Golden Horn. Isfahan, far from the sea, was only occasionally visited by Europeans. Most of its trade was in the hands of Jews, Hindus, and especially a colony of Armenian Christians brought in by Shah Abbas.

Beneath these superficial differences, the two capitals had much in common. Wheeled vehicles were scarce in hilly Istanbul and nonexistent in Isfahan. Both cities were built for walking and, aside from the royal plaza in Isfahan, lacked the open spaces common in contemporary European cities. Streets were narrow and irregular. Houses crowded against each other in dead-end lanes. Residents enjoyed their privacy in interior courtyards. Artisans and merchants organized themselves into guilds that had strong social and religious as well as economic bonds. The shops of each guild adjoined each other in the markets.

Women were seldom seen in public, even in Istanbul's mazelike covered market or in Isfahan's long, serpentine bazaar. At home, the women's quarters—called *anderun*°, or "interior," in Iran and *harem,* or "forbidden area," in Istanbul—were separate from the public rooms where the men of

Isfahan (is-fah-HAHN)

anderun (an-deh-ROON)

the family received visitors. In both areas, low cushions, charcoal braziers for warmth, carpets, and small tables constituted most of the furnishings.

The private side of family life has left few traces, but it is apparent that women's society—consisting of wives, children, female servants, and sometimes one or more eunuchs—was not entirely cut off from the outside world. Ottoman court records reveal that women, using male agents, were very active in the urban real estate market. Often they were selling inherited shares of their father's estate, but some both bought and sold real estate on a regular basis and even established religious endowments for pious purposes. The fact that Islamic law, unlike some European codes, permitted a wife to retain her property after marriage gave some women a stake in the general economy and a degree of independence from their spouses. Women also appeared in other types of court cases, where they often testified for themselves, for Islamic courts did not recognize the role of attorney. Although comparable Safavid court records do not survive, historians assume that a parallel situation prevailed in Iran.

European travelers commented on the veiling of women outside the home, but miniature paintings indicate that ordinary female garb consisted of a long, ample dress with a scarf or long shawl pulled tight over the forehead to conceal the hair. Lightweight trousers, either close-fitting or baggy, were often worn under the dress. This mode of dress was not far different from that of men. Poor men wore light trousers, a long shirt, a jacket, and a hat or turban. Wealthier men wore over their trousers ankle-length caftans, often closely fitted around the chest. The norm for both sexes was complete coverage of arms, legs, and hair.

Public life was almost entirely the domain of men. Poetry and art, both somewhat more elegantly developed in Isfahan than in Istanbul, were as likely to extol the charms of beardless boys as pretty women. Despite religious disapproval of homosexuality, attachments to adolescent boys were neither unusual nor hidden. Women who appeared in public—aside from non-Muslims, the aged, and the very poor—were likely to be slaves. Miniature paintings frequently depict female dancers, musicians, and even acrobats in attitudes

and costumes that range from decorous to decidedly erotic.

Despite social similarities, the overall flavors of Isfahan and Istanbul were not the same. Isfahan had its prosperous Armenian quarter across the river from the city's center, but it was not a truly cosmopolitan capital, just as the peoples of the Safavid realm were not remarkably diverse. Like other rulers of extensive land empires, Shah Abbas located his capital toward the center of his domain within comparatively easy reach of any threatened frontier. Istanbul, in contrast, was a great seaport and crossroads located on the straits separating the sultan's European and Asian possessions. People of all sorts lived or spent time in Istanbul: Venetians, Genoese, Arabs, Turks, Greeks, Armenians, Albanians, Serbs, Jews, Bulgarians, and more. In this respect, Istanbul conveyed the cosmopolitan character of major seaports from London to Canton (Guangzhou) and belied the fact that its prosperity rested on the vast reach of the sultan's territories rather than on the voyages of its merchants.

Economic Crisis and Political Collapse

The silk fabrics of northern Iran were the mainstay of the Safavid Empire's foreign trade. However, the manufacture that eventually became most powerfully associated with Iran was the deep-pile carpet made by knotting colored yarns around stretched warp threads. Different cities produced distinctive carpet designs. Women and girls did much of the actual knotting work.

Overall, Iran's manufacturing sector was neither large nor notably productive. Most of the shah's subjects, whether Iranians, Turks, Kurds, or Arabs, lived by subsistence farming or herding. Neither area of activity recorded significant technological advances during the Safavid period.

The Safavids, like the Ottomans, had difficulty finding the money to pay troops armed with firearms. This crisis occurred somewhat later in Iran because of its greater distance from Europe. By the end of the sixteenth century, it was evident that a more systematic adoption of cannon and firearms in the Safavid Empire would be needed to hold off the Ottomans and the Uzbeks° (Turkish rulers who had succeeded the Timurids on Iran's Central Asian frontier; see Map 18.1). Like the Ottoman cavalry a century earlier, the warriors furnished by the nomad leaders were not inclined to trade in their bows for firearms. Shah Abbas responded by establishing a slave corps of year-round soldiers and arming them with guns. The Christian converts to Islam who initially provided the manpower for the new corps were mostly captives taken in raids on Georgia in the Caucasus°.

In the late sixteenth century, the inflation caused by cheap silver spread into Iran; then overland trade through Safavid territory declined because of mismanagement of the silk monopoly after Shah Abbas's death in 1629. As a result, the country faced the unsolvable problem of finding money to pay the army and bureaucracy. Trying to unseat the nomads from their lands to regain control of taxes was more difficult and more disruptive militarily than the piecemeal dismantlement of the land-grant system in the Ottoman Empire. The nomads were still a cohesive military force, and pressure from the center simply caused them to withdraw to their mountain pastures until the pressure subsided. By 1722, the government had become so weak and commanded so little support from the nomadic groups that an army of marauding Afghans was able to capture Isfahan and effectively end Safavid rule.

THE MUGHAL EMPIRE

What distinguished the Indian empire of the Mughal° sultans from the empires of the Ottomans and Safavids was the fact that India was a land of Hindus ruled by a Muslim minority. Muslim dominion in India was the result of repeated military campaigns from the early eleventh century onward, and the Mughals had to contend with the Hindus' long-standing resentment of the destruc-

tion of their culture by Muslims. Thus, the challenge facing the Mughals was not just conquering and organizing a large territorial state but also finding a formula for Hindu-Muslim coexistence.

Political Foundations

Babur° (1483–1530), the founder of the **Mughal Empire,** was a Muslim descendant of both Timur and Genghis Khan (*Mughal* is Persian for "Mongol"). Invading from Central Asia, Babur defeated the last Muslim sultan of Delhi in 1526. Babur's grandson **Akbar** (r. 1556–1605), a brilliant but mercurial man, established the central administration of the expanding state. Under him and his three successors—the last of whom died in 1707—all but the southern tip of India fell under Mughal rule, administered first from Agra and then from Delhi°.

Akbar granted land revenues to military officers and government officials in return for their service. Ranks, called *mansabs°,* some high and some low, entitled their holders to revenue assignments. As in the other Islamic empires, revenue grants were not considered hereditary, and the central government kept careful track of their issuance.

With a population of 100 million, a thriving trading economy based on cotton cloth, and a generally efficient administration, India under Akbar was probably the most prosperous empire of the sixteenth century. He and his successors faced few external threats and experienced generally peaceful conditions in their northern Indian heartland.

Foreign trade boomed at the port of Surat in the northwest, which also served as an embarkation point for pilgrims on their way to Mecca. Like the Safavids, the Mughals had no navy or merchant ships. The government saw the Europeans—after Akbar's time, primarily Dutch and English, the Portuguese having lost most of their Indian ports—less as enemies than as shipmasters whose naval support could be procured as needed in return for trading privileges.

Uzbeks (UHZ-bex) Caucasus (CAW-kuh-suhs)
Mughal (MOH-guhl)

Babur (BAH-bur) Delhi (DEL-ee) *mansabs* (MAN-sabz)

New Year Celebration at the Court of Shah Jahan (r. 1628–1658) The pre-Islamic Iranian tradition of celebrating the New Year (in Persian *No Ruz*, "New Day") on March 21, the vernal equinox, spread with Islamic rule. The dancing girls are a characteristic Indian aspect of the celebration. (The Royal Collection © Her Majesty Queen Elizabeth II)

Hindus and Muslims

The Mughal state inherited traditions of unified imperial rule from both the Islamic caliphate and the more recent examples of Genghis Khan and Timur. Those traditions did not necessarily mean religious intolerance. Seventy percent of the *mansabdars°* (officials holding land revenues) appointed under Akbar were Muslim soldiers born outside India, but 15 percent were Hindus. Most of the Hindu appointees were warriors from the north called **Rajputs°,** one of whom rose to be a powerful revenue minister.

Akbar, the most illustrious ruler of his dynasty, differed from his Ottoman and Safavid counterparts—Suleiman the Magnificent and Shah Abbas the Great—in his striving for social harmony and not just for more territory and revenue. His marriage to a Rajput princess signaled his desire for reconciliation and even intermarriage between Muslims and Hindus. The birth of a son in 1569 ensured that future rulers would have both Muslim and Hindu ancestry.

Akbar ruled that in legal disputes between two Hindus, decisions would be made according to village custom or Hindu law as interpreted by local Hindu scholars. Shari'a law was in force for Muslims. Akbar made himself the legal court of last resort, creating an appeals process not usually present in Islamic jurisprudence.

Akbar also made himself the center of a new "Divine Faith" incorporating Muslim, Hindu, Zoroastrian, Sikh°, and Christian beliefs. He was strongly attracted by Sufi ideas, which permeated the religious rituals he instituted at his court. To promote serious consideration of his religious principles, he oversaw, from a catwalk high above the audience, debates among scholars of all religions assembled in his octagonal private audience chamber. When courtiers uttered the Muslim exclamation "Allahu Akbar"—"God is great"—they also understood it in its second grammatical meaning: "God is Akbar."

Akbar's religious views did not survive him, but the court culture he fostered, reflecting a mixture of Muslim and Hindu traditions, flourished until his zealous great-grandson Aurangzeb° (r. 1658–1707) reinstituted many restrictions on Hindus. Mughal and Rajput miniature paintings reveled in precise portraits of political figures and depictions of scantily clad women, even though they brought frowns to the faces of pious Muslims, who deplored the representation of human beings. Most of the leading painters were Hindus. In addition to the florid style of Persian verse favored at court, a

---

mansabdars (man-sab-DAHRZ)

Rajputs (RAHJ-putz)   **Sikh** (sick)
Aurangzeb (ow-rang-ZEB)

new taste developed for poetry and prose in the popular language of the Delhi region. The modern descendant of this language is called *Urdu* in Pakistan and *Hindi* in India.

Central Decay and Regional Challenges

Mughal power did not long survive Aurangzeb's death in 1707. Some historians consider the land-grant system a central element in the rapid decline of imperial authority, but other factors were at play as well. Aurangzeb's additions to Mughal territory in southern India were not all well integrated into the imperial structure, and strong regional powers arose to challenge Mughal military supremacy. A climax came in 1739 when Nadir Shah, the warlord who had seized power in Iran after the fall of the Safavids, invaded the Mughal capital and carried off to Iran the "peacock throne," the priceless jewel-encrusted symbol of Mughal grandeur. Another throne was found for the later Mughals to sit on; but their empire, which survived in name to 1857, was finished.

In 1723, Nizam al-Mulk°, the powerful vizier of the Mughal sultan, gave up on the central government and established his own nearly independent state at Hyderabad in the eastern Deccan. Other officials bearing the title *nawab*° became similarly independent in Bengal and Oudh° in the northeast, as did the Marathas in the center. In the northwest, simultaneous Iranian and Mughal weakness allowed the Afghans to establish an independent kingdom.

Some of these regional powers, and the smaller princely states that arose on former Mughal territory, were prosperous and benefited from the removal of the sultan's heavy hand. Linguistic and religious communities, freed from the religious intolerance instituted during the reign of Aurangzeb, similarly enjoyed greater opportunity for political expression. However, this disintegration of central power favored the intrusion of European adventurers.

Joseph François Dupleix° took over the presidency of the French stronghold of Pondicherry° in 1741 and began a new phase of European involvement in India. He captured the English trading center of Madras and used his small contingent of European and European-trained Indian troops to become a power broker in southern India. Though offered the title *nawab,* Dupleix preferred to operate behind the scenes, using Indian princes as puppets. His career ended in 1754 when he was called home. Deeply involved in wars in Europe, the French government was unwilling to pursue further adventures in India. Dupleix's departure opened the way for the British, whose ventures in India are described in Chapter 22.

TRADE EMPIRES IN THE INDIAN OCEAN

Although the Ottomans, Safavids, and the Mughals did not seriously contest the growth of Portuguese and then Dutch, English, and French maritime power, the majority of non-European shipbuilders, captains, sailors, and traders were Muslim. Groups of Armenian, Jewish, and Hindu traders were also active, but they remained almost as aloof from the Europeans as the Muslims did. The presence in every port of Muslims following the same legal traditions and practicing their faith in similar ways cemented the Muslims' trading network. Islam, from its very outset in the life and preachings of Muhammad (570–632), was always congenial to trade and traders. Unlike Hinduism, it was a proselytizing religion, a factor that encouraged the growth of coastal Muslim communities as local non-Muslims were drawn into Muslim commercial activities, converted, and intermarried with Muslims from abroad.

Although European missionaries, particularly the Jesuits, tried to extend Christianity into Asia and Africa (see Chapters 15 and 17), most Europeans, the Portuguese excepted, were less inclined than the Muslims were to treat local converts or the

---

Nizam al-Mulk (nee-ZAHM al-MULK)   *nawab* (NAH-wab)
Oudh (OW-ad)

Dupleix (doo-PLAY)   **Pondicherry** (pon-dih-CHER-ree)

offspring of mixed marriages as full members of their communities. As a consequence, Islam spread extensively into East Africa and Southeast Asia during precisely the time of rapid European commercial expansion. Even without the support of the Muslim land empires, Islam became a source of resistance to growing European domination.

Muslims in the East Indies

Historians disagree about the chronology and manner of Islam's spread in Southeast Asia. Arab traders were well known in southern China as early as the eighth century, so Muslims probably reached the East Indies at a similarly early date. Nevertheless, the dominance of Indian cultural influences in the area for several centuries thereafter indicates that early Muslim visitors had little impact on local beliefs. Clearer indications of conversion and the formation of Muslim communities date from roughly the fourteenth century. The strongest overseas linkage is to the port of Cambay in India (see Map 18.2) rather than to the Arab world. Islam took root first in port cities and in some royal courts and spread inland slowly, possibly transmitted by itinerant Sufis.

Although appeals to the Ottoman sultan for support against the Europeans ultimately proved of little use, Islam as a political ideology strengthened resistance to Portuguese, Spanish, and Dutch intruders. When the Spaniards conquered the Philippines during the decades following the establishment of their first fort in 1565, they encountered Muslims on the southern island of Mindanao° and the nearby Sulu archipelago. They called them "Moros," the Spanish term for their old enemies, the Muslims of North Africa. In the ensuing Moro wars, the Spaniards portrayed the Moros as greedy pirates who raided non-Muslim territories for slaves. In fact, they were political, religious, and commercial competitors whose perseverance enabled them to establish the Sulu Empire based in the southern Philippines, one of the strongest states in Southeast Asia from 1768 to 1848.

Other local kingdoms that looked on Islam as a force to counter the aggressive Christianity of the Europeans included the actively proselytizing Brunei° Sultanate in northern Borneo and the **Acheh° Sultanate** in northern Sumatra. At its peak in the early seventeenth century, Acheh succeeded Malacca as the main center of Islamic expansion in Southeast Asia. It prospered from trade in pepper and cotton cloth from Gujarat in India. Acheh declined after the Dutch seized Malacca from Portugal in 1641.

How well Islam was understood in these Muslim kingdoms is open to question. In Acheh, for example, a series of women ruled between 1641 and 1699. This practice came to an end when local Muslim scholars obtained a ruling from scholars in Mecca and Medina that Islam did not approve of female rulers. This ruling became a turning point after which scholarly understandings of Islam gained greater prominence in the East Indies.

Historians have theorized that the first propagators of Islam in Southeast Asia were merchants, Sufi preachers, or both. The scholarly vision of Islam, however, took root in the sixteenth century by way of pilgrims returning from years of study in Mecca and Medina. Islam was the primary force in the dissemination of writing in the region. Some of the returning pilgrims wrote in Arabic, others in Malay or Javanese. As Islam continued to spread, *adat,* a form of Islam rooted in pre-Muslim religious and social practices, retained its preeminence in rural areas over practices centered on the Shari'a, the religious law. But the royal courts in the port cities began to heed the views of the pilgrim teachers, as in their condemnation of female rulers. Though different in many ways, both varieties of Islam provided believers with a firm basis of identification in the face of the growing European presence. Christian missionaries gained most of their converts in regions that had not yet converted to Islam, such as the northern Philippines.

Muslims in East Africa

The East African ports that the Portuguese began to visit in the fifteenth century were governed by Muslim rulers but were not linked politically

Mindanao (min-duh-NOW)

Brunei (BROO-nie)   Acheh (AH-cheh)

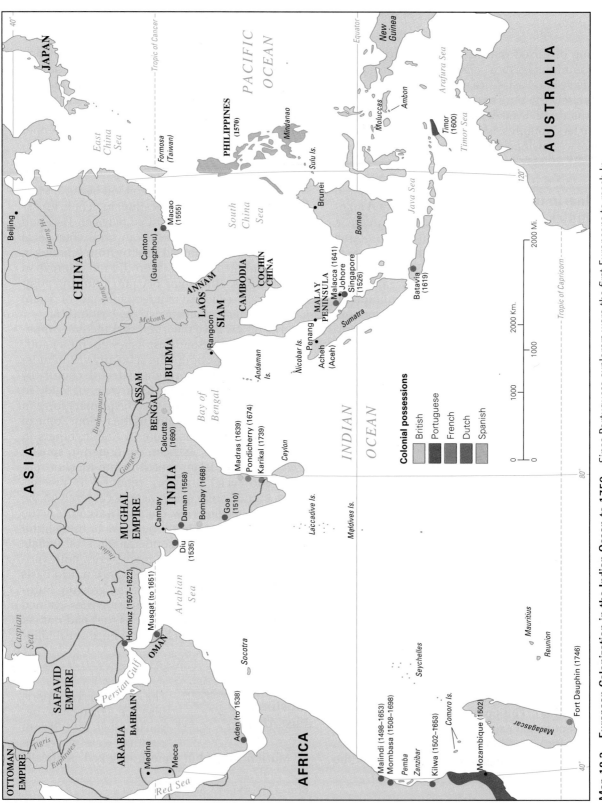

Map 18.2 European Colonization in the Indian Ocean to 1750 Since Portuguese explorers were the first Europeans to reach India by rounding Africa, Portugal gained a strong foothold in both areas. Rival Spain was barred from colonizing the region by the Treaty of Tordesillas in 1494, which limited Spanish efforts to lands west of a line drawn through the mid-Atlantic Ocean. The line carried around the globe provided justification of Spanish colonization in the Philippines. French, British, and Dutch colonies date from after 1600 when joint stock companies provided a new stimulus for overseas commerce.

Colonial possessions

British
Portuguese
French
Dutch
Spanish

(see Map 18.2). People living in the millet and rice lands of the Swahili Coast—from the Arabic *sawahil*° meaning "coasts"—had little contact with those in the dry hinterlands. Throughout this period, the East African lakes region and the highlands of Kenya witnessed unprecedented migration and relocation of peoples because of drought conditions that persisted from the late sixteenth through most of the seventeenth century.

Cooperation among the trading ports of Kilwa, Mombasa, and Malindi was hindered by the thick bush country that separated the cultivated tracts of coastal land and by the fact that the ports competed with one another in the export of ivory; ambergris° (a whale by-product used in perfumes); and forest products such as beeswax, copal tree resin, and wood (Kilwa also exported gold). In the eighteenth century, slave trading, primarily to Arabian ports but also to India, increased in importance. Because Europeans—the only peoples who kept consistent records of slave-trading activities—played a minor role in this slave trade, few records have survived to indicate its extent. Perhaps the best estimate is that 2.1 million slaves were exported between 1500 and 1890, a little over 12.5 percent of the total traffic in African slaves during that period (see Chapter 17).

The Portuguese conquered all of the coastal ports from Mozambique northward except Malindi, with whose ruler Portugal cooperated. A Portuguese description of the ruler indicates some of the cloth and metal goods that Malindi imported, as well as some local manufactures:

> The King wore a robe of damask trimmed with green satin and a rich [cap]. He was seated on two cushioned chairs of bronze, beneath a rough sunshade of crimson satin attached to a pole. An old man, who attended him as a page, carried a short sword in a silver sheath. There were many players on [horns], and two trumpets of ivory richly carved and of the size of a man, which were blown through a hole in the side, and made sweet harmony with the [horns].[1]

Initially, the Portuguese favored the port of Malindi, which caused the decline of Kilwa and Mombasa. Repeatedly plagued by local rebellion, Portuguese power suffered severe blows when the Arabs of **Oman** in southeastern Arabia captured their south Arabian stronghold at Musqat (1650) and then went on in support of African resistance to seize Mombasa (1698), which had become the Portuguese capital in East Africa. The Portuguese briefly retook Mombasa but lost control permanently in 1729. From then on, the Portuguese had to content themselves with Mozambique in Africa and a few remaining ports in India (Goa) and farther east (Macao and Timor).

The Omanis created a maritime empire of their own, but one that worked in greater cooperation with the African populations. The Bantu language of the coast, broadened by the absorption of Arabic, Persian, and Portuguese loan words, developed into **Swahili**°, which was spoken throughout the region. Arabs and other Muslims who settled in the region intermarried with local families, giving rise to a mixed population that played an important role in developing a distinctive Swahili culture.

Islam also spread in the southern Sudan in this period, particularly in the dry areas away from the Nile River. This growth coincided with a waning of Ethiopian power as a result of Portugal's stifling of trade in the Red Sea. Yet no significant contact developed between the emerging Muslim Swahili culture and that of the Muslims in the Sudan, to the north.

The Coming of the Dutch

The Dutch played a major role in driving the Portuguese from their possessions in the East Indies. They were better organized than the Portuguese through the Dutch East India Company (see Chapter 17). Just as the Portuguese had tried to dominate the trade in spices, so the Dutch concentrated at first on the spice-producing islands of Southeast Asia. The Portuguese had seized Malacca, a strategic town on the narrow strait at the end of the Malay Peninsula, from a local Malay ruler in 1511. The Dutch took it away from them in

---

sawahil (suh-WAH-hil)   **ambergris** ((AM-ber-grees)

Swahili (swah-HEE-lee)

1641, leaving Portugal little foothold in the East Indies except the islands of Ambon° and Timor (see Map 18.2).

Although the United Netherlands was one of the least autocratic countries of Europe, the governors-general appointed by the Dutch East India Company deployed almost unlimited powers in their efforts to maintain their trade monopoly. They could even order the execution of their own employees for "smuggling"—that is, trading on their own. Under strong governors-general, the Dutch fought a series of wars against Acheh and other local kingdoms on Sumatra and Java. In 1628 and 1629, their new capital at **Batavia,** now the city of Jakarta on Java, was besieged by a fleet of fifty ships belonging to the sultan of Mataram°, a Javanese kingdom. The Dutch held out with difficulty and eventually prevailed when the sultan was unable to get effective help from the English.

Suppressing local rulers, however, was not enough to control the spice trade once other European countries adopted Dutch methods, became more knowledgeable about where goods might be acquired, and started to send more ships to Southeast Asia. In the course of the eighteenth century, therefore, the Dutch gradually turned from being a middleman for Southeast Asian producers and European buyers to being a producer of crops in areas they controlled, notably in Java. Javanese teak forests yielded high-quality lumber, and coffee, transplanted from Yemen, grew well in the hilly regions of western Java. In this new phase of colonial export production, Batavia developed from being the headquarters town of a far-flung enterprise to being the administrative capital of a conquered land.

Beyond the East Indies, the Dutch utilized their discovery of a band of powerful eastward-blowing winds (called the "Roaring Forties" because they blow throughout the year between 40 and 50 degrees south latitude) to reach Australia in 1606. In 1642 and 1643, Abel Tasman became the first European to set foot on Tasmania and New Zealand and to sail around Australia, signaling European involvement in that region.

Ambon (am-BOHN)   **Mataram** (MAH-ah-ram)

CONCLUSION

It is no coincidence that the Mughal, Safavid, and Ottoman Empires declined simultaneously in the seventeenth and eighteenth centuries. The complex changes in military technology and in the world economy that were underway in smaller European countries either passed them by or affected them adversely. Despite their efforts on conquering more and more land, these land-based empires faced increasing difficulty in maintaining traditional military forces paid through land grants.

The opposite was true for seafaring countries intent on turning trade networks into maritime empires. Improvements in ship design, navigation accuracy, and the use of cannon gave an ever-increasing edge to European powers competing with local seafaring peoples. In contrast to the age-old Asian tradition that imperial wealth came from control of broad expanses of agricultural land, European countries promoted joint-stock companies and luxuriated in the prosperity gained from their ever increasing control of Indian Ocean commerce.

That a major shift in world economic and political alignments was well under way by the late seventeenth century was scarcely perceivable in those parts of Asia and Africa ruled by the Ottoman and Mughal sultans and the Safavid shahs. They relied mostly on land taxes, usually indirectly collected via holders of land grants or tax farmers, rather than on customs duties or control of markets to fill the government coffers. With ever-increasing military expenditures, these taxes fell short of the rulers' needs. Oblivious to the fundamental problem basic with the entire economic system, imperial courtiers pursued their luxurious ways, poetry and the arts continued to flourish, and the quality of manufacturing and craft production remained generally high. Eighteenth-century European observers marveled no less at the riches and industry of these eastern lands than at the fundamental weakness of their political and military systems.

■ Key Terms

Ottoman Empire	Akbar
Suleiman the Magnificent	*mansabs*
Janissaries	Rajputs
Safavid Empire	Acheh Sultanate
Shi'ite	Oman
Hidden Imam	Swahili
Shah Abbas I	Batavia
Mughal Empire	

■ Suggested Reading

The best comprehensive and comparative account of the post-Mongol Islamic land empires, with an emphasis on social history, is Ira Lapidus, *A History of Islamic Societies* (1988). For a brief, general introduction to the relations between the Muslim land empires and the development of Indian Ocean trade, see Patricia Risso, *Merchants and Faith: Muslim Commerce and Culture in the Indian Ocean* (1995).

On the Ottoman Empire, the standard political history is Stanford J. Shaw, *History of the Ottoman Empire and Modern Turkey,* vol. 1, *Empire of the Ghazis: The Rise and Decline of the Ottoman Empire, 1280–1808* (1976). Jason Goodwin, *Lords of the Horizons: A History of the Ottoman Empire* (1999), offers a more readable and journalistic account.

The most comprehensive treatment of the history of Safavid Iran is in the articles in Peter Jackson and Laurence Lockhart, eds., *The Cambridge History of Iran,* vol. 6, *The Timurid and Safavid Periods* (1986). For the artistic side of Safavid history, abundantly illustrated, see Anthony Welch, *Shah Abbas and the Arts of Isfahan* (1973).

A highly readable work that situates the Mughal Empire within the overall history of the subcontinent is Stanley Wolpert, *A New History of India,* 4th ed. (1993). For a broad treatment of the entire development of Islamic society in India with emphasis on the Mughal period, see S. M. Ikram, *History of Muslim Civilization in India and Pakistan* (1989). Wheeler Thackston has made a lively translation of Babur's autobiography in *The Baburnama: Memoirs of Babur, Prince and Emperor* (1996). For a comprehensive history of the Mughals, see John F. Richards, *The Mughal Empire* (1993).

■ Note

1. Esmond Bradley Martin and Chryssee Perry Martin, *Cargoes of the East: The Ports, Trade and Culture of the Arabian Seas and Western Indian Ocean* (London: Elm Tree Books, 1978), 17.

EASTERN EURASIA,

1500–1800

—*A*—

**New Relations in Eurasia • The Russian Empire • The Later Ming
and Early Qing Empires • Tokugawa Japan, to 1800**
SOCIETY AND CULTURE: Style and Conversion: Christian Rivalries in Beijing

n the 1650s, two expanding empires battled for control of Siberia, the Amur° River basin, and the Pacific coast of northern Asia. Hardy Russian scouts, mostly Cossacks, came east across the tundra, hoping to stake an early claim to the great Amur waterway. They built wooden forts on its northern bank, but they were countered by Manchu agents of the Qing° Empire based in China, which hoped to secure the same stretch of Pacific coast the Russians sought. The Manchus built wooden forts on the southern bank of the Amur.

Neither empire sent large forces into the Amur territories, and the contest was mostly a struggle for the goodwill of the local Evenk and Dagur peoples. The Qing emperor emphasized the importance of treading lightly in the struggle and well understood the principles of espionage:

Upon reaching the lands of the Evenks and the Dagurs you will send to announce that you have come to hunt deer. Meanwhile, keep a careful record of the distance and go, while hunting, along the northern bank of the Amur until you come by the shortest route to the town of Russian settlement at Albazin. Thoroughly reconnoitre its location and situation. I don't think the Russians will take a chance on attacking you. If they offer you food, accept it and show your gratitude.[1]

That delicacy gives a false impression of the intensity of the struggle between these two great empires. The contest was partly for dominance in the new northeast Asian economy of furs, timber, and metals concentrated in Siberia, Manchuria, and Yakutsk. But even without the attraction of those specific resources, the Amur River would have been critical in the interplay of the two empires, because each had an overriding need to protect itself against the other. The kingdoms of Europe, and even Europe's emerging sea-based empires, were small in comparison

---

Amur (AH-moor)   **Qing** (ching)

with these titanic Eurasian empires. Where the Russian and Qing Empires faced each other—in Central Asia, in Mongolia, and in Northeast Asia—they had to expend great resources conquering and defending lands that in the long run yielded very little profit. But for either to have flinched would have meant disaster at the hands of the other.

In 1689, the Qing and Russian Empires formalized their stand-off with a treaty establishing a border and a set of customs regulations. Russia was denied access to the Pacific coast east of the Amur, but the Russians exploited a more northerly route to explore the North Pacific and colonize the northwestern coast of North America.

For the Russian and Qing Empires, size, agriculture, and infrastructure for overland communication and transport were of the greatest importance. When challenged by the new empires of Europe, the Russian and Qing Empires faced common problems and experienced similar outcomes. The response of Japan was spectacularly different. That small, relatively remote nation had been a minor player in Asian affairs but was able to withstand economic and political changes more effectively than Asia's greatest empires.

As you read this chapter, ask yourself the following questions:

- What did the Russian and Qing Empires have in common? How do their similarities explain the tensions between them?

- What were the Russian and Qing attitudes toward Europe in the times of Peter the Great and Emperor Kangxi? What were the long-term consequences of these attitudes?

- What explains the greater speed of Japanese economic and technological development in the 1700s?

NEW RELATIONS IN EURASIA

After 1500, no single power controlled all of Central Asia, and no unified economic policy protected and promoted trade. Large and ambitious empires based in the Middle East, in Russia, and in China competed for control of parts of Central Asia, and this competition deepened their conflicts with the remaining Mongol groups and further depressed both travel and profitable trade. As the 1500s passed, the transporting of many goods by caravan between East Asia and the Middle East was neither cheap nor reliable. Oasis cities that had been rich and cosmopolitan in the days when overland trade was vigorous became isolated. Their governors were often hostile to outside influences.

Along the southern and eastern coasts of Eurasia, merchants from Europe, the Middle East, and Asia were taking advantage of the new global trade connections. Seaborne trade was now cheaper, faster, and more reliable than overland trade.

Ancient Asian ports that had become rich from centuries of trade found new economic stimulation from the development of European commerce. China, and later Japan, were also beneficiaries of this new trade and sought means of cushioning the effects of globalization on their own economies and societies. Russia, in contrast, had to enter a period of renewed and more militant expansion or risk being left out of the Pacific trade.

The Land-Based Empires of Eurasia

The Portuguese, Spanish, and Dutch Empires relied on the sea for contact with their colonies. For the Ottoman, Russian, Mughal, and Ming Empires, things were very different. They were land-based empires and much larger than the sea-based empires of Europe. Their self-defense was extremely expensive. They had fewer choices than their smaller European contemporaries about where to expand and how to enrich themselves after they expanded.

Central Asia remained the strategic center of competition for the land-based Eurasian empires. Much of Central Asia, however, was arid steppes or desert, and its commercial importance had declined steeply by 1500. Maintaining garrisons in these regions was extremely expensive, for food, weapons, animals, and even building materials had to be brought in from far away. The best hope of eventually making these territories self-supporting lay in the development of agriculture and mining, which required the introduction of large-scale irrigation, crops able to thrive in cold and dry climates, extensive new roads, and large numbers of settlers or prisoners to serve as laborers. The Russian and Qing Empires achieved some success in agriculture and mining, but the costs were steep.

The challenge to make large, unprofitable areas in the land-based Eurasian empires self-supporting reinforced the emphasis on agriculture as the predominant source of wealth and government tax revenues. It also reinforced the tendency toward political centralization. If the herculean task of environmental transformation across Central Asia and parts of northern Asia was to be achieved, imperial governments had to be in full command of the massive resources necessary for development of the infrastructure. Forced labor by the domestic population persisted in the Russian and Qing Empires after it was abandoned in Europe; in Russia, serfdom became more brutal and widespread in the seventeenth and eighteenth centuries than ever before.

In the long run, these empires were at a disadvantage in the competition with the sea-based empires of Europe. The Europeans concentrated on the colonization of profitable areas, linked the development of commerce to the enrichment of their central governments, and enlisted the aid of joint-stock companies to acquire and develop territories. Between 1500 and about 1800, the land-based empires of Eurasia were the largest administrative and economic systems in the world, but they posed more of a danger to each other than they faced from any of the sea-based empires of Europe.

New Global Influences

The European entities that first challenged Russia and the Qing were not states. In the sixteenth and seventeenth centuries, the Society of Jesus and the East India companies created ties between Asia and Europe. One of the first **Jesuits,** Francis Xavier, went to India in the mid-sixteenth century looking for converts and later traveled throughout Southeast and East Asia. He spent two years in Japan and died in 1552 in China. Following Xavier, other Jesuits had a significant influence in China and presented Europeans with an intriguing picture of Asian life.

China reaped some material benefits from contact with the Jesuits. Chinese converts to Catholicism were important in introducing European techniques of crop production, irrigation, and engineering. The outstanding Jesuit of late Ming China, Matteo Ricci° (1552–1610), became expert in the Chinese language and an accomplished scholar of the Confucian classics. He and other Jesuits in China made a deep impression on the Ming elites at Beijing° and also in the wealthy, cosmopolitan cities of the Yangzi River delta and the southern China coast. The Society of Jesus was the most prominent transmitter of European science and technology to China and of Chinese philosophy and literature to Europe.

European merchant ships carried the Jesuits to East Asia. First came the Portuguese, who after 1500 dominated the spice trade of the Moluccas and Java and the trade routes around India. The Spanish also were interested in the trade and established a small base on the island of Taiwan, off the coast of southeast China. Soon after 1600, the Dutch dislodged the Portuguese and Spanish from Taiwan. To secure their influence in East Asia and to discredit their rivals, representatives of the Dutch East India Company (VOC) willingly complied with Chinese rituals by which foreigners were supposed to acknowledge the moral superiority of the emperor of China. The Dutch also got along well with the rulers of Japan and retained exclusive permission to live on an island off Nagasaki°, after other Europeans were banned from the country. Outside Japan, however, the VOC faced a strong

Matteo Ricci (ma-TAY-o REE-chee)   **Beijing** (bay-JING)
Nagasaki (nah-gah-SAH-kee)

CHRONOLOGY

	Russia	China and Central Asia	Korea and Japan
1500	**1547** Ivan IV tsar		
	1582 Cossacks conquer Khanate of Sibir		**1582** Japanese invasion of Korea
1600	**1613–1645** Rule of Mikhail, the first Romanov tsar	**1601** Matteo Ricci active in Ming China	**1600** Decisive battle begins Tokugawa Shogunate
		1644 Qing conquest of Beijing	**1649** Closing of Japan
		1662–1722 Rule of Emperor Kangxi	
	1689–1725 Rule of Peter the Great	**1689** Treaty of Nerchinsk with Russia	
		1691 Qing control of Inner Mongolia	
1700	**1712** St. Petersburg becomes Russia's capital	**1736–1795** Rule of Emperor Qianlong	
		1755 Qing conquest of Turkestan	
	1762–1796 Rule of Catherine the Great		
	1799 Alaska becomes a Russian colony		

rival in the East India Company of England, chartered by Queen Elizabeth I in 1600.

The European trading companies and the Jesuits are examples of the global organizations that became conduits between Asia and Europe. But in the 1700s, these organizations were viewed with suspicion by imperial authorities in Europe as well as in Asia.

selves on their southern border with Turkestan. Instead, they could turn their attention toward eastern Eurasia, including Mongolia and **Siberia,** and even to the Pacific coast. The expanding European empires diminished the need to maintain western and southern boundaries against the Ottoman Empire somewhat, because the Europeans held the line against further Ottoman expansion in the Balkans and began to challenge and distract the Ottomans in the eastern Mediterranean.

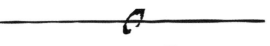

THE RUSSIAN EMPIRE

The shift toward the seas and away from inland Asia presented both challenges and opportunities to the rising Russian Empire. The fragmentation of political power in Central Asia lessened the pressure on the Russian rulers to defend them-

The Rise of Romanov Power

After the dissolution of Mongol power in Russia, the city of Moscow became the foundation for a new state, **Muscovy°**. By 1500, Muscovy dominated the lands that had been controlled by the

Muscovy (MUSS-koe-vee)

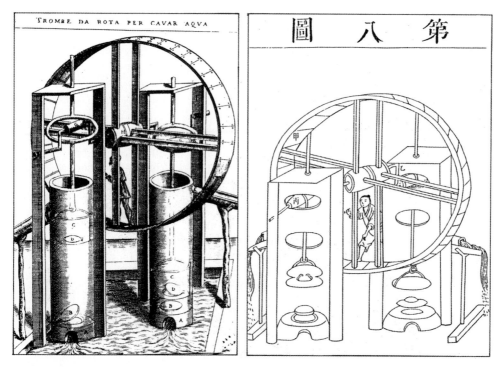

TROMBE DA ROTA PER CAVAR AQVA

圖 八 第

From the Jesuit Library at Beijing   Jesuits such as Matteo Ricci were willing to share books on technology and science with Chinese scholars. But without firsthand experience, it was impossible for Chinese translators to convey how the devices actually worked. Here, a man walking in a wheel drives a shaft that changes the pressure inside two pumps. In the Chinese translation of the drawing, the mechanisms were all lost.   (Left: From Zonca, *Trombe da Rota per Vavar Aqua* [1607]. Right: "Diagram Number Eight" from *Qi tushuo* [*Illustrations on Energy*] [1627]. Both courtesy of Joseph Needham, *Science and Civilization in China*, vol. 4)

Kievan state. By the mid-sixteenth century, Novgorod, which had been independent since the twelfth century, was absorbed. To mark the extension of Muscovy and of his personal power, the Muscovite ruler Ivan IV ("the Terrible") assumed the title **tsar** (from "caesar") in 1547. Within a few years, Ivan expanded Russia's borders far to the east through the conquest of the Khanates of Kazan and Astrakhan and the northern Caucasus region (see Map 19.1).

The westward extension of the territories ruled by Ivan IV and his successors did not progress much thereafter. Instead, Russia had to defend itself more strenuously on the European front. In the early seventeenth century, Swedish and Polish forces briefly occupied Moscow on separate occa-

sions. In the midst of this "Time of Troubles," the old line of Muscovite rulers was finally deposed, and the Russian aristocracy—the *boyars*°—allowed one of their own, **Mikhail Romanov°,** to become tsar (r. 1613–1645).

The early Romanov rulers realized that consolidation of their own authority and successful competition with neighboring powers went together. Options for Russian expansion were limited. The Ottoman Empire controlled the Balkans and Black Sea, the Safavid rulers of Iran dominated southern Central Asia, and Sweden controlled the Baltic Sea. The obvious direction for expansion was east.

---

boyar (BOY-ar)   **Romanov** (ROE-man-off or roe-MAN-off)

Map 19.1   The Expansion of Russia, 1500–1800   Sweden and Poland initially blocked Russian expansion in Europe, while the Ottoman Empire blocked the southwest. In the sixteenth century, Russia began to expand east, toward Siberia and the Pacific Ocean. By the end of the rule of Catherine the Great in 1796, Russia encompassed all of northern and northeastern Eurasia.

Russians and Turks

Under the Romanov dynasty, the divisions between Russians and Turks tended to be represented as conflicts between Christians and "infidels" or between the civilized and the "barbaric." Despite this rhetoric, it is important to understand that the interplay of Turkic (Central Asian) and Russian (Slavic) influences was what produced the Russian Empire. These cultural groups were defined not by blood ties but by the way in which they lived.

A revealing example is the **Cossacks.** Their name comes from a Turkic word for a warrior or mercenary and is related to the modern name *Kazakh.* The word *Cossack* in various forms seems to have first emerged in the Ukraine, where it referred to bands of people living on the steppes, herding or robbing for their livelihoods. But the Cossacks of the Ukraine were a diverse group. Many were escaped serfs from Muscovy or Lithuania; others were wandering Turks or Cumans, Poles, Hungarians, or Mongols. Who their ancestors were was irrelevant. What mattered was that they lived in close-knit bands, were superb riders and fighters, and were feared by both the villagers and the legal authorities.

The Muscovite and early Romanov rulers decided to take no chances with the Cossacks, but Russia also desired to exploit the Cossacks' extraordinary military spirit and skills. The empire reached an accommodation with them, enrolling them in special military regiments and allowing them to live in autonomous villages. In return, the Cossacks performed distinctive service for Russia, defending against Swedish and Ottoman incursions in the west and leading campaigns for exploration, conquest, and settlement in the east.

The Cossacks were an example of the ways in which Russia combined elements considered "Turk" with those considered "Russian." They displayed the military skills of Asian horsemen but were Russian speakers, Christians, and in most cases willing participants in the building of the Russian Empire.

Peter the Great

Peter the Great, who ruled Russia from 1689 to 1725, was determined to secure a warm-water port on the Black Sea. Peter described his wars with the Ottoman Empire as a new crusade to liberate Constantinople (now Istanbul) from the Muslim sultans. He also claimed the right to function as the legal protector of Orthodox Christians living in the Balkan territories under Ottoman rule. Peter's forces seized the port of Azov in 1696, but the fortress was lost again in 1713, and Russian expansion southward was blocked for the rest of Peter's reign.

Peter was more successful in his campaigns in the west. In the long and costly Great Northern War (1700–1721), his modernized armies broke Swedish control of the Baltic Sea, establishing direct contacts between Russia and Europe. Peter's victory forced the European powers to recognize Russia as a major power for the first time. Taking advantage of his new prestige in Europe, he built a new city, St. Petersburg, on land captured from Sweden. In 1712, the city became Russia's capital. Peter intended St. Petersburg to be a model to Russian elites seeking to absorb European culture and a demonstration to Europeans of Russian sophistication. Houses were to be built in the baroque style then fashionable in western Europe. Nobles were ordered to wear western styles and shave their beards. Peter attempted to end the traditional seclusion of upper-class Russian women by requiring officials, officers, and merchants to bring their wives to the social gatherings he organized in the capital.

There was also a political objective in building the new capital: Peter intended to break the power of the boyars by sharply reducing their traditional roles in government and the army. The old boyar council of Moscow was replaced by a group of advisers in St. Petersburg whom the tsar appointed. Members of the traditional nobility continued to serve as generals and admirals, but officers in Peter's modern, professional army and navy were promoted according to merit, not birth.

Peter admired European technology and culture, but he had no intention of following the movement of the Netherlands and Britain toward political liberalization. The goal of Westernization was to strengthen the Russian state and the institutions of personal power that the Russians called **autocracy.** A decree of 1716 proclaimed that the tsar "is not obliged to answer to anyone in the world for his doings, but possesses power and authority over his kingdom and land, to rule them at his will and pleasure as a Christian ruler." Under this expansive definition of his role, Peter brought the Russian Orthodox Church firmly under state control, built factories and iron and copper foundries to provide munitions and supplies for the military, and increased the burdens of taxes and forced labor on the serfs. **Serfs**—the great mass of Russian people, forced by law and custom to work the land of their overlords—could have been freed as part of Peter's reform. But there was no move to abolish serf status, because the Russian Empire was dependent on serfs for the production of basic foodstuffs.

The Russian Drive Eastward

Long before Peter's time, Russian rulers realized that the eastern frontier was wide open to Russian expansion because no other great empire controlled the northern tier of Asia. Russian exploration of Siberia began in the time of Ivan IV and was led by a Cossack, Yermak Timofeyovich°. By force of their rifles, Yermak's troops attacked the only political power in the region, the Khanate of Sibir in 1582. Yermak himself did not survive to return to Moscow, but Cossacks remained in the forefront of Russian campaigns to conquer and settle Siberia.

Siberian furs and timber were the first valued resources; after 1700, gold, coal, and iron also became important. By the 1650s, Cossack explorers had claimed the Amur Valley for the Russian Empire, and many villages along the Amur River were rendering tribute to Russian officials. Through the 1650s, clashes occurred between these soldiers and soldiers of the Qing Empire stationed near the river. To deprive the Russians of the goods rendered by the Amur villagers, the Qing Empire forcibly resettled native peoples westward in Qing territory.

By the late 1600s, the Russian and Qing rulers saw that their interests lay in a diplomatic agree-

Yermak Timofeyovich (YAIR-mak tih-mo-FAY-oh-vich)

ment that would delineate their borders in Mongolia, Siberia, and the Amur River Valley, as well as fix trade and tariff regulations across their borders. The Treaty of Nerchinsk in 1689 was a strategic coup for both empires, and it was reinforced in the Treaty of Kiakhta in 1727.

The immediate results were two. First, Mongol groups lost the leverage they had gained by exploiting Russian and Qing competition. Thereafter, the Mongols steadily declined as a power, and the Qing Empire quickly consolidated its control over Mongolia and Central Asia. Second, with a fixed boundary and Siberia inside it, Russia could concentrate on further eastern expansion, all the way to the Pacific and into North America. When Catherine the Great (r. 1762–1796) died, Russian reach extended from Poland in the west to Alaska in the east and was still growing.

THE LATER MING AND EARLY QING EMPIRES

The economic and cultural achievements of the **Ming Empire** continued until 1600. An international market eager for Ming porcelain (called "china"), as well as for silk and lacquered furniture, stimulated the commercial development of East Asia, the Indian Ocean, and Europe.

The End of the Ming

This apparent golden age, however, was beset by serious problems that by the year 1600 left the Ming Empire economically exhausted, politically deteriorating, and technologically lagging behind both its East Asian neighbors and Europe. Some of these problems were the result of natural disasters associated with climate change. Average temperatures dropped, reached a low point about 1645, then remained low until the early 1700s. The resulting agricultural distress and famine fueled large uprisings that speeded the end of the Ming Empire. The devastation caused by these uprisings and the

Power and Youth   Emperor Kangxi (left) and Peter the Great (right) were contemporaries, great rulers, and rivals for control of Central and Northeast Asia. Both were child-emperors who outwitted their elders to achieve personal rule and then pursued all avenues of knowledge to strengthen their empires. But their youthful portraits show differences: Peter is depicted here while he was a student in Holland in 1697, learning engineering and shipbuilding. Kangxi, in a portrait from about 1690, preferred to be portrayed as a refined scholar.   (left: The Palace Museum, Beijing; right: Collection, Countess Bobrinskoy/Michael Holford)

spread of epidemic diseases resulted in steep declines in local populations.

Other kinds of global change also affected China. American silver flooded into China in exchange for goods sold to Europe. As the amount of silver in circulation rose, its relative value fell. Nevertheless, the Ming government maintained a strict ratio in price between silver coins and copper coins. As silver declined in value, more and more copper was needed to make purchases and pay taxes. In a time of worsening economic and population conditions, the consequent inflation hit the rural population especially hard.

Environmental and economic stress do not in themselves destroy societies. Indeed, both the eastern Mongols and the Manchus centralized their political systems and increased the territories under their control in the 1600s, all at the expense of the Ming Empire. The importance of global factors in the demise of the Ming must be placed in the context of the special factors operating on China.

For the entire later Ming period, the boundaries of the empire were critical to its health. The Mongols remained strong in the north. The **Manchus** grew stronger in the northeast. In the southwest, there were repeated uprisings among native peoples crowded by the immigration of Chinese farmers. Pirates based in Okinawa and in Taiwan frequently looted the southeastern coastal towns. Ming military resources, concentrated against the Mongols and the Manchus in the north, could not be deployed to defend the coasts. As a result, many southern Chinese migrated to Southeast Asia to profit from the sea trading networks of the Indian Ocean.

After decades of weakening control, the Ming ruler was deposed when rebellious forces captured Beijing. The imperial family left the city, but a Ming general entered into an agreement with Manchu leaders, inviting them to take Beijing from the rebels. The Manchu did so in the summer of 1644 but did not restore the Ming. They claimed China for their own and began a forty-year conquest of the rest of the Ming territories.

Power and Trade in the Early Qing

The new **Qing Empire** was ruled by a Manchu imperial family, and Manchus were the leaders of the military forces. But Manchus were a very small portion of the population, and from its beginnings, the empire was dependent on diverse peoples for its achievements. Though the Qing style of rule was multilingual and international, the overwhelming majority of officials, soldiers, merchants, and farmers were Chinese.

Before the year 1700, the Qing gained south China, and for the first time the island of Taiwan was incorporated into an empire based in China (see Map 19.2). The Qing Empire also conquered

Map 19.2   The Qing Empire, 1644–1783   The Qing Empire began in Manchuria and captured north China in 1644. Between 1644 and 1783, the Qing conquered all the former Ming territories and added Taiwan, the lower Amur River basin, Inner Mongolia, eastern Turkestan, and Tibet. The resulting state was more than twice the size of the Ming Empire.

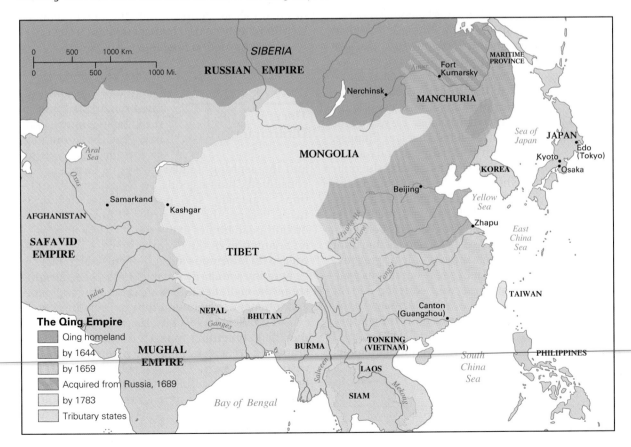

Mongolia and Central Asia. The seventeenth and eighteenth centuries in China—particularly the reigns of the Kangxi° (r. 1662–1722) and Qianlong° (r. 1736–1796) emperors—were a period of great economic, military, and cultural achievement.

The early Qing emperors wished to foster economic and demographic recovery in China. They repaired the roads and waterworks, lowered transit taxes, mandated comparatively low rents and interest rates, and helped resettle the areas devastated during the peasant rebellions of the late Ming period. Foreign trade was encouraged. Korea, Vietnam, Burma, and Nepal sent regular embassies to the Qing tribute court and carried the latest Chinese fashions back home. Overland routes of communication were revived.

Emperor Kangxi

The early Qing conquest of Beijing and north China was carried out under the leadership of a group of Manchu aristocrats who dominated the first Qing emperor based in China and were regents for his young son, who was declared emperor in 1662. This child-emperor, Kangxi, spent several years doing political battle with his regents, and in 1669 he gained real as well as formal control of the government by executing his chief regent. **Kangxi** was then sixteen. He was an intellectual prodigy who mastered classical Chinese, Manchu, and Mongolian at an early age and memorized the Chinese classics. He was a successful military commander who personally led troops in the great campaigns that brought Mongolia under Qing control by 1691. He battled with and then made peace with the Russian Empire and negotiated complex domestic political crises. His reign, lasting until his death in 1722, was marked not only by great expansion of the empire but by great stability as well.

As the Qing conquest was consolidated in north China, south China, and Northeast Asia, maps in the European style—reflecting the century of Jesuit influence at the Ming court—were created as practical guides to the newly conquered regions

and as symbols of Qing dominance. Kangxi considered introducing the European calendar, but protests were so strong that the plan was dropped. The emperor himself remained friendly with the Jesuits and frequently discussed scientific and philosophical issues with them (see Society and Culture: Style and Conversion: Christian Rivalries in Beijing). When he fell ill with malaria in the 1690s, he relied on Jesuit medical expertise (in this case, the use of quinine) for his recovery. He ordered the creation of illustrated books in Manchu detailing European anatomical and pharmaceutical knowledge.

The exchange of information between the Qing and the Europeans that Kangxi had fostered was never one-way. When the Jesuits informed the Qing court on matters of anatomy, for instance, the Qing were able to demonstrate to the Jesuits an early form of inoculation, called **variolation,** that had been used to stem the spread of smallpox after the Qing conquest of Beijing. Similarly, the enormous imperial factories that produced porcelain inspired the industrial management of practices of Josiah Wedgwood in England.

Tea and Diplomacy

The brilliant successes of the Qing in conquest and trade excited admiration in Europe. The wealthy and the aspiring middle classes of Europe avidly consumed Chinese goods, both genuine and imitations, especially silk, porcelain, and decorative items. Perhaps the most striking Chinese influence on European homes in this period was wallpaper—an adaptation of the Chinese practice of covering walls with enormous loose-hanging watercolors or calligraphy scrolls. By the mid-1700s, special workshops throughout China were producing wallpaper and other consumer items for export to Europe.

In political philosophy, too, the Europeans felt they had something to learn from the early Qing emperors. In the late 1770s, poems supposedly written by Emperor Qianlong were translated into French and disseminated through the intellectual circles of western Europe. These works depicted the Qing emperors as benevolent despots who

---

Kangxi (KAHNG-shee)   Qianlong (chee-YEN-loong)

Style and Conversion: Christian Rivalries in Beijing

The Treaty of Nerchinsk (1689) presented new opportunities for Russian missionaries in Beijing to continue their work of ministering to Russians in Beijing as well as spreading Orthodox Christianity in China. They failed to gain converts, largely because they did not learn Chinese. But they believed their failure was due to the interference of the Jesuits, who had arrived before them, knew Chinese, and made themselves indispensable in diplomatic communications between the Qing and Russian courts. In 1722, leaders of the Orthodox Church wrote the following comment to the new head of the Russian mission in Beijing.

I t would be prudent if you kept your rank of bishop a secret, because your status might arouse opposition among our enemies—especially our main enemies, the Jesuits. They are constantly creating troubles between us and others, as well as strife among ourselves, in order to frustrate our good works. Of course it could not be otherwise, for remember that Jesus cried out to the Father, "Lord, have I not sown good seed? Where have these weeds come from?" And the Lord said, "The Devil has done this."

For their part, the Jesuits considered the Russian missionaries hopelessly unpersuasive, not only because of their limitations of language but also because of their poverty. Russians traveled overland, by caravan, to Beijing, which was very expensive. Once there, they lived on a very small allowance from the Qing court, and they were often short of food and fuel, not to mention new clothes. The relatively independent and wealthy Jesuits considered the Russian missionaries unprepared for international experience, as Matteo Ripa made clear in his report to the Vatican on the Russian mission in Beijing, probably in 1718.

I sent a present to the head of the mission, then visited him. His manners were courteous and dignified, and his dress remarkably neat. With me, he pretended to be a Roman Catholic (despite the fact he was obviously Orthodox), speaking just enough Latin to be understood. He told me that a priest who was ill and in bed could speak Latin, and so I went to visit him, but all I could get out of him was the word "intelligit, intelligit, [he understands, he understands]" over and over. The head of the mission told me that the congregation is limited to descendants of Russian prisoners of war. They cannot convert the Chinese because they don't speak Chinese, and besides they have so few priests that they have no time for any but their flock of Russians.

The truth is, their church services have no ceremony at all, and they allow men and women to worship together, which in China is considered abominable. And though the head of the mission looks elegant, the priests on his staff look very shabby. To make matters worse, the priests play in the streets in front of the mission. In China this is absolutely uncouth, and no respectable person would do it.

What do you think accounts for the tensions between the Jesuits and Russian Orthodox churchmen in China? What were they really competing for?

Source: Eric Widmer, *The Russian Ecclesiastical Mission in Peking During the Eighteenth Century* (Cambridge, MA: Harvard East Asian Research Center, 1976), 44, 63. © The President and Fellows of Harvard College 1976. Reproduced by permission of the Harvard University Asia Center.

campaigned against superstition and ignorance, curbed the excesses of the aristocracy, and patronized science and the arts. Voltaire proclaimed the Qing emperors model philosopher-kings and advocated such rulership as a protection against the growth of aristocratic privilege. Though Jesuit interest in China was in decline by this time, the works of the Jesuits stimulated interest in the languages and civilizations of East Asia.

The Qing were eager to expand China's economic influence but were determined to control the trade very strictly. Europeans were permitted to trade only at Canton. This system worked well enough for European traders until the late 1700s, when Britain became worried about its massive trade deficit with China. Because the Qing Empire rarely bought anything from Britain, British silver poured into China to pay for the imported tea and other products. In 1792, George Macartney was dispatched to China to open diplomatic relations with the Qing Empire and attempt to revise the trade system.

The **Macartney mission** to China, which extended into 1793, was a fiasco. Qing officials were not expecting Macartney and would not allow him to travel from Canton to Beijing. Moreover, they did not accept his credentials, and Macartney did not know how to make any headway through the Qing bureaucracy. There were prolonged disputes about rituals. The basic issues were unresolvable. Britain wished the Qing Empire to abandon its trade system and to open Chinese ports to a wide range of competing British firms to reverse the trade imbalance. The Qing, however, had no interest in changing the system that provided revenue to the imperial family and lessened serious piracy problems. Macartney left China humiliated by his inability to persuade the Qing to make changes.

Dutch, French, and Russian embassies soon attempted to achieve what Macartney had failed to do. When they failed also, European frustration with the Qing mounted. The great European admiration for China of the early 1700s faded, and China was considered despotic, self-satisfied, and unrealistic. Political solutions seemed impossible because the Qing court would not communicate with foreign envoys or observe the simplest rules of the diplomatic system familiar to Europeans.

Population and Social Stress

The early Qing population exploded from about 100 million under the Ming to between 350 million and 400 million by the end of the 1700s. Despite the efficiency of Chinese agriculture, population growth created economic and environmental decline. Whatever woodlands remained in China were rapidly diminishing. Even though his deforestation led to serious erosion and the danger of flooding grew, government corruption and general inefficiency limited efforts to prevent flooding or recover from its effects. Dams and dikes were not maintained, and silted-up river channels were not dredged. By the end of the eighteenth century, the Grand Canal was nearly unusable, and the towns that bordered it were starved for commerce.

The result was localized misery in many parts of interior China by the year 1800. Environmental deterioration and the decline of agriculture prompted many people to move. They sought seasonal jobs in better-off agricultural areas, or they worked in low-status jobs such as barge puller, charcoal burner, or nightsoil carrier. Many drifted to the cities to make their way by begging, prostitution, or theft. In central and southwestern China, where farmers had been impoverished by serious flooding, rebellions became endemic.

The Qing Empire was outgrowing the state's control. The Qing government employed about the same number of officials as the Ming even though the Qing Empire was twice the size of the Ming geographically and nearly four times its size in terms of population. To maintain local control, the Qing depended on working alliances with local elites, including gentry and aspiring official families. But this dependence undercut the government's ability to enforce tax regulations and to control standards for admission to government service, resulting in widespread corruption and shrinking government revenues.

In addition, the Qing fell victim to some of the basic characteristics of the land-based empires. To defend itself against Russia, it had conquered a huge stretch of territory, and the costs of maintaining it were enormous. Population growth and the need to transport food to nonagricultural areas stressed the food and grain systems. The need to invest in agriculture and in transport infrastructure limited investment in new industries and heightened government interest in taxing foreign trade. Russia was attempting to move out of that mode by turning toward European-style imperialism and industrialization. Japan, China's neighbor, was poised for an entirely different response.

TOKUGAWA JAPAN, TO 1800

Like East Asia under the Qing rulers, Japan under the Tokugawa° shoguns moved from the intense militarization of the early 1600s to the comparative peace of the 1700s, while at the same time facing a decrease in state revenues and mounting European pressure. In nearly every respect, the Japanese reaction to these problems was more successful than the Qing response.

Shogunate and Economy

After the imperial collapse of the twelfth century, Japan was ruled by a series of decentralized military governments—the shogunates. Following a civil war during the later 1500s, a new shogun, Tokugawa Ieyasu°, declared victory. Though Japan was brought under a single military government, the structure of the **Tokugawa Shogunate** had a very important influence over the development of the Japanese economy in the early modern period.

The emperor of Japan had no political power; he remained at Kyoto°, the medieval capital. The Tokugawa shoguns built a new capital for themselves at Edo° (now Tokyo). A well-maintained road connected Kyoto and Edo, and trade and trading centers developed along this route.

Each regional lord maintained a castle town, a small bureaucracy, a population of warriors—*samurai*°—and military support personnel, and often an academy. Between these towns there was

frequent traffic. Because Tokugawa shoguns required the lords to visit Edo frequently, good roads linked Edo to three of the four main islands of Japan.

The domestic peace of the Tokugawa era forced the warrior class to adapt itself to the growing bureaucratic needs of the state. As the samurai became better educated, more attuned to the tastes of the civil elite, and more interested in conspicuous consumption, merchants were well positioned to exploit the new opportunities. The state attempted—unsuccessfully—to curb the independence of the merchants when the economic well-being of the samurai was threatened, particularly when rice prices went too low or interest rates on loans were too high.

The 1600s and 1700s were centuries of high achievement in artisanship and commerce. Japanese skills in steel making, pottery, and lacquerware were joined by excellence in the production and decoration of porcelain, thanks in no small part to Korean experts brought back to Japan after the invasion of 1582. In the early 1600s, manufacturers and merchants amassed enormous family fortunes. Several of the most important industrial and financial companies had their origins in *sake*° or beer breweries of the early Tokugawa period, then branched out into manufacturing, finance, and transport.

Wealthy industrial families usually cultivated close alliances with their regional lords and, if possible, with the shogun himself. In this way, they could weaken the strict control of merchant activity that was an official part of Tokugawa policy. By the end of the 1700s, the industrial families of Tokugawa Japan held the key to modernization and the development of heavy industry, particularly in the prosperous provinces.

The "Closing" of Japan

Like China, Japan at the end of the 1500s was a target of missionary activity by the Jesuits. But converts to Catholic Christianity among the Japanese elite were comparatively few. Generally, Christianity was more successful among farmers in

---

Tokugawa (toe-koo-GAH-wah)   Ieyasu (ee-yeh-YAH-soo)
Kyoto (kee-YO-toe)   Edo (ED-doe)
samurai (SAH-moo-rie)

---

sake (SAH-kay)

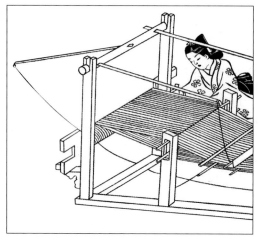

Silk Weaving by Japanese Women   Before the emergence of large factories, this sort of work could be done in the home or at a shared village site.   (From Hishikawa Mornobu, *Wakoku hyakujo* [1895]. Reproduced courtesy of the Harvard-Yenching Library)

the southern and eastern regions of Japan. But when these regions were the scenes of massive uprisings in the late 1630s by impoverished farmers, the rebellions were blamed on Christian influence. Hundreds of Japanese Christians were crucified as a warning to others; belief in Christianity was banned by law.

In 1649, the shogunate ordered the closing of the country, making it illegal and punishable by death for foreigners to come in or for Japanese to leave to prevent the spread of foreign influence in Japan. A few Europeans, primarily the Dutch, were permitted to reside on a small island near Nagasaki, and a few Japanese were licensed to supply their needs. The knowledge that these intermediaries acquired and eventually spread was known as "Dutch studies." It included information about European weapons, technology, shipbuilding, mathematics and astronomy, anatomy and medicine, and geography.

The closing of Japan was ignored by some of the regional lords whose fortunes depended on overseas trade with Korea, Okinawa°, Taiwan, China, and Southeast Asia. The "outer" lords at the northern and southern extremes of Japan tended to be under less control by the shoguns.

Okinawa (oh-kee-NAH-wah)

Elite Decline and Social Crisis

In the 1700s, population growth was putting a great strain on the well-developed lands of central Japan. In the remote provinces, where the lords had sponsored programs to settle and develop new agricultural lands, the rate of economic growth far outstripped the growth rate in centrally located domains. Also weakening the Tokugawa government in the 1700s was the shogunate's inability to halt the economic decline of the samurai, whose salaries paid in rice were being destabilized by the rice brokers. Laws designed to regulate the price of rice and the rate of interest had been passed early in the Tokugawa period, but these laws were not always enforced, sometimes because neither the lords nor the samurai wished them to be. By the early 1700s, members of both groups were dependent on the willingness of merchants to provide them credit.

The Tokugawa shoguns, like governments throughout East Asia, accepted the Confucian idea that agriculture should be the basis of state wealth and that merchants should occupy lowly positions in society because of their reputed lack of moral character. However, the Tokugawa government's decentralized system limited its ability to regulate merchant activities and actually stimulated the growth of commercial activities. Despite official disapproval, merchants and others involved in the growing economy enjoyed relative freedom and influence in eighteenth-century Japan. They produced a vivid culture of their own, fostering the development of *kabuki* theater, colorful woodblock prints and silkscreened fabrics, and restaurants.

The Tokugawa Shogunate put into place a political and economic system that fostered innovation, but the government itself could not exploit it. Thus, the government remained quite traditional during the Tokugawa period, while other segments of society developed new methods of productivity and management.

CONCLUSION

In the early eighteenth century, Eurasia was dominated by the enormous Russian and the Qing land-based empires. Both depended on large transportation systems and intense agricultural production, and they often competed for the same resources. At the center of their political structures were powerful emperors with the economic and legal resources to command armies. Each empire had its most brilliant period—under Peter the Great and Emperor Kangxi—when the throne was occupied by a talented, energetic, and far-sighted ruler.

There were also distinct differences between these empires. Although the Qing court was generally open to many kinds of foreign influences, distance and circumstance limited Qing contact with Europe. The European merchants did not make much of an impression. The Jesuits were influential in philosophy, mathematics, astronomy, and other issues of concern to them, but they were not an inexhaustible resource. From the Jesuits, the Kangxi emperor got very little insight into the emergence of European empires, their tactics, or their goals.

Russia's location and circumstances were different. St. Petersburg gave Peter the Great a "window" into Europe, and from that vantage point he gathered architecture, engineering, shipbuilding,

and military technologies of all kinds. He understood the meaning of the new European use of the sea, and set Russia on a path tending toward European practices of diplomacy and imperialism and away from the static values of the huge land empires.

These variations on an imperial pattern were not shared by Japan. Instead of pursuing centralization, standardization, and strengthening of the ruler, Japan was decentralized. Local lords had great incentive to develop their lands, and merchants worked with the regional lords to develop local enterprises, sustain local samurai, and outfit local soldiers. Many regions of Tokugawa Japan created innovative means of financing local industry and developed unique relationships with other countries, despite the official decision to limit Western contacts.

■ Key Terms

Jesuits	Ming Empire
Siberia	Manchus
Muscovy	Qing Empire
tsar	Kangxi
Mikhail Romanov	variolation
Cossacks	Macartney mission
Peter the Great	Tokugawa Shogunate
autocracy	*samurai*
serfs	

■ Suggested Reading

There is a great deal of literature focused on the Jesuits' history in various countries. For East Asia in the sixteenth and seventeenth centuries, see Michael Coopers, S.J., *Rodrigues the Interpreter: An Early Jesuit in Japan and China* (1974). For China, see David E. Mungello, *Curious Land: Jesuit Accommodation and the Origins of Sinology* (1985), and Jonathan D. Spence, *The Memory Palace of Matteo Ricci* (1984). For Japan, see C. R. Boxer, *The Christian Century in Japan, 1549–1650* (1951).

On early modern Russian history, see W. E. Brown, *A History of Eighteenth-Century Russia* (1980), and Robert O. Crummey, *Aristocrats and Servitors: The Boyar Elite in Russia, 1613–1689* (1983). Among the best-known books on Peter the Great are Matthew Smith Anderson, *Peter the Great* (1978); Robert K. Massie, *Peter the Great: His Life and World* (1980); and Lindsey Hughes, *Russia in the Age of Peter the Great: 1682–1725* (1998).

For China during the transition from the Ming to Qing periods, see James W. Tong, *Disorder Under Heaven: Collective Violence in the Ming Dynasty* (1991); Frederic Wakeman, *The Great Enterprise* (1985); and Lynn Struve, *Voices from the Ming-Qing Cataclysm: In Tiger's Jaws* (1993). On the history of the Manchus and of the Qing Empire, see Evelyn Sakakida Rawski, *The Last Emperors* (1999), and Pamela Kyle Crossley, *The Manchus* (1997).

There is a great deal published on the Macartney mission, much of it originating in the diaries and memoirs of the participants. See the exhaustively detailed Alain Peyrefitte, *The Immobile Empire*, trans. Jon Rothschild

(1992). For a more theoretical discussion, see James L. Hevia, *Cherishing Men from Afar: Qing Guest Ritual and the Macartney Embassy of 1793* (1995).

On Japan in this period, see Chie Nakane and Shinzaburo Oishi *Tokugawa Japan: The Social and Economic Antecedents of Modern Japan*, trans. Conrad Totman (1990), and Tessa Morris-Suzuki, *The Technological Transformation of Japan from the Seventeenth to the Twenty-First Century* (1994).

■ Note

1. Adapted from G. V. Melikhov, "Manzhou Penetration into the Basin of the Upper Amur in the 1680s," in S. L. Tikhvinshii, ed., *Manzhou Rule in China* (Moscow: Progress Publishers, 1983).

REVOLUTIONS RESHAPE THE WORLD,
1750–1870

CHAPTER 20
REVOLUTIONARY CHANGES IN THE ATLANTIC WORLD, 1750–1850
CHAPTER 21
THE EARLY INDUSTRIAL REVOLUTION, 1760–1851
CHAPTER 22
AFRICA, INDIA, AND CHINA, 1750–1870

Between 1750 and 1870, dramatic political, economic, and social changes affected nearly every part of the world. In the West, the American, French, and Haitian Revolutions unleashed forces of nationalism and social reform. At this time, the Industrial Revolution introduced technologies and patterns of work that made industrial societies wealthier, more socially fluid, and militarily more powerful than nonindustrial, traditional societies. Even while Europe's colonial empires in the Western Hemisphere were being dismantled, the Industrial Revolution was fueling European economic expansion, which undermined traditional producers in distant places such as Asia and Africa. When this economic penetration was resisted, as it was in East Asia, the industrializing nations of the West used military force to open markets.

Great Britain expanded its empire by establishing colonial rule in distant Australia, New Zealand, and India. India alone had a population larger than the combined populations of all the colonies that Europe lost in the Americas. The Atlantic slave trade was ended by an international abolitionist movement and by Great Britain's use of diplomacy and naval power. European economic influence expanded in Africa.

442

Invigorated by this exchange, some African states created new institutions and introduced new economic sectors.

The Ottoman Empire, the Qing Empire, and Japan were deeply influenced by the expansion of Europe and the United States. Each society met the Western challenge with reform programs that preserved traditional structures while adopting elements of Western technology and organization. The Ottoman court introduced reforms in education, the military, and law and created the first constitution in an Islamic state. The Qing Empire survived the period of European expansion, but a series of military defeats and civil war seriously compromised China's centralization efforts. Japan experienced the most revolutionary change, abolishing its ancient political system and initiating radical top-down transformations.

The economic, political, and social revolutions that began in the mid-eighteenth century shook the foundations of European culture and led to the expansion of Western power across the globe. Societies throughout Asia, Africa, and Latin America responded to cross-cultural contacts. Some resisted foreign intrusion by using local culture and experience as a guide. Others adopted Western commercial policies, industrial technologies, and government institutions.

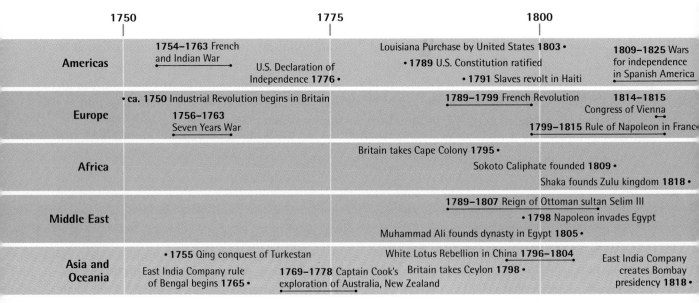

	1750	1775	1800
Americas	1754–1763 French and Indian War	U.S. Declaration of Independence 1776 •	Louisiana Purchase by United States 1803 • • 1789 U.S. Constitution ratified • 1791 Slaves revolt in Haiti	1809–1825 Wars for independence in Spanish America
Europe	• ca. 1750 Industrial Revolution begins in Britain 1756–1763 Seven Years War		1789–1799 French Revolution 1799–1815 Rule of Napoleon in France	1814–1815 Congress of Vienna
Africa		Britain takes Cape Colony 1795 •	Sokoto Caliphate founded 1809 • Shaka founds Zulu kingdom 1818 •	
Middle East			1789–1807 Reign of Ottoman sultan Selim III • 1798 Napoleon invades Egypt Muhammad Ali founds dynasty in Egypt 1805 •	
Asia and Oceania	• 1755 Qing conquest of Turkestan East India Company rule of Bengal begins 1765 •	1769–1778 Captain Cook's exploration of Australia, New Zealand	White Lotus Rebellion in China 1796–1804 Britain takes Ceylon 1798 •	East India Company creates Bombay presidency 1818 •

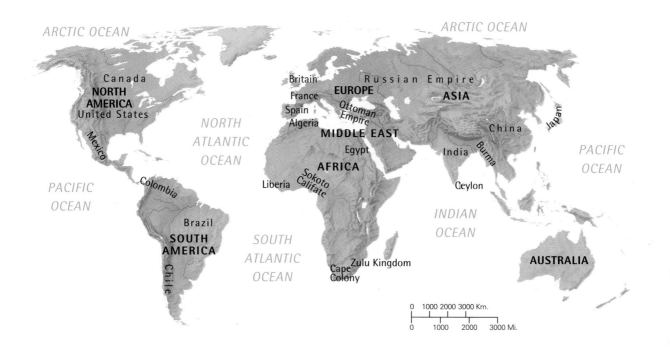

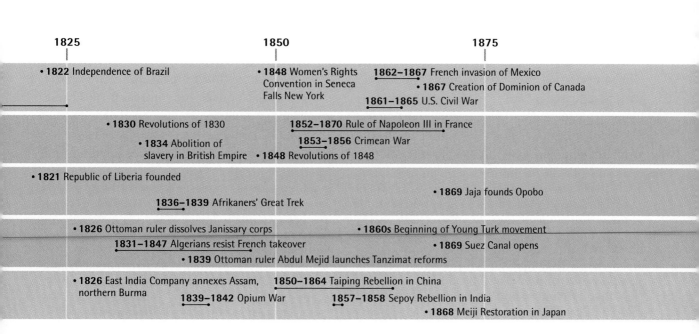

1825	1850	1875

- **1822** Independence of Brazil
- **1848** Women's Rights Convention in Seneca Falls New York
- **1862–1867** French invasion of Mexico
- **1867** Creation of Dominion of Canada
- **1861–1865** U.S. Civil War

- **1830** Revolutions of 1830
- **1834** Abolition of slavery in British Empire
- **1848** Revolutions of 1848
- **1852–1870** Rule of Napoleon III in France
- **1853–1856** Crimean War

- **1821** Republic of Liberia founded
- **1836–1839** Afrikaners' Great Trek
- **1869** Jaja founds Opobo

- **1826** Ottoman ruler dissolves Janissary corps
- **1831–1847** Algerians resist French takeover
- **1839** Ottoman ruler Abdul Mejid launches Tanzimat reforms
- **1860s** Beginning of Young Turk movement
- **1869** Suez Canal opens

- **1826** East India Company annexes Assam, northern Burma
- **1839–1842** Opium War
- **1850–1864** Taiping Rebellion in China
- **1857–1858** Sepoy Rebellion in India
- **1868** Meiji Restoration in Japan

REVOLUTIONARY CHANGES IN THE ATLANTIC WORLD, 1750–1850

Prelude to Revolution: War and the Enlightenment • The American Revolution • The French Revolution • Revolution in Haiti and Latin America • Economic and Social Liberation Movements
ENVIRONMENT AND TECHNOLOGY: The Pencil

On the evening of August 14, 1791, more than two hundred slaves and black freedmen met in secret in the plantation district of northern Saint Domingue° (present-day Haiti) to set the date for an armed uprising against local slave owners. Although the delegates agreed to delay the attack for a week, violence began almost immediately. During the following decade, the Haitian rebels abolished slavery, defeated military forces from Britain and France, and gained independence.

News and rumors about revolutionary events in France that had spread through the island incited the slave community and divided the island's white population between royalists (supporters of France's King Louis XVI) and republicans (supporters of democracy). The free mixed-race population initially gained some political rights from the French Assembly but was then forced to rebel when the slave-owning elite reacted violently.

Among those planning the insurrection was Toussaint L'Ouverture°, a black freedman. This remarkable revolutionary organized the rebels into a potent military force, negotiated with the island's royalist and republican factions and, with representatives of Great Britain and France, wrote his nation's first constitution. Throughout the Western Hemisphere, Toussaint became a towering symbol of resistance to oppression for slaves and a fiend for slave owners.

The Haitian slave rebellion was an important episode in the long and painful political and cultural transformation of the modern Western world. Economic expansion and the growth of trade were creating unprecedented wealth. Intellectuals were questioning the traditional place of monarchy and slavery in society. An emerging class of merchants, professionals, and manu-

Saint Domingue (san doe-MANG)

Toussaint L'Ouverture (too-SAN loo-ver-CHORE)

facturers began to press for a larger political role, and economies were increasingly opened to competition.

Imperial powers resisted the loss of colonies, and monarchs and nobles struggled to retain their ancient privileges. Revolutionary steps forward were often matched by reactionary steps backward. The liberal and nationalist ideals of the eighteenth-century revolutionary movements were only imperfectly realized in Europe and the Americas in the nineteenth century.

As you read this chapter, ask yourself the following questions:

- How did imperial wars among European powers provoke revolution?

- How did revolution in one country help to incite revolution elsewhere?

- Why were the revolutions in France and Haiti more violent than the American Revolution?

- How were political revolts linked to the abolition of slavery?

PRELUDE TO REVOLUTION: WAR AND THE ENLIGHTENMENT

In large measure, the cost of wars fought among Europe's major powers over colonies and trade precipitated the revolutionary era that began in 1775 with the American Revolution. The struggle of Britain, France, and Spain for political preeminence in western Europe and overseas produced many violent conflicts during the eighteenth century. In the Seven Years War (1756–1763), known as the French and Indian War in America, Britain gained dominance in North America and in India. All parties suffered from the enormous costs of these conflicts.

New Western ideas and political environments also made people much more critical of any effort to

extend the power of a monarch or impose new taxes, and raised questions about the rights of individuals. As Chapter 16 recounted, the **Enlightenment** applied the methods and questions of the Scientific Revolution to the study of human society. Some thinkers challenged long-established religious and political institutions. They argued that if scientists could understand the laws of nature, then surely similar forms of disciplined investigation might reveal laws of human nature. Others wondered whether society and government might be better regulated and more productive if guided by reason rather than by hereditary rulers and the church.

These new perspectives and the intellectual optimism that fed them were to help guide the English political philosopher John Locke (1632–1704). Locke argued in 1690 that governments were created to protect life, liberty, and property and that the people had a right to rebel when a monarch violated these natural rights. In *The Social Contract,* published in 1762, the French-Swiss intellectual Jean-Jacques Rousseau° (1712–1778) asserted that the will of the people was sacred and that the legitimacy of the monarch depended on the consent of the people. Although both men believed that government rested on the will of the people rather than divine will, Locke emphasized the importance of individual rights, and Rousseau envisioned the people acting collectively because of their shared historical experience.

The Enlightenment is commonly associated with hostility toward monarchy, but Voltaire, one of the Enlightenment's most critical intellects, believed that Europe's monarchs were likely agents of political and economic reform, and he wrote favorably of China's Qing° emperors. Indeed, some sympathetic members of the nobility and reforming monarchs in Spain, Russia, Austria, and Prussia actively sponsored and promoted the dissemination of new ideas, providing patronage for many intellectuals. They recognized that elements of the Enlightenment critique of the ancien régime° buttressed their own efforts to expand royal authority at the expense of religious institutions, the nobility, and regional autonomy. Monarchs also understood that the era's passion for science and technology

Jean-Jacques Rousseau (zhahn-zhock roo-SOE)
Qing (ching)   *ancien régime* (ahn-see-EN ray-ZHEEM)

held the potential of fattening national treasuries and improving economic performance (see Environment and Technology: The Pencil).

The Western Hemisphere shared in the debates of Europe. In colonial societies where political rights were even more limited than in Europe, the idea that government authority ultimately rested on the consent of the governed was potentially explosive. The efforts of ordinary men and women to resist the growth of government power and the imposition of new cultural forms provide an important political undercurrent to much of the revolutionary agitation and conflict from 1750 to 1850. But spontaneous popular uprisings gained revolutionary potential only when they coincided with ideological divisions and conflicts within the governing class itself.

THE AMERICAN REVOLUTION

After defeating the French in the French and Indian War, the British government faced two related problems in its North American colonies. One was the likelihood of armed conflict with Amerindian peoples as settlers quickly pushed west of the Appalachian Mountains and across the Ohio River. Already burdened with war debts, Britain desperately wanted to avoid additional expenditures for frontier defense. The other problem was how to get the colonists to shoulder more of the costs of imperial defense and colonial administration. Every effort to impose new taxes or prevent the settlement of the trans-Appalachian frontier provoked angry protests in the colonies. The confrontational and impolitic way in which a succession of weak British governments responded made the situation politically explosive.

Frontiers and Taxes

The British Proclamation of 1763, which sought to establish an effective western limit for settlement, threw into question the claims of thousands of already established farmers without effectively protecting Amerindian land. The Quebec Act of 1774 annexed disputed lands to the province of Quebec, thus denying eastern colonies the authority to distribute lands claimed as a result of original charters. Colonists saw the Quebec Act as punitive and tyrannical, and Amerindian peoples received no relief from the continuous assault on their land.

New commercial regulations that increased the cost of foreign molasses and endangered New England's profitable trade with Spanish and French Caribbean sugar colonies provoked widespread boycotts of British goods. The Stamp Act of 1765, which imposed a tax on all legal documents, newspapers, pamphlets, and other types of printed material, led to violent protest and more effective boycotts. Parliament imposed new taxes and duties soon after repealing the Stamp Act in 1766, even sending British troops to quell urban riots. Unable to control the streets of Boston, British authorities reacted by threatening traditional liberties, dissolving the colonial legislature of Massachusetts, and dispatching a warship and two regiments of soldiers to reestablish control. Support for a complete break with Britain grew when a British force fired on an angry Boston crowd on March 5, 1770, killing five civilians. This "Boston Massacre," which seemed to expose the naked force on which colonial rule rested, radicalized public opinion throughout the colonies.

Parliament attempted to calm public opinion by repealing some of the taxes and duties, then stumbled into another crisis by granting the British East India Company a monopoly for importing tea to the colonies, which raised anew the constitutional issue of Parliament's right to tax the colonies. It also offended wealthy colonial merchants, who were excluded from this profitable commerce. The crisis came to a head in the already politically overheated port of Boston when tea worth £10,000 was dumped into the harbor by protesters disguised as Amerindians.

The Course of the Revolution

As the crisis mounted, patriots created new governing bodies, effectively deposed many British governors and other officials, passed laws, appointed

CHRONOLOGY

	The Americas	Europe
1750		
	1756–1763 French and Indian War	**1756–1763** Seven Years War
1775	**1770** Boston Massacre **1776** American Declaration of Independence **1778** United States alliance with France **1783** Treaty of Paris ends American Revolution **1789** U.S. Constitution ratified **1791** Slaves revolt in Saint Domingue (Haiti)	**1789** Storming of Bastille begins French Revolution **1793–1794** Reign of Terror in France **1795–1799** The Directory rules France
1800	**1798** Toussaint L'Ouverture defeats British in Haiti **1804** Haitians defeat French invasion and declare independence **1808** Portuguese royal family arrives in Brazil **1808–1809** Revolutions for independence begin in Spanish South America	**1799** Napoleon overthrows the Directory **1804** Napoleon crowns himself emperor
1825	**1822** Brazil gains independence	**1814** Napoleon abdicates; Congress of Vienna opens **1830** Greece gains independence; revolution in France
1850	**1838** End of slavery in British Caribbean **1848** Women's Rights Convention in Seneca Falls, New York **1861–1865** American Civil War	**1848** Revolutions in France, Austria, Germany, Hungary, and Italy
1875	**1865** End of slavery in United States **1886** End of slavery in Cuba **1888** End of slavery in Brazil	

judges, and even took control of colonial militias. Simultaneously, radical leaders organized crowds to intimidate loyalists—people who were pro-British—and to enforce the boycott of British goods.

Events were propelling the colonies toward revolution. Elected representatives, meeting in Philadelphia as the Continental Congress in 1775, assumed the powers of government, creating a currency and organizing an army. **George Washington** (1732–1799), a Virginia planter who had served in the French and Indian War, was named commander. On July 4, 1776, Congress approved the Declaration of Independence, the document that proved to be the most enduring statement of the revolutionary era's ideology:

We hold these truths to be self evident: That all men are created equal; that they are endowed by their creator with certain unalienable rights; that among these are life, liberty and the pursuit of happiness; that, to secure these rights, governments are instituted among men, deriving their just powers from the consent of the governed.

This affirmation of popular sovereignty and individual rights influenced the language of revolution and popular protest around the world.

To shore up British authority, Great Britain sent more than 400 ships, 50,000 soldiers, and 30,000 German mercenaries. But this military commitment proved futile. Although British forces won most of the battles, Washington slowly built a competent Continental army and civilian support

The Pencil

From early times, Europeans had used sharp points, lead, and other implements to sketch, make marks, and write brief notes. At the end of the seventeenth century, a source of high-quality graphite was discovered at Borrowdale in northwestern England. Borrowdale graphite gained acceptance among artists, artisans, and merchants. At first, pure graphite was simply wrapped in string. By the eighteenth century, pieces of graphite were being encased in wooden sheaths and resembled modern pencils. Widespread use of this useful tool was retarded by the limited supply of high-quality graphite from the English mines.

The English crown periodically closed the Borrowdale mines or restricted production to keep prices high and maintain adequate supplies for future needs. As a result, artisans in other European nations developed alternatives that used lower-quality graphite or, most commonly, graphite mixed with sulfur and glues.

The major breakthrough occurred in 1793 in France when war with England ruptured trade links. The government of revolutionary France responded to the shortage of graphite by assigning a thirty-nine-year-old scientist, Nicolas-Jacques Conté, to find an alternative. Conté had earlier promoted the military use of balloons and conducted experiments with hydrogen. He also had had experience using graphite alloys in the development of crucibles for melting metal.

Within a short period, Conté produced a graphite that is the basis for most lead pencils today. He succeeded by mixing finely ground graphite with potter's clay and water. The resulting paste was dried in a long mold, sealed in a ceramic box, and fired in an oven. The graphite strips were then placed in a wooden case. Although some believed the Conté pencils were inferior to the pencils made from Borrowdale graphite, Conté

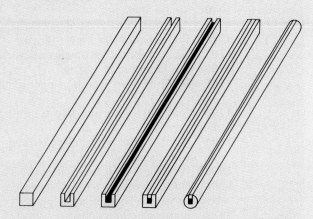

Pencils Wartime necessity led to invention of the modern pencil in France. (Drawing by Fred Avent for Henry Petroski. Reproduced by permission)

produced a very serviceable pencil that could be produced in uniform quality and unlimited amounts.

Henry Petroski, summarizing the achievement of Conté in his *The Pencil*, wrote: "The laboratory is really the modern workshop. And modern engineering results when the scientific method is united with experience with the tools and products of craftsmen. . . . Modern engineering, in spirit if not in name, would come to play a more and more active role in turning the craft tradition into modern technology, with its base of research and development."

Source: This discussion depends on Henry Petroski, *The Pencil: A History of Design and Circumstance* (New York: Knopf, 1990); the quotation is from pp. 50–78.

networks that provided supplies and financial resources. In the final decisive battle, fought at Yorktown, Virginia (see Map 20.1), an American army, supported by French soldiers, besieged a British army led by General Charles Cornwallis. With escape cut off by a French fleet, Cornwallis surrendered to Washington as the British military band played "The World Turned Upside-Down."

New Republican Institutions

Ignoring the British example of an unwritten constitution, representatives in each of the newly independent states drafted formal charters and submitted the results to voters for ratification. Europeans were fascinated by these written constitutions and by their formal ratification by the people. Here was the social contract of Locke and Rousseau made manifest. The state constitutions also placed severe limits on executive authority

Map 20.1   The American Revolutionary War   The British army won most of the major battles, and British troops held most of the major cities. Even so, the American revolutionaries eventually won a comprehensive military and political victory.

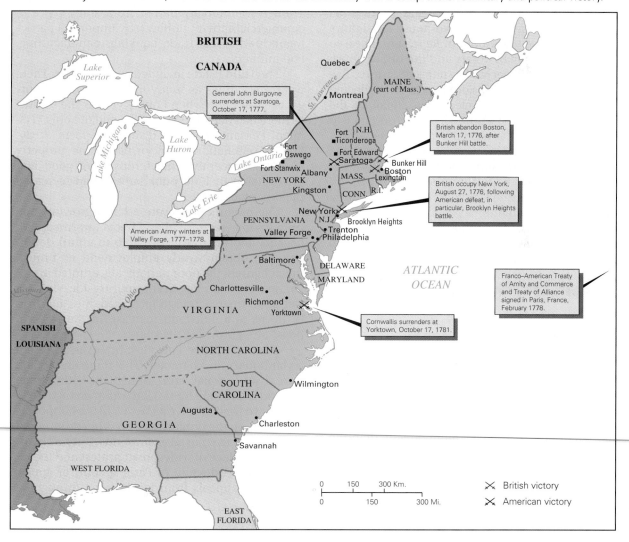

but granted legislatures greater powers than in colonial times. Many states also inserted in their constitutions a bill of rights to provide further protection against government tyranny.

An effective constitution for the new national government was developed more slowly and hesitantly. The Articles of Confederation—the first constitution of the United States—were not accepted by all the states until 1781. With the coming of peace in 1783, there was an effort to fashion a new constitution.

Debate at the **Constitutional Convention,** which began meeting in May 1787, focused on several issues: representation, electoral procedures, executive powers, and the relationship between the federal government and the states. The final compromise provided for a two-house legislature: the lower house (the House of Representatives) to be elected directly by voters and the upper house (the Senate) to be elected by state legislatures. The chief executive—the president—was to be elected indirectly by "electors" selected by ballot in the states (each state had a number of electors equal to the number of its representatives and senators).

Although the U.S. Constitution created the most democratic government of the era, only a minority of the adult population was given full rights. Southern leaders were able to protect the institution of slavery by counting three-fifths of the slave population in the calculations that determined their states' congressional representatives. Although women had led prewar boycotts and had organized relief and charitable organizations during the war, they were denied political rights in the new republic.

THE FRENCH REVOLUTION

The French Revolution confronted the entrenched privileges of an established church, monarchy, and aristocracy more directly than the American Revolution did. It also expanded mass participation in political life and radicalized the democratic tradition. But in the end, the passions unleashed in France by revolutionary events could not be sustained.

French Society and Fiscal Crisis

French society was divided into three groups. The clergy, the First Estate, numbered about 130,000 in a nation of 28 million. The Catholic Church owned about 10 percent of the nation's land and extracted substantial amounts of wealth from the economy in the form of tithes and ecclesiastical fees. Despite its substantial wealth, the church was exempted from nearly all taxes.

The 300,000 members of the nobility, the Second Estate, controlled about 30 percent of the land and retained ancient rights on much of the rest. Nobles held the vast majority of high administrative, judicial, military, and church positions. Though traditionally barred from some types of commercial activity, nobles were important participants in wholesale trade, banking, manufacturing, and mining.

The Third Estate included everyone else. There were three times as many members of the bourgeoisie°, in 1774, when Louis XVI took the throne, as there had been in 1715, at the end of Louis XIV's reign. Peasants accounted for 80 percent of the French population. They owned some property and lived decently when crops were good and prices stable. By 1780, poor harvests had decreased their incomes.

The nation's poor were a large, growing, and troublesome sector. Urban streets swarmed with beggars and prostitutes. Unable to afford decent housing, obtain steady employment, or protect their children, the poor periodically erupted in violent protest and rage. In the countryside, violence was often the reaction to increased dues and fees. In towns and cities, an increase in the price of bread often provided the spark.

These explosive episodes, however, were not revolutionary in character. The remedies sought were conventional and immediate rather than structural and long term. That was to change when the Crown tried to solve its fiscal crisis by imposing new taxes on the nobility and on other groups that in the past had enjoyed exemptions. But this effort failed in the face of widespread protest and the refusal of the Parlement of Paris, a court of appeal that heard appeals from local courts throughout

bourgeoisie (boor-zwah-ZEE)

France, to register the new tax. In 1768, frustrated authorities exiled the members of that Parlement and pushed through a series of unpopular fiscal measures. Despite the worsening fiscal crisis, the French took on the heavy burden of supporting the American Revolution, delaying collapse by borrowing enormous sums. By the end of the war with Britain, more than half of France's national budget was required to service the debt alone. In 1787, the desperate king called an Assembly of Notables to approve a radical and comprehensive reform of the economy and fiscal policy. Despite the fact that the members of this assembly were selected by the king's advisers from the high nobility, the judiciary, and the clergy, it proved unwilling to act as a rubber stamp for the proposed reforms or new taxes. Instead, these representatives of France's most privileged classes sought to protect their interests by questioning the competence of the king and his ministers to supervise the nation's affairs, thus creating the conditions for political revolution.

Protest Turns to Revolution

Unable to extract needed tax concessions from the notables, King Louis XVI was forced to call the **Estates General,** the French national legislature, which had not met since 1614. Traditionally, the three estates met separately, and a positive vote by two of the three was required for action. Tradition, however, was quickly overturned when the Third Estate refused to conduct business until the king ordered the other two estates to sit with it in a single body. During a six-week period of stalemate, many parish priests deserted the First Estate to meet with them.

When this expanded Third Estate declared itself the **National Assembly,** the king and his advisers recognized that the reformers intended to force them to accept a constitutional monarchy. Louis's agenda for fiscal reform was being displaced by the central ideas of the era: the people were sovereign, and the legitimacy of political institutions and individual rulers ultimately depended on their carrying out the people's will. Louis prepared for a confrontation with the National Assembly by moving military forces to Versailles. But before he could act, the people of Paris intervened.

A succession of bad harvests beginning in 1785 had propelled bread prices upward throughout France and provoked an economic depression. By the time the Estates General met, nearly a third of the Parisian work force was unemployed. Hunger and anger marched hand in hand through working-class neighborhoods.

When the people of Paris heard that the king was massing troops to arrest their representatives, crowds of common people began to seize arms and mobilize. On July 14, 1789, a crowd searching for military supplies attacked the Bastille°, a medieval fortress used as a prison. The futile defense of the Bastille cost ninety-eight lives before its garrison surrendered. Enraged, the attackers hacked the commander to death and then paraded through the city with his head and that of Paris's chief magistrate stuck on pikes.

These events coincided with uprisings in the country. Peasants sacked manor houses and destroyed documents that recorded their traditional obligations. They refused to pay taxes and dues to landowners and seized common lands. Forced to recognize the fury raging through rural areas, the National Assembly voted to end traditional obligations and to reform the tax system. Having forced acceptance of their narrow agenda, the peasants ceased their revolt.

These popular uprisings strengthened the hand of the National Assembly in its dealings with the king. One manifestation of this altered relationship was passage of the **Declaration of the Rights of Man.** The French declaration, however, was more sweeping in its language than the American Declaration of Independence. Among the enumerated natural rights were "liberty, property, security, and resistance to oppression." The Declaration of the Rights of Man also guaranteed free expression of ideas, equality before the law, and representative government.

While delegates debated political issues in Versailles, the economic crisis worsened in Paris. Because the working women of Paris faced high food prices every day as they struggled to feed their families, their anger had a hard edge. On October 5,

---

Bastille (bass-TEEL)

Parisian Stocking Mender The poor lived very difficult lives. This woman uses a discarded wine barrel as a shop where she mends socks. (Private collection)

market women organized a crowd of thousands to march the 12 miles (19 kilometers) to Versailles°. Once there, they forced their way into the National Assembly to demand action from the frightened representatives: "The point is that we want bread." The crowd then entered the royal apartments, killed some of the king's guards, and searched for Queen Marie Antoinette°, whom they loathed as a symbol of extravagance. Eventually, the crowd demanded that the royal family return to Paris. Preceded by the heads of two aristocrats carried on pikes and hauling away the palace's supply of flour, the triumphant crowd escorted the royal family to Paris.

The National Assembly achieved a radically restructured French society in the next two years. It passed a new constitution that dramatically limited monarchical power and abolished the nobility as a hereditary class. Economic reforms swept away monopolies and trade barriers within France. The Legislative Assembly created by the new constitution seized church lands to use as collateral for a new paper currency, and priests, who were to be elected, were put on the state payroll. When the government tried to force priests to take a loyalty oath, however, many Catholics joined a growing counterrevolutionary movement.

At first, many European monarchs had welcomed the weakening of the French king, but by 1791 Austria and Prussia threatened to intervene in support of the monarchy. The Legislative Assembly responded by declaring war. Although the war went badly at first for French forces, people across France responded patriotically to foreign invasions, forming huge new volunteer armies and mobilizing national resources to meet the challenge. By the end of 1792, French armies had gained the upper hand everywhere.

In this period of national crisis and foreign threat, the French Revolution entered its most radical phase. A failed effort by the king and queen to escape from Paris and find foreign allies cost the king any remaining popular support. As foreign armies crossed into France, his behavior was increasingly viewed as treasonous. In August 1792, the Legislative Assembly suspended the king, ordered his imprisonment, and called for the formation of a new National Convention to be elected by the vote of all men. Swept along by popular passion, the newly elected National Convention convicted Louis XVI of treason, sentencing him to death and proclaiming France a republic.

The guillotine ended the king's life in January 1793. Invented in the spirit of the era as a more humane way to execute the condemned, this machine was to become the bloody symbol of the revolution. During the period of repression called the Reign of Terror (1793–1794), approximately 40,000 people were executed or died in prison. This radical phase ended in July 1794 when the Terror's leaders were executed by guillotine.

Versailles (vuhr-SIGH)   **Antoinette** (ann-twah-NET)

Parisian Women Marching on Versailles   When the market women of Paris marched to Versailles and forced the royal family to return to Paris with them, they altered the course of the French Revolution. In this drawing, the women are armed with pikes and swords and drag a cannon. Only the woman on the far left is clearly middle class, and she is pictured hesitating or turning away from the resolute actions of the poor women around her.   (Bibliothèque nationale de France)

Reaction and Dictatorship

Purged of the radicals, the National Convention—the new legislative assembly of the French republic—began to undo the radical reforms. It removed many of the emergency economic controls that had been holding down prices and protecting the working class. When the Paris working class rose in protest in 1795, the Convention approved the use of overwhelming military force. The Convention also permitted the Catholic Church to regain much of its former influence, but would not return the Church's confiscated wealth. Finally, it ratified a more conservative constitution, which protected property, established a voting process that reduced the power of the masses, and created a new executive authority, the Directory. Once installed in power, however, the Directory proved unable to end the foreign wars or solve domestic economic problems.

After losing the election of 1797, the Directory suspended the results. The republican phase of the Revolution was clearly dead. Legitimacy was now based on coercive power rather than on elections. Two years later, **Napoleon Bonaparte** (1769–1821), a brilliant young general in the French army, seized power. Just as the American and French Revolutions had been the start of the modern democratic tradition, the military intervention that brought Napoleon to power in 1799 marked the advent of another modern form of government: popular authoritarianism.

In contrast to the National Convention, Napoleon proved capable of realizing France's dream of dominating Europe and providing effective protection for persons and property at home. Negotiations with the Catholic Church led to the Concordat of 1801, which gave French Catholics the right to practice their religion freely. Napoleon's Civil Code of 1804 asserted two basic principles inherited from the moderate first stage of the French Revolution: equality in law and protection of property. Even some members of the nobility became supporters after Napoleon declared himself emperor and France an empire in 1804.

While providing personal security, the Napoleonic system denied or restricted many individual rights. Women were denied basic political rights. Free speech and free expression were limited. Criticism of the government, viewed as subversive, was proscribed, and most opposition newspapers disappeared.

Ultimately, the Napoleonic system depended on the success of French arms and French diplomacy (see Map 20.2). From Napoleon's assumption of power until his fall, no single European state could defeat the French military. Austria and Prussia were forced to become allies of France. Only Britain, protected by its powerful navy, remained able to thwart Napoleon's plans to dominate Europe. In June 1812, Napoleon made the fateful decision to invade Russia with the largest army ever assembled in Europe, approximately 600,000 men. Five weeks after occupying Moscow, he was forced to retreat. The brutal Russian winter and attacks by Russian forces destroyed his army. A broken and battered fragment of 30,000 men returned home to France.

After the debacle in Russia, Austria and Prussia deserted Napoleon and entered an alliance with Britain and Russia. Unable to defend Paris, Napoleon was forced to abdicate the French throne in April 1814. The allies exiled Napoleon to the island of Elba off the coast of Italy and restored the French monarchy.

Retrenchment, Reform, and Revolution

The French Revolution and Napoleon's imperial ambitions had threatened the very survival of the European old order. Ancient monarchies had been overturned and long-established political institutions tossed aside. The very existence of the nobility and church had been put at risk. Under the leadership of the Austrian foreign minister, Prince Klemens von Metternich° (1773–1859), Britain, Russia, Austria, and Prussia worked together in Vienna to create a comprehensive peace settlement that they hoped would safeguard the conservative order. Because the participants in the **Congress of Vienna** believed that a strong and stable France was the best guarantee of future peace, the French monarchy was reestablished. Metternich sought to offset French strength with a balance of power.

Despite the power of the conservative monarchs, popular support for national self-determination and democratic reform grew throughout Europe. In 1821, Greek patriots launched a movement for independence from Ottoman control. In 1830, Russia, France, and Great Britain forced the Ottoman Empire to recognize Greek independence. That same year, the people of Paris rose up and forced King Charles X to abdicate. His successor, Louis Philippe° (r. 1830–1848), reestablished the constitution and extended voting privileges.

Despite limited political reform, conservatives continued to hold the upper hand in Europe. Finally, in 1848, the desire for democratic reform and national self-determination and the frustrations of urban workers led to upheavals across Europe. The **Revolutions of 1848** began in Paris, where members of the middle class and workers united to overthrow the regime of Louis Philippe and create the Second French Republic. Adult men were given voting rights, slavery was abolished in French colonies, the death penalty was ended, and a ten-hour workday was legislated for Paris. But Parisian workers' demand for programs to reduce unemployment and lower prices provoked conflicts with the middle class, which wanted to protect property rights. Desiring the reestablishment of order, the French elected Louis Napoleon, nephew of the former emperor, president in December 1848. Three years later, he overturned the constitution as a result of popular plebiscite and, after ruling briefly as dictator, became Emperor Napoleon III. He remained in power until 1871.

Despite their heroism on the barricades of Vienna, Rome, and Berlin, the revolutionaries of 1848 also failed to gain either their nationalist or their republican objectives. Metternich, the symbol of reaction, fled Vienna in disguise, but little lasting

---

Metternich (MET-uhr-nik)

Louis Philippe (loo-EE fee-LEEP)

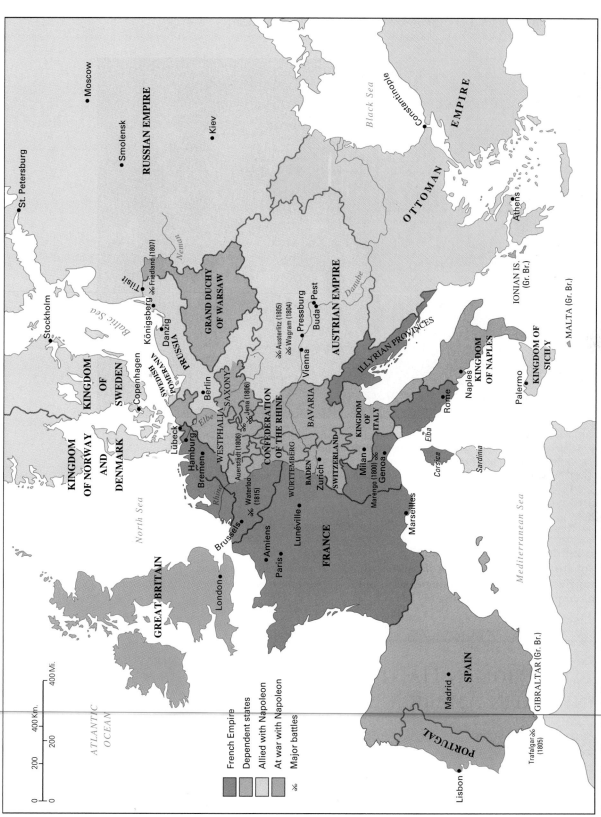

Map 20.2 Napoleon's Europe, 1810 By 1810, Great Britain was the only remaining European power at war with Napoleon. Because of the loss of the French fleet at the Battle of Trafalgar in 1805, Napoleon was unable to threaten Britain with invasion, and Britain was able to assist the resistance movements in Spain and Portugal, thereby helping to weaken French power.

French Empire
Dependent states
Allied with Napoleon
At war with Napoleon
Major battles

ATLANTIC OCEAN

GREAT BRITAIN
London
Brussels
Amiens
Paris
Lunéville
FRANCE
Marseilles

North Sea

KINGDOM OF NORWAY AND DENMARK
Copenhagen
Stockholm
St. Petersburg

Baltic Sea

KINGDOM OF SWEDEN

SWEDISH POMERANIA
PRUSSIA
Königsberg
Danzig
Lübeck
Hamburg
Bremen
Berlin
WESTPHALIA
SAXONY
Auerstädt (1806)
Jena (1806)
CONFEDERATION OF THE RHINE
WÜRTTEMBERG
BADEN
Zurich
SWITZERLAND
Waterloo (1815)
Elbe
Rhine

Tilsit
Friedland (1807)
Neman

GRAND DUCHY OF WARSAW

RUSSIAN EMPIRE
Moscow
Smolensk
Kiev

BAVARIA
KINGDOM OF ITALY
Milan
Marengo (1800)
Genoa

AUSTRIAN EMPIRE
Vienna
Pressburg
Buda
Pest
Austerlitz (1805)
Wagram (1804)
Danube

ILLYRIAN PROVINCES

Black Sea

OTTOMAN EMPIRE
Constantinople
Athens

IONIAN IS. (Gr. Br.)
MALTA (Gr. Br.)

Rome
Naples
KINGDOM OF NAPLES
Palermo
KINGDOM OF SICILY

Elba
Corsica
Sardinia

Mediterranean Sea

SPAIN
Madrid

PORTUGAL
Lisbon
Trafalgar (1805)

GIBRALTAR (Gr. Br.)

400 Mi.
400 Km.
200
200
0
0

The Revolution of 1830 in Belgium After the 1830 uprising that overturned the restored monarchy in France, Belgians rose up to declare their independence from Holland. In Poland and Italy, similar uprisings, combining nationalism and a desire for self-governance, failed. This painting by Baron Gustaf Wappers romantically illustrates the popular nature of the Belgian uprising by bringing to the barricades men, women, and children drawn from both the middle and the working classes. (Musées royaux des Beaux-Arts de Belgique, Brussels)

change occurred. Monarchs retained the support not only of aristocrats but also of professional militaries, largely recruited from among peasants who had little sympathy for urban workers.

REVOLUTION IN HAITI AND LATIN AMERICA

In the Americas, the revolutionary ideology of the American and French Revolutions was spreading and taking hold. On the island of Hispaniola, a revolution ended slavery and French rule in Saint Domingue. The same economic and political forces that had undermined British rule in the colonies that became the United States were present in Spanish America and Brazil.

The Haitian Revolution

The French colony of Saint Domingue produced two-thirds of France's tropical imports and generated nearly one-third of all French foreign trade. This impressive wealth depended on a brutal slave regime. Saint Domingue's harsh punishments and high mortality were notorious throughout the Caribbean.

In 1789, when news of the calling of France's Estates General arrived on the island, wealthy white planters sent a delegation to Paris charged with seeking more home rule and greater economic freedom. The *gens de couleur*° also sent representatives. Mostly small planters or urban merchants, these free mixed-race delegates focused on ending race discrimination and political inequality. They did not seek freedom for slaves, because the most prosperous gens de couleur were slave owners themselves.

The political turmoil in France weakened colonial authority, permitting rich planters, poor whites, gens de couleur, and slaves to pursue their narrow interests, in an increasingly bitter and confrontational struggle. By 1791, whites and the gens de couleur were engaged in open warfare. This breach between the two groups of slave owners gave the slaves an opening. Their rebellion began on the plantations of the north and spread throughout the colony. Plantations were destroyed, masters and overseers killed, and crops burned.

The rebellious slaves eventually gained the upper hand under the military leadership of **Toussaint L'Ouverture,** a former domestic slave. Politically strengthened in 1794 when the radical National Convention in Paris abolished slavery in all French possessions, Toussaint overcame his rivals in Saint Domingue, defeated a British expeditionary force in 1798, and then led an invasion of neighboring Santo Domingo, freeing the slaves there. Toussaint continued to assert his loyalty to France but gave the French government no effective role in local affairs.

In 1802, Napoleon sent a large military force to Saint Domingue to reestablish both French authority and slavery. At first, the French forces were successful. Toussaint was captured and sent to France, where he died in prison. Eventually, however, French losses to yellow fever and the resistance of the revolutionaries turned the tide. Few slave women had taken up arms during the early stages of the Haitian Revolution, but now they joined the armed resistance. In 1804, the free republic of Haiti joined the United States as the second independent nation in the Western Hemisphere. But independence and emancipation were achieved at a terrible price. Tens of thousands had died, and the economy was destroyed.

Latin American Revolutions

The great works of the Enlightenment as well as revolutionary documents like the Declaration of Independence and the Declaration of the Rights of Man circulated widely in Latin America. But it was Napoleon's decision to invade Portugal (1807) and Spain (1808), not revolutionary ideas, that ignited Latin America's struggle for independence.

In 1808, the royal family of Portugal fled to Brazil and maintained court there for over a decade. In Spain, in contrast, Napoleon forced King Ferdinand VII to abdicate and placed his own brother, Joseph Bonaparte, on the throne. When Spanish patriots fighting against the French created a new political body, the Junta° Central, and claimed the right to exercise the king's powers over Spain's colonies, a vocal minority of powerful colonists objected. In late 1808 and 1809, popular movements overthrew Spanish colonial officials in Venezuela, Mexico, and Bolivia and created local juntas. In each case, Spanish officials' harsh repression gave rise to a greater sense of a separate American nationality. By 1810, Spanish colonial authorities were facing a new round of revolutions more clearly focused on the achievement of independence.

In Caracas (the capital city of modern Venezuela), a revolutionary junta led by creoles (colonial-born whites) declared independence in 1811. Its leaders were large landowners who espoused popular sovereignty and representative democracy, defended slavery, and opposed full citizenship for the black and mixed-race majority. The junta's narrow agenda spurred loyalists in the colonial administration and church hierarchy to rally thousands of free blacks and slaves to defend the Spanish Empire. **Simón Bolívar°** (1783–1830) became the preeminent leader of the independence movement in Spanish South America.

Between 1813 and 1817, military advantage shifted back and forth between the patriots and loyalists, but by 1820, momentum swung irreversibly to the patriots. After liberating present-day Venezuela, Colombia, Ecuador, Peru, and Bolivia, Bolívar's army defeated the last Spanish armies in

---

gens de couleur (zhahn deh koo-LUHR)

Junta (HUN-tah)
Simón Bolívar (see-MOAN bow-LEE-varh)

1824. But Bolívar's attempt to draw the former Spanish colonies into a formal confederation failed (see Map 20.3).

Buenos Aires (the capital city of modern Argentina) was the second important center of revolutionary activity in Spanish South America. In the south, a coalition of militia commanders, merchants, and ranchers declared independence as the United Provinces of the Río de la Plata in 1816. Patriot leaders in Buenos Aires at first sought to retain control over the old Viceroyalty of Río de la Plata, but a separatist movement defeated these ambitions. A mixed force of Chileans and Argentines, led by José de San Martín° (1778–1850), liberated Chile in 1820. Simón Bolívar overcame final Spanish resistance in Peru in 1824.

The arrival of the Portuguese royal family in Brazil in 1808 had helped to maintain the loyalty of the colonial elite and to stimulate the local economy. But when King John VI returned to Portugal in 1821, Brazilians began to reevaluate Brazil's relationship with Portugal and to talk openly of independence.

Unwilling to return to Portugal and committed to maintaining his family's hold on Brazil, King John's son Pedro aligned himself with the rising tide of independence sentiment. In 1822, he declared Brazilian independence. Unlike its neighbors, which became constitutional republics, Brazil gained independence as a constitutional monarchy with Pedro I, heir to the throne of Portugal, as emperor. The monarchy lasted until 1889, when it was overthrown by republicans.

Mexico

In 1810, Mexico was Spain's richest and most populous colony. But the sharp distinctions among its creole, native, and Spanish populations made it ripe for revolution. The first stage of the revolution against Spain occurred in central Mexico, where wealthy ranchers and farmers had aggressively forced many Amerindian communities from their traditional agricultural lands. By the time news of Napoleon's invasion of Spain reached the region, crop failures and epidemics had further afflicted the poor.

On September 16, 1810, **Miguel Hidalgo y Costilla°,** parish priest of the small town of Dolores, rang the church bells, attracting thousands. In a fiery speech, he urged the crowd to rise up against the oppression of Spanish officials. Tens of thousands of the rural and urban poor joined his movement. They lacked military discipline and adequate weapons but knew who their oppressors were. At first sympathetic to Hidalgo's objectives, wealthy Mexicans eventually turned against Hidalgo, who was captured, tried, and executed in 1811.

Although insurgents continued to wage war against Spanish forces, colonial rule seemed secure in 1820. However, news of the military revolt in Spain unsettled the conservative groups and church officials who had defended Spanish rule against Hidalgo and Morelos. In 1821, Colonel Agustín de Iturbide° and other loyalist commanders forged an alliance with remaining insurgents and declared Mexico's independence. The conservative origins of Mexico's transition to independence were highlighted by the decision to create a monarchical form of government and crown Iturbide as emperor. In early 1823, however, the army overthrew Iturbide and Mexico became a republic.

ECONOMIC AND SOCIAL LIBERATION MOVEMENTS

During the nineteenth century, the newly independent nations of the Western Hemisphere struggled to realize the Enlightenment ideals of freedom and individual liberty. The persistence of slavery and women's inequality raised troubling questions about these ideals. By century's end, reform movements in many of the hemisphere's nations had made significant progress, but much remained to be done.

José de San Martín (hoe-SAY deh san mar-TEEN)

Miguel Hidalgo y Costilla (mee-GEHL ee-DAHL-go ee cos-TEA-ah)
Agustín de Iturbide (ah-goos-TEEN deh ee-tur-BEE-deh)

Map 20.3 Latin America by 1830 By 1830, patriot forces had overturned the Spanish and Portuguese Empires of the Western Hemisphere. Regional conflicts, local wars, and foreign interventions challenged the survival of many of these new nations following independence.

Within the image:

OREGON COUNTRY (Joint U.S.-British occupation)

BRITISH NORTH AMERICA (Gr. Br.)

UNITED STATES

Colorado

Mississippi

Rio Grande

MEXICO 1821

San Antonio

ATLANTIC OCEAN

Gulf of Mexico

Havana

Mexico City • Veracruz

BAHAMA IS. (Gr. Br.)

CUBA (Spain)

HAITI 1804

PUERTO RICO (Spain)

JAMAICA (Gr. Br.)

BRITISH HONDURAS (Gr. Br.)

GUATEMALA
Guatemala

Caribbean Sea

UNITED PROVINCES OF CENTRAL AMERICA 1823—1839

Panama

Caracas

TRINIDAD (Gr. Br.)

VENEZUELA

BR. GUIANA (Gr. Br.)

DUTCH GUIANA (Neth.)

FRENCH GUIANA (France)

Socorro
Bogotá

Magdalena

GRAN COLOMBIA 1819—1830

Quito

ECUADOR

Galápagos Islands

Amazon

EMPIRE OF BRAZIL 1822

PERU 1824

Lima

Bahia

PACIFIC OCEAN

BOLIVIA 1825

La Paz

Sucre

Paraná

PARAGUAY 1811

São Paulo

Rio de Janeiro

CHILE 1817

UNITED PROVINCES OF THE RÍO DE LA PLATA 1816

Valparaíso
Santiago

ARGENTINA

Buenos Aires

URUGUAY 1828

Montevideo

Bahía Blanca

1811 Year independence gained

Colony

0   500   1000 Km.

0   500   1000 Mi.

PATAGONIA (Disputed between Argentina and Chile)

Islas Malvinas (Falkland Islands)

Benito Juárez's Triumph over the French   Benito Juárez overcame humble origins to lead the overthrow of French imperialism. He remains a powerful symbol of secularism and republican virtue in Mexico. In this 1948 mural by José Clemente Orozco, Juárez's face dominates a scene of struggle that pits Mexican patriots against the allied forces of the Catholic Church, Mexican conservatives, and foreign invaders.   (Museo Nacional de Historia/CENIDIAP-INBA)

The Abolition of Slavery

In both the United States and Latin America, strong antislavery sentiments were expressed during the struggles for independence. In nearly all the new nations of the Western Hemisphere, revolutionary leaders asserted universal ideals of freedom and citizenship that contrasted sharply with the reality of slavery. Men and women who wanted to outlaw slavery were called **abolitionists.** Despite the efforts of abolitionists, slavery survived in much of the hemisphere until the 1850s. In regions where the export of plantation products was most important—such as the United States, Brazil, and Cuba—the abolition of slavery was achieved with great difficulty.

In the United States, some northern states had abolished slavery after the revolution, and Congress banned the importation of new slaves in 1808. But this progress was stalled by the profitable expansion of cotton agriculture after the War of 1812. In Spanish America, tens of thousands of slaves gained freedom by joining revolutionary armies during the wars for independence. After independence, most Spanish American republics prohibited the slave trade. Counteracting that trend was the growing international demand for sugar and coffee, products traditionally produced on plantations by slaves. As prices rose for plantation products in the first half of the nineteenth century, Brazil and Cuba (a Spanish colony until 1899) increased their imports of slaves.

During the long struggle to end slavery in the United States, American abolitionists argued that slavery offended both morality and the universal rights asserted in the Declaration of Independence. Two groups denied full rights of citizenship under the Constitution, women and free African-Americans, played important roles in the abolition of slavery. Women served on the executive committee of the American Anti-Slavery Society and produced some of the most effective propaganda against slavery. Many women abolitionists advocated female suffrage as well. Frederick Douglass, a former slave, became one of the most effective abolitionist speakers and writers. More radical black leaders saw civil war or slave insurrection as necessary for ending slavery.

During the Civil War, pressure for emancipation rose as tens of thousands of black freemen and escaped slaves joined the Union army. Hundreds of thousands of other slaves fled their masters' plantations and farms for the protection of advancing northern armies. In 1863, in the midst of the Civil War, President Lincoln began the abolition of slavery by issuing the Emancipation Proclamation, which ended slavery in rebel states not occupied by the Union army. Final abolition was accomplished in 1865, by the Thirteenth Amendment to the Constitution.

After Britain ended its participation in the slave trade in 1807, it negotiated treaties with Spain, Brazil, and other importers of slaves to eliminate the slave trade to the Americas. But enforcement proved difficult. For example, Brazil, despite its treaty of 1830, illegally imported over a half-million more African slaves before the British navy finally forced compliance in the 1850s. The Brazilian parliament passed legislation abolishing slavery in 1888.

Slavery lasted longest in Cuba. Despite strong British pressure, the Spanish colony continued to import large numbers of African slaves until the 1860s. More important, however, was the growth of support for abolition in these colonies. Both Cuba and Puerto Rico had larger white and free colored populations than did the Caribbean colonies of Britain and France. As a result, there was less fear in Cuba and Puerto Rico that abolition would lead to the political ascendancy of former slaves (as had occurred in Haiti). In Puerto Rico, where slaves numbered approximately thirty thousand, local reformers sought and gained the abolition of slavery in 1873. Eventually, during a decade-long war to defeat forces seeking the independence of Cuba, the Spanish government moved toward gradual abolition. Finally, in 1886, slavery was abolished.

Equal Rights for Women and Blacks

The abolition of slavery in the Western Hemisphere did not end racial discrimination or provide full political rights for every citizen. Not only blacks but also women suffered political and economic discrimination during the nineteenth century.

In 1848, a group of women angered by their exclusion from an international antislavery meeting issued a call for a meeting to discuss women's rights. The **Women's Rights Convention** at Seneca Falls, New York, issued a statement that said in part, "We hold these truths to be self-evident: that all men and women are equal." While moderates focused on the issues of greater economic independence and full legal rights, increasing numbers of women demanded the right to vote. Others lobbied to provide better conditions for women working outside the home, especially in textile factories.

Progress toward equality between men and women was equally slow in Canada and Latin America. Canada's first women doctors received their training in the United States because no woman was able to receive a medical degree in Canada until 1895. Argentina and Uruguay were among the first Latin American nations to provide public education for women. Both nations introduced coeducation in the 1870s. Chilean women gained access to some careers in medicine and law in the 1870s. In Brazil, where many women were active in the abolitionist movement, four women graduated in medicine by 1882. Throughout the hemisphere, more rapid progress was achieved in lower-status careers that threatened male economic power less directly, and by the end of the century, women dominated elementary school teaching throughout the Western Hemisphere.

From Canada to Argentina and Chile, the majority of working-class women had no direct involvement in these reform movements, but in their daily lives, they succeeded in transforming gender relations. By the end of the nineteenth century, large numbers of poor women worked outside the home on farms, in markets, and, increasingly, in factories.

Throughout the hemisphere, there was little progress toward eliminating racial discrimination. Blacks were denied the vote throughout the southern United States and subjected to the indignity of segregation. Racial discrimination against men and women of African descent was also common in Latin America, though seldom spelled out in legal codes. Latin Americans tended to view racial identity across a continuum of physical characteristics rather than in the narrow terms of black and white that defined race relations in the United States.

CONCLUSION

The revolutions of the late eighteenth century hastened the transformation of Western society. Royal governments attempting to impose new taxes to pay war debts collided with ideas of elections and representative institutions. French officers who took part in the American Revolution helped ignite the French Revolution. Black freemen from Haiti traveled to France to seek their rights and returned to spread revolutionary passions. Napoleon's invasion of Portugal and Spain then helped initiate the movement toward independence in Latin America. The promises of universal citizenship were only partially achieved.

Each revolution had its own character. The revolutions in France and Haiti were more violent and destructive than the mainland American revolutions. In many places, monarchy, multinational empires, and the established church contested with liberal and nationalist sentiments well into the nineteenth century. Only a minority gained full political rights. Democratic institutions often failed. Slavery endured in the Americas past the mid-1800s.

■ Key Terms

Enlightenment
George Washington
Constitutional Convention
Estates General
National Assembly
Declaration of the
   Rights of Man
Napoleon Bonaparte
Congress of Vienna

Revolutions of 1848
gens de couleur
Toussaint L'Ouverture
Simón Bolívar
Miguel Hidalgo y Costilla
abolitionists
Women's Rights
   Convention

■ Suggested Reading

Eric Hobsbawm's *The Age of Revolution* (1962) provides a clear analysis of the class issues that appeared during this era. The American Revolution has received a great amount of attention from scholars. Colin Bonwick, *The American Revolution* (1991), and Edward Countryman, *The American Revolution* (1985), provide excellent introductions.

François Furet, *Interpreting the French Revolution* (1981), breaks with interpretations that emphasize class and ideological interpretations. Georges Lefebve, *The Coming of the French Revolution,* trans. R. R. Palmer (1947), presents the classic class-based analysis. George Rudé, *The Crowd in History: Popular Disturbances in France and England* (1981), remains the best introduction to the role of mass protest in the period. The recently published *The Women of Paris and Their French Revolution* (1998) by Dominique Godineau; Felix Markham, *Napoleon* (1963); and Robert B. Holtman, *The Napoleonic Revolution* (1967), provide reliable summaries of the period. For a brief survey of the revolutions of 1830 and 1848, see Arthur J. May, *The Age of Metternich, 1814–48,* rev. ed. (1963).

The classic study of the Haitian Revolution is C. L. R. James, *The Black Jacobins,* 2d ed. (1963). For the independence era in Latin America, see John Lynch, *The Spanish American Revolutions, 1808–1826,* 2d ed. (1986); Jay Kinsbruner, *Independence in Spanish America* (1994); and A. J. R. Russell-Wood, ed., *From Colony to Nation: Essays on the Independence of Brazil* (1976).

On the issue of slavery, see David Brion Davis, *Slavery and Human Progress* (1984); George M. Frederickson, *The Black Image in the White Mind: The Debate on Afro-American Character and Destiny, 1817–1914* (1971); and Benjamin Quarles, *Black Abolitionists* (1969). For abolition in Latin America and the Caribbean, see Rebecca Scott, *Slave Emancipation in Cuba: The Transition to Free Labor, 1860–1899* (1985); Robert Conrad, *The Destruction of Brazilian Slavery, 1850–1888* (1973); and William A. Green, *British Slave Emancipation: The Sugar Colonies and the Great Experiment, 1830–1865* (1976).

An excellent history of immigration is Walter Nagent, *Crossings: The Great Transatlantic Migrations, 1870–1914* (1992). For the women's rights movement see Ellen Carol DuBois, *Feminism and Suffrage: The Emergence of an Independent Women's Movement in America, 1848–1869* (1999).

THE EARLY INDUSTRIAL REVOLUTION,

1760–1851

—*e*—

**Causes of the Industrial Revolution • The Technological
Revolution • The Impact of the Industrial Revolution • Responses
to Industrialization • The Effects of Industrialization in Russia
and the Ottoman Empire**
**SOCIETY AND CULTURE: Charles Babbage, Ada Lovelace,
and the "Analytical Engine"**

n January 1840, a shipyard in Britain launched a radically new ship. The *Nemesis* had an iron hull, a flat bottom so it could navigate in shallow waters, and a steam engine to power it upriver and against the wind. The ship was heavily armed. In November, it arrived off the coast of China. Though ships from Europe had been sailing to China for three hundred years, the *Nemesis* was the first steam-powered iron gunboat seen in Asian waters. A Chinese observer noted: "Iron is employed to make it strong. The hull is painted black, weaver's shuttle fashion. On each side is a wheel, which by the use of coal fire is made to revolve as fast as a running horse. . . . At the vessel's head is a Marine God, and at the head, stern, and sides are cannon, which give it a terrific appearance. Steam vessels are a wonderful invention of foreigners, and are calculated to offer delight to many."[1]

Instead of offering delight, the *Nemesis* and other steam-powered warships that soon joined it steamed up the Chinese rivers, bombarded forts and cities, and brought in troops and supplies. With this new weapon, Britain, a small island nation half a world away, was able to defeat the largest and most populated country in the world in its own heartland.

The *Nemesis* was no isolated invention. Its outstanding features—steam power and cheap iron—were part of a larger phenomenon, the **Industrial Revolution,** that involved dramatic innovations in manufacturing, mining, transportation, and communications and equally rapid changes in society and commerce. New technologies and new social and economic arrangements allowed the industrializing countries—first Britain, followed by western Europe and the United States—to unleash massive increases in production and productivity, exploit the world's natural resources as never before, and transform the environment and human life in unprecedented ways.

The distribution of this power and wealth was very uneven within industrializing countries and around the world. The first countries to industrialize grew in wealth and power. China and other regions without industry were easily taken advantage of. Russia and eastern Europe managed their own industrial revolutions by the end of the nineteenth century. But in Egypt, India, and a few other non-Western countries, the economic and military power of the European countries soon stifled the tentative beginnings of industrialization.

As you read this chapter, ask yourself the following questions:

- What caused the Industrial Revolution?
- What were the key innovations that increased productivity and drove industrialization?
- What was the impact of these changes on the society and environment of the industrializing countries?
- How did the Industrial Revolution affect the relations between the industrialized and the nonindustrialized parts of the world?

CAUSES OF THE INDUSTRIAL REVOLUTION

What caused the Industrial Revolution, and why did it begin in England in the late eighteenth century? The basic precondition of this momentous event seems to have been economic development propelled by population growth, an agricultural revolution, the expansion of trade, and an openness to innovation.

Preconditions for Industrialization

The population of Europe rose in the eighteenth century—slowly at first, faster after 1780, then even faster in the early nineteenth century. The population of England and Wales rose unusually fast—from 5.5 million in 1688 to 18 million by 1851. Industrialization and the population boom reinforced each other. A high birthrate meant a large percentage of children, which explains both the vitality of the British people in that period and the widespread use of child labor.

This population explosion and urbanization could only have taken place alongside an **agricultural revolution** that provided food for city dwellers and forced poorer peasants off the land. Long before the eighteenth century, the introduction and acceptance of the potato and maize from the Americas had increased food supplies in Europe. In the cool and humid regions of Europe, from Ireland to Russia, potatoes yielded two or three times more food per acre than grain. Maize (American corn) was grown across Europe from southwestern France to the Balkans.

During the seventeenth century, rich English landowners began draining marshes, improving the soil, and introducing crop rotation using turnips, legumes, and clover that did not deplete the soil and could be fed to cattle. Additional manure from improved breeds of livestock fertilized the soil for other crops. Some also "enclosed" land—that is, consolidated their holdings, including commons that in the past had been open to all. This "enclosure movement" also turned tenants and sharecroppers into landless farm laborers. Many moved to the cities to seek work; others became homeless migrants and vagrants; still others emigrated.

The growth of the population and food supply was accompanied by the growth of trade. Most of it was local, but a growing share consisted of imports from other parts of the world like tea and sugar and simple goods that even middle-class people could afford, such as cotton textiles, iron hardware, and pottery.

Trade was accompanied by a growing interest in technology and innovation among educated people throughout Europe and eastern North

CHRONOLOGY

	Technology	Economy, Society, and Politics
1750		
	1759 Josiah Wedgwood opens pottery factory	
	1764 Spinning jenny	
	1769 Richard Arkwright's water frame; James Watt patents steam engine	**1776** Adam Smith's *Wealth of Nations*
		1776–1783 American Revolution
	1779 First iron bridge	
	1785 Boulton and Watt sell steam engines; Samuel Crompton's mule	**1789–1799** French Revolution
	1793 Eli Whitney's cotton gin	
1800	**1800** Alessandro Volta's battery	
	1807 Robert Fulton's *Clermont*	**1804–1815** Napoleonic Wars
	1820s Construction of Erie Canal	**1820s** U.S. cotton industry begins
	1829 *Rocket,* first steam-powered locomotive	
		1833 Factory Act in Britain
	1837 Wheatstone & Cooke's telegraph	**1834** German Zollverein; Robert Owen's Grand National Consolidated Trade Union
	1838 First ships steam across the Atlantic	
	1840 *Nemesis* sails to China	
	1843 Samuel Morse's Baltimore-to-Washington telegraph	**1846** Repeal of British Corn Laws
		1847–1848 Irish famine
1850	**1851** Crystal Palace opens in London	**1848** Collapse of Chartist movement; revolutions in Europe
		1853–1856 Crimean War

America. They read descriptions of new techniques and inventions in many publications, and some experimented on their own.

Britain's Advantages

These changes were widespread, but Britain in the eighteenth century had the fastest-growing population, food supply, and overseas trade. The British also put inventions into practice more quickly than other people. In the eighteenth century, Britain became the world's leading exporter of tools, guns, hardware, and other craft goods. Its mining and metal industries employed engineers willing to experiment with new ideas. It had the largest merchant marine and produced more ships, naval supplies, and navigation instruments than other countries.

Moreover, Britain had a more fluid society than the rest of Europe. Political power was not as centralized as on the European continent, and the government employed fewer bureaucrats and officials. Class lines eased as members of the gentry, and even some aristocrats, married into merchant families. Intermarriage among the families of petty merchants, yeoman farmers, and town craftsmen was common.

At a time when transportation by land was very costly, Great Britain had good water transportation, thanks to its indented coastline, navigable rivers, and growing network of canals (see Map 21.1). It had a unified internal market, with none of the duties and tolls that goods had to pay every few miles in France. This encouraged specialization and trade. More people there were involved in production for export and in trade and finance than in any other major country. It had financial and

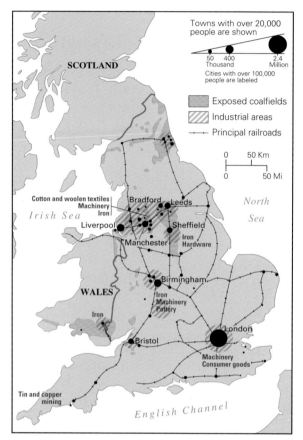

Map 21.1 **The Industrial Revolution in Britain, ca. 1850** The first industries arose in northern and western England. These regions had abundant coal and iron-ore deposits for the iron industry and a moist climate and fast-flowing rivers, factors important for the cotton-textile industry.

insurance institutions able to support growing business enterprises and a patent system that offered inventors the hope of rich rewards.

By 1830, the political climate in western Europe was as favorable to business as Britain's had been a half-century earlier. Industrialization first took hold in Belgium and northern France, as their businessmen visited Britain to observe the changes and to spy out industrial secrets. In spite of British laws forbidding the emigration of skilled workers and the export of textile machinery, many slipped through, setting up machines, training workers in the new methods, and even starting

their own businesses. European governments created technical schools; eliminated internal tariff barriers, tolls, and other hindrances to trade; and encouraged the formation of joint-stock companies and banks to channel private savings into industrial investments. On the European continent, as in Britain, cotton was the first industry to industrialize.

THE TECHNOLOGICAL REVOLUTION

Five revolutionary innovations spurred industrialization: (1) mass production through the division of labor, (2) new machines and mechanization, (3) a great increase in the supply of iron, (4) the steam engine and the changes it made possible in industry and transportation, and (5) the electric telegraph.

Mass Production and Mechanization

The pottery industry offers a good example of **mass production,** the making of many identical items by breaking the process into simple repetitive tasks. **Josiah Wedgwood** opened a pottery business in 1759 that was able to produce porcelain cheaply, by means of the **division of labor.** He subdivided the work into highly specialized and repetitive tasks, such as unloading the clay, mixing it, pressing flat pieces, dipping the pieces in glaze, putting handles on cups, packing kilns, and carrying things from one part of his plant to another. He substituted the use of molds for the potter's wheel wherever possible, a change that not only saved labor but created identical plates and bowls that could be stacked. These radical departures from the age-old methods of craftsmanship allowed Wedgwood to lower the cost of his products while improving their quality. As a result, his factory grew far larger than his competitors' factories and employed several hundred workers. His own salesmen traveled throughout England touting his goods.

Wedgwood's Potteries   In Staffordshire, England, Josiah Wedgwood established a factory to mass-produce beautiful and inexpensive china. The bottle-shape buildings are kilns in which thousands of pieces of china could be fired at one time. Kilns, factories, and housing were all mixed together in pottery towns, and smoke from burning coal filled the air.   (Mary Evans Picture Library)

Wedgwood was also interested in new technologies. He invested in toll roads and canals so that clay could be shipped economically from southwestern England to his factories in the Midlands. In 1782, to mix clay and grind flint, he purchased one of the first steam engines to be used in industry. Wedgwood's interest in applying technology to manufacturing was connected with his membership in the Birmingham Lunar Society, a group of manufacturers, scientists, and inventors who met when the moon was full so they could see their way home after dark. This critical mass of creative thinkers willing to exchange ideas and discoveries encouraged the atmosphere of experimentation and innovation that characterized late-eighteenth-century England. Similar societies throughout Britain were creating a vogue for science and giving the word *progress* a new meaning: "change for the better" (see Society and Culture: Charles Babbage, Ada Lovelace, and the "Analytical Engine").

The cotton industry, the largest industry in this period, illustrates the role of **mechanization,** the use of machines to do work previously done by hand. The cotton plant did not grow in Europe, but the cloth was so much cooler, softer, and cleaner than wool that wealthy Europeans developed a liking for this costly import. When the powerful English woolen industry persuaded Parliament to forbid the import of cotton cloth into England, it stimulated attempts to import cotton fiber and make the cloth locally. Here was an opportunity for enterprising inventors to reduce costs with labor-saving machinery.

Beginning in the 1760s, a series of inventions—the spinning jenny, the water frame, and the mule—revolutionized the spinning of cotton thread and allowed British industry to undersell high-quality handmade cotton cloth from India. British cotton output increased tenfold between 1770 and 1790.

When the boom in thread production and the soaring demand for cloth created bottlenecks in weaving, inventors in England rose to the challenge with power looms, carding machines, chlorine bleach, and cylindrical printing presses. By the 1830s, large English textile mills powered by steam engines were turning raw cotton into printed cloth. This was a far cry from the cottage industries of the previous century.

Mechanization offered two advantages: (1) productivity for the manufacturer and (2) price for the consumer. Whereas in India it took 500 hours to spin a pound of cotton, the improved mule of 1830 required only 80 minutes. Cotton mills needed very few skilled workers, and managers often hired children to tend the spinning machines. Mechanization and cheap labor allowed the price of cloth to fall by 90 percent from 1782 to 1812, and it kept on dropping.

The industrialization of Britain made cotton into America's most valuable crop. In 1793, the American Eli Whitney patented his cotton gin, a simple device that separated the bolls from the fiber and made the growing of short-staple cotton

Charles Babbage, Ada Lovelace, and the "Analytical Engine"

In the early nineteenth century, many professions relied on tables of numbers such as logarithms, astronomical positions, and actuarial data. Calculated by hand, these tables were full of arithmetic and typographical errors. In 1820, while correcting such a table, the English mathematician Charles Babbage exclaimed: "I wish to God these calculations had been executed by steam." Babbage went on to devise a machine—he called it the "Difference Engine"—to perform calculations and print out the results as flawlessly as a power loom produced cloth. While a prototype was being built, he designed the "Analytical Engine," which could interpret instructions inserted on punched cards and could alter its calculations in response to the results of previous calculations.

One of Babbage's assistants, Ada, the countess of Lovelace, translated an article by the Italian military engineer L. F. Menabrea about the Analytical Engine for the magazine Taylor's Scientific Memoirs. In his autobiography, published in 1864, Babbage recalled: "The late Countess of Lovelace informed me that she had translated the memoir of Menabrea. I asked why she had not herself written an original paper on a subject with which she was so intimately acquainted? To this Lady Lovelace replied that the thought had not occurred to her. I then suggested that she should add some notes to Menabrea's memoir; an idea which was immediately adopted. . . . The notes of the Countess of Lovelace extend to about three times the length of the original memoir. Their author has entered fully into almost all the very difficult and abstract questions concerned with the subject.

In the notes that she added to Menabrea's article, Ada Lovelace wrote the following:

The distinctive characteristic of the Analytical Engine, and that which has rendered it possible to endow mechanism with such extensive faculties as bid fair to make this engine the executive right-hand of abstract algebra, is the introduction into it of the principle which Jacquard devised for regulating, by means of punched cards, the most complicated patterns in the fabrication of brocaded stuffs [fabrics]. . . .

The bounds of *arithmetic* were outstepped the moment the idea of applying the cards had occurred; and the Analytical Engine does not occupy common ground with mere "calculating machines." It holds a position wholly its own; and the considerations it suggests are most interesting in their nature. . . . A new, a vast, and a powerful language is developed for the future use of analysis, in which to wield its truths so that these may become of more speedy and accurate practical application for the purposes of mankind than the means hitherto in our possession have rendered possible. Thus not only the mental and the material, but the theoretical and the practical in the mathematical world, are brought into more intimate and effective connexion with each other. We are not aware of its being on record that anything partaking in the nature of what is so well designated the *Analytical Engine* has been hitherto proposed, or even thought of, as a practical possibility, any more than the idea of a thinking or of a reasoning machine.

In short, Babbage invented the computer.

The first working computers were not built until a hundred years later, but Babbage is honored as the first person to imagine such a machine. And the widely used programming language Ada is named after his friend, the countess of Lovelace.

Is "a thinking or . . . a reasoning machine" a good description of a computer? Because Babbage's Analytical Engine did not use electricity, can it really be called a computer?

Source: From Philip Morison and Emily Morison, eds., *Charles Babbage and His Calculating Engines: Selected Writings by Charles Babbage and Others* (New York: Dover, 1961), 68, 251–252. © Copyright 1961. Reprinted by permission of Dover Publications.

economical. This invention permitted the spread of cotton farming into Georgia, then into Alabama, Mississippi, and Louisiana, and finally as far west as Texas. By the late 1850s, the southern states were producing a million tons of cotton a year, five-sixths of the world's total.

With the help of British craftsmen who introduced jennies, mules, and power looms, Americans developed a cotton industry in the 1820s. By 1840, the United States had 1,200 cotton mills, two-thirds of them in New England, powered by water rather than steam. Americans so excelled at the use of interchangeable parts in mass-producing guns that Europeans called it the "American system of manufactures." In the next hundred years, the use of machinery to mass-produce consumer items was to become the hallmark of American industry.

Iron and Steam

Iron making also was transformed during the Industrial Revolution. Iron had been in use for thousands of years for tools, swords and other weapons, and household items such as knives, pots, hinges, and locks. Wherever it was produced, however, deforestation eventually drove up the cost of charcoal (used for smelting) and restricted output. Furthermore, iron had to be repeatedly heated and hammered to drive out impurities, a difficult and costly process. Then in 1709, Abraham Darby discovered that coke (coal from which the impurities have been cooked out) could be used in place of charcoal. The resulting metal was of lower quality than charcoal iron but much cheaper to produce, for coal was plentiful. Britain's iron production began rising fast, from 17,000 tons in 1740 to 3 million tons in 1844, as much as in the rest of the world put together.

Opening of the Saltash Bridge over the Tamar River in England in 1859   During the celebrations, a steam locomotive pulled a train over the bridge while a steam-powered paddle wheeler passed underneath.   (Elton Collection, Ironbridge Gorge Museum Trust)

Even more important than the mechanization of manufacturing was the invention of the **steam engine.** Thomas Newcomen developed a crude and inefficient steam engine between 1702 and 1712 for use in coal mines, where its voracious appetite for fuel mattered little. Then **James Watt,** an instrument maker at Glasgow University in Scotland, developed an improved version and patented his idea in 1769. Seven years later, he and Matthew Boulton began selling steam engines to manufacturers of iron, pottery, and cotton.

Watt's steam engine was the most celebrated invention of the eighteenth century. Because there seemed almost no limit to the amount of coal in the ground, steam-generated energy seemed an inexhaustible source of power, and steam engines could be used where animal, wind, and water power were lacking. Without the steam engine, industrialization would have been a limited phenomenon.

Inspired by the success of Watt's engine, inventors in France in 1783, in the United States in 1787, and in England in 1788 put steam engines on boats. The first commercially successful steamboat was Robert Fulton's *Clermont,* which steamed between New York City and Albany in 1807. The first steam engines used so much coal that no ship could carry more than a few days' worth, but engineers soon developed more efficient engines, and in 1838 two steamers, the *Great Western* and the *Sirius,* crossed the Atlantic on steam power alone.

On land as on water, the problem was not imagining uses for steam-powered vehicles but building ones that worked, for steam engines were too heavy and weak to pull any weight. After Watt's patent expired in 1800, inventors experimented with lighter, more powerful high-pressure engines and in the early 1800s built several steam-powered vehicles able to travel on roads or rails. Between 1830 and 1850, a railroad-building mania swept Britain. The first lines linked towns and mines with the nearest harbor or waterway. As passenger traffic soared, entrepreneurs built lines between the major cities and then to small towns as well. Railroads were far cheaper, faster, and more comfortable than stagecoaches, and millions of people got in the habit of traveling.

In the United States, entrepreneurs built railroads as fast and cheaply as possible. By the 1840s,

The *De Witt Clinton* Locomotive, 1835–1840   The *De Witt Clinton* was the first steam locomotive built in the United States. The high smokestack let the hot cinders cool so they would not set fire to nearby trees, an important consideration at a time when eastern North America was still covered with forests. The three passenger cars are clearly horse-carriages fitted with railroad wheels.   (Corbis)

6,000 miles (10,000 kilometers) of track radiated westward from Boston, New York, Philadelphia, and Baltimore. The boom of the 1840s was dwarfed by the mania of the 1850s, when 21,000 miles (34,000 kilometers) of new track were laid, much of it westward across the Appalachians to Memphis, St. Louis, and Chicago. The trip from New York to Chicago, which once took three weeks by boat and on horseback, could be made in forty-eight hours. The railroads opened up the Midwest, turning the vast prairie into wheat fields and pasture for cattle to feed the industrial cities of the eastern United States.

Railways triggered the industrialization of Europe. Belgium, independent since 1830, quickly copied the British. State-planned and -supervised railroad construction in the mid-1840s in France and Prussia not only satisfied the long-standing need for transportation, but also stimulated the iron, machinery, and construction industries. In the 1850s and 1860s, the states of Germany also experienced an industrial boom.

Borsig Ironworks in Germany in the 1840s
This foundry was built to supply rails, locomotives, and other iron products to the German railroads, then under construction. (Deutsches Technikmuseum Berlin. Photo: Hans-Joachim Bartsch. Bildarchiv Preussischer Kulturbesitz)

Communication over Wires

The advent of railroads coincided with the development of the **electric telegraph.** After the Italian scientist Alessandro Volta invented the battery in 1800, making it possible to produce an electric current, many inventors tried to apply electricity to communication. The first practical telegraphy systems were developed almost simultaneously in England and America. In England, Wheatstone and Cooke introduced a five-needle telegraph in 1837; it remained in use until the early twentieth century. That same year, the American Samuel Morse introduced a code of dots and dashes that could be transmitted with a single wire; in 1843, he erected a line between Washington and Baltimore.

By the late 1840s, telegraph wires were being strung throughout the eastern United States and western Europe. In 1851, the first submarine telegraph cable was laid across the English Channel from England to France; it was the beginning of a network that eventually enclosed the entire globe. The world was rapidly shrinking, to the applause of Europeans and Americans for whom speed was a clear measure of progress. No longer were communications limited to the speed of which a ship could sail or a horse could gallop.

THE IMPACT OF THE INDUSTRIAL REVOLUTION

Although inventions were the most visible aspect of the Industrial Revolution, many other changes in society, politics, and the economy took place. Early changes—smoky cities, slum neighborhoods, polluted water, child labor in mines and textile mills—were being alleviated by the mid-nineteenth century. But by then national or even international problems were replacing these local ones: business cycles, labor conflicts, and the transformation of entire regions into industrial landscapes.

New Industrial Cities

The most dramatic environmental changes brought about by industrialization occurred in the towns. Never before had towns grown so fast. London, one of the largest cities in Europe in 1700 with 500,000 inhabitants, grew to 959,000 by 1800 and to 2,363,000 by 1850, by then the largest city in the world. Smaller towns grew even faster. Manchester's population increased eightfold in a century. Liverpool grew sixfold in the first sixty years of the nineteenth century. New York City, already 100,000 strong in 1815, reached 600,000 (including Brooklyn) in 1850. In some areas, towns merged and formed megalopolises, such as Greater London, the English Midlands, central Belgium, and the Ruhr district of Germany.

People who prospered greatly from industrialization poured their new wealth into fine new homes, churches, museums, and theaters. Yet by all accounts, the industrial cities grew much too fast. As poor migrants streamed in from the countryside, developers built cheap, shoddy row houses for them to rent. These tenements were dangerously overcrowded. Often, several families had to live in one small room. Town dwellers recently arrived from the country brought country ways with them. People threw their sewage and trash out the windows to be washed down the gutters in the streets. The poor kept pigs and chickens, the rich kept horses, and pedestrians stepped into the street at their own risk. Air pollution from burning coal got steadily worse. People drank water drawn from wells and rivers contaminated by sewage and industrial runoff. The River Irwell, which ran through Manchester, was, in the words of one visitor, "considerably less a river than a flood of liquid manure."

To the long list of preindustrial urban diseases such as smallpox, dysentery, and tuberculosis, industrialization added new ailments. Rickets, a bone disease caused by lack of sunshine, became endemic in dark and smoky industrial cities. Steamships brought cholera from India, causing great epidemics that struck the poor neighborhoods especially hard. In the 1850s, when the average life expectancy in England was forty years, it was only twenty-four years in Manchester, and around seventeen years in Manchester's poorest neighborhoods, because of the high infant mortality. Shocking reports of slum life led to municipal reforms, such as garbage removal, water and sewage systems, and parks and schools. These measures began to alleviate the ills of urban life after the mid-nineteenth century.

Rural Environments

Long before the Industrial Revolution began, practically no wilderness areas were left in Britain and very few in western Europe. Human activity had turned almost every piece of land into fields, forests, pastures, or towns. The most serious problem was deforestation. People cut timber to build ships and houses, to heat homes, and to manufacture bricks, iron, glass, beer, bread, and many other items.

Americans transformed their environment even faster than Europeans did. Settlers viewed forests not as a valuable resource but as a hindrance to development. In their haste to "open up the West," pioneers felled trees and burned them, built houses and abandoned them when they moved on. The cultivation of cotton was especially harmful. Planters cut down forests, grew cotton for a few years until it depleted the soil, and then moved west, abandoning the land to scrub pines. The American idea of nature as an obstacle to be overcome and dominated persisted long after the entire continent was occupied.

To contemporaries, the new transportation systems brought the most obvious changes in rural life. Governments and private trusts built numerous roads. Canal building boomed in Britain, France, and the Low Countries in the late eighteenth century. Canals were marvels of construction, with deep cuts, tunnels, and even aqueducts that carried barges over rivers. They also were a sort of school where engineers learned skills they were able to apply to the next great transportation system: the railroads. They laid track across rolling country by cutting deeply into hillsides and erecting daringly long bridges of stone and iron across valleys. Soon, clanking trains pulled by puffing, smoke-belching locomotives were invading long-isolated districts.

Thus, in the century after industrialization began, the landscape of industrializing countries was transformed more rapidly than ever before. But the ecological changes, like the technological and economic changes that caused them, were only beginning.

The McCormick Reaper
In the nineteenth century, the machine age arrived in the countryside. The McCormick reaper increased productivity and also promoted the concentration of land in grain-producing regions of the United States. (Navistar International Harvester Archives)

Working Conditions

Most industrial jobs were unskilled, repetitive, and boring. Factory work did not vary with the seasons or the time of day but began and ended by the clock. Workdays were long, there were few breaks, and foremen watched constantly. Workers who performed one simple task over and over had little sense of achievement or connection to the final product. Industrial accidents were common and could ruin a family. Unlike even the poorest preindustrial farmer or artisan, factory workers had no control over their tools, jobs, or working hours.

Women workers were concentrated in textile mills, partly because of ancient traditions, partly because textile work required less strength than metalworking, construction, or hauling. On average, women earned one-third to one-half as much as men. Young unmarried women worked to support themselves or to save for marriage. Married women took factory jobs when their husbands were unable to support the family. Mothers of infants faced a hard choice: whether to leave their babies with wet nurses at great expense and danger or to bring them to the factory and keep them quiet with opiates. Rather than working together as family units, husbands and wives increasingly worked in different places.

Factory work was never the main occupation of working women. Most young women who sought paid employment in the early years of industrialization became domestic servants in spite of the low pay, drudgery, and risk of sexual abuse. Other women with small children tried hard to find work they could do at home, such as laundry, sewing, embroidery, millinery, or taking in lodgers.

Even with both parents working, poor families found it hard to make ends meet. As in preindustrial societies, parents thought children should contribute to their upkeep as soon as they were able to. The first generation of workers brought their children with them to the factories and mines as early as age five or six; they had little choice, since there were no public schools or day care centers. Employers encouraged the practice and even hired orphans. They preferred children because they were cheaper and more docile than adults and were better able to tie broken threads or crawl under machines to sweep the dust. Mine operators used children to pull coal carts along the low passageways from the coal face to the mine shaft. In the mid-nineteenth century, when the British government began restricting child labor, mill owners increasingly recruited Irish immigrants.

American industry began on a somewhat different note than the British. When Francis Cabot Lowell built a cotton mill in Massachusetts, he deliberately hired the unmarried daughters of New England farmers, promising decent wages and housing in dormitories under careful moral supervision. Other manufacturers eager to combine profits with morality followed his example. But soon the profit motive won out, and manufacturers imposed longer hours, harsher working conditions, and lower wages. When the young women went on strike, the factory owners replaced them with Irish immigrant women willing to accept lower pay and worse conditions.

The rising demand for cotton and the abolition of the African slave trade in the United States in 1808 caused an increase in the price of slaves. As the "Cotton Kingdom" expanded, the number of slaves rose through natural increase, from 700,000 in the 1790s to 3,200,000 slaves by 1850. Similarly, Europe's and North America's surging demand for tea and coffee prolonged slavery on sugar plantations in the West Indies and caused it to spread to the coffee-growing regions of southern Brazil. Slavery was part and parcel of the Industrial Revolution, just as much as child labor in Britain, the clothes that people wore, and the beverages they drank.

Changes in Society

Industrialization accentuated the polarization of society and disparities of income. In Britain, the worst-off were those who clung to an obsolete skill or craft, such as hand-loom weavers in a time of power looms. Even by working more hours, they could not escape destitution.

The wages and standard of living of factory workers did not decline steadily like those of hand-loom weavers; they fluctuated wildly with the cycles of economic growth and contraction. During the war years 1792 to 1815, the poor suffered hardship when the price of food rose faster than wages. Then, in the 1820s, real wages and public health began to improve, as industrial production grew at over 3 percent a year, pulling the rest of the economy along. Prices fell so that even the poor could afford comfortable, washable cotton clothes.

Overall, the benefits of industrialization—cheaper food, clothing, and utensils—did not improve workers' standard of living until the 1850s. The real beneficiaries of the early Industrial Revolution were the entrepreneurs whose money came from manufacturing. Most were the sons of middling shopkeepers, craftsmen, or farmers who had a little capital to start a cotton-spinning or machine-building business. Many tried and some succeeded, largely by plowing their profits back into the business. A generation later, in the nineteenth century, some newly rich industrialists bought their way into high society. With industrialization came a "cult of domesticity" that removed middle-class women from contact with the business world and left them responsible for the home, the servants, the education of children, and the family's social life.

RESPONSES TO INDUSTRIALIZATION

Changes as profound as the Industrial Revolution could not occur without political ferment and ideological conflict. So many other momentous events took place during those years—the American Revolution (1776–1783), the French Revolution (1789–1799), the Napoleonic Wars (1804–1815), the reactions and revolts that periodically swept over Europe after 1815—that we cannot neatly separate out the consequences of industrialization from the rest. But it is clear that the Industrial Revolution strengthened the ideas of laissez faire° and socialism and sparked workers' protests.

---

laissez faire (lay-say fair)

Laissez Faire

The most celebrated exponent of **laissez faire** ("let them do") was Adam Smith (1723–1790), a Scottish economist. In *The Wealth of Nations* (1776), Smith argued that if individuals were allowed to seek their personal gain, the effect, as though guided by an "invisible hand," would be to increase the general welfare. Except to protect private property, the government should refrain from interfering in business; it should even allow duty-free trade with foreign countries.

Although it was true that governments at the time were incompetent at regulating their national economies, it was becoming obvious that industrialization was not improving the general welfare but was for some causing great misery. Other thinkers blamed the workers' plight on the population boom, which outstripped the food supply and led to falling wages. The workers' poverty, they claimed, was as much a result of "natural law" as the wealth of successful businessmen, and the only way the working class could avoid mass famine was to delay marriage and practice self-restraint and sexual abstinence.

Laissez faire provided an ideological justification for a special kind of capitalism: banks, stock markets, and chartered companies allowed investors to obtain profits with reasonable risks but with much less government control and interference than in the past. But not everyone accepted the grim conclusions of the "dismal science," as economics was then known. Jeremy Bentham (1748–1832) believed that it was possible to maximize "the greatest happiness of the greatest number," if only a Parliament of enlightened reformers would study the social problems of the day and pass appropriate legislation; his philosophy became known as utilitarianism.

Positivism and Utopian Socialism

Some French social thinkers, moved by sincere concern for the poor, offered a more radically new vision of a just civilization. Espousing a philosophy called **positivism,** the count of Saint-Simon (1760–1825) argued that the scientific method could solve social as well as technical problems. He recommended that the poor, guided by scientists and artists, form workers' communities under the protection of benevolent business leaders. These ideas found no following among workers, but they attracted the enthusiastic support of bankers and entrepreneurs, inspired by visions of railroads, canals, and other symbols of progress.

Meanwhile, the **utopian° socialism** of Charles Fourier (1768–1837), who loathed capitalists, imagined an ideal society in which groups of sixteen hundred workers would live in dormitories and work together on the land and in workshops where music, wine, and pastries would soften the hardships of labor. For this idea, critics called him "utopian"—a dreamer.

The person who came closest to creating a utopian community was the Englishman Robert Owen (1771–1858), a successful cotton manufacturer who believed that industry could provide prosperity for all. Conscience-stricken by the appalling plight of the workers, Owen took over the management of New Lanark, a mill town south of Glasgow. He improved the housing and added schools, a church, and other amenities. He also testified before Parliament against child labor and for government inspection of working conditions, thereby angering his fellow industrialists.

Protests and Reforms

Workers benefited little from the ideas of these middle-class philosophers. Instead, they resisted the harsh working conditions in their own ways. They changed jobs frequently and were often absent, especially on Mondays. Periodically, workers rioted or went on strike. Such acts of resistance did nothing, however, to change the nature of industrial work. Not until workers learned to act together could they hope to have much influence.

Gradually, they formed benevolent societies and organizations to demand universal male suffrage and shorter workdays. In 1834, Robert Owen organized the Grand National Consolidated Trade Union to lobby for an eight-hour workday; it gained half a million members but failed a few months later in the face of government prosecution of trade union activities. The Chartist

utopian (you-TOE-pee-uhn)

movement had more success, gathering petitions by the thousands to present to Parliament. Although Chartism collapsed in 1848, it left a legacy of labor organizing. Eventually, mass movements persuaded political leaders to look into the abuses of industrial life, despite the prevailing laissez-faire philosophy.

In the 1820s and 1830s, the British Parliament began investigating conditions in the factories and mines. The Factory Act of 1833 prohibited the employment of children under age nine in textile mills and limited the working hours of children between the ages of nine and eighteen. The Mines Act of 1842 prohibited the employment of all women and of boys under age ten underground. Several decades passed before the government appointed enough inspectors to enforce the new laws.

The British learned to seek reform through accommodation. On the European continent, in contrast, the revolutions of 1848 (see Chapter 20) revealed widespread discontent with repressive governments but failed to soften the hardships of industrialization.

Emigration

Another response to growing population, rural crises, and business cycles was emigration. Many poor Irish emigrated to England in search of work in construction and factories. After the potato crop failed in Ireland in 1847–1848, one-quarter of the Irish population died in the resulting famine, and another quarter emigrated to England and America. On the European continent, the negative effects of economic downturns were tempered by the existence of small family farms to which urban workers could return when they were laid off, but vast numbers still left Europe in search of better opportunities in the Western Hemisphere.

The United States received approximately 600,000 European immigrants in the 1830s, 1.5 million in the 1840s, and then 2.5 million per decade until 1880. In the 1890s, an astonishing total of 5.2 million immigrants arrived. European immigration to Latin America also increased dramatically after 1880. Immigrants from Europe faced prejudice and discrimination from those who believed they threatened the well-being of na-

tive-born workers by accepting low wages, and they threatened national culture by resisting assimilation.

Asian immigration to the Western Hemisphere also increased after 1850. Between 1849 and 1875, approximately 570,000 Chinese immigrants arrived in the Americas, half in the United States. India also contributed more than a half-million immigrants to the Caribbean region. Asians faced more obstacles to immigration than did Europeans and were often victims of violence and more extreme forms of discrimination in the New World.

Despite discrimination, most immigrants were also motivated to assimilate. Many intellectuals and political leaders wondered if the evolving mix of culturally diverse populations could sustain a common citizenship. As a result, efforts were directed toward compelling immigrants to assimilate. They learned the language spoken in their adopted countries as fast as possible in order to improve their earning capacity.

Union movements and electoral politics in the hemisphere also felt the influence of new arrivals who aggressively sought to influence government and improve working conditions. Immigrants also introduced new languages, foods, and customs. Mutual benevolent societies and less formal ethnic associations pooled resources to help immigrants open businesses, aid the immigration of their relatives, or bury their family members, sometimes worsening the fears of the native-born that immigration posed a threat to national culture. They also established links with political movements, sometimes exchanging votes for favors.

THE EFFECTS OF INDUSTRIALIZATION IN RUSSIA AND THE OTTOMAN EMPIRE

For most places in the world, trade with the industrial countries of western Europe and North America meant exporting raw materials. In the few countries whose governments were tempted to imitate the West, cheap Western imports, backed by the power of Great Britain, thwarted the spread of industry for a century or more.

Two factors inhibited the spread of the industrial revolution. One was the active opposition of Great Britain and other industrial nations, whose tactics in Asia and Africa, ranging from military invasion to financial manipulation, are described in the chapters that follow. The other factor was that most parts of the world were ill prepared politically, socially, and/or economically to undertake industrial modernization. Russia and the Ottoman Empire illustrate how difficult it was to overcome both of these problems even in places that had long observed and copied changes underway in western Europe.

Russia

Eighteenth-century Russian tsars had actively promoted the Westernization of their giant land's armies and elite. Its aristocrats spoke French, its army was modeled on the armies of western Europe, and it participated in European wars and diplomacy. Yet Russia differed from western Europe in one important aspect: it had almost no middle class. Thus, industrialization there arose not from the initiative of local entrepreneurs but by government decree and through the work of foreign engineers.

Tsar Nicholas I (r. 1825–1855) built the first railroad in Russia from St. Petersburg, the capital, to his summer palace in 1837. A few years later, he insisted that the trunk line from St. Petersburg to Moscow run in a perfectly straight line. American engineers built locomotive workshops in Russia, and British engineers set up textile mills. These projects, though well publicized, were oddities in a society where most people were serfs tied to the estates of powerful noble landowners and towns were few and far apart.

Until the late nineteenth century, the Russian government's interest in industry was limited and hesitant. An industrial revolution, to be successful, required large numbers of educated and independent-minded artisans and entrepreneurs. Suspicious of Western ideas, especially anything smacking of liberalism, socialism, or revolution, the Russian government feared the spread of liter-

acy and of modern education beyond the minimum needed to train the officer corps and the bureaucracy. Rather than run the risk of allowing a middle class and a working class to arise that might challenge its control, the regime of Nicholas I kept the peasants in serfdom and preferred to import most industrial goods and pay for them with exports of grain and timber.

Russia aspired to Western-style economic development. But fear of political change caused the country to fall further behind western Europe, economically and technologically, than it had been a half-century before. When France and Britain went to war against Russia in 1854, they faced a Russian army equipped with obsolete weapons and bogged down for lack of transportation.

The Ottoman Empire

The Ottoman rulers were earlier than the rulers of other Eurasian empires to experiment with financial and military modernization. However, entrenched opposition kept the Ottoman government from putting most reforms into place until the mid-1800s. The reforms came too late to preserve the empire's independence from western Europe, but they added momentum for centralization, helped promote nationalism in the late nineteenth century, and created a practical base for the creation of a Turkish republic in the twentieth century.

When Sultan Selim° III (r. 1789–1807) introduced reforms at the end of the eighteenth century to strengthen the military and increase the control of the central government, a massive military uprising overthrew and executed him. In 1826, Selim's cousin Sultan Mahmud° II (r. 1808–1839) cautiously revived the reform movement. First he announced the creation of a new army corps. When the traditional military corps (the Janissaries) rose in revolt, he ordered loyal troops to attack the Janissary barracks and obliterate the force.

Mahmud also sought to secularize the state and reduce the political power of the Muslim religious elite. He brought education and law under the authority of the civil government and established

Selim (seh-LEEM)   **Mahmud** (MACH-mood)

a uniform code of civil law. One important proclamation called for public trials and equal protection under the law for all, whether Muslim, Christian, or Jew. No Islamic country had ever produced anything so nearly approaching a constitution, and the Ottoman Empire enjoyed a renewed reputation as a progressive influence in the Middle East.

In the 1830s, an Ottoman imperial school of military sciences was established at Istanbul. Instructors imported from western Europe taught chemistry, engineering, mathematics, and physics in addition to military history. In 1838, the first medical school was established, for army doctors and surgeons. Reforms in military education became the model for more general educational reforms. Urban elites in Istanbul, the capital, embraced European language and culture, as well as military professionalism and progressive political reform. Newspapers—most of them in French—were founded at Istanbul, and travel to Europe—particularly to England and France—by wealthy Turks became more common. European dress became the fashion for progressive men in the Ottoman cities of the later 1800s; traditional dress became a symbol of the religious, the rural, and the parochial.

Interest in importing European military, industrial, and communications technology remained strong through the 1800s, but the Ottoman rulers quickly learned that limited improvements in military technology had unforeseen cultural and social effects. The introduction of modern weapons and drill required a change in traditional military dress. Beards, deemed unhygienic and a fire hazard, were restricted, along with the wearing of loose trousers and turbans. The adoption of European military caps, which had leather bills on the front to protect against the glare of the sun, became controversial because they interfered with Muslim soldiers' touching their foreheads to the ground during daily prayers. The compromise was the brimless cap now called the *fez*.

The new public rights and political participation were explicitly restricted to men. Private life, including everything connected to marriage and divorce, was left within the sphere of religious law, and at no time was there a question of political participation or reformed education for women.

Indeed, the reforms actually decreased the influence of women.

The Crimean War, 1853–1856

Since the reign of Peter the Great (r. 1689–1725), the Russian Empire had been attempting to expand southward at the Ottomans' expense. By 1815, Russia had pried the Georgian region of the Caucasus away from the Ottomans, and the threat of Russian intervention in Serbia had prevented the Ottomans from crushing a Serbian independence effort (see Map 21.2).

Between 1853 and 1856, the **Crimean° War** raged on the Black Sea and its northern shore. Nominally a war between the Russian and Ottoman Empires about whether Russia could claim to protect Christians in the Ottoman domains, this extremely destructive conflict also involved in the dispute Austria, Britain, France, and the Italian kingdom of Sardinia-Piedmont, all of which sided—actively or passively—with the Ottoman Empire because they feared any expansion of Russia's power and influence.

During the prolonged sea conflict, Britain and France trapped the Russian fleet in the Black Sea. Russia's lack of railways hampered attempts to supply both its land and its sea forces. Tsar Alexander II (r. 1855–1881) abandoned the key fortress of Sevastopol in 1855 and sued for peace. The terms of peace blocked Russian expansion into eastern Europe and the Middle East but also gave the Ottoman Empire protection from western European imperialism, since Britain and France agreed that neither would take Ottoman territory for its exclusive use.

The Crimean War brought significant changes to all the combatants. The tsar and his government, already beset by demands for the reform of serfdom, education, and the military, plunged into reforms that slightly improved Russia's economy but profoundly destabilized its political system. The Ottoman rulers also continued their reform agendas after the war, but no reform could repair the chronic insolvency of the imperial government due to declining revenues from agricultural yields

---

Crimean (cry-ME-uhn)

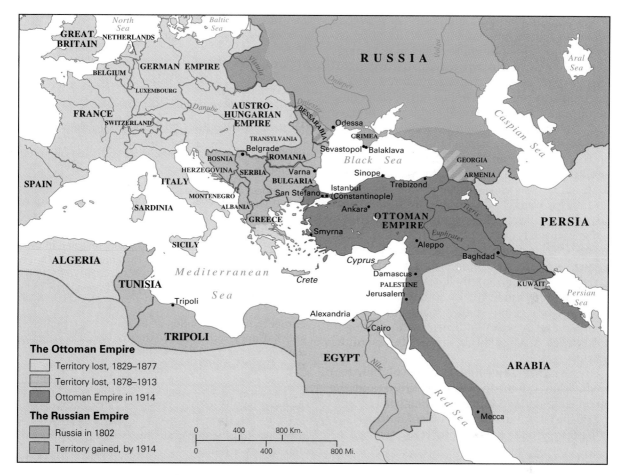

Map 21.2   Disintegration of the Ottoman Empire, 1829–1914   At its height, the Ottoman Empire controlled most of the perimeter of the Mediterranean Sea. But in the 1800s, Ottoman territory shrank as many countries gained their independence—frequently with the aid of France or Russia. The Black Sea, which left the Turkish coast vulnerable to assault by the Russian navy, was a weak spot that was intensely contested in the Crimean dispute.

and widespread corruption. From the conclusion of the Crimean War in 1856 on, the Ottoman government became heavily dependent on foreign loans and European imports.

Militarily, the Crimean War marked the transition from traditional to modern industrial warfare. Although all the combatant nations used cavalry in the Crimean War, the famous British "Light Brigade" and many other cavalry units were destroyed by the rapid and relatively accurate fire of new **breech-loading rifles.** Cavalry were not the only victims of the new speed of the guns. Many traditional infantry units came to grief attempting to use ranks of marching, brightly coated soldiers to overwhelm lines of rapidly firing riflemen.

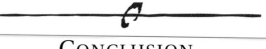

CONCLUSION

In the period from 1760 to 1851, the new technologies of the Industrial Revolution greatly increased humans' power over nature. Goods could be manufactured in vast quantities at low cost. People and messages could travel at unprecedented speeds. In addition to utilizing the energy produced by muscle power, wind, and water, humans gained access to the energy stored in coal. Faster than ever before, humans turned woodland into farmland, dug canals and laid tracks, bridged rivers and cut through mountains, and covered the countryside with towns and cities.

This newfound power over nature, far from benefiting everyone, increased the disparities between individuals and societies. Some people acquired great wealth, while others lived in poverty and squalor. Middle-class women were restricted to the care of their homes and children. Many working-class women had to leave home to earn wages in factories or as domestic servants. These changes in work and family life provoked intense debates among intellectuals. Some defended the disparities in the name of laissez faire; others criticized the injustices that industrialization brought. Society was slow to bring these abuses under control.

By the 1850s, the Industrial Revolution had spread from Britain to western Europe and the United States, and its impact was being felt by Russia and the Ottoman Empire. Industrial Britain was on the move, as the next chapter recounts.

■ Key Terms

Industrial Revolution	James Watt
agricultural revolution (eighteenth century)	electric telegraph
	laissez faire
mass production	positivism
Josiah Wedgwood	utopian socialism
division of labor	Crimean War
mechanization	breech-loading rifles
steam engine	

■ Suggested Reading

General works on the history of technology give pride of place to industrialization. For an optimistic overview, see Joel Mokyr, *The Lever of Riches: Technological Creativity and Economic Progress* (1990). Other important recent works include James McClellan III and Harold Dorn, *Science and Technology in World History* (1999); David Landes, *The Wealth and Poverty of Nations* (1998); and Ian Inkster, *Technology and Industrialization: Historical Case Studies and International Perspectives* (1998).

There is a rich literature on the British industrial revolution, beginning with T. S. Ashton's classic *The Industrial Revolution, 1760–1830,* published in 1948 and often reprinted.

The impact of industrialization on workers is the theme of E. P. Thompson's classic work, *The Making of the English Working Class* (1963), but see also E. R. Pike, *"Hard Times": Human Documents of the Industrial Revolution* (1966). The role of women is most ably revealed in Lynn Y. Weiner, *From Working Girl to Working Mother: The Female Labor Force in the United States, 1820–1980* (1985), and in Louise Tilly and Joan Scott, *Women, Work, and Family* (1978).

European industrialization is the subject of J. Goodman and K. Honeyman, *Gainful Pursuits: The Making of Industrial Europe: 1600–1914* (1988); John Harris, *Industrial Espionage and Technology Transfer: Britain and France in the Eighteenth Century* (1998); and David Landes, *The Unbound Prometheus: Technological Change and Industrial Development in Western Europe from 1750 to the Present* (1972). On the beginnings of American industrialization, see David Jeremy, *Artisans, Entrepreneurs and Machines: Essays on the Early Anglo-American Textile Industry, 1770–1840* (1998).

On the environmental impact of industrialization, see Richard Wilkinson, *Poverty and Progress: An Ecological Perspective on Economic Development* (1973), and Richard Tucker and John Richards, *Global Deforestation in the Nineteenth-Century World Economy* (1983).

The first book to treat industrialization as a global phenomenon is Peter Stearns, *The Industrial Revolution in World History* (1993); see also Louise Tilly's important article "Connections," *American Historical Review* (February 1994). On the Ottoman Empire, see Huri Islamoglu-Inan, ed., *The Ottoman Empire and the World Economy* (1987). On Russia, see David Saunders, *Russia in the Age of Reaction and Reform, 1801–1881* (1993).

■ Note

1. *Nautilus Magazine* 12 (1843): 346.

AFRICA, INDIA, AND CHINA, 1750–1870

Changes and Exchanges in Africa • India Under British Rule •
The Qing Empire
ENVIRONMENT AND TECHNOLOGY: Whaling

n 1782, Tipu Sultan inherited the throne of Mysore°, which his father had made the most powerful state in south India. The ambitious and talented new ruler also inherited a healthy distrust of the British East India Company's territorial ambitions. Before the company could invade Mysore, Tipu Sultan launched his own attack in 1785. He then sent an embassy to France in 1788 seeking an alliance against Britain. Neither of these ventures was immediately successful.

Not until a decade later did the French agree to a loose alliance with Tipu Sultan to challenge Britain's colonial and commercial supremacy in the Indian Ocean. General Napoleon Bonaparte invaded Egypt in 1798 to threaten British trade routes to India and hoped to use the alliance with Tipu Sultan to drive the British out of India. The French invasion of Egypt went well enough

at first, but a British naval blockade and the ravages of disease crippled the French force. When the French withdrew, another military adventurer, Muhammad Ali, commander of the Ottoman army in Egypt, took advantage of the situation to revitalize Egypt and expand its rule.

Meanwhile, Tipu's alliance with France did not protect him from the East India Company, whose military victory in 1792 deprived him of most of his seacoast. Tipu lost his life in 1799 while defending his capital against another British assault. Mysore was divided between the British and their Indian allies.

As these events illustrate, talented local leaders and European powers were both vying to expand their influence in South Asia and Africa between 1750 and 1870. Midway through that period, it was by no means clear who would gain the upper hand. Britain and France were as likely to fight each other as they were to fight any Asian or African state. In 1800, the two nations were engaged in their third major war for

---

Mysore (my-SORE)

overseas supremacy since 1750. By 1870, how-ever, Britain had gained a decisive advantage over France and had established commercial dominance in trade in Africa, the Indian Ocean, and East Asia. Moreover, Britain created a new colonial empire in the East.

As you read this chapter, ask yourself the following questions:

• Why were the British able to gain decisive advantages in distant lands?

• Why were Asians and Africans so divided, some choosing to cooperate with the Europeans while others resisted their advances?

• Why was even the Qing Empire unable to stop the European advance?

• How important an advantage were Britain's weapons, ships, and economic motives?

• How much of the outcome was the result of advance planning, and how much was due to particular individuals or to chance?

CHANGES AND EXCHANGES IN AFRICA

During the century before 1870, Africa underwent dynamic political changes and a great expansion of foreign trade. Indigenous African leaders as well as Middle Eastern and European imperialists built powerful new states or expanded old ones. As the continent's external slave trades to the Americas and to Islamic lands died slowly under British pressure, trade in goods such as palm oil, ivory, timber, and gold grew sharply. In return, Africans imported large quantities of machine-made textiles and firearms. These complex changes are best understood by looking at African regions separately.

New African States

Internal forces produced clusters of new states in two parts of sub-Saharan Africa in the early nineteenth century (see Map 22.1). In the fertile coastlands of southeastern Africa (in modern South Africa), a serious drought at the beginning of the nineteenth century led to conflict for grazing and farming lands among the small, independent chiefdoms of the region. An upstart named Shaka emerged in 1818 as head of a new **Zulu** kingdom, whose military discipline and courage soon made them the most powerful and most feared fighters in southern Africa. Shaka's regiments raided his African neighbors, seized their cattle, and captured their women and children. To protect themselves from the Zulu, some neighboring Africans created their own states.

Although Shaka ruled for little more than a decade, he successfully instilled a new national identity into his newly conquered subjects. He grouped all the young people into regiments that lived together and were taught Zulu customs and fighting methods. At public festivals, regiments of young men and women, paraded, danced, and pledged their loyalty to Shaka.

Meanwhile, Islamic reform movements were creating another powerful state in the savannas of West Africa. The reformers followed a classic Muslim pattern: a *jihad* (holy war) added new lands, spreading Islamic beliefs and laws among conquered people. The largest reform movement was led by Usuman dan Fodio° (1745–1817), whose armed supporters conquered and combined the older Hausa states into a new empire ruled by a caliph (sultan) in the city of Sokoto. The **Sokoto Caliphate** (1809–1906) was the largest state in West Africa since the fall of Songhai in the sixteenth century.

In addition to being a center of Islamic learning and reform, the Sokoto Caliphate became a center of slavery. Many captured in the wars were enslaved and put to work in the empire or sold away across the Sahara or the Atlantic.

Usuman dan Fodio (OO-soo-mahn dahn FOH-dee-oh)

CHRONOLOGY

	Africa	India	China
1750		**1756** Black Hole of Calcutta **1765** East India Company (EIC) rule of Bengal begins	
	1798 Napoleon invades Egypt	**1798** Britain annexes Ceylon **1799** EIC defeats Mysore	**1794–1804** White Lotus Rebellion
1800	**1805** Muhammad Ali seizes Egypt **1806** Britain takes Cape Colony **1808** Britain outlaws slave trade and takes over Sierra Leone **1809** Sokoto Caliphate founded **1818** Shaka founds Zulu kingdom **1821** Foundation of Republic of Liberia; Egypt takes control of Sudan	**1818** EIC creates Bombay presidency **1826** EIC annexes Assam and northern Burma **1828** Brahmo Samaj founded	
	1831–1847 Algerians resist French takeover **1834** Britain abolishes slavery **1840** Omani sultan moves capital to Zanzibar		**1839–1842** Opium War
1850		**1857–1858** Sepoy Rebellion leads to end of EIC rule and Mughal rule	**1850–1864** Taiping Rebellion **1860** Sack of Beijing
	1867 End of Atlantic slave trade **1869** Jaja founds Opobo	**1877** Queen Victoria becomes empress of India **1885** First Indian National Congress	
	1889 Menelik unites modern Ethiopia		

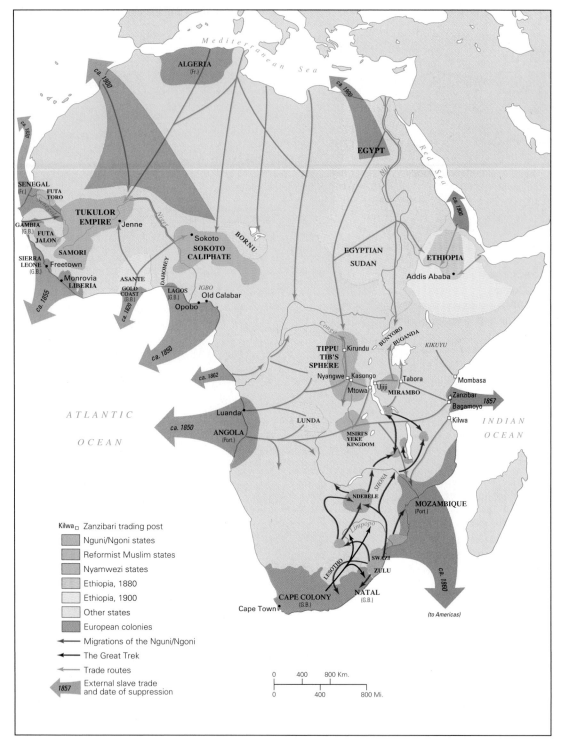

Mediterranean Sea

ALGERIA
(Fr.)

ca. 1900

ca. 1900

EGYPT

Red Sea

ca. 1820

ca. 1900

SENEGAL
(Fr.)
FUTA
TORO

TUKULUR
EMPIRE
• Jenne

Niger

EGYPTIAN
SUDAN

ETHIOPIA

Nile

Addis Ababa •

GAMBIA
(G.B.)
FUTA
JALON

SOKOTO
• Sokoto
CALIPHATE

BORNU

SAMORI

SIERRA
LEONE
(G.B.)
• Freetown

• Monrovia
LIBERIA

ASANTE

DAHOMEY

GOLD
COAST
(G.B.)

LAGOS
(G.B.)
Old Calabar
Opobo

IGBO

ca. 1855

ca. 1820

ca. 1850

ca. 1862

Congo

BUNYORO
BUGANDA

KIKUYU

TIPPU
TIB'S
SPHERE
Kirundu

Nyangwe
Kasongo
Mtowa
Ujiji
MIRAMBO

Tabora

Mombasa

Zanzibar
Bagamoyo
1857

Kilwa

ATLANTIC

OCEAN

Luanda

ca. 1850

LUNDA

ANGOLA
(Port.)

MSIRI'S
YEKE
KINGDOM

INDIAN

OCEAN

SHONA

NDEBELE

MOZAMBIQUE
(Port.)

Kilwa □ Zanzibari trading post

Limpopo

ca. 1860

Nguni/Ngoni states

Reformist Muslim states

Nyamwezi states

Ethiopia, 1880

Ethiopia, 1900

Other states

European colonies

Migrations of the Nguni/Ngoni

The Great Trek

Trade routes

1857 External slave trade
and date of suppression

LESOTHO

SWAZI

ZULU

CAPE COLONY
(G.B.)
Cape Town

NATAL
(G.B.)

(to Americas)

0   400   800 Km.

0   400   800 Mi.

Map 22.1   Africa in the Nineteenth Century   Expanding internal and overseas trade drew
much of Africa into global networks, but foreign colonies in 1870 were largely confined to Algeria
and southern Africa. Growing trade, Islamic reform movements, and other internal forces created
important new states throughout the continent.

Modernization in Egypt and Ethiopia

In northeastern Africa, the ancient African states of Egypt and Ethiopia were undergoing a period of growth and **modernization.** Napoleon's invasion of Egypt ended in 1801, but the shock of this display of European strength and Egyptian weakness prompted **Muhammad Ali,** who eliminated his rivals and ruled Egypt from 1805 to 1848, to begin the political, social, and economic reforms.

Muhammad Ali's central aim was to give Egypt sufficient military strength to prevent another European conquest, but he was pragmatic enough to make use of European experts and techniques to achieve that goal. His reforms transformed Egyptian landholding, increased agricultural production, and created a modern administration and army. To pay for these ventures and for the European experts and equipment that he imported, he required Egyptian peasants to cultivate cotton and other crops for export.

By the end of Muhammad Ali's reign in 1848, the modernization of Egypt was well under way. The trade with Europe had expanded by almost 600 percent, and a new class of educated Egyptians had begun to replace the old ruling aristocracy. Egyptians were replacing many of the foreign experts, and the fledgling program of industrialization was providing the country with its own textiles, paper, weapons, and military uniforms. The demands on peasant families for labor and military service, however, were acutely disruptive.

Ali's grandson Ismail° (r. 1863–1879) placed even more emphasis on Westernizing Egypt. "My country is no longer in Africa," Ismail declared, "it is in Europe."[1] A huge increase in cotton exports during the American Civil War helped finance a network of new irrigation canals, 800 miles (1,300 kilometers) of railroads, a modern postal service, and the dazzling new capital city of Cairo.

State building and reform also were under way in the ancient Christian kingdom of Ethiopia. Beginning in the 1840s, Ethiopian rulers purchased modern weapons from European sources and created strong armies loyal to the ruler. Emperor Téwodros° II (r. 1833–1868) and his successor, Yohannes° IV (r. 1872–1889), brought back under imperial rule large areas of ancient Ethiopia. When King Menelik of Shoa succeeded Yohannes as emperor in 1889, the merger of their separate realms created the modern boundaries of Ethiopia.

European Penetration

France's long and difficult war to conquer the North African country of Algeria from 1830 to 1848 was a rare example of European use of force in Africa before 1870. More typical was the peaceful penetration of European explorers, missionaries, and traders.

Small expeditions of adventurous explorers, using their own funds or financed by private geographical societies, were seeking to uncover the mysteries of inner Africa that had eluded earlier Europeans. Many of the explorers sought to map the course of Africa's great rivers: the Niger, the Nile, and the Congo.

In contrast to these heavily financed expeditions with hundreds of African porters, the Scottish missionary David Livingstone (1813–1873) organized modest treks through southern and Central Africa to scout out locations for Christian missions. His several expeditions in southern and equatorial Africa made him a celebrity. In 1871, he was met by the Welsh-American journalist Henry Morton Stanley (1841–1904) on a publicity-motivated search for the "lost" missionary doctor. On an expedition from 1874 to 1877, Stanley descended the Congo River to its mouth.

The most significant European influence in Africa between 1750 and 1870 was commercial. No sooner was the mouth of the Niger River discovered in 1830 than eager entrepreneurs began to send expeditions up the river to scout out its potential for trade. The value of trade between Africa and the other Atlantic continents more than doubled between the 1730s and the 1780s, then doubled again by 1870. Before about 1825, the slave trade accounted for most of that increase, but thereafter African exports of vegetable oils, gold, ivory, and other goods drove overseas trade to new heights.

Ismail (is-MAH-eel)   **Téwodros** (tay-WOH-druhs)

Yohannes (yoh-HAHN-nehs)

Téwodros's Mighty Cannon Like other modernizers in the nineteenth century, Emperor Téwodros of Ethiopia sought to reform his military forces. In 1861, he forced resident European missionaries and craftsmen to build guns and cannon, including this 7-ton behemoth nicknamed "Sebastopol" after the Black Sea port that had been the center of the Crimean War. It took five hundred men to haul the cannon across Ethiopia's hilly terrain. (From Hormuzd Rassam, *Narrative of the British Mission to Theodore, King of Abyssinia, II*, London 1869, John Murray)

As Chapter 20 recounted, the successful revolutions in the United States, France, Saint Domingue, and Latin America helped turn Western opinion against the slave trade and slavery. Once the world's greatest slave traders, the British became the most aggressive abolitionists. During the half-century after 1815, Britain spent some $60 million (£12 million) in its efforts to end the slave trade through naval patrols, a sum equal to the profits British slave traders had made in the fifty years before 1808. Although British patrols captured 1,635 slave ships and liberated over 160,000 enslaved Africans, continued demand for slaves in Cuba and Brazil kept the trade going until 1867.

The demand for slaves in the Americas claimed the lives and endangered the safety of untold numbers of Africans, but the exchanges also satisfied other Africans' desires for cloth, metals, and other goods. To continue their access to those imports, Africans expanded their **"legitimate" trade** (exports other than slaves). The most successful of the new exports from West Africa was palm oil, a vegetable oil used by British manufacturers for soap, candles, and lubricants. From the mid-1830s, the trading states of the Niger Delta emerged as the premier exporters of palm oil. Coastal Africans there grew rich and used their wealth to buy large numbers of male slaves to paddle the giant dugout canoes that transported palm oil from inland markets along the narrow delta creeks to the trading ports.

Another effect of the suppression of the slave trade was the spread of Western cultural influences in West Africa. To serve as a base for their anti–slave trade naval squadron, in 1808 the British had taken over the small colony of Sierra Leone°. Over the next several years, 130,000 men, women, and chil-

Sierra Leone (see-ER-uh lee-OWN)

King Jaja of Opobo   This talented man rose from slavery in the Niger Delta port of Bonny to head one of the town's major palm oil trading firms, the Anna Pepple House, in 1863. Six years later, Jaja founded and ruled his own trading port of Opobo.   (Reproduced from *West Africa: An Introduction to Its History*, by Michael Crowder, by courtesy of the publishers, Addison Wesley Longman)

of distinguished graduates. For example, Samuel Adjai Crowther (1808–1891), freed as a youth from a slave ship in 1821 by the British squadron, became the first Anglican bishop in West Africa in 1864, administering a pioneering diocese along the lower Niger River. James Africanus Horton (1835–1882), the son of a slave liberated in Sierra Leone, became a doctor and the author of many studies of West Africa.

Other Western cultural influences came from people of African birth or descent returning to their ancestral homeland in this era. In 1821, to the south of Sierra Leone, free black Americans began a settlement that grew into the Republic of Liberia, a place of liberty at a time when slavery was illegal and flourishing in the United States. Free blacks from Brazil and Cuba chartered ships to return to their West African homelands, bringing with them Roman Catholicism, architectural motifs, and clothing fashions from the New World. Although the number of Africans exposed to Western culture in 1870 was still small, this influence grew rapidly.

Secondary Empires in Eastern Africa

When British patrols hampered the slave trade in West Africa, slavers moved southward and then around the tip of southern Africa to eastern Africa. There the Atlantic slave trade joined an existing trade in slaves to the Islamic world that also was expanding. Two-thirds of the 1.2 million slaves exported from eastern Africa in the nineteenth century went to markets in North Africa and the Middle East; the other third went to European plantations in the Americas and the Indian Ocean.

Slavery within eastern Africa also grew between 1800 and 1873, as Arab and Swahili owners purchased some 700,000 slaves from inland eastern Africa to do the labor-intensive work of harvesting cloves on plantations on Zanzibar Island and the neighboring coast. These territories belonged to the sultan of Oman, an Arabian kingdom on the Persian Gulf. The sultan moved his court to Zanzibar in 1840. Zanzibar also was an important market for ivory, most of which was shipped to India, where much of it was carved into decorative objects for middle-class Europeans.

dren taken from "captured" vessels were liberated in Sierra Leone. Christian missionaries helped settle these impoverished and dispirited **recaptives** in and around Freetown, the capital. In time, the mission churches and schools made many willing converts among such men and women.

Sierra Leone's schools also produced a number

Caravans led by African and Arab merchants brought ivory from hundreds of miles inland. Some of these merchants created large personal empires by using capital they had borrowed from Indian bankers and modern firearms they had bought from Europeans and Americans. These modern rifles felled countless elephants for their ivory tusks and inflicted widespread devastation and misery on the inland people.

One can blame the Zanzibari traders for the pillage and havoc in the once-peaceful center of Africa. However, the circle of responsibility was still broader. Europeans supplied the weapons used by the invaders and were major consumers of ivory and cloves. For this reason, histories have referred to the states carved out of eastern Africa as "secondary empires," in contrast to the empire that Britain was establishing directly. At the same time, Britain was working to bring the Indian Ocean slave trade to an end in eastern Africa. British officials pressured the sultan of Oman into halting the Indian Ocean slave trade from Zanzibar in 1857 and ending the import of slaves into Zanzibar in 1873.

INDIA UNDER BRITISH RULE

The people of South Asia felt the impact of European commercial, cultural, and colonial expansion more immediately and profoundly than did the people of Africa. While Europeans were laying claim to only small parts of Africa between 1750 and 1870, nearly all of India (with three times the population of all of Africa) came under Britain's direct or indirect rule. After the founding of East India Company in 1600, it took British interests 250 years to commandeer the colonies and trade of the Dutch, fight off French and Indian challenges, and pick up the pieces of the decaying Mughal° Empire. By 1763 the French were stymied, in 1795 the Dutch company was dissolved, and in 1858 the last Mughal emperor was dethroned, leaving the vast subcontinent in British hands.

Company Men

As Mughal power weakened in the eighteenth century, British, Dutch, and French companies expanded into India (see Map 22.2). Such far-flung European trading companies were speculative and risky ventures. Their success depended on hard-drinking and ambitious young "Company Men," who used hard bargaining, and hard fighting when necessary, to persuade Indian rulers to allow them to establish trading posts at strategic points along the coast. To protect their fortified warehouses from attack by other Europeans or by native states, the companies hired and trained Indian troops known as **sepoys°**. In divided India, these private armies came to hold the balance of power.

In 1691, the East India Company (EIC) had convinced the **nawab°** (the term used for Mughal governors) of the large state of Bengal in northeast India to let the company establish a fortified outpost at the fishing port of Calcutta. A new nawab, pressing claims for additional tribute from the prospering port, overran the fort in 1756 and imprisoned a group of EIC men in a cell so small that many died of suffocation. To avenge their deaths in this "Black Hole of Calcutta," a large EIC force from Madras overthrew the nawab. The weak Mughal emperor was persuaded to acknowledge the EIC's right to rule Bengal in 1765. Fed by the tax revenues of Bengal as well as by profits from trade, the EIC was on its way. Calcutta grew into a city of 250,000 by 1788.

In southern India, EIC forces secured victory for the British Indian candidate for nawab of Arcot during the Seven Years War, thereby gaining an advantage over French traders who had supported the loser. The defeat of Tipu Sultan of Mysore at the end of the century (described at the start of the chapter) secured south India for the company and prevented a French resurgence.

Along with Calcutta and Madras, the third major center of British power in India was Bombay, on

---

Mughal (MOO-guhl)

sepoy (SEE-poy)　nawab (NAH-wab)

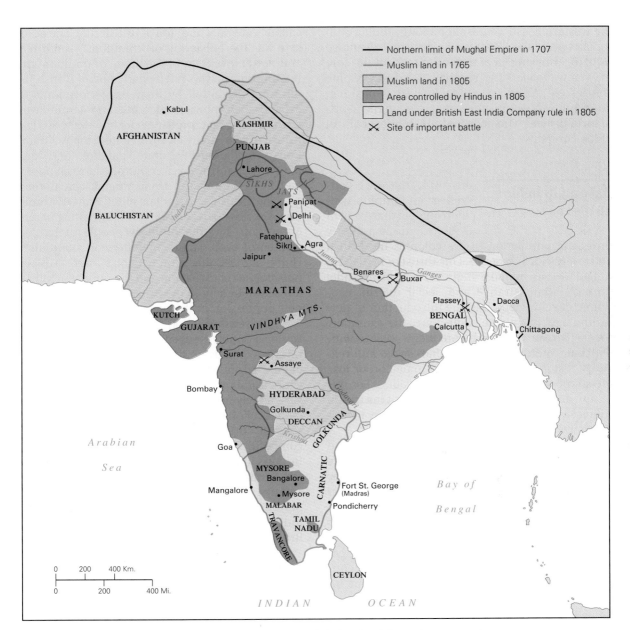

Map 22.2   India, 1707–1805   As Mughal power weakened during the eighteenth century, other Indian states and the British East India Company expanded their territories.

the western coast. There, after a long conflict with Indian rulers, the EIC gained a decisive advantage in 1818, annexing large territories to form the core of what was called the "Bombay Presidency." Some states were taken over completely, as Bengal had been, but very many others remained in the hands of local princes who accepted the political control of the company.

Raj and Rebellion, 1818–1857

In 1818, the EIC controlled an empire with more people than in all of western Europe and fifty times the population of the colonies the British had lost in North America. One thrust of **British raj** (reign) was to remake India on a British model through administrative and social reform, economic development, and the introduction of new technology. But at the same time, the Company Men—like the Mughals before them—had to temper their interference with Indian social and religious customs lest they provoke rebellion or lose the support of their Indian princely allies. For this reason and because of the complexity of the task of ruling such a vast empire, there were many inconsistencies in Britain's policies toward India.

The main policy was to create a powerful and efficient system of government. British rule before 1850 relied heavily on military power—170 sepoy regiments and 16 European regiments. Another policy was to disarm approximately 2 million warriors who had served India's many states and turn them to civilian tasks, mostly cultivation. A third policy gave freer rein to Christian missionaries eager to convert and uplift India's masses. Few converts were made, but the missionaries kept up steady pressure for social reforms.

Another key British policy was to turn India's complex and overlapping patterns of landholding into private property. In Bengal, this reform worked to the advantage of large landowners, but in Mysore, the peasantry gained. Private ownership made it easier for the state to collect the taxes that were needed to pay for the costs of administration, the army, and economic reform.

Such policies of "Westernization, Anglicization, and modernization," as they have been

called, were only one side of British rule. The other side was the bolstering of "traditions"—both real and newly invented. In the name of tradition, the Indian princes who ruled nearly half of British India were permitted by their British overlords to expand their power, splendor, and tenure well beyond what their predecessors had ever had. The British rulers themselves invented many "traditions"—including elaborate parades and displays—half borrowed from European royal pomp, half freely improvised from Mughal ceremonies.

The British and Indian elites danced sometimes in close partnership, sometimes in apparent opposition. But the ordinary people of India—women of every status, members of subordinate Hindu castes, the "untouchables" and "tribals" outside the caste system, and the poor generally—found less benefit in the British reforms and much new oppression in the new taxes and "traditions."

The transformation of British India's economy was also doubled-edged. On the one hand, British raj created many new jobs as a result of the growth of internal and external trade and the expansion of agricultural production, such as in opium in Bengal—largely for export to China—coffee in Ceylon (an island off the tip of India), and tea in Assam (a state in northeastern India). On the other hand, competition from cheap cotton goods produced in Britain's industrial mills drove many Indians out of the handicraft textile industry. In the eighteenth century, India had been the world's greatest exporter of cotton textiles; in the nineteenth century, India increasingly shipped raw cotton fiber to Britain.

Even the beneficial economic changes introduced under British rule were disruptive, and there were no safety nets for the needy. Thus, local rebellions by displaced ruling elites, disgruntled religious traditionalists, and the economically dispossessed were almost constant during the first half of the nineteenth century. The greatest concern was over the continuing loyalty of Indian sepoys in the EIC's army.

Discontent was growing among Indian soldiers. In the early decades of EIC rule, most sepoys came from Bengal, one of the first states the company had annexed. The Bengali sepoys resented the active recruitment of other ethnic groups into the army after 1848, such as Sikhs° from Punjab and Gurkhas from Nepal. Many high-caste Hindus objected to a new law in 1856 requiring new recruits to be available for service overseas in the growing Indian Ocean empire, for their religion prohibited ocean travel. The replacement of the standard military musket by the far more accurate Enfield rifle in 1857 also caused problems. Soldiers were ordered to use their teeth to tear open the ammunition cartridges, which were greased with animal fat. Hindus were offended by this order if the fat came from cattle, which they considered sacred. Muslims were offended if the fat came from pigs, which they considered unclean.

Although the cartridge-opening procedure was quickly changed, the initial discontent grew into rebellion by Hindu sepoys in May 1857. British troubles mushroomed when Muslim sepoys, peasants, and discontented elites joined in. The rebels asserted old traditions to challenge British authority: sepoy officers in Delhi proclaimed their loyalty to the Mughal emperor; others rallied behind the Maratha leader Nana Sahib. The rebellion was put down by March 1858, but it shook this piecemeal empire to its core.

Historians have attached different names and meanings to the events of 1857 and 1858. Concentrating on the technical fact that the uprising was an unlawful action by soldiers, nineteenth-century British historians labeled it the **"Sepoy Rebellion"** or the "Mutiny," and these names are still commonly used. Seeing in these events the beginnings of the later movement for independence, some modern Indian historians have termed it the "Revolution of 1857." In reality, it was much more than a simple mutiny, because it involved more than soldiers, but it was not yet a nationalist revolution, for the rebels' sense of a common Indian national identity was weak.

Political Reform and Industrial Impact

Whatever it is called, the rebellion of 1857–1858 was a turning point in the history of modern India. In its wake, Indians gained a new centralized government, entered a period of rapid economic growth, and began to develop a new national consciousness.

The changes in government were immediate. In 1858, Britain eliminated the last traces of Mughal and EIC rule. In their place, a new secretary of state for India in London oversaw Indian policy, and a new governor-general in Delhi acted as the British monarch's viceroy on the spot. A proclamation by Queen Victoria in November 1858 guaranteed all Indians equal protection of the law and the freedom to practice their religions and social customs; it also assured Indian princes that so long as they were loyal to the queen, British India would respect their control of territories and "their rights, dignity and honour."[2]

A powerful and efficient bureaucracy controlled the Indian masses. Members of the elite **Indian Civil Service** (ICS), mostly graduates of Oxford and Cambridge Universities, held the senior administrative and judicial posts. Only a thousand men at the end of the nineteenth century, they visited the villages in their districts, heard lawsuits and complaints, and passed judgments. Beneath them were a far greater number of Indian officials and employees. Recruitment into the ICS was by open examination given only in England and thus inaccessible to most Indians. In 1870, only one Indian was a member of the ICS. Subsequent reforms led to fifty-seven Indian appointments by 1887, but the process stalled.

A second transformation of India after 1857 resulted from involvement with industrial Britain. The government invested millions of pounds sterling in harbors, cities, irrigation canals, and other public works. British interests felled forests to make way for tea plantations, persuaded Indian farmers to grow cotton and jute for export, and created great irrigation systems to alleviate the famines that periodically decimated whole provinces. As a result, India's trade expanded rapidly.

Most of the exports were agricultural commodities for processing elsewhere: cotton fiber, opium, tea, silk, and sugar. In return, India imported manufactured goods from Britain, including the flood of machine-made cotton textiles that severely undercut Indian hand-loom weavers. The

Sikh (seek)

effects on individual Indians varied enormously. Some women found new jobs, though at very low pay, on plantations or in the growing cities, where prostitution flourished. Others struggled to hold families together or ran away from abusive husbands. Everywhere in India, poverty remained the norm.

The Indian government also promoted the introduction of new technologies into India not long after their appearance in Britain. Earlier in the century, there were steamboats on the rivers and a massive program of canal building for irrigation. Beginning in the 1840s, a railroad boom (paid for out of government revenues) gave India its first national transportation network, followed shortly by telegraph lines. Indeed, in 1870, India had the greatest rail network in Asia and the fifth largest in the world.

The freer movement of Indians and rapid urban growth promoted the spread of cholera°, a disease transmitted through water contaminated by human feces. In 1867, officials demonstrated the close connection between cholera and pilgrims who bathed in and drank from sacred pools and rivers. The installation of a new sewerage system (1865) and a filtered water supply (1869) in Calcutta dramatically reduced cholera deaths there. Similar measures in Bombay and Madras also led to great reductions, but most Indians lived in small villages, where famine and lack of sanitation kept cholera deaths high. Only after 1900 did sanitary improvements lower the death rate from cholera.

Rising Indian Nationalism

Both the successes and the failures of British rule stimulated the development of Indian nationalism. The failure of the rebellion of 1857 led some thoughtful Indians to argue that the only way to regain control of their destiny was to reduce their country's social and ethnic divisions.

Individuals such as Rammohun Roy (1772–1833) had promoted pan-Indian nationalism a generation earlier. A Western-educated Bengali from a Brahmin family, Roy was a successful administrator for the EIC and a thoughtful student of comparative religion. His Brahmo Samaj° (Divine Society), founded in 1828, attracted Indians who sought to reconcile the values they found in the West with the ancient religious traditions of India. They backed the British outlawing of widow burning (sati°) in 1829 and of slavery in 1843 and sought to correct other abuses of women and female infanticide. Roy and his followers advocated reforming the caste system, and urged a return to the founding principles set out in the Upanishads, ancient sacred writings of Hinduism.

Although Brahmo Samaj remained an influential movement, a growing number of Indian intellectuals based their nationalism on the secular values they absorbed in Western schools. European and American missionaries played a prominent role in the spread of Western education. In 1870, there were 790,000 Indians in over 24,000 elementary and secondary schools, and India's three universities (established in 1857) awarded 345 degrees.

Many of the new nationalists came from the Indian middle class. Hoping to increase their influence and improve their employment opportunities in the Indian government, they convened the first **Indian National Congress** in 1885. The members sought a larger role for Indians in the civil service and called for more money to be spent on alleviating the poverty of the Indian masses. The Indian National Congress effectively voiced the opinions of elite, Western-educated Indians, but it would need the support of the masses to challenge British rule.

Colonies and Commerce

India was not only Britain's largest colony; it was also an increasingly important center of trade. British trade to India grew 350 percent between 1841 and 1870, while India's exports increased 400 percent. In addition to cotton fiber and indigo dye for Europe, India became a major producer of opium, largely destined for China. In the 1830s and 1840s, opium was 40 percent of India's exports.

---

cholera (KAHL-uhr-uh)

Brahmo Samaj (BRAH-moh suh-MAHJ)   *sati* (suh-TEE)

Indian Railroad Station, 1866   British India built the largest network of railroads in Asia. People of every social class traveled by train.   (Eyre and Hobbs House Art Gallery)

This new commercial expansion was closely tied to the needs of Britain's growing industrial economy and reflected a new philosophy of overseas trade. Rather than rebuilding the closed, mercantilist network of trade with its colonies, Britain sought to trade freely with all parts of the world, including the independent states of the Americas, Africa, and Asia.

To protect these valuable trade links, Britain acquired some new colonies. The Cape Colony at the tip of Africa was acquired from the Dutch in 1806 to serve ships on the long voyages from Europe to Asia. Other possessions were added in Southeast Asia. In 1824, the East India Company established a free port at Singapore, on the site of a small Malay fishing village with a superb harbor. Singapore soon became the center of trade and shipping between the Indian Ocean and China.

The shipbuilding revolution underway in the nineteenth century made global commerce easier. Merchant ships in the eighteenth century rarely exceeded 300 tons, but after 1850, swift **clipper ships** of 2,000 tons were commonplace in the British merchant fleet. Shipbuilders used iron to fasten American and tropical timbers together to make these larger vessels. The clippers' huge canvas sails and streamlined hulls cut voyage times between India and Europe from six months to three months, which lowered shipping costs and further stimulated maritime trade. Although the middle decades of the nineteenth century were the golden age of the sailing ship, industrial technology was also beginning to produce steam-powered iron vessels that found military uses in Britain's commercial penetration of China (see Environment and Technology: Whaling).

ENVIRONMENT + TECHNOLOGY

Whaling

The rapid expansion of whaling aptly illustrates the growing power of technology over nature in this period. Many contemporaries, like many people today, were sickened by the killing of the planet's largest living mammals. American novelist Herman Melville captured the conflicting sentiments in his epic whaling story, *Moby Dick* (1851). One of his characters enthusiastically explains why the grisly and dangerous business existed:

> But, though the world scorns us as whale hunters, yet does it unwittingly pay us the profoundest homage; yea, an all abounding adoration! for almost all the tapers, lamps, and candles that burn around the globe, burn, as before so many shrines, to our glory!

Melville's character overstates the degree to which whale oil dominated illumination and does not mention its many other industrial uses and the importance of whale meat for food in some countries. Whalebone

(baleen) was the plastic of its day. Whalebone was used for umbrella stays, carriage springs, fishing rods, suitcase frames, combs, and brushes, and its use in corsets allowed Western women to achieve the hourglass shape that fashion dictated.

New manufacturing technologies went hand in hand with new hunting technologies. The revolution in ship design enabled whalers from Europe and North America to extend the hunt into the southern oceans off New Zealand. By the nineteenth century, whaling ships were armed with guns that shot a steel harpoon armed with vicious barbs deep into the whale. In the 1840s, explosive charges on harpoon heads ensured the whale's immediate death. Yet as this depiction of Japanese whaling shows, simple tools and weapons remained part of the dangerous work.

Another century of extensive hunting devastated many whale species before international agreements finally limited the killing of these giant sea creatures.

Netting Whales   During the Tokugawa, whaling became an important new industry in parts of Japan.   (Courtesy Rizzoli)

THE QING EMPIRE

The Qing Empire, created by the Manchus, had distinguished itself in the 1600s for its adept maneuverings, both strategic and diplomatic, against Russia. The Qing rulers had earned the admiration of the Jesuits, who transmitted to Europe a very appealing image of the emperors in China as enlightened philosopher-kings. But the failure in 1793 of the British attempt to establish diplomatic and trade relations with the Qing—the Macartney mission (see Chapter 19)—turned European opinion against China, and in the very early 1800s few Europeans apart from traders based in Canton had much contact with or interest in China. For their part, the Qing rulers and bureaucrats were embroiled in serious domestic crises: rebellions by displaced indigenous peoples and the poor and protests against the injustice of the local magistrates. The Qing rulers of 1800 believed that Europe was remote and only casually interested in trade. Only slowly did officials learn that Britain was passionate about foreign trade and already had colonies in India, a major naval base at Singapore.

Economic and Social Disorder

The Qing conquest in the 1600s brought stability to central China, previously subjected to decades of rebellion and agricultural shortages. The result was a great expansion of the agricultural base, together with a doubling of the population between about 1650 and about 1800. By 1800, population strain on the land had caused serious environmental damage in some parts of central and western China. Deforestation, erosion, and soil exhaustion left swollen populations stranded on rapidly deteriorating land.

Many groups had serious grievances against the government. Minority peoples in central and southwestern China resented having been driven off their lands during the boom of the 1700s. Mongols resisted the appropriation of their grazing lands and the displacement of their traditional

elites. Many people mistrusted the government, suspecting that all officials were corrupt. The growing presence of foreign merchants and missionaries in coastal cities added to their discontent.

As the nineteenth century opened, the White Lotus Rebellion (1794–1804)—partly inspired by a mystical ideology that predicted the restoration of the Chinese Ming dynasty and the coming of the Buddha—was raging across central China. The White Lotus was the first in a series of large internal conflicts that continued through the 1800s. Ignited by deepening social instabilities, these movements were sometimes intensified by local ethnic conflicts and by unapproved religions.

The Opium War, 1839–1842

For more than a century, British officials had been frustrated by the enormous trade deficit caused by the British demand for tea and the Qing refusal to facilitate the importation to China of any British product. In opium, British merchants discovered an extremely profitable trade. Despite a Qing law of 1729 making it illegal to import opium, European merchants and their Chinese partners were smuggling in growing quantities of the highly addictive drug that was grown in British India. By the 1830s, as many as 30,000 chests of opium were being imported. For a time, the Qing emperor and his officials debated whether to legalize and tax opium or to enforce the existing ban on the drug more strictly. They decided to root out the use and the importation of opium, and in 1839 they sent an official to Canton to deal with the matter.

Britain considered the Qing ban on the importation of opium an intolerable restraint of trade and a direct threat to Britain's economic health, and indirectly a cause for war. When British naval and marine forces arrived at the south China coast in late 1839 and negotiations broke down, the **Opium War** (1839–1842) broke out. The British kept most confrontations on the sea, where they had a distinct technological advantage. British ships landed marines who pillaged coastal cities and then returned to their ships and sailed to new destinations (see Map 22.3). The Qing had no

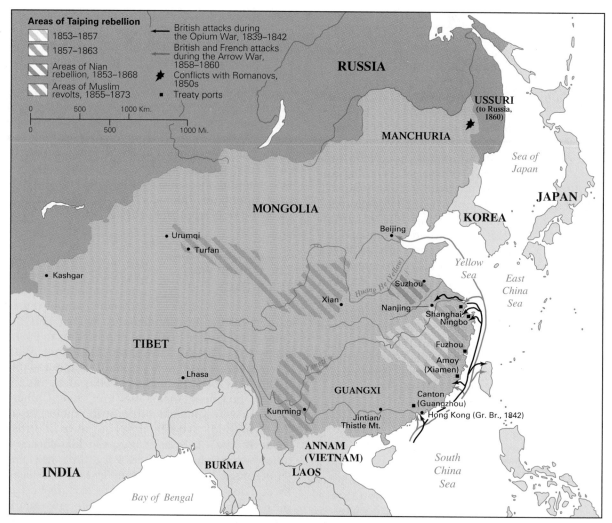

Map 22.3 Conflicts in the Qing Empire, 1839–1870 In the Opium War of 1839–1842 the seacoasts saw most of the action. Since the Qing had no imperial navy, the well-armed British ships encountered little resistance as they shelled the southern coasts. In inland conflicts, such as the Taiping Rebellion, the opposing armies were massive and slow moving. Battles on land were often prolonged attempts by one side to starve out the other side before making a major assault.

imperial navy, and even in the land engagements, the traditional, hereditary soldiers, the **Bannermen,** proved woefully inadequate. The British could quickly transport their forces by sea along the coast. Qing troops, in contrast, moved primarily on foot. Moving Qing reinforcements from central to eastern China took more than three months, and when the defense forces arrived, they were exhausted and basically without weapons.

Against the British invaders, the Bannermen used the few muskets the Qing had imported during the 1700s. Firing these obsolete weapons was slow and dangerous. A majority of the Bannermen, however, had no guns and fought with swords, knives, spears, and clubs. Soldiers under British command—many of them Indians—carried percussion-cap rifles, which were far quicker, safer, and more accurate than the matchlocks. In addition, the British deployed new gunboats able to proceed up the shallow water of the Yangzi River.

When the invaders approached Nanjing, the revered former Ming capital, the Qing decided to negotiate an end to the war. In 1842, the **Treaty of Nanking** (Nanjing) increased the number of **treaty ports**—cities opened to foreign residents—from one (Canton) to five, lowered tariffs to 5 percent, and made the island of Hong Kong a permanent British colony. British residents in China were granted the rights of extraterritoriality. The Qing government had to pay an indemnity of 21 million ounces of silver to Britain as a penalty for having started the war.

Later treaties expanded the privileges of foreign traders and missionaries in China. The number of treaty ports, where foreign merchants enjoyed the rights of extraterritoriality, grew to more than ninety by 1900. In Canton, Shanghai°, and other coastal cities, Europeans and Americans built comfortable housing in zones where Chinese were not permitted to live, and they entertained themselves in exclusive restaurants and bars. Some of the work of Christian missionaries was benevolent: hospitals, shelters, and soup kitchens. The missionaries themselves also undermined Confucian beliefs and condemned long-standing customs, such as footbinding. The foreigners and their privileges became a target of resentment.

The Taiping Rebellion, 1850–1864

The most startling demonstration of the inflammatory mixture of social unhappiness and foreign intrusion was the great civil war usually called the **Taiping Rebellion.** In Guangxi, where the Taiping movement originated, social problems had been generating disorders for half a century. Agriculture in the region was unstable, and many people made their living from arduous and despised trades such as disposing of human waste, making charcoal, and mining. Ethnic divisions complicated economic distress. A minority group, the Hakkas, were frequently found in the lowliest trades, and tensions between them and the majority were rising. Also, the area was close enough to Canton to feel the cultural and economic impact of the growing number of Europeans and Americans.

The founder of the movement, Hong Xiuquan°, came from a humble Hakka background. He saw himself as the younger brother of Jesus, commissioned by God to found a new kingdom on earth and drive the Manchu conquerors, the Qing, out of China. Hong called his new religious movement the "Heavenly Kingdom of Great Peace."

Hong quickly attracted a community of believers, primarily Hakkas like himself. When news of the heresy reached the government, Qing troops were sent to arrest the leaders. But after the Taipings soundly repelled the imperial troops, their numbers multiplied, and they began to enlarge their domain into eastern and northern China. Women participated fully in work, and military teams organized separately by sex.

Panic preceded the Taipings. Villagers feared being forced into Taiping units, and Confucian elites recoiled in horror from the bizarre ideology of foreign gods, totalitarian rule, and walking, working, warring women. But the huge numbers the Taipings were able to muster overwhelmed attempts at local defense. When the rebel army conquered Nanjing in 1853, the Taiping leaders decided to settle there and make it the capital of the new "Heavenly Kingdom of Great Peace."

By then, Qing military commanders were becoming more successful in halting the Taiping advances. The Qing court agreed to special taxes to fund the new armies and acknowledged the new combined leadership of the civilian and professional force. The new Qing armies surrounded Nanjing, hoping to starve out the rebels. The Taipings, however, mobilized enormous campaigns in nearby parts of eastern China, scavenging supplies, and Nanjing held out for more than a decade

In 1856, the British and French launched a series of swift, brutal coastal attacks—a second opium war, because the Qing had not observed the provisions of the treaties signed after the first Opium War. Their troops invaded Beijing, sacked

Shanghai (shahng-hie)

Hong Xiuquan (hoong shee-OH-chew-an)

Nanjing Encircled   For a decade, the Taipings held the city of Nanjing as their capital. For years, Qing and international troops attempted to break the Taiping hold. By the summer of 1864, Qing forces had built tunnels leading to the foundations of Nanjing's city walls and had planted explosives. The detonation of explosives signaled the final Qing assault on the rebel capital. As shown here, the common people of the city, along with their starving livestock, were caught in the cross-fire. Many of the Taiping leaders escaped the debacle at Nanjing, but nearly all were hunted down and executed.   (Roger-Viollet)

the Summer Palace in 1860, and imposed new treaties that punished the Qing for not enacting all the provisions of the Treaty of Nanking. Having secured their principal objective, the British and French forces now joined the Qing in the campaign against the Taipings. The injection of European weaponry and money aided in the quelling of the Taiping and other rebels during the 1860s.

The Taiping Rebellion ranks as the world's bloodiest civil war and the greatest armed conflict before the twentieth century. Estimates of deaths range from 20 million to 30 million. The loss of life was due primarily to starvation and disease, for most engagements consisted of surrounding the enemy holed up in fortified cities and waiting until they died, surrendered, or were so weakened that they could be easily defeated. Many of the most intensely cultivated regions of central and eastern China were depopulated and laid barren. Cities, too, were hard hit. Major cultural centers in eastern China lost masterpieces of art and architecture, imperial libraries were burned or their collections exposed to the weather, and the printing blocks used to make books were destroyed.

Decentralization at the End of the Qing Empire

The Qing government emerged from the 1850s with no hope of achieving solvency. The treasury had been bankrupted by decades of corruption, the indemnities demanded by Europeans after the Opium Wars, and the huge costs of the Taiping rebellion. To ensure that the Qing government began repaying its debt to Britain, Robert Hart was installed as inspector-general of a newly created Imperial Maritime Customs Service. The revenues he collected were split between Britain and the Qing. Britons and Americans put themselves in the employ of the Qing government as advisers and ambassadors, attempting to smooth communications between the Qing, Europe, and the United States while the imperial government started up the diplomatic machinery demanded by Europe in its latest treaties.

The real work of the recovery, however, was managed by the provincial governors who had come to the forefront in the struggle against the Taipings and who continued to levy their own taxes, raise their own troops, and run their own bureaucracies. Some became so powerful that they were managing Qing foreign policy as well as domestic affairs. From the 1860s forward, the Qing Empire disintegrated into a set of large power zones in which provincial governors handed over leadership to their protégés.

CONCLUSION

What is the global significance of these complex political and economic changes in Asia and Africa? One perspective stresses the continuing exploitation of the weak by the strong, of African, Asian, and Pacific peoples by aggressive Europeans. In this view, the emergence of Britain as the dominant imperial power continues the European expansion that the Portuguese and the Spanish pioneered and the Dutch continued. Yet even though the balance of power was shifting in the Europeans' favor between 1750 and 1870, Asian and African cultures were still vibrant, and most people were free of European control. Islamic reform movements and the rise of the Zulu nation had greater significance for their respective regions of Africa than did Western forces. Despite some ominous concessions to European power, the Chinese were still largely in control of their own destinies. Even in India, most people's lives and beliefs showed more continuity with the past than the change due to British rule.

From another perspective, what was most important about this period was not the political and military strength of the Europeans but their growing dominance of the world's commerce, especially through long-distance ocean shipping. In this view, like other Europeans, the British were drawn to Africa and southern Asia by a desire to obtain new materials. However, trade was similarly two-sided. Asians and Africans welcomed the industrial manufactures and other imports brought on European ships. The opium trade is a stark example of how harmful this trade could be, as are its effects on the weavers of India. But one should not overlook the beneficial side. Consumers found industrially produced goods far cheaper and sometimes better than the handicrafts these imports replaced or supplemented. Global trade also created larger markets for African and Asian goods, such as vegetable oil trade from West Africa, cotton from Egypt and India, and tea from China.

In short, it must not be imagined that Asians and Africans were powerless in dealing with European expansion. The Indian princes who extracted concessions from the British in return for their cooperation and the Indians who rebelled against the raj both forced the system to accommodate their needs. Moreover, some Asians and Africans were beginning to use European education, technology, and methods to transform their own societies. In 1870, no one could say how long and how difficult that learning process would be, but Africans and Asians would continue to shape their own futures.

■ Key Terms

Zulu	Sepoy Rebellion
Sokoto Caliphate	Indian Civil Service
modernization	Indian National Congress
Muhammad Ali	clipper ships
"legitimate" trade	Opium War
recaptives	Bannermen
sepoys	Treaty of Nanking
nawab	treaty ports
British raj	Taiping Rebellion

■ Suggested Reading

Volumes 2 and 3 of *The Oxford History of the British Empire,* edited by William Roger Louis, (1998, 1999), are the most up-to-date global surveys of this period. Less Anglo-centric in its interpretation is Immanuel Wallerstein's *The Modern World-System III: The Second Era of Great Expansion of the Capitalist World-Economy, 1730–1840s* (1989).

For more on African topics, see Roland Oliver and Anthony Atmore, *Africa Since 1800,* 4th ed. (1994); J. D. Omer-Cooper, *The Zulu Aftermath* (1966); Murray Last, *The Sokoto Caliphate* (1967); A. G. Hopkins, *An Economic History of West Africa* (1973); and Norman R. Bennett, *Arab Versus European: War and Diplomacy in Nineteenth Century East Central Africa* (1985).

Very readable introductions to India in this period are Sugata Bose and Ayeshia Jalal, *Modern South India* (1998); Burton Stein, *A History of India* (1998); and Stanley Wolpert, *A New History of India,* 6th ed. (1999). See also Daniel Headrick, *The Tentacles of Progress: Technology Transfer in the Age of Imperialism, 1850–1940* (1988).

On the later Qing Empire, see Pamela Kyle Crossley, *Orphan Warriors: Three Manchu Generations and the End of the Qing World* (1990); Peter Ward Fay, *The Opium War, 1840–1842: Barbarians in the Celestial Empire in the Early Part of the Nineteenth Century and the War by Which They Forced Her Gates Ajar* (1975); Christopher Hibbert, *The Dragon Wakes: China and the West, 1793–1911* (1970); and Jonathan D. Spence, *God's Chinese Son: The Taiping Heavenly Kingdom of Hong Xiuquan* (1996).

■ Notes

1. Quoted in P. J. Vatikiotis, *The History of Modern Egypt: From Muhammad Ali to Mubarak,* 4th ed. (Baltimore: Johns Hopkins University Press, 1991), 74.
2. Quoted by Bernard S. Cohn, "Representing Authority in Victorian England," in *The Invention of Tradition,* ed. Eric Hobsbawm and Terence Ranger (Cambridge: Cambridge University Press, 1983), 165.

GLOBAL DOMINANCE AND DIVERSITY,
1850–1949

CHAPTER 23
THE NEW POWER BALANCE, 1850–1900
CHAPTER 24
THE NEW IMPERIALISM, 1869–1914
CHAPTER 25
THE CRISIS OF THE IMPERIAL ORDER, 1900–1929
CHAPTER 26
THE COLLAPSE OF THE OLD ORDER, 1929–1949
CHAPTER 27
STRIVING FOR INDEPENDENCE: AFRICA, INDIA, AND LATIN AMERICA,
1900–1949

etween 1850 and 1950, Europe, the United States, and Japan industrialized and became powerful. One cause of the power of Europe, the United States, and Japan was nationalism, a bond uniting people on the basis of a common culture or shared historical experiences. In some nations, public participation resulted in basic freedoms and strong parliamentary institutions. In others, authoritarian leaders used nationalist feelings to mobilize mass support.

Another cause of Western and Japanese power in this period was industrialization itself. New technologies and economic arrangements transformed the lives of people of all classes and professions. Work increasingly took place in factories and offices, separating employment from home life, husbands from wives, children from parents. A growing proportion of married women became housewives, and compulsory education systems took over the care of children. Intensifying industrial activities transformed the natural environment. Pollution from manufacturing, long a local problem, began to affect entire regions.

Industrialization led to the creation of increasingly destructive weapons that enabled the Western powers to extend their commercial and political influence over Africa, most of Asia, and Latin America. By 1914, Britain, France, and the

United States dominated over half of the area and peoples of the world. By the time Germany and Japan entered the competition for overseas colonial empires, few unconquered territories remained.

Germany's desire to become a global power was a major cause of the First World War. The defeat of Germany did not restore the prewar equilibrium, as the victorious Allied nations had hoped. The Russian Revolution of 1917 led to the establishment of the world's first communist state. The collapse of the Ottoman Empire sparked changes in Middle Eastern societies, most dramatically in Turkey itself.

When the world economy collapsed in the 1930s, social disruption in Germany and Japan brought to power extremist politicians who sought to solve their countries' economic woes by seizing neighboring territories. Nationalism assumed its most hideous form in World War II. The war led to the massacre of millions of innocent people and the destruction of countless cities.

Domination by the great powers inspired a new generation of leaders to embrace the politics of national liberation. After decades of struggle, India achieved independence in 1947. Two years later, Communists led by Mao Zedong overthrew a Chinese government they denounced as too subservient to the West. In Latin America, leaders turned to nationalist economic and social politics.

The year 1945 marked the end of western European dominance. Only the United States and the Soviet Union remained to compete for global influence. Meanwhile, nationalism was rapidly spreading to the rest of the world, bringing with it the urge to acquire the benefits and power of industrial technology.

	1850	1870	1890
Americas	Creation of Dominion of Canada 1867 •	U.S. Civil War 1861–1865 British build railroads in Brazil and Argentina 1880s •	• 1890 U.S. is leading steel producer Spanish-American War 1898 • 1880–1914 Immigration from southern & eastern Europe surges
Europe	• 1851 Majority of British population living in cities • 1856 Transformation of steel and chemical industries begins	1870–1914 Era of the New Imperialism • 1871 Unification of Germany, Italy	1894–1906 Dreyfus affair in France
Africa	1853–1877 Livingstone, Stanley expeditions in central Africa End of transatlantic slave trade 1867 • Gold discovered in southern Africa 1884–1886	• 1880s West Africa conquered by France and Britain 1884–1885 Berlin Africa Conference Nigeria becomes British protectorate 1899 •	• 1896 Ethiopians defeat Italian army at Adowa
Middle East	Suez Canal opens 1869 •	1863–1879 Ismail westernizes Egypt • 1882 British occupy Egypt • 1878 Ottoman Empire loses most of its European territories	• 1904 Young Turk reforms in Ottoman Empire
Asia and Oceania	Direct British rule in India 1858 •	• 1862 French conquer Indochina Meiji Restoration in Japan 1868 • First Indian National Congress 1885 • Russia conquers Central Asia 1884–1887	Boxer Rebellion in China 1900 • Sino-Japanese War 1894 • 1904–1905 Russo-Japanese War

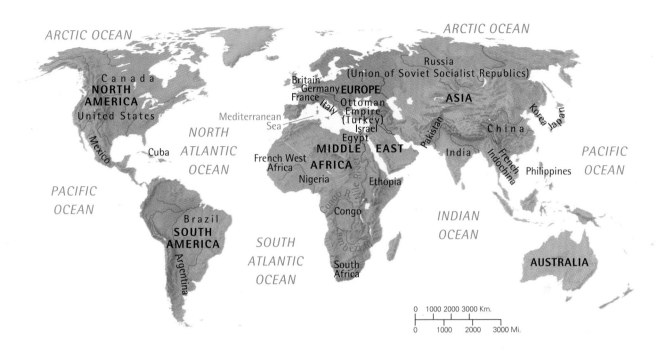

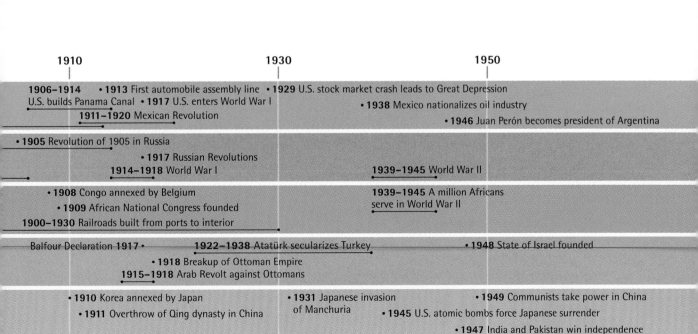

1910	1930	1950

1906–1914 • **1913** First automobile assembly line • **1929** U.S. stock market crash leads to Great Depression
U.S. builds Panama Canal • **1917** U.S. enters World War I • **1938** Mexico nationalizes oil industry
1911–1920 Mexican Revolution • **1946** Juan Perón becomes president of Argentina

• **1905** Revolution of 1905 in Russia
• **1917** Russian Revolutions
1914–1918 World War I **1939–1945** World War II

• **1908** Congo annexed by Belgium **1939–1945** A million Africans
• **1909** African National Congress founded serve in World War II
1900–1930 Railroads built from ports to interior

Balfour Declaration 1917 • **1922–1938** Atatürk secularizes Turkey • **1948** State of Israel founded
• **1918** Breakup of Ottoman Empire
1915–1918 Arab Revolt against Ottomans

• **1910** Korea annexed by Japan • **1931** Japanese invasion • **1949** Communists take power in China
• **1911** Overthrow of Qing dynasty in China of Manchuria • **1945** U.S. atomic bombs force Japanese surrender
• **1947** India and Pakistan win independence

THE NEW POWER BALANCE,

1850–1900

—f—

**New Technologies and the World Economy • Social
Transformations • Nationalism and the Unification of Germany •
The Great Powers of Europe, 1871–1900 • New Great Powers:
The United States and Japan**

SOCIETY AND CULTURE: Demonstrating for Women's Rights

On January 18, 1871, in the Hall of Mirrors of the palace of Versailles, King Wilhelm I of Prussia was proclaimed emperor of Germany before a crowd of officers and other German rulers. This ceremony marked the unification of many small German states into one nation. Off to one side stood Prussian chancellor Otto von Bismarck°, the man most responsible for the creation of a united Germany. A few years earlier, he had declared, "The great issues of the day will be decided not by speeches and votes of the majority—that was the great mistake of 1848 and 1849—but by iron and blood." Indeed it was "blood"—that is, victories on the battlefield—rather than popular participation that had led to the unification of Germany; among the dignitaries in the Hall of Mirrors that day, only two or three were civilians. As for "iron," it meant not

only weapons but, more important, the industries required to produce weapons. Thus, after 1871, nationalism, once a dream of revolutionaries and romantics, became ever more closely associated with military force and with industry.

This chapter deals with a small group of countries—Germany, France, Britain, Russia, the United States, and Japan—that we call "great powers." In the next chapter, which deals with the era of the "New Imperialism" (1870–1914), we will see how these nations used their power to conquer colonial empires in Asia and Africa and to control Latin America. Together, Chapters 23 and 24 describe an era in which a handful of wealthy industrialized nations—all but one of them of European culture—imposed on the other peoples of the world a domination more powerful than any experienced before or since.

As you read this chapter, ask yourself the following questions:

Otto von Bismarck (UTT-oh fun BIS-mark)

- What new technologies and industries appeared between 1850 and 1900, and how did they affect the world economy?
- How did the societies of the industrial countries change during this period?
- Why do we call certain countries "great powers" but not others?

♆

NEW TECHNOLOGIES AND THE WORLD ECONOMY

After 1850, industrialization took off in new directions. Germany and the United States surpassed Great Britain as the world's leading industrial powers by 1890. Small companies were overshadowed by large corporations owned by wealthy capitalists or (especially in Russia and Japan) by governments. New technologies based on advances in physics and chemistry revolutionized everyday life and transformed the world economy.

The Steel and Chemical Industries

Steel is a special form of iron, both hard and elastic. A series of inventions in the 1850s made steel the cheapest and most versatile metal ever known. As a result, world steel production rose from a half-million tons in 1870 to 28 million in 1900, of which the United States produced 10 million, Germany 8, and Britain 4.9. Steel became cheap and abundant enough to make rails, bridges, ships, and even "tin" cans meant to be used once and thrown away.

The new steel mills were hungry consumers of coal, iron ore, limestone, and other raw materials. They took up as much space as whole towns, belched smoke and particulate night and day, and left behind huge hills of slag and other waste products. Environmental degradation affected steel-producing regions such as the English Midlands, the German Ruhr, and parts of Pennsylvania.

The chemical industry followed a similar pattern. By the early nineteenth century, only soda, sulfuric acid, and chlorine bleach (used in the cotton industry) were manufactured on a large scale, especially in Britain. Then in 1856, the development of the first synthetic dye, aniline purple, from coal tar launched the mass production of organic chemicals—compounds containing carbon atoms. These bright, long-lasting colors delighted consumers but hurt tropical countries, such as India, that produced indigo, a blue vegetable dye.

Chemistry also made important advances in the manufacture of explosives. In 1866, the Swedish scientist Alfred Nobel found a way to turn nitroglycerin into a stable solid—dynamite. This and other new explosives were very useful in mining and the construction of railroads and canals. They also enabled the armies and navies of the great powers to arm themselves with increasingly accurate and powerful rifles and cannon.

The growing complexity of industrial chemistry made it one of the first fields where science and technology interacted on a daily basis. This development gave a great advantage to Germany, which had the most advanced engineering schools and scientific institutes of its time. By the end of the nineteenth century, Germany was the world's leading producer of dyes, drugs, synthetic fertilizers, ammonia, and nitrates used in making explosives.

Electricity

The third great innovation of the late nineteenth century was **electricity.** In the 1870s, inventors devised efficient generators that turned mechanical energy into electric current and opened the way to a host of new applications. Arc lamps lit up public squares, theaters, and stores. Then in 1879, **Thomas Edison** in the United States developed an incandescent lamp well suited to lighting small rooms and in 1882 created the world's first electrical distribution network, in New York City. By the turn of the century, electric lighting was rapidly replacing dim and smelly gas lamps in the cities of Europe and North America.

Other uses of electricity quickly appeared. Electric streetcars and, later, subways helped reduce the traffic jams that clogged large cities. Electric motors replaced steam engines and power belts, increasing productivity and improving workers' safety. As demand for electricity grew, engineers learned to use waterpower to produce electricity, and hydroelectric plants were built.

Electricity helped alleviate some environmental problems, since electric motors and lamps did not pollute the air. Power plants were built at a distance from cities. As electric trains and streetcars replaced horse-drawn trolleys and coal-burning locomotives, cities became noticeably cleaner and healthier. At the same time, electricity created a huge demand for copper, bringing Chile, Montana, and southern Africa into the world economy as never before.

Shipping and Telegraph Cables

At midcentury, a series of developments radically transformed ocean shipping. Iron and steel took the place of wood. Propellers replaced paddle wheels and sails. By the turn of the century, more efficient engines could convert the heat produced by burning a single sheet of paper into the power to move 1 ton over half a mile. The average size of freighters increased from 200 tons in 1850 to 7,500 tons in 1900. The Suez Canal, constructed in 1869, shortened the distance between Europe and Asia and triggered a massive switch from sail power to steam.

The world's fleet of merchant ships grew from 9 million to 35 million tons between 1850 and 1910, as passengers, mail, and perishable freight traveled on fast and reliable scheduled liners. To control their ships around the globe, shipping companies used a new medium of communications: **submarine telegraph cables** laid on the ocean floor linking the continents. Cables were laid across the Atlantic in 1866, and by the turn of the century, cables connected every country and almost every inhabited island.

Railroads

The fifty years after 1850 saw a tremendous expansion of the world's **railroad** networks. At the end of its Civil War in 1865, the United States already had 35,000 miles (over 56,000 kilometers) of track, three times as much as Britain, and still growing. Germany, France, Canada, Russia, and Japan also built large networks.

Railroads were not confined to industrialized nations, but were constructed around the world. The British built the fourth largest rail network in the world in India (see Chapter 22). Many old cities doubled in size to accommodate railroad stations, sidings, tracks, warehouses, and repair shops. In the countryside, railroads consumed vast amounts of land and timber for ties to hold the rails and for bridges. Throughout the world, they opened new land to agriculture, mining, and other uses.

World Trade and Finance

Thanks to the growing speed and falling cost of transportation between 1850 and 1913, world trade expanded tenfold, transforming the economies of different parts of the world in different ways. The capitalist economics of western Europe and North America grew more prosperous and diversified, despite deep depressions in which workers lost their jobs and investors their fortunes.

Long after German and American industries surpassed the British, Britain continued to dominate the flow of trade, finance, and information. In 1900, two-thirds of the world's submarine cables were British or passed through Britain. Over half of the world's shipping was British owned. Britain invested one-fourth of its national wealth overseas, much of it in the United States and Argentina.

Nonindustrial areas were more vulnerable to changes in price and demand than were the industrialized nations, for many of them produced raw materials that could be replaced by synthetic substitutes or alternative sources of supply. Nevertheless, until World War I, the value of exports from the tropical countries generally remained high.

SOCIAL TRANSFORMATIONS

The technological and economic changes of the late nineteenth century sparked profound social changes in the industrial nations. A fast-growing population swelled cities to unprecedented size, and millions of Europeans emigrated to the Americas. Workers spawned labor move-

CHRONOLOGY

	Europe	United States	East Asia
1850	**1851** Majority of British population living in cities **1856** Bessemer converter; first synthetic dye **1859** Charles Darwin, *On the Origin of Species* **1861** Emancipation of serfs (Russia) **1866** Alfred Nobel develops dynamite **1867** Karl Marx, *Das Kapital*		**1853** Commodore Perry "opens" Japan
		1865 Civil War ends; economic expansion begins **1865–1914** Surge of immigration from southern and eastern Europe	
1875	**1871** Unification of Germany; unification of Italy **1875** Social Democratic Party founded in Germany **1882** Married Women's Property Act (Britain)	**1879** Thomas Edison develops incandescent lamp **1890** United States is the world's leading producer of steel **1890s** "Jim Crow" laws enforce segregation in southern states **1899** United States acquires Puerto Rico and the Philippines	**1868** Meiji Restoration begins modernization drive in Japan **1894** Sino-Japanese War
1900	**1905** Revolution of 1905 (Russia)		**1904–1905** Russo-Japanese War **1910** Japan annexes Korea

ments and new forms of radical policies, and women's lives were dramatically altered.

Population and Migrations

The population of Europe grew faster from 1850 to 1914 than ever before or since, almost doubling from 265 million to 468 million, despite mass migrations of Europeans to the United States, Canada, Australia, New Zealand, and Argentina. Between 1850 and 1900, on average, 400,000 Europeans migrated overseas every year; between 1900 and 1914, the flood rose to over 1 million a year. People of European ancestry rose from one-fifth to one-third in the world's population.

Much of the increase came from a drop in the death rate, as epidemics and starvation became less common. The Irish famine of 1847–1848 was the last peacetime famine in European history. North American wheat supplemented Europe's food. Year-round supplies of meat, fruit, vegetables, and oils improved the diet of European and North American city dwellers.

Urbanization and Social Structures

In 1851, Britain became the first nation to have a majority of its population living in towns and cities. By 1914, 80 percent of its population was urban, as were 60 percent of the German and 45 percent of the French populations. London grew from 2.7 million in 1850 to 6.6 million in 1900. New York

Urban Growth: Vienna in 1873 During the nineteenth century, European cities grew with unprecedented speed. This bird's-eye view of the Austro-Hungarian capital shows the transformation. The densely populated inner city surrounded the cathedral. In 1857, high walls that once had protected the old city from attack were torn down to make room for the Ringstrasse, a broad, tree-shaded boulevard lined with public buildings, museums, churches, and a university. Beyond the Ring, the newly wealthy bourgeoisie built new neighborhoods of large houses and apartment buildings. (Museen der Stadt, Vienna)

reached 3.4 million by 1900, a fifty-fold increase in the century. In the English Midlands, in the German Ruhr, and around Tokyo Bay, towns fused into one another, filling in the fields and woods that once had separated them.

In early industrial cities, the poor crowded together in unsanitary tenements. New urban technologies transformed city life for most residents. Pipes brought in clean water and carried away sewage. First gas and then electric lighting made cities safer and more pleasant at night. By the end of the century, municipal governments provided police and fire departments, schools, parks, and other amenities unheard of a century earlier.

As sanitation improved, urban death rates fell below birthrates for the first time. Confident that

their children would survive infancy, couples began to limit the number of children they had. To accommodate the growing population, planners laid out new cities, such as Chicago, on a rectangular grid, and middle-class families moved to new developments on the edges of cities. In Paris, older neighborhoods with narrow, crooked streets and rickety tenements were replaced with broad boulevards and modern apartment buildings. Brilliantly lit by gas and electricity, Paris became the "city of lights," a model for city planners from New Delhi to Buenos Aires. By 1900, electric streetcars and subways allowed working-class people to live miles from their workplaces.

In fast-growing cities such as London, New York, and Chicago, newcomers arrived so quickly that housing construction and municipal services could not keep up. Immigrants who saved their money to reunite their families could not afford costly municipal services. As a result, the poorest neighborhoods remained as overcrowded, unhealthy, and dangerous as they had been since the early decades of industrialization.

While urban environments improved in many ways, air quality worsened. Coal, burned to power steam engines and heat buildings, polluted the air, coating everything with a film of grimy dust. And the thousands of horses that pulled the carts and carriages covered the streets with their wastes, causing a terrible stench.

Labor Movements and Socialist Politics

Industrialization combined with the revolutionary ideas of the late eighteenth century to produce two kinds of movements—socialism and labor movements—calling for further changes. **Socialism** was an ideology developed by radical thinkers who questioned the sanctity of private property and argued in support of industrial workers against their employers. **Labor unions** were organizations formed by industrial workers to defend their interests in negotiations with employers. The socialist and labor movements were never identical. Most of the time they were allies; occasionally they were rivals.

Labor unions sought not only better wages but also improved working conditions and insurance against illness, accidents, disability, and old age. They grew slowly because strikes were illegal and hard to sustain. When laws were relaxed, British, German, and American labor grew rapidly.

By far the best-known socialist was **Karl Marx** (1818–1883), a German journalist who lived most of his life in England. The ideas he expressed succinctly in the *Communist Manifesto* (1848) and in great detail in *Das Kapital°* (1867) provided an intellectual framework for the growing dissatisfaction with raw industrial capitalism. He argued that the capitalists unfairly extracted the "surplus value" of workers' labor—that is, the difference between workers' wages and the value of the goods

they manufactured. The concentration of wealth in a few hands convinced Marx that class struggle between workers and owners was inevitable. But the International Working Man's Association Marx helped found in 1864 attracted more intellectuals than workers. Workers found other means of redressing their grievances, such as the vote and labor unions.

The nineteenth century saw a gradual extension of the right to vote throughout Europe and North America. Universal male suffrage became law in the United States in 1870, in France and Germany in 1871, in Britain in 1885, and in the rest of Europe soon after. With universal male suffrage, socialist politicians could expect to capture many seats in their nations' parliaments, because the newly enfranchised working class was so numerous. Democratic socialist parties sought to use voting power to gain concessions from government and eventually even to win elections.

Working-Class Women and Men

Working-class women led lives of toil and pain, considerably harder than the lives of their menfolk. Although the worst abuses of child labor had been banned in most European countries by 1850, parents expected girls as young as ten to contribute to the household. Many became domestic servants, commonly working sixteen or more hours a day, six and a half days a week, for little more than room and board. Their living quarters, usually in the attic or basement, contrasted with the luxurious quarters of their masters. Female servants were vulnerable to sexual abuse by their masters or their masters' sons.

Young women often preferred work in a factory to domestic service. Men worked in construction, iron and steel, heavy machinery, or on railroads; women worked in textiles and the clothing trades, two extensions of traditional women's household work. Most industrial countries passed legislation limiting the hours or forbidding the employment of women in the hardest and most dangerous occupations, such as mining and foundry work. Such legislation also reinforced gender divisions in industry, keeping women in low-paid, subordinate positions.

Das Kapital (DUSS cop-ee-TALL)

Married women with children were expected to stay home, even if their husbands did not make enough to support the family. In addition to the work of child rearing and housework, married women of the working class contributed to the family's income by taking in boarders, sewing, or weaving baskets. The hardest and worst-paid work was washing other people's clothes. Since electric lighting and indoor plumbing cost more than most working-class families could afford, even ordinary household duties like cooking and washing remained heavy burdens.

The poorest of the poor were orphans and single women with children. Unable to find jobs or support themselves at home, many turned to prostitution. The wealth of middle-class men made it easy for them to take advantage of the poverty of working-class women.

The Victorian Age and Women's "Separate Sphere"

In English-speaking countries, the period from about 1850 to 1914 is known as the **Victorian Age.** The expression refers not only to the reign of Queen Victoria of England (r. 1837–1901) but to rules of behavior and to an ideology surrounding the family and the relations between men and women. The Victorians contrasted the masculine ideals of strength and courage with the feminine virtues of beauty and kindness, and they idealized the home as a peaceful and loving refuge from the dog-eat-dog world of competitive capitalism.

Victorian morality claimed to be universal, yet it best fit the European upper- and middle-class family. Men and women were thought to belong in **"separate spheres."** Successful businessmen spent their time at work or relaxing in men's clubs. They put their wives in charge of rearing the children, running the household, and spending the family money to enhance the family's social status.

The most important duty of middle-class women was rearing children. Unlike the rich of previous eras, who handed their children over to wet nurses and tutors, Victorian mothers nursed their own babies and showered their children with love and attention. Even those who could afford nannies and governesses remained personally in-volved in their children's education. While boys were being prepared for the business world or the professions, girls were taught such skills as embroidery, drawing, and music, which offered no monetary reward or professional preparation but enhanced their social graces and marriage prospects.

Young women could work until they got married, but only in genteel occupations such as retail and office work. Jobs that required higher education, especially jobs in the professions, were closed to women. Until late in the century, few universities granted degrees to women. The first profession open to women was teaching, as more and more countries passed laws calling for universal compulsory education. Women were considered well suited to teaching young children and girls—an extension of the duties of Victorian mothers. Teaching, however, was judged suitable only for single women; married women were expected to stay home, taking care of their own children.

Governments enforced legal discrimination against women. Until the end of the century, most European countries considered women minors for life—that is, subject to their fathers before marriage and to their husbands after. Even Britain, among the most progressive countries, did not give women the right to control their own property until 1882, with passage of the Married Women's Property Act.

Some middle-class women organized to fight prostitution, alcohol, and child labor. By the turn of the century, a few were challenging male domination of politics and the law. By 1914, women had won the right to vote in twelve states of the United States. British women did not vote until 1918. (See Society and Culture: Demonstrating for Women's Rights.)

NATIONALISM AND THE UNIFICATION OF GERMANY

The most influential idea of the nineteenth century was **nationalism.** The French revolutionaries had defined people, previously considered the subjects of a sovereign, as the citizens

Demonstrating for Women's Rights

Before the First World War, no country allowed all women to vote. In Britain, women who demonstrated for voting rights were known as "suffragettes." When petitions to Parliament and peaceful demonstrations had no effect, Emmeline Pankhurst, the leader of the movement, concluded that more forceful measures were required. In the following passage, she describes the tactics she devised to call attention to the cause of women's suffrage.

Whatever preparations the police department were making to prevent the demonstration, they failed because, while as usual, we were able to calculate exactly what the police department were going to do, they were utterly unable to calculate what we were able to do. We had planned a demonstration for March 4th, and this one we announced. We planned another demonstration for March 1st, but this one we did not announce. Late on the afternoon of Friday, March 1st, I drove in a taxicab, accompanied by the Hon. Secretary of the Union, Mrs. Tuke and another of our members, to No. 10 Downing Street, the official residence of the Prime Minister. It was exactly half past five when we alighted from the cab and threw our stones, four of them, through the window panes. As we expected we were promptly arrested and taken to Cannon Row police station. The hour that followed will long be remembered in London. At intervals of fifteen minutes relays of women who had volunteered for the demonstration did their work. The first smashing of glass occurred in the Haymarket and Picadilly, and greatly startled and alarmed both pedestrians and po-

lice. A large number of women were arrested, and everybody thought that this ended the affair. But before the excited populace and the frustrated shop owners' first exclamation had died down, before the police had reached the station with their prisoners, the ominous crashing and splintering of plate glass began again, this time along both sides of Regent Street and the Strand. A furious rush of police and people toward the second scene of action ensued. While their attention was taken up with occurrences in this quarter, the third relay of women began breaking the windows in Oxford Circus and Bond Street. The demonstration ended for the day at half past six with the breaking of many windows in the Strand. . . .

The demonstration had taken place in the morning, when a hundred or more women had walked quietly into Knightsbridge and walking singly along the streets demolished nearly every pane of glass they passed. Taken by surprise the police arrested as many as they would reach, but most of the women escaped.

For that two days' work something like two hundred suffragettes were taken to the various police stations, and for days the long procession of women streamed through the courts.

If the goal was to obtain the right to vote, why did the demonstrators break store windows? And why did they do so at fifteen-minute intervals?

Source: Emmeline Pankhurst, *My Own Story* (London, 1914), pp. 211–219.

of a *nation*—a concept identified with a territory, the state that ruled it, and the culture of its people. Because the most widely spoken language in nineteenth-century Europe was German, the unification of most German-speaking people into a single state in 1871 had momentous consequences for the world.

National Identity Before 1871

The idea of redrawing the boundaries of states to accommodate linguistic, religious, or cultural differences was revolutionary. Language was usually the crucial element in creating a feeling of national unity, but language and citizenship seldom coincided. The fit between France and the French language was exceptional. The Italian- and German-speaking peoples were divided among many small states. Living in the Austrian Empire were peoples who spoke German, Czech, Slovak, Hungarian, Polish, and other languages. Even where people spoke a common language, they could be divided by religion or institutions. The Irish, though English speaking, were mostly Catholic, whereas the English were primarily Protestant.

Until the 1860s, nationalism was associated with **liberalism,** the revolutionary middle-class ideology that emerged from the French Revolution (see Chapter 20) and asserted the sovereignty of the people and demanded constitutional government, a national parliament, and freedom of expression. The most famous nationalist of the early nineteenth century, Giuseppe Mazzini° (1805–1872), led a failed liberal revolution of 1848 in Italy that sought to unify the Italian peninsula. Although the revolutions of 1848 failed except in France, their strength convinced conservative governments that they could not forever keep their citizens out of politics and that mass politics, if properly managed, could strengthen rather than weaken the state. A new generation of conservative political leaders learned how to preserve the social status quo through public education, universal military service, and colonial conquests, all of which built a sense of national unity.

Giuseppe Mazzini (jew-SEP-pay mat-SEE-nee)

The Unification of Germany

Some German nationalists wanted to unite all Germans under the Catholic Austrian throne. Others wanted to exclude Austria with its many non-Germanic peoples and unite all other German-speaking areas under Lutheran Prussia. The Prussian state had two advantages: (1) the newly developed industries of the Rhineland and (2) the first European army to make use of railroads, telegraphs, breechloading rifles, steel artillery, and other products of modern industry. The king of Prussia, Wilhelm I (r. 1861–1888), had entrusted the running of his government to his chancellor, the brilliant and authoritarian aristocrat **Otto von Bismarck** (1815–1898), who was determined to use Prussian military and German nationalism to advance the interests of the Prussian state.

In 1864, after a quick victory against Denmark, he set his sights on Austria, which surrendered in 1866. To everyone's surprise, Prussia took no Austrian territory. Instead, Prussia and some smaller states formed the North German Confederation, the nucleus of a future Germany. Then in 1870, Bismarck provoked a war with France. In this "Franco-Prussian War," German armies used their superior firepower and tactics to achieve a quick victory.

The spoils of victory included a large indemnity and two provinces of Alsace and Lorraine. To the Germans, this region was German because a majority of its inhabitants spoke German. To the French, it was French because it had been so when the nation of France was forged in the Revolution and because most of its inhabitants considered themselves French. These two conflicting definitions of nationalism kept enmity between France and Germany smoldering for decades.

Nationalism After 1871

The Franco-Prussian War changed the political climate of Europe. France became wholeheartedly liberal. The Italian peninsula became unified as the kingdom of Italy. Germany, Austria-Hungary (as the Austrian Empire had renamed itself in 1867), and Russia remained conservative.

All politicians tried to manipulate public opinion to bolster their governments. The spread of literacy allowed politicians and journalists to appeal to the emotions of the poor, diverting their anger from their employers to foreigners and their votes from socialist to nationalist parties.

In many countries, the dominant group used nationalism to justify the imposing of its language, religion, or customs on minority populations. The Russian Empire attempted to "Russify" its diverse ethnic populations. The Spanish government made the Spanish language compulsory in the schools, newspapers, and courts of its Basque- and Catalan-speaking provinces. Immigrants to the United States were expected to learn English.

Some people looked to science for support of political dominance. One of the most influential scientists of the century, and the one whose ideas were most widely cited and misinterpreted, was the English biologist **Charles Darwin** (1809–1882), who had spent years traveling through South America and the South Pacific studying plant and animal life. His famous book, *On the Origin of Species by Means of Natural Selection* (1859), argued that over hundreds of thousands of years, living beings had either evolved in the struggle for survival or become extinct. The philosopher Herbert Spencer (1820–1903) and others took up Darwin's ideas of "natural selection" and "survival of the fittest" and applied them to human society. Extreme Social Darwinists developed elaborate pseudo-scientific theories of racial differences, claiming that they were the result not of history but of biology.

THE GREAT POWERS OF EUROPE, 1871–1900

After 1871, politicians and journalists discovered how easily they could whip up popular frenzy against neighboring countries. Rivalries over colonial territories, ideological differences between liberal and conservative governments, and even minor border incidents or trade disagreements contributed to a growing atmosphere of international tension.

Germany at the Center of Europe

International relations revolved around a united Germany, because Germany was located in the center of Europe and had the most powerful army on the European continent. After creating a unified Germany in 1871, Bismarck worked to maintain peace in Europe. To isolate France, he forged a loose coalition with Austria-Hungary and Russia, which he was able to keep together for twenty years.

Bismarck proved equally adept at manipulating mass politics at home. To weaken the influence of middle-class liberals, he extended the vote to all adult men. By imposing high tariffs on manufactured goods and wheat, he gained the support of both the wealthy industrialists of the Rhineland and the great landowners of eastern Germany. He stole the thunder of the socialists by introducing social legislation—medical, unemployment, and disability insurance and old-age pensions—long before other industrial countries did. Under his leadership, the German people developed a strong sense of national unity and pride in their industrial and military power.

In 1888, Wilhelm I was succeeded by his grandson Wilhelm II (r. 1888–1918), who dismissed Chancellor Bismarck. Wilhelm II talked about his "global policy" and demanded that Germany, with the mightiest army and the largest industrial economy in Europe, have a colonial empire, "a place in the sun."

The Liberal Powers: France and Great Britain

France, once the dominant nation in Europe, had difficulty reconciling itself to being in second place. Its population and its army lagged far behind Germany's. French industry was growing much slower than Germany's, due to the loss of the iron and coal mines of Lorraine. The French people were deeply divided over the very nature of the state: some were monarchists and Catholics; a growing number held republican and anticlerical views. Despite these problems, a long tradition of popular participation in politics and a strong sense of nationhood, reinforced by a fine system of universal public education, gave the French people a deeper cohesion than appeared on the surface.

Great Britain was the only other country in Europe with a democratic tradition. The British government alternated smoothly between the Liberal and Conservative Parties, and the income gap between rich and poor gradually narrowed. Nevertheless, Britain had problems that grew more apparent as time went on.

One problem was Irish resentment of English rule as a foreign occupying force. Another problem was the British economy. Once the workshop of the world, Great Britain had fallen behind the United States and Germany in such important industries as iron and steel, chemicals, electricity, and textiles. Even in shipbuilding and shipping, Britain's traditional specialties, Germany was catching up. Britain was also preoccupied with its enormous and fast-growing empire. Though a source of wealth for investors and the envy of other imperialist nations, the empire was a constant drain on Britain's finances.

After the Crimean War of 1854–1856 (see Chapter 21), Britain turned its back on Europe and pursued a policy of "splendid isolation." Britain's preoccupation with India led British statesmen to exaggerate the Russian threat to the shipping routes through the Mediterranean and Central Asia.

The Conservative Powers: Russia and Austria-Hungary

The forces of nationalism weakened rather than strengthened Russia and Austria-Hungary. The reason for this effect was that their populations were far more divided, socially and ethnically, than were the German, French, or British peoples.

Nationalism was most divisive in the Austrian Empire. The decision to rename itself the Austro-Hungarian Empire in 1867 appeased its Hungarian critics but alienated its Slavic-speaking minorities. The Austro-Hungarian Empire still thought of itself as a great power and attempted to dominate the Balkans. This strategy irritated Russia, which thought of itself as the protector of Slavic peoples everywhere, and it eventually led to war.

Russia was the most misunderstood country in Europe. Its enormous size and population led many Europeans to exaggerate its military potential, but Russia was weakened by national and social divisions. All in all, only 45 percent of the peoples of the tsarist empire spoke Russian.

To strengthen the bonds between the monarchy and the Russian people and promote industrialization by enlarging the labor pool, the moderate conservative Tsar Alexander II (r. 1855–1881) emancipated the peasants from serfdom in 1861. That measure, however, did not create a modern society but only turned serfs into communal farmers with few skills and little capital. Though technically "emancipated," the great majority of Russians had little education, few legal rights, and no say in their government. After Alexander's assassination in 1881, his successors Alexander III (r. 1881–1894) and Nicholas II (r. 1894–1917) opposed all forms of social change. Industrialization consisted largely of state-sponsored projects, such as railroads, iron foundries, and armament factories, and led to social unrest among urban workers. Wealthy landowning aristocrats continued to dominate the Russian court and administration and succeeded in blocking most reforms.

The weaknesses in Russia's society and government became glaringly obvious after Russia's defeat in the Russo-Japanese War of 1904–1905 (see below). The shock of defeat caused a popular uprising, the Revolution of 1905, that forced Tsar Nicholas II to grant a constitution and an elected Duma (parliament). But as soon as he was able to rebuild the army and the police, he reverted to the traditional despotism of his forefathers. Small groups of radical intellectuals, angered by the contrast between the wealth of the elite and the poverty of the common people, began plotting the violent overthrow of the tsarist autocracy.

The Doss House   Late-nineteenth-century cities showed more physical than social improvements. This painting by Makovsky of a street in St. Petersburg contrasts the broad avenue and impressive buildings with the poverty of the crowd.   (The state Russian Museum/Smithsonian Institution Traveling Exhibit)

NEW GREAT POWERS: THE UNITED STATES AND JAPAN

Europeans had come to regard their continent as the center of the universe and their states as the only great powers in the world. The rest of the world was either ignored or used as bargaining chips in the game of power politics. The late nineteenth century marked the high point of European power and arrogance, yet at that very moment, two nations outside Europe were becoming great powers. One of them, the United States, was inhabited mainly by people of European origin, and its rise to great-power status had been predicted early in the nineteenth century by astute observers like the French statesman Alexis de Tocqueville. The other one, Japan, seemed so distant and exotic in 1850 that no European had guessed it would join the ranks of the great powers.

The United States, 1865–1900

After the Civil War ended in 1865, the United States entered a period of vigorous growth. Hundreds of thousands of immigrants arrived every year, mainly from Russia, Italy, and Central Europe, raising the population to 63 million in 1891. Although many settled on the newly opened lands west of the Mississippi (see Map 23.1), most of the migrants moved to the towns, which mushroomed

Emigrant Waiting Room The opening of the western region of the United States attracted settlers from the east coast and from Europe. These migrants are waiting for a train to take them to the Black Hills of Dakota during one of the gold rushes of the late nineteenth century. (Library of Congress)

into cities in a few years. In the process, the nation became an industrial giant. By 1900, the United States had overtaken Britain and Germany as the world's leading industrial power.

This explosive growth was accomplished with few government restrictions and much government help, such as free land for railroads and protective tariffs. In this atmosphere of unfettered free enterprise, the nation got rich fast, as did its upper and middle classes.

Expansion created many victims. First among them were the American Indians. When the railroads penetrated the west after the Civil War, they brought white colonists eager to start farming, ranching, or mining. The indigenous Indians whose lands they invaded fought back with great courage but were outnumbered and outgunned. In Canada, the government tried to protect the Indians from the whites. The United States Army, how-

ever, always sided with the settlers. The U.S. government had signed numerous treaties with the Indians but tore them up when settlers demanded land. After decades of warfare, massacres, and starvation, the government confined the remaining Indians to reservations on the poorest lands.

The U.S. government also abandoned African-Americans in 1877, after the end of Reconstruction, especially in the defeated southern states. Though freed from slavery in 1865, most of them became sharecroppers who were at the mercy of their landowners. In the 1890s, the southern states instituted "Jim Crow" laws segregating blacks in public transportation, jobs, and schools. Not only did southern judges apply harsh laws in a biased manner, but black Americans were also subject to the lawless violence of mobs, which lynched an average of fifty blacks a year until well into the twentieth century.

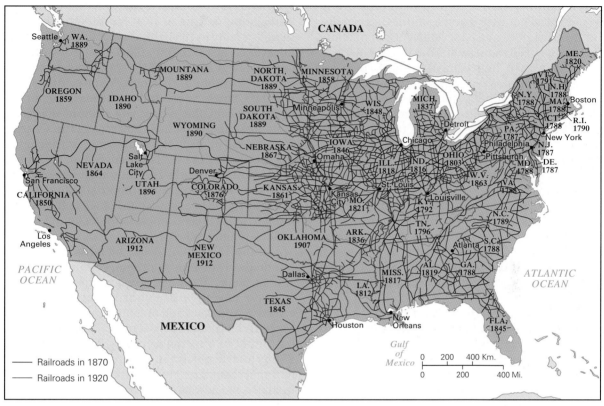

Map 23.1   The United States, 1850–1920   This map shows the expansion of the United States from the coasts into the interior of the continent. In the western half of the continent, only California and Texas were states in 1850; territories located farther from the coasts became states later. The economic development, shown by the railroad lines, followed much the same pattern, radiating west and south from the northeastern states and—to a lesser extent—eastward from California.

Racism also affected Asian immigrants, many of whom had come to the United States to build railroads in the western states. In 1882, the U.S. government barred the Chinese from immigrating by enacting the first of many racial exclusion laws.

Working-class whites benefited little from the booming economy. Economic depressions in 1873 and 1893 caused more distress in the United States than in Europe, because the United States had few labor laws and no unemployment compensation to soften the hardships. Police or the army repressed strikes and unions. The courts consistently supported employers against their employees, capital against labor, and business against government.

Working-class women bore the brunt of repressive labor practices because they earned less

than men, had more responsibilities, and seldom were members of labor unions. As in Britain, activist middle-class women organized to demand female suffrage and to fight against alcohol, prostitution, and other social evils.

The booming economy and the waves of immigrants radically transformed the environment. Timber companies clear-cut large areas of Michigan, Wisconsin, and the Appalachian Mountains to provide lumber for railroad ties and frame houses, pulp for paper, and fuel for locomotives and iron foundries. Farmers cleared the forests and plowed the prairies. Buffalo, the dominant animals of the western territories, were massacred by the hundreds of thousands to starve out the Indians and clear the land for cattle. In the west, the government began massive irrigation projects. In the industrial northeast, iron foundries, steel mills, and steam engines caused severe local air pollution.

In spite of all the assaults, the North American continent was so huge that large parts of it remained unspoiled. A few especially beautiful areas were declared national parks, beginning with Yellowstone in Wyoming in 1872, thereby marking a new stage in Americans' attitude toward nature. Thanks to the efforts of naturalist John Muir and President Theodore Roosevelt (1901–1909), large parts of the western states were set aside as national forests.

Most citizens showed little interest in foreign affairs. Patriots tended to celebrate American freedom and democracy, the conquest of a huge continent, and the country's remarkable technological achievements. In this period, the inventor Thomas Edison was probably the most admired man in America.

The expansionism of the United States and its businesses did not stop at the borders but exerted a strong influence on Mexico and the Caribbean. Naval officers, bankers, and politicians urged active intervention in the Western Hemisphere. In 1899, the United States defeated Spain, annexed Puerto Rico and the Philippines, and turned Cuba into an American protectorate (see Chapter 24). Long recognized as the leading power in the Americas, the United States found itself involved in Asian affairs as well. Nevertheless, although their country was fast becoming a global power, most Americans still preferred George Washington's policy of "no European entanglements."

The Rise of Japan, 1850–1900

China and Japan both felt the influence of the Western powers as never before in the late nineteenth century, but their responses were completely opposite. As Chapter 22 explained, China resisted Western influence and became weaker. Japan transformed itself into a major industrial and military power (see Map 23.2).

In 1853, the arrival of a small U.S. fleet with demands for an opening of Japan to trade with the United States sparked a crisis in the Tokugawa Shogunate that governed Japan. Aware of China's humiliating defeats in the Opium Wars, officials signed a treaty in 1858. But the treaty sparked a political crisis in the country that led to the overthrow of the Shogunate in 1868 and proclaimed the "Meiji° Restoration." The new Japanese rulers, unlike the Chinese, were under no illusion that they could fend off the Westerners without changing their institutions or their society. In the Charter Oath issued in 1868, the young emperor included the prophetic phrase: "Knowledge shall be sought throughout the world and thus shall be strengthened the foundation of the imperial polity." It was to be the motto of a new Japan, which embraced all foreign ideas, institutions, and techniques that could strengthen the nation.

In the 1870s and 1880s, the government sent hundreds of students to Britain, Germany, and the United States and hired foreign experts to teach Japanese how to build railroads, organize a modern army and navy, and operate a bureaucracy. The Meiji leaders created a government structure similar to that of imperial Germany. They introduced Western-style posts and telegraphs, railroads and harbors, banking, clocks, and calendars. They modeled the new Japanese navy on the British and the army on the Prussian. They even encouraged foreign clothing styles and pastimes. In 1889, Japan promulgated a new and authoritarian constitution modeled on that of Germany, with a bicameral legislature and a cabinet led by a prime minister. But the army and navy remained free of civilian control, only wealthy men were allowed to vote, and important decisions were made without popular input or even knowledge.

The government was especially interested in Western technology. It opened vocational, technical, and agricultural schools and founded four imperial universities. It brought in foreign experts to advise on medicine, science, and engineering. The Japanese government also encouraged industrialization. It taxed farmers heavily to pay for the purchase of ships, machines, and other capital goods. It set up state-owned enterprises to manufacture cloth and inexpensive consumer goods for sale abroad. In 1881, to pay off its debts, the govern-

Meiji (MAY-gee)

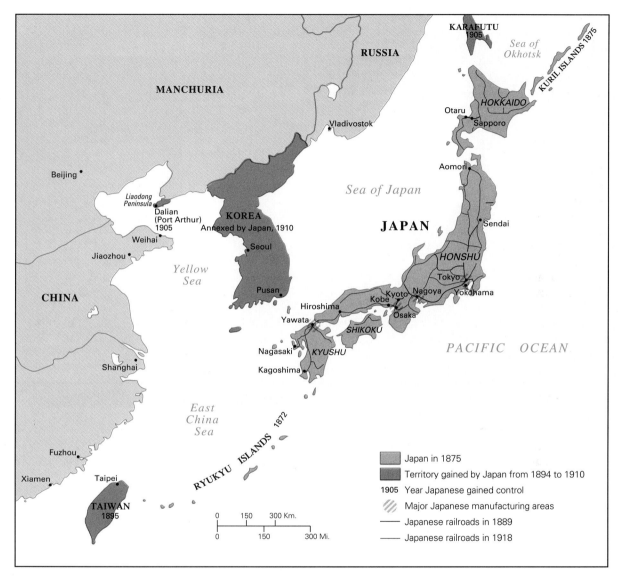

Map 23.2   Expansion and Modernization of Japan, 1868–1918   As Japan acquired modern industry, it followed the example of the European powers in seeking overseas colonies. Its colonial empire grew at the expense of its neighbors: Taiwan was taken from China in 1895, Karafutu (now Sakhalin) from Russia in 1905, and all of Korea became a colony in 1910.

Arrivals from the East In 1853, Commodore Matthew Perry's ships surprised the Tokugawa Shogunate by appearing not in Kyushu or southern Honshu, where European ships previously had been spotted, but at Uraga on the coast of eastern Honshu. The Japanese soon learned that Perry had come not from the south but across the Pacific from the east. The novelty of the threat unsettled the provincial leaders, who were largely responsible for their own defense. In this print done after the Meiji Restoration, the traditionally dressed local samurai go out to confront the mysterious "black ships." (Courtesy of the Trustees of the British Museum)

ment sold these enterprises to private investors, mainly large *zaibatsu*°, or conglomerates.

Japan began to define its own "sphere of influence" that would include Korea, Manchuria, and part of China. In 1894, Japan went to war with China over Korea, defeating its much larger but weaker adversary in less than six months. China had to evacuate Korea, cede Taiwan and the Liaodong Peninsula, and pay a heavy indemnity. By 1900, Japan was sufficiently Westernized that the Western powers rescinded the unequal treaties

they had imposed forty years earlier, although they did make Japan return the Liaodong Peninsula to China.

Emboldened by China's obvious weakness, Japan and Russia competed for possession of the mineral-rich Chinese province of Manchuria. In 1905, Japan surprised the world by defeating Russia in the Russo-Japanese War. In spite of Western attempts to restrict it to the role of junior partner, Japan continued to increase its influence. It gained control of southern Manchuria, with its industries and railroads, and established a protectorate over Korea. In 1910, it finally annexed Korea, joining the ranks of the world's colonial powers.

zaibatsu (zye-BOT-soo)

CONCLUSION

After World War I broke out in 1914, many people, especially in Europe, looked back on the period from 1850 to 1914 as a golden age. For some, and in certain ways, it was. Industrialization was a powerful torrent changing Europe, North America, and East Asia. While other technologies like shipping and railroads increased their global reach, new ones—electricity, the steel and chemical industries, and the global telegraph network—contributed to the enrichment and empowerment of the industrial nations. Memories of the great scourges—famines, wars, and epidemics—faded. Clean water, electric lights, and railways began to improve the lives of city dwellers, even the poor. Goods from distant lands, even travel to other continents, came within the reach of millions.

European and American society seemed to be heading toward better organization and greater security. Municipal services made city life less dangerous and chaotic. Through labor unions, workers achieved some measure of recognition and security. By the turn of the century, liberal political reforms had taken hold in western Europe and the United States and seemed about to triumph in Russia as well. Morality and legislation aimed at providing security for women and families, though equality between the sexes was still beyond reach.

The framework for all these changes was the nation-state. The world economy, international politics, even cultural and social issues revolved around a handful of countries—the great powers—that believed themselves in control of the destiny of the world. These included the most powerful European nations of the previous century, as well as two newcomers—the United States and Japan—that were to play important roles in the future. Seldom in history had there been such a concentration of wealth, power, and self-confidence.

The success of the great powers rested on their ability to extract resources from nature and from other societies, especially in Asia, Africa, and Latin America. In a global context, the counterpart of the rise of the great powers is the story of imperialism and colonialism. To complete our understanding of the period before 1914, let us turn now to the relations between the great powers and the rest of the world.

■ Key Terms

steel	Karl Marx
electricity	Victorian Age
Thomas Edison	"separate spheres"
submarine telegraph cables	nationalism
railroads	liberalism
socialism	Otto von Bismarck
labor unions	Charles Darwin

■ Suggested Reading

Industrialization is the subject of Peter Stearns, *The Industrial Revolution in World History* (1993), and David Landes, *The Unbound Prometheus: Technological Change and Industrial Development in Western Europe from 1750 to the Present* (1969). Two interesting works on nationalism are E. J. Hobsbawm, *Nation and Nationalism Since 1780* (1990), and Benedict Anderson, *Imagined Communities: Reflections on the Origin and Spread of Nationalism* (1991).

Barrington Moore, *The Social Origins of Dictatorship and Democracy* (1966), is a classic essay on European society. On European women, see Renate Bridenthal, Claudia Koonz, and Susan Stuard, eds., *Becoming Visible: Women in European History* (1987); Patricia Branca, *Silent Sisterhood: Middle-Class Women in the Victorian Home* (1975); Louise Tilly and Joan Scott, *Women, Work, and Family* (1987); and Theresa McBride, *The Domestic Revolution: The Modernization of Household Service in England and France, 1820–1920* (1976). The history of family life is told in Beatrice Gottlieb, *The Family in the Western World from the Black Death to the Industrial Age* (1993). Albert Lindemann, *A History of European Socialism* (1983), covers the labor movements as well.

There are many excellent histories of individual countries. Germany in the late nineteenth century is well treated in Erich Eyck, *Bismarck and the German Empire* (1964). On Britain, see Donald Read, *The Age of Urban Democracy: England, 1868–1914* (1994), and David Thomson, *England in the Nineteenth Century, 1815–1914*

(1978). On France, Eugen Weber, *Peasants into Frenchmen* (1976), and Roger Price, *A Social History of Nineteenth-Century France* (1987), are especially recommended. A good introduction to Russian history is Hans Rogger, *Russia in the Age of Modernization and Revolution, 1881–1917* (1983).

Three very different aspects of American life are described in Carl Degler, *Out of Our Past: The Forces That Shaped Modern America* (1970); Thomas Hughes, *American Genesis: A Century of Invention and Technological Enthusiasm* (1989); and John Opie, *Nature's Nation: An Environmental History of the United States* (1998).

There are several interesting books on Japan, in particular Peter Duus, *The Rise of Modern Japan*, 2d ed. (1998), and Tessa Morris-Suzuki, *The Technological Transformation of Japan* (1994). Two fine books cover the history of modern China: John King Fairbank, *The Great Chinese Revolution, 1800–1985* (1987), and Jonathan D. Spence, *The Search for Modern China* (1990).

THE NEW IMPERIALISM,
1869–1914

The New Imperialism: Motives and Methods • The Scramble for Africa • Asia and Western Dominance • Imperialism in Latin America • The World Economy and the Global Environment

ENVIRONMENT AND TECHNOLOGY: Imperialism and Tropical Ecology

n November 1869, Empress Eugénie of France, Emperor Francis Joseph of Austria-Hungary, and sixteen hundred other dignitaries from the Middle East and Europe assembled at Port Said° in Egypt to celebrate the inauguration of the greatest construction project of the century: the **Suez Canal.** Ismail°, the khedive° (ruler) of Egypt, had invited all the Christian princes of Europe and all the Muslim princes of Asia and Africa, except the Ottoman sultan, his nominal overlord. He wanted to show that Egypt was not only independent but an equal of the great powers.

Ismail used this occasion to emphasize the harmony and cooperation between the peoples of Africa, Asia, and Europe. A French journalist wrote:

> This multitude, coming from all parts of the world, presented the most varied and singular spectacle. All races were represented. . . . We

saw, coming to attend this festival of civilization, men of the Orient wearing clothes of dazzling colors, chiefs of African tribes wrapped in their great coats, Circassians in war costumes, officers of the British army of India with their shakos [hats] wrapped in muslin, Hungarian magnates wearing their national costumes.[1]

To bless the inauguration, Ismail also had invited clergy of the Muslim, Orthodox, and Catholic faiths. A reporter noted: "The Khedive . . . wished to symbolize thereby the unity of men and their brotherhood before God, without distinction of religion; it was the first time that the Orient had seen such a meeting of faiths to celebrate and bless together a great event and a great work."[2]

The canal was a great success, but not in the way Ismail intended it to be. Ships using it could travel between Europe and India in less than two weeks—much less time than the month or longer consumed by sailing around Africa and into the Indian Ocean. By lowering freight costs, the canal stimulated shipping and the construction of steamships, giving an

---

Port Said (port sah-EED)   Ismail (is-mah-EEL)
khedive (kuh-DEEV)

Opening of the Suez Canal   When the canal opened in 1869, thousands of dignitaries and ordinary people gathered to watch the ships go by.   (Bildarchiv Preussischer Kulturbesitz)

advantage to nations that had heavy industry and a large maritime trade over land-based empires and countries that had few merchant ships. Great Britain, which long opposed construction of the canal for fear that it might fall into enemy hands, benefited more than any other nation. France, which provided half of the capital and most of the engineers, came in a distant second, for it had less trade with Asia than Britain did. Egypt, which contributed the other half of the money and most of the labor, was the loser in this affair. Instead of making Egypt powerful and independent, the Suez Canal provided the excuse for a British invasion and occupation of Egypt. Far from inaugurating an era of harmony among the peoples of three continents and three faiths, the canal triggered a wave of European domination over Africa and Asia.

Between 1869 and 1914 Germany, France, Britain, Russia, and the United States used industrial technology to impose their will on the nonindustrial parts of the world. Historians use the expression **New Imperialism** to describe this exercise of power.

As you read this chapter, ask yourself the following questions:

CHRONOLOGY

	The Scramble for Africa	Asia and Western Dominance	Imperialism in Latin America
1870	**1869** Opening of the Suez Canal **1874** British warfare against the Asante (Gold Coast) **1877–1879** British wars against the Xhosa and the the Zulu (South Africa) **1882** British forces occupy Egypt **1884–1885** Berlin Conference; Leopold II obtains Congo Free State	**1862–1895** French conquer Indochina **1865–1876** Russian forces advance into Central Asia **1878** United States obtains Pago Pago Harbor (Samoa) **1885** Britain completes conquest of Burma **1887** United States obtains Pearl Harbor (Hawaii) **1894–1895** China defeated in Sino-Japanese War **1895** France completes conquest of Indochina	**1870–1910** Railroad building boom: British companies in Argentina and Brazil; U.S. companies in Mexico.
1890			
			1895–1898 Cubans revolt against Spanish rule
	1899–1902 South African War between Afrikaners and the British **1902** First Aswan Dam completed (Egypt)	**1898** United States annexes Hawaii and purchases Philippines from Spain **1899–1902** U.S. forces conquer and occupy Philippines **1903** Russia completes Trans-Siberian Railway **1904–1905** Russia defeated in Russo-Japanese War	**1898** Spanish-American War; United States annexes Puerto Rico and Guam **1903** United States backs secession of Panama from Colombia **1904–1907, 1916** U.S. troops occupy Dominican Republic **1904–1914** United States builds Panama Canal **1912** U.S. troops occupy Nicaragua and Honduras
1910	**1908** Belgium annexes Congo		

- What motivated the industrial nations to conquer new territories, and what means did they use?

- Which parts of the world were annexed to the new empires, and which ones became economic dependencies?

- How did the environment change in the lands subjected to the New Imperialism?

THE NEW IMPERIALISM: MOTIVES AND METHODS

The New Imperialism was characterized by an explosion of territorial conquests. Between 1869 and 1914, Europeans seized territories in Africa and Central Asia, and both Europeans and Americans took territories in Southeast Asia and the Pacific. Approximately 10 million square miles (26 million square kilometers) and 150 million people fell under the rule of Europe and the United States in this period. The New Imperialism, however, was more than a land grab. The imperial powers used economic and technological means to reorganize dependent regions and bring Africa, Latin America, and other parts of the world into the world economy as suppliers of foodstuffs and raw materials and as consumers of industrial products.

What inspired Europeans and Americans to venture overseas and impose their will on other societies? There is no simple answer to this question. Economic, cultural, and political motives were involved in each case.

Political and Economic Motives

The great powers of the late nineteenth century, as well as less powerful countries like Italy, Portugal, and Belgium, were competitive and hypersensitive about their status. French leaders, humiliated by their defeat by Prussia in 1871 (see Chapter 23), sought to reestablish their nation's prestige through territorial acquisitions overseas. Great Britain, already in possession of the world's largest and richest empire, felt the need to protect India, its "jewel in the crown," by acquiring colonies in East Africa and Southeast Asia. Many Germans believed that a country as important as theirs required an impressive empire overseas.

Political motives were not limited to statesmen in the capital cities. Colonial governors, even officers posted to the farthest colonial outposts, practiced their own diplomacy. They often decided on their own to claim a piece of land before some rival got it. Armies fighting frontier wars found it easier to defeat their neighbors than to make peace with them. In response to border skirmishes with neighboring states, colonial agents were likely to send in troops, take over their neighbors' territories, and then inform their home governments. Governments felt obligated to back up their men-on-the-spot in order not to lose face. The great powers of Europe acquired much of West Africa, Southeast Asia, and the Pacific islands in this manner.

Industrialization had stimulated the demand for minerals, such as copper, tin, chrome, manganese, coal, and, most of all, gold and diamonds. The demand for such industrial crops as cotton and rubber and for stimulants such as sugar, coffee, tea, and tobacco also grew. These products were found in the tropics, but never in sufficient quantities. European merchants, manufacturers, and shippers secured sources of tropical raw materials and protected markets for their industries. Entrepreneurs and investors looked for profits from mines, plantations, and railroads in Asia, Africa, and Latin America.

Cultural Motives

The late nineteenth century saw a Christian revival in Europe and North America. Both Catholics and Protestants founded new missionary societies for purposes that were not just religious but more broadly cultural. They sought to export their own norms of "civilized" behavior. They were determined to abolish slavery in Africa and bring Western education, medicine, hygiene, and monogamous marriage to all the world's peoples.

The sense of moral duty and cultural superiority was not limited to missionaries. Many others,

Religion and Imperialism   European penetration into Africa was accompanied by enthusiastic efforts to convert the Africans to Christianity. European missionaries built schools and clinics as well as churches. Here, African schoolchildren are shown a picture of the Virgin Mary holding the baby Jesus, an image designed to replace traditional African religious objects. Mary and Jesus are represented as Europeans.   (USGP)

equating technological innovations with "progress" and "change for the better," believed that Western technology proved the superiority of Western ideas, customs, and culture. This attitude at least included the idea that non-Western peoples could achieve, through education, the same cultural level as Europeans and Americans. More harmful were racist ideas of Social Darwinists (see Chapter 23) that relegated non-Europeans to a status of permanent inferiority. Caucasians—whites—were always at the top of this ranking, which was often an excuse for permanent rule over Africans and Asians.

Imperialism soon attracted young men, finding few opportunities for adventure and glory at home in an era of peace. A few easy victories in the 1880s helped to overcome the indifference of the European public and parliaments. By the 1890s, imperialism was a popular cause, an overseas extension of European and American nationalism.

These motives alone do not explain the events of that time. What made it possible to conquer a piece of Africa, to convert the "heathen," or to start a plantation was the sudden increase in the power that industrial peoples could wield over nonindustrial peoples and over the forces of nature. Technological advances explain both the motives and the outcome of the New Imperialism.

The Tools of the Imperialists

The Industrial Revolution provided the means to achieve imperial objectives at a reasonable cost. More efficient steamships, the Suez Canal, and a global network of submarine telegraph cables became parts of a new technology of imperialism.

In 1854, a British doctor discovered that the drug quinine could prevent the deadly malaria that had hampered European penetration of tropical Africa. This and a few sanitary precautions sharply reduced European death rates in West Africa and opened the continent to more merchants, officials, and missionaries. The development of new and much deadlier firearms in the 1860s and 1870s shifted the balance of power on land between Westerners and other peoples. By the 1870s, armies in Europe and the United States had all switched to new breechloader rifles. Two more innovations appeared in the 1880s: smokeless powder, which did not foul the gun or reveal the soldier's position, and repeating rifles, which could shoot fifteen rounds in fifteen seconds. In the 1890s, European and American armies began using machine guns, which could fire eleven bullets per second. European-led forces of a few hundred could thereby defeat non-European armies of thousands.

Colonial Agents and Administration

Once colonial agents took over a territory, their home government expected them to cover their own costs and, if possible, return some profit to the home country. In some cases, such as along the West African coast or in Indochina, there was already a considerable trade that could be taxed. In other places, profits could come only from investments and a thorough reorganization of the indigenous societies.

The impact of colonial rule depended most on economic and social conditions. One important factor was the presence of European settlers. Where European settlers were numerous but still a minority of the population, as in Algeria and South Africa, settlers and the home country struggled for control over the indigenous population. In colonies with few white settlers, the European governors ruled autocratically.

Nowhere could colonialism operate without the cooperation of indigenous elites, because no colony was wealthy enough to pay the salaries of more than a handful of European officials. In most cases, the colonial governors exercised power through traditional rulers willing to cooperate, as in India (see Chapter 22). In addition, colonial governments educated a few local youths as clerks, nurses, policemen, customs inspectors, and the like.

THE SCRAMBLE FOR AFRICA

Until the 1870s, African history was largely shaped by internal forces and local initiatives. Outside Algeria and southern Africa, European countries possessed only small enclaves on the coasts. Then within a decade, Africa was invaded and divided among the European powers in a movement often referred to as the **"scramble" for Africa** (see Map 24.1). This invasion affected all regions of the continent.

Egypt

Throughout the mid-nineteenth century, the khedives of Egypt had tried to modernize their armed forces; build canals, harbors, railroads, and other public works; and reorient agriculture toward export crops, especially cotton (see Chapter 22). Their interest in the Suez Canal was also part of this modernization policy. These ambitions cost vast sums of money,

which the khedives borrowed from European creditors at high interest rates.

By 1876, interest payments on the large foreign debt consumed one-third of Egypt's foreign export earnings. To avoid bankruptcy, the Egyptian government sold its shares in the Suez Canal to Great Britain and accepted four foreign "commissioners of the debt" to oversee its finances. Still not satisfied, French and British bankers lobbied their governments to appoint a Frenchman as minister of public works and a Briton as minister of finance and, when high taxes caused hardship and popular discontent, to depose Ismail.

When this foreign intervention provoked a military uprising, the British sent an army into Egypt in 1882. In the name of defending the Suez Canal, this occupation lasted for seventy years, during which the British maintained the Egyptian government and the fiction of Egyptian sovereignty but retained real power in their own hands.

Eager to develop Egyptian cotton production, the British completed a dam across the Nile, at Aswan in upper Egypt in 1902, which doubled the effective acreage. This economic development enriched a small elite of landowners and merchants, many of them foreigners. Egyptian peasants got little relief from the heavy taxes collected to pay for their country's crushing foreign debt and the expenses of the British army of occupation. Muslim religious leaders objected to Western ways, such as the drinking of alcohol and the relative freedom of women. By the 1890s, Egyptian politicians and intellectuals were demanding that the British leave, but to no avail.

Western and Equatorial Africa

While the British were taking over Egypt, the French were planning to extend their empire into the interior of West Africa. In 1879, **King Leopold II** of Belgium used his personal fortune to lay claim to the giant Congo basin in equatorial Africa, while a French agent was laying claims to territory north of the river. These events sparked a flurry of diplomatic activity.

At the **Berlin Conference** on Africa in 1884 and 1885, the major powers agreed that henceforth,

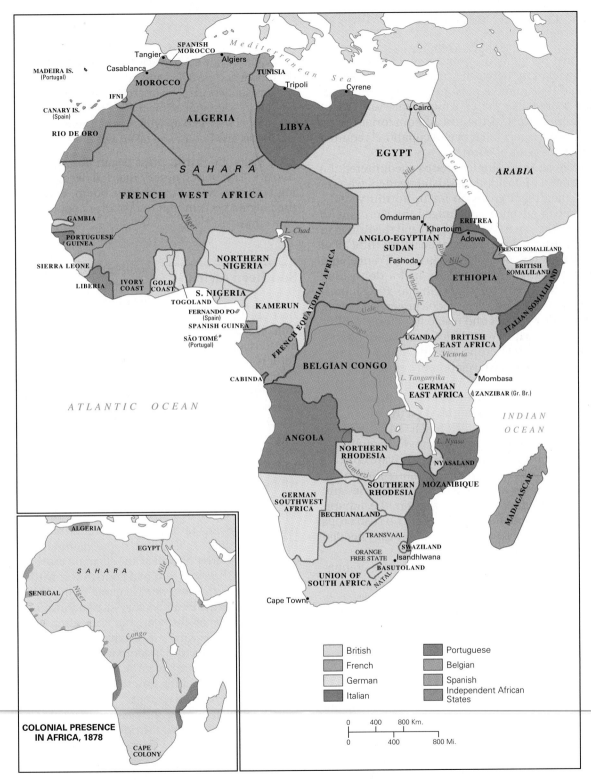

Map 24.1 Africa in 1878 and 1914 In 1878, the European colonial presence was limited to a few coastal enclaves, plus portions of Algeria and South Africa. By 1914, Europeans had taken over all of Africa except Ethiopia and Liberia.

"effective occupation" would replace the former trading relations between Africans and Europeans. Leopold II acquired a personal domain under the name "Congo Free State," while France and Portugal claimed most of the rest of equatorial Africa, at least on paper. "Effective occupation" required many more years of effort.

In West Africa, French troops encountered the determined opposition of Muslim leaders who resisted the French invasion for up to thirty years. The French advance encouraged the Germans to stake claims to parts of the region and the British to move north from their coastal enclaves, until all of West Africa was occupied by Britain, France, and Germany. West Africa had long had a flourishing trade. In the Gold Coast (now Ghana), British trading companies bought the cocoa grown by African farmers at low prices and resold it for large profits. Although French West Africa produced cotton, peanuts, and other crops, the difficulties of transportation limited its development before 1914.

Compared to West Africa, equatorial Africa had few inhabitants and little trade. Rather than try to govern these vast territories directly, authorities in the Congo Free State, the French Congo, and the Portuguese colonies of Angola and Mozambique farmed out huge pieces of land to private concession companies, offering them a monopoly on the natural resources and trade of their territories and the right to employ soldiers and tax the inhabitants. The inhabitants, however, had no cash crops that they could sell to raise the money they needed to pay their taxes.

Freed from outside supervision, the companies forced the African inhabitants at gunpoint to produce cash crops and carry them, on their heads or backs, to the nearest railroad or navigable river. The worst abuses took place in the Congo Free State, where a rubber boom lasting from 1895 to 1905 made it profitable for private companies to coerce Africans to collect latex from vines that grew in the forests. One Congolese refugee told the British consul Roger Casement, who investigated the atrocities:

> We begged the white men to leave us alone, saying we could get no more rubber, but the white men and their soldiers said: "Go. You are only beasts yourselves, you are only *nyama* (meat)."

> We tried, always going further into the forest, and when we failed and our rubber was short, the soldiers came to our towns and killed us. Many were shot, some had their ears cut off; others were tied up with ropes around their necks and bodies and taken away.[3]

After 1906, the British press began publicizing the horrors. The public outcry that followed, coinciding with the end of the rubber boom, convinced the Belgian government to take over Leopold's private empire in 1908.

Southern Africa

Southern Africa had long attracted European settlers because of its location on the sea route to India and because of its mild climate. By the 1850s, minorities of **Afrikaners** (descendants of early Dutch settlers), British settlers from the 1820s, and Indians brought by the British coexisted in four separate colonies with the indigenous African farmers and pastoralists. There were also independent African states, of which the Zulu kingdom was the most powerful (see Chapter 22).

The discovery of diamonds in 1868 and gold in 1886 lured thousands of new English-speaking white settlers as well as Africans looking for work. It also raised the region's importance to Great Britain, which fought a series of wars to subdue the independent Africans and the two Afrikaner republics. By 1879, Britain had annexed the diamond area around Kimberley as well as the separate territories of the Xhosa° people and had gone to war with the Zulu. Despite the superior weapons of the British, the Zulu scored a major victory at Isandhlwana° in the first battle of the war, but thereafter British might prevailed. King Cetshwayo° was captured and sent into exile, his kingdom was dismembered, and Zulu lands were given to white ranchers. Yet throughout those bitter times, the Zulu's sense of nationhood remained strong.

The British mining and railroad magnate **Cecil Rhodes** (1853–1902) led the political crusade to ex-

Xhosa (KOH-sah) Cetshwayo (set-SHWAH-yo)
Isandhlwana (ee-sawn-dull-WAH-nah)

pand British influence in the region. He also led a concession company, the British South Africa Company, and founded two new colonies: Southern Rhodesia (now Zimbabwe) and Northern Rhodesia (now Zambia). When the Ndebele° and Shona people who inhabited the region resisted, British machine guns defeated them.

However, the gold mines lay firmly in Afrikaner territory. Efforts by Rhodes and the British government to annex the two Afrikaner republics, Transvaal° and Orange Free State, led to the South African War (1899–1902). At first, the well-armed Afrikaners had the upper hand, but Great Britain brought in 450,000 troops and crushed the Afrikaner armies. Nevertheless, Afrikaners emerged as the ruling element in the Union of South Africa, founded in 1910 by the four European settlers states. The clear loser was the African majority of this new state whose laws curtained their rights to land, the vote, and equal status with the white minority.

| **Political and Cultural Responses** | Many African states and communities fought to preserve their independence, but only one succeeded in withstanding |

the power of European weaponry. By 1910, not only the Zulu and Ndebele, but the ancient kingdoms of **Asante°** and Benin and the newer Sokoto Caliphate and other new West Africa Muslim states (see Chapter 22) had met defeat. The one exception was **Emperor Menelik**'s newly enlarged kingdom of Ethiopia, whose well-armed and well-trained armies defeated a large Italian invasion in 1896.

Despite the imperialists' military victories, European control was weak in 1910, and most Africans continued living much as before. Gradually, they had to pay taxes by selling cash crops or migrate to places of employment. Such migrations were most disruptive in colonies that lost land to European settlers who took over African lands.

More Africans came into contact with missionaries than with any other Europeans. Missionaries, both men and women, opened schools to teach

reading, writing, and arithmetic to village children. Boys were taught crafts such as carpentry, while girls learned domestic skills such as cooking, laundry, and child care. Along with basic skills, the first generation of Africans educated in mission schools acquired Western ideas of justice and progress. Samuel Ajayi Crowther, a Yoruba rescued from slavery as a boy and educated in mission schools in Sierra Leone, went on to become an Anglican minister and, in 1864, the first African bishop.

Christianity proved successful in converting followers of traditional religions but made no inroads among Muslims. Instead, European colonialism unwittingly helped the diffusion of Islam, which spread along busier and safer trade routes. The number of Muslims in sub-Saharan Africa probably doubled between 1869 and 1914. In addition to new religious beliefs, colonial rule brought an end to fighting and slave raiding.

ASIA AND WESTERN DOMINANCE

During the period from 1869 to 1914, the pressure of the industrial powers was felt throughout Asia, the East Indies, and the Pacific islands. As trade with these regions grew in the late nineteenth century, so did their attractiveness to imperialists eager for economic benefits and national prestige (see Map 24.2).

| **Central Asia** | Between 1865 and 1876, Russian forces with modern rifles and artillery ad- |

vanced into Central Asia. Nomads like the Kazakhs, who lived east of the Caspian Sea, fought bravely but in vain. The fertile agricultural land of Kazakhstan attracted 200,000 Russian settlers. Despite government policies of not interfering in indigenous customs, by the end of the nineteenth century, the nomads were fenced out and reduced to starvation.

As the Qing Empire was losing control over Central Asia south of the Kazakh steppe land (see

Ndebele (en-duh-BELL-ay)   Transvaal (trans-VAHL)
Asante (uh-SAWN-tay)

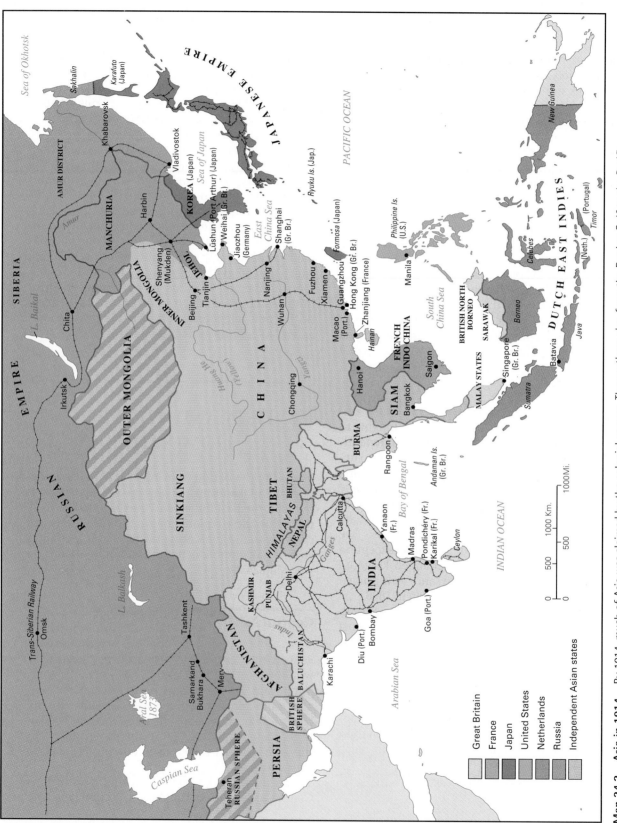

Map 24.2 Asia in 1914 By 1914, much of Asia was claimed by the colonial powers. The southern rim, from the Persian Gulf to the Pacific, was occupied by Great Britain, France, the Netherlands, and the United States. Central Asia had been incorporated into the Russian Empire. Japan, now industrialized, had joined the Western imperialist powers in expanding its territory and influence at the expense of China.

Chapter 22), Russia acquired land suitable for cotton, along with a large and growing Muslim population. Russian rule brought few benefits to the peoples of the Central Asian oases. The Russians abolished slavery, built railroads to link the region with Europe, and planted hundreds of thousands of acres of cotton. Unlike Europeans in Africa, they did not attempt to change the customs, languages, or religious beliefs of their subjects.

Southeast Asia and Indonesia

The peoples of the Southeast Asian peninsula and the Indonesian archipelago came under intense imperialist pressure during the nineteenth century. Burma (now Myanmar) and Malaya (now Malaysia) were gradually taken over by the British. Indochina fell piece by piece under French control. By the early 1900s, the Dutch had subdued northern Sumatra, the last part of the Dutch East Indies to be conquered. Only Siam (now Thailand) remained independent.

Despite their varied political histories, all of these regions had rich potential for agricultural cash crops, such as cinchona° (an antimalarial drug), natural rubber, sugar, tea, coffee, and palm oil (see Environment and Technology: Imperialism and Tropical Ecology). In exchange for these valuable exports, the inhabitants of the region received two benefits from colonial rule: peace and a reliable food supply. As a result, their numbers increased at an unprecedented rate.

Colonialism and the growth of population brought many social changes. The more numerous agricultural and commercial peoples gradually moved into mountainous and forest areas, displacing the earlier inhabitants who practiced hunting and gathering or shifting agriculture. The migrations of the Javanese to Borneo and Sumatra are but one example. Immigrants from China and India changed the ethnic composition and culture of every country in the region. Thus, the population of the Malay Peninsula became one-third Malay, one-third Chinese, and one-third Indian.

As in Africa, European missionaries attempted to spread Christianity under the colonial umbrella. Islam, however, was much more successful in gaining new converts, for it had been established in the region for centuries and people did not consider it a religion imposed on them by foreigners.

Hawaii and the Philippines, 1878–1902

By the 1890s, the United States had a fast-growing population and industries that produced more manufactured goods than they could sell at home. Merchants and bankers began to look for export markets. The political mood was also expansionist, and many echoed the feelings of naval strategist Alfred T. Mahan°: "Whether they will or no, Americans must now begin to look outward. The growing production of the country requires it."

Some Americans had been looking outward for quite some time, especially across the Pacific to China and Japan. In 1878, the United States obtained the harbor of Pago Pago in Samoa as a coaling and naval station, and in 1887 it secured the use of Pearl Harbor in Hawaii for the same purpose. Six years later, American settlers in Hawaii deposed Queen Liliuokalani (1838–1917) and offered the Hawaiian Islands to the United States. At the time, President Grover Cleveland (1893–1897) was opposed to annexation, and the settlers had to content themselves with an informal protectorate. By 1898, however, the United States under President William McKinley (1897–1901) had become openly imperialistic. It annexed Hawaii as a strategic steppingstone to Asia.

While large parts of Asia were falling under colonial domination, the people of the Philippines were chafing under their Spanish rulers. The movement for independence began among young Filipinos studying in Europe, but soon shifted to the Philippines, where **Emilio Aguinaldo,** leader of a secret society, rose in revolt and proclaimed a republic in 1898. The revolutionaries had a good chance of winning independence, for Spain had its hands full with a revolution in Cuba (see below).

cinchona (sin-CHO-nuh)

Mahan (muh-HAN)

ENVIRONMENT + TECHNOLOGY

Imperialism and Tropical Ecology

Like all conquerors before them, the European imperialists of the nineteenth century exacted taxes and rents from the peoples they conquered. But they also sent botanists and agricultural experts to their tropical colonies to increase the production of commercial crops. In doing so, they radically changed the landscapes of their tropical dependencies.

The most dramatic effects were brought about by the deliberate introduction of new crops—an acceleration of the Columbian Exchange that had begun in the fifteenth century. In the early nineteenth century, tea was transferred from China to India and Ceylon. In the 1850s, British and Dutch botanists smuggled seeds of the cinchona tree from the Andes in South America to India and Java. They had to operate in secret, because the South American republics, knowing the value of this crop, prohibited the export of seeds. With the seeds, the British and Dutch established cinchona plantations in Ceylon and Java, respectively, to produce quinine, which was essential as an antimalarial drug and a flavoring for tonic water. Similarly, in the 1870s, British agents stole seeds of the rubber tree from the Amazon rain forest and transferred them to Malaya and Sumatra.

Before these transfers, vast forests covered the highlands of India, Southeast Asia, and Indonesia, precisely the lands where the new plants grew best. So European planters had the forests cut down and replaced with thousands of acres of commercially profitable trees and bushes, all lined up in perfect rows and tended by thousands of indigenous laborers to satisfy the demands of customers in faraway lands. The crops that poured forth from the transformed environments brought great wealth to the European planters and the imperial powers. In 1909, the British botanist John Willis justified the transformation in these terms:

Whether planting in the tropics will always continue to be under European management is another question, but the northern powers will not permit that the rich and as yet comparatively undeveloped countries of the tropics should be entirely wasted by being devoted merely to the supply of the food

Unfortunately for Aguinaldo and his followers, the United States acquired the Philippines after the Spanish-American War lest the islands go to another imperialist power such as Japan or Germany. In 1899, Aguinaldo rose up again and proclaimed the independence of his country. In spite of protests by anti-imperialists in the United States, the U.S. government decided that its global interests outweighed the interests of the Filipino people. In rebel areas, a U.S. army of occupation tortured prisoners, burned villages and crops, and forced the inhabitants into "reconcentration camps." Many American soldiers tended to look on Filipinos with the same racial contempt with which Europeans viewed their colonial subjects. By the end of the insurrection in 1902, the war had cost the lives of 5,000 Americans and 200,000 Filipinos.

After the end of the insurrection, the United States attempted to soften its rule with public works and economic development projects. New buildings went up in the city of Manila; roads, harbors, and railroads were built; and the Philippine economy was tied ever more closely to that of the United States. In 1907, Filipinos were allowed to elect representatives to a legislative assembly; however, ultimate authority remained in the hands of a governor appointed by the president of the United States. In 1916, the Philippines were the first U.S. colony to be promised independence, a promise fulfilled thirty years later.

and clothing wants of their own people, when they can also supply the wants of the colder zones in so many indispensable products.

This quotation raises important questions about trade versus self-sufficiency. If a region's economy supplies the food and clothing wants of its own people, is its output "entirely wasted"? What is the advantage of trading the products of one region (such as the tropics) for those of another (such as the colder zones)? Is this trade an obligation? Should one part of the world (such as the "northern powers") let another refuse to develop and sell its "indispensable products"? Can you think of a case where a powerful country forced a weaker one to trade?

Source: The quotation is from John Christopher Willis, *Agriculture in the Tropics: An Elementary Treatise* (Cambridge: Cambridge University Press, 1909), 38–39.

Branch of a Cinchona Tree   The bark of the cinchona tree was the source of quinine, the only antimalarial drug known before 1940. Quinine made it much safer for Europeans to live in the tropics.   (From Bentley & Trimen's *Medicinal Plants.* Hunt Institute for Botanical Documentation, Carnegie Mellon University)

IMPERIALISM IN LATIN AMERICA

In the Western Hemisphere, therefore, the New Imperialism manifested itself not by a "scramble" for territories but in a form of economic dependence called **free-trade imperialism.** In the larger republics of South America, the pressure was mostly financial and economic. In Central America and the Caribbean, it also included military intervention by the United States.

Railroads and the Imperialism of Free Trade

Latin America's economic potential was huge, for the region could produce many agricultural and mineral products in demand in the industrial countries. What was needed was a means of opening the interior to development. Railroads seemed the perfect answer.

Starting in the 1870s, almost every country in Latin America acquired railroads, usually connecting mines or agricultural regions with the nearest port rather than linking up the different parts of the interior. Since Latin America did not have any steel or mechanical industries, all the equipment and building material came from Britain or the United States. So did the money to build the

Railroads Penetrate South America   The late nineteenth century saw the construction of several railroad networks in South America, often through rugged and dangerous terrain. This photograph shows the opening of a bridge on the Transandine Railroad in Peru. Flags were raised in honor of American construction and British ownership of the railroad.   (Tony Morrison/South American Pictures)

networks, the engineers who designed and maintained them, and the managers who ran them.

Argentina, a land of rich soil that produced wheat, beef, and hides, gained the longest and best-developed rail network south of the United States. By 1914, 86 percent of the railroads in Argentina were owned by British firms, 40 percent of the employees were British, and the official language of the railroads was not Spanish but English. The same was true of mining and industrial enterprises and public utilities throughout Latin America.

In many ways, the situation resembled that of India or Ireland, which also obtained a rail network in exchange for raw materials and agricultural products. The difference was that the Indians and Irish had little say in the matter because they were under British rule. But in Latin America, the political elites encouraged foreign companies with generous concessions as the most rapid way to modernize their countries and enrich the property owners.

American Expansionism and the Spanish-American War

After 1865, the European powers used their financial power to penetrate Latin America. But there was no need for territorial acquisitions, because the Latin American governments provided the political backing for the economic arrangements and Latin Americans had shown themselves capable of resisting invasions. In addition, by the Monroe Doctrine (1823), the United States closed the entire Western Hemisphere to all outside intervention—except its own.

The United States had long had interests in Cuba, the closest and richest of the Caribbean islands. American businesses invested great sums of money in the Spanish colony's sugar and tobacco industries. In 1895, the Cuban nationalist José Martí started a revolution against Spanish rule. American newspapers thrilled readers with lurid stories of Spanish atrocities, businessmen worried about their investments, and politicians demanded that the U.S. government help liberate Cuba.

On February 15, 1898, the U.S. battleship *Maine* accidentally blew up in Havana harbor, killing 266 American sailors. The U.S. government immediately blamed Spain and issued an ultimatum that the Spanish evacuate Cuba. Spain agreed to the ultimatum, but the American press and Congress were eager for war, and President McKinley did not restrain them.

The Spanish-American War was over quickly. On May 1, 1898, U.S. warships destroyed the Spanish fleet at Manila in the Philippines. Two months later, the United States Navy sank the Spanish Atlantic fleet off Santiago, Cuba. By mid-August, Spain was suing for peace. The United States purchased the Philippines from Spain and took over Puerto Rico and Guam as war booty. Cuba became an independent republic, subject, however, to American interference.

American Intervention in the Caribbean and Central America

The nations of the Caribbean and Central America were small and poor, and their governments were corrupt, unstable, and often bankrupt. They seemed to offer an open invitation to foreign interference. To ward off European intervention or for other reasons, the United States occupied Cuba, the Dominican Republic, Nicaragua, Honduras, and Haiti on one or more occasions before 1920. The United States was especially forceful in Panama, which was a province of Colombia. Here, the issue was not corruption or debts but a more vital interest: the construction of a canal across the isthmus of Panama to speed shipping between the east and west coasts of the United States. In 1878, the Frenchman Ferdinand de Lesseps, builder of the Suez Canal, had obtained a concession from Colombia to construct a canal across the isthmus, which lay in Colombian territory. Financial scandals and yellow fever, however, doomed his project.

When the United States acquired Hawaii and the Philippines, it recognized the strategic value of a canal that would allow warships to move quickly between the Atlantic and Pacific Oceans. The main obstacle was Colombia, whose senate refused to give the United States a piece of its territory. In 1903, the U.S. government supported a Panamanian rebellion against Colombia and quickly recognized the independence of Panama. In exchange, it obtained the right to build a canal and to occupy a zone 5 miles (8 kilometers) wide on either side of it. Work began in 1904, and the **Panama Canal** opened on August 15, 1914.

THE WORLD ECONOMY AND THE GLOBAL ENVIRONMENT

Although the New Imperialists' conquests were much larger that those of the Spanish conquistadors, their aim was not only to extend their power over new territories and peoples but to control both the natural world and indigenous societies and put them to work more efficiently than had ever been done before. They expressed their belief in progress and their good intentions in the clichés of the time: "the conquest of nature," "the annihilation of time and space," "the taming of the wilderness," and "our civilizing mission." The New Imperialism set in motion global environmental flows that were larger and more deliberate than the "Columbian Exchange" of that earlier imperial era.

Expansion of the World Economy

For centuries, spices, sugar, silk, and other exotic or tropical products had found a ready market in Europe. The Industrial Revolution vastly expanded this demand. Imports of foods and stimulants such as tea, coffee, and cocoa increased substantially during the nineteenth century. The trade in industrial raw materials grew even faster. Some were the products of agriculture, such as cotton, jute for bags, and palm oil for soap and lubricants. Others were minerals such as diamonds, gold, and copper. There also were wild forest products that only later came to be cultivated: timber for buildings and railroad ties, cinchona bark, rubber for rainwear and tires, and gutta-percha° to insulate electric cables.

The growing needs of the industrial world could not be met by the traditional methods of production and transportation of the nonindustrial world. When the U.S. Civil War interrupted the export of cotton to England in the 1860s, the British turned to India. But they found that Indian cotton was ruined by exposure to rain and dust during the long trip on open carts from the interior of the country to the harbors. To prevent the expansion of their industry from being stifled by the technological backwardness of their newly conquered territories, the imperialists made every effort to bring those territories into the mainstream of the world market.

One great change was in transportation. The Suez and Panama Canals cut travel time and lowered freight costs dramatically. Steamships became more numerous, and as their size increased, new, deeper harbors were needed. The Europeans also built railroads throughout the world; India alone had 37,000 miles (nearly 60,000 kilometers) of track by 1915, almost as much as Germany or Russia. Railroads reached into the interior of Latin America, Canada, China, and Australia. In 1903, the Russians completed the Trans-Siberian Railway from Moscow to Vladivostok on the Pacific. Visionaries even made plans for railroads from Europe to India and from Egypt to South Africa.

Transformation of the Global Environment

In addition to the vast exchange of natural products and manufactured goods that flowed through the speedy transportation networks of the industrial world, imperial botanists applied agricultural science to every promising plant species. In the nineteenth century, they founded botanical gardens in Java, India, Mauritius°, Ceylon, Jamaica, and other tropical colonies. These gardens not only collected local plants but also exchanged plants with other gardens. They were especially active in systematically transferring commercially valuable plant species from one tropical region to another. Cinchona, tobacco, sugar, and other crops were introduced, improved, and vastly expanded in the colonies of Southeast Asia and Indonesia (see Environment and Technology: Imperialism and Tropical Ecology). Cocoa and coffee growing spread over large areas of Brazil and Africa; oil-palm plantations were established in Nigeria and the Congo Basin. Rubber, used to make waterproof garments and bicycle tires, originally came from the latex of Hevea trees growing wild in the Brazilian rain forest. Then in the 1870s, British agents smuggled seedlings from Brazil to the Royal Botanic Gardens at Kew near London, and from there to the Botanic Garden of Singapore. These plants formed the nucleus of the enormous rubber economy of Southeast Asia.

Throughout the tropics, land once covered with forests or devoted to shifting slash-and-burn agriculture was transformed into permanent farms and plantations. Even in areas not developed to export crops, growing populations put pressure on the land. In Java and India, farmers felled trees to obtain arable land and firewood. They terraced hillsides, drained swamps, and dug wells.

Irrigation and water control transformed the dry parts of the tropics as well. In the 1830s, British engineers in India had restored ancient canals that had fallen into disrepair. Their success led them to build new irrigation canals, turning thousands of previously barren acres into well-watered, densely populated farmland. The migration of European experts spread the newest techniques of irrigation

---

gutta-percha (gut-tah–PER-cha)

Mauritius (maw-REE-shuss)

engineering around the world. By the turn of the century, irrigation projects were under way wherever rivers flowed through dry lands. In Egypt and Central Asia, irrigation brought more acres under cultivation in one forty-year span than in all previous history.

Railroads had voracious appetites for land and resources. They cut into mountains, spanned rivers and canyons with trestles, and covered as much land with their freight yards as whole cities had needed in previous centuries. They also consumed vast quantities of iron, timber for ties, and coal or wood for fuel. Most important of all, railroads brought people and their cities, farms, and industries to areas previously occupied by small, scattered populations.

Prospectors looking for valuable minerals opened the earth to reveal its riches: gold in South Africa, Australia, and Canada; tin in Nigeria, Malaya, and Bolivia; copper in Chile and Central Africa; iron ore in northern India; and much else. Where mines were dug deep inside the earth, the dirt and rocks brought up with the ores formed huge mounds near mine entrances. Open mines dug to obtain ores lying close to the surface created a landscape of lunar craters, and runoff from the minerals poisoned the water for miles around. Refineries that processed the ores fouled the environment with slag heaps and more toxic runoff.

The transformation of the land by human beings, a constant throughout history, accelerated sharply. Only the changes occurring since 1914 can compare with the transformation of the global environment that took place between 1869 and 1914.

CONCLUSION

The opening of the Suez Canal in 1869 was the symbolic beginning of the New Imperialism. It demonstrated the power of modern industry to subdue nature by carving the land. It stimulated shipping and trade between the industrial countries and the tropics. It deepened the involvement of Europeans in the affairs of the Middle East, Africa, and Asia. From that year until 1914, not only the great powers but smaller countries too—even,

in some cases, individual Europeans or Americans—had the power to decide the fate of whole countries. The motivation to conquer or control other lands surely helps explain the New Imperialism. But the means at the disposal of the imperialists—that is, the gap that opened between their technologies and forms of organization and those available to Asians, Africans, and Latin Americans—is equally important.

The new technological means and the enhanced motivations of the imperialists resulted in the most rapid conquest of territories in the history of the world. In less than half a century, almost all of Africa and large parts of Asia and Oceania were added to the colonial empires, while Latin America was turned into an economic colony of the industrial powers. In the process of developing the economic potential of their empires, the colonial powers transformed natural environments around the world.

The opening of the Panama Canal in August 1914 confirmed the new powers of the industrializing nations—but with a twist, for it was the United States, a latecomer to the game of imperialism, that created the canal. In that same month, the other imperialist nations turned their weapons against one another and began a life-or-death struggle for supremacy in Europe. That conflict is the subject of the next chapter.

■ Key Terms

Suez Canal	Cecil Rhodes
New Imperialism	Asante
"scramble" for Africa	Emperor Menelik
King Leopold II (Belgium)	Emilio Aguinaldo
Berlin Conference	free-trade imperialism
Afrikaners	Panama Canal

■ Suggested Reading

Two good introductions to imperialism are D. K. Fieldhouse, *Colonialism, 1870–1945* (1981), and Scott B. Cook, *Colonial Encounters in the Age of High Imperialism* (1996). The debate on the theories of imperialism is presented in Roger Owen and Robert Sutcliffe, *Studies in the Theory of Imperialism* (1972), and in Winfried Baumgart,

Imperialism (1982). The British Empire is the subject of Bernard Porter, *The Lion's Share: A Short History of British Imperialism, 1850–1970* (1976).

On Africa in this period, see Roland Oliver and Anthony Atmore, *Africa Since 1800*, new ed. (1994). Adam Hochschild's *King Leopold's Ghost: A Story of Greed, Terror, and Heroism in Colonial Africa* (1998) is a very readable account of imperialism in the Belgian Congo. The classic novel about the impact of colonial rule on African society is Chinua Achebe's *Things Fall Apart* (1958).

Imperial rivalries in Asia are the subject of Akira Iriye, *Across the Pacific: An Inner History of American–East Asian Relations*, rev. ed. (1992); David Gillard, *The Struggle for Asia, 1828–1914: A Study in British and Russian Imperialism* (1977); and Peter Hopkirk, *The Great Game: The Struggle for Empire in Central Asia* (1994). On other aspects of imperialism in Asia, see Clifford Geertz, *Agricultural Involution: The Process of Ecological Change in Indonesia* (1963), especially chapters 4 and 5, and Stanley Karnow, *In Our Image: America's Empire in the Philippines* (1989).

On Latin America in this period, see David Bushnell and Neill Macauley, *The Emergence of Latin America in the Nineteenth Century* (1994). Free-trade imperialism is the subject of D. C. M. Platt, *Latin America and British Trade, 1806–1914* (1973). On American expansionism, see David Healy, *Drive to Hegemony: The United States in the Caribbean, 1898–1917* (1989), and Walter LaFeber, *The Panama Canal*, rev. ed. (1990).

On race relations in the colonial world, see Robert Huttenback, *Racism and Empire: White Settlers and Colored Immigrants in the British Self-Governing Colonies, 1830–1910* (1976). Gender relations are the subject of Caroline Oliver, *Western Women in Colonial Africa* (1982), and Cheryl Walker, ed., *Women and Gender in Southern Africa to 1945* (1990). David Northrup's *Indentured Labor in the Age of Imperialism, 1834–1922* (1995), discusses migrations and labor.

The impact of technology on the New Imperialism is the subject of Daniel R. Headrick, *The Tools of Empire: Technology and European Imperialism in the Nineteenth Century* (1981) and *The Tentacles of Progress: Technology Transfer in the Age of Imperialism, 1850–1940* (1988), and Clarence B. Davis and Kenneth E. Wilburn, Jr., eds., *Railway Imperialism* (1991).

■ Notes

1. *Journal officiel* (November 29, 1869), quoted in Georges Douin, *Histoire du règne du khédive Ismaïl* (Rome: Real Societá di geografia d'Egritto, 1933), 453.
2. E. Desplaces in *Journal de l'Union des Deux Mers* (December 15, 1869), quoted ibid., 453.
3. "Correspondence and Report from His Majesty's Consul at Boma respecting the Administration of the Independent State of the Congo," *British Parliamentary Papers, Accounts and Papers,* 1904 (Cd. 1933), lxii, 357.

THE CRISIS OF THE IMPERIAL ORDER,

1900–1929

**The Crisis in Europe and the Middle East • The "Great War" and
the Russian Revolutions • Peace and Dislocation in Europe •
China and Japan: Contrasting Destinies • The New Middle East •
Science and Technology in the Industrialized World**
SOCIETY AND CULTURE: The Experience of Battle

On June 28, 1914, Archduke Franz Ferdinand, heir to the throne of Austria-
Hungary, was riding in an open carriage
through Sarajevo, capital of the province of
Bosnia-Herzegovina, which Austria had annexed six years before. When the carriage
stopped momentarily, Gavrilo Princip, a member of a pro-Serbian conspiracy, fired his pistol
twice, killing the archduke and his wife.

Those shots ignited a war that spread
throughout Europe, then turned into a global
war as the Ottoman Empire fought against
Britain in the Middle East and Japan attacked
German positions in China. France and Britain
involved their empires in the war and brought
Africans, Indians, Australians, and Canadians to
Europe to fight and labor on the front lines. Finally, in 1917, the United States entered the fray.

The next three chapters tell a story of violence and hope. This chapter looks at the causes
of war between the great powers; the consequences of that conflict in Europe, the Middle

East, and Russia; and the upheavals in China
and Japan. It also reviews the accelerating rate of
technological change that made the first half of
the twentieth century so violent and so hopeful.
Entirely new technologies made war more dangerous yet allowed far more people to live
healthier, more comfortable, and more interesting lives than ever before.

As you read this chapter, ask yourself the following questions:

- How did the First World War lead to revolution
in Russia and the disintegration of other empires?
- What role did the war play in eroding European dominance in the world?
- Why did China and Japan follow such diver-
gent paths in this period?
- How did European and North American society and technology change in the aftermath of
the war?

THE CRISIS IN EUROPE AND THE MIDDLE EAST

When the twentieth century opened, the world seemed firmly under the control of the great powers. Its first decade saw peace and economic growth in most of the world. New technologies—airplanes, automobiles, radio, and cinema—aroused much excitement. With their colonial conquests over, the great powers seemed matched and likely to maintain peace. The only international war of the period, the Russo-Japanese War (1904–1905), ended quickly with a decisive Japanese victory.

However, two major changes were undermining the apparent stability of the world. In Europe, tensions mounted as Germany challenged Britain at sea and France in Morocco. As the Ottoman Empire grew weaker, the resulting chaos in the Balkans gradually drew the European powers into its hostilities.

The Ottoman Empire and the Balkans

By 1900, economic, technological, and military decline had made the once-great Ottoman Empire the "sick man of Europe," and it was losing its outlying provinces. Between 1902 and 1912, Macedonia rebelled, Austria-Hungary annexed Bosnia, Crete merged with Greece, Albania became independent, and Italy conquered Libya, the Ottomans' last foothold in Africa. In 1912–1913, Serbia, Bulgaria, Romania, and Greece chased the Turks out of the Balkans, except for a small enclave around Constantinople.

The European powers meddled in the internal affairs of the Ottoman Empire. Russia and Austria-Hungary competed to become the protector of the Slavic peoples of the Balkans. France and Britain, posing as protectors of Christian minorities, controlled Ottoman finances, taxes, railroads, mines, and public utilities.

In reaction, Turks began to assert themselves against rebellious minorities and meddling foreigners. In 1909, the group known as the Young Turks overthrew the sultan and replaced him with his brother. The new regime began to reform the police, the bureaucracy, and the education system and hired a German general to modernize Turkey's armed forces. At the same time, it cracked down on Greek and Armenian minorities.

Nationalism, Alliances, and Military Strategy

Nationalism was deeply rooted in European culture. It united the citizens of France, Britain, and Germany behind their respective governments and gave them tremendous cohesion and strength of purpose. But nationalism could also be a dividing rather than a unifying force. In the large but fragile multinational Russian, Austro-Hungarian, and Ottoman Empires, ethnic and religious minorities, repressed for centuries, were stirring. The easy victories in the wars of the New Imperialism led some in power to believe that only war could heal the divisions in their societies.

What turned assassination of the Archduke Franz Ferdinand in a small town in the Balkans into a conflict involving all the great powers was the system of alliances that had grown up over the previous decades. At the center of Europe stood Germany, the most heavily industrialized country in Europe and yearning to dominate. Its army was the best trained and equipped, and its heavily armed battleships were challenging Great Britain's naval supremacy. Germany joined Austria-Hungary and Italy in the Triple Alliance in 1882. When in 1907 Britain, France, and Russia formed an Entente° ("understanding"), Europe was divided into two blocs of roughly equal power (see Map 25.1).

The alliance system was cursed by inflexible military planning. In the years before World War I, military planners in France and Germany had worked out elaborate railroad timetables to mobilize their respective armies in a few days. Other countries were less well prepared. Russia, a large country with an underdeveloped rail system,

---

Entente (on-TONT)

CHRONOLOGY

	Europe and North America	Middle East	East Asia
1900			**1900** Boxer Rebellion in China
	1904 British-French Entente		**1904–1905** Russo-Japanese War
	1907 British-Russian Entente	**1909** Young Turks overthrow Sultan Abdul Hamid	
1910	**1912–1913** Balkan Wars		**1911** Chinese revolutionaries led by Sun Yat-sen overthrow Qing dynasty
	1914 Assassination of Archduke Franz Ferdinand sparks World War I		**1915** Japan presents Twenty-One Demands to China
	1916 Battles of Verdun and the Somme	**1916** Arab Revolt in Arabia	
	1917 Russian Revolutions; United States enters the war	**1917** Balfour Declaration	
	1918 Armistice ends World War I		
	1919 Treaty of Versailles	**1919–1922** War between Turkey and Greece	**1919** May Fourth Movement in China
1920	**1920** First commercial radio broadcast (United States)		
	1921 New Economic Policy in Russia	**1922** Egypt nominally independent	
		1923 Mustafa Kemal proclaims Turkey a republic	
	1927 Charles Lindbergh flies alone across the Atlantic		**1927** Guomindang forces occupy Shanghai and expel Communists

needed several weeks to mobilize its forces. Britain, with only a tiny volunteer army, had no mobilization plans. German generals, believing that the British would stay out of a future European war, made war plans to defeat France in a matter of days, then transport their entire army by train across Germany to the Russian border before Russia could fully mobilize.

On July 28, 1914, emboldened by the backing of Germany, Austria-Hungary declared war on Serbia, triggering the mobilization plans of Russia, France, and Germany. On July 29, the Russian government ordered general mobilization to force Austria to back down. On August 1, France honored its treaty obligation to Russia and ordered general mobilization. Minutes later, Germany did the same. Because of the rigid railroad timetables, war was now automatic.

The German General Staff expected France to capitulate before the British could get involved. But on August 3, when German troops entered Belgium, Britain demanded their withdrawal. When Germany refused, Britain declared war on Germany.

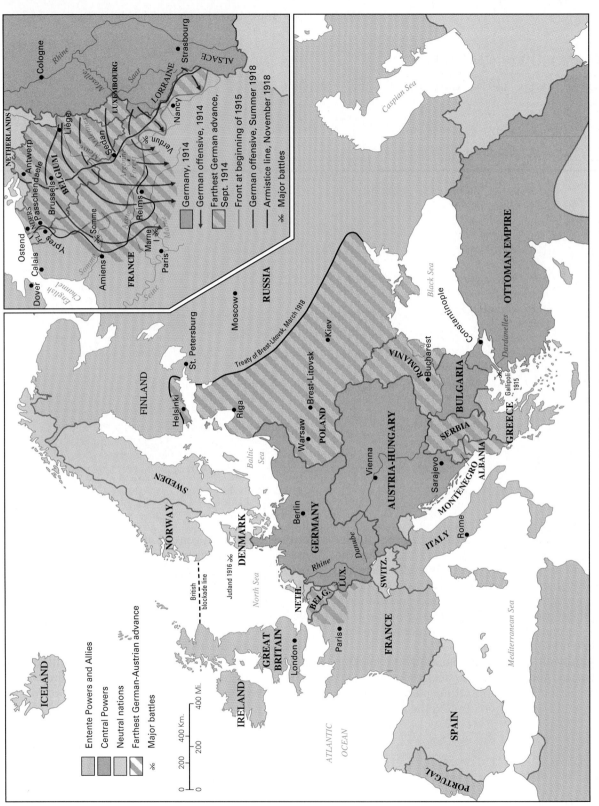

Map 25.1 The First World War in Europe Most of the fighting in World War I took place on two fronts. After an initial surge through Belgium into northern France, the German offensive bogged down for four years along the Western Front. To the east, the German armies conquered a large part of Russia during 1917 and early 1918. Despite spectacular victories in the east, Germany lost the war because its armies collapsed along the strategically important Western Front.

Entente Powers and Allies
Central Powers
Neutral nations
Farthest German-Austrian advance
Major battles

Germany, 1914
German offensive, 1914
Farthest German advance, Sept. 1914
Front at beginning of 1915
German offensive, Summer 1918
Armistice line, November 1918
Major battles

ICELAND
NORWAY
SWEDEN
FINLAND
IRELAND
GREAT BRITAIN
London
DENMARK
NETH.
BELG.
LUX.
GERMANY
Berlin
Paris
FRANCE
SWITZ.
ITALY
Rome
SPAIN
PORTUGAL
POLAND
Warsaw
AUSTRIA-HUNGARY
Vienna
RUSSIA
Moscow
St. Petersburg
Helsinki
Riga
Brest-Litovsk
Kiev
ROMANIA
Bucharest
SERBIA
Sarajevo
MONTENEGRO
ALBANIA
BULGARIA
GREECE
OTTOMAN EMPIRE
Constantinople
Dardanelles
Gallipoli 1915
Caspian Sea
Black Sea
Baltic Sea
North Sea
ATLANTIC OCEAN
Mediterranean Sea
Danube
Rhine
Treaty of Brest-Litovsk, March 1918
Jutland 1916
British blockade line

Cologne
Rhine
Strasbourg
ALSACE
LORRAINE
LUXEMBOURG
Nancy
Verdun
Argonne Forest
Saar
Moselle
NETHERLANDS
Antwerp
Passchendaele
BELGIUM
Liège
Sedan
Brussels
FLANDERS
Ypres
Ostend
Calais
Dover
Reims
Somme
Amiens
Marne I
Marne
FRANCE
Paris
Seine
English Channel
Somme

THE "GREAT WAR" AND THE RUSSIAN REVOLUTIONS

Throughout Europe, people greeted the outbreak of war with parades and hopes for a quick victory. The German sociologist Max Weber wrote: "This war, with all its ghastliness, is nevertheless grand and wonderful. It is worth experiencing." Very few imagined that their side might not win, and no one foresaw that everyone would lose. The effect of the war was especially devastating in Russia, for it destroyed the old society, introduced a radical new political system, and put professional revolutionaries in charge of Russia's industrialization.

Stalemate, 1914–1917

In 1914, the generals' carefully drawn-up plans went awry from the start. Believing that a spirited attack would always prevail, French generals hurled their troops, dressed in bright blue-and-red uniforms, against the well-defended German border and suffered a crushing defeat. By early September, the German armies held Belgium and northern France and were fast approaching Paris.

German victory seemed assured. But when Russia attacked, German troops needed for the final push into France were shifted to the Russian front. A gap opened between two German armies along the Marne River, into which France's last reserves moved. At the Battle of the Marne, the Germans were thrown back several miles.

During the next month, both sides spread out until they formed an unbroken line extending over 300 miles (some 500 kilometers) from the North Sea to the border of Switzerland. All along this **Western Front,** machine guns provided an almost impenetrable defense against advancing infantry but were useless for the offensive because they were too heavy for one man to carry and took too much time to set up. To escape the deadly streams of bullets, soldiers dug holes for themselves in the ground, connected the holes to form shallow trenches, then dug communications trenches to the rear. Within weeks, the battlefields were scarred with lines of trenches several feet deep, their tops protected by sandbags and their floors covered with planks (see Society and Culture: The Experience of Battle).

For four years, generals on each side again and again ordered their troops to attack. In battle after battle, thousands of young men on one side climbed out of their trenches, raced across the open fields, and were mowed down by enemy machine-gun fire. Poison gas added to the horror of battle.

The year 1916 saw the bloodiest and most futile battles of the war. The Germans attacked French forts at Verdun, losing 281,000 men and causing 315,000 French casualties. In retaliation, the British attacked the Germans at the Somme River and suffered 420,000 casualties—60,000 on the first day alone—while the Germans lost 450,000 and the French 200,000.

This was not warfare as it had ever been waged before; it was mass slaughter. Neither side could win, for the armies were stalemated by trenches and machine guns. During four years of the bloodiest fighting the world had ever seen, the Western Front moved no more than a few miles one way or another.

At sea, the war was just as inconclusive. As soon as the war broke out, the British cut the German overseas telegraph cables, blockaded the coasts of Germany and Austria-Hungary, and set out to capture or sink all enemy ships still at sea. The German High Seas Fleet, built at enormous cost, seldom left port. Only once, in May 1916, did it confront the British Grand Fleet. At the Battle of Jutland, off the coast of Denmark, the two fleets lost roughly equal numbers of ships, and the Germans escaped back to their harbors.

In early 1915, in retaliation for the British naval blockade, Germany announced a blockade of Britain by submarines. German submarines attacked every vessel they could. One attack sank the British ocean liner *Lusitania,* killing 1,198 people, 139 of them Americans. When the United States protested, Germany ceased its submarine campaign, hoping to keep America neutral.

Trench Warfare in World War I   German and Allied soldiers on the Western Front faced each other from elaborate networks of trenches. Attacking meant jumping out of the trenches and racing across a no man's land of mud and barbed wire. Here we see Princess Patricia's Canadian Light Infantry repelling a German attack near Ypres, in northern France, in March 1915, using machine guns, rifles, and hand grenades.   (Courtesy, The Princess Patricia's Canadian Light Infantry, Regimental Museum and Archives)

The Home Front and the War Economy

The war economy transformed civilian life. In France and Britain, food rations were allocated according to need, improving nutrition among the poor. Unemployment vanished. Thousands of Africans, Indians, and Chinese were recruited for heavy labor in Europe. Employers hired women to fill jobs in steel mills, mines, and munitions plants vacated by men off to war. Women became streetcar drivers, mail carriers, and police or found work in government bureaucracies. Many joined auxiliary military services as doctors, nurses, mechanics, and ambulance drivers. These positions gave thousands of women a sense of participation and a taste of independence.

German civilians paid an especially high price because of the British naval blockade. The German chemical industry developed synthetic explosives and fuel, but synthetic food was not an option. Wheat flour disappeared, replaced first by rye, then by potatoes and turnips, then by acorns and chestnuts, and finally by sawdust. After the failure of the potato crop in 1916 came the "turnip winter," when people had to survive on 1,000 calories per day, half of the normal amount that an active adult needed. Women, children, and the elderly were especially hard hit.

During the war, the British and French overran German's African colonies except for German East Africa, which remained undefeated until the end of the war (see Map 24.1). The war brought hardships

The Experience of Battle

What is it like to be a soldier in the midst of a battle? Here is how the German writer Erich Maria Remarque, a veteran of World War I, described a battle from a soldier's point of view in his classic war novel, All Quiet on the Western Front *(1928).*

Night again. We are deadened by the strain—a deadly tension that scrapes along one's spine like a gapped knife. Our legs refuse to move, our hands tremble, our bodies are a thin skin stretched painfully over repressed madness, over an almost irresistible, bursting roar. We have neither flesh nor muscles any longer, we dare not look at one another for fear of some incalculable thing. So we shut our teeth—it will end—it will end—perhaps we will come through.

Suddenly the nearer explosions cease. The shelling continues but it has lifted and falls behind us, our trench is free. We seize the hand-grenades, pitch them out in front of the dug-out and jump after them. The bombardment has stopped and a heavy barrage now falls behind us. The attack has come.

No one would believe that in this howling waste there could still be men; but steel helmets now appear on all sides of the trench, and fifty yards from us a machine-gun is already in position and barking.

The wire entanglements are torn to pieces. Yet they offer some obstacle. We see the storm-troops coming.

Our artillery opens fire. Machine-guns rattle, rifles crack. The charge works its way across. Haie and Kropp begin with the hand-grenades. They throw as fast as they can, others pass them the handles with the strings already pulled. . . .

We recognize the smooth distorted faces, the helmets: they are French. They have already suffered heavily when they reach the remnants of the barbed wire entanglements. A whole line has gone down before our machine-guns; then we have a lot of stoppages and they come nearer.

I see one of them, his face upturned, fall into a wire cradle. His body collapses, his hands remain suspended as though he were praying. Then his body drops clean away and only his hands with the stumps of his arms, shot off, now hang in the wire.

How successful is Remarque in conveying a soldier's experiences to readers who have never been to war? How do you explain what makes men willing to fight such battles?

Source: Erich Maria Remarque, *All Quiet on the Western Front*, trans. A. W. Wheen (Boston: Little, Brown, 1958), 98–99. *Im Westen Nichts Neues*, copyright 1928 by Ullstein A. G. Copyright renewed © 1956, 1957, 1958 by Erich Maria Remarque. *All Quiet on the Western Front*, copyright © 1929, 1930 by Little, Brown and Company. All rights reserved.

to many African colonies, whose inhabitants faced heavy taxes, low prices for requisitioned export crops, and forced recruitment. Many Europeans stationed in Africa left to join the war, leaving large areas with little or no European presence. Over a million Africans served in the various armies, and perhaps three times that number were drafted as porters to carry army equipment. In some places, these impositions provoked African uprisings that lasted for years.

One country grew rich during the war: the United States, which for two and a half years stayed technically neutral while businesses engaging in war production did a roaring business supplying France and Britain. After the United States entered the war in 1917, civilians were exhorted to help the war effort by investing their savings in war bonds and growing food in backyard "victory gardens." Employment created by the war opened up jobs for hired women and African-Americans.

The Ottoman Empire at War

On August 2, 1914, the Turks signed a secret alliance with Germany. In November, they joined the fighting, hoping to gain land at Russia's expense. But the campaign in the Caucasus proved disastrous for both armies and for the civilian populations. Suspecting the Armenians of being pro-Russian, the Turks forced them to march from their homelands across the mountains in the winter. Hundreds of thousands of Armenians died of hunger and exposure, an omen of even ghastlier tragedies to come.

The Turks also closed the Dardanelles, the strait between the Mediterranean and Black Seas (see Map 25.1). When a British attempt to force open the Dardanelles failed, the British tried to subvert the Ottoman Empire from within by promising the emir (prince) of Mecca, Hussein ibn Ali, a kingdom of his own. In 1916, Hussein started an Arab revolt against the Turks. His son **Faisal**° led an Arab army in support of the British advance from Egypt into Palestine and Syria that contributed to the Ottoman defeat.

The British made promises to Chaim Weizmann°, leader of the British Zionists, that a Jewish homeland in Palestine would be carved out of the Ottoman Empire and placed under British protection. In November, as British armies were advancing on Jerusalem, Foreign Secretary Sir Arthur Balfour wrote that "His Majesty's Government view with favor the establishment in Palestine of a national home for the Jewish people and will use their best endeavours to facilitate the achievement of that object, it being clearly understood that nothing shall be done which may prejudice the civil and religious rights of existing non-Jewish communities in Palestine." The British did not foresee that this statement, known as the **Balfour Declaration,** would lead to conflicts between Palestinians and Jewish settlers.

Double Revolution in Russia, 1917

At the beginning of the war, Russia had the largest army in the world, but its generals were incompetent, supplies were lacking, and soldiers were poorly trained and equipped. In August 1914, two Russian armies invaded eastern Germany but were thrown back. Several times the Russians defeated the Austro-Hungarian army, only to be defeated by the Germans. In 1916, after a string of defeats, the Russian army ran out of ammunition and other essential supplies. Soldiers were ordered into battle unarmed and told to pick up the rifles of fallen comrades.

With so many men in the army, railroads broke down for lack of fuel and parts, and crops rotted in the fields. Civilians faced shortages and widespread hunger. In the cities, food and fuel became scarce. During the bitterly cold winter of 1916–1917, factory workers and housewives had to line up in front of grocery stores before dawn in order to get something to eat. The court of Tsar° Nicholas II, however, remained as extravagant and corrupt as ever.

When food ran out in Petrograd, the capital, in early March 1917, housewives and women factory workers staged mass demonstrations. Soldiers mutinied and joined striking workers to form soviets (councils) to take over factories and barracks. A few days later, the tsar abdicated, and leaders of the parliamentary parties formed a Provisional Government. Thus began what Russians called the "February Revolution" because their calendar was two weeks behind the one in use elsewhere.

Revolutionary groups came out of hiding. Most numerous were the Social Revolutionaries, who advocated the redistribution of land to the peasants. The Social Democrats, a Marxist party, were divided. The Mensheviks, who advocated electoral politics and reform in the tradition of European Socialists, had a large following among intellectuals and factory workers. The rival **Bolsheviks** were a small but tightly disciplined group dedicated to radical revolution. **Vladimir Lenin** (1870–1924), the Bolshevik leader, became a revolutionary in his teens when his older brother was executed for plotting to kill the tsar. His goal was to

---

Faisal (fie-SAHL) **Chaim Weizmann** (hi-um VITES-mun)

tsar (zahr)

create a party that would lead the revolution rather than wait for it.

In early April 1917, the German government, hoping to destabilize Russia, allowed Lenin to travel from exile in Switzerland to Russia in a sealed railway car. As soon as he arrived in Petrograd, he announced his program: immediate peace, all power to the soviets, and transfers of land to the peasants and factories to the workers. This plan proved immensely popular among soldiers and workers exhausted by the war.

When the Provisional Government ordered another offensive against the Germans a few months later, Russian soldiers began to desert by the hundreds of thousands, throwing away their rifles and walking back to their villages. The Bolsheviks, meanwhile, were gaining support among the workers of Petrograd and the soldiers and sailors stationed there. On November 6, 1917 (October 24 in the Russian calendar), they rose up and took over the city. This "October Revolution" overthrew the Provisional Government and arrested Mensheviks, Social Revolutionaries, and other rivals.

The Bolsheviks nationalized all private land and ordered the peasants to hand over their crops without compensation. The peasants, having seized their landlords' estates, resisted. In the cities, the Bolsheviks took over the factories and drafted the workers into compulsory labor brigades. To enforce his rule, Lenin created the Cheka, a secret police force with powers to arrest and execute opponents. The Bolsheviks also sued for peace with Germany and Austria-Hungary. By the Treaty of Brest-Litovsk, signed on March 3, 1918, Russia lost territories containing a third of its population and wealth.

The End of the War in Western Europe, 1917–1918

Like many other Americans, President **Woodrow Wilson** wanted to stay out of the European conflict. For nearly three years, he kept the United States neutral and tried to persuade the belligerents to compromise. But in late 1916, German leaders decided to starve the British into submission by using submarines to sink merchant ships carrying food supplies to Great Britain. The Germans knew that unrestricted submarine warfare was likely to bring the United States into the war, but they were willing to gamble that Britain and France would collapse before the United States could send enough troops to help them.

The submarine campaign resumed on February 1, 1917, but the German gamble failed. The British organized their merchant ships into convoys protected by destroyers, and on April 6, President Wilson asked the United States Congress to declare war on Germany.

On the Western Front, the two sides were so evenly matched in 1917 that the war seemed unlikely to end until one side or the other ran out of young men. Losing hope of winning, soldiers began to mutiny. In May 1917, before the arrival of U.S. forces, fifty-four of one hundred French divisions along the Western Front refused to attack. During the summer, Italian troops also mutinied, panicked, or deserted.

Between March and August 1918, General Erich von Ludendorff launched a series of surprise attacks that broke through the front at several places and pushed to within 40 miles (64 kilometers) of Paris. But victory eluded him. Meanwhile, every month was bringing another 250,000 American troops to the front. In August, the Allies counterattacked, and the Germans began a retreat that could not be halted, for German soldiers, many of them sick with the flu, had lost the will to fight.

In late October, Ludendorff resigned, and sailors in the German fleet mutinied. Two weeks later, Kaiser Wilhelm fled to Holland as a new German government signed an armistice. On November 11 at 11 A.M., the guns on the Western Front went silent.

PEACE AND DISLOCATION IN EUROPE

The Great War lasted four years. It took almost twice as long for Europe to recover. Millions of people had died or been disabled, political tensions lingered, and national economies remained depressed until the mid-1920s. But the return of peace and prosperity soon proved illusory.

The Impact of the War

The war left more dead and wounded and more physical destruction than any previous conflict. It is estimated that between 8 million and 10 million people died, almost all of them young men. Perhaps twice that many returned home wounded, gassed, or shell-shocked, many of them injured for life. In addition, the war created millions of refugees.

Many refugees found shelter in France, which welcomed 1.5 million people, but the preferred destination was the United States. About 800,000 immigrants succeeded in reaching it before U.S. immigration laws passed in 1921 and 1924 closed the door to eastern and southern Europeans. Canada, Australia, and New Zealand adopted similar restrictions on immigration. The Latin American republics welcomed European refugees, but their poverty discouraged potential immigrants.

One unexpected by-product of the war was the great influenza epidemic of 1918–1919, which started among soldiers heading for the Western Front. This was no ordinary flu but a virulent strain that infected almost everyone on earth and killed one person in every forty. It caused the largest number of deaths in so short a time in the history of the world. Half a million Americans perished in the epidemic—five times as many as died in the war. Worldwide, some 30 million people died, 20 million in India alone.

The war also caused serious damage to the environment. No place on earth was ever so completely devastated as the scar across France and Belgium known as the Western Front. The fighting ravaged forests and demolished towns. The earth was gouged by trenches, pitted with craters, and littered with ammunition, broken weapons, chunks of concrete, and the bones of countless soldiers. After the war, it took a decade to clear away the debris and create military cemeteries with neat rows of crosses stretching for miles. The war also hastened the buildup of industry, with mines, factories, and railroad tracks.

The Peace Treaties

In early 1919, delegates of the victorious Allies met in Paris. The defeated powers were kept out until the treaties were ready for signing. Russia, in the throes of civil war, was not invited.

From the start, three men dominated the Paris Peace Conference: United States president Wilson, British prime minister David Lloyd George, and French premier Georges Clemenceau°. They ignored the Italians, who had joined the Allies in 1915, and paid even less attention to the delegates of smaller European nations. They rejected the Japanese proposal that all races be treated equally and ignored the call of the Pan-African Congress for attention to the concerns of African peoples around the world. They also ignored the ten thousand other delegates of various nationalities who did not represent sovereign states—the Arab leader Faisal, the Zionist Chaim Weizmann, and several Armenian delegations—who came to Paris to lobby for their causes.

Each man had his own agenda. Wilson wanted to apply the principle of self-determination, by which he meant creating nations that reflected European ethnic or linguistic divisions. He proposed a **League of Nations,** a world organization to safeguard the peace and foster international cooperation. His idealism clashed with the more hard-headed and self-serving nationalism of the Europeans. Lloyd George insisted that Germany pay a heavy indemnity. Clemenceau wanted Germany to give back Alsace and Lorraine, cede the industrial Saar region to France, and make the Rhineland a buffer state.

The result was a series of compromises that satisfied no one (see Map 25.2). The European powers formed a League of Nations, but the United States Congress, reflecting the isolationist feelings of the American people, refused to join. France recovered Alsace and Lorraine but was unable to detach the Rhineland and had to content itself with vague promises of British and American protection if Germany ever rebuilt its army. Britain acquired new territories in Africa and the Middle East but was greatly weakened by human losses and the disruption of its trade.

On June 28, 1919, the German delegates reluctantly signed the **Treaty of Versailles°.** Germany

---

Georges Clemenceau (zhorzh cluh-mon-SO)
Versailles (vuhr-SIGH)

Map 25.2 Territorial Changes in Europe After World War I   Although the heaviest fighting took place in western Europe, the territorial changes there were relatively minor; two provinces taken by Germany in 1871, Alsace and Lorraine, were returned to France. In eastern Europe, in contrast, the changes were enormous. The disintegration of the Austro-Hungarian Empire and the defeat of Russia allowed a belt of new countries to arise, stretching from Finland in the north to Yugoslavia in the south.

was forbidden to have an air force and was permitted only a token army and navy. It gave up large parts of its eastern territory to a newly reconstituted Poland. The Allies made Germany promise to pay reparations, but they did not set a figure or a period of time for payment. A "guilt clause," which was to rankle for years to come, obliged the Germans to accept "responsibility for causing all the loss and damage" of the war. The Treaty of Versailles left Germany humiliated but largely intact and potentially the most powerful nation in Europe. Establishing a peace neither of punishment nor of reconciliation, the treaty was one of the great failures in history.

In eastern Europe, the Allies created new national states in the lands lost by the old Russian, German, and Austro-Hungarian empires. Austria and Hungary became separate states; Poland was resurrected after over a century; Czechoslovakia and Yugoslavia were created from parts of Austria-Hungary. These small nations all contained disaffected minorities and were safe only as long as Germany and Russia remained weak.

Russian Civil War and the New Economic Policy

Fighting continued in Russia for another three years after the end of the Great War. The Bolshevik Revolution had provoked Allied intervention, and, in December 1918, civil war broke out in Russia. The Communists, as the Bolsheviks now called themselves, held central Russia, but all the surrounding provinces rose up against them. Counterrevolutionary armies led by former tsarist officers obtained weapons and supplies from the Allies. By 1921, the superior discipline of their Red Army, led by Leon Trotsky, gave the Communists victory over their enemies.

Gradually, the Communists reunited most of the rebellious provinces of the old Russian Empire. In 1920, Ukrainian Communists declared the independence of a Soviet republic of Ukraine; then in 1922, it merged with Russia to create the Union of Soviet Socialist Republics (USSR), or Soviet Union. In 1920–1921, the Red Army reconquered the oil-rich Caucasus and reestablished Soviet control of Central Asia. In 1922, the new Soviet republics of Georgia, Armenia, and Azerbaijan joined the USSR.

Years of warfare, revolution, and mismanagement had ruined the Russian economy. Factories and railroads had shut down. Farmland had been devastated and livestock killed, causing hunger in the cities. Lenin decided to release the economy from party and government control. In March 1921, he announced the **New Economic Policy** (N.E.P.), which allowed peasants to own land and sell their crops, private merchants to trade, and private workshops to produce goods and sell them on the free market. Only the biggest businesses, such as banks, railroads, and factories, remained under government ownership.

The relaxation of controls had an immediate effect. Production began to climb, and food and other goods became available. In the cities, food remained scarce because farmers used their crops to feed their livestock rather than sell them. But the N.E.P. reflected no change in the goal of the Communist Party to create a modern industrial economy without private property, under party guidance. It merely provided breathing space—what Lenin called "one step back to advance two steps forward." This meant investing in heavy industry and electrification, moving farmers to the new industries, while providing food for the urban workers. In other words, it meant making the peasants, the great majority of the Soviet people, pay for the industrialization of Russia.

When Lenin died in January 1924, his associates jockeyed for power. Leon Trotsky, commander of the Red Army, had the support of many "Old Bolsheviks" who had joined the party before the Revolution, but Joseph Stalin, general secretary of the Communist Party, got the support of the majority and filled the party bureaucracy with individuals loyal to himself. In January 1929, he forced Trotsky to flee the country. Then, as absolute master of the party, he prepared to industrialize the Soviet Union at breakneck speed.

An Ephemeral Peace

The decade after the end of the war can be divided into two distinct periods: five years of painful recovery and readjustment (1919–1923), followed by six years of growing peace and prosperity (1924–

1929). One of the big adjustments in many Western societies was granting political rights to women. Women in Norway were the first to obtain the vote in Europe, in 1915. Russian women followed in 1917 and Canadian and German women in 1918. Britain gave women over age thirty the vote in 1918 and later extended it to younger women. The Nineteenth Amendment to the U.S. Constitution granted suffrage to American women in 1920. To many people's surprise, the new women voters tended to vote just as their male relatives did.

Changes in international politics and economics were more upsetting. In the first period, the German government had printed money recklessly to fund reparations payments, causing the most severe inflation the world had ever seen. As Germany teetered on the brink of civil war, radical nationalists called for revenge and tried to overthrow the government. Finally, the German government issued a new currency and promised to resume reparations payments, and the French agreed to withdraw their troops from the Ruhr.

Then in 1924, the vexed issue of reparations vanished as Germany borrowed money from New York banks to make its payments to France and Britain, which used the money to repay their wartime loans from the United States. This triangular flow of money stimulated the rapid recovery of the European economies. France began rebuilding its war-torn northern zone, Germany recovered from its hyperinflation and joined the League of Nations, and in the United States a boom began that was to last over five years.

While their economies flourished, governments grew more cautious and businesslike. Yet neither Germany nor the Soviet Union accepted its borders with the small nations that had arisen between them. In 1922, they signed a secret pact allowing the German army to conduct maneuvers in Russia (in violation of the Versailles treaty) in exchange for German help in building up Russian industry.

For a time, the League of Nations proved adept at resolving issues pertaining to health, labor relations, and postal and telegraph communications. But without U.S. participation, sanctions against states that violated League rules carried little weight.

CHINA AND JAPAN: CONTRASTING DESTINIES

China and Japan took different directions in the early twentieth century. Still in need of deep internal reform, giant China went through a revolution but soon collapsed into chaos. Japan's reforms before 1900 had gained it industry and a powerful military, which it used to take advantage of China's weakness.

Revolution in China

China's population—about 400 million in 1900—was the largest of any other country in the world and growing fast, but China's society and government were falling behind. Most Chinese worked incessantly, survived on a diet of grain and vegetables, and spent their lives in fear of floods, bandits, and tax collectors. Peasant plots averaged half as large as they had been two generations earlier. Landowners lived off the rents of their tenants. Officials, chosen through an elaborate examination system, enriched themselves from taxes and the government's monopolies on salt, iron, and other products. Wealthy merchants handled China's growing import-export trade in collaboration with foreign companies. The contrast between the squalor in which most urban residents lived and the luxury of the foreigners' enclaves in the treaty ports sharpened the resentment of educated Chinese.

In 1900, China's **Empress Dowager Cixi°,** who had seized power in a palace coup two years earlier, encouraged a secret society, the Righteous Fists, or Boxers, to rise up and expel all the foreigners from China. When the Boxers threatened the foreign legation in Beijing, an international force from the Western powers and Japan captured the city and forced China to pay a huge indemnity. Shocked by these events, many Chinese students became convinced that China needed a revolution to get rid of the Qing dynasty and modernize their country.

Cixi (tsuh-shee)

Rice Paddies in China   After irrigating all the level land, Chinese farmers turned to the hillsides. To grow rice even on the steepest slopes, they terraced the land and controlled the flow of water so that each field received the optimum amount that the rice shoots required.   (Julia Waterlow/Eye Ubiquitous)

When Cixi died in 1908, the Revolutionary Alliance led by **Sun Yat-sen°** (Sun Zhongshan, 1867–1925) prepared to take over. Sun had spent much of his life in Japan, England, and the United States, plotting the overthrow of the Qing dynasty. His ideas, a mixture of nationalism, socialism, and Confucian philosophy, and his tenacious spirit attracted a large following. A revolutionary assembly elected Sun president of China in December 1911, and the last Qing ruler, the boy-emperor Puyi, abdicated the throne. But Sun had no military forces at his command. To avoid a clash with the army, he resigned after a few weeks, and a new national assembly elected **Yuan Shikai°**, the most powerful of the regional generals, president of the new Chinese republic.

Yuan was an able military leader, but he had no political program. When Sun reorganized his followers into a political party called **Guomindang°** (National People's Party), Yuan quashed every attempt at creating a Western-style government and harassed Sun's followers. Victory in the first round of the struggle to create a new China went to the military.

Japan and World War I

Japan's population reached 60 million in 1925 and was increasing by a million a year. The crash program of industrialization begun in 1868 by the Meiji oligarchs (see Chapter 23) accelerated during the First World War, when Japan exported textiles, consumer goods, and munitions. In the

---

Sun Yat-sen (soon yot-SEN)   **Yuan Shikai** (you-AHN she-KIE)

Guomindang (gwo-min-dong)

war years, its economy grew four times as fast as western Europe's and eight times faster than China's. Blessed with a rainy climate and many fast-flowing rivers, Japan quickly expanded its hydroelectric capacity. By the mid-1930s, 89 percent of Japanese households had electric lights, compared with 44 percent of British households.

The main beneficiaries of prosperity were the *zaibatsu*°, four giant corporations—Mitsubishi, Sumitomo, Yasuda, and Mitsui—that controlled most of Japan's industry and commerce. Farmers, who constituted half of the population, remained poor; some, in desperation, sold their daughters to textile mills or into domestic service, where young women formed the bulk of the labor force. Labor unions were weak and repressed by the police.

The Japanese were quick to join the Allied side in World War I. They saw the war as a golden opportunity to advance their interests while the Europeans were occupied elsewhere. The war created an economic boom, as the Japanese suddenly found their products in greater demand than before.

The Japanese soon conquered the German colonies in the northern Pacific and on the coast of China, then turned their attention to the rest of China. In 1915, Japan presented China with Twenty-One Demands, which would have turned it into a virtual protectorate. Britain and the United States persuaded Japan to soften the demands but could not prevent it from keeping the German coastal enclaves and extracting railroad and mining concessions at China's expense. Thus began a bitter struggle between the two countries that was to last for thirty years.

China in the 1920s

To many educated Chinese, the great powers' decision at the Paris Peace Conference to go along with Japan's seizure of the German enclaves in China was a cruel insult. On May 4, 1919, students demonstrated in front of the Forbidden City of Beijing. Despite a government ban, the May Fourth Movement spread to other parts of China. A new generation was growing up to challenge the old officials, the regional generals, and the foreigners.

China's regional generals—the warlords—still supported their armies through plunder and arbitrary taxation. They frightened off trade and investment in railroads, industry, and agricultural improvement. While neglecting the dikes and canals on which the livelihood of Chinese farmers depended, they fought one another and protected the gangsters who ran the opium trade. During the warlord era, China grew poorer, and only the treaty ports prospered.

Sun Yat-sen tried to make a comeback in Canton (Guangzhou) in the early 1920s. Though not a Communist, he was impressed with the efficiency of Lenin's revolutionary tactics and let a Soviet adviser reorganize the Guomindang along Leninist lines. He also welcomed members of the newly created Chinese Communist Party into the Guomindang.

When Sun died in 1925, the leadership of his party passed to Chiang Kai-shek° (1887–1975). An officer and director of the military academy, Chiang trained several hundred young officers, who remained loyal to him thereafter. In 1927, he determined to crush the regional warlords. As his army moved north from its base in Canton, he briefly formed an alliance with the Communists. Once his troops had occupied Shanghai, however, he allied himself with local gangsters to crush the labor unions and decimate the Communists, whom he considered a threat. He then defeated or co-opted most of the other warlords and established a dictatorship.

Chiang's government issued ambitious plans to build railroads, develop agriculture and industry, and modernize China from the top down. However, his followers were neither competent administrators like the Japanese officials of the Meiji Restoration nor ruthless modernizers like the Russian Bolsheviks. Instead, the government attracted thousands of opportunists whose goal was to "become an official and get rich" by taxing and plundering businesses. In the countryside, tax collectors and landowners squeezed the peasants ever harder. What little money reached the government went

---

zaibatsu (zie-BOT-soo)

Chiang Kai-shek (chang kie-shek)

to the military. Twenty years after the fall of the Qing, China remained mired in poverty, subject to corrupt officials and the whims of nature.

THE NEW MIDDLE EAST

At the Paris Peace Conference, France, Britain, Italy, and Japan proposed to divide the territories of the Ottoman Empire among themselves, but their ambitions clashed with President Wilson's ideal of national self-determination. Turkish nationalists made modern Turkey a new independent country. The Arab-speaking territories of the old Ottoman Empire became part of the League of Nations' new **mandate system,** run by French and British administrations that were accountable to the League of Nations for "the material and moral well-being and the social progress of the inhabitants." In the midst of these territories, Zionists were encouraging Jewish immigration (see Map 25.3).

The Rise of Modern Turkey

At the end of the First World War, the Allied forces occupied the Ottoman Empire and made the sultan give up most of his lands. But they had to reckon with Mustafa Kemal, a war hero who had formed a nationalist government in central Anatolia with the backing of fellow army officers. His armies reconquered Anatolia and the area around Constantinople in 1922 and expelled hundreds of thousands of Greeks. In response, the Greek government expelled all Muslims from Greece.

As a war hero and proclaimed savior of his country, Kemal was able to impose wrenching changes on his people faster than any other reformer would have dared. An outspoken modernizer, he was eager to bring Turkey closer to Europe as quickly as possible. He abolished the sultanate, in 1923 declared Turkey a secular republic, and introduced European laws. In a radical break with Islamic tradition, he suppressed Muslim courts,

schools, and religious orders and replaced the Arabic alphabet with the Latin alphabet.

Kemal attempted to Westernize the traditional Turkish family. Women received civil equality, including the right to vote and be elected to the national assembly. Kemal forbade polygamy and instituted civil marriage and divorce. He even changed people's clothing, strongly discouraging women from veiling their faces and ordered Turkish men to wear European brimmed hats instead of the fez. He ordered everyone to take a family name, choosing the name Atatürk ("father of the Turks") for himself.

Arab Lands and the Question of Palestine

Among the Arab people, the thinly disguised colonialism of the mandate system set off protests and rebellions. Arabs viewed the European presence not as "liberation" from Ottoman "oppression" but as foreign occupation.

The British attempted to control the Middle East with a mixture of bribery and intimidation. They helped Faisal, leader of the Arab Revolt, become king of Syria. When the French ousted him, the British made him king of Iraq. They used bombers to quell rural insurrections in Iraq. In 1931, they reached an agreement with King Faisal's government: official independence for Iraq in exchange for the right to keep two air bases, a military alliance, and an assured flow of petroleum. France, meanwhile, sent thousands of troops to Syria and Lebanon to crush nationalist uprisings.

In Egypt as in Iraq, the British substituted a phony independence for official colonialism. They declared Egypt independent in 1922 but reserved the right to station troops along the Suez Canal to secure their link with India in the event of war. Despite nationalist opposition, Britain was successful in keeping Egypt in limbo—neither independent nor a colony—thanks to an alliance with King Farouk and conservative Egyptian politicians who feared both secular and religious radicalism.

As soon as Palestine became a British mandate in 1920, Jewish immigrants arrived, encouraged by the Balfour Declaration of 1917. Most settled in the cities, but some purchased land to establish *kib-*

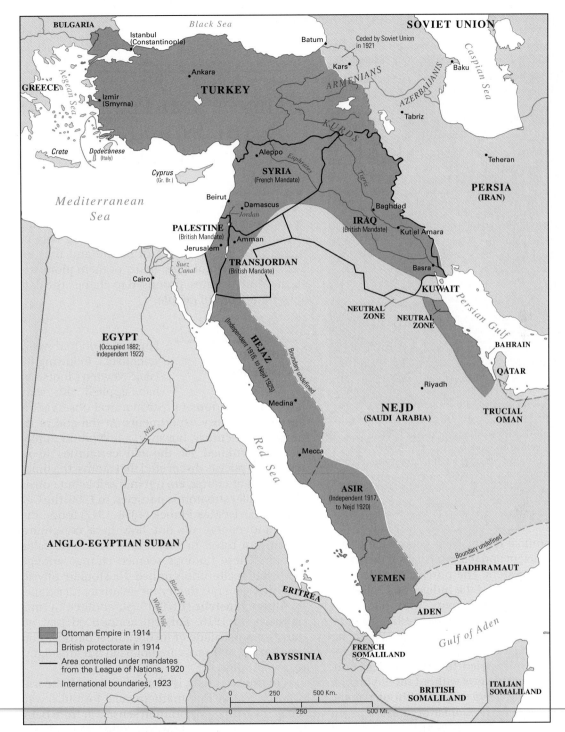

Map 25.3 Territorial Changes in the Middle East After World War I   The defeat and dismemberment of the Ottoman Empire at the end of World War I resulted in an entirely new political map of the region. The Turkish Republic inherited Anatolia and a small piece of the Balkans, while the Ottoman Empire's Arab provinces were divided between France and Great Britain. The French acquired Syria and Lebanon and the British got Palestine (now Israel), Transjordan (now Jordan), and Iraq. Only Iran and Egypt remained as they had been.

Mustafa Kemal Atatürk   After World War I, Mustafa Kemal was determined to modernize Turkey on the Western model. Here he is shown wearing a European-style suit and teaching the Latin alphabet.   (Stock Montage)

butzim, communal farms. Their goals were to become self-sufficient and reestablish their ties to the land of their ancestors. The purchases of land by Jewish agencies angered the indigenous Palestinians, especially tenant farmers who had been evicted to make room for settlers. In 1920–1921, riots erupted between Jews and Arabs. When far more Jewish immigrants arrived than they had anticipated, the British tried to limit immigration, thereby alienating the Jews without mollifying the Arabs. Increasingly, Jews arrived without papers, smuggled in by militant Zionist organizations. In the 1930s, the country was torn by strikes and guerrilla warfare that the British could not control. In the process, Britain earned the hatred of both sides and of much of the Arab world as well.

SCIENCE AND TECHNOLOGY IN THE INDUSTRIALIZED WORLD

With the signing of the peace treaties, the countries that had fought for four years turned their efforts toward building a new future. Advances in science offered astonishing new insights into the mysteries of nature and the universe. New technologies, many of them pioneered in the United States, promised to change the daily lives of millions of people.

Revolution in the Sciences

For two hundred years, scientists, following in Isaac Newton's footsteps, had applied the same laws and equations to astronomical observations and to laboratory experiments. At the end of the nineteenth century, however, a revolution in physics undermined all the old certainties about nature. Physicists discovered that atoms, the building blocks of matter, are not indivisible but consist of far smaller subatomic particles. In 1900, the German physicist **Max Planck** (1858–1947) found that light and energy do not flow in a continuous stream but travel in small units, which he called *quanta.* These findings seemed strange enough, but what really undermined Newtonian physics was the general theory of relativity developed by **Albert Einstein** (1879–1955), another German physicist. In 1916, Einstein announced that not only is matter made of insubstantial particles, but time, space, and mass are not fixed but are relative to one another.

To nonscientists, it seemed as though theories expressed in arcane mathematical formulas were replacing truth and common sense. Far from being mere speculation, however, the new physics promised to unlock the secrets of matter and provide humans with plentiful—and potentially dangerous—new sources of energy.

The new social sciences were even more unsettling than the new physics, for they challenged Victorian morality, middle-class values, and notions of Western superiority. Sigmund Freud (1856–1939), a Viennese physician, developed a technique—psychoanalysis—to probe the minds of his patients. He found not only rationality but also hidden layers of emotion and desire repressed by social restraints. "The primitive, savage and evil impulses have not vanished from any individual, but continue their existence, although in a repressed state," he warned. Meanwhile, sociologists and anthropologists had begun the empirical study of societies, both Western and non-Western. Before the war, the French sociologist Emile Durkheim (1858–1917) had come to the then-shocking conclusion that "there are no religions that are false. All are true in their own fashion."

If the words *primitive* and *savage* applied to Europeans as well as to other peoples, and if religions were all equally "true," then what remained of the superiority of Western civilization? Cultural relativism, as the new approach to human societies was called, was as unnerving as relativity in physics.

Wartime experiences helped call into question the West's faith in reason and progress. Some people accepted the new ideas with enthusiasm. Others condemned and rejected them, clinging to the sense of order and faith in progress that had energized European and American culture before the war.

The New Technologies of Modernity

Some Europeans and Americans viewed the new sciences with mixed feelings, but new technologies aroused almost universal excitement. In North America, even working-class people could afford some of the new products of scientific research, inventors' ingenuity, and industrial production. Mass consumption lagged in Europe, but science and technology were just as advanced, and public fascination with the latest inventions—the cult of the modern—was just as strong.

No other innovation attracted public interest as much as airplanes. In 1903, two young American mechanics, Wilbur and Orville Wright, built the first aircraft that was heavier than air and could be maneuvered in flight. From that moment on, wherever they appeared, airplanes fascinated people. During the war, the exploits of air aces relieved the tedium of news from the front. In the 1920s, aviation became a sport and a form of entertainment, and flying daredevils achieved extraordinary fame by pushing their planes to the very limit—and often beyond. Among the most celebrated pilots were three Americans: Amelia Earhart, the first woman to fly across the Atlantic Ocean; Richard Byrd, the first to fly over the North Pole, in 1926; and Charles Lindbergh, the first person to fly alone across the Atlantic, in 1927. The heroic age of flight lasted until the late 1930s, when aviation became a means of transportation.

Electricity's impact on home life was more sweeping. The first home use of electricity was for lighting, thanks to the economical and long-lasting tungsten bulb. Then, having persuaded people to wire their homes, electrical utilities joined manufacturers in advertising electric irons, fans, washing machines, hot plates, radios, and other electric appliances. After the war, radio moved from the battlefield into the home. The first commercial station began broadcasting in Pittsburgh in 1920. By 1930, hundreds of stations were broadcasting news, sports, soap operas, and advertising to 12 million homes in North America. In Europe, radio spread more slowly because governments reserved the airwaves for cultural and official programs and taxed radio owners to pay for the service.

Another medium that spread explosively in the 1920s was film. Motion pictures had begun in France in 1895 and flourished in Europe. In the United States, filmmaking started at almost the same time, but American filmmakers saw the medium's potential to entertain audiences rather than preserve outstanding theatrical performances. After World War I, filmmaking took root and flourished in Japan, India, Turkey, Egypt, and a suburb of Los Angeles, California, called Hollywood. American and European movie studios were both successful in exporting films, since silent movies presented no language problems. In 1927, the United States had introduced the first "talking" motion picture, *The Jazz Singer,* which changed all the rules. The number of Americans who went to see their favorite stars in thrilling adventures and heart-breaking romances rose from 40 million in 1922 to 100 million in 1930, at a time when the population of the country was about 120 million. Europeans had the technology and the art but neither the wealth nor the huge market of the United States. Hollywood studios began the diffusion of American culture that has continued to this day.

Advances in medicine—some learned in the war—were another important—and life-saving—technology. Wounds were regularly disinfected, and x-ray machines helped diagnose fractures. After the war, cities built costly water supply and sewage treatment systems. By the 1920s, indoor plumbing and flush toilets were becoming common even in working-class neighborhoods. Interest in cleanliness altered private life. Soap and appliance manufacturers filled women's magazines with advertisements for products to help housewives keep their family's homes and clothing spotless and their meals fresh and wholesome. The decline in infant mortality and improvements in general health and life expectancy in this period owe as much to the cult of cleanliness as to advances in medicine.

Technology and the Environment

Two new technologies—the skyscraper and the automobile—transformed the urban environment even more radically than the railroad had done in the nineteenth century. At the end of the nineteenth century, architects had begun to design ever-higher buildings using load-bearing steel frames and passenger elevators. Major corporations in Chicago and New York competed to build the most daring buildings in the world, such as New York's 55-story Woolworth Building (1912) and Chicago's 34-story Tribune Tower (1923). A building boom in the late 1920s produced dozens of skyscrapers, culminating with the 86-story, 1,239-foot (377-meter) Empire State Building in New York City, completed in 1932.

European cities restricted the height of buildings to protect their architectural heritage; Paris forbade buildings over 56 feet (17 meters) high. In innovative designs, however, European architects led the way. In the 1920s, the Swiss architect known as Le Corbusier° outlined a new approach to architecture that featured simplicity of form, absence of surface ornamentation, easy manufacture, and inexpensive materials. Among his influential designs were the main buildings of Chandigarh, the new capital of the Indian state of Punjab. Other architects—including the Finn Eero Saarinen, the Germans Ludwig Mies van der Rohe° and Walter Gropius, and the American Frank Lloyd Wright—advanced his lines of thought and added their own to create what became known as the International Style.

While central business districts were reaching for the sky, outlying areas were spreading far out into the countryside, thanks to the automobile. The assembly line pioneered by Henry Ford mass-produced vehicles in ever-greater volume and at falling prices. By 1929, the United States had one car for every five people, five-sixths of the world's automobiles. Far from being blamed for their exhaust emissions, automobiles were praised as the solution to urban pollution. As cars replaced carts and carriages, horses disappeared from city streets, as did tons of manure.

The most important environmental effect of automobiles was suburban sprawl. Middle-class families could now live in single-family homes too spread apart to be served by public transportation. By the late 1920s, paved roads rivaled rail networks both in length and in the surface they occupied. As middle- and working-class families bought cars, cities acquired rings of automobile suburbs. Los Angeles, the first true automobile city, consisted of suburbs spread over hundreds of square miles and linked together by broad avenues. In those sections of the city where streetcar lines went out of business, the automobile, at first a plaything for the wealthy, became a necessity for commuters. Many Americans saw Los Angeles as the portent of a glorious future when everyone would have a car; only a few foresaw the congestion and pollution that would ensue.

Le Corbusier (luh cor-booz-YEH)
Ludwig Mies van der Rohe (LOOD-vig MEES fon der ROW-uh)

The Archetypal Automobile City   As Los Angeles grew from a modest town into a sprawling metropolis, broad avenues, parking lots, and garages were built to accommodate automobiles. By 1929, most families owned a car, and streetcar lines had closed for lack of passengers. This photograph shows a street in the downtown business district.   (Ralph Morris Archives/Los Angeles Public Library)

Farmers began buying cars and light trucks, using them to transport produce as well as passengers. Governments obliged by building new roads and paving old ones to make automobile travel smoother and safer. In 1915, Ford introduced a gasoline-powered tractor, and by the mid-1920s, these versatile machines began replacing horses. Tractors hastened the end of agriculture as a family enterprise.

CONCLUSION

The Great War caused a major realignment among the nations of the world. France and Britain, the two leading colonial powers, emerged economically weakened despite their victory. The war brought defeat and humiliation to Germany but did not reduce its military or industrial potential. It destroyed the old regime and the aristocracy of Russia, leading to civil war and revolution from which the victorious powers sought to isolate themselves. Two other old empires—the Austro-Hungarian and the Ottoman—were divided into many smaller and weaker nations. For a while, the Middle East seemed ripe for a new wave of imperialism. But there and throughout Asia, the war unleashed revolutionary nationalist movements that challenged European influence.

Only two countries benefited from the war. Japan took advantage of the European conflict to develop its industries and press its demands on a China weakened by domestic turmoil and social unrest. The United States emerged as the most prosperous and potentially most powerful nation, restrained only by the isolationist sentiments expressed by many Americans.

Modern technology and industrial organization had long been praised in the name of "progress" for their ability to reduce toil and disease and improve living standards. The war showed that they possessed an equally awesome destructive potential. In the late 1920s, it seemed as though the victors in the Great War might restore the prewar prosperity and European dominance of the globe. But the spirit of the 1920s was an illusion—not real peace but the eye of a hurricane. The prosperity of the late 1920s in most industrial states also proved illusory.

■ Key Terms

Western Front	New Economic Policy
Faisal	Cixi, Empress Dowager
Balfour Declaration	Sun Yat-sen
Bolsheviks	Yuan Shikai
Vladimir Lenin	Guomindang
Woodrow Wilson	mandate system
League of Nations	Max Planck
Treaty of Versailles	Albert Einstein

■ Suggested Reading

Bernadotte Schmitt and Harold C. Bedeler, *The World in the Crucible, 1914–1918* (1984), and John Keegan, *The First World War* (1999), are two engaging overviews of World War I. Imanuel Geiss, *July 1914: The Outbreak of the First World War* (1967), argues that Germany caused the conflict. Barbara Tuchman's *The Guns of August* (1962) and Alexander Solzhenitsyn's *August 1914* (1972) recount the first month of the war in detail. Keegan's *The Face of Battle* (1976) vividly describes the Battle of the Somme from the soldiers' perspective.

For the background to the Russian Revolution, read Theodore von Laue's *Why Lenin? Why Stalin?* 2d ed.

(1971); but see also Richard Pipes, *The Russian Revolution* (1990), and Orlando Figes, *A People's Tragedy: The Russian Revolution, 1891–1924* (1996). The classic eyewitness account of the Revolution is John Reed's *Ten Days That Shook the World* (1919).

John Maynard Keynes's *The Economic Consequences of the Peace* (1920) is a classic critique of the Paris Peace Conference. Arno Mayer's *Political Origins of the New Diplomacy, 1917–1918* (1959) analyzes the tensions and failures of great-power politics. The 1920s are discussed in Raymond Sontag's *A Broken World, 1919–1939* (1971).

The best recent book on Japan in the twentieth century is Daikichi Irokawa's *The Age of Hirohito: In Search of Modern Japan* (1995). See also Richard Storry, *A History of Modern Japan* (1982), and Tessa Morris-Suzuki, *The Technological Transformation of Japan* (1994). In the large and fast-growing literature on twentieth-century China, two general introductions are especially useful: John K. Fairbank, *The Great Chinese Revolution, 1800–1985* (1986), and Jonathan Spence, *The Search for Modern China* (1990).

On the war and its aftermath in the Middle East, see David Fromkin, *A Peace to End All Peace* (1989), and M. E. Yapp, *The Near East Since the First World War* (1991). Bernard Lewis, *The Emergence of Modern Turkey* (1968), is a good introduction.

The towering intellectuals of the era are the subject of Peter Gay, *Freud: A Life for Our Time* (1988), and Abraham Pais, *Subtle Is the Lord: The Science and Life of Albert Einstein* (1982). Three books capture the enthusiastic popular response to technological innovations: David E. Nye, *Electrifying America: Social Meanings of a New Technology* (1990); Peter Fritzsche, *A Nation of Fliers: German Aviation and the Popular Imagination* (1992); and the sweeping overview by Thomas Hughes, *American Genesis: A Century of Invention and Technological Enthusiasm, 1870–1970* (1989).

THE COLLAPSE OF THE OLD ORDER,

1929–1949

Stalin's Revolution • The Depression • The Rise of Fascism •
East Asia, 1931–1945 • The Second World War •
The Character of Warfare
ENVIRONMENT AND TECHNOLOGY: Biomedical Technologies

efore the First World War, the Italian futurist poets exalted violence as a noble and manly idea. Filippo Marinetti defined their creed in these words: "We want to glorify war, the world's only hygiene—militarism, deed, destroyer of anarchisms, the beautiful ideas that are death-bringing, and the subordination of women." His friend Gabriele d'Annunzio said: "If it is a crime to incite citizens to violence, I shall boast of this crime."

The war taught most survivors to abhor violence. During the 1920s, the world seemed to return to what United States president Warren Harding called "normalcy": prosperity in Europe and America, European colonialism in Asia and Africa, paternalistic U.S. domination of Latin America, and peace almost everywhere. But for a few, war and domination became a creed and a goal.

In 1929, the artificial normalcy of the 1920s began to come apart. The Great Depression caused governments to turn against one another in a desperate attempt to protect their people's livelihood. As the economic crisis spread around the world, businesses went bankrupt, prices fell, factories closed, and workers were laid off. Even wholly agricultural nations and colonies suffered as markets for their exports shriveled.

Some countries chose to solve their problems by violent means. When nations shut their doors to Japan's products, the Japanese military tried to save their country by conquering China. In Germany, the Depression reawakened resentments against the victors of the Great War; people who feared communism or blamed Jews for their troubles turned to Hitler and the Nazis, who promised to save their society by dominating others. In the Soviet Union, Stalin used energetic and murderous means to force his country into a communist version of the Industrial Revolution.

The result was war. The Second World War engulfed more lands and peoples and caused far more deaths and destruction than any previous conflict. At the end of it, much of Europe and East Asia lay in ruins, and millions of destitute refugees sought safety in other lands. The European colonial powers were either defeated or so weakened that they could no longer hold onto their empires when Asian and African peoples asserted their desire for independence.

As you read this chapter, ask yourself the following questions:

- How did the Soviet Union change under Stalin, and at what cost?

- What were the main causes of the Second World War?

- How was the war fought, and why did Japan and Germany lose?

STALIN'S REVOLUTION

After **Joseph Stalin** (1879–1953) achieved total mastery over the USSR in early 1929 (see Chapter 25), he led it through another revolution: an economic and social transformation that turned it into a great industrial and military power and intensified both admiration for and fear of communism throughout the world.

Five-Year Plans

Stalin's ambition to turn the USSR into an industrial nation was not intended initially to produce consumer goods for a mass market, much less enrich individuals as in Britain and the United States. Instead, his aim was to increase the power of the Communist Party domestically and the power of the Soviet Union in relation to other countries. By building up Russia's industry, Stalin was determined to prevent a repetition of the humiliating defeat Russia had suffered at the hands of Germany in 1917.

Stalin encouraged rapid industrialization through a series of **Five-Year Plans,** a system of centralized control copied from the German experience of World War I. The goal of the first five-year plan was to quintuple the output of electricity and double that of heavy industry: iron, steel, coal, and machinery. Beginning in October 1928, the Communist government created whole industries and cities from scratch, then recruited millions of peasants and trained them to work in the new factories and mines and offices. In every way except actual fighting, Stalin's Russia resembled a nation at war.

Rapid industrialization hastened environmental changes. Hydroelectric dams turned rivers into strings of reservoirs. Roads, canals, and railroad tracks cut the landscape. Forests and grassland were turned into farmland. From an environmental perspective, the outcome of the Five-Year Plans resembled the transformation that had occurred in the United States and Canada a few decades earlier.

Collectivization of Agriculture

Since the Soviet Union was still a predominantly agrarian country, the only way to pay for these massive investments, provide the labor, and feed the millions of new industrial workers was to squeeze the peasantry. Stalin therefore proceeded with the most radical social experiment conceived up to that time: the collectivization of agriculture.

Collectivization meant consolidating small private farms into vast collectives and making the farmers work together in commonly owned fields. Each collective was expected to supply the government with a fixed amount of food and distribute what was left among its members. Collectives were to become outdoor factories through the use of machinery and techniques of mass production. Collectivization was expected to bring the peasants once and for all under government control so they never again could withhold food supplies as they had done during the period of Lenin's New Economic Policy (see Chapter 25).

The government mounted a massive propaganda campaign to enlist the farmers' support. At

CHRONOLOGY

	Europe and North Africa	Asia and the Pacific
1930	**1931** Great Depression reaches Europe **1933** Hitler comes to power in Germany	**1931** Japanese forces occupy Manchuria
1935	**1936** Hitler invades the Rhineland	
		1937 Japanese troops invade China, conquer coastal provinces; Chiang Kai-shek flees to Sichuan
		1937–1938 Japanese troops take Nanjing
	1939 (Sept. 1) German forces invade Poland	
1940	**1940 (March–April)** German forces conquer Denmark, Norway, the Netherlands, and Belgium	
	1940 (May–June) German forces conquer France	
	1940 (June–Sept.) Battle of Britain	
	1941 (June 21) German forces invade USSR	**1941 (Dec. 7)** Japanese aircraft bomb Pearl Harbor
	1942–1943 Allies and Germany battle for control of North Africa; Soviet victory in Battle of Stalingrad (1943)	**1942 (Jan–March)** Japanese conquer Thailand, Philippines, Malaya
		1942 (June) United States Navy defeats Japan at Battle of Midway
	1943–1944 Red Army slowly pushes Wehrmacht back to Germany	
	1944 (June 6) D-day: U.S., British, and Canadian troops land in Normandy	
1945	**1945 (May 7)** Germany surrenders	**1945 (Aug. 6)** United States drops atomic bomb on Hiroshima
		1945 (Aug. 14) Japan surrenders
		1945–1949 Civil war in China
		1949 Communists defeat Guomindang; Mao proclaims People's Republic (Oct. 1)

first, all seemed to go well, but soon *kulaks*° ("fists"), the better-off peasants, began to resist giving up all their property. When soldiers came to force them into collectives at gunpoint, the kulaks burned their own crops, smashed their own equipment, and slaughtered their own livestock. Within a few months, they slaughtered half of the Soviet Union's horses and cattle and two-thirds of its sheep and goats. In retaliation, Stalin ruthlessly ordered the "liquidation of kulaks as a class" and incited the poor peasants to attack their wealthier

neighbors. Over 8 million kulaks were arrested. Many were executed. The rest were sent to slave labor camps, where most starved to death.

The peasants who were left had been the least successful before collectivization and proved to be the least competent after. Many were sent to work in factories. The rest were forbidden to leave their farms. With half of their draft animals gone, they could not plant or harvest enough to meet the swelling demands of the cities. Yet government agents took whatever they could find, leaving little or nothing for the farmers themselves. After bad harvests in 1933 and 1934, a famine swept through

---

kulaks (COO-lox)

the countryside, killing some 5 million people, about one in every twenty farmers.

Stalin's second Five-Year Plan, designed to run from 1933 to 1937, was originally intended to increase the output of consumer goods. But when the Nazis took over Germany in 1933 (see below), Stalin changed the plan to emphasize heavy industries that could produce armaments. Between 1927 and 1937, the Soviet output of metals and machines increased fourteen-fold while consumer goods became scarce and food was rationed. After a decade of Stalinism, the Soviet people were more poorly clothed, fed, and housed than they had been during the years of the New Economic Policy.

Terror and Opportunities

The 1930s brought both terror and new opportunities to the Soviet people. The forced pace of industrialization, the collectivization of agriculture, and the uprooting of millions of people could be accomplished only under duress. To prevent any possible resistance or rebellion, the NKVD, Stalin's secret police force, created a climate of suspicion and fear. The terror that pervaded the country was a reflection of Stalin's own paranoia, for he distrusted everyone and feared for his life.

First "Old Bolsheviks" and high officials were put on trial; then the terror spread steadily downward. The government regularly made demands on people that they could not meet, so everyone was guilty of breaking some regulation. People from all walks of life were arrested—sometimes on a mere suspicion or because of a false accusation by a jealous coworker or neighbor, sometimes for expressing a doubt or working too hard or not hard enough, sometimes for being related to someone previously arrested, sometimes for no reason at all. Millions of people were sentenced without a trial. At the height of the terror, some 8 million were sent to *gulags*° (labor camps), where perhaps a million died each year of exposure or malnutrition. To its victims, the terror seemed capricious and random.

Yet Stalin's regime received the support of many Soviet citizens. Suddenly, with so many people gone and new industries and cities being built everywhere, there were opportunities for those who remained, especially the poor and the young. Women entered careers and jobs previously closed to them, such as steelworkers, physicians, and office managers; but they retained their household and child-rearing duties, receiving little help from men. People who moved to the cities, worked enthusiastically, and asked no questions could hope to rise into the upper ranks of the Communist Party, the military, the government, or the professions, where the privileges and rewards were many.

Stalin's brutal methods helped the Soviet Union industrialize faster than any country had ever done. By the late 1930s, the USSR was the world's third largest industrial power, after the United States and Germany. To foreign observers, it seemed to be booming with construction projects, production increases, and labor shortages. Even anti-Communist observers admitted that only a planned economy subject to strict government control could avoid the Depression. To millions of Soviet citizens who took pride in the new strength of their country, and to many foreigners who contrasted conditions in the Soviet Union with the unemployment and despair in the West, Stalin's achievement seemed worth any price.

THE DEPRESSION

On October 24, 1929—"Black Thursday"—the New York stock market went into a dive. Within days, stocks lost half their value, and their value continued to fall for three years. Thousands of banks and businesses collapsed. Millions of workers lost their jobs. The stock-market crash started the deepest and most widespread depression in history.

Economic Crisis

As consumers reduced their purchases, businesses cut production. General Motors, for example, saw its sales drop by half between 1929 and 1931. Companies laid off thousands of workers, throwing them onto public charity. Business and government agencies re-

gulag (GOO-log)

placed their women workers with men, arguing that men had to support their families, whereas women worked only for "pin money." Jobless men deserted their families. As farm prices fell, small farmers went bankrupt and lost their land. By mid-1932, the American economy had fallen by half, and 25 percent of the work force was unemployed. Government spending on welfare and public works was unable to restore prosperity. Many observers thought the free-enterprise system would be replaced by bread lines, soup kitchens, men selling apples on street corners, and hoboes riding freight trains.

Frightened by the stock market collapse, the New York banks called in their loans to Germany and Austria. Without American money, Germany and Austria stopped paying reparations to France and Britain, which then could not repay their war loans to America. By 1931, the Depression had spread to Europe. Governments canceled both reparations payments and war loans, but it was too late to save the world economy.

In 1930, the U.S. government, hoping to protect domestic industries from foreign competition, imposed the highest import duty in American history. In retaliation, other countries raised their tariffs. As a result, global industrial production declined by 36 percent between 1929 and 1932, while world trade dropped by a breathtaking 62 percent.

Depression in Industrial Nations

This massive economic upheaval had profound political repercussions. In the United States, Franklin D. Roosevelt was elected president in 1932 on a "New Deal" platform of government programs to stimulate and revitalize the economy. British and French governments also intervened in their economies and escaped the worst of the Depression by making their colonial empires purchase their products. In the Soviet Union, the five-year plans continued to provide jobs and economic growth.

Nations that relied on exports to pay for imported food and fuel, in particular Japan and Germany, suffered much more. In Germany, unemployment reached 6 million by 1932, twice as high as in Britain. Half the German population lived in poverty. In Japan, the burden of the Depression fell on the farmers and fishermen, who saw their incomes drop sharply. Some, in desperation, revived the ancient practice of selling their daughters. As economic grievances worsened, radical politicians took over the governments in Germany and Japan, manipulated the economies, and turned their nations' military might to acquire empires large enough to support a self-sufficient economy.

Depression in Nonindustrial Regions

The Depression affected Asia, Africa, and Latin America in different ways. A wall of new import duties protected India's infant industries from foreign competition; living standards stagnated but did not drop. The Depression added little to China's problems, except in coastal regions.

Countries that depended on exports were hard hit by the Depression. When automobile production dropped by half in the United States and Europe, so did imports of rubber, devastating the economies of Southeast Asia. When the Depression hit, American tourists vanished from Cuba's beaches and bars, and with them went Cuba's prosperity. The industrialization of Argentina and Brazil was set back a decade or more by the loss of their export markets. In response, military officers seized power in several Latin American countries, consciously imitating dictatorships emerging in Europe.

Southern and central Africa recovered from the Depression quickly, because falling prices made their gold and other minerals more valuable. But this mining boom benefited only a small number of mine owners and investors. For Africans, it was at best a mixed blessing, for mining offered jobs and cash wages to men, while women had to manage without them in the villages.

THE RISE OF FASCISM

The Depression sharpened the polarization of European society that had been underway for decades. Many underpaid or unemployed workers saw in the seeming collapse of the capitalist economy an opportunity as well as temporary suffering. They urged the establishment of a socialist society through the ballot box and strikes instead of the violent revolution that had torn Russia apart.

Frightened investors and factory owners, along with conservative elements in society such as the church and the military, feared the consequences of this political shift to the left. In the democracies of western Europe and North America, middle-income voters kept politics in balance. But in some societies, the war and the Depression left people vulnerable to the appeals of ultra-nationalist politicians who became adept at using propaganda to appeal to people's fears. They promised to bring back full employment, stop the spread of communism, and achieve the territorial conquests that World War I had denied them.

vided social security and public services. On the whole, they proved to be neither ruthless radicals nor competent administrators.

What Mussolini and the Fascist movement really excelled at was publicity: bombastic speeches, spectacular parades, news bulletins full of praise for *Il Duce*° ("the leader"), and signs everywhere proclaiming "Il Duce is always right!" Mussolini's genius was to apply the techniques of modern mass communications and advertisement to political life. Billboards, movie footage, and radio news bulletins galvanized the masses in ways never before seen in peacetime. Although his rhetoric was filled with words like *war, violence,* and *struggle,* his foreign policy was cautious. But his techniques of whipping up public enthusiasm were not lost on other radicals. By the 1930s, fascist movements had appeared in most European countries, as well as in Latin America, China, and Japan.

Mussolini's Italy

The first country to seek radical answers was Italy. World War I, which had never been popular, left thousands of veterans who found neither pride in their victory nor jobs in the postwar economy. Unemployed veterans and violent youths banded together into *fasci di combattimento* (fighting units) to demand action and intimidate politicians. When socialist unions threatened to strike, factory and property owners hired gangs of these *fascisti* to defend them.

Benito Mussolini (1883–1945), a spellbinding orator, quickly became the leader of the **Fascist Party,** which glorified warfare and the Italian nation. By 1921, the party had 300,000 members, many of whom used violent methods to repress strikes, intimidate voters, and seize municipal governments. A year later, when the Fascists failed to win an election, Mussolini threatened to march on Rome if he was not appointed prime minister. The government gave in.

Mussolini proceeded to install Fascist Party members in all government jobs, crush all opposition parties, and jail anyone who criticized him. The party took over the press, public education, and youth activities and gave employers control over their workers. The Fascists lowered living standards but reduced unemployment and pro-

Hitler's Germany

Like Mussolini, **Adolf Hitler** (1889–1945) had served in World War I and looked back fondly on the clear lines of authority and the camaraderie he had experienced in battle. After the war, he too recreated that experience in a paramilitary group, the National Socialist German Workers' Party—**Nazis** for short. Hitler used his gifts as an orator to appeal to Germans disappointed at Germany's humiliation after the war and the hyperinflation of 1923. In 1924, he too led an uprising, but the attempted seizure of Munich was a failure. Germany was not yet ready to follow Italy's path.

The Depression changed that. While serving a jail sentence for the coup attempt, Hitler wrote *Mein Kampf*° (*My Struggle*), but when it was published in 1925, no one took the book or its author's extreme nationalist, racist, and anti-Jewish ideas seriously. Hitler believed that Germany should incorporate all German-speaking people, even those who lived in neighboring countries. He distinguished among a "master race" of Aryans (he meant Germans, Scandinavians, and Britons), a degenerate "Alpine" race of French and Italians,

---

Il Duce (eel DOO-chay)   *Mein Kampf* (mine compf)

Hitler the Orator A masterful public speaker, Adolf Hitler often captivated mass audiences at Nazi Party rallies. (Roger Viollet)

and an inferior race of Russian and eastern European Slavs, who, he believed, were fit only to be slaves of the master race. He reserved his most intense hatred for Jews, on whom he blamed every disaster that had befallen Germany, especially the defeat of 1918. He glorified violence, which would enable the "master race" to defeat and subjugate all others.

When the Depression hit, the Nazis gained supporters among the unemployed who believed Nazi promises of jobs for all and among property owners frightened by the growing popularity of Communists. In March 1933, as leader of the largest party in Germany, Hitler became chancellor.

Once in office, he quickly assumed dictatorial power, just as Mussolini had done. He expelled the Communist Party from the Reichstag° (parliament), intimidated it to give him dictatorial powers, and then put Nazis in charge of all government agencies, educational institutions, and professional organizations. He banned all other political parties and threw their leaders into concentration camps. The Nazis deprived Jews of their citizenship and civil rights, prohibited them from marrying "Aryans," ousted them from the professions, and confiscated their property. In August 1934, Hitler proclaimed himself *Führer*° ("leader") and called Germany the "Third Reich" (empire)—the third after the Holy Roman Empire and the German Empire of 1871 to 1918.

The Nazis' economic and social policies were spectacularly effective. The government undertook massive public works projects. Businesses got contracts to manufacture weapons for the armed forces. Women, who had entered the work force during and after World War I, were urged to return to *"Kinder, Kirche, Küche"* (children, church, kitchen), releasing jobs for men. By 1936, business was booming, unemployment was at its lowest level since the 1920s, and living standards were rising. Hitler's popularity soared because most Germans believed their economic well-being outweighed the loss of liberty.

The Road to War, 1933–1939

Hitler sought not prosperity or popularity, but conquest. As soon as he came to office, he began to build up the armed forces with conquest in mind. Meanwhile, he tested the reactions of the other powers through a series of surprise moves followed by protestations of peaceful intent.

In 1933, Hitler withdrew Germany from the League of Nations. France and Britain hesitated to retaliate by blockading or invading Germany. Two

---

Reichstag (RIKES-tog) *Führer* (FEW-rer)

years later, he announced that Germany was going to introduce conscription, build up its army, and create an air force—in violation of the Versailles treaty. Instead of protesting, Britain signed a naval agreement with Germany. The message was clear: neither Britain nor France was willing to risk war by standing up to Germany. The United States, absorbed in its own domestic economic problems, had reverted to isolationism.

Emboldened by the weakness of the democracies, Italy in 1935 invaded Ethiopia, the last independent state in Africa and a member of the League of Nations. The League and the democracies protested but refused to close the Suez Canal to Italian ships or impose an oil embargo. The following year, when Hitler sent troops into the Rhineland on the borders of France and Belgium, the other powers merely protested.

By 1938, Hitler decided his rearmament plans were far enough advanced that he could escalate his demands. In March, Germany invaded and soon annexed Austria, with little protest from its German-speaking citizens. Then came the turn of Czechoslovakia. Hitler demanded autonomy for its German-speaking borderlands, then their annexation. At the Munich Conference of September 1938, the leaders of France, Britain, and Italy gave Hitler everything he wanted to keep him from starting a war. Once again, Hitler learned that aggression paid off and that the democracies always gave in.

The democracies' policy of "appeasement" ran counter to the European balance-of-power tradition for three reasons. The first was the deep-seated fear of war among all people who had lived through World War I. The second was fear of communism. The conservative politicians who ruled France and Britain were more afraid of Stalin than of Hitler, for Hitler claimed to respect Christianity and private property. Rather than revive the pre–World War I alliance of Britain, France, and Russia, they sold out the Czechs. The third cause was the very novelty of fascist tactics. Britain's prime minister, Neville Chamberlain, assumed that political leaders (other than the Bolsheviks) were honorable men and that an agreement was as valid as a business contract. Thus, when Hitler said he had "no further territorial demands," Chamberlain believed him.

After Munich, it was too late to stop Hitler, short of war. Germany and Italy were now united in an alliance called the Axis. In March 1939, Germany invaded what was left of Czechoslovakia. Belatedly realizing that Hitler could not be trusted, France and Britain sought Soviet help. Stalin, however, distrusted the "capitalists" as much as they distrusted him. Hitler, meanwhile, offered to divide Poland between Germany and the Soviet Union. On August 23, Stalin accepted. The Nazi-Soviet Pact freed Hitler from the fear of a two-front war and gave Stalin two more years of peace to build up his armies. One week later, on September 1, 1939, German forces swept into Poland across the Eastern Front. The war was on.

EAST ASIA, 1931–1945

When the Depression ruined Japan's export trade, ultranationalists, including young army officers, resented their country's dependence on foreign trade. If only Japan had a colonial empire, they thought, it would not be beholden to the rest of the world. But Europeans and Americans had already taken most potential colonies in Asia. Japan had only Korea, Taiwan, and a railroad in Manchuria. Japanese nationalists saw China, with its vast population and resources, as the solution to their country's problems.

The Manchurian Incident of 1931

Meanwhile, the Guomindang° was becoming stronger in China and preparing to challenge the Japanese presence in Manchuria, a province rich in coal and iron ore. Junior officers in the Japanese army guarding the South Manchurian Railway, frustrated by the caution of their superiors, determined to take action. In September 1931, an explosion on a railroad track, probably staged, gave them an excuse to conquer the entire

Guomindang (gwo-min-dong)

German Dive–Bomber over Eastern Europe   In this painting, a German ME-100 fighter plane attacks a Soviet troop convoy on the Eastern Front.   (AKG London)

province. In Tokyo, weak civilian ministers acquiesced to the attack to avoid losing face and shortly recognized the "independence" of Manchuria under the name "Manchukuo°."

The U.S. government condemned the Japanese conquest. The League of Nations refused to recognize Manchukuo and urged the Japanese to remove their troops from China. Persuaded that the Western powers would not fight, Japan resigned from the League.

During the next few years, the Japanese built railways and heavy industries in Manchuria and northeastern China and sped up their rearmament. The government grew more authoritarian, jailing thousands of dissidents. On several occasions, superpatriotic junior officers who mutinied or assassinated leading political figures received mild punishments, and generals and admirals sympathetic to their views replaced more moderate civilian politicians.

The Chinese Communists and the Long March

Until the Japanese seized Manchuria, the Chinese government seemed to be consolidating its power and creating the conditions for a national recovery. The main challenge to the government of **Chiang Kai-shek°** came from the Chinese Communists, who were organizing industrial workers and who worked in alliance with the Nationalists until in 1927, when

---

Manchukuo (man-CHEW-coo-oh)

Chiang Kai-shek (chang kie-shek)

Chiang Kai-shek arrested and executed Communists and labor leaders alike.

The few Communists who escaped the mass arrests fled to the remote mountains of Jiangxi°, in southeastern China. Among them was **Mao Zedong°** (1893–1976), a farmer's son who had left home to study philosophy. In the early 1920s, Mao discovered the works of Karl Marx, joined the Communist Party, and soon became one of its leaders. In Jiangxi, Mao began studying conditions among the peasants, in whom Communists had previously shown no interest. He planned to redistribute land from the wealthier to the poorer peasants, thereby gaining adherents for the coming struggle with the Guomindang army.

Mao's reliance on the peasantry was a radical departure from Marxist-Leninist ideology, which stressed the backwardness of the peasants and pinned its hopes on industrial workers. Mao was also an advocate of women's equality. Before 1927, the Communists had organized the women who worked in Shanghai's textile mills, the most exploited of all Chinese workers. Later, in their mountain stronghold in Jiangxi, they organized women farmers, allowed divorce, and banned arranged marriages and footbinding.

The Guomindang army pursued the Communists into the mountains, building small forts throughout the countryside. Rather than risk direct confrontations, Mao responded with guerrilla warfare. Government troops often mistreated civilians, but Mao insisted that his soldiers help the peasants, pay a fair price for food and supplies, and treat women with respect. In spite of their good relations with the peasants of Jiangxi, the Communists decided to break out of the southern mountains and trek to Shaanxi°, an even more remote province in northwestern China. The so-called **Long March** took them 6,000 miles (nearly 9,700 kilometers) in one year, 17 miles (27 kilometers) a day over desolate mountains and through swamps and deserts, pursued by the army and bombed by Chiang's aircraft. Of the 100,000 Communists who left Jiangxi in October 1934, only 4,000 reached Shaanxi a year later.

Jiangxi (jang-she)   Mao Zedong (ma-oh zay-dong)
Shaanxi (SHAWN-she)

Mao on the Long March   In 1934–1935, Mao Zedong led his rag-tag army of guerrillas across the rugged mountains of southern and western China. In this romanticized painting, young Mao is speaking to a group of soldiers in spotless uniforms who look up at him with worshipful expressions.   (Library of Congress)

The Sino-Japanese War, 1937–1945

On July 7, 1937, Japanese troops attacked Chinese forces near Beijing. As in 1931, the junior officers who ordered the attack quickly obtained the support of their commanders and then, reluctantly, of the government. Within weeks, Japanese troops seized Beijing, Tianjin, Shanghai, and other coastal cities, and the Japanese navy blockaded the entire coast of China.

Once again, the United States and the League of Nations denounced the Japanese atrocities. Yet the Western powers were too preoccupied with events in Europe and with their own economic problems to risk a military confrontation in Asia. When the Japanese sank a U.S. gunboat and shelled a British ship on the Yangzi River, the U.S. and British governments responded only with righteous indignation and pious resolutions.

The large Chinese armies were poorly led and armed and lost every battle. Within a year, Japan controlled the coastal provinces of China and the lower Yangzi and Yellow River Valleys, China's richest and most populated regions, but the Chinese people continued to resist, either in the army or, increasingly, with the Communist guerrilla forces. Japan's periodic attempts to turn the tide by conquering one more piece of China only pushed Japan deeper into the quagmire.

Warfare between Chinese and Japanese was incredibly violent. In the winter of 1937–1938, Japanese troops took Nanjing, raped 20,000 women, killed 200,000 prisoners and civilians, and looted and burned the city. To slow them down, Chiang ordered the Yellow River dikes blasted open, causing a flood that destroyed 4,000 villages, killed 890,000 people, and made 12.5 million homeless. Two years later, when the Communists ordered a massive offensive, the Japanese retaliated with a "kill all, burn all, loot all" campaign, destroying hundreds of villages down to the last person, building, and farm animal.

The Chinese government, led by Chiang Kai-shek, escaped to the mountains of Sichuan in the center of the country. There he built up a huge army, not to fight Japan but to prepare for a future confrontation with the Communists. The army drafted over 3 million men, even though it had only a million rifles and could not provide food or clothing for all its soldiers. The Guomindang raised farmers' taxes, even when famine forced farmers to eat the bark of trees. Such taxes were not enough to support both a large army and the thousands of government officials and hangers-on who had fled to Sichuan. To avoid taxing its wealthy supporters, the government printed money, causing inflation, hoarding, and corruption.

From his capital of Yan'an in Shaanxi province, Mao also built up his army and formed a government. Unlike the Guomindang, the Communists listened to the grievances of the peasants, especially the poor, to whom they distributed land confiscated from wealthy landowners. Because they could present themselves as the only group in China that was serious about fighting the Japanese, the Communists obtained support and intelligence from farmers in Japanese-occupied territory.

THE SECOND WORLD WAR

The Second World War was much bigger and deadlier than the First in every way. It was fought around the world, from Norway to New Guinea, from Hawaii to Egypt, and on every ocean. It was a total war that showed how effectively industry, science, and nationalism could be channeled into mass destruction.

The War of Movement

Defensive maneuvers had dominated in World War I. In World War II, motorized weapons gave back the advantage to the offensive. Opposing forces moved fast, their victories hinging as much on the aggressive spirit of their commanders and the military intelligence they obtained as on numbers of troops or firepower.

The Wehrmacht°, or German armed forces, was the first to learn this lesson. It not only had tanks, trucks, and fighter planes but perfected their combined use in a tactic called *blitzkrieg*° (lightning war): fighter planes scattered enemy troops and disrupted communications, and tanks punctured the enemy's defenses and then, with the help of the infantry, encircled and captured enemy troops. At sea, the navies of both Japan and the United States had developed aircraft carriers that could launch planes against targets hundreds of miles away.

The very size and mobility of the opposing forces made the fighting far different from any the world had ever seen. Countries were conquered in a matter of days or weeks. The belligerents mobilized the economies of entire continents, squeezing them for every possible resource. They tried not only to defeat their enemies' armed forces

---

Wehrmacht (VAIR-mokt) *blitzkrieg* (BLITS-creeg)

but—by means of blockades, submarine attacks on shipping, and bombing raids on industrial areas—to damage the economies that supported those armed forces. They thought of civilians not as innocent bystanders but as legitimate targets and, later, as vermin to be exterminated.

War in Europe and North Africa

It took less than a month for the Wehrmacht to conquer Poland. Britain and France declared war on Germany but took no military action. Meanwhile, the Soviet Union invaded eastern Poland and the Baltic republics of Lithuania, Latvia, and Estonia. Although the Poles fought bravely, the Polish infantry and cavalry were no match for German or Russian tanks. During the winter of 1939–1940, Germany and the Western democracies faced each other in what soldiers called a "phony war" and watched as the Soviet Union attacked Finland, which resisted for many months.

In March 1940, Hitler went on the offensive again, conquering Denmark, Norway, the Netherlands, and Belgium in less than two months. In May, he attacked France. Although the French army had as many soldiers, tanks, and aircraft as the Wehrmacht, its morale was low, and it quickly collapsed. By the end of June, Hitler was master of all of Europe between Russia and Spain.

Germany still had to face one enemy: Britain. The British had no army to speak of, but they had other assets: the English Channel, the Royal Navy and Air Force, and a tough new prime minister, Winston Churchill. The Germans knew they could invade Britain only by gaining control of the airspace over the Channel, so they launched a massive air attack—the Battle of Britain—lasting from June through September. They failed, however, because the Royal Air Force had better fighters and used radar and code breaking to detect approaching German planes.

Frustrated, Hitler turned his attention eastward against the Soviet Union. Within five months, the Wehrmacht conquered the Baltic states, Ukraine, and half of European Russia; captured a million prisoners of war; and stood at the very gates of Moscow and Leningrad (now St. Petersburg). The USSR seemed on the verge of collapse when suddenly the weather turned cold, machines froze, and the fighting came to a halt. Like Napoleon, Hitler had ignored the environment of Russia at his peril.

The next spring, the Wehrmacht renewed its offensive. It surrounded Leningrad in a siege that was to cost a million lives. Leaving Moscow aside, it turned toward the Caucasus and its oil wells. In August, the Germans attacked **Stalingrad** (now Volgograd), the key to the Volga River and the supply of oil. For months, German and Soviet soldiers fought over every street and every house. When winter came, the Red Army counterattacked and encircled the city. In February 1943, the remnants of the German army in Stalingrad surrendered. Hitler had lost his greatest gamble (see Map 26.1).

From Europe, the war spread to Africa. During 1941, British forces conquered Italian East Africa and invaded Libya as well. The Italian rout in North Africa brought the Germans to their rescue. During 1942, the German army and the forces of the British Empire seesawed back and forth across the deserts of Libya and Egypt. Because the British could decode German messages and had more weapons and supplies, they were finally able to expel the Germans from Africa in May 1943.

War in Asia and the Pacific

The war presented Japan with the opportunity to take over European colonies in Southeast Asia, with their abundant oil, rubber, and other strategic materials. After Japanese forces occupied French Indochina in July 1941, the United States and Britain cut off shipments of steel, scrap iron, oil, and other products that Japan desperately needed. This left Japan with three alternatives: accept the shame and humiliation of giving up its conquests, as the Americans insisted; face economic ruin; or widen the war. Japan chose war.

On December 7, 1941, Japanese planes bombed the U.S. naval base at **Pearl Harbor,** Hawaii, sinking or damaging scores of warships. Then, between January and March 1942, the Japanese bombed Hong Kong and Singapore and in-

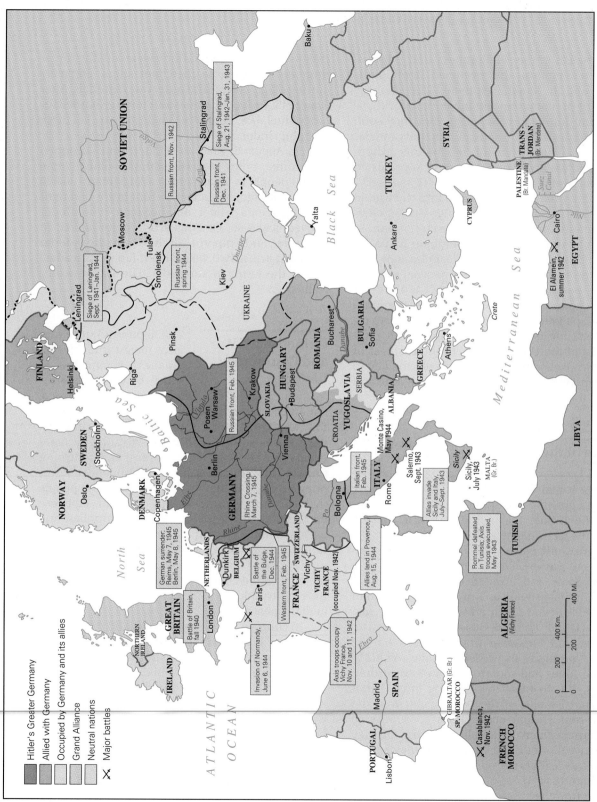

Map 26.1 World War II in Europe and North Africa In a series of quick and decisive campaigns from September 1939 to December 1941, German forces overran much of Europe and North Africa. There followed three years of bitter fighting as the Allies slowly pushed the Germans back. This map shows the maximum extent of Germany's conquests and alliances, as well as the key battles and the front lines at various times.

Hitler's Greater Germany
Allied with Germany
Occupied by Germany and its allies
Grand Alliance
Neutral nations
X Major battles

Siege of Stalingrad, Aug. 21, 1942–Jan. 31, 1943
Russian front, Nov. 1942
Russian front, Dec. 1941
Russian front, spring 1944
Siege of Leningrad, Sept. 1941–Jan. 1944
Russian front, Feb. 1945
German surrender: Reims, May 7, 1945 Berlin, May 8, 1945
Rhine Crossing, March 7, 1945
Battle of the Bulge, Dec. 1944
Western front, Feb. 1945
Invasion of Normandy, June 6, 1944
Battle of Britain, fall 1940
Axis troops occupy Vichy France, Nov. 10 and 11, 1942
Allies land in Provence, Aug. 15, 1944
Italian front, Feb. 1945
Monte Cassino, May 1944
Salerno, Sept. 1943
Allies invade Sicily and Italy, July–Sept. 1943
Sicily, July 1943
Rommel defeated in Tunisia; Axis troops evacuated, May 1943
El Alamein, summer 1942
Casablanca, Nov. 1942

SOVIET UNION
Baku
Stalingrad
Moscow
Tula
Smolensk
Leningrad
Helsinki
FINLAND
Pinsk
Kiev
Riga
UKRAINE
Warsaw
Posen
Kraków
SLOVAKIA
HUNGARY
Budapest
ROMANIA
Bucharest
BULGARIA
Sofia
SERBIA
YUGOSLAVIA
CROATIA
ALBANIA
GREECE
Athens
Crete
TURKEY
Ankara
CYPRUS
SYRIA
TRANS-JORDAN (Br. Mandate)
PALESTINE (Br. Mandate)
Cairo
EGYPT
LIBYA
Mediterranean Sea
Black Sea
Yalta
MALTA (Gr. Br.)
Sicily
ITALY
Rome
Bologna
Vienna
Berlin
GERMANY
SWITZERLAND
FRANCE
VICHY FRANCE (occupied Nov. 1942)
Paris
Dunkirk
BELGIUM
NETHERLANDS
London
GREAT BRITAIN
IRELAND
NORTHERN IRELAND
DENMARK
Copenhagen
NORWAY
Oslo
SWEDEN
Stockholm
Baltic Sea
North Sea
ATLANTIC OCEAN
PORTUGAL
Lisbon
SPAIN
Madrid
GIBRALTAR (Gr. Br.)
SP. MOROCCO
FRENCH MOROCCO
ALGERIA (Vichy France)
TUNISIA
Elbe
Danube
Rhine
Ebro
Po
Vistula
Volga
Don
Dnieper
Dniester
Suez Canal
Nile

0   200   400 Km.
0   200   400 Mi.

vaded Thailand, the Philippines, and Malaya. Within a few months, they occupied all of Southeast Asia and the Dutch East Indies. The Japanese claimed to be liberating the inhabitants of these lands from European colonialism. But they soon began to confiscate food and raw materials and demand heavy labor from the inhabitants, whom they treated with contempt. Those who protested were brutally punished.

The entry of the United States into the war, in alliance with Britain and the Soviet Union, challenged Japan's dream of an East Asian empire. In April 1942, American planes bombed Tokyo. In May, the United States Navy defeated a Japanese fleet in the Coral Sea, ending Japanese plans to conquer Australia. A month later, at the **Battle of Midway,** Japan lost four of its six largest aircraft carriers. Japan did not have enough industry to replace them, for its war production was only one-tenth that of the United States. In the vastness of the Pacific Ocean, aircraft carriers held the key to victory, and without them, Japan faced a long and hopeless war (see Map 26.2).

The End of the War

Its new American ally also helped the Soviet Union capitalize on the advantage it had won in the Battle of Stalingrad. Aided by a growing stream of supplies from factories in the United States, the Red Army began pushing the Wehrmacht back toward Germany.

The Western powers, meanwhile, staged two invasions of Europe. Beginning in July 1943, they captured Sicily and invaded Italy. Mussolini resigned, and Italy signed an armistice, but German troops held off the Allied advance for two years. Then on D-day (June 6, 1944), 156,000 British, American, and Canadian troops landed on the coast of Normandy in western France. Within a week, the Allies had more troops in France than Germany did. To meet this growing force, Hitler had to transfer part of the Wehrmacht from the Eastern Front. Despite advancing armies on three sides, Germany held out for almost a year. On May 7, 1945, a week after Hitler committed suicide, German military leaders surrendered.

By June 1944, U.S. bombers were also attacking Japan from newly captured island bases in the Pacific, and U.S. submarines were sinking larger numbers of Japanese merchant ships, gradually cutting off Japan's oil and other raw materials. After May 1945, with the Japanese air force grounded for lack of fuel, U.S. planes began destroying Japanese shipping, industries, and cities at will.

On August 6, 1945, the United States dropped an atomic bomb on **Hiroshima,** killing some 80,000 people in a flash and leaving about 120,000 more to die agonizing deaths from burns and radiation. Three days later, another atomic bomb destroyed Nagasaki. On August 14, Japan offered to surrender, and Emperor Hirohito gave the order to lay down arms. Two weeks later, Japanese leaders signed the terms of surrender. The war was officially over.

Chinese Civil War and Communist Victory

The Japanese surrender also meant the end of Japanese occupation of much of China, but instead of bringing peace, it marked an intensification of the contest between the Guomindang and the Communists. Guomindang forces started with many advantages: more troops and weapons, U.S. support, and control of China's cities. But their behavior eroded whatever popular support they had. They taxed the people they "liberated" more heavily than the Japanese had, looted businesses, confiscated supplies, and enriched themselves at the expense of the population. To pay its bills, Chiang's government printed money so fast that it soon lost all its value, ruining merchants and causing hoarding and shortages. In the countryside, the Guomindang's brutality alienated the peasants.

In contrast, the Communists' land reform programs had won them popular support, which was even more important than the heavy equipment brought by Guomindang soldiers, who began deserting by the thousands, and the Japanese equipment seized by the Soviets in the last weeks of the war. By 1949, the Guomindang armies were collapsing everywhere, defeated more by their own greed and ineptness than by the Communists. As the Communists advanced, high-ranking members of the Guomindang fled to Taiwan, protected from the mainland by the United States Navy. On

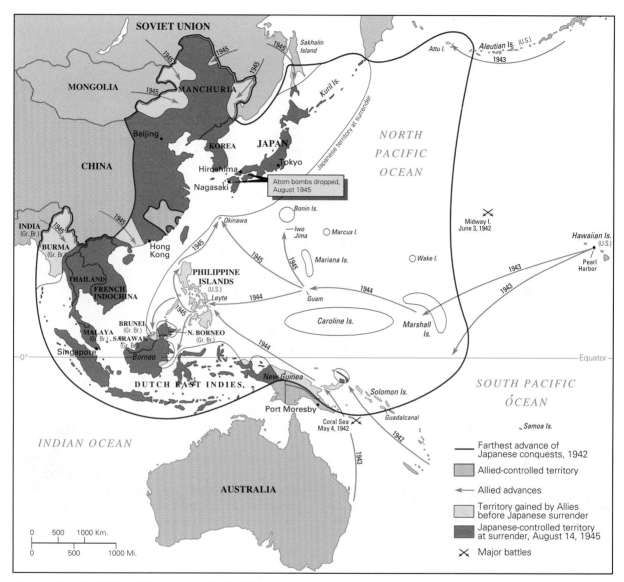

Map 26.2   World War II in Asia and the Pacific   After having conquered much of China between 1937 and 1941, Japanese forces launched a sudden attack on Southeast Asia, Indonesia, and the Pacific in late 1941 and early 1942. American forces slowly reconquered the Pacific islands and the Philippines until August 1945, when the atomic bombing of Hiroshima and Nagasaki forced Japan's surrender.

Hiroshima After the Atomic Bomb   On August 6, 1945, an atomic bomb destroyed the city, killing over fifty thousand people. This photo shows the devastation of the city center, where only a few concrete buildings remained standing.   (Wide World Photos)

October 1, 1949, Mao Zedong announced the founding of the People's Republic of China.

THE CHARACTER OF WARFARE

The war left an enormous death toll. Recent estimates place the figure at close to 60 million deaths, six to eight times more than in World War I. Over half of the dead were civilian victims of massacres, famines, or bombs. The Soviet Union lost between 20 million and 25 million people, more than any other country. China suffered 15 million deaths; Poland lost some 6 million, of whom half were Jewish; the Jewish people lost another 3 million outside Poland. Over 4 million Germans and over 2 million Japanese died. In much of the world, almost every family mourned one or more of its members. In contrast, Great Britain lost 400,000 people, the United States 300,000.

One reason for the terrible toll in human lives and suffering was a change in moral values, as belligerents identified not just soldiers but entire peoples as enemies. Another reason for the devastation was the appearance of new technologies that carried destruction deep into enemy territory far beyond the traditional battlefields.

The War of Science   Scientists made many contributions to the technology of warfare. Chemists found ways to make synthetic rubber from coal or oil. Physicists perfected radar, which warned of approaching enemy aircraft and submarines. Others broke enemy codes and developed antibiotics that saved the lives of countless wounded soldiers (see Environment and Technology: Biomedical Technologies).

Aircraft development was especially striking. As war approached, German, British, and Japanese aircraft manufacturers developed fast, maneuverable fighter planes. U.S. industry produced aircraft of every sort but was especially noted for its heavy bombers designed to fly in huge formations and drop tons of bombs on enemy cities. The Japanese developed the Mitsubishi "Zero" fighter plane—light, fast, and agile. Unable to produce heavy planes in large numbers, Germany responded with radically new designs, including the first jet fighters, low-flying buzz bombs, and fearful V-2 missiles.

In October 1939, President Roosevelt received a letter from physicist Albert Einstein, a Jewish refugee from Nazism, warning of the dangers of nuclear power. Fearing that Germany might develop a nuclear bomb first, Roosevelt placed the vast resources of the U.S. government at the disposal of physicists and engineers, both Americans and refugees from Europe. By 1945, they had built two atomic bombs, each one powerful enough to annihilate an entire city.

Bombing Raids

The Germans began the war from the air, but it was the British and Americans who excelled at large-scale urban bombardment. Since it was very hard to pinpoint individual buildings, especially at night, such raids were aimed at weakening the morale of the civilian population.

In May 1942, 1,000 British planes dropped incendiary bombs on Cologne, setting fire to most of the old city. Between July 24 and August 2, 1943, 3,330 British and Americans bombers set fire to Hamburg, killing 50,000 people. Later raids destroyed Berlin, Dresden, and other German cities. All in all, the bombing raids against Germany killed 600,000 people—more than half of them women and children—and injured 800,000. If the air strategists had hoped thereby to break the morale of the German people, they failed. The only effective bombing raids were those directed against oil depots and synthetic fuel plants; by early 1945, they had almost brought the German war effort to a standstill.

American bombing raids on Japanese cities were even more devastating than the fire-bombing of German cities, for Japanese cities were built of wood. In March 1945, a large raid set Tokyo ablaze, killing 80,000 people and leaving a million homeless. Five months later, single atomic bombs did something similar.

The Holocaust

The Nazis killed defenseless civilians on an even larger scale. Their murders were not the by-products of some military goal but a calculated policy of extermination.

Their first targets were Jews. Soon after Hitler came to power, he deprived German Jews of their citizenship and legal rights. When eastern Europe fell under Nazi rule, the Nazis herded its large Jewish population into ghettos in the major cities, where many died of starvation and disease. Then, in early 1942, the Nazis decided to carry out Hitler's "final solution to the Jewish problem" by applying modern industrial methods to the slaughter of human beings. German companies built huge extermination camps in eastern Europe. Every day, trainloads of cattle cars arrived at the camps and disgorged thousands of captives and the corpses of those who had died of starvation or asphyxiation along the way. The strongest survivors were put to work and fed almost nothing until they died. Women, children, the elderly, and the sick were shoved into gas chambers and asphyxiated with poison gas. **Auschwitz,** the biggest camp, was a giant industrial complex designed to kill up to twelve thousand people a day. Most horrifying of all were the tortures inflicted on prisoners selected by Nazi doctors for "medical experiments." This mass extermination, now called the **Holocaust** ("burning"), claimed some 6 million Jewish lives.

Besides the Jews, the Nazis also killed 3 million Polish Catholics—especially professionals, army officers, and the educated—in an effort to reduce the Polish people to slavery. They also exterminated

Biomedical Technologies

Life expectancy at birth has nearly doubled in the past 150 years. Even in the poorest countries, life expectancy has risen from forty to sixty or seventy years. The cause of this remarkable change is threefold: clean water, immunizations, and antibiotics.

The realization that drinking water can spread disease came first to Dr. Charles Snow, who noticed the correlation between deaths from cholera and the water from a particular pump in London during an epidemic in 1854. Since then, public health officials have been very conscious of the quality of drinking water, although only wealthy cities can afford to purify and chlorinate water for all their inhabitants.

The practice of immunization goes back to the eighteenth century, when physicians in Turkey and in Europe applied infected pus from a person with smallpox (variolation) or an animal with cowpox (vaccination) to healthy persons to build up their resistance to smallpox. By the end of the nineteenth century, it became clear that immunity to many diseases could be conferred by injections of weakened bacteria. Immunizations offer the single most effective way to prevent childhood diseases and thereby increase life expectancy.

Antibiotics are more recent. In 1928, Dr. Alexander Fleming discovered that a certain mold, *Penicillin notatum,* could kill bacteria. Antibiotics were first used in large quantities in the Second World War. Along with two other innovations—synthetic antimalarial drugs and blood transfusions—antibiotics helped cut the fatality of battlefield wounds from 11 percent in World War I to 3 percent in World War II.

The remarkable success of these technologies has led people to consider good health their natural birthright. Unfortunately, the victory over disease is temporary at best. The abuse of antibiotics and of antibacterial products encourages the growth of new

Biotechnology in Action   Campaigns to immunize children against diseases reached even remote villages, as here in Thailand.   (Peter Charlesworth/Saba)

strains of old diseases, such as tuberculosis, which can resist all known antibiotics. And although bacterial diseases are no longer as prevalent as they once were, humans are still susceptible to viral afflictions such as influenza and AIDS.

homosexuals, Jehovah's Witnesses, Gypsies, the disabled, and the mentally ill—all in the interests of "racial purity." Whenever a German was killed in an occupied country, the Nazis retaliated by burning a village with all its inhabitants. After the invasion of Russia, the Wehrmacht was given orders to execute all captured communists, government employees, and officers. They also worked millions of prisoners of war to death or let them die of starvation.

The Home Front

Rapid military movements and air power carried the war to people's homes in China, Japan, Southeast Asia, and Europe. Armies swept through the land, confiscating food, fuel, and anything else of value. Bombers and heavy artillery pounded cities into rubble, leaving only the skeletons of buildings, while survivors cowered in cellars. Air-raid sirens awakened people throughout the night. Millions fled their homes in terror. Of all the major belligerents, only Americans escaped such nightmares, and war production ended the deprivations of the Depression years.

The war demanded an enormous production effort from civilians. In the face of advancing Germans in 1941, the Soviets dismantled over fifteen hundred factories and rebuilt them in the Ural Mountains and Siberia, where workers soon turned out more tanks and artillery than the Axis. American factories produced an unending supply of ships, aircraft, trucks, tanks, and other materiel for the Allied effort. The Axis Powers also could not compete.

With so many men mobilized for war, women were responsible for much of this production. For example, 6 million women entered the American labor force during the war, 2.5 million of them in manufacturing jobs previously considered "men's work." Soviet women took over half of all industrial and three-quarters of all agricultural jobs. In the other belligerent countries, women also played a major role in the war effort, replacing men in fields, factories, and offices. The Nazis, in contrast, believed that German women should stay home and bear children, and they imported 7 million "guest workers"—a euphemism for war prisoners and captured foreigners.

War and the Environment

As in World War I, battles scarred the landscape, leaving behind spent ammunition and damaged equipment. Retreating armies flooded large areas of China and the Netherlands. The bombing of cities left ruins that remained visible for a generation or more. The main cause of environmental stress, however, was not the fighting but the economic development that sustained it.

As war industries boomed—the United States increased its industrial production fourfold during the war—so did the demand for raw materials. Mining companies opened new mines and towns in Central Africa to supply strategic minerals. Brazil, Argentina, and other Latin American countries deprived of manufactured imports began building their own steel mills, factories, and shipyards. In India, China, and Europe, timber felling accelerated far beyond forest regrowth.

We must keep the environmental effects of the war in perspective. From the vantage point of the present, the environmental impact of the war seems quite modest in comparison with the damage inflicted on the earth by the long consumer boom that began in the post–World War II years.

CONCLUSION

Between 1929 and 1949, the old global order—conservative, colonialist, and dominated by Great Britain and France—was shattered by the Depression, the politics of violence, and the most devastating war in history. Stalin transformed the Soviet Union into an industrial giant at enormous human cost. Reacting to the Depression, which weakened the Western democracies, Hitler in Germany and military leaders in Japan prepared for a war of conquest. Though Germany and Japan achieved stunning victories at first, their forces soon faltered in the face of the greater industrial production of the United States and the Soviet Union.

The war was so destructive and spread to so much of the globe because rapidly advancing technology was readily converted from civilian to military production. Machines that had made cars could also manufacture bombers or tanks. Engineers could design factories to kill people with maximum efficiency. The accelerating technology of missiles and nuclear bombs made the entire planet vulnerable to human destruction for the first time in history.

Into the power vacuum left by the collapse of Germany and Japan stepped the two superpowers: the United States and the USSR. When the war ended, U.S. soldiers were stationed in Australia, Japan, and western Europe, and the Red Army occupied all of eastern Europe and parts of northern China. Within months of their victory, these one-time allies became ideological enemies.

The global impact of World War II was drastic and almost immediate, because the war weakened the European colonial powers and because so much of the fighting took place in North Africa, Southeast Asia, and other colonial areas. Within fifteen years of the end of the war, almost every European colonial empire had disappeared. As the long era of European domination receded, Asians and Africans began reclaiming their independence.

■ Key Terms

Joseph Stalin	Long March
Five-Year Plans	Stalingrad
Benito Mussolini	Pearl Harbor
Fascist Party	Battle of Midway
Adolf Hitler	Hiroshima
Nazis	Auschwitz
Chiang Kai-shek	Holocaust
Mao Zedong	

■ Suggested Reading

The literature on the period from 1929 to 1945 is enormous and growing fast. The following list is but a very summary introduction.

Charles Kindelberger's *The World in Depression, 1929–39* (1973) and Robert McElvaine's *The Great Depression: America, 1929–1941* (1984) provide a sophisticated economic analysis of the Depression. A. J. H. Latham's *The*

Depression and the Developing World, 1914–1939 (1981) gives a global perspective.

The best recent book on Japan in the twentieth century is Daikichi Irokawa's *The Age of Hirohito: In Search of Modern Japan* (1995). On Japanese expansion, see W. G. Beasley, *Japanese Imperialism, 1894–1945* (1987). The race to war is covered in Akira Iriye, *The Origins of the Second World War in Asia and the Pacific* (1987). Michael Barnhart, *Japan Prepares for Total War* (1987), is short and well written.

In the large and fast-growing literature on twentieth-century China, two general introductions are especially useful: John K. Fairbank, *The Great Chinese Revolution, 1800–1985* (1986), and Jonathan Spence, *The Search for Modern China* (1990). On the warlord and Guomindang periods, see Lucien Bianco, *Origins of the Chinese Revolution, 1915–1949* (1971). The Japanese invasion of China is the subject of Iris Chang, *The Rape of Nanking: The Forgotten Holocaust of World War II* (1997), and of James Hsiung and Steven Levine, eds., *China's Bitter Victory: The War with Japan, 1937–1945* (1992). Jung Chang, *Wild Swans: Three Daughters of China* (1991), is a fascinating account of women's experiences during the Revolution and the Mao era by the daughter of two Communist officials.

Among recent biographies of Stalin, see Dmitrii Volkogonov's *Stalin: Triumph and Tragedy* (1991) and Robert Tucker's *Stalin as Revolutionary, 1879–1929* (1973) and *Stalin in Power: The Revolution from Above, 1928–1941* (1990). On the transformation of the USSR, see Roy Medvedev's *Let History Judge: The Origins and Consequences of Stalinism* (1989) and Stephen Kotkin's *Magnetic Mountain: Stalinism as Civilization* (1995). Stalin's collectivization of agriculture is vividly portrayed in Robert Conquest's *Harvest of Sorrow* (1986); see also Sheila Fitzpatrick's *Stalin's Peasants: Resistance and Survival in the Russian Village After Collectivization* (1994). Conquest's *The Great Terror: A Reassessment* (1990) describes the purges of the 1930s. Alexander Solzhenitsyn, a veteran of Stalin's prisons, explores them in a detailed history, *The Gulag Archipelago, 1918–1956* (3 vols., 1974–1978), and in a short, brilliant novel, *One Day in the Life of Ivan Denisovich* (1978).

Alexander De Grand provides an excellent interpretation of fascism in *Italian Fascism: Its Origins and Development,* 2d ed. (1989). William Shirer's *The Rise and Fall of the Third Reich* (1960) is a long but very dramatic eyewitness description of Nazi Germany by a journalist. The dictators are the subject of two fine biographies: Denis Mack Smith's *Mussolini* (1982) and Alan Bullock's *Hitler: A Study in Tyranny* (1965). See also A. J. P. Taylor's controversial classic, *The Origins of the Second World War* (1966).

Two very detailed books on World War II are John Keegan, *The Second World War* (1990), and Gerhard Weinberg, *A World at Arms: A Global History of World War II* (1994). Particular aspects of the war in Europe are covered in Alexander Werth, *Russia at War, 1941–1945* (1965), and Conrad Crane, *Bombs, Cities, and Civilians* (1993). One of the most readable accounts of the war in Asia and the Pacific is Ronald Spector's *Eagle Against the Sun* (1988). Also see Akira Iriye, *Power and Culture: The Japanese-American War, 1941–1945* (1981), and James Hsiung and Steven Levine, eds., *China's Bitter Victory: The War with Japan, 1937–1945* (1992).

The terror of life under Nazi rule is the subject of two powerful memoirs: Anne Frank's *The Diary of a Young Girl* (1953) and Eli Wiesel's *Night* (1960). On the Holocaust, see Lucy Dawidowicz, *The War Against the Jews,* *1933–1945,* 2d ed. (1986); Leni Yahil, *The Holocaust: The Fate of European Jewry* (1990); and a controversial book by Daniel Goldhagen, *Hitler's Willing Executioners: Ordinary Germans and the Holocaust* (1996).

Among the many books that capture the scientific side of warfare, two are especially recommended: Richard Rhodes's long but fascinating *The Making of the Atomic Bomb* (1986) and F. H. Hinsley and Alan Stripp, eds., *Code Breakers* (1993).

Among the many books on the home front in the United States, the most vivid is Studs Terkel, *"The Good War": An Oral History of World War Two* (1984). Margaret Higonnet et al., eds., *Behind the Lines: Gender and the Two World Wars* (1987), discusses the role of women in the war.

STRIVING FOR INDEPENDENCE: AFRICA, INDIA, AND LATIN AMERICA, 1900–1949

Sub-Saharan Africa, 1900–1945 • The Indian Independence Movement, 1905–1947 • Latin America, 1900–1949
SOCIETY AND CULTURE: Self-Government in Africa

miliano Zapata°, leader of a peasant rebellion in the Mexican Revolution, liked to be photographed on horseback, carrying a sword and a rifle and draped with bandoliers of bullets. Mahatma Gandhi°, who led the independence movement in India, preferred to be seen sitting at a spinning wheel, dressed in a *dhoti*°, the simple loincloth worn by Indian farmers. The images they liked to project and the methods they used could not have been more opposed. Yet their goals were similar: each wanted social justice and a better life for the poor in a country free of foreign domination.

The previous two chapters focused on a world convulsed by war and revolution. The world wars involved Europe, East Asia, the Middle East, and the United States, and they sparked

violent revolutions in Russia and China. They accelerated the development of aviation, electronics, nuclear power, and other technologies. Although these momentous events dominate the history of the first half of the twentieth century, parts of the world that were little touched by war also underwent profound changes in this period, partly for internal reasons and partly because of the influence of warfare and revolution in other parts of the world.

In this chapter, we examine the changes that took place in three regions: sub-Saharan Africa, India, and three major countries of Latin America—Mexico, Brazil, and Argentina. These three regions were very distinct culturally, yet they had much in common. Africa and India were colonies of Europe, both politically and economically. Though politically independent, the Latin American republics were dependent on Europe and the United States for the sale of raw

---

Zapata (zeh-PAH-teh)   **Gandhi** (GAHN-dee)
dhoti (DOE-tee)

materials and commodities and for imports of manufactured goods, technology, and capital. In all three regions, independence movements tried to wrest control from distant foreigners and improve the livelihood of their peoples. Their success was partial at best.

As you read this chapter, ask yourself the following questions:

- How did wars and revolutions in Europe and East Asia affect people in the tropics and farther south?
- Why did educated Indians and Africans want independence?
- How compatible were Latin American goals of social justice and economic development?

SUB-SAHARAN AFRICA, 1900–1945

Of all the continents, Africa was the last to be subject to European colonization (see Chapter 24). The first half of the twentieth century, when nationalist movements threatened European rule in Asia, was Africa's classic period of colonialism. After World War I, Britain, France, Belgium, and South Africa divided Germany's African colonies among themselves. In the 1930s, Italy invaded Ethiopia. The colonial empires reached their peak shortly before World War II.

Colonial Africa: Economic and Social Changes

Outside of Algeria, Kenya, and South Africa, few Europeans lived in Africa. In 1930, Nigeria, with a population of 20 million, was ruled by 386 British officials and 8,000 policemen and military, of whom 150 were European. Yet the presence of even a small number of Europeans stimulated deep changes.

From the turn of the century, the colonial powers built railroads from coastal cities to mines and plantations in the interior in order to provide raw materials to the industrial world. In many places, the economic boom of the interwar years benefited few Africans, because colonial governments sold or leased African communal lands to European companies or, in eastern and southern Africa, to white settlers. Where land was divided into small farms, some Africans benefited from the boom. Farmers in the Gold Coast (now Ghana°) profited from the high prices of cocoa, as did palm oil producers in Nigeria and coffee growers in East Africa.

In most of Africa, women played a major role in the retail trades, selling pots and pans and other hardware, toys, cloth, and food in the markets. Many maintained their economic independence and kept their household finances separate from those of their husbands, following a custom that predated the colonial period. However, they faced new competition from large European wholesalers and immigrant Indian, Greek, and Syrian retail traders.

For many Africans, economic development meant working in European-owned mines and plantations, often under compulsion. Eager to develop the resources of the territories under their control, colonial governments used their police powers to force Africans to work under harsh conditions for little or no pay. In the 1920s, when the government of French Equatorial Africa decided to build a railroad from Brazzaville to the Atlantic coast, a distance of 312 miles (502 kilometers), it drafted 127,000 men to carve a roadbed across mountains and through rain forests. For lack of food, clothing, and medical care, 20,000 of them died, an average of 64 deaths per mile of track.

Europeans prided themselves on bringing modern health care to Africa; yet before the 1930s, there was too little of it to help the majority of Africans, and other aspects of colonialism actually worsened public health. Migrants to cities, mines, and plantations and soldiers moving from post to post spread syphilis, gonorrhea, tuberculosis, and malaria. Sleeping sickness and smallpox epidemics raged throughout Central Africa. In

Ghana (GAH-nuh)

Diamond Mining in Southern Africa The discovery of diamonds in the Transvaal in 1867 attracted prospectors to the area around Kimberley. The first wave of prospectors consisted of individual "diggers," including a few Africans. By the late 1870s, surface deposits had been exhausted, and further mining required complex and costly machinery. After 1889, one company, De Beers Consolidated, owned all the diamond mines. This photograph shows the entrance to a mine shaft and mine workers surrounded by heavy equipment. (Royal Commonwealth Society. By permission of the Syndics of Cambridge University Library)

recruiting men to work, colonial governments depleted rural areas of farmers needed to plant and harvest crops. Forced requisitions of food taken to feed the workers left the remaining populations undernourished and vulnerable to diseases. Not until the 1930s did colonial governments realize the negative consequences of their labor policies and begin to invest in agricultural development and health care for Africans.

Africans migrated to cities because they offered the hope of jobs and excitement and, for a few, the chance to become wealthy. In 1900, Ibadan° in Nigeria was the only city in sub-Saharan Africa with more than 100,000 inhabitants; fifty years later, dozens of cities had reached that size, including Nairobi° in Kenya, Johannesburg in South Africa, Lagos in Nigeria, Accra in Gold Coast, and Dakar in Senegal.

However, migrations damaged the family life of those involved, for almost all the migrants were men, leaving women in the countryside to farm and raise children. Cities built during the colonial period reflected the colonialists' attitudes with

Ibadan (ee-BAH-dahn) **Nairobi** (nie-ROE-bee)

CHRONOLOGY

	Africa	India	Latin America
1900	**1900s** Railroads connect ports to the interior	**1905** Viceroy Curzon splits Bengal; mass demonstrations **1906** Muslims found All-India Muslim League	**1876–1910** Porfirio Díaz, dictator of Mexico **1911–1919** Mexican Revolution; Emiliano Zapata and Pancho Villa against the Constitutionalists **1917** New constitution proclaimed in Mexico
1920	**1920s** J. E. Casely Hayford organizes political movement in British West Africa	**1919** Amritsar Massacre **1929** Gandhi leads March to the Sea **1930s** Gandhi calls for independence; he is repeatedly arrested	**1928** Plutarco Elías Calles founds Mexico's National Revolutionary Party **1930–1945** Getulio Vargas, dictator of Brazil **1934–1940** Lázaro Cárdenas, president of Mexico **1938** Cárdenas nationalizes Mexican oil industry; Vargas proclaims Estado Novo in Brazil
1940		**1939** British bring India into World War II **1940** Muhammad Ali Jinnah demands a separate nation for Muslims **1947** Partition and independence of India and Pakistan	**1943** Juan Perón leads military coup in Argentina **1946** Perón elected president of Argentina

their racially segregated housing, clubs, restaurants, hospitals, and other institutions. Patterns of racial discrimination were most rigid in the white-settler colonies of eastern and southern Africa.

Religious and Political Changes The dislocations caused by foreign rule, migration, and sudden economic change buffeted Africans' traditional beliefs. Many turned to one of the two universal religions, Christianity and Islam, for guidance. A major attraction of the Christian denominations was their mission schools, which provided access to employment as clerks, teachers, clergy, or shopkeepers. These schools educated a new elite, many of whom learned not only skills and literacy but Western political ideas as well.

Islam also emphasized literacy—in Arabic rather than in a European language—and was less disruptive of traditional African customs such as polygamy. Muslim traders spread Islam inland in East Africa and southward toward the West African coast.

The contrast between the liberal ideas imparted by Western education and the realities of racial discrimination under colonial rule contributed to the rise of nationalism among educated

Africans. These nationalist movements were also inspired by the ideas of pan-Africanists from America, who advocated the unity of African peoples around the world. These movements were small and had little influence until World War II (see Society and Culture: Self-Government in Africa). One of the most successful would be the **African National Congress,** which Western-educated lawyers and journalists founded in 1909 to defend the interests of Africans in South Africa.

The Second World War (1939–1945) had a profound effect on the peoples of Africa, even those far removed from the theaters of war. The war brought hardships, such as increased forced labor, inflation, and requisitions of raw materials. Yet it also brought hope. During the campaign to oust the Italians from Ethiopia, Emperor **Haile Selassie°** (r. 1930–1974) led his own troops into his capital, Addis Ababa, and reclaimed his title. Many Africans who served as soldiers and carriers in Burma, North Africa, and Europe listened to Allied propaganda in favor of European liberation movements and against Nazi racism. They returned to their countries with new and radical ideas.

THE INDIAN INDEPENDENCE MOVEMENT, 1905–1947

In British India, decades of economic transformations had already awakened nationalist ideas among the educated middle class. In response, the British gradually granted India a limited amount of political autonomy while maintaining overall control. But unresolved religious and communal tensions among the Indian peoples led to violent conflicts after the withdrawal of the British in 1947 (see Map 27.1).

The Land and the People

Economic development—what the British called the "moral and material progress of India"—hardly benefited the average Indian. To produce timber for construction and railroad ties and to clear land for tea and rubber plantations, government foresters cut down most of the tropical hardwood forests that had covered the subcontinent in the nineteenth century. In spite of deforestation and extensive irrigation, the amount of land available to peasant families shrank with each successive generation, because the Indian population grew from 250 million in 1900 to 389 million in 1941. Landless young men converged on the cities, exceeding the number of jobs available in the slowly expanding industries.

Indians were divided into many classes. Peasants, the great majority, paid rents to the landowner, interest to the village moneylender, and taxes to the government and had little left to improve their land or raise their standard of living. The government protected property owners, from village moneylenders all the way up to the princes and maharajahs°, who owned huge tracts of land. The cities were crowded with craftsmen, traders, and workers of all sorts, mostly very poor.

The peoples of India spoke many different languages. As a result of British rule and increasing trade and travel, English became, like Latin in medieval Europe, the common medium of communication of the Western-educated middle class. This new class of English-speaking government bureaucrats, professionals, and merchants was to play a leading role in the independence movement.

The majority of Indians practiced Hinduism and were subdivided into hundreds of castes, each affiliated with a particular occupation. Hinduism discouraged intermarriage and other social interactions among the castes and with people who were not Hindus. Muslims constituted one-quarter of the people of India but formed a majority in the northwest and in eastern Bengal. More reluctant than Hindus to learn English, Muslims felt discriminated against by both British and Hindus.

Haile Selassie (HI-lee seh-LASS-ee)

maharajah (mah-huh-RAH-juh)

SOCIETY & CULTURE

Self-Government in Africa

Colonialism rested on the presumption of European superiority. Nowhere was that presumption more evident than in Africa, where colonialists argued that Africans had not evolved politically and therefore would not be ready for self-rule for a long time. Here is an expression of such thinking from the pamphlet African Opportunity, *by Lord Milverton, a former governor of Nigeria.*

The African has had self-government. Until about fifty years ago he had had it for countless centuries, and all it brought him was blood-stained chaos, a brief, insecure life, haunted by fear, in which evil tradition and custom held him enslaved to superstition, hunger, disease, squalor and ruthless cruelty, even to his family and friends. For countless centuries, while all the pageant of history swept by, the African remained unmoved—in primitive savagery.

The Gold Coast nationalist J. E. Casely Hayford responded to that sort of attack by giving examples of progressive and beneficial government in precolonial Africa.

A people who could, indigenously, and without a literature, evolve the orderly representative government which obtained in Ashanti and the Gold Coast before the advent of the foreign interloper, are a people to be respected and shown consideration when they proceed to discuss questions of self-government.

How do these quotations illustrate the importance of history in an argument about the future?

Source: Quotations from Thomas Hodgkin, *Nationalism in Colonial Africa* (New York: New York University Press, 1957), 172–173.

British Rule and Indian Nationalism

Colonial India was ruled by a viceroy appointed by the British government; the country was administered by a few thousand members of the Indian Civil Service. These men, imbued with a sense of duty toward their subjects, formed one of the most honest (if not the most efficient) bureaucracies of all time. Drawn mostly from the English gentry, they liked to think of India as a land of lords and peasants. They considered it their duty to protect the Indian people from the dangers of industrialization and radical politics.

At the turn of the century, the majority of Indians—especially the peasants, landowners, and princes—accepted British rule. But the Europeans' racist attitude toward dark-skinned people increasingly offended those Indians who had learned English and absorbed English ideas of freedom and representative government and then discovered that thinly disguised racial quotas excluded them from the Indian Civil Service, the officer corps, and prestigious country clubs.

In 1885, a small group of English-speaking Hindu professionals had founded a political organization called the **Indian National Congress.** For twenty years, its members respectfully petitioned the government for access to the higher administrative positions and for a voice in official decisions, but they had little influence outside intellectual circles. Then, in 1905, Viceroy Lord Curzon divided the province of **Bengal** in two to improve the efficiency of its administration. This decision, made without consulting anyone, angered not only educated Indians, who saw it as a step taken to lessen their influence, but also millions of uneducated Hindu

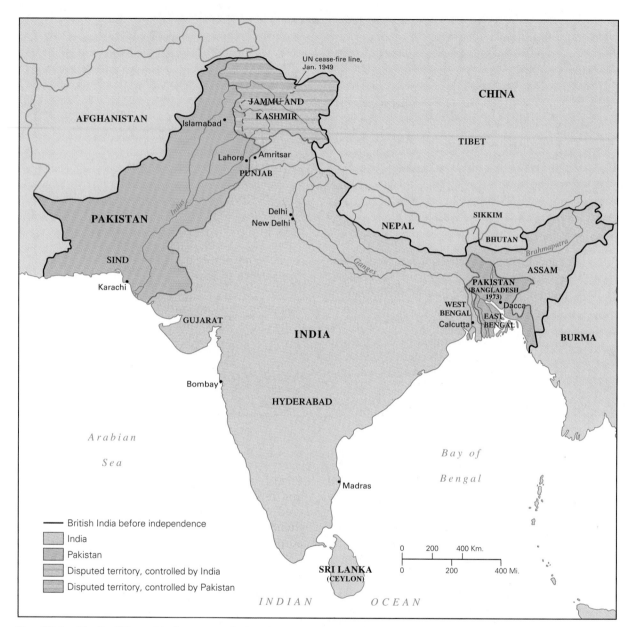

Map 27.1   The Partition of India, 1947   Before the British, India was divided among many states, ethnic groups, and religions. When the British left in 1947, the subcontinent split along religious lines. The predominantly Muslim regions of Sind and Punjab in the northwest and East Bengal in the east formed the new nation of Pakistan. The predominantly Hindu center became the Republic of India. Jammu and Kashmir remained disputed territories and poisoned relations between the two new countries.

Bengalis, who suddenly found themselves outnumbered by Muslims in East Bengal. Soon Bengal was the scene of demonstrations, boycotts of British goods, and even incidents of violence against the British. Meanwhile, fearful of Hindu dominance elsewhere in India, Muslims founded the **All-India Muslim League** in 1906. Politics, once primarily the concern of Westernized intellectuals, turned into two mass movements: one by Hindus and one by Muslims.

To maintain their commercial position and prevent social upheavals, the British resisted the idea that India could, or should, industrialize. Their geologists looked for minerals, such as coal or manganese, that British industry required. However, when the only Indian member of the Indian Geological Service, Pramatha Nath Bose, wanted to prospect for iron ore, he had to resign because the government wanted no part of an Indian steel industry that could compete with that of Britain. Bose joined forces with Jamsetji Tata, a Bombay textile magnate who decided to produce steel in spite of British opposition. With the help of German and American engineers and equipment, Tata's son Dorabji opened the first steel mill in India in 1911, in a town called Jamshedpur in honor of his father. Although it produced only a fraction of the steel that India required, Jamshedpur

Construction Site in Colonial India   British civil engineers were active throughout India building roads, railroads, and canals. Here, a British official supervises Indian workers building a bridge.   (The Billie Love Collection)

became a powerful symbol of Indian national pride. It prompted Indian nationalists to ask why did a country that could produce its own steel need foreigners to run its government.

During World War I, Indians supported Britain enthusiastically; 1.2 million men volunteered for the army, and millions more Indians voluntarily contributed money to the government. Many expected that the British would reward such loyalty with political concessions. Others organized to demand such concessions and began demanding a voice in the government. In 1917, in response to the agitation, the British government announced "the gradual development of self-governing institutions with a view to the progressive realization of responsible government in India as an integral part of the British Empire." This sounded like a promise of self-government, but the timetable was left so vague that nationalists denounced it as a devious maneuver to postpone India's independence.

The dreadful toll of the influenza epidemic of 1918 and 1919 increased the mounting political tensions. Leaders of the Indian National Congress declared that the British reform proposals were too little too late. On April 13, 1919, in the city of Amritsar in Punjab, General Reginald Dyer ordered his troops to fire into a peaceful crowd of some 10,000 demonstrators, killing at least 379 and wounding 1,200. As waves of angry demonstrations swept over India, the period of gradual accommodation between the British and the Indians came to a close.

Mahatma Gandhi and Militant Nonviolence

For the next twenty years, India teetered on the edge of violent uprisings and harsh repression, possibly even war. That it did not succumb was due to **Mohandas K. Gandhi** (1869–1948), a man known to his followers as "Mahatma," the "great soul."

Gandhi began life with every advantage. His family was wealthy enough to send him to England for his education. After his studies, he lived in southern Africa, where he practiced law for the small Indian community living there and developed his tactics of nonviolent protest. During World War I, he returned to India and joined the Indian National Congress.

Gandhi had some unusual political ideas. He denounced the popular ideals of violent struggle. Instead, inspired by both Hindu and Christian concepts, he preached the virtues of *ahimsa*° (nonviolence) and *satyagraha*° (the search for truth). He refused to countenance violence among his followers, and several times he called off demonstrations when they turned violent.

Gandhi had an affinity for the poor that was unusual even among socialist politicians. In 1921, he gave up the Western-style suits worn by lawyers and the fine raiment of wealthy Indians and henceforth wore simple peasant garb: a length of homespun cloth below his waist and a shawl. He attracted ever-larger numbers of followers among the poor and the illiterate, who soon began to revere him, and he transformed the cause of Indian independence from an elite movement of the educated into a mass movement with a quasi-religious aura.

Gandhi was a brilliant political tactician and a master of public relations gestures. In 1929, for instance, he led a few followers on an 80-mile (129-kilometer) walk, camped on a beach, and gathered salt from the sea in a blatant and well-publicized act of civil disregard for the government's monopoly of salt. But he discovered that unleashing the power of popular participation was one thing; controlling its direction was quite another. Within days of his "Walk to the Sea," demonstrations of support broke out all over India, in which the police killed 100 demonstrators and arrested over 60,000.

Many times during the 1930s, Gandhi threatened to fast "unto death," and several times he did come close to death, to protest the violence of both the police and his followers and to demand independence for India. He was repeatedly arrested and spent a total of six years in jail. But every arrest made him more popular. He became a cult figure not only in his own country but also in the Western media. He never won a battle or an election; instead, in the words of historian Percival Spear, he made the British "uncomfortable in their cherished field of moral rectitude," and he gave Indi-

ahimsa (uh-HIM-sah)   *satyagraha* (suh-TYAH-gruh-huh)

ans the feeling that theirs was the ethically superior cause.

India Moves Toward Independence

In the 1920s, slowly and reluctantly, the British began to give in to the pressure of the Indian National Congress and the Muslim League. They handed over to Indians control of "national" areas such as education, the economy, and public works. They also gradually admitted more Indians into the Civil Service and the officer corps.

Indian politicians obtained the right to erect high tariff barriers against imports in order to protect India's infant industries from foreign, even British, competition. Behind these barriers, Indian entrepreneurs built plants to manufacture iron and steel, cement, paper, cotton and jute textiles, sugar, and other products. Besides creating jobs, this early industrialization helped create a class of wealthy Indian businessmen who supported the Indian National Congress and its demands for independence. Though paying homage to Gandhi, they preferred his successor as leader of the Indian National Congress, **Jawaharlal Nehru°** (1889–1964). A highly educated nationalist and subtle thinker, Nehru, in contrast to Gandhi, looked forward to creating a modern industrial India.

When Viceroy Lord Linlithgow took India into World War II without consulting a single Indian, the Congress-dominated provincial governments resigned in protest and found that boycotting government office increased their popular support. Gandhi called Britain's offer of independence after the end of the war a "postdated cheque on a failing bank" and demanded full independence immediately. His "Quit India" campaign aroused popular demonstrations against the British and provoked a wave of arrests, including his own.

As in World War I, Indians contributed heavily to the Allied war effort, supplying 2 million soldiers and enormous amounts of resources, especially timber needed for emergency construction. The Second World War divided the Indian people. Most Indian soldiers felt they were fighting to defend their country rather than to support the British Empire. A small number of Indians, meanwhile, were so anti-British that they joined the Japanese side.

Partition and Independence

When the war ended, Britain's new Labour Party government prepared for Indian independence, but deep suspicions between Hindus and Muslims complicated the process. The break between the two communities had started in 1937, when the Indian National Congress won the provincial elections and refused to share power with the Muslim League. In 1940, the leader of the League, **Muhammad Ali Jinnah°** (1876–1948), demanded what many Muslims had been dreaming of for years: a country of their own, to be called Pakistan.

As independence approached, talks between Jinnah and Nehru broke down, and battle lines were drawn. Violent rioting between Hindus and Muslims broke out in Bengal and Bihar despite Gandhi's appeals for tolerance and cooperation. By early 1947, the Indian National Congress had accepted the idea of a partition of India into two states, one secular but dominated by Hindus, the other Muslim. In June, Lord Mountbatten, the last viceroy, decided that independence must come immediately. On August 15, British India gave way to a new India and Pakistan. The Indian National Congress, led by Nehru, formed the first government of India; Jinnah and the Muslim League established a government for the provinces that made up Pakistan.

The rejoicing over independence was marred by violent outbreaks between Muslims and Hindus. Throughout the land, Muslim and Hindu neighbors turned on one another, and armed members of one faith hunted down people of the other faith. Leaving all their possessions behind, Hindus fled from predominantly Muslim areas, and Muslims fled from Hindu areas, but trainloads of desperate refugees of one faith were attacked and massacred. Within a few months, some 12 million people had abandoned their ancestral homes

Nehru (NAY-roo)

Jinnah (jee-NAH)

and a half-million lay dead. In January 1948, Gandhi died too, gunned down by an angry Hindu refugee.

LATIN AMERICA, 1900–1949

Latin America achieved independence from Spain and Portugal but did not industrialize or resolve the huge gap between wealthy landowners and desperately poor peasants. Throughout the nineteenth century, ideological divisions, unstable governments, and violent upheavals were common, and Latin American states became economically dependent on the wealthier countries, especially the United States and Great Britain.

Three Latin American republics—Mexico, Brazil, and Argentina—contained well over half of Latin America's land, population, and wealth. Mexico underwent a traumatic social revolution, while Argentina and Brazil evolved more peaceably.

The Mexican Revolution, 1910–1920

Mexico gained its independence in 1821. At the beginning of the twentieth century, Mexican society was so deeply divided between rich and poor that only a revolution could move the country toward prosperity and democracy. A few very wealthy families of Spanish origin, less than 1 percent of the population, owned 85 percent of Mexico's land, mostly in huge haciendas (estates). Closely tied to this elite were the handful of American and British companies that controlled most of Mexico's railroads, silver mines, plantations, and other productive enterprises. At the other end of the social scale were Indians and mestizos°, people of mixed Indian and European ancestry. Most of them were peasants who worked on the haciendas or farmed small communal plots near their ancestral villages.

Despite many upheavals in Mexico in the nineteenth century, the government in 1910 seemed in control; no one expected a revolution. For thirty-four years, General Porfirio Díaz° (1830–1915) had ruled Mexico under the motto "Liberty, Order, Progress." To Díaz, "liberty" meant freedom for rich hacienda owners and foreign investors to acquire more land. The government imposed "order" through rigged elections and a policy of *pan o palo* (bread or the stick)—that is, bribes for Díaz's supporters and summary justice for those who opposed him. And "progress" meant mainly the importing of foreign capital, machinery, and technicians to take advantage of Mexico's labor, soil, and natural resources.

Though a mestizo himself, Díaz discriminated against the nonwhite majority of Mexicans. He and his supporters tried to eradicate what they saw as Mexico's embarrassingly rustic traditions. On many middle- and upper-class tables, French cuisine replaced traditional Mexican dishes. The wealthy replaced sombreros and ponchos with European garments, and they preferred horse racing and soccer to the traditional bullfighting and cockfighting. To the educated middle class— the only group with a strong sense of Mexican nationhood—this devaluation of Mexican culture became a symbol of the Díaz regime's failure to defend national interests against foreign influences.

When uprisings broke out in 1911, Días resigned and was replaced by a series of reform-minded governments. Unlike the independence movement in India, the Mexican Revolution was not the work of one party with a well-defined ideology. Instead, it developed haphazardly, led by a series of ambitious but limited leaders, each representing a different segment of Mexican society.

As early as 1911, **Emiliano Zapata** (1879–1919), an Indian farmer, had led a revolt against the haciendas in the mountains of Morelos, south of Mexico City (see Map 27.2). His soldiers were peasants, some of them women, mounted on horseback and armed with pistols and rifles. For several years, they periodically came down from the mountains, burned hacienda buildings, and returned land to the Indian villages.

---

mestizo (mess-TEE-zoh)

Díaz (DEE-as)

dustrial workers. Calling themselves Constitutionalists, their leaders organized private armies and in 1914 succeeded in taking control of the government. By then, the revolution had spread to the countryside.

Zapata and Villa were part agrarian rebels, part social revolutionaries. They enjoyed tremendous popular support but could never rise above their regional and peasant origins and lead a national revolution. The Constitutionalists had fewer soldiers than Zapata and Villa; but they held the major cities, controlled the country's exports of oil, and used the proceeds of oil sales to buy modern weapons. Fighting continued for years, and gradually the Constitutionalists took over most of Mexico. In 1919, they defeated and killed Zapata; Villa was assassinated four years later. An estimated 2 million people lost their lives in the civil war, and much of Mexico lay in ruins.

During their struggle to win support against Zapata and Villa, the Constitutionalists adopted many of their rivals' agrarian reforms and also proposed social programs designed to appeal to workers and the middle class. The Constitution of 1917 promised universal suffrage and a one-term presidency; state-run education to free the poor from the hold of the Catholic Church; the end of debt peonage; restrictions on foreign ownership of property; and laws specifying minimum wages and maximum hours to protect laborers. Although these reforms were too costly to implement right away, they had important symbolic significance, for they enshrined the dignity of Mexicans and the equality of Indians, mestizos, and whites, as well as of peasants and city people.

Emiliano Zapata   Zapata, the leader of a peasant rebellion in southern Mexico during the Mexican Revolution, stands in full revolutionary regalia: sword, rifles, bandoliers, boots, and sombrero.   (Brown Brothers)

Another leader appeared in Chihuahua, a northern state where seventeen individuals owned two-fifths of the land and 95 percent of the people had no land at all. Starting in 1913, **Francisco "Pancho" Villa** (1877–1923), a former ranch hand, mule driver, and bandit, organized an army of three thousand men, most of them cowboys. They too seized land from the large haciendas, not to rebuild traditional communities but to create family ranches.

The inequities of Mexican society and foreign intervention angered Mexico's middle class and in-

The Mexican Revolution Institutionalized, 1920–1940

In the early 1920s, after a decade of violence that exhausted all classes, the Mexican Revolution lost momentum. Only in Morelos did peasants receive land. Nevertheless, the revolution changed the social makeup of the governing class in important ways. For the first time in Mexico's history, representatives of rural communities, unionized workers, and public employees were admitted to the inner circle.

Map 27.2   The Mexican Revolution   The Mexican Revolution began in two distinct regions of the country. One was the mountainous and densely populated area south of Mexico City, particularly Morelos, homeland of Emiliano Zapata. The other was the dry and thinly populated ranch country of the north, such as Chihuahua, home of Pancho Villa. The fighting that ensued crisscrossed the country along the main railroad lines, shown on the map.

In 1928, the establishment of the National Revolutionary Party, or PNR, gave the Mexican Revolution a second wind. **Lázaro Cárdenas°,** who became president in 1934, brought peasants' and workers' organizations into the party, renamed it the Mexican Revolutionary Party (PRM), and removed the generals from government positions. Then he set to work implementing the reforms promised in the Constitution of 1917. Cárdenas redistributed 44 million acres (17.6 million hectares) to peasant communes. He closed church-run schools, replacing them with government schools. He nationalized the railroads and numerous other businesses. Cárdenas's most dramatic move was

the expropriation of foreign-owned oil companies without provoking foreign intervention.

When Cárdenas's term ended in 1940, Mexico, like India, was still a land of poor farmers with a small industrial base. The revolution had brought great changes, however. The political system was free of both chaos and dictatorships. A small group of wealthy people no longer monopolized land and other resources. The military was tamed, the Catholic Church no longer controlled education, and the nationalization of oil had demonstrated Mexico's independence from foreign corporations and military intervention.

Lázaro Cárdenas (LAH-sah-roe KAHR-dih-nahs)

***The Agitator*, a Mural by Diego Rivera**   Diego Rivera (1886–1957) was politically committed to the Mexican Revolution and widely admired as an artist. This mural, painted at the National Agricultural School at Chapingo near Mexico City, shows a political agitator addressing peasants and workers. With one hand, the speaker points to miners laboring in a silver mine; with the other, to a hammer and sickle.   (Universidad Autonoma de Chapingo/CENIDIAP-INBA)

The Transformation of Argentina

At the end of the nineteenth century, railroads and refrigerator ships, which allowed the safe transportation of meat, changed not only the composition of Argentina's exports but also the way they were produced—in other words, the land itself. European consumers preferred the soft flesh of Lincoln sheep and Hereford cattle to the tough, sinewy meat of creole cattle and merino sheep. The valuable Lincolns and Herefords could not be allowed to roam and graze on the *pampas°* (grassy plains). To safeguard them, the pampas had to be divided, plowed, cultivated, and fenced with barbed wire to keep out predators and other unwelcome animals. Once fenced, the land could be used to produce wheat as well as beef and mutton. Within a few years, grasslands that had stretched to the horizon were transformed into farmland. Like the North American midwest, the pampas became one of the world's great producers of wheat and meat.

Argentina's government represented the interests of the *oligarquía°*, a very small group of wealthy landowners. Members of this elite controlled enormous haciendas where they grew rich raising cattle and sheep and growing wheat for export to Europe and the United States. Little interested in any business other than farming, they were content to let foreign companies, mainly British, build Argentina's railroads, processing plants, and public utilities. So important were British interests in the Argentinean economy that the language used on the railroads was not Spanish but English.

Brazil and Argentina, to 1929

Before the First World War, Brazil's elite produced most of the world's coffee and cacao, grown on vast estates, and natural rubber, gathered by Indians from rubber trees growing wild in the Amazon rain forest. Like their Argentinean counterparts, they had little interest in other forms of

pampas (POM-pus)

oligarquía (oh-lee gar-KEE-ah)

development; let British companies build railroads, harbors, and other infrastructure; and imported all manufactured goods. At the time, this situation seemed to offer a rational division of labor that allowed each country to do what it did best. If the British did not grow coffee, why should Brazil build locomotives?

Rubber exports collapsed after 1912, replaced by cheaper plantation rubber from Southeast Asia. The outbreak of war in 1914 put an end to imports from Europe. To a certain extent, the United States replaced the European countries as suppliers of machinery, but European immigrants in Argentina and Brazil also built factories to manufacture textiles and household goods.

The disruption of the old trade patterns weakened the landowning class. In Argentina, the urban middle class obtained the secret ballot and universal male suffrage in 1916 and elected a liberal politician, Hipólito Irigoyen°, as president. In Brazil, junior officers rebelled periodically against the government but accomplished little. In neither country did the urban middle class take power away from the wealthy landowners. Instead, the two classes shared power at the expense of both the landless peasants and the urban workers.

The 1920s were a period of peace and prosperity in South America, in contrast to Mexico. Trade with Europe resumed, prices received for agricultural exports remained high, and both Argentina and Brazil used profits accumulated during the war to industrialize and improve their transportation systems and public utilities. Yet as they were moving forward, new technologies again left them dependent on the advanced industrial countries.

Right after the war, the major powers scrambled to build powerful transmitters on every continent to compete with the telegraph cable companies and to take advantage of the boom in international business and news reporting. No Latin American country then possessed the knowledge or funds to build its own transmitters. So a cartel of British, French, German, and American communications companies set up a national radio company in each Latin American republic, installing a prominent local politician as its president, but the cartel held all the stock and therefore

received all the profits. Thus, even as Brazil and Argentina were taking over their railroads and older industries, the major industrial countries controlled the diffusion of the newer aviation and radio technologies.

The Depression and the Vargas Regime in Brazil

The Depression hit Latin America as hard as it hit Europe and the United States; in many ways, it marks a more important turning point for the region than either of the world wars. The sharp fall in the value of agricultural and mineral exports undermined the shaky political systems. Like European countries, Argentina and Brazil veered toward authoritarian regimes that promised to solve their economic problems.

In 1930, **Getulio Vargas°** (1883–1953), a state governor, staged a coup and proclaimed himself president of Brazil. He proved to be a masterful politician. He wrote a new constitution that broadened the franchise and limited the president to one term. He raised import duties and promoted national firms and state-owned enterprises, culminating in the construction of the Volta Redonda steel mill in the 1930s. By 1936, industrial production had doubled, especially in textiles and small manufactures. Brazil was on its way to becoming an industrial country. Vargas's policy, called **import-substitution industrialization,** became a model for other Latin American countries as they attempted to break away from neocolonial dependency.

The industrialization of Brazil brought all the familiar environmental consequences. Powerful new machines allowed the reopening of old mines and the digging of new ones. Cities grew as poor peasants looking for work arrived from the countryside. Around the older neighborhoods of Rio de Janeiro° and São Paulo°, the poor turned steep hillsides and vacant lands into immense slums.

The countryside also was transformed. Scrubland was turned into pasture, and new acreage was

---

Hipólito Irigoyen (ee-POH-lee-toe ee-ree-GO-yen)

Getulio Vargas (jay-TOO-lee-oh VAR-gus)
Rio de Janeiro (REE-oh day zhuh-NAIR-oh)
São Paulo (sow PAL-oh)

planted in wheat, corn, and sugar cane. Even the Amazon rain forest—half of the land area of Brazil—was affected. American industrialist Henry Ford invested $8 million to clear land for the world's largest rubber plantation. Although Brazilian opposition and rubber-tree diseases forced Ford to abandon the project, the project was a forerunner of the degradation that the Amazon forest would suffer later in the century.

Vargas instituted many reforms favorable to urban workers, such as labor unions, pension plans, and disability insurance, but he refused to take any measures that might help the millions of landless peasants or harm the interests of the great landowners. Because the benefits of Brazil's economic recovery were so unequally distributed, communist and fascist movements demanded even more radical changes.

In 1938, prohibited by his own constitution from being reelected, Vargas staged another coup, abolished the constitution, and instituted the Estado Novo°, or "New State," with himself as supreme leader. He abolished political parties, jailed opposition leaders, and turned Brazil into a fascist state. When the Second World War broke out, however, Vargas aligned Brazil with the United States and contributed troops and ships to the Allied war effort. Vargas was himself overthrown in 1945 by a military coup.

Argentina After 1930

Economically, the Depression hurt Argentina almost as badly as it hurt Brazil. Politically, it triggered a military overthrow of the popularly elected President Irigoyen in 1930. The new government represented the large landowners and big business interests. For thirteen years, the generals and the oligarquía ruled, doing nothing to lessen the poverty of the workers or the frustrations of the middle class. When World War II broke out, Argentina sympathized with the Axis but remained officially neutral.

In 1943, another military revolt, led by Colonel **Juan Perón°** (1895–1974), took place. Once in power, the officers took over the highest positions in government and business. Inspired by Nazi victories, their goal was nothing less than the conquest of South America. As the war turned against the Nazis, the officers saw their popularity collapse.

Perón, however, had other plans. Inspired by his charismatic wife **Eva Duarte Perón** (1919–1952), he appealed to the urban workers. Eva Perón became the champion of the *descamisados*°, or "shirtless ones," and campaigned tirelessly for social benefits and for the cause of women and children. With his wife's help, Perón won the presidency in 1946 and created a populist dictatorship in imitation of the Vargas regime in Brazil.

Like Brazil, Argentina industrialized rapidly under state sponsorship. Perón spent lavishly on social welfare projects as well as on the military, depleting the capital that Argentina had earned during the war. Though a skillful demagogue who played off the army against the navy and both against the labor unions, Perón could not create a stable government out of the chaos of coups and conspiracies. After Eva died in 1952, he lost his political skills (or perhaps they were hers), and soon Perón was overthrown in yet another military coup.

CONCLUSION

Sub-Saharan Africa, India, and Latin America lay outside the theaters of war that engulfed most of the Northern Hemisphere, but they were deeply affected by global events and by the demands of the industrial powers. Sub-Saharan Africa and India were still under colonial rule, and their political life revolved around the yearnings of their elites for political independence and their masses for social justice. Mexico, Argentina, and Brazil were politically independent, but economically they were also closely tied to the industrial nations with which they traded. Their deeply polarized societies and the stresses caused by their dependence on

Estado Novo (esh-TAH-doe NO-vo)
Juan Perón (hoo-AHN pair-OWN)

descamisados (des-cah-mee-SAH-dohs)

the industrial countries clashed with the expectations of ever larger numbers of their peoples.

In Mexico, these stresses brought about a long and violent revolution, out of which Mexicans forged a lasting sense of national identity. Argentina and Brazil moved toward greater economic independence, but at the price of militarism and dictatorship. In India, the conflict between growing expectations and the reality of colonial rule produced both a movement for independence and an ethnic split that tore the nation apart. In sub-Saharan Africa, demands for national self-determination and economic development were only beginning to be voiced by 1949.

Nationalism and the yearning for social justice were the two most powerful forces for change in the early twentieth century. These ideas originated in the industrialized countries but resonated in the independent countries of Latin America as well as in colonial regions such as the Indian subcontinent and sub-Saharan Africa. However, they did not always unite people against their colonial rulers or foreign oppressors; instead, they often divided them along social, ethnic, or religious lines. Western-educated elites looked to industrialization as a means of modernizing their country and ensuring their position in it, while peasants and urban workers supported nationalist and revolutionary movements in the hope of improving their lives. Often these goals were not compatible.

■ Key Terms

African National Congress	Emiliano Zapata
Haile Selassie	Francisco "Pancho" Villa
Indian National Congress	Lázaro Cárdenas
Bengal	Getulio Vargas
All-India Muslim League	import-substitution
Mohandas K. (Mahatma) Gandhi	industrialization
	Juan Perón
Jawaharlal Nehru	Eva Duarte Perón
Muhammad Ali Jinnah	

■ Suggested Reading

Two excellent general introductions to Africa are Roland Oliver and Anthony Atmore, *Africa since 1800*, 4th ed. (1994), and A. E. Afigbo et al., *The Making of Modern Africa*, vol. 2, *The Twentieth Century* (1986). Outstanding novels about Africa in the colonial era include Chinua Achebe, *Arrow of God* (1964); Buchi Emecheta, *The Joys of Motherhood* (1980); and Peter Abraham, *Mine Boy* (1946).

For a general introduction to Indian history, see Sumit Sarkar, *Modern India, 1885–1947* (1983), and Percival Spear, *India: A Modern History*, rev. ed. (1972). On the influenza epidemic of 1918–1919, see Alfred W. Crosby, *America's Forgotten Pandemic: The Influenza of 1918* (1989). The Indian independence movement has received a great deal of attention. Judith M. Brown's most recent book on Gandhi is *Gandhi: Prisoner of Hope* (1989). *Gandhi's Truth: On the Origin of Militant Nonviolence* (1969), by noted psychoanalyst Erik Erikson, is also recommended. The environment is discussed in M. Gadgil and R. Guha, *This Fissured Land: An Ecological History of India* (1993).

Thomas Skidmore and Peter Smith, *Modern Latin America*, 3d ed. (1992), offer the best brief introduction. On the Mexican Revolution, two books are essential: Alan Knight, *The Mexican Revolution*, 2 vols. (1986), and John M. Hart, *Revolutionary Mexico: The Coming and Process of the Mexican Revolution* (1987). The standard work on Brazil is E. Bradford Burns, *A History of Brazil*, 3d ed. (1993). The history of modern Argentina is ably treated in David Rock, *Argentina, 1517–1987: From Spanish Colonization to Alfonsín* (1987). Mark Jefferson, *Peopling the Argentine Pampas* (1971), and Jeremy Adelman, *Frontier Development: Land, Labour and Capital on the Wheatlands of Argentina and Canada, 1890–1914* (1994), describe the transformation of the Argentinean environment.

THE PERILS AND PROMISES OF A GLOBAL COMMUNITY, 1945–2001

CHAPTER 28
THE COLD WAR AND DECOLONIZATION, 1945–1975

CHAPTER 29
CRISIS, REALIGNMENT, AND THE DAWN OF THE POST–COLD WAR WORLD, 1975–1991

CHAPTER 30
THE END OF A GLOBAL CENTURY, 1991–2001

he notion of a postwar era in which all the world's peoples could rejoice in the defeat of totalitarianism became increasingly hollow as the Cold War set in between the United States and the Soviet Union and more and more peoples engaged in struggles for national independence. From 1945 to 1991, conflicts between communist and noncommunist forces in emerging nations repeatedly involved the superpowers, sometimes as arms suppliers or allies, sometimes as combatants. The Korean War and the Vietnam War engaged American troops; the Soviet Union became bogged down in a war in Afghanistan. Leaders of the Third World,

a group of states proclaiming nonalignment in the Cold War, tried to advance their state-building programs by playing off the United States against the Soviet Union and gaining favors from both sides.

A turning point of sorts arrived around 1975. Escalating oil prices, provoked by conflicts in the Middle East, shook the world's economic foundations. The major nuclear powers began to recognize the futility of the arms race. The countries of East Asia rapidly industrialized. And the attitudes of young people around the world increasingly clashed with those of the parental, World War II, generation.

602

In the relatively nonindustrialized parts of the world, population grew rapidly. Governments in Latin America, Africa, South Asia, China, and the Middle East faced serious problems in providing the necessities of life. The extension of agriculture and other pressures on resources sped the deterioration of the environment.

The dissemination of new technologies, ranging from "green revolution" agricultural practices to consumer electronics, transformed daily life. Regional cultures, many of them religiously based, felt threatened by the spread of Western consumer society and entertainment. The vision of a global culture excited some people while repelling others.

Formal relations among groups of states—the United Nations, Cold War alliances, and free trade agreements—brought the world's peoples closer together than ever before. With the emergence of a truly global community, peacekeeping, human rights, and gender equality became international issues.

The rapid collapse of the Soviet Empire beginning in 1989 also ended the overarching political and economic struggles of the Cold War. Global debates refocused variously on the global expansion of trade and high technology, on the widening gap between the rich nation of the North and the miserably poor South, and on growing degradation of the environment. Another perspective on globalization seized the world's attention on September 11, 2001, when Islamic terrorists attacked the symbols of America's global economic and political power. Was this another turning point? If so, only time would tell in what direction.

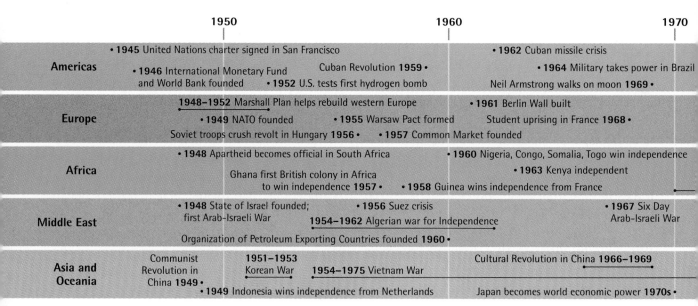

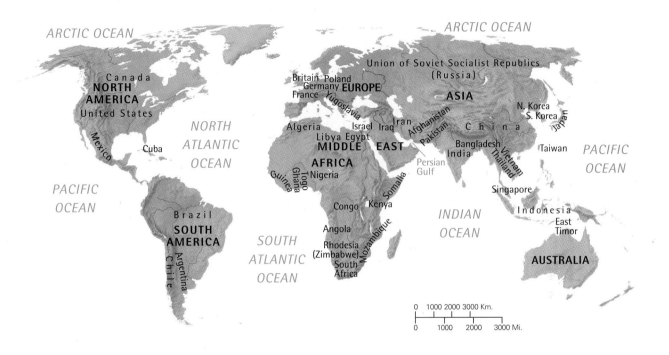

THE COLD WAR AND DECOLONIZATION, 1945–1975

**Decolonization and Nation Building • The Cold War •
Beyond a Bipolar World**
ENVIRONMENT AND TECHNOLOGY: The Green Revolution

n 1946, in a speech at Fulton, Missouri, Great Britain's wartime leader Winston Churchill declared that "an iron curtain has descended across the Continent [of Europe]. . . . I am convinced there is nothing they [the communists] so much admire as strength, and there is nothing for which they have less respect than weakness, especially military weakness." The phrase **"iron curtain"** became a watchword of the **Cold War,** the state of political tension and military rivalry that was then beginning between the United States and its allies and the Soviet Union and its allies.

In the early years of World War II, Churchill and President Franklin Roosevelt had looked forward to a postwar world of economic cooperation and restoration of sovereignty to peoples suffering Axis occupation and, above all, to a world where war and territorial conquest would not be tolerated. By the time Churchill delivered his "iron curtain" speech, however, Britain's electorate had voted him out of power, Harry S

Truman had succeeded to the presidency after Roosevelt's death, and the Soviet Union was dominating eastern Europe and supporting communist movements in China, Iran, Turkey, Greece, and Korea. Although Soviet diplomats sat with their former allies in the newly founded United Nations Organization, confrontation rather than cooperation was the hallmark of relations between East and West.

The intensity of the Cold War sometimes obscured a postwar phenomenon of even greater importance. Western domination of Asia, Africa, and Latin America was largely ended, and the colonial empires of the New Imperialism were gradually dismantled. A new generation of national leaders sometimes skillfully played Cold War antagonism to their own advantage. Their real business, however, was the difficult task of nation building.

Each land freeing itself from imperialism had its own specific history and conditions. After independence, some new nations sided openly with the United States and some with the Soviet Union. Others banded together in a posture of neutrality and spoke with one voice about their need for economic and technical assistance and the obligation of the wealthy nations to satisfy those needs.

The Cold War military rivalry stimulated extraordinary advances in weaponry and associated technologies, but many new nations struggled to educate their citizens, nurture industry, and escape the economic constraints imposed by their former imperialist masters. The environment suffered severe pressures, whether from oil exploration and transport to feed the growing economies of the wealthy nations or from deforestation in poor regions challenged by the need for cropland. Neither rich nor poor realized the costs associated with environmental change.

As you read this chapter, ask yourself the following questions:

• What impact did economic philosophy have on both the Cold War and the decolonization movement?

• How was a third world war averted?

• Was world domination by the superpowers good or bad for the rest of the world?

DECOLONIZATION AND NATION BUILDING

Whereas the losing countries in World War I were stripped of colonies, it was primarily countries on the winning side in World War II that ended up losing their colonies (see Map 28.1). Circumstances differed profoundly from place to place. In some Asian countries, where colonial rule was of long standing, newly independent states found themselves in possession of viable industries, communications networks, and education systems. In other countries, notably in Africa, decolonization gave birth to nations facing dire economic problems and internal disunity. In Latin America, where political independence already had been achieved, the quest was for freedom from foreign economic domination, particularly by the United States.

New Nations in Southern Asia

Newly independent India and Pakistan were strikingly dissimilar. Muslim Pakistan defined itself according to religion and quickly fell under the control of military leaders. Though 90 percent Hindu, the much larger republic of India, led by Prime Minister Jawaharlal Nehru, was secular. It inherited most of the considerable industrial and educational resources the British had developed, along with the larger share of trained civil servants and military officers.

The decision of the Hindu ruler of the northwestern state of Jammu and Kashmir to join India without consulting his overwhelmingly Muslim subjects led to a war between India and Pakistan in 1947 that ended with an uneasy truce, only to resume briefly in 1965. Though Kashmir remains a flashpoint of patriotic feeling, the two countries managed to avoid further warfare.

Despite recurrent predictions that multi-lingual India might break up into a number of linguistically homogeneous states, most Indians recognized that unity benefited everyone; and the country pursued a generally democratic and socialist line of development. Pakistan, in contrast, did break up. In 1971, its Bengali-speaking eastern section seceded to become the independent country of Bangladesh.

Elsewhere in the region, nationalist movements won independence as well. Britain granted independence to Burma (now Myanmar°) in 1948 and established the Malay Federation that same year. (Singapore, once a member of the federation, became an independent city-state itself in 1965.)

Myanmar (myahn-MAH)

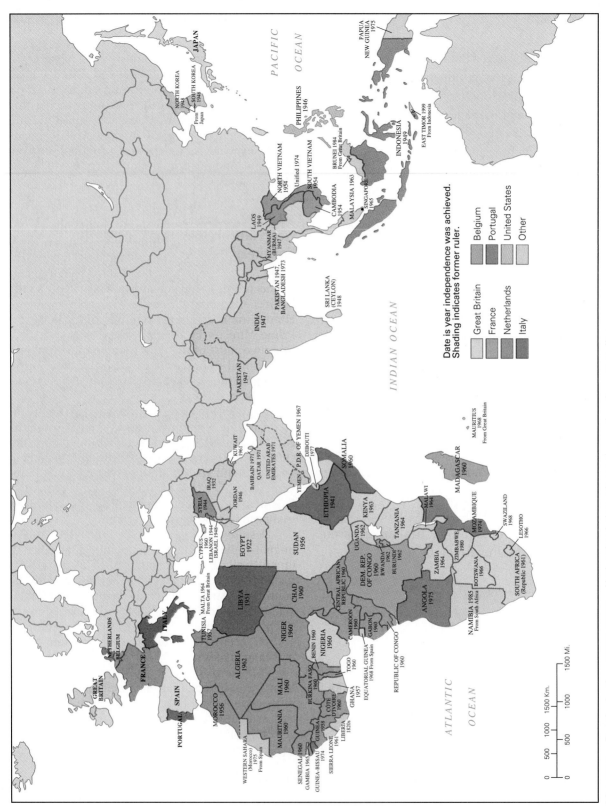

Map 28.1 Decolonization, 1947–1990 Notice that independence came a decade or so earlier in South and Southeast Asia than in Africa. Numerous countries that gained independence after World War II in the Caribbean, in South and Central America, and in the Pacific are not shown.

Date is year independence was achieved.
Shading indicates former ruler.

Great Britain
France
Netherlands
Italy
Belgium
Portugal
United States
Other

PACIFIC
OCEAN

JAPAN

NORTH KOREA 1948
SOUTH KOREA 1948 From Japan

PAPUA NEW GUINEA 1975

PHILIPPINES 1946

INDONESIA 1949

EAST TIMOR 1999 From Indonesia

NORTH VIETNAM 1954
Unified 1974
SOUTH VIETNAM 1954

BRUNEI 1984 From Great Britain

MYANMAR (BURMA) 1947

LAOS 1949

CAMBODIA 1954

MALAYSIA 1963

SINGAPORE 1965

PAKISTAN 1947
BANGLADESH 1973

SRI LANKA (CEYLON) 1948

INDIA 1947

PAKISTAN 1947

INDIAN OCEAN

KUWAIT 1961

BAHRAIN 1971
QATAR 1971
UNITED ARAB EMIRATES 1971

YEMEN, P.D.R. OF 1967
DJIBOUTI 1977

SOMALIA 1960

MAURITIUS 1968 From Great Britain

IRAQ 1932
JORDAN 1946

SYRIA 1944

CYPRUS 1960
LEBANON 1944
ISRAEL 1948

ETHIOPIA 1941

KENYA 1963

MALAWI 1964

MADAGASCAR 1960

EGYPT 1922

SUDAN 1956

UGANDA 1962
RWANDA 1962
BURUNDI 1962

TANZANIA 1964

ZAMBIA 1964

MOZAMBIQUE 1975

SWAZILAND 1968

LESOTHO 1966

LIBYA 1951

CHAD 1960

CENTRAL AFRICAN REPUBLIC 1960

DEM. REP. OF CONGO 1960

ZIMBABWE 1980

BOTSWANA 1966

SOUTH AFRICA (Republic 1961)

NETHERLANDS
BELGIUM

FRANCE

ITALY

GREAT BRITAIN

SPAIN

PORTUGAL

TUNISIA 1956

MALTA 1964 From Great Britain

NIGER 1960

NIGERIA 1960

CAMEROON 1960

GABON 1960

ANGOLA 1975

NAMIBIA 1985 From South Africa

MOROCCO 1956

ALGERIA 1962

MALI 1960

BENIN 1960

TOGO 1960

EQUATORIAL GUINEA 1968 From Spain

REPUBLIC OF CONGO 1960

WESTERN SAHARA (Morocco) 1975 From Spain

MAURITANIA 1960

SENEGAL 1960

GAMBIA 1965

GUINEA-BISSAU 1974

GUINEA 1958

SIERRA LEONE 1961

LIBERIA 1820s

COTE D'IVOIRE 1960

GHANA 1957

BURKINA FASO 1960

ATLANTIC
OCEAN

0   500   1000   1500 Mi.
0   500   1000   1500 Km.

CHRONOLOGY

	Cold War	Decolonization
1945		
	1948–1949 Berlin airlift	**1947** Partition of India
	1949 NATO formed	**1949** Dutch withdraw from Indonesia
	1950–1953 Korean War	
	1952 United States detonates first hydrogen bomb	**1954** CIA intervention in Guatemala; defeat at Dienbienphu ends French hold on Vietnam
1955	**1955** Warsaw Pact concluded	**1955** Bandung Conference
	1956 Soviet Union suppresses Hungarian revolt	
	1957 Soviet Union launches first artificial satellite into earth orbit	**1957** Ghana becomes first British colony in Africa to gain independence
		1959 Fidel Castro leads revolution in Cuba
		1960 Shootings in Sharpeville intensify South African struggle against apartheid; Nigeria becomes independent
	1961 East Germany builds Berlin Wall	
		1962 Algeria wins independence
1965		
1975	**1975** Helsinki Accords; end of Vietnam War	**1971** Bangladesh secedes from Pakistan

In 1946, the United States kept its promise of postwar independence for the Philippine Islands but retained close economic ties and leases on military bases. In the Dutch East Indies, Sukarno (1901–1970) had cooperated with the Japanese occupation in hopes that the Dutch would never return. After a military confrontation, Dutch withdrawal was finally negotiated in 1949, and Sukarno went on to become the dictator of his resource-rich but underdeveloped nation of Indonesia.

In all these cases, communist insurgents plagued the departing colonial powers and the newly formed governments. The most important postwar communist movement arose in the part of Southeast Asia known as French Indochina. There, Ho Chi Minh° (1890–1969), who had spent several years in France during World War I, played the piv-

otal role. After training in Moscow, he returned to Vietnam to found the Indochina Communist Party in 1930.

Ho Chi Minh's nationalist coalition, then called the Viet Minh, fought the French with help from the People's Republic of China. After a brutal struggle, the French stronghold of Dienbienphu° fell in 1954, marking the doom of France's colonial enterprise. Ho's Viet Minh government took over in the north, and a noncommunist nationalist government ruled in the south. Fighting between North and South Vietnam eventually became a major Cold War conflict.

Ho Chi Minh (hoe chee min)   **Dienbienphu** (dyen-byen-phu)

The Struggle for Independence in Africa

In the quarter-century between 1955 and 1980, African nationalists succeeded in ending European colonial rule. Mostly they gained their independence peacefully, but where European settlers were numerous, violence became the norm.

Algeria rebelled in 1954. The French government was as determined to hold on to Algeria as it had been to keep Vietnam. Ten percent of the Algerian population was European, and Algeria's economy was strongly oriented toward France. Both sides pursued the revolt with great brutality. When the Algerians finally won independence in 1962, the flood of angry colonists returning to France undermined the Algerian economy because very few Arabs had received technical training or acquired management experience.

None of the independence movements in sub-Saharan Africa matched the Algerian struggle in scale. Some of the politicians who led the nationalist movements had devoted their lives to ridding their homelands of foreign occupation. An example is Kwame Nkrumah° (1909–1972), who in 1957 became prime minister of Ghana (formerly the Gold Coast), the first British colony in Africa to achieve independence. Only a few hundred Ghanaian children of Nkrumah's generation had graduated each year from the seven-year elementary schools, and he was one of only a handful who made it through teacher training college. After graduation, he spent a decade reading philosophy and theology in the United States and absorbing ideas about black pride and independence then being propounded by black leaders W. E. B. Du Bois and Marcus Garvey.

After a brief stay in Britain, Nkrumah returned in 1947 to the Gold Coast to work for independence. The time was right. Great Britain had already freed its Asian colonies, and Nkrumah quickly united the people of Ghana behind him. Independence thus came without war or protracted bloodshed. Nkrumah turned out to be more effective internationally as a spokesman for colonized peoples than he was at home as an ad-

French Soldiers on Patrol in Algeria The Algerian war was one of the most savage struggles for independence in the era of decolonization. The French held out a more secular, Western-style view of life but did not hesitate to intrude into homes and residential areas in search of their enemies. At independence in 1961, most Algerian leaders spoke French more readily than Arabic. (Marc Riboud/Magnum Photos, Inc.)

ministrator. In 1966, a group of army officers ousted him.

Jomo Kenyatta (ca. 1894–1978) traveled a more difficult road in Kenya, where a substantial number of European coffee planters strengthened Britain's desire to retain control. A movement the settlers called Mau Mau, formed mostly by the Kikuyu° people, became active in 1952. As violence between settlers and movement fighters escalated, British troops hunted down the leaders and reset-

---

Kwame Nkrumah (KWAH-mee nn-KROO-muh)

Kikuyu (kih-KOO-you)

tled the Kikuyu. The British charged Kenyatta with being a Mau Mau leader and held him in prison and then in internal exile for eight years during a declared state of emergency. They released him in 1961, and negotiations with the British to write a constitution for an independent Kenya followed. In 1964, Kenyatta was elected the first president of the Republic of Kenya. He proved to be an effective, though autocratic, ruler.

In contrast, African leaders in the French colonies of sub-Saharan Africa were slow to call for independence. They visualized change in terms of promises of greater political and civil rights made in 1944 by the Free French movement of General Charles de Gaulle. This Brazzaville Conference also had promised to expand French education at the village level, to improve health services, and to open more lower-level administrative positions to Africans, but the word *independence* was never mentioned.

African politicians also realized that some French colonies—such as Ivory Coast with its coffee and cacao exports, fishing, and hardwood forests—had good economic prospects and others, such as land-locked, desert Niger, did not. As a Malagasy politician said in 1958, "When I let my heart talk, I am a partisan of total and immediate independence [for Madagascar]; when I make my reason speak, I realize that it is impossible." Ultimately, however, the heart prevailed everywhere. Guinea, under the dynamic leadership of Sékou Touré°, led the way in 1958. By the time Nigeria, the most populous West African state, achieved independence from Great Britain in 1960, the leaders of many former French colonies in West Africa could attend the celebrations as independent heads of state.

European settlers fought hard to hold on in southern Africa. The African struggle against Portuguese rule in Angola and Mozambique dragged on until frustrated Portuguese military commanders overthrew the government of Portugal in 1974 and granted the African colonies independence the following year. After a ten-year fight, European settlers in the British colony of Southern Rhodesia ceded power in 1980 to the African majority, who renamed the country Zimbabwe. The change had been swift; a century after the "scramble" for Africa began, European colonial rule in Africa had ended.

Only South Africa and neighboring Southwest Africa remained in the hands of European minorities. After World War II, the white minority government had reconstructed South Africa along extreme racial separation, or *apartheid*°. The cities, the best jobs, and most of the land were reserved for Europeans. Africans and others classified as "nonwhites" were subjected to strict limitations on place of residence, right to travel, and access to jobs and public facilities.

The African National Congress (ANC), formed in 1912, led the fight against apartheid and in favor of a nonracial society. After police fired on demonstrators in the African town of Sharpeville in 1960, an African lawyer named Nelson Mandela (b. 1918) organized guerrilla resistance by the ANC. Mandela was sentenced to life in prison in 1964 (see in Chapter 30 Society and Culture: Nelson Mandela) and the government outlawed the ANC and other opposition organizations. For a time, things were quiet, but in 1976 young students reignited the bloody and prolonged struggle that would force an end to apartheid.

The Quest for Economic Freedom in Latin America

In Latin America, the postwar decades saw continuing struggles over foreign ownership and social inequality. American and European companies dominated Chile's copper, Cuba's sugar and resort hotels, Colombia's coffee, Guatemala's bananas, and the communications networks of several countries. Even in a country like Mexico, where the ruling Institutional Revolutionary Party, or PRI, was officially committed to revolutionary independence and economic development, a yawning gulf between rich and poor, urban and rural, persisted. According to one estimate from the mid-1960s, not more than 300 foreign and 800 Mexican companies dominated the country, and some 2,000 families made up the

---

Sékou Touré (SAY-koo too-RAY)

apartheid (uh-PART-hate)

industrial-financial elite. At the other end of the economic scale were peasants and the 14 percent of the population classified as Indian.

Jacobo Arbenz Guzmán, elected president of Guatemala in 1951, was typical of Latin American leaders who tried to confront the power of foreign interests. His expropriation of large estates angered the United Fruit Company, a U.S. corporation that dominated banana exports and held vast tracts of land in reserve. Reacting to reports that Arbenz was becoming friendly toward communism, the United States Central Intelligence Agency (CIA) prompted a takeover by the Guatemalan military in 1954. CIA intervention removed Arbenz from the scene; it also condemned Guatemala to decades of governmental instability and growing violence between leftist and rightist elements in society.

In Cuba, U.S. companies owned 40 percent of raw sugar production, 23 percent of nonsugar industry, 90 percent of telephone and electrical services, and 50 percent of public service railways. The needs of the U.S. economy largely determined Cuban foreign trade and held back development. Profits went north to the United States or to a small class of wealthy Cubans, many of foreign origin. Cuba's ruler during that period, Fulgencio Batista, became a symbol of corruption, repression, and foreign economic domination.

In 1959, a popular rebellion forced Batista to flee the country. Fidel Castro, the lawyer leader of the rebels, his brother Raoul Castro, and Ernesto "Che" Guevara°, who was the main theorist of communist revolution in Latin America, created a new regime. Within a year, Fidel Castro's government redistributed land, lowered urban rents, and raised wages, effectively transferring 15 percent of the national income from rich to poor. Within twenty-two months, the Castro government seized almost all U.S. property in Cuba and most Cuban corporations. This action resulted in a blockade by the United States, the flight of middle-class and technically trained Cubans, a drop in foreign investment, and the beginning of chronic food shortages.

Little evidence supports the view that Castro undertook his revolution to install a communist government. But at that time, the East-West rivalry of the Cold War was increasingly influencing international politics, and Castro soon turned to the Soviet Union for economic aid. In doing so, he unwittingly committed his nation to economic stagnation and dependence on a foreign power as damaging as the previous relationship with the United States had been.

In April 1961, some fifteen hundred Cuban exiles, whom the CIA had trained for a year in Guatemala, landed at the Bay of Pigs in an effort to overthrow Castro. The Cuban army defeated the attempted invasion in a matter of days, partly because the new U.S. president, John F. Kennedy, decided not to provide all the air support that the plan originally called for. The failure of the Bay of Pigs invasion tarnished the reputation of the United States and the CIA and provoked Castro into declaring that he and his revolution were and always had been Marxist-Leninist.

THE COLD WAR

As decolonization was altering one set of old relationships, relations among powerful nations were also changing. The wartime alliance between the United States, Great Britain, and the Soviet Union had been an uneasy one. American and British leaders committed to free markets and untrammeled capital investment had loathed socialism in its several forms for more than a century. After World War II, the iron curtain in Europe and communist insurgencies in China and elsewhere seemed to confirm the threat of worldwide revolution.

To protect themselves from the Soviet Union, which they perceived as the nerve center of world revolution and as a military power capable of launching a terrible new war, the United States and the countries of western Europe established the **North Atlantic Treaty Organization (NATO)** military alliance in 1949. But Soviet leaders felt themselves surrounded by hostile forces just when they

---

Che Guevara (chay guh-VAHR-uh)

were trying to recover from the terrible losses sustained in the war. The distrust and suspicion between the two sides played out on a worldwide stage.

The United Nations

In 1944, representatives from the United States, Great Britain, the Soviet Union, and China met and drafted specific charter proposals that finally bore fruit in the United Nations Charter, a treaty ratified on October 24, 1945. Like the League of Nations, the **United Nations** had two main bodies: the General Assembly, with representatives from all member states; and the Security Council, with five permanent members—China, France, Great Britain, the United States, and the Soviet Union—and seven rotating members. Various United Nations agencies focused on specialized international problems—for example, UNICEF (United Nations Children's Emergency Fund), FAO (Food and Agriculture Organization) and UNESCO (United Nations Educational, Scientific and Cultural Organization) (see Environment and Technology: The Green Revolution). The United Nations operated by majority vote, except that the five permanent members of the Security Council had veto power in that chamber.

All signatories to the United Nations Charter renounced war and territorial conquest. Nevertheless, peacekeeping, the sole preserve of the Security Council, became a vexing problem. The permanent members often exercised their veto to protect their friends and interests, though from time to time they authorized the United Nations to send observers or peacekeeping forces to monitor truces or agreements.

The decolonization of Africa and Asia greatly swelled the size of the General Assembly but not the Security Council. Many of the new nations looked to the United Nations for material assistance and access to a wider political world. While the vetoes of the Security Council's permanent members often stymied actions touching even indirectly on Cold War concerns, the General Assembly became an arena for expressing opinions on many issues involving decolonization, a movement that the Soviet Union strongly encouraged but the Western colonial powers resisted.

In the early years of the United Nations, General Assembly resolutions carried great weight. An example is a 1947 resolution that sought to divide Palestine into sovereign Jewish and Arab states. Gradually, though, the flood of new members produced a voting majority concerned more with poverty, racial discrimination, and the struggle against imperialism than with the Cold War. As a result, the Western powers increasingly disregarded the General Assembly, allowing the new nations of the world to have their say but not to act collectively.

Capitalism and Communism

In July 1944, with Allied victory a forgone conclusion, economic specialists representing over forty countries met at Bretton Woods, a New Hampshire resort, to devise a new international monetary system. The signatories eventually agreed to fix exchange rates. They also created the International Monetary Fund (IMF) to use currency reserves from member nations to finance temporary trade deficits and the **World Bank** to provide funds for reconstructing Europe and helping needy countries.

The Soviet Union attended the Bretton Woods Conference and signed the agreements, but by 1946, suspicion between the Soviet Union and the United States and Britain had deepened. While the rest of the world moved to a monetary system that relied for stability on most countries holding reserves of dollars and the United States holding reserves of gold, the Soviet Union established a closed monetary system for itself and the new communist regimes in eastern Europe. In the Western countries, supply and demand determined prices; in the Soviet command economy, government priorities and agencies allocated goods and set prices, irrespective of market forces.

Many leaders from the newly independent states preferred the Soviet Union's socialist example to the capitalism of their former colonizers. Thus, the relative success of economies patterned on Eastern or Western models became an element

The Green Revolution

Concern about world food supplies grew directly out of the serious shortages that many nations faced because of the devastation and trade disruptions of World War II. The Food and Agriculture Organization of the United Nations, the Rockefeller Foundation, and the Ford Foundation took leading roles in fostering crop research and educating farmers about agricultural techniques. In 1966, the International Rice Research Institute (established in 1960–1962) began distributing seeds for an improved rice variety known as IR-8. Crop yields from this and other new varieties, along with improved farming techniques, were so impressive that the term *Green Revolution* was coined to describe a new era in agricultural history.

On the heels of the successful new rice strains came new varieties of corn and wheat. Building on twenty years of Rockefeller-funded research in Mexico, the Centro Internacional de Mejoramiento de Maiz y Trigo (International Center for the Improvement of Maize and Wheat) was established in 1966 under Norman Borlaug, who was awarded the Nobel Peace Prize four years later. This organization distributed around the world short, stiff-strawed varieties of wheat that were resistant to disease and responsive to fertilizer.

By 1970, other centers for research on tropical agriculture had been established in Ibadan, Nigeria, and Cali, Colombia. But the success of the Green Revolution and the growing need for its products called for a more comprehensive effort. The Consultative Group on International Agricultural Research brought together World Bank expertise, private foundations, international organizations, and national foreign aid agencies to undertake worldwide support of efforts to increase food productivity and improve natural resource management.

Miracle Rice   New strains of so-called miracle rice made many nations in South and Southeast Asia self-sufficient in food production after decades of worry about the growth of population outstripping agricultural productivity.
(Victor Englebert)

in the Cold War rivalry. Each side trumpeted economic successes measured by such things as industrial output, changes in per capita income, and productivity gains as evidence of its superiority.

During World War II, increased military spending and the draft brought full employment and high wages to the United States. With peace, the United States enjoyed prosperity and an international competitive advantage, while European economies were still heavily damaged from the war. To support European reconstruction, the U.S. **Marshall Plan** provided $12.5 billion to friendly countries between 1948 and 1952. By 1963, a resurgent European economy had doubled 1940 output.

Western European governments generally increased their role in economic management during this period. In Great Britain, the Labour Party government of the 1950s nationalized coal, steel, railroads, and health care. The French government nationalized public utilities; the auto, banking, and insurance industries; and parts of the mining industry.

In 1948, European governments also promoted economic cooperation and integration with the creation of the Organization of European Economic Cooperation (OEEC). After cooperative policies on coal and steel proved successful, some OEEC countries were ready to begin lowering tariffs to encourage the movement of goods and capital. In 1957, France, West Germany, Italy, the Netherlands, Belgium, and Luxembourg signed a treaty creating the European Economic Community, also known as the Common Market. By the 1970s, the Common Market nations had nearly overtaken the United States in industrial production. The economic alliance expanded after 1970, as Great Britain, Denmark, Greece, Ireland, Spain, Portugal, Finland, Sweden, and Austria joined. The enlarged alliance called itself the **European Community (EC).**

Prosperity brought dramatic changes to European society. Average wages increased, unemployment fell, and social welfare benefits were expanded. Governments increased spending on health care, unemployment benefits, old age pensions, public housing, and grants to poor families with children. The combination of economic growth and income redistribution raised living standards and fueled demand for consumer goods.

The Soviet experience provided a dramatic contrast. The economy of the Soviet Union was just as devastated at the end of the Second World War as those of western Europe. However, with enormous natural resources, a large population, and abundant energy at its disposal, Soviet recovery was rapid at first. Moreover, Soviet planners had made large investments in technical and scientific education, and the Soviet state had developed heavy industry in the 1930s and during the war years. But as the postwar period progressed, bureaucratic control of the economy grew less efficient. In the 1970s, the gap with the West widened. The Soviet economy failed to meet domestic demand for clothing, housing, food, automobiles, and consumer electronics. Agricultural inefficiency forced the Soviet Union to rely on food imports.

The socialist nations of eastern Europe were compelled to follow the Soviet economic model, although some national differences appeared. Poland and Hungary, for example, implemented agricultural collectivization more slowly than did Czechoslovakia. Significant growth occurred among the socialist economies, but the inefficiencies and failures that plagued the Soviet economy troubled them as well.

The United States and the Soviet Union competed in providing loans and grants and in supplying arms (at bargain prices) to countries willing to align with them politically. Thus, the relative success or failure of capitalism and communism in Europe and the United States was not necessarily the strongest consideration in other parts of the world when the time came to construct new national economies.

West Versus East in Europe and Korea

For many countries, peace brought foreign military occupation and new governments installed and controlled by the occupiers. The Soviet Union's military occupation facilitated communist victories in eastern Europe. The United States occupied Japan. Korea and Germany were divided among the Allies.

For the United States, the shift from viewing the Soviet Union as an ally against Germany to seeing it as a worldwide enemy took two years. In the waning days of World War II, the United States had seemed amenable to the Soviet desire for freer access to the Mediterranean through Turkish straits. But in July 1947, the **Truman Doctrine** offered military aid to help both Turkey and Greece resist Soviet military pressure and subversion. In 1951, Greece and Turkey were admitted to NATO. NATO's Soviet counterpart, the **Warsaw Pact,** emerged in 1955 in response to the Western powers' decision to allow West Germany to rearm within limits set by NATO (see Map 28.2).

The Soviet Union tested Western resolve in 1948–1949 by blockading the areas of Berlin occupied by British, French, and American forces, which were surrounded by Soviet-controlled East Germany. Airlifts of food and fuel defeated the blockade. In 1961, the East German government accentuated Germany's political division by building the Berlin Wall, as much to prevent its citizens from fleeing to the noncommunist western part of that city as to keep Westerners from entering East German territory. The West tested the East, in turn, by encouraging a rift between the Soviet Union and Yugoslavia. Western aid and encouragement resulted in Yugoslavia's signing a defensive treaty with Greece and Turkey (but not with NATO) and deciding against joining the Warsaw Pact.

Soviet power set clear limits on how far any eastern European country might stray from Soviet domination. In 1956, Soviet troops crushed an anti-Soviet revolt in Hungary. Czechoslovakia suffered Hungary's fate in 1968. The West, a passive onlooker, had no recourse but to acknowledge that the Soviet Union had the right to intervene in the domestic affairs of any Soviet-bloc nation whenever it wished.

A more explosive crisis erupted in Korea, where the Second World War had left Soviet troops in control north of the thirty-eighth parallel and American troops in control to the south. When no agreement could be reached on holding country-wide elections, communist North Korea and noncommunist South Korea became independent states in 1948. Two years later, North Korea invaded South Korea. The United Nations Security Council, in the absence of the Soviet delegation, voted to condemn the invasion and called on members of the United Nations to come to the defense of South Korea. The United States was the primary ally of South Korea. The People's Republic of China supported North Korea. The **Korean War** lasted until 1953 when the two sides eventually agreed to a truce along the thirty-eighth parallel, but no peace treaty was concluded.

Japan benefited from the Korean War in an unexpected way. Massive purchases of supplies by the United States and spending by American servicemen on leave provided a financial stimulus to the Japanese economy similar to the stimulus that Europe received from the Marshall Plan.

U.S. Defeat in Vietnam

A shooting war also developed in Vietnam. In 1954, United States president Dwight D. Eisenhower (1953–1961) and his foreign policy advisers decided not to aid France in its effort to sustain colonial rule in Vietnam, perceiving that the days of the European colonial empires were numbered. After winning independence, however, communist North Vietnam supported a guerrilla movement—the Viet Cong—against the noncommunist government of South Vietnam.

When John F. Kennedy became president (1961–1963), he and his advisers decided to support the South Vietnamese government of President Ngo Dinh Diem°. They realized that the Diem government was corrupt and unpopular, but they feared that a communist victory would encourage communist movements throughout Southeast Asia and alter the Cold War balance of power. Kennedy steadily increased the number of American military advisers from 685 to almost 16,000 while secretly encouraging the overthrow and execution of Diem in hopes of seeing a more popular and honest government come to power.

Lyndon Johnson, who became president (1963–1969) after Kennedy was assassinated, gained support from Congress for unlimited expansion of U.S. military deployment. By the end of 1966, 365,000 U.S. troops were engaged in the

Diem (dee-EM)

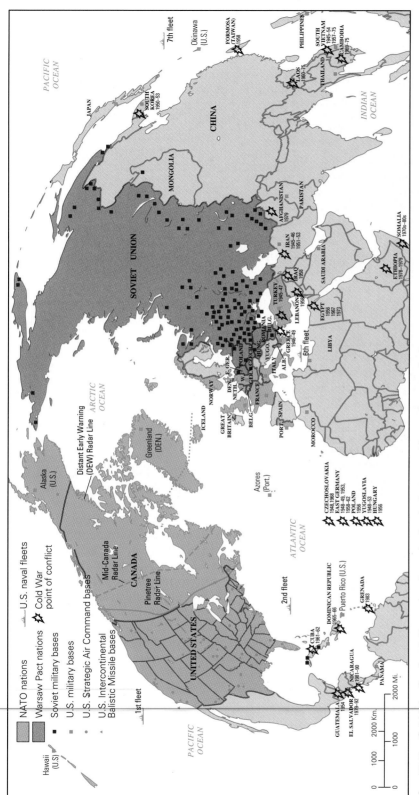

Map 28.2 Cold War Confrontation   A polar projection is shown on this map because Soviet and U.S. strategists planned to attack one another by missile in the polar region, hence the Canadian-American radar lines. Military installations along the southern border of the Soviet Union were directed primarily at China.

The Vietnamese People at War American and South Vietnamese troops burned many villages to deprive the enemy of civilian refuges. This policy undermined support for the South Vietnamese government in the countryside. (Dana Stone/ Black Star)

Vietnam War. Nothing the Americans tried, however, succeeded in stopping the Viet Cong guerrillas and their North Vietnamese allies. Diem's successors turned out to be just as corrupt and unpopular as he was, and the heroic nationalist image of North Vietnam's leader, Ho Chi Minh, evoked strong sympathies among many South Vietnamese.

In 1973, a treaty between North Vietnam and the United States ended U.S. involvement in the war and promised future elections. Two years later, in violation of the treaty, Viet Cong and North Vietnamese troops overran the South Vietnamese army and captured the southern capital of Saigon, re-

naming it Ho Chi Minh City. The two parts of Vietnam were reunited in a single state ruled from the north. The war was bloody and traumatic. The Vietnamese had over a million casualties. The deaths of fifty-eight thousand Americans overseas and the vigorous antiwar movement at home ensured that the United States would not easily be drawn into another shooting war.

The Race for Nuclear Supremacy

The devastation of Hiroshima and Nagasaki with atomic weapons had ushered in a new era. After the Soviet Union exploded its first nuclear device in 1949, fears of a worldwide holocaust grew and then became even greater when the United States exploded a far more powerful weapon, the hydrogen bomb, in 1952 and the Soviet Union followed suit less than a year later. The conviction that the nuclear superpowers were willing to use their terrible weapons if their vital interests were threatened spread despair around the world.

In 1954, President Eisenhower warned Soviet leaders against attacking western Europe. In response to such an attack, he said, the United States would reduce the Soviet Union to "a smoking, radiating ruin at the end of two hours." A few years later, the Soviet leader Nikita Khrushchev° offered an equally stark promise: "We will bury you." His reference was to economic competition, but the image produced in Americans was of literal burial.

Everyone's worst fears seemed about to be realized in the **Cuban missile crisis** of 1962. When the Soviet Union deployed nuclear-tipped missiles in Cuba in response to the U.S. installation of similar missiles in Turkey, the world held its breath. Confronted by unyielding diplomatic pressure and military threats from President Kennedy, Khrushchev backed down and pulled the missiles from Cuba. Subsequently, the United States removed its missiles from Turkey.

Arms limitation also saw progress. In 1963, Great Britain, the United States, and the Soviet Union agreed to ban the testing of nuclear

---

Khrushchev (KROOSH-chef)

weapons in the atmosphere, in space, and under water, thus reducing the environmental danger of radioactive fallout. In 1968, the United States and the Soviet Union together proposed a world treaty against further proliferation of nuclear weapons. It was signed by 137 countries. Not until 1972, however, did the two superpowers truly recognize the futility of squandering their wealth on ever-larger missile forces.

In Europe, the Soviet-American arms race outran the economic ability of atomic powers France and Britain to keep pace. Instead, the European states sought to relax tensions. Between 1972 and 1975, the Conference on Security and Cooperation in Europe (CSCE) brought delegates from thirty-seven European states, the United States, and Canada to Helsinki. The goal of the Soviet Union was to gain European acceptance of the political boundaries of the Warsaw Pact nations. The **Helsinki Accords** affirmed that no boundaries should be changed by military force. It also contained formal (but nonbinding) declarations calling for economic, social, and governmental contacts across the iron curtain, and for cooperation in humanitarian fields, a provision that paved the way for dialogue about human rights.

Space exploration was another offshoot of the nuclear arms race. The contest to build larger and more accurate missiles for delivery of warheads prompted the superpowers to prove their skills in rocketry by launching space satellites. The Soviet Union placed a small *Sputnik* satellite into orbit around the earth in October 1957. The United States responded with its own satellite three months later. The space race was on, a contest in which accomplishments in space were understood to signify equivalent achievements in the military sphere. *Sputnik* administered a deep shock to American pride and confidence, but in 1969 two Americans, Neil A. Armstrong and Edwin E. "Buzz" Aldrin, became the first humans to walk on the moon.

Despite rhetorical Cold War saber-rattling by Soviet and American leaders, the threat of nuclear war forced a measure of restraint on the superpower adversaries. Because fighting each other directly would have risked escalation to the level of nuclear exchange, they carefully avoided crises that might provoke such confrontations.

BEYOND A BIPOLAR WORLD

Although the East-West superpower rivalry dominated world affairs, newly independent states had concerns that were primarily domestic and regional. The challenge they faced was to find a way to pursue their ends within the bipolar structure of the Cold War—and possibly to take advantage of the East-West rivalry. In short, the superpowers dominated the world but did not control it. And as time progressed, they dominated it less and less.

The Third World

As one of the most successful leaders of the decolonization movement, Indonesia's President Sukarno was an appropriate figure to host a meeting in 1955 of twenty-nine African and Asian countries at Bandung, Indonesia. The conferees proclaimed solidarity among all peoples fighting against colonial rule. The Bandung Conference marked the beginning of an effort by the many new, poor, mostly non-European nations emerging from colonialism to gain more weight in world affairs by banding together. The terms **nonaligned nations** and **Third World,** which became commonplace in the following years, signaled these countries' collective stance toward the rival sides in the Cold War. If the West, led by the United States, and the East, led by the Soviet Union, represented two worlds locked in mortal struggle, the Third World consisted of everyone else.

Leaders of the so-called Third World countries preferred the label *nonaligned,* which signified freedom from membership on either side. However, because the Soviet Union supported national liberation movements and the nonaligned movement included communist countries such as China and Yugoslavia, many Western leaders did not take the term *nonaligned* seriously. They saw Sukarno, Nehru, Nkrumah, and Egypt's Gamal Abd al-Nasir° as stalking horses for a communist

Gamal Abd al-Nasir (gah-MAHL AHB-d al-NAH-suhr)

takeover of the world. This may also have been the hope of some Soviet leaders, who were quick to offer some of these countries military and financial aid.

For the movement's leaders, however, nonalignment was a means to extract money and support from one or both superpowers. By flirting with the Soviet Union, the United States, or the People's Republic of China, a country could get military and economic aid.

Some skillful nonaligned leaders were able to gain from both sides. Nasir, who ruled Egypt from 1952 to 1970, and his successor, Anwar al-Sadat°, played the game well. The United States offered to build a dam at Aswan°, on the Nile River, to increase Egypt's electrical generating and irrigation capacity. When Egypt turned to the Soviet Union for arms, the United States reneged on the dam project in 1956. The Soviet Union then picked it up and in the 1960s brought it to conclusion. In 1956, Israel, Great Britain, and France conspired to invade Egypt. Their objective was to overthrow Nasir, regain the Suez Canal (he had recently nationalized it), and secure Israel from any Egyptian threat. The invasion succeeded militarily, but both the United States and the Soviet Union pressured the invaders to withdraw, thus saving Nasir's government. In 1972, Sadat evicted his Soviet military advisers but a year later used his Soviet weapons to attack Israel. After he lost that war, he announced his faith in the power of the United States to solve Egypt's political and economic problems.

Numerous other countries adopted similar balancing strategies. In each case, local leaders were trying to develop their nation's economy and assert or preserve their nation's interests. Manipulating the superpowers was simply a means toward those ends and implied very little about true ideological orientation.

Japan and China

No other countries took better advantage of the opportunities presented by the superpowers' preoccupation than did Japan and China. Japan signed a peace treaty with most of its former enemies in 1951 and regained independence from American occupation the following year. Renouncing militarism and its imperialist past, Japan remained on the sidelines throughout the Korean War. Its new constitution, written under American supervision in 1946, allowed only a limited self-defense force, banned the deployment of Japanese troops abroad, and gave the vote to women.

The Japanese turned their talents and energies to rebuilding their industries and engaging in world commerce. By isolating Japan from most world political issues, the Cold War provided an exceptionally favorable environment for Japan to develop its economic strength.

Three industries that took advantage of government aid and the newest technologies paved the way for Japan's emergence as an economic superpower after 1975. Projects producing 60 million kilowatts of electricity were completed between 1951 and 1970, almost a third through dams on Japan's many rivers. Between 1960 and 1970, steel production more than quadrupled, reaching 15.7 percent of the total capacity of countries outside the Soviet bloc. The shipbuilding industry produced six times as much tonnage in 1970 as in 1960, almost half of the new tonnage produced outside the Soviet bloc.

While Japan benefited from being outside the Cold War, China was deeply involved in Cold War politics. When Mao Zedong° and the communists defeated the nationalists in 1949 and established the People's Republic of China (PRC), their main ally and source of arms was the Soviet Union. By 1956, however, the PRC and the Soviet Union were beginning to diverge politically, partly in reaction to the Soviet rejection of Stalinism and partly because of China's reluctance to be cast forever in the role of student. Mao had his own notions of communism, focusing strongly on the peasantry, whom the Soviets ignored in favor of the industrial working class.

Mao's Great Leap Forward in 1958 was supposed to vault China into the ranks of world industrial powers by maximizing the use of labor in small-scale, village-level industries. The policy failed but demonstrated Mao's willingness to carry

---

al-Sadat (al-seh-DAT)   Aswan (AS-wahn)

Mao Zedong (maow dzuh-dong)

out massive economic and social projects of his own devising.

In 1966, Mao instituted another radical nationwide program, the **Cultural Revolution.** He ordered the mass mobilization of Chinese youth into Red Guard units. His goal was to kindle revolutionary fervor in a new generation and to ward off the stagnation and bureaucratization he saw in the Soviet Union. Red Guard units criticized and purged teachers, party officials, and intellectuals for "bourgeois values." Internal party conflict continued until 1971, when Mao admitted that attacks on individuals had gotten out of hand. Meanwhile, small-scale industrialization resulted in record levels of agricultural and industrial production. The last years of the Cultural Revolution were dominated by radicals led by Mao's wife, Jiang Qing°, who focused on restrictions on artistic and intellectual activity.

In the meantime, the rift between the PRC and the Soviet Union had opened so wide that United States President Richard Nixon (1969–1974), by reputation a staunch anticommunist, dropped objections to the PRC's joining the United Nations. In 1971, the PRC occupied China's permanent seat on the Security Council, displacing the Chinese nationalist government on Taiwan. The following year, Nixon visited Beijing, making dramatically clear the new cooperation between the People's Republic of China and the United States.

The Middle East

Independence had come gradually to the Arab countries of the Middle East. Britain granted Syria and Lebanon independence after World War II. Other Arab countries—Iraq, Egypt, Jordan—enjoyed nominal independence during the interwar period but remained under indirect British control until the 1950s.

Overshadowing all Arab politics, however, was the struggle with the new state of Israel. British policy on Palestine between the wars oscillated between favoring Zionist Jewish immigrants and the indigenous Palestinian Arabs. After the war, under intense pressure to resettle European Jewish re-

fugees, Britain turned the Palestine problem over to the United Nations. In November 1947, the General Assembly voted in favor of partitioning Palestine into two states, one Jewish and one Arab. The Jewish community made plans to declare independence while the Palestinians, who felt the proposed land division was unfair, reacted in horror and took up arms. When Israel declared its independence in May 1948, neighboring Arab countries sent armies to help the Palestinians crush the newborn state.

Israel, however, prevailed on all fronts. Some 700,000 Palestinians became refugees. They found shelter in United Nations refugee camps in Jordan, Syria, Lebanon, and the Gaza Strip (a bit of coastal land on the Egyptian-Israeli border). The right of these refugees to return home remains a focal point of Arab politics. In 1967, Israel responded to threatening military moves by Egypt's Nasir by preemptively attacking Egyptian and Syrian air bases. In six days, Israel won a smashing victory. Israel won control of Jerusalem, previously split with Jordan, the West Bank, the Gaza Strip, the strategic Golan Heights in southern Syria, and the entire Sinai Peninsula. Acquiring all of Jerusalem satisfied Jews' deep longing to return to their holiest city, but Palestinians continued to regard Jerusalem as their destined capital, and Muslims in many countries protested Israeli control of the Dome of the Rock, a revered Islamic shrine located in the city. These acquisitions resulted in a new wave of Palestinian refugees.

The rival claims to Palestine continued to plague Middle Eastern politics. The Palestine Liberation Organization (PLO), headed by Yasir Arafat°, waged guerrilla war against Israel, frequently engaging in acts of terrorism. The militarized Israelis were able to blunt or absorb these attacks and launch counterstrikes that likewise involved assassinations and bombings. Though the United States proved a firm friend of Israel and the Soviet Union armed the Arab states, neither superpower saw the struggle between Zionism and Palestinian nationalism as a vital concern—until oil became a political issue.

Jiang Qing (jyahn ching)

Arafat (AR-uh-fat)

The phenomenal concentration of oil wealth in the Persian Gulf states—Iran, Iraq, Kuwait, Saudi Arabia, Qatar, Bahrain, and the United Arab Emirates—was not fully realized until after World War II when demand for oil rose sharply as civilian economies recovered. As a world oversupply diminished in the face of rising demand, oil-producing states in 1960 formed the **Organization of Petroleum Exporting Countries (OPEC)** to promote their collective interest in higher revenues.

Oil politics and the Arab-Israeli conflict intersected in October 1973. A surprise Egyptian attack across the Suez Canal threw the Israelis into temporary disarray. Within days, the war turned in Israel's favor, and an Egyptian army was trapped at the canal's southern end. The United States then arranged a cease-fire and the disengagement of forces. But before that could happen, the Arab oil-producing countries voted to embargo oil shipments to the United States and the Netherlands as punishment for their support of Israel.

The implications of oil as an economic weapon profoundly disturbed the worldwide oil industry. Prices rose—along with feelings of insecurity. In 1974, OPEC responded to the turmoil in the oil market by quadrupling prices, setting the stage for massive transfers of wealth to the producing countries and provoking a feeling of crisis throughout the consuming countries.

The Emergence of Environmental Concerns

Skyrocketing oil prices focused new attention on natural resource issues. Before the mid-1960s, only a few people noticed that untested technologies and all-out drives for industrial productivity were rapidly degrading the environment. The superpowers were particularly negligent of the environmental impact of pesticide and herbicide use, automobile exhaust, industrial waste disposal, and radiation hazards.

New youth activism focused awareness on environmental problems. In 1968, a wave of student unrest swept many parts of the world. Earth Day was first celebrated in 1970, the year in which the United States established its Environmental Protection Agency.

After 1974, making gasoline engines and home heating systems more efficient and lowering highway speed limits to conserve fuel became matters of national debate in the United States while

Oil Crisis at the Gas Station   Dislocations in the oil industry caused by OPEC price rises that began in 1974 produced long lines at gas pumps and local shortages. The crisis brought Middle East politics home to consumers and created a negative stereotype of "oil sheikhs."   (Keza/Liaison)

poorer countries struggled to find the money to import oil. A widely read 1972 study, *The Limits of Growth,* forecast a need to cut back on consumption of natural resources in the twenty-first century. Thus, as the most dangerous moments of the Cold War seemed to be passing, ecological and environmental problems of worldwide impact vied with the superpower rivalry and Third World nation building for public attention.

CONCLUSION

The Cold War and the decolonization movement seemed to arise as logical extensions of World War II. The question of who would control the parts of Europe and Asia liberated from Axis occupation led to Churchill's notion of an iron curtain dividing East and West. The war exhaustion of the European imperialist powers encouraged Asian and African peoples to seek independence and embark on building their own nations.

Intellectuals often framed their understanding of the period in terms of a philosophical struggle between capitalism and socialism dating back to the nineteenth century. But for leaders facing the challenge of governing new nations and creating viable economies, ideology became intertwined with questions of how to profit from the Cold War rivalry between the United States and the Soviet Union.

Historians do not all agree on the year 1975 as the end of the postwar era. The end of the Vietnam War, the beginning of the world oil crisis, and the signing of the Helsinki Accords that brought a measure of agreement among Europeans on both sides of the iron curtain were pivotal events for some countries. But the number of independent countries in the world had grown enormously, and each was in the process of working out its own particular problems. What marks the mid-1970s as the end of an era, therefore, is not a single event so much as the emergence of new concerns. Young people with no memories of World War II were less concerned with the Cold War and the specter of nuclear annihilation than with newly recognized threats to the world environment and with making their own way in the world. In the wealthier nations, this meant taking advantage of economic growth and increasing technological sophistication. In the developing world, it meant seeking the education and employment needed for playing active roles in the drama of nation building.

■ Key Terms

iron curtain	Warsaw Pact
Cold War	Korean War
North Atlantic Treaty Organization (NATO)	Vietnam War
	Cuban missile crisis
United Nations	Helsinki Accords
World Bank	nonaligned nations
Marshall Plan	Third World
European Community (EC)	Cultural Revolution (China)
Truman Doctrine	
	Organization of Petroleum Exporting Countries (OPEC)

■ Suggested Reading

The period since 1945 has been particularly rich in memoirs by government leaders. Some that are particularly relevant to the Cold War and decolonization are Dean Acheson (United States secretary of state under Truman), *Present at the Creation* (1969); Nikita Khrushchev, *Khrushchev Remembers* (1970); and Anthony Eden (British prime minister), *Full Circle* (1960).

Geoffrey Barraclough, *An Introduction to Contemporary History* (1964), is a remarkable early effort at understanding the broad sweep of history during this period.

Scholarship on the origins of the Cold War is extensive and includes Akira Iriye, *The Cold War in Asia: A Historical Introduction* (1974); Bruce Kuniholm, *The Origins of the Cold War in the Middle East* (1980); Madelaine Kalb, *The Congo Cables: The Cold War in Africa—From Eisenhower to Kennedy* (1982); and Michael J. Hogan, *A Cross of Iron: Harry S Truman and the Origins of the National Security State* (1998). For a recent reconsideration of earlier historical viewpoints, see Melvyn P. Leffler and David S. Painter (eds.), *Origins of the Cold War: An International History* (1994).

Good general histories of the Cold War include Martin Walker, *The Cold War: A History* (1993), and Walter Lafeber, *America, Russia, and the Cold War, 1945–1992* (1993). The latter puts emphasis on how the Cold War eroded American democratic values. For a look at the Cold War from the Soviet perspective, see William Taubman, *Stalin's America Policy* (1981); for the American perspective, see John Lewis Gaddis, *Strategies of Containment: A Critical Appraisal of Postwar American National Security Policy* (1982).

The nuclear arms race and the associated Soviet-U.S. competition in space are well covered by McGeorge Bundy, *Danger and Survival: Choices About the Bomb in the First Fifty Years* (1988), and Walter MacDougall, *The Heavens and the Earth: A Political History of the Space Age* (1985). Among the many novels illustrating the alarming impact of the arms race on the general public are Philip Wylie, *Tomorrow!* (1954), and Nevil Shute, *On the Beach* (1970). At a technical and philosophical level, Herman Kahn's *On Thermonuclear War* (1961) had a similar effect.

The end of the European empires is broadly treated by D. K. Fieldhouse, *The Colonial Empires* (1982); for the British Empire in particular, see Brian Lapping, *End of Empire* (1985). For a critical view of American policies toward the decolonized world, see Gabriel Kolko, *Confronting the Third World: United States Foreign Policy, 1945–1980* (1988).

For books on some of the specific episodes of decolonization treated in this chapter, see, on Algeria, Alistaire Horne, *A Savage War of Peace: Algeria, 1954–1962* (1987); on Cuba, Hugh Thomas, *Cuba: The Pursuit of Freedom* (1971); on the Suez crisis of 1956, Keith Kyle, *Suez 1956* (1991); on Britain's role in the Middle East over the period of the birth of Israel, William Roger Louis, *The British Empire in the Middle East, 1945–1951* (1984); on Vietnam, George Herring, *America's Longest War: The United States and Vietnam, 1950–1975* (1986), and Stanley Karnow, *Vietnam: A History* (1991); and on Latin America, Eric Wolf, *The Human Condition in Latin America* (1972).

The special cases of Japan and China in this period are covered by Takafusa Nakamura, *A History of Showa Japan, 1926–1989* (1998); Marius B. Jansen, *Japan and China: From War to Peace, 1894–1972* (1975); and Maurice Meisner, *Mao's China and After: A History of the People's Republic* (1986). John Merrill, *Korea: The Peninsular Origins of the War* (1989), presents the Korean War as a civil and revolutionary conflict as well as an episode of the Cold War. Among the hundreds of books on the Arab-Israeli conflict, Charles D. Smith, *Palestine and the Arab-Israel Conflict* (1992), and Trevor N. Dupuy, *Elusive Victory: The Arab-Israeli Wars, 1947–1974* (1978), stand out.

CRISIS, REALIGNMENT, AND THE DAWN OF THE POST–COLD WAR WORLD,

1975–1991

Postcolonial Crises and Asian Economic Expansion, 1975–1990 •
The End of the Bipolar World, 1989–1991 • The Challenge of
Population Growth • Unequal Development and the Movement of
Peoples • Technological and Environmental Change
SOCIETY AND CULTURE: China's Family–Planning Needs

On Thursday, July 22, 1993, police officers in Rio de Janeiro's banking district attempted to arrest a young boy caught sniffing glue. In the resulting scuffle, one police officer was injured by stones thrown by a group of homeless children who lived in nearby streets and parks. Late the following night, hooded vigilantes in two cars fired hundreds of shots at a group of these children sleeping on the steps of a church. The attackers, later identified as off-duty police officers, killed five children there and two more in a park.

At that time, more than 350,000 abandoned children lived in Rio's streets and parks and resorted to begging, selling drugs, stealing, and prostitution to survive. In 1993 alone, death squads and drug dealers killed more than four hundred of them. Few people sympathized with the victims. One person living near the scene of the July shootings said, "Those street kids are bandits, and bandits have to die. They are a rotten branch that has to be pruned."[1]

At the end of the twentieth century, the brutality of those children's lives was an increasingly common feature of life in the developing world, where rapid population growth was outstripping economic resources. Similar problems of violence, poverty, and social breakdown could be found in most developing nations.

In wealthy industrialized nations as well, politicians and social reformers worried about the effects of unemployment, family breakdown, substance abuse, and homelessness. As had been true during the eighteenth-century Industrial Revolution (see Chapter 21), dramatic economic growth, increased global economic integration, and rapid technological progress in the post–World War II period coincided with growing social dislocation and inequality. Among the most important events of the period were the emergence of new industrial powers in Asia and the precipitous demise of the Soviet Union and its socialist allies.

New challenges also appeared in the form of world population growth and large-scale migrations. Population grew most rapidly in the world's poorest nations, worsening social and economic problems and undermining fragile political institutions. In the industrialized nations, the arrival of large numbers of culturally and linguistically distinct immigrants fueled economic growth but also led to the appearance of anti-immigrant political movements and, in some cases, violent ethnic conflict.

As you read this chapter, ask yourself the following questions:

- How did the Cold War affect politics in Latin America and the Middle East in the 1970s and 1980s?
- What forces led to the collapse of the Soviet Union?
- What is the relationship between the rate of population growth and the wealth of nations?
- How has technological change affected the global environment in the recent past?

POSTCOLONIAL CRISES AND ASIAN ECONOMIC EXPANSION, 1975–1989

Between 1975 and 1991, wars and revolutions provoked by a potent mix of ideology, nationalism, ethnic hatred, and religious fervor spread death and destruction through many of the world's least developed regions. Although often tied to earlier colonialism and foreign intervention, each conflict reflected a specific set of historical experiences. In many cases, conflicts provoked by local and regional causes tended to become more deadly and long lasting because the United States and the Soviet Union intervened. Conflicts in which the rival superpowers financed and armed competing factions or parties were called **proxy wars.**

Local and regional conflicts and proxy wars were not universal. During this same period, Japan gained a position among the world's leading industrial powers, while a small number of other Asian economies quickly entered the ranks of industrial and commercial powers. By the early 1990s, the collapse of the Soviet system in eastern Europe had ended the Cold War. As former socialist nations opened their markets to foreign investment and competition, economic transformation was often accompanied by wrenching social change. Other challenges facing the late twentieth century included growing inequalities among nations and within nations, rapid population expansion, and degradation of the environment.

Revolutions, Repression, and Democratic Reform in Latin America

After the Cuban Revolution, Fidel Castro sought to end the domination of the United States and uplift the Cuban masses by changing the economy in fundamental ways. Both objectives led to confrontation with the United States. The Cuban Revolution was the first revolution in the Western Hemisphere to nationalize foreign investment, redistribute the wealth of the elite, and forge an alliance with the Soviet Union. The fact that a communist government could come to power and thwart efforts by the United States to overthrow it energized the revolutionary left throughout Latin America (see Chapter 28). Unable to overthrow Castro and fearful that revolution would spread across Latin America, the United States mobilized its political and military allies in Latin America to defeat communism at all costs.

Brazil was the first to experience the full effects of the conservative reaction to the Cuban Revolution. Claiming that Brazil's civilian political leaders

CHRONOLOGY

	The Americas	Middle East	Asia	Eastern Europe
1970	**1964**　Military takeover in Brazil **1970**　Salvador Allende elected president of Chile **1973**　Allende overthrown **1976**　Military takeover in Argentina **1979**　Sandinistas overthrow Anastasio Somoza in Nicaragua **1983–1990** Democracy returns in Argentina, Brazil, and Chile			
1980		**1979**　Islamic Revolution overthrows shah of Iran **1980–1988**　Iran-Iraq War	**1975**　Vietnam war ends **1978**　China opens its economy **1986**　Average Japanese income overtakes income in United States	**1978**　USSR sends troops to Afghanistan **1985**　Mikhail Gorbachev becomes Soviet head of state
	1989　United States invades Panama		**1989**　Tiananmen Square confrontation	**1989**　USSR withdraws troops from Afghanistan; Berlin Wall falls **1989–1991**　End of communism in eastern Europe **1990**　Reunification of Germany
1990	**1990**　Sandinistas defeated in elections in Nicaragua	**1990**　Iraq invades Kuwait **1991**　Persian Gulf War		

could not protect the nation from communist subversion, the army overthrew the democratically elected government in 1964. The military suspended the constitution, outlawed all existing political parties, and exiled former presidents and opposition leaders. Death squads—illegal paramilitary organizations sanctioned by the government—detained, tortured, and executed thousands of citizens. The dictatorship also undertook an ambitious economic program that promoted industrialization through import substitution, using tax and tariff policies to compel foreign-owned companies to increase investment in manufacturing.

Elements of this "Brazilian Solution" were imposed across much of Latin America in the 1970s and early 1980s. In 1970, Chile's new president, **Salvador Allende°,** undertook an ambitious program of socialist reforms to redistribute wealth from the elite and middle classes to the poor. He also nationalized most of Chile's heavy industry and

---

Salvador Allende (sal-vah-DOR ah-YEHN-day)

mines, including the American-owned copper companies that dominated the Chilean economy. From the beginning of Allende's presidency, the administration of United States President Richard Nixon (1969–1973) worked in Chile to organize opposition to Allende's reforms. After Chile's economy weakened, Allende was overthrown in 1973 by a military uprising led by General Augusto Pinochet° and supported by the United States. President Allende and thousands of Chileans died in this uprising, and thousands of others were illegally seized, tortured, and imprisoned without trial. Once in power, Pinochet rolled back Allende's reforms, reduced state participation in the economy, and encouraged foreign investment. In 1976, Argentina followed Brazil and Chile into military dictatorship. During the next seven years, the military fought what it called the **Dirty War** against terrorism. More than nine thousand Argentines lost their lives, and thousands of others endured arrest, terrible tortures, and the loss of property.

The flow of U.S. arms to regimes with the worst human rights records stopped during the four-year term of United States President Jimmy Carter (1977–1980). Carter championed human rights in the hemisphere and sought to placate Latin American resentment for past U.S. interventions by renegotiating the Panama Canal treaty, agreeing to the reestablishment of Panamanian sovereignty in the Canal Zone at the end of 1999. He also tried, but failed, to find some common ground with the **Sandinistas°,** a revolutionary movement in Nicaragua that overthrew the corrupt dictatorship of Anastasio Somoza in 1979. The Sandinistas received significant political and financial support from Cuba and, once in power, sought to imitate the command economies of Cuba and the Soviet Union. The Nicaraguan Revolution nationalized properties owned by members of the Nicaraguan elite and U.S. citizens.

In 1981, Ronald Reagan became president and replaced Carter's policy of conciliation with efforts at reversing the results of the Nicaraguan Revolution and defeat a revolutionary movement in neighboring El Salvador. His options, however, were limited by the U.S. Congress, which feared that Central America might become another Vietnam. The Reagan administration sought to roll back the Nicaraguan Revolution by the use of punitive economic measures and by supporting anti-Sandinista Contras (counterrevolutionaries), using both legal and illegal funds.

The Contras were unable to defeat the Sandinistas, but they did gain a bloody stalemate by the end of the 1980s. Confident that they were supported by the majority of Nicaraguans and assured that the U.S. Congress was close to cutting off aid to the Contras, the Sandinistas called for free elections in 1990. But they had miscalculated and lost the election. Exhausted by more than a decade of violence, a majority of Nicaraguan voters rejected the Sandinistas and elected a middle-of-the-road coalition led by Violeta Chamorro°.

The military dictatorships established in Brazil, Chile, and Argentina all came to an end between 1983 and 1990. In each case, reports of kidnappings, tortures, and corruption by military governments undermined public support. In Argentina, the military junta foolishly decided in 1982 to seize the Falkland Islands—the Argentines called them the "Malvinas." The Argentine junta had helped President Reagan support the Contras in Nicaragua and believed he would keep Britain's prime minister, Margaret Thatcher, from taking military action. When the Argentine garrison in the Falklands surrendered, military rule in Argentina itself collapsed.

In Chile and Brazil, the military dictatorships ended without the drama of foreign war. Despite significant economic growth under Pinochet, Chileans resented the violence and corruption of the military. In 1988, Pinochet called a plebiscite to extend his authority, but the majority vote went against him. Brazil's military initiated a gradual transition to civilian rule in 1985. By 1991, nearly 95 percent of Latin America's population lived under civilian rule.

Islamic Revolutions in Iran and Afghanistan

The Middle East was another region where the superpowers were involved in local revolutions. The United States was motivated to act in

---

Augusto Pinochet (ah-GOOS-toh pin-oh-CHET)
Sandinistas (sahn-din-EES-tahs)

Violeta Chamorro (vee-oh-LET-ah cha-MOR-roe)

The Nicaraguan Revolution Overturns Somoza   A revolutionary coalition that included Marxists drove the dictator Anastasio Somoza from power in 1979. The Somoza family had ruled Nicaragua since the 1930s and maintained a close relationship with the United States.   (Susan Meiselas/Magnum Photos, Inc.)

support of Israel and to protect access to petroleum from the region. The Soviet Union wished to prevent the spread of radical Islamic movements across the border into its own Muslim regions.

The Iranian Revolution of 1979 proved enormously frustrating to the United States. In 1953, covert intervention by the United States Central Intelligence Agency (CIA) helped Shah Muhammad Reza Pahlavi° retain his throne in the face of a movement to usurp royal power. Even when he finally nationalized the foreign-owned oil industry, the shah continued to enjoy special American support. As oil revenues increased following the price increases of the 1970s, the United States encouraged the shah to spend his nation's growing wealth on equipping the Iranian army with advanced

American weaponry. By the 1970s, there was mounting popular resentment against the shah's dependence on the United States, the ballooning wealth of the elite families that supported him, and the inefficiency, malfeasance, and corruption of his government, which led to mass opposition.

Ayatollah Ruhollah Khomeini°, a Shi'ite° philosopher-cleric who had spent most of his eighty-plus years in religious and academic pursuits, became the voice and symbolic leader of the opposition. Massive street demonstrations and crippling strikes forced the shah to flee Iran and ended the monarchy in 1979. In the Islamic Republic of Iran, which replaced the monarchy, Ayatollah Khomeini was supreme arbiter of disputes and

---

Reza Pahlavi (REH-zah PAH-lah-vee)

Ayatollah Ruhollah Khomeini (eye-uh-TOLL-uh ROOH-ol-LAH ko-MAY-nee)   Shi'ite (SHE-ite)

guarantor of religious legitimacy. Elections were held, but monarchists, communists, and other groups opposed to the idea of an Islamic Republic were barred from running for office. Shi'ite clerics with little training for government service emerged in many of the highest posts, and stringent measures were taken to replace Western styles and culture with Islamic norms. Universities were temporarily closed, and their faculties were purged of secularists and monarchists. Women were compelled to wear modest Islamic garments outside the house, and semi-official vigilante committees policed public morals.

The United States under President Carter had criticized the shah's repressive regime, but the overthrow of a long-standing ally and the creation of the Islamic Republic were blows to American prestige. Khomeini saw the United States as a "Great Satan" opposed to Islam, and he helped to foster Islamic revolutionary movements elsewhere, which threatened the interests of both the United States and Israel. In November 1979, Iranian radicals seized the U.S. embassy in Tehran and then held fifty-two diplomats hostage for 444 days. Americans felt humiliated by their inability to do anything, particularly after the failure of a military rescue attempt.

In the fall of 1980, shortly after negotiations for the release of the hostages began, **Saddam Husain°,** the ruler of neighboring Iraq, invaded Iran to topple the Islamic Republic. His own dictatorial rule rested on a secular Arab nationalist philosophy and long-standing friendship with the Soviet Union, which had provided him with advanced weaponry. He feared that the fervor of Iran's revolutionary Shi'ite leaders would infect his own country's Shi'ite majority and threaten his power. The war pitted American weapons in the hands of the Iranians against Soviet weapons in the hands of the Iraqis, but the superpowers avoided overt involvement during eight years of bloodshed. Covertly, however, the Reagan administration sent arms to Iran, hoping to gain the release of other American hostages held by radical Islamic groups in Lebanon and to help finance the Contra war against the Sandinista government of Nicaragua. When this deal came to the light in 1986, the result-

---

Saddam Husain (sah-DAHM who-SANE)

ing political scandal intensified American hostility toward Iran. Openly tilting toward Iraq, President Reagan sent the United States Navy to the Persian Gulf, ostensibly to protect nonbelligerent shipping. The move helped persuade Iran to accept a cease-fire in 1988.

While the United States faced anguish and frustration in Iran, the Soviet Union found itself facing even more serious problems in neighboring Afghanistan. Since World War II, the Soviet Union had succeeded in staying out of shooting wars by using proxies to challenge the United States. But in 1978, the Soviet Union sent its army to Afghanistan to support a fledgling communist regime against a hodgepodge of local, religiously inspired guerrilla bands that had taken control of much of the countryside.

With the United States, Saudi Arabia, and Pakistan paying, equipping, and training the Afghan rebels, the Soviet Union found itself in the same kind of unwinnable war the United States had stumbled into in Vietnam. Unable to justify the continuing drain on manpower, morale, and economic resources and facing widespread domestic discontent over the war, Soviet leaders finally withdrew their troops in 1989. The Afghan communists held on for another three years. But once rebel groups took control of the entire country, they began to fight among themselves over who should rule.

Asian Transformation

Japan has few mineral resources and is dependent on oil imports, but the Japanese economy weathered the oil price shocks of the 1970s better than did the economies of Europe and the United States. In fact, Japan experienced a faster rate of economic growth in the 1970s and 1980s than did any other major developed economy, growing at about 10 percent a year. Average income also increased rapidly, overtaking that of the United States in 1986.

There are some major differences between the Japanese industrial model and that of the United States. During the American occupation, Japanese industrial conglomerates, *zaibatsu* (see Chapter 25), were broken up. Although ownership of major

Muslim Women Mourning the Death of Ayatollah Khomeini in 1989 An Islamic revolution overthrew the shah of Iran in 1979. Ayatollah Khomeini sought to lead Iran away from the influences of Western culture and challenged the power of the United States in the Persian Gulf. (Alexandra Avakian/Woodfin Camp & Associates)

industries became less concentrated as a result, new industrial alliances appeared. There are now six major *keiretsu*° that each include firms in industry, commerce, construction, and a major bank tied together in an interlocking ownership structure. There are also minor keiretsu dominated by a major corporation, like Toyota, and including its major suppliers. These combinations of companies have close relationships with government. Government assistance in the form of tariffs and import regulations inhibiting foreign competition was crucial in the early stages of the development of Japan's automobile and semiconductor industries, among others.

Through the 1970s and 1980s, Japanese success at exporting manufactured goods produced

keiretsu (kay-REHT-soo)

huge trade surpluses with other nations, prompting the United States and the European Community to try to pry open the Japanese market through tough negotiating. These efforts had only limited success. In 1990, Japan enjoyed a trade surplus with the rest of the world that was twice as large as in 1985. Many experts assumed that the competitive advantages that Japan enjoyed in the 1980s would propel Japan past the United States as the world's preeminent industrial economy. But the Japanese economy began to stall at the end of the decade.

The Japanese model of close cooperation between government and industry was imitated by a small number of other Asian states. The most important of them was South Korea, which overcame the devastation of the Korean War in little more than a decade through a combination of inexpensive labor, strong technical education, and substantial domestic capital reserves. Despite large defense expenditures, South Korea developed heavy industries such as steel and shipbuilding, as well as consumer industries such as automobiles and consumer electronics. Japanese investment and technology transfers accelerated this process. Hyundai was typical of the four giant corporations that accounted for nearly half of South Korea's gross domestic product (GDP) in manufacturing products ranging from supertankers and cars to electronics and housing.

Taiwan, Hong Kong, and Singapore also developed modern industrial and commercial economies so rapidly that these three nations and South Korea were often referred to as the **Asian Tigers.** All shared many characteristics that helped explain their rapid industrialization. All had disciplined and hard-working labor forces, and all invested heavily in education. For example, as early as 1980, Korea had as many engineering graduates as Germany, Britain, and Sweden combined. All had high rates of personal saving that allowed them to fund investment in new technology generously. In 1987, the saving rates in Taiwan and South Korea were three times higher than in the United States. All emphasized outward-looking export strategies. And, like Japan, all of these dynamic Pacific Rim economies benefited from government sponsorship and protection. All were beneficiaries of the extraordinary expansion in world trade and international communication that permitted technology to be disseminated more rapidly than at any other time in the past. As a result, newly industrializing nations began with current technologies.

In China after Mao Zedong's death in 1976, the communist leadership introduced a comprehensive economic reform that allowed more individual initiative and permitted individuals to accumulate wealth. Beginning in 1978, the Communist Party in Sichuan province freed more than six thousand firms to compete for business outside the state planning process. The results were remarkable. Under China's leader, **Deng Xiaoping°**, these reforms were expanded across the nation. China also began to permit foreign investment for the first time since the communists came to power in 1949.

Between 1978 and the end of the 1990s, foreign investors committed more than $180 billion to the Chinese economy, and McDonald's, Coca-Cola, Airbus, and other foreign companies opened for business. But more than 100 million workers were still employed in state-owned enterprises, and most foreign-owned companies were segregated in special economic zones. The result was a dual industrial sector—one modern and efficient and connected to international markets, the other dominated by government and directed by political decisions.

In the countryside, Deng Xiaoping permitted the contracting of land to individuals and families, who were free to consume or sell whatever they produced. By 1984, 93 percent of China's agricultural land was in effect in private hands and producing for the market, tripling agricultural output.

Perhaps the best measure of the success of Deng's reforms is that between 1980 and 1993, China's per capita output more than doubled, averaging more than 8 percent growth per year in comparison with the world average of slightly more than 1 percent and Japan's average of 3.3 percent. This growth was overwhelmingly the result of exports to the developed nations of the West, especially the United States. Nevertheless, per capita measures of wealth indicated that China remained a poor nation. China's per capita GDP was roughly the same as Mexico's—about $3,600 per year. By comparison, Taiwan had a per capita GDP of $14,700.

Deng Xiaoping's strategy of balancing change and continuity helped China avoid some of the social costs and political consequences experienced by Russia and other European socialist countries that abruptly plunged into capitalism and democracy. As Chinese officials put it, China was "changing a big earthquake into a thousand tremors." The nation's leadership faced a major challenge in 1989. Responding to mass movements in favor of democracy across the globe and to inflation, Chinese students and intellectuals, many of whom had studied outside China, led a series of protests demanding more democracy and an end to inflation and corruption. This movement culminated in a massive occupation of **Tiananmen Square°** by

---

Deng Xiaoping (dung show-ping)

Tiananmen (tee-yehn-ahn-men)

protestors, in the heart of Beijing. After weeks of standoff, tanks pushed into the square, killing hundreds, perhaps thousands. Many more were arrested. Although the Communist party survived this challenge, it was not clear whether rapid economic growth, increasing inequality, high levels of unemployment, and massive migration from the countryside to the cities could occur without triggering a political transformation.

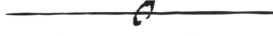

THE END OF THE BIPOLAR WORLD, 1989–1991

Few in 1980 predicted the startling collapse of the Soviet Union and the socialist nations of the Warsaw Pact. The once-independent nations and ethnic groups that had been brought within the Soviet Union and the eastern European nations seemed securely transformed by the experiences and institutions of communism. By 1990, however, nationalism was resurgent, and communism was nearly finished.

Crisis in the Soviet Union

Under United States President Ronald Reagan and the Soviet Union's General Secretary, Leonid Brezhnev°, the rhetoric of the Cold War remained intense. Massive new U.S. investments in armaments, including a space-based missile protection system that never became operational, placed heavy burdens on the Soviet economy, which was unable to absorb the cost of developing similar weapons. Soviet economic problems were systemic. Obsolete industrial plants and centralized planning stifled initiative and responsiveness to market demand. Government bureaucrats and Communist Party favorites received special privileges, including permission to shop in stores that stocked Western goods, but the average citizen faced long lines and waiting lists for goods. Soviet citizens contrasted their lot with the free and prosperous life of the West depicted in the increasingly accessible Western media. The arbitrariness of the bureaucracy, the cynical manipulation of information, and deprivations created a generalized crisis in morale.

Despite the unpopularity of the war in Afghanistan and growing discontent, Brezhnev refused to modify his rigid and unsuccessful policies. But he was unable to contain an underground current of protest. Self-published underground writings by critics of the regime circulated widely despite government efforts to suppress them. The physicist Andrei Sakharov and his wife, Yelena Bonner, protested the nuclear arms race and human rights violations and were condemned to banishment within the country. Some Jewish dissidents spoke out against anti-Semitism, but many more left for Israel or the United States.

By the time **Mikhail Gorbachev°** took up the reins of the Soviet government in 1985, war weariness, economic decay, and vocal protest had reached critical levels. Casting aside Brezhnev's hard line, Gorbachev authorized major reforms in an attempt to stave off total collapse. His policy of political openness (*glasnost*) permitted criticism of the government and the Communist Party. His policy of ***perestroika*°** ("restructuring") was an attempt to address long-suppressed economic problems by moving away from central state planning and toward a more open economic system. In 1989, he ended the war in Afghanistan, which had cost many lives and much money.

The Collapse of the Socialist Bloc

Events in eastern Europe were very important in forcing change on the Soviet Union. In 1980, protests by Polish shipyard workers in the city of Gdansk led to the formation of **Solidarity,** a labor union that soon enrolled 9 million members. The Roman Catholic Church in Poland, strengthened by the elevation of a Pole, Karol Wojtyla°, to the papacy as John Paul II in 1978, gave strong moral support to the protest movement. As Gorbachev

---

Leonid Brezhnev (leh-oh-NEED BREZ-nef)

Gorbachev (GORE-beh-CHOF)
perestroika (per-ih-STROY-kuh)
Karol Wojtyla (KAH-rol voy-TIL-ah)

loosened political controls in the Soviet Union after 1985, communist leaders elsewhere lost confidence in Soviet resolve, and critics and reformers in Poland and throughout the rest of eastern Europe were emboldened (see Map 29.1).

Beleaguered Warsaw Pact governments vacillated between relaxation of control and the suppression of dissent. As the Catholic clergy in Poland had supported Solidarity, Protestant and Orthodox religious leaders aided the rise of opposition groups elsewhere. This combination of nationalism and religion provided a powerful base for opponents of the communist regimes. Threatened

by these forces, communist governments sought to quiet the opposition by seeking solutions to their severe economic problems. They turned to the West for trade and financial assistance and opened their nations to travelers, ideas, styles, and money from Western countries, all of which accelerated the demand for change.

By the end of 1989, communist governments across eastern Europe had fallen. The dismantling of the Berlin Wall, the symbol of a divided Europe and the bipolar world, vividly represented this transformation. In Poland, Hungary, Czechoslovakia, and Bulgaria, communist leaders decided that

Map 29.1   The End of Soviet Domination in Eastern Europe   The creation of new countries out of Yugoslavia and Czechoslovakia and the reunification of Germany marked the most complicated changes of national borders since World War I. The Czech Republic and Slovakia separated peacefully, but Slovenia, Croatia, Macedonia, and Bosnia and Herzegovina achieved independence only after bitter fighting.

change was inevitable and initiated political reforms. When Romanian dictator Nicolae Ceausescu° refused to surrender power, he provoked a rebellion that ended with his arrest and execution. The comprehensiveness of these changes became clear in 1990, when Solidarity leader Lech Walesa° was elected president of Poland and dissident playwright Vaclav Havel° was elected president of Czechoslovakia. That same year, East and West Germany were reunited, and the eastern Baltic states of Lithuania, Estonia, and Latvia declared their independence of the Soviet Union.

The end of the Soviet Union came suddenly in 1991 (see Map 29.2). Gorbachev's efforts to transform the Soviet system could not keep up the tide of change sweeping through the region. After Communist hardliners botched a poorly conceived coup against Gorbachev, disgust with communism boiled over. Boris Yeltsin, the president of the Russian Republic and long-time member of the Communist Party, led popular resistance to the coup in Moscow and emerged as the most powerful leader in the country. Russia, the largest republic in the Soviet Union, was effectively taking the place of the disintegrating USSR. In September 1991, the Congress of People's Deputies voted to dissolve the union. Mikhail Gorbachev went into retirement.

The ethnic and religious passions that fueled the breakup of the Soviet Union soon challenged the survival of Yugoslavia and Czechoslovakia. The dismemberment of Yugoslavia began with declarations of independence in Slovenia and Croatia in 1991. A year later, Czechoslovakia peacefully divided into the Czech Republic and Slovakia.

The Persian Gulf War, 1990–1991

The breakup of the Soviet Union and the end of the Cold War did not bring an end to international conflict. The Persian Gulf War began when Iraq's ruler, Saddam Husain, invaded Kuwait in August 1991. Husain had failed to get Kuwait's royal family to reduce the size of Iraq's debt to the oil-rich nation. He was also eager to gain control of Kuwait's oil

Nicolae Ceausescu (neh-koh-LIE chow-SHES-koo)
Lech Walesa (leck wah-LEN-suh)
Vaclav Havel (vah-SLAV hah-VEL)

fields. Husain believed that the smaller and militarily weaker nation could be quickly defeated and suspected, as a result of a conversation with an American diplomat, that the United States would not react.

Saudi Arabia, a key regional ally of the United States and a major oil producer, felt threatened by Iraq's action and helped draw the United States into the conflict. Soon the United States and its allies had concentrated an imposing military force of 500,000 in the region. With his intention to use force endorsed by the United Nations and with many Islamic nations supporting military action, President George Bush ordered an attack in early 1991. Iraq proved incapable of countering the sophisticated weaponry of the coalition. The missiles and bombs of the United States destroyed not only military targets but also "relegated [Iraq] to a preindustrial age," reported the United Nations after the war. Although Iraq's military defeat was comprehensive, Husain remained in power, and the country was not occupied. Husain, in fact, crushed an uprising in the months following this defeat. In the wake of this event, the United States and its key allies imposed "no fly" zones that denied Iraq's military aircraft access to the northern and southern regions of the country.

In the United States, the results of the war were interpreted to mean that the U.S. military defeat in the Vietnam War could be forgotten and that U.S. military capability was unrivaled. Unable to deter military action by the U.S.-led coalition or to meaningfully influence the diplomacy that surrounded the war, Russia had been of little use to its former ally Iraq, and its impotence was clear.

THE CHALLENGE OF POPULATION GROWTH

For most of human history, population growth was viewed as beneficial, and human beings were seen as a source of wealth. Since the late eighteenth century, however, population growth has been viewed with increasing alarm. Some feared that food supplies could not keep up with population growth.

Worker Unrest in Eastern Europe   After the collapse of the Soviet Union, workers such as these angry women surrounding plant managers in Minsk, capital of Belarus, demanded improvements in their working conditions.   (Yuri Ivanoff)

Others foresaw class and ethnic struggle as numbers overwhelmed resources. By the second half of the twentieth century, population growth was increasingly seen as a threat to the environment.

Demographic Transition

World population exploded in the twentieth century (see Table 29.1). At current rates of growth, world population increases by a number equal to the total population of the United States every three years. Unlike population growth in the eighteenth and nineteenth centuries, when much of the increase occurred in the wealthiest nations, population growth at the end of the twentieth century was overwhelmingly in the poorest nations. Fertility rates had dropped in most developing nations but remained much higher than rates in the industrialized nations. At the same time, improvements in hygiene and medical treatment caused mortality rates to fall. The result has been rapid population growth.

Educated Europeans of the nineteenth century had been ambivalent about the rapid increase in human population. Some saw it as a blessing that would promote economic well-being. Others warned that the seemingly relentless increase would bring disaster. Best known of these pessimists was the English cleric **Thomas Malthus,** who in 1798 argued convincingly that unchecked population growth would outstrip food production. When Malthus looked at Europe's future, he used a prejudiced image of China's huge population to terrify his European readers.

The generation that came of age in the years immediately following World War II inherited a world in which the views of Malthus were casually dismissed. Industrial and agricultural productivity had multiplied supplies of food and other necessities. Cultural changes associated with expanded fe-

Map 29.2 The End of the Soviet Union   When Communist hardliners failed to overthrow Gorbachev in 1991, popular anti-Communist sentiment swept the Soviet Union. Following Boris Yeltsin's lead in Russia, the republics that constituted the Soviet Union declared their independence.

male employment, older age at marriage, and more effective family planning had combined to slow the rate of population increase. And by the late 1960s, Europe and other industrial societies had made what was called the **demographic transition** to lower fertility rates (average number of births per woman) and reduce mortality. The number of births in the developed nations was just adequate for the maintenance of current population levels. Thus, many experts argued that the population growth then occurring in developing nations was a short-term phenomenon that would be ended by the combination of economic and social changes that had altered European patterns.

When the demographic transition failed to occur in the Third World by the late 1970s, the issue of population growth had become politicized.

The leaders of some developing nations actively promoted large families, arguing that larger populations would increase national power. Industrialized, mostly white, nations raised concerns about rapid population growth in Asia, Africa, and Latin America. Populist political leaders in those regions asked whether these concerns were not fundamentally racist.

However, once the economic shocks of the 1970s and 1980s revealed the vulnerability of developing economies, governments in the developing world jettisoned pronatalist policies. In the 1970s, Mexico's government had encouraged high fertility, and population growth in Mexico rose to 3 percent per year. By the 1980s, Mexico started to promote birth control, and the annual population growth rate fell to 2.3 percent.

Table 29.1 Population for World and Major Areas, 1750–2050

Population Size (Millions)							
Major Area	1750	1800	1850	1900	1950	1998	2050
World	791	978	1,262	1,650	2,521	5,901	8,909
Africa	106	107	111	133	221	749	1,766
Asia	502	635	809	947	1,402	3,585	5,268
Europe	163	203	276	408	547	729	628
Latin America and the Caribbean	16	24	38	74	167	504	809
North America	2	7	26	82	172	305	392
Oceania	2	2	2	6	13	30	46
Percentage Distribution							
Major Area	1750	1800	1850	1900	1950	1998	2050
World	100	100	100	100	100	100	100
Africa	13.4	10.9	8.8	8.1	8.8	12.7	19.8
Asia	63.5	64.9	64.1	57.4	55.6	60.8	59.1
Europe	20.6	20.8	21.9	24.7	21.7	12.4	7.0
Latin America and the Caribbean	2.0	2.5	3.0	4.5	6.6	8.5	9.1
North America	0.3	0.7	2.1	5.0	6.8	5.2	4.4
Oceania	0.3	0.2	0.2	0.4	0.5	0.5	0.5

Source: J. D. Durand, "Historical Estimates of World Population: An Evaluation" (Philadelphia: University of Pennsylvania, Population Studies Center, 1974, mimeographed); United Nations, *The Determinants and Consequences of Population Trends,* vol. 1 (New York: United Nations, 1973); United Nations, *World Population Prospects as Assessed in 1963* (New York: United Nations, 1966); United Nations, *World Population Prospects: The 1998 Revision* (New York: United Nations, 1999); United Nations Population Division, Department of Economic and Social Affairs, http://www.popin.org/pop1998/4.htm.

The Industrialized Nations

In much of Europe and Japan at the beginning of the twenty-first century, fertility levels are so low that population will fall unless immigration increases. In Japan, women have an average of 1.39 children; in Italy, the number is 1.2. Sweden provides cash payments, tax incentives, and job leaves to families with children, but the average number of births there fell to 1.4 in recent years. The low fertility found in mature industrial nations is tied to higher levels of female education and employment, the material values of consumer culture, and access to contraception and abortion. Educated women now defer marriage and child rearing until they are established in careers.

As fertility declined in the industrialized nations of western Europe, life expectancy has improved due to more abundant food, improved hygiene, and better medical care. Italy, for example, soon will have more than twenty adults fifty years old or over for each five-year-old child. Japan faces an even more drastic aging of its population. This demographic transformation presents a challenge very different from the one foreseen by Malthus. These nations generally offer a broad array of social services, including retirement income, medical services, and housing supplements for the elderly. As the number of retirees increases relative to the number of people who are employed, the costs of these services may become unsustainable.

In contrast, in Russia and some former socialist nations, life expectancy and birthrates have both fallen. Life expectancy for Russian men is now only fifty-seven years, down almost ten years since 1980. In the Czech Republic, Hungary, and Poland, life expectancy is improving in response to improved economic conditions, but in most of the rest of eastern Europe, the Russian pattern of declining life expectancy is found. High unemployment, low incomes, food shortages, and the dismantling of the social welfare system of the communist era have all contributed to this decline.

The Developing Nations

Population pyramids generated by demographers clearly illustrate the profound transformation in human reproductive patterns and life expectancy in the years since World War II. Figure 29.1 shows the 1985 age distributions in Pakistan, South Korea, and Sweden—nations at three different stages of economic development. Sweden is a mature industrial nation. South Korea is a rapidly industrializing nation that has surpassed many European nations in both industrial output and per capita wealth. Pakistan is a poor, traditional Muslim nation with rudimentary industrialization, low educational levels, and little effective family planning.

These demographic changes are transforming the global balance of population. At current rates, 95 percent of all future population growth will be in developing nations (see Table 29.1). A comparison between Europe and Africa illustrates these changes. In 1950, Europe had twice the population of Africa. By 1985, Africa had drawn even. According to projections, by 2025 Africa's population will be three times larger than Europe's. The populations of Latin America and Asia also were expanding dramatically, but at rates slower than those in sub-Saharan Africa and the Muslim world.

In Asia, the populations of India and China continued to grow despite government efforts to reduce family size (see Society and Culture: China's Family-Planning Needs). In China, efforts to enforce a limit of one child per family led to large-scale female infanticide as rural families sought to produce male heirs. India's policies of forced sterilization created widespread outrage and led to the electoral defeat of the ruling Congress Party. Yet both countries achieved some successes. Between 1960 and 1982, India's birthrate fell from 48 to 34 per thousand, while China's rate declined even more sharply—from 39 to 19. Still, by 2025, China and India will each have some 1.5 billion people.

UNEQUAL DEVELOPMENT AND THE MOVEMENT OF PEOPLES

Two characteristics of the postwar world should now be clear. First, despite decades of experimentation with state-directed economic development, most nations that were poor in 1960 were as poor or poorer at the end of the 1990s. The only exceptions were a few rapidly developing Asian industrial nations and an equally small number of

Figure 29.1   Age Structure Comparison: Islamic Nation (Pakistan), Non–Islamic Developing Nation (South Korea), and Developed Nation (Sweden), 1985   *Source:* Data from the World Bank.

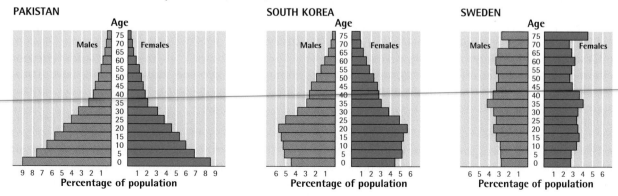

China's Family-Planning Needs

China has the world's largest population: over a billion people. Although China enjoyed rapid economic growth in the closing years of the twentieth century, population pressures continued to present severe problems. In 1993, the Chinese economy became the world's tenth largest. Nevertheless, China's per capita gross domestic product of $370 remained at Third World levels. Heavy pressure on families to have only one child resulted in the killing of female infants and the abandonment of children with disabilities. Peng Yu, vice minister of the State Family Planning Commission, explained the need for efforts at population control.

China is a developing country with a huge population but limited cultivated land, inadequate per capita resources and a weak economic foundation. . . . Despite continuous efforts in family planning, the huge base has created an annual net increase of around 14 million in recent years, equal to the total population of a medium-sized country. At present, per capita cultivated land in China has declined to less than 0.1 hectare, equivalent to only one-fourth the world average as are [its] per capita freshwater resources. . . . Although national income has been climbing by 25 percent annually, the increase has been eaten up by new population growth, resulting in reduced fund accumulation and also holding up the speed of economic construction. A fast-growing population has also created great difficulties in employment, education, housing, transportation, and health care. Confronted by such grim realities, to guarantee basic living conditions and constantly improve standards of living, China cannot follow the Western mode under which natural falling birth rates coincide with gradual economic growth.

The Chinese government's family-planning practices have been harshly criticized. Why has the Chinese government sought to control population growth? What effect has population growth had on the environment and economic development? What ethical questions are raised by the effort of any government to limit population growth?

oil-exporting nations. Second, world population increased to startlingly high levels, and most of the increase was in the poorest nations.

The combination of intractable poverty and growing population generated a surge in international immigration, both legal and illegal. Few other issues stirred more controversy. Even moderate voices sometimes framed the discussion of immigration as a competition among peoples. One commentator summarized his analysis this way: "As the better-off families of the northern hemisphere individually decide that having only one or at the most two children is sufficient, they may not recognize that they are in a small way vacating future space (that is, jobs, parts of inner cities, shares of population, shares of market preferences) to faster-growing ethnic groups both inside and out-side their boundaries. But that, in fact, is what they are doing."[2]

The Problem of Growing Inequality

Since 1945, global economic productivity has expanded more rapidly than at any other time in the past. Faster, cheaper communications and transportation have combined with improvements in industrial and agricultural technologies to create levels of material abundance that would have amazed those who experienced the first Industrial Revolution (see Chapter 21). Despite this remarkable economic expansion and growing market integration, the majority of the world's population remains in poverty. The industrialized nations of the Northern Hemisphere now enjoy a larger share of the world's wealth than they did a century ago. As a result, the gap between rich and poor nations has grown much wider. The thousands of homeless street children who live among the gleaming glass and steel towers of Rio's banking district can be seen as a metaphor for the social consequences of postwar economic development.

Wealth inequality within nations also grew. In the United States, for example, the south and southwest grew richer in the past three decades relative to the older industrial regions of the midwest. Regional inequalities also appeared in developing nations. Generally, capital cities such as Buenos Aires, in Argentina, and Lagos, in Nigeria, attracted large numbers of migrants from rural areas because they offered more opportunities, even if those opportunities could not compare to the ones available in developed nations.

Even in the industrialized world, people were divided into haves and have-nots. During the presidency of Ronald Reagan (1981–1989), wealth inequality in the United States reached its highest level since the 1929 stock market crash. Some scholars estimated that the wealthiest 1 percent of households in the United States controlled more than 30 percent of the nation's total wealth. Even in Europe, where tax and inheritance laws redistributed wealth, unemployment, homelessness, and substandard housing were increasingly common.

Internal Migration: The Growth of Cities

Migration from rural areas to urban centers in developing nations increased threefold from 1925 to 1950. After that, the pace accelerated. Shantytowns sprawling

Garbage Dump in Manila, Philippines Garbage pickers are a common feature of Third World urban development. Thousands of poor families in nearly every Third World city sort and sell bottles, aluminum cans, plastic, and newspapers to provide household income. (Geoff Tompkinson/Aspect Picture Library Ltd.)

around major cities in developing nations are commonly seen as signs of social breakdown and economic failure. Nevertheless, city life was generally better than life in the countryside. A World Bank study estimated that three out of four migrants to cities made economic gains. Residents of cities in sub-Saharan Africa, for example, were six times more likely than rural residents to have safe water. An unskilled migrant from the depressed northeast of Brazil could triple his or her income by moving to Rio de Janeiro.

As the scale of rural-to-urban migration grew, these benefits proved more elusive, however. In many West African cities, basic services were crumbling under the pressure of rapid population growth. In 1990 in Mexico City, one of the world's largest cities, more than thirty thousand people lived in garbage dumps, where they scavenged for food and clothing. Worsening conditions and the threat of crime and political instability led many governments to try to slow migration to cities and, in some cases, to return people to the countryside. Indonesia, for example, has relocated more than half a million urban residents since 1969. Despite some successes with slowing the rate of internal migration, nearly every poor nation still faces the challenge of rapidly growing cities.

Global Migration

Each year, hundreds of thousands of men and women leave the developing world to emigrate to industrialized nations. After 1960, this movement increased in scale, and ethnic and racial tensions in the host nations worsened. By the 1990s, levels of immigration posed daunting social and cultural challenges for both host nations and immigrants.

Many European nations actively promoted guest worker programs and other inducements to immigration in the 1960s when an expanding European economy first confronted labor shortages. However, attitudes toward immigrants changed as the size of the immigrant population grew and as European economies slowed in the 1980s. Facing higher levels of unemployment, native-born workers saw immigrants as competitors willing to work for lower wages and less likely to support unions.

Because immigrants generally are young adults and commonly retain the positive attitudes toward early marriage and large families dominant in their native cultures, immigrant communities in Europe and the United States tended to have fertility rates higher than the rates of the host populations. In Germany in 1975, for example, immigrants made up about 7 percent of the population but accounted for nearly 15 percent of all births. Although the fertility of the Hispanic population in the United States is lower than the rates in Mexico and other Latin American nations, Hispanic groups will contribute well over 20 percent of all population growth in the United States during the next twenty-five years.

As the Muslim population in Europe and the Asian and Latin American populations in the United States expand in the twenty-first century, cultural conflicts will test definitions of citizenship and nationality. The United States will have some advantages in meeting these challenges because of long experience with immigration and relatively open access to citizenship. Yet in the 1990s, the United States was moving slowly in the direction of European efforts to restrict immigration and defend a culturally conservative definition of nationality.

TECHNOLOGICAL AND ENVIRONMENTAL CHANGE

Technological innovation powered the economic expansion that began after World War II by increasing productivity and disseminating human creativity. Because most of the economic benefits were concentrated in the advanced industrialized nations, technology increased the power of those nations relative to the developing world. Even within developed nations, postwar technological innovations did not benefit all classes, industries, and regions equally.

The multiplication of farms and factories intensified environmental threats. Loss of rain forest, soil erosion, global warming, pollution of air and water, and extinction of species imperiled human societies. Environmental protection measures, like the acquisition of new technology, progressed furthest in societies with the most economic resources.

New Technologies and the World Economy

Nuclear energy, jet engines, radar, and tape recording were among the many World War II developments that later had an impact on consumers' lives. When applied to industry, new technology increased productivity, reduced labor requirements, and improved the flow of information. As the Western economies recovered from the war and incomes rose, consumers purchased new products that reduced their workloads or provided entertainment.

Improvements in existing technologies accounted for much of the developed world's productivity increases during the 1950s and 1960s. Larger and faster trucks, trains, and airplanes cut transportation costs. Both capitalist and socialist governments expanded highway systems, improved railroad track, and constructed airports and nuclear power plants.

No other technology had greater significance in this period than the computer. Only large corporations, governments, and universities could afford the first computers. But by the mid-1980s, desktop computers had replaced typewriters in most of the developed world's offices, and technological advances continued. Each new generation of computers was faster and more powerful than the one before.

Computers also altered manufacturing. Small dedicated computers were used to control and monitor machinery in some industries. European and Japanese companies were the first to introduce such robots into the factory. The United States introduced robots more slowly because it enjoys lower labor costs.

The transnational corporation became the primary agent of these technological changes. In the post–World War II years, many companies with multinational ownership and management invested in and marketed products throughout the world. International trade agreements and open markets furthered the process.

As transnational manufacturers, agricultural conglomerates, and financial giants became wealthier and more powerful, they increasingly escaped the controls imposed by national governments. If labor costs were too high in Japan, antipollution measures too intrusive in the United States, or taxes too high in Great Britain, transnational companies relocated—or threatened to do so. Governments in the developing world were often hard-pressed to control the actions of these powerful enterprises. As a result, the worst abuses of labor or of the environment usually occurred in poor nations.

Conserving and Sharing Resources

In the 1960s, environmental activists and political leaders began warning about the devastating environmental consequences of population growth, industrialization, and the expansion of agriculture onto marginal lands. Assaults on rain forests and redwoods, the disappearance of species, and the poisoning of streams and rivers raised public consciousness. Environmental damage occurred in the advanced industrial economies and in the poorest of the developing nations. Perhaps the worst environmental record was achieved in the former Soviet Union, where industrial and nuclear wastes were often dumped with little concern for environmental consequences. The accumulated effect of scientific studies and public debate led to national and international efforts to slow, if not undo, damage to the environment.

The expanding global population required increasing quantities of food, housing, energy, and other resources as the twentieth century ended. In the developed world, the consumer-driven economic expansion of the post–World War II years became an obstacle to addressing environmental problems. How could the United States, Germany, or Japan change consumption patterns to protect the environment without endangering corporate profits, wages, and employment levels?

Many developing countries saw exploitation of their environmental resources and industrialization as the solution to their rapidly growing populations. The results were predictable: erosion and pollution.

Responding to Environmental Threats

Despite the gravity of environmental threats, there were many successful efforts to preserve and protect the environment. The Clean Air Act, the Clean Water Act, and the Endangered Species Act were passed in the United States in the 1970s as part of an environmental effort that included the nations of the European Community and Japan. Environmental awareness spread by means of the media and grassroots political movements, and most nations in the developed world enforced strict antipollution laws and sponsored massive recycling efforts. Many also encouraged resource conservation by rewarding energy-efficient factories and the manufacturers of fuel-efficient cars and by promoting the use of alternative energy sources such as solar and wind power.

These efforts produced significant results. In western Europe and the United States, air quality improved dramatically. In the United States, smog levels were down nearly a third from 1970 to 2000 even though the number of automobiles increased more than 80 percent. Emissions of lead and sulfur dioxide were down as well. The Great Lakes, Long Island Sound, and Chesapeake Bay were all much cleaner at the end of the century than they had been in 1970. The rivers of North America and Europe also improved. Still, more than thirty thousand deaths each year in the United States are attributed to exposure to pesticides and other chemicals.

New technologies made much of this improvement possible. Pollution controls on automobiles, planes, and factory smokestacks reduced harmful emissions. Similar progress was made in the chemical industry. Scientists identified the chemicals that threaten the ozone layer, and the phase-out of their use in new appliances and cars began.

Clearly the desire to preserve the natural environment was growing around the world. In the developed nations, continued political organization and enhanced awareness of environmental issues seemed likely to lead to step-by-step improvements in environmental policy. In the developing world and most of the former Soviet bloc, however, population pressures and weak governments were major obstacles to effective environmental policies. In China, for example, respiratory disease caused by pollution was the leading cause of death. Thus, it was likely that the industrialized nations would have to fund global improvements, and the cost was likely to be high.

CONCLUSION

The world was profoundly altered between 1975 and 1991. The Cold War dominated international relations to the end of the 1980s. Every conflict threatened to provoke a confrontation between the nuclear-armed superpowers, for both the United States and the Soviet Union feared that every conflict and every regime change represented a potential threat to their strategic interests. As a result, the superpowers were drawn into a succession of civil wars and revolutions. The costs in lives and property were terrible, the gains small. As defense costs escalated, the Soviet system crumbled. By 1991, the Soviet Union and the socialist Warsaw Pact had disappeared, transforming the international stage.

Latin America was pulled into the violence of the late Cold War period and paid a terrible price. The 1970s and 1980s witnessed a frontal assault on democratic institutions, a denial of human rights, and economic decline. This was the period of death squads and Dirty War. With the end of the Cold War, peace returned there, and democracy began to replace dictatorship.

In the Persian Gulf, the end of the Cold War did not lead to peace. Iran and Iraq have experienced deep cycles of political turmoil, war, and foreign threats since the late 1970s.

The world also was altered by economic growth and integration, by population growth and movement, and by technological and environmental change. Led by the postwar recovery of the industrial powers and the remarkable economic expansion of Japan and the Asian Tigers, the world economy grew dramatically. The development and application of new technology contributed significantly to this process. International markets were more open and integrated than at any other time. The new wealth and exciting technologies of the postwar era were not shared equally, however.

Population growth in the developing world was one reason for this divided experience. Unable to find adequate employment or, in many cases, bare subsistence, people in developing nations migrated across borders hoping to improve their lives. These movements often provided valuable labor in the factories and farms of the developed world, but they also provoked cultural, racial, and ethnic tension. Problems of inequality, population growth, and international migration would continue to challenge the global community in the coming decades.

Technology seemed to offer some hope for meeting these challenges. Engineering, financial services, education, and other professions developed an international character thanks to the communications revolution. Ambitious and talented people in the developing world could now fully participate in global intellectual and economic life. However, most people working in the developing world remained disconnected from this liberating technology by poverty. Technology also bolstered efforts to protect the environment, providing the means to clean auto and factory emissions, even while it helped produce much of the world's pollution. Technology has been intertwined with human culture since the beginning of human history. Our ability to control and direct its use will determine the future.

■ Key Terms

proxy wars	Asian Tigers
Salvador Allende	Deng Xiaoping
Dirty War	Tiananmen Square
Sandinistas	Mikhail Gorbachev
Ayatollah Ruhollah Khomeini	*perestroika*
	Solidarity
Saddam Husain	Thomas Malthus
keiretsu	demographic transition

■ Suggested Reading

Among the works devoted to postwar economic performance are W. L. M. Adriaasen and J. G. Waardensburg, eds., *A Dual World Economy: Forty Years of Development Experience* (1989); P. Krugman, *The Age of Diminished Expectations: U.S. Economic Policy in the 1990s* (1990); B. J. McCormick, *The World Economy: Patterns of Growth and Change* (1988); and H. van der Wee, *Prosperity and Upheaval: The World Economy, 1945–1980* (1986).

For Latin America, Thomas E. Skidmore and Peter H. Smith, *Modern Latin America,* 4th ed. (1996), provides an excellent general introduction to the period 1975 to 1991.

For the Pacific Rim, see Jonathan Spence, *The Search for Modern China* (1990); Edwin O. Reischauer, *The Japanese* (1988); H. Patrick and H. Rosovsky, *Asia's New Giant: How the Japanese Economy Works* (1976); and Staffan B. Linder, *Pacific Century: Economic and Political Consequences of Asian-Pacific Dynamism* (1986).

Focused examinations of the Soviet bloc are provided in K. Dawisha, *Eastern Europe, Gorbachev and Reform: The Great Challenge* (1988); Barbara Engel and Christine Worobec, eds., *Russia's Women: Accommodation, Resistance, Transformation* (1990); David Remnick, *Lenin's Tomb: The Last Days of the Soviet Empire* (1993); and Charles Maier, *Dissolution: The Crisis of Communism and the End of East Germany* (1997).

The story of the Iranian Revolution and the early days of the Islamic Republic of Iran is well told by Shaul Bakhash, *The Reign of the Ayatollahs: Iran and the Iranian Revolution* (1990). Barnet Rubin, *The Fragmentation of Afghanistan* (1995), provides excellent coverage of the struggle between Soviet forces and the Muslim resistance in that country.

A number of studies examine the special problems faced by women in the postwar period. See, for example, Elisabeth Croll, *Feminism and Socialism in China* (1978); J. Ginat, *Women in Muslim Rural Society: Status and Role in Family and Community* (1982); June Hahner, *Women in Latin America* (1976); P. Hudson, *Third World Women Speak Out* (1979); A. de Souza, *Women in Contemporary India and South Asia* (1980); and M. Wolf, *Revolution Postponed: Women in Contemporary China* (1985).

For general discussions of economic, demographic, and environmental problems facing the world, see R. N. Gwynne, *New Horizons? Third World Industrialization in an International Framework* (1990); P. R. Ehrlich and A. E. Ehrlich, *The Population Explosion* (1990); Paul M.

Kennedy, *Preparing for the Twenty-First Century* (1993); and J. L. Simon, *Population Matters: People, Resources, Environment and Immigration* (1990).

For issues associated with technological and environmental change, see M. Feshbach and A. Friendly, *Ecocide in the U.S.S.R.* (1992); John Bellamy Foster, *Economic History of the Environment* (1994); S. Hecht and A. Cockburn, *The Fate of the Forest: Developers, Destroyers, and Defenders of the Amazon* (1989); K. Marton, *Multinationals, Technology, and Industrialization: Implications and Impact in Third World Countries* (1986); S. P. Huntington,

The Third Wave: Demoralization in the Late Twentieth Century (1993); L. Solomon, *Multinational Corporations and the Emerging World Order* (1978); and B. L. Turner II et al., eds., *The Earth as Transformed by Human Action: Global and Regional Changes in the Biosphere over the Past 300 Years* (1990).

■ Notes

1. *New York Times,* July 24, 1993, 1.
2. Paul Kennedy, *Preparing for the Twenty-First Century* (New York: Random House, 1993), 45.

THE END OF
A GLOBAL CENTURY,
1991–2001

A Fragmented World • Elements of a Global Culture
SOCIETY AND CULTURE: **Nelson Mandela**

As the year 1999 ended, *Time* magazine, in keeping with its long-standing tradition of choosing a "Person of the Year," decided to name the "Person of the Century." Instead of simply consulting among themselves or hiring a polling company to conduct a statistically sound survey, the editors conducted a poll over the Internet. Individuals with access to the Internet—well under half of the U.S. population—could vote for whomever they liked as many times as they wished. After deleting the names they considered frivolous, the editors came up with several lists of winners, ranging from revolutionaries to sports heroes. At the very top of the list was Albert Einstein; Franklin D. Roosevelt and Mahatma Gandhi were the first and second runners-up.

Time's winners encapsulated how many people viewed the world around them. Albert Einstein opened the door to the scientific wonders of the Atomic Age and inadvertently made possible the Cold War's "balance of terror."

Franklin D. Roosevelt led the military alliance that crushed fascism in World War II, leaving the United States the world's most powerful nation. Mahatma Gandhi pioneered nonviolence in the face of injustice as a technique for winning rights and in the process helped set in motion the wave of decolonization of the post–World War II decades. And the Internet, *Time*'s technological collaborator, symbolized a revolution in communication that promised to bring the peoples of the world into ever closer contact.

Despite these emblems of the twentieth century's achievements, the twenty-first century dawned on a world deeply concerned about ethnic conflicts, human rights violations, environmental problems, and economic uncertainties. While powerful economic and cultural forces pushed for greater globalization, peoples in many lands sought ways to preserve or achieve autonomy and identity and safeguard human rights. While affluent individuals in the most developed countries enjoyed unprecedented prosperity, growing disparities between rich and poor, both within and among countries, cast a shadow on the future.

As you read this chapter, ask yourself the following questions:

- How did technology contribute to the process of globalization in the late twentieth century?
- What are the main sources of conflict in the post–Cold War world?
- What role does the struggle for human rights play in the contemporary world?

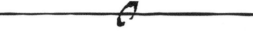

A FRAGMENTED WORLD

Religion, ethnicity, and race took stage center with the fading of the Cold War. In the era of decolonization, most governments in the newly independent states were too preoccupied with the problems of governance and economic development to put much effort into attempts to redraw boundaries, despite their lack of relationship to ethnic and linguistic realities. This generally conservative attitude toward change was reinforced by a number of violent episodes that aroused fears that the world order somehow might dissolve.

Challenges to the Nation-State

The modern idea of the world as a community of sovereign nation-states wielding absolute authority within recognized borders began with the Peace of Westphalia in 1648 that ended Europe's Wars of Religion. But international commitment to the concept of the sovereign nation-state did not erase the passions of groups within states who felt alienated from their rulers or their rulers' religion.

The conflicts were many, extending even to countries with only small religious minorities (see Map 30.1). The Tamil-speaking Hindu population in Sri Lanka fought a prolonged and merciless guer-

rilla struggle throughout the 1980s and 1990s against the dominant Singhalese-speaking Buddhists. Dissidents in mostly Catholic East Timor fought for separation from Muslim Indonesia from the moment Portuguese rule ended in 1975 down to 1999, when their goal was finally achieved by popular referendum. In East Africa, Eritrea fought for and won independence from religiously and linguistically different Ethiopia in 1993. The ethnic hatreds between the Hutu people and the Tutsi people that repeatedly wracked Rwanda and Burundi spilled over into Congo (then Zaire) in 1998, overturning the long-standing dictatorship of President Joseph Mobutu. Even constitutionally secular India saw instances of violence against Muslims and Christians in the name of Hindu nationalism.

In some instances, large-scale violence was avoided. Czechs and Slovaks agreed to divide post-communist Czechoslovakia into the Czech Republic and the Republic of Slovakia in 1993. A brief uprising among the Maya population of southern Mexico in 1994 drew needed government attention and aid to that part of the country. And Malay-Chinese animosities in Malaysia and Indonesia were largely submerged in prosperity until economic calamity struck those countries in 1997. In Yugoslavia, a population that had seemed harmonious until 1991 dissolved into a morass of separatist and warring groups. Industrial and urban Slovenia and agricultural Croatia, the most northerly parts of Yugoslavia, were recognized as independent states in 1992 after brief struggles with federal Yugoslav forces.

The Yugoslavian province of Bosnia and Herzegovina faced greater difficulties. The people living there spoke Serbo-Croatian, but 40 percent were Muslims, 30 percent Eastern Orthodox Serbs, and 18 percent Croatian Catholics. The murderous three-sided fighting that broke out with the declaration of Bosnian national independence in 1992 gave rise to **ethnic cleansing,** an effort by one racial, ethnic, or religious group to eliminate the people and culture of a different group.

The Bosnia crisis challenged the international community to consider whether one country could rightly intervene in another nation's civil war when the intervening power had no national interests at stake. Since the territories that retained the

CHRONOLOGY

	Politics	Economics and Society
1991		**1991** CNN covers Persian Gulf War live from Baghdad
	1992 Yugoslavia disintegrates—Croatia and Slovenia become independent states	
	1992–1995 Bosnia crisis	**1993** Nobel Peace Prize to Nelson Mandela
	1994 Maya uprising in southern Mexico	
1995	**1995** Nerve gas released in Tokyo subway	**1995** World Trade Organization founded
		1997 Asian financial crisis
	1998 Terrorist bombings of U.S. embassies in Kenya and Tanzania; India and Pakistan test atomic bombs	
	1999 Kosovo crisis; East Timor secedes from Indonesia	**1999** Nobel Peace Prize to Doctors Without Borders
2000		
	2001 Terrorists attack World Trade Center and Pentagon; United States ousts Taliban government of Afghanistan	

name Yugoslavia—the southern regions centered on the heavily populated province of Serbia—were helping the Bosnian Serbs and independent Croatia was helping the Croatians of Bosnia, the question was whether anyone was going to come to the aid of the Muslims, Bosnia's largest ethnic group. No Muslim state had the capability to intervene in a major way. Finally, after much indecision—and extensive television coverage of atrocities and wanton destruction—the United States made a cautious intervention and eventually brokered a tentative settlement in 1995.

The shooting had hardly stopped in Bosnia when tension began to heighten in Kosovo, a southern province of Yugoslavia populated mostly by Albanian-speaking Muslims. The North Atlantic Treaty Organization (NATO) alliance repeatedly urged Serbia to stop mistreating the Kosovars (that is, the Albanian-speaking Muslims of Kosovo) and to permit them to participate in Yugoslavia's federal government as they had done before 1989, when Kosovo was an autonomous province within Yugoslavia. When NATO's warnings went unheeded, the United States, Britain, and France, acting under the NATO umbrella, launched an aerial war against Serbia in 1999.

In the aftermath of the air attacks, no one was certain whether new principles of international action had been established. Having nearly single-handedly won the Kosovo war without losing any American lives to enemy fire, the United States had again proven its might. But it was unclear when and where future U.S. or NATO interventions might occur.

Problems of the Global Economy

Issues of foreign intervention and national sovereignty also surfaced in the economic realm. World economic development after World War II at first favored industry in Europe and commodity production elsewhere. But unprecedented new avenues for the international flow of money helped once-poor East Asian countries such as Japan, Taiwan, and South Korea reach levels of industrial prosperity previously enjoyed only in Europe and North America.

Other factors similarly altered the world pattern of wealth distribution (see Map 30.2). During the decade of high oil prices starting in 1974, the oil-producing states became rich, but foreign debt

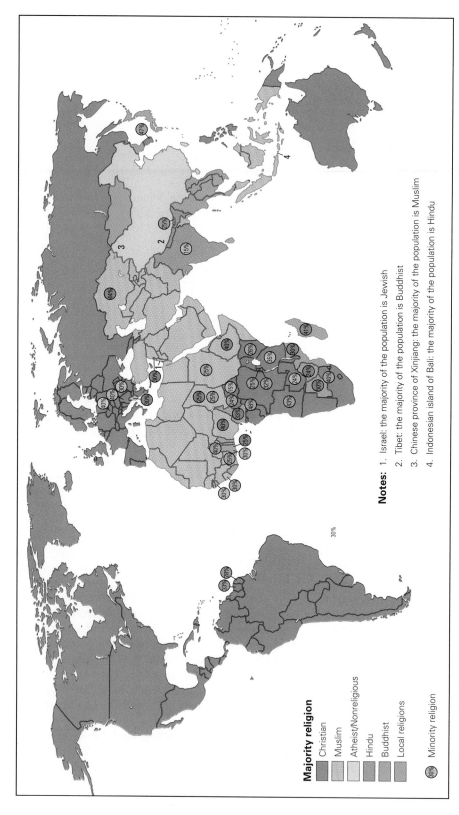

Map 30.1   World Religions   Believers in Islam, Christianity, and Buddhism make up large percentages of the population in many countries. Differing forms of these religions seldom coincide with national boundaries. As religion revives as a source of social identity or a rationale for political assertion or mass mobilization, the possibility of religious activism spreading across broad geographic regions becomes greater, as does the likelihood of domestic discord in multireligious states.

became a major problem for some of the world's biggest countries, including Mexico and Brazil (see Chapter 29). After the collapse of the Soviet Union in 1991, the newly independent republics in eastern Europe required enormous investment to adapt their inefficient command economies to the global marketplace. By century's end, it was still unclear whether Russia's faltering economy would make a successful transition to capitalism.

At the same time, Southeast Asia boomed. Benefiting from investment and technical expertise from Japan and other industrial nations, Thailand, Malaysia, and Indonesia experienced rapid economic growth. Malaysia built the world's tallest skyscraper. Like other tropical countries, Indonesia cut down and sold its tropical hardwood trees on the world market. Groups concerned with protecting animal habitats and saving species from extinction protested these assaults, but quick profits and a national interest in economic development proved of greater weight.

The fevered pace of economic growth in Asia exploded in 1997. A financial crisis sent currency and stock values plummeting first in Thailand and then in neighboring countries, eventually triggering serious recession in Japan.

Such financial crises exemplified the tight interconnections within the global economy and raised the question of whether prosperous nations were obliged to rescue failing economies. A financial bailout for Mexico became a heated political issue in the United States in 1995, the year after the North American Free Trade Agreement (NAFTA), eliminating tariffs among the United States, Canada, and Mexico, went into effect. Arguing that Mexican prosperity was in the U.S. national interest, President Bill Clinton (1993–2001) pushed through a rescue plan that turned out to be successful. Other countries went to the International Monetary Fund and World Bank for assistance. These bodies made their assistance conditional on internal economic reforms that were often politically difficult, such as terminating government subsidies for basic foodstuffs and liberalizing investment.

Economic sanctions—embargoes, boycotts, freezing of assets, and restrictions on investment, all intended to harm another country's economy—became popular as a weapon, though one that only rich nations could wield. The United States, some-

times with the collaboration of its European allies, imposed severe sanctions on Iraq, Libya, Iran, Yugoslavia, and a number of other countries it had disputes with.

In 1995, in an effort to bring order to international trade, the world's major trading powers established the **World Trade Organization (WTO)** as the climax of a final round of negotiations under the rubric General Agreement on Tariffs and Trade (GATT). Charged with enforcing GATT agreements hammered out during periodic negotiating sessions over forty-seven years, the WTO seeks to reduce barriers to world trade. Despite a membership of 110 nations, however, the WTO is not without enemies, and its meetings have become the focus of protest demonstrations.

Old Threat, New Dangers

On September 11, 2001, the festering problems of the Middle East erupted in new danger for the United States and the rest of the world when nineteen terrorists hijacked four airliners and succeeded in crashing two of them into the twin skyscrapers of the World Trade Center in New York City and one into the Pentagon building in Washington, D.C. Over three thousand civilians perished. In response, the United States sent bombs and troops against a dictatorial and intolerant Islamic regime in Afghanistan, the Taliban. With the help of indigenous Afghan opposition groups, they overthrew that government. The Taliban had defiantly harbored and assisted the man accused of the suicide attacks, Usama bin Laden°, a Saudi engineer from a wealthy family. He had volunteered to fight the Soviet Union in Afghanistan but subsequently transferred his animosity to the United States after the Saudi regime permitted American troops to be stationed on "sacred" Saudi soil during and after the Gulf War of 1991.

Bin Laden's attacks, beginning with the bombing of the American embassies in Kenya and Tanzania in 1998 and the destroyer *USS Cole* making a port call in Yemen in 2000, raised an old tactic to a new level. **Terrorism** rests on the belief that

---

Usama bin Ladin (oo-SAH-mah bin LAH-din)

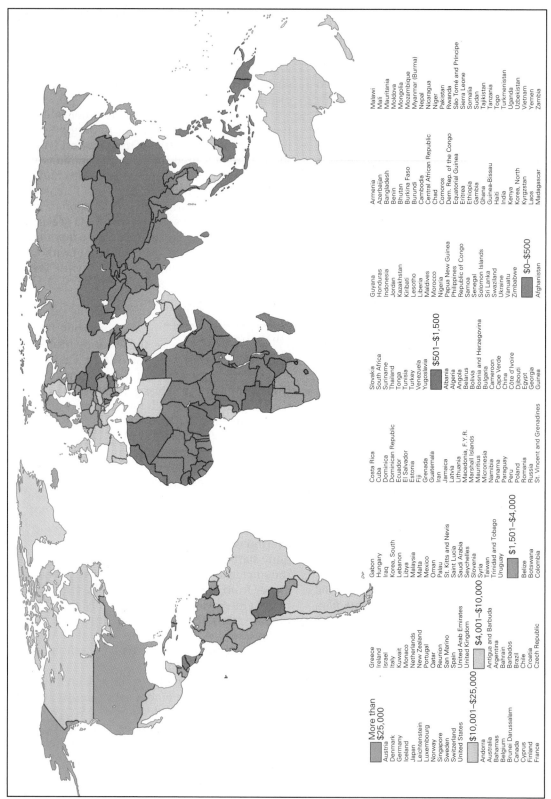

Map 30.2   Estimated GNP per Capita, 1990s   Since World War II, wealth has increasingly been concentrated in a small number of industrialized nations in the Northern Hemisphere. The cost of developing and acquiring new technologies has widened the gap between rich and poor nations.

Terrorist Attack on World Trade Center   The airline striking the tower ignited an intense fire that collapsed the entire building. The fire from a slightly earlier collision destroyed the twin tower. Over 300 fire fighters and police officers died evacuating the buildings before their collapse. A third hijacked airliner struck the Pentagon building in Washington D.C. A fourth crashed in Pennsylvania when passengers fought with the terrorists.   (Associated Press, AP)

horrendous acts of violence can provoke harsh reprisals or demonstrate such government incompetence that existing regimes will lose legitimacy and people will look to the terrorists for leadership. Global television broadcasts enhanced the impact of such attacks and made them more effective.

While anti-Israeli Palestinian groups set the tone for media-centered terrorism, hijacking airplanes in 1968 and killing Israeli athletes during the Munich Olympic Games of 1972, Bin Laden

went beyond their short-range political objectives by urging Muslims throughout the world to see terrorist attacks as part of a jihad, or holy war, waged against non-Muslim enemies, the United States and Israel in particular. However, since the carefully planned and effective American counterstrike against Bin Laden's Taliban protectors took few civilian lives and the United States proclaimed its intent of assisting the Afghans in building a better government and at last repair the ravages of their struggle against the Soviet Union, Bin Laden's hope that Muslims would flock to his banner in response to American overreaction proved hollow.

With the declaration by President George W. Bush of a "war on terrorism," the future of this tactic, whether by Basque separatists in Spain, Tamil militants in Sri Lanka, or anti-Israeli Islamic extremists in the West Bank and Gaza Strip, became doubtful. Much seemed to hinge on the ability of the United States to identify and disrupt terrorist plans without generating intolerable levels of outrage in the Muslim world or unwarranted persecution of peaceful American citizens of Muslim faith. The challenge marked the end of a post–Cold War decade during which the United States had seemed uncertain of its role as the world's only superpower, and its foreign policy had garnered strong criticism—and not just in the Muslim world—for arrogance, selfishness, and failure to consult with allies.

Fear that nuclear devices might come into the possession of someone like Usama bin Laden reinvigorated the world community's determination to stem their spread. The sense of impending nuclear doom that had shadowed the world during the Cold War had quickly subsided after communism collapsed in Europe in 1991. Yet nuclear weapons remained, safeguards against their being sold or stolen seemed inadequate, and disposal of radioactive materials posed difficult technical problems.

In addition, a number of countries undertook nuclear programs in secret. The Cold War balance of nuclear forces between the United States and the Soviet Union had eventually proved an element of stability since neither side could have started a nuclear war without facing total annihilation. A small number of weapons in an unbalanced situation seemed more perilous. The difficulty of **nuclear nonproliferation**—prevention of countries with nuclear programs, like North Korea and Iraq, from deploying weapons—became evident when India and Pakistan openly tested nuclear bombs and missile delivery systems in 1998. Pakistan's program later evoked particular concern because of the sympathy of many Pakistanis for Usama bin Laden and the Taliban.

Chemical and biological weapons, which could kill massively and indiscriminately and be delivered in missile warheads, posed a similar threat. But where nuclear weapons required advanced technology and large investments in factories and equipment, seemingly ordinary chemical and pharmaceutical plants using standard equipment could produce lethal chemicals and biological agents. United Nations inspections of Iraqi warmaking potential (carried out as part of the settlement of the 1991 Persian Gulf War) uncovered and destroyed extensive stocks of chemical munitions and plants for producing nerve gas and lethal germs. In 1995, an apocalyptic Buddhist sect released nerve gas—ineffectively—in the Tokyo subway system; and after the 1991 attack on the World Trade Center and the Pentagon, an unknown terrorist sent letters through the U.S. mail containing spores of anthrax, a lethal disease. Assigning responsibility for terrorism raised worries of countries or religious groups being punished unfairly.

Human Rights

In addition to maintaining peaceful relations between states, the United Nations also aimed to protect the rights of individuals (see Society and Culture: Nelson Mandela). A General Assembly resolution passed on December 10, 1948, called the **Universal Declaration of Human Rights,** contained thirty articles that it proclaimed to be "a common standard of achievement for all peoples and nations."[1] It condemned slavery, torture, cruel and inhuman punishment, and arbitrary arrest, detention, or exile. It called for freedom of movement, assembly, and thought. It asserted rights to life, liberty, and security of person; to impartial public trials; and to education, employment, and leisure. The declaration ringingly asserted the principle of equality, most fully set forth in Article 2:

> Everyone is entitled to all the rights and freedoms set forth in this Declaration, without distinction of any kind, such as race, color, sex, language, religion, or political or other opinion, national or social origin, property, birth or other status.[2]

Religious tolerance had emerged from Europe's bloody religious wars of the sixteenth and seventeenth centuries. The idea of inalienable rights came from the U.S. Constitution (1788) and Bill of Rights (1791) and the French Declaration of

Nelson Mandela

The drama of decolonization in Africa climaxed in 1994 when Nelson Rolihlahla Mandela was elected president of South Africa in the first election open to citizens of all races. Born in 1918, Mandela became an active protester for civil rights as a college student in 1940. While working for a law degree, he helped found the Youth League of the African National Congress (ANC) in 1944.

After violent racial clashes in 1960 prompted the banning of the ANC, Mandela became its underground leader, challenging the apartheid regime (see Chapter 28) and calling for a new constitution based on democratic principles. Facing the full military mobilization of the apartheid state, he organized armed resistance and was arrested in 1962. While serving a life sentence, he refused several offers of freedom that would have required recognition of government racial policies.

In 1990, when it became evident that apartheid could not be maintained, Mandela was released and the next year elected president of the ANC. In 1993, he was awarded the Nobel Peace Prize, and in the following year he was elected president of South Africa. The following excerpt comes from his inauguration address.

Our daily deeds as ordinary South Africans must produce an actual South Africa that will reinforce humanity's belief in justice, strengthen its confidence in the nobility of the human soul and sustain all our hopes for a glorious life for all. . . .

To my compatriots, I have no hesitation in saying that each one of us is as intimately attached to the soil of this beautiful country as are the jacaranda trees of Pretoria and the mimosa trees of the bushveld. . . .

That spiritual and physical oneness we all share with this common homeland explains the depth of the pain we all carried in our hearts as we saw our country tear itself apart in a terrible conflict, and as we saw it spurned, outlawed and isolated by the peoples of the world, precisely because it had become the universal base of the pernicious ideology and practice of racism and racial oppression.

We, the people of South Africa, feel fulfilled that humanity has taken us back into its bosom, that we, who were outlaws not so long ago, have today been given the rare privilege to be host to the nations of the world on our own soil. . . .

The time for the healing of wounds has come.

The moment to bridge the chasms that divide us has come.

Why was Mandela's election considered a great victory for human rights? What is the significance of Mandela's use of the word compatriot?

Source: Inauguration Address of Nelson Mandela as State President of South Africa, May 10, 1994.

the Rights of Man (1789). The struggle against slavery and the woman suffrage movement in the nineteenth and twentieth centuries extended the concept of tolerance to all races and both sexes (see Chapters 25 and 28). The concept of social justice steadily advanced in Europe and America with the legalization of labor unions, the spread of universal education, and the establishment of government programs to care for the needy and ensure adequate standards of living for all citizens.

Although the ideological roots of the declaration lay mostly in European and American history, not all the countries that voted for the declaration in 1948 shared this heritage. Most countries later joining the United Nations willingly signed the declaration because it implicitly condemned the persistence of discriminatory European colonial regimes. Despite this apparent agreement, however, some people had philosophical reservations about the declaration's formulation of human rights.

Human rights activists, often working through international philanthropic bodies known as **nongovernmental organizations (NGOs),** focused their efforts on combating torture, imprisonment without trial, and summary execution by government death squads, as well as providing famine relief and refugee assistance. NGOs devoted to relieving hunger and oppression and bringing human rights abuses to world attention proliferated in the 1970s. Amnesty International, founded in 1961 and numbering a million members in 162 countries by the 1990s, concentrated on gaining freedom for people illegally imprisoned. Médecins Sans Frontières (Doctors Without Borders), founded in 1971, was awarded the Nobel Peace Prize in 1999 for the medical assistance it offered in scores of crisis situations. Even entertainers became involved in relieving suffering through Live Aid, a 1985 rock concert in London and Philadelphia that raised millions of dollars for famine assistance.

Such efforts raised the prominence of human rights as a global concern and put pressure on governments to consider human rights when making foreign policy decisions. Skeptics observed, however, that a Western country could prod a non-Western country to improve its human rights performance—for example, by barring the government from cutting off a thief's hand as stipulated by Islamic law—but reverse criticism of a Western country—for example, condemnation of persistent racial discrimination in the United States—often fell on deaf ears. Thus, the human rights movement was sometimes seen as another form of Western cultural imperialism, a club with which to beat former colonial societies into submission.

Women's Rights

No other issue exemplified this dichotomy of views so clearly as women's rights. Inspired by parallel efforts to combat racial discrimination and end the war in Vietnam, feminist activism revived in the United States in the 1960s and spread around the world. The movement focused on equal access to education and jobs and on quality-of-life matters such as ending sexual exploitation, gaining control of reproduction, and abandoning confining clothing styles. Ironically, the decades in which the feminist movement (followed by movements for gay and lesbian rights in North America and Europe) became a major force also saw sexuality become a more explicit and prominent aspect of commercial, artistic, and social life.

Feminists in the West decried the oppression of women in other parts of the world. At the same time, some non-Western women complained about the deterioration of morality and family life in the West and what they considered to be the feminists' misplaced concern with matters such as clothing. As with human rights, non-Western peoples disputed the West's definition of priorities. Western women and many secularized Muslim women protested Islam's requirement that a woman cover her head and wear loose-fitting garments to conceal the shape of her body, practices enforced by law in countries such as Iran and Saudi Arabia. Nevertheless, many outspoken Muslim women voluntarily donned concealing garments as expressions of personal belief, statements of resistance to secular dictatorship, or defenses against coarse male behavior. Some African women saw their real problems as deteriorating economic conditions, AIDS, and the customary practice of circumcising girls, a form of genital mutilation that could cause chronic infections or permanently impair sexual enjoyment.

Efforts to coordinate the struggle for women's rights internationally gained momentum in the 1970s with a series of highly publicized international conferences. The search for a universally accepted women's rights agenda proved elusive, but a rising global tide of women's education, access to employment, political participation, and control of fertility augured well for the eventual achievement of gender equality.

ELEMENTS OF A GLOBAL CULTURE

In many quarters, people voiced concerns about **cultural imperialism** that went beyond the issue

Beijing Women's Conference in 1995   This gathering of women, under United Nations auspices, from every part of the world illustrated the challenges posed by women's search for equality. The Chinese government, consistent with its policies of suppressing dissent and closely regulating social life, tried to limit press access to the conference. As in many other instances, these efforts to silence or control women's voices on issues like abortion and family planning proved ineffective.   (Alesandra Boulat/Sipa Press)

idea that the United States was the primary culprit in cultural imperialism rested in part on the fact that Americans invented and developed much of the technology that formed and spread popular culture in the twentieth century. A close analysis of cultural trends reveals a diversity of voices that the case for cultural imperialism overlooks.

The Medium and the Message

With much of Europe's and Japan's industry in ruins after World War II, the United States became the world's main exporter of movies. Hollywood exported an image of the United States as a land of gangsters and cowboys, luxurious living, and—from the 1970s on—explicit sexuality. Although filmmakers in many other nations began to produce films of high artistic merit, they did not cut deeply into Hollywood's mass international audiences.

In contrast, the new medium of television outside the United States usually became a government monopoly, following the pattern of telegraph and postal service and radio broadcasting. However, many state broadcasters eventually turned to American and other foreign sources to meet the demand for shows because broadcasting American soap operas, adventure series, and situation comedies was cheaper than producing them locally. The United States, however, was not the only external source of programming.

American producers realized that satellite transmission provided an opening to an international market. Specializing in rock music videos aimed at a youth audience, MTV (Music Television) became an international enterprise offering special editions in different parts of the world. CNN (Cable News Network) became the most viewed and informative news source during the 1991 Persian Gulf War, when it broadcast live from Baghdad. Providing news around the clock, CNN began to supplant other commercial and government news programming as the best source of information about rapidly developing events.

At first, the computer industry, which mushroomed for defense and business purposes in the post–World War II decades, had little connection with television or movies. But as computers'

of human rights. Critics complained that conglomerates were flooding the world with Western images, styles, and goods. In this view, global marketing was an especially insidious effort not only to overwhelm the world with a single Western outlook shaped by capitalist ideology, but also to suppress or devalue traditional cultures and alternative ideologies.

But in truth, technology, not ideology, played the central role in spreading Western culture. The electronic storage capacity and speed increased, their media uses expanded. In the 1990s, Japan introduced the first digital television broadcasting at about the time that disks containing digitized movies and computer programs with movie-like action became increasingly available.

More widespread was communication over the Internet, a linkage of academic, government, and business computer networks. Developed originally for U.S. defense research in the 1960s, the Internet became a major cultural phenomenon with the proliferation of personal computers in the 1980s. With the establishment of the World Wide Web as an easy-to-use graphic interface in the 1990s, the number of Internet users skyrocketed. Myriad new companies formed to explore "e-commerce," the commercial dimension of the Internet. By century's end, many American college students were spending less time studying conventional books and scholarly resources than they were spending to explore the Web for entertainment and to accomplish class assignments.

As in earlier eras, technological developments had unanticipated consequences. The new telecommunications and entertainment technologies derived disproportionately from American invention, industry, and cultural creativity. Thus, they could be seen as portents of Western, especially American, cultural domination. But the American input was rather uneven, and the more widespread the new technologies became, the greater the opportunities they afforded to people around the world to adapt them to their own purposes.

The Spread of Popular Culture

The new technologies changed perceptions of culture. At the end of the nineteenth century, sophisticated Europeans and Americans, like earlier elite groups from imperial Rome to Ming China, valued most what they considered **high culture:** paintings, literature, and other works created to satisfy their tastes. They sneered at **popular culture** as localized entertainment for villagers and common folk—vigorous, picturesque, and quaint, but essentially vulgar. Influenced by the preferences of the European imperialist powers, mod-

Japanese Adult Male Comic Book Comic magazines emerged after World War II as a major form of publication in Japan and a distinctive product of Japanese culture. Different series are directed to different age and gender groups. Issued weekly and running to some 300 pages in black and white, the most popular magazines sell as many copies as major news magazines do in the United States. (Private Collection)

ernizing elite groups around the world turned their backs on their own artistic traditions.

In fact, illustrious European composers and choreographers had been turning to folk tunes and dances for inspiration since the eighteenth century. And the search for fresh sounds and images intensified with the advent of modernism in Europe in the mid-nineteenth century. Some were captivated by the sounds and images of Europe's new industrial society; others drew inspiration from popular culture. Spanish artist Pablo Picasso (1881–1973), for example, borrowed the imagery of

African masks in some of his paintings, circuses and carnivals in others, and newspaper typography in still others.

The phonograph, invented by Thomas Edison in 1878, was the key that opened popular culture to global audiences. Phonograph records spread American popular music around the world. Jazz recordings and jazz musicians became popular in Europe in the 1920s. The driving force behind jazz was the creative skill of black musicians such as Duke Ellington, Louis Armstrong, Ella Fitzgerald, and Billie Holiday. Orchestral composers such as the Russian Igor Stravinsky and the Frenchman Maurice Ravel utilized jazz rhythms and themes. However, jazz remained the music of nightclubs and dance parties instead of concert halls. By World War II, black jazz musicians had become so much a part of the international image of the United States that Nazi propaganda frequently incorporated vile racial caricatures of them. Ironically, while jazz was widely perceived abroad as quintessential American popular culture, it remained largely the preserve of the African-American minority at home.

The international popularity of jazz derived from the appeal of its rhythms and naturalness—that is, from the music itself—not from its approval by a colonial ruling class. The same was true of rock 'n' roll, a dynamic, sensual, and audacious popular music that arose in the 1950s and became even more widespread than jazz. Rock grew out of black rhythm-and-blues and derived initially from innovative black American performers like Chuck Berry. The rise to international stardom in the 1960s of Britain's Beatles helped make rock 'n' roll a worldwide phenomenon. The core of rock remained American and British, but popular musicians from all over the world recorded in rock-influenced styles. Some achieved broad acclaim, as did Jamaica's Bob Marley with his Caribbean reggae style. Others gained strong local followings by blending rock with traditional forms, as happened with Malagasy music in Madagascar and Rai music in Algeria.

In the 1970s and 1980s, critics around the world identified the United States as the chief propagator of a worldwide consumer culture. This judgment seemed to be confirmed by the international cachet of American brand names like Levi's, Coca-Cola, Marlboro, Gillette, McDonald's, and Kentucky Fried Chicken. But names blazoned in neon atop the skyscrapers of Tokyo—Hitachi, Sony, Sanyo, and Mitsubishi—also commanded instant recognition, as did such European names as Nestlé, Mercedes, Pirelli, and Benetton. The concept of a globe-girdling American consumer culture had been overtaken by internationalization. Yet, on balance, the overall direction of change in popular culture and consumer taste during the decades following World War II was indeed toward the United States.

Some Marxist intellectuals interpreted the spread of American products as simply another form of imperialism, inevitably destroying local crafts, styles, and cultural traditions. But most young Turks, Nigerians, Taiwanese, and others who liked to wear Levis's jeans, drink Coke, smoke Camels, and listen to rock 'n' roll had little sense of being under the thumb of the imperialists. Although their nations' economies may have been in thrall to transnational business concerns, they themselves generally felt free to condemn American foreign policy and considered their personal style preferences simply a result of living within an increasingly global culture. Thus, the reality of cultural imperialism was far more ambiguous than European imperialism had been in the days of colonial viceroys and gunboat diplomacy.

Global Connections and Elite Culture

While the globalization of popular culture became a subject of dispute, cultural links across national and ethnic boundaries at a more elite level generated less controversy. The end of the Cold War reopened intellectual and cultural contacts between former adversaries, making possible such things as Russian-American collaboration on space missions and extensive business contacts among former rivals. Graduate education became increasingly global.

Spurred by American economic, political, and cultural eminence in the second half of the century, English spread as a global language even as the British Empire faded away. English became the most commonly taught second language in the world, and a number of technology-intensive industries, including air transportation and computers, used it extensively. In newly independent countries, even universities that took pride in teaching in the national language often had science faculties that operated in English.

Architectural design and engineering afford another example of globalization at the higher cultural level. The International Style pioneered by European architects in the 1920s (see Chapter 25) was the guiding aesthetic for the austere, ornament-free skyscrapers sheathed in glass that began to rise in world capitals in the 1960s.

The International Style was criticized, however, for neglecting local architectural traditions. In the United States, this criticism formed the foundation of **postmodernism,** a movement that called for abandoning the rigid rules of architectural modernism and showing greater sensitivity to history and local context and for allowing diverse voices, such as those of minorities, to be heard. Some architects, including a growing number from non-Western countries, responded to the postmodern critique. Conventional glass and steel skyscrapers continued to be built, but liberation from the International Style permitted architects in different countries to follow their own inclinations and experiment with a broad array of forms, surface decoration, and references to earlier architectural traditions.

Dance, music, literature, and cultural theory were all affected by postmodernist impulses, though the forms they took differed from one area to another. Common to much postmodernist thought was a sense that the modernist styles that composed the artistic avant-garde between 1850 and 1950 reflected the limited perspective of an elite, white, male European-American intelligentsia preoccupied with individualism and innovation. Against this background, postmodernism championed an aesthetic based on multiculturalism, social inclusion, historical continuity, and styles and forms from everyday life.

Postmodernism was not the only indicator of cultural change on a global scale. Among the ten winners of the Nobel Prize for literature between 1982 and 1991 were writers from Colombia, Nigeria, Egypt, Mexico, and the West Indies. By contrast, the previous decade's winners had included only one non-European. The prize committee thus helped the world recognize the growing strength of its cultural diversity.

The West, for good or ill, dominated the early postimperialist era because the web of international contact made possible by advanced technologies had yet to reach its full extent or become accessible to most people. According to one estimate, at the end of the century, half of the world's people had never spoken on a telephone. The cultural changes spurred by technology were only in midcourse, and technology seemed likely to offer a means of releasing profound creative energies in unexpected locales.

The Endurance of Cultural Diversity

Diverse cultural traditions persisted at the twentieth century's end despite globalization. Japan demonstrated that a country with a non-Western culture could perform at a high economic level. The efficiency, pride in workmanship, and group solidarity of Japanese workers, supported by closely coordinated government and corporate policies, played a major role in transforming Japan from a defeated nation with a demolished industrial base in 1945 to an economic power by the 1980s.

Japan's success in the modern industrial world called into question an assumption common in the immediate postwar era. Since industrialization was pioneered by Europeans and Americans, many Westerners thought that the spread of industrialization to different parts of the world would require the adoption of Western culture in every area of life. As awareness of the economic impact of Japanese culture and society began to spread, however, it became apparent that Taiwan and South Korea, along with Singapore and Hong Kong (a British colony before being reunited with China in 1997), were developing dynamic industrial economies of their own. Until the Asian financial crisis of 1997, Muslim Malaysia and Buddhist Thailand had appeared to be embarking on the same road to development. Had Japan been unique, or would cultural variety prove fully compatible with industrial growth and prosperity worldwide?

Clearly, the long-standing Western assumption of European and American exceptionalism—the belief that all of world history culminated in the exceptional convergence of political freedom, secularism, and industrialization in the West—needed to be abandoned. So, too, did the corollary that the twenty-first century would be as thoroughly dominated by Western culture and economic and political power as the previous two centuries had been.

Also coming into question was whether industrialization offered the only viable route to prosperity. As computer technology continued to change almost all aspects of life, perhaps countries could achieve prosperity in the twenty-first century primarily through their control of information and telecommunications.

The lesson to be drawn from the success of Japan and the other rising economic powers of Asia was not that Western technology pointed the way to universal well-being, but rather that human ingenuity and adaptability are endlessly fertile and creative. Human cultural achievement has historically followed unpredictable paths, reaching one sort of climax in one time and place and a different sort in another. In the same spirit, the future locus of spiritual and cultural achievement remained essentially unpredictable at the start of a new millennium.

CONCLUSION

The final decade of the twentieth century witnessed a burgeoning of computer and telecommunications technology that fostered the worldwide spread of popular culture while at the same time enabling businesses and financial markets to operate on a truly global scale. It also witnessed an intensification of world concerns for human rights as fears of international conflicts between great powers faded into the past. But in some respects, it was more strongly marked by things that came to an end than by things that had their start.

For nearly eight decades, from the outbreak of World War I to the dissolution of the Soviet Union, a world whose economic and political destiny had seemed firmly in the grip of European imperialism witnessed an increasingly lethal struggle between competing European ideologies. The outcome of the struggle, in which all the peoples of the world eventually became principals or pawns, was often in doubt. Each camp accused the other of leading humanity down the road to slavery—slavery to fascist or communist dictators according to one side, slavery to the insatiable greed of capitalist profiteers according to the other. Each camp similarly had a vision of how it would organize the world in the event of victory. Adolf Hitler visualized a "thousand year Reich [empire]" serving the desires of an Aryan superrace. Communists spoke of a "workers' paradise" of equality and brotherhood. Responding to these oppressive visions, Western leaders extolled the virtues of "freedom," a world order that would permit all peoples to elect their own governments and allow every individual to pursue his or her individual destiny in an open and competitive market environment.

Victory, when it came, proved far more complicated and puzzling than Western ideologues had anticipated. Though "democratization" and "economic liberalization" became watchwords of Western, and particularly American, foreign policy, many of the world's peoples proved less concerned with liberal ideology than with ethnic, linguistic, and religious quarrels or with simply maintaining life and hope in circumstances of increasing poverty and overpopulation. Developing countries and post-communist countries alike looked to the United States, Europe, and Japan for financial salvation, introducing democratic institutions and open markets only to the degree necessary to gain Western support.

The United States and the other major industrial countries recognized that they could not meet all of the world's demands, but they were reluctant to put too much trust in international bodies such as the United Nations, which had no financial resources beyond the dues paid by its member states. Thus, the end of the global contest among European ideologies did not produce a workable model of a world community. To the contrary, local conflicts and atrocities proliferated in the 1990s, and more and more countries debated whether to seek

Millennium Celebration in Sydney, Australia   Uncertainties about what lay ahead for the world in the twenty-first century took a backseat to exuberant festivities as the millennium ended. The sleek modern silhouette of Sidney's opera house and the neon signs of major corporations epitomized the hopes of many.   (Sydney Morning Herald/Sipa Press)

nuclear weapons or other weapons of mass destruction in anticipation of future confrontations.

Yet while world order seemed as unattainable as ever before, economic, technological, and cultural forces drew the world's peoples ever closer together. Since the victors in the world struggle had been the capitalists rather than the fascists or communists, private business and consumer economics expanded aggressively into every region of the globe, checked only by market conditions and rearguard efforts by authoritarian governments, such as that of China, to control the pace and direction of change.

For most of the world's population, the 1990s brought greater desire for and access to consumer goods, and a globalized culture became more and more a reality. But the logic of global economic growth, with its immense demands on clean water,

clear air, and nonrenewable resources, made it clear that some of the world's greatest problems, including how to preserve the shared global environment for future generations of humanity, had no obvious solutions and had only begun to be addressed.

■ Key Terms

ethnic cleansing

economic sanctions

World Trade Organization (WTO)

terrorism

nuclear nonproliferation

Universal Declaration of Human Rights

nongovernmental organizations (NGOs)

cultural imperialism

high culture

popular culture

postmodernism

■ Suggested Reading

Many of the subjects in this chapter are covered by thematic essays in Richard W. Bulliet, ed., *The Columbia History of the Twentieth Century* (1998).

The Bosnian crisis is well covered in Susan L. Woodward, *Balkan Tragedy: Chaos and Dissolution After the Cold War* (1995). Other world crises involving international intervention are treated in William J. Durch, ed., *UN Peacekeeping, American Policy, and the Uncivil Wars of the 1990s* (1996). Terrorism is well covered by Bruce Hoffman, *Inside Terrorism* (1998). Gilles Kepel, *The Revenge of God: The Resurgence of Islam, Christianity, and Judaism in the Modern World* (1994), deals with recent religio-political movements. Human rights are well surveyed by Jack Donnelly, *International Human Rights,* 2d ed. (1998).

A seminal book in the awakening of the feminist movement in the 1970s is Betty Friedan, *The Feminine Mystique* (1974). For the revival of feminism in Europe, see Gisela Kaplan, *Contemporary Western European Feminism* (1992). For non-Western perspectives, see Phyllis Andors, *The Unfinished Liberation of Chinese Women, 1949–1980* (1983), and Chandra Talpade Mohanty, Ann Russo, and Lourdes Torres, eds., *Third World Women and the Politics of Feminism* (1991).

The interrelationships between high culture and popular culture during the twentieth century are treated from very different perspectives by Greil Marcus, *Lipstick Traces: A Secret History of the Twentieth Century* (1989), and Kurt Varnedoe, *High and Low: Modern Art and Popular Culture* (1991). The former concentrates on the avant-garde from dada to punk rock, the latter on images from popular culture used in art. Two very readable books by James B. Twitchell, *Carnival Culture: The Trashing of Taste in America* (1992) and *Adcult USA: The Triumph of Advertising in American Culture* (1996), detail the rise of popular culture in the United States and present various reactions to this phenomenon.

Many interpretations of and approaches to postmodernism are sampled in Thomas Docherty, ed., *Postmodernism: A Reader* (1993). These may be compared with a classic early statement of modernism: Amédée Ozenfant's *Foundations of Modern Art* (1931).

Thomas P. Hughes, *American Genesis: A Century of Invention and Technological Enthusiasm, 1870–1970* (1989), offers a far-ranging account of the American role in twentieth-century technological change by an outstanding historian of technology. Books on films and the film industry around the world are legion. A good place to start is Gerald Mast, *A Short History of the Movies* (1986). A similar survey of jazz music is available from Marshall W. Stearns, *The Story of Jazz* (1970). For the rock video phenomenon, see E. Ann Kaplan, *Rocking Around the Clock: Music Television, Postmodernism, and Consumer Culture* (1987).

Some noteworthy novels that have attempted to visualize the near future on the basis of current perceptions of technological change, environmental deterioration, and growth of transnational corporations are David Brin, *Earth* (1990), and Bruce Sterling, *Islands in the Net* (1988). See too William Gibson's "Sprawl" trilogy: *Neuromancer* (1984), *Count Zero* (1987), and *Mona Lisa Overdrive* (1988).

■ Notes

1. "Universal Declaration of Human Rights," in *Twenty-Five Human Rights Documents* (New York: Center for the Study of Human Rights, Columbia University, 1994), 6.
2. Ibid.

GLOSSARY

The glossary for *The Earth and Its Peoples,* 2/e Brief is for the complete text, Chapters 1 through 30.

Abbasid Caliphate Descendants of the Prophet Muhammad's uncle, al-Abbas, the Abbasids overthrew the **Umayyad Caliphate** and ruled an Islamic empire from their capital in Baghdad (founded 762) from 750 to 1258. *(p. 181)*

abolitionists Men and women who agitated for a complete end to slavery. British abolitionists achieved the abolition of the transatlantic slave trade in 1808 and slavery in 1834. American abolitionist activities were one factor leading to the Civil War (1861–1865). *(p. 460)*

absolutism The theory of unlimited royal power popular in France and other early modern European monarchies. *(p. 371)*

Acheh Sultanate Muslim kingdom in northern Sumatra. Main center of Islamic expansion in Southeast Asia in the early seventeenth century, it declined after the Dutch seized **Malacca** from Portugal in 1641. *(p. 419)*

Aden Port city in the modern south Arabian country of Yemen. A major center in Indian Ocean trade. *(p. 315)*

African National Congress An organization seeking equal voting and civil rights for black inhabitants of South Africa. Founded in 1912 as the South African Native National Congress, it changed its name in 1923. Though it was banned and its leaders were jailed, it helped bring majority rule to South Africa. *(p. 588)*

Afrikaners South Africans descended from Dutch and French settlers of the seventeenth century. Their Great Trek founded new colonies in the nineteenth century. A minority among South Africans, they held political power after 1910, imposing racial segregation (apartheid) after 1949. *(p. 530)*

Agricultural Revolution(s) (ancient) The change from food gathering to food production that occurred between ca. 8000 and 2000 B.C.E. Also known as the Neolithic Revolution. *(p. 8)*

Agricultural Revolution (eighteenth century) The transformation of farming resulting from the spread of new crops, improvements in cultivation and livestock breeding, and consolidation of small holdings into large farms from which tenants and sharecroppers were forcibly expelled. *(p. 464)*

Aguinaldo, Emilio (1869–1964) Leader of the Filipino independence movement against Spain (1895–1898). He proclaimed independence in 1899. His movement was crushed and he was captured by the United States Army in 1901. *(p. 533)*

Akbar (1542–1605) Most illustrious sultan of the Mughal Empire in India (r. 1556–1605). He expanded the empire and pursued a policy of conciliation with Hindus. *(p. 416)*

Akhenaten Egyptian pharaoh (r. 1353–1335 B.C.E.). He built a new capital at Amarna, fostered a new style of naturalistic art, and imposed worship of the sun-disk. The Amarna letters, largely from his reign, preserve official correspondence with subjects and neighbors. *(p. 47)*

Alexander (356–323 B.C.E.) King of Macedonia in northern Greece. Between 334 and 323 B.C.E. he conquered the Persian Empire, reached the Indus Valley, and founded many Greek-style cities. Later known as Alexander the Great. *(p. 105)*

Alexandria City on the Mediterranean coast of Egypt founded by Alexander. The capital of the Hellenistic kingdom of the **Ptolemies**, it contained the famous Library and the Museum—a center for science and literature. Its merchants traded in the Mediterranean and the Indian Ocean. *(p. 106)*

Allende, Salvador (1908–1973) Socialist politician elected president of Chile in 1970 and overthrown by the military in 1973. He died during the military attack. *(p. 625)*

All-India Muslim League Organization founded in India in 1906 to defend the interests of India's Muslim minority. Led by Muhammad Ali Jinnah, it negotiated with the **Indian National Congress.** In 1940, the League began demanding a separate state for Muslims, to be called Pakistan. (See also **Jinnah, Muhammad Ali.**) *(p. 591)*

amulet Charm meant to protect the bearer from evil. Amulets reflect the religious practices of the common people. *(p. 19)*

Anasazi Important culture of what is now the southwest of the United States (1000–1300 C.E.). Centered on Chaco Canyon in New Mexico and Mesa Verde in Colorado, the Anasazi culture built multistory residences and worshipped in subterranean buildings called kivas. *(p. 248)*

aqueduct A conduit, either elevated or under ground, using gravity to carry water from a source to a city. *(p. 134)*

Arawak Amerindian peoples who inhabited the Greater Antilles of the Caribbean at the time of Columbus. (*p. 345*)

Armenia Areas in eastern Anatolia and the western Caucasus occupied by speakers of the Armenian language. One of the earliest Christian kingdoms. (*p. 168*)

Asante African kingdom on the **Gold Coast** that expanded rapidly after 1680. Asante traded gold, slaves, and ivory and resisted British imperial ambitions for a quarter century before being absorbed into Britain's Gold Coast colony in 1902. (*p. 531*)

Ashikaga Shogunate (1336–1573) The second of Japan's military governments headed by a shogun (a military ruler). Sometimes called the Muromachi Shogunate. (*p. 298*)

Ashoka Third ruler of the **Mauryan Empire** in India (r. 270–232 B.C.E.). He converted to Buddhism and broadcast his precepts on inscribed stones and pillars, the earliest surviving Indian writing. (*p. 116*)

Ashur Chief deity of the Assyrians and bringer of victory in war. Also the name of an important Assyrian religious and political center. (*p. 70*)

Asian Tigers Collective name for South Korea, Taiwan, Hong Kong, and Singapore—nations that became economic powers in the 1970s and 1980s. (*p. 630*)

Atahualpa (1502?–1533) Last ruling Inca emperor of Peru. He was executed by the Spanish. (*p. 358*)

Atlantic system The trade network that after 1500 moved goods, people, and cultures around the Atlantic Ocean. (*p. 383*)

Augustus (63 B.C.E.–14 C.E.) Honorific name of Octavian, founder of the **Roman Principate,** the military dictatorship that replaced the failing rule of the **Roman Senate.** After defeating rivals, between 31 B.C.E. and 14 C.E. he laid the groundwork for stability and prosperity in the Roman Empire. (*p. 129*)

Auschwitz Nazi extermination camp in Poland, the largest center of mass murder during the **Holocaust.** Close to a million Jews, Gypsies, Communists, and others were killed there. (*p. 579*)

autocracy Strong, centralized rule, such as by the **tsar** in Russia or **Haile Selassie** in Ethiopia. Autocrats did not rely on the aristocracy or the clergy for legitimacy. (*p. 431*)

ayllu Andean lineage group or kin-based community. (*p. 250*)

Aztecs Also known as Mexica, the Aztecs created a powerful empire in central Mexico (1325–1521 C.E.). They forced defeated peoples to provide goods and labor as a tax. (*p. 245*)

Babylon The largest and most important city in Mesopotamia, the capital of the Amorite king **Hammurabi** in the eighteenth century B.C.E. and the Neo-Babylonian king Nebuchadnezzar in the sixth century B.C.E. (*p. 14*)

balance of power Political strategy by which, beginning in the eighteenth century, the European states acted together to prevent any from becoming too powerful. (*p. 373*)

Balfour Declaration Statement issued by Britain's Foreign Secretary Arthur Balfour in 1917 favoring the establishment of a Jewish national home in Palestine. (*p. 548*)

Bannermen Hereditary military servants of the **Qing Empire,** whose ancestors of various origins had fought for the founders of the empire. (*p. 496*)

Bantu Name of a large group of sub-Saharan African languages and of the peoples speaking them. (*p. 167*)

Batavia Fort established ca. 1619 as headquarters of Dutch East India Company operations in Indonesia; today the city of Jakarta. (*p. 422*)

Battle of Midway U.S. naval victory over the Japanese fleet in June 1942. The Japanese lost four of their best aircraft carriers, making it a turning point in World War II. (*p. 576*)

Beijing China's northern capital, first used as an imperial capital in 906 and now the capital of the People's Republic of China. (*p. 283*)

Bengal Region of northeastern India, the first to be conquered by the British in the eighteenth century. It remained the center of British India throughout the nineteenth century. The 1905 split of the province into predominantly Hindu West Bengal and predominantly Muslim East Bengal (now Bangladesh) sparked anti-British riots. (*p. 589*)

Berlin Conference (1884–1885) Conference that German chancellor Otto von Bismarck called to set rules for the partition of Africa. It led to the creation of the Congo Free State under King **Leopold II** of Belgium. (See also **Bismarck, Otto von.**) (*p. 528*)

Bhagavad-Gita The most important work of Indian sacred literature, a dialogue between the warrior Arjuna and the god Krishna on duty and the fate of the spirit. (*p. 117*)

Bismarck, Otto von (1815–1898) Chancellor (prime minister) of Prussia from 1862 until 1871, when he became chancellor of Germany. A conservative nationalist, he led Prussia to victory against Austria (1866) and France (1870) and was responsible for the creation of the German Empire in 1871. (*p. 512*)

Black Death An outbreak of **bubonic plague** that spread across Asia, North Africa, and Europe in the mid-fourteenth century, carrying off vast numbers of persons. (*p. 326*)

Bolívar, Simón (1783–1830) The most important military leader in the struggle for independence in South America. Born in Venezuela, he led military forces there and in Colombia, Ecuador, Peru, and Bolivia. (*p. 457*)

Bolsheviks Marxist party founded by Vladimir Lenin in 1903. Under Lenin's leadership, they seized power in November 1917 during the Russian Revolution. (See also **Lenin, Vladimir.**) (*p. 548*)

Bonaparte, Napoleon. See **Napoleon I.**

Borobudur A massive stone monument on the Indonesian island of Java, erected by the Sailendra kings around 800 C.E. (*p. 160*)

bourgeoisie In early modern Europe, the class of well-off town dwellers whose wealth came from manufacturing, finance, commerce, and allied professions. (*p. 375*)

breech-loading rifle Gun into which bullets were individually inserted at the end of the barrel above the trigger. Later guns had magazines, a compartment holding multiple bullets. (*p. 479*)

British raj The rule over much of South Asia between 1765 and 1947 by the East India Company and then by the British government. (*p. 490*)

bubonic plague A bacterial disease transmitted by flea bites to rodents and humans; humans in late stages of the illness can spread the bacteria by coughing. Highly lethal and hard to prevent, major plague epidemics have created crises in many parts of the world. (See also **Black Death.**) (*pp. 223, 268*)

Buddha (563–483 B.C.E.) An Indian prince named Siddhartha Gautama, who renounced his social position. After becoming "enlightened" (the meaning of *Buddha*) he enunciated the principles of Buddhism. (See also **Mahayana Buddhism; Theravada Buddhism.**) (*p. 112*)

Byzantine Empire Historians' name for the eastern portion of the Roman Empire from the fourth century onward, taken from "Byzantion," an early name for Constantinople, the Byzantine capital city. The empire fell to the Ottomans in 1453. (See also **Ottoman Empire.**) (*p. 196*)

caliphate Office established in succession to the Prophet Muhammad, to rule the Islamic empire; also the name of that empire. (See also **Abbasid Caliphate; Sokoto Caliphate; Umayyad Caliphate.**) (*p. 179*)

capitalism The economic system of investment in business in return for a share of the profits that first developed in early modern Europe. *Commercial capitalism*, the trading system of the early modern economy, is often distinguished from *industrial capitalism*, the system based on machine production. (*p. 397*)

caravel A small, highly maneuverable three-masted ship used by the Portuguese and Spanish in the exploration of the Atlantic. (*p. 348*)

Cárdenas, Lázaro (1895–1970) President of Mexico (1934–1940). He changed Mexican life by distributing land to the peasants, bringing representatives of workers and farmers into politics, and nationalizing the oil industry. (*p. 596*)

Carthage City located in present-day Tunisia, founded by **Phoenicians** ca. 800 B.C.E. It became a major commercial center and naval power in the western Mediterranean until defeated by Rome in the third century B.C.E. (*p. 81*)

Catholic Reformation Religious reform movement within the Latin Christian Church, begun in response to the **Protestant Reformation**. It clarified Catholic theology and reformed clerical training and discipline. (*p. 366*)

Celts Peoples sharing a common language and culture that originated in Central Europe in the first half of the first millennium B.C.E. After 500 B.C.E. they spread as far as Anatolia, Spain, and the British Isles. Later overtaken by Roman conquest and Germanic invasions, their descendants survive on the western fringe of Europe (Brittany, Wales, Scotland, Ireland). (*p. 68*)

Champa A state located in what is now southern Vietnam. It was hostile to Annam and was annexed by Annam and destroyed as an independent entity in 1500. (*p. 299*)

Champa rice Quick-maturing rice that yields two harvests in one growing season. Originally introduced into Champa from India, it was later sent to China as a tribute gift by the Champa state. (See also **tributary system.**) (*p. 235*)

Chang'an City in the Wei Valley in eastern China. It became the capital of the Zhou kingdom and the Qin and early Han Empires. (*p. 141*)

Charlemagne (742–814) King of the Franks (r. 768–814); emperor (r. 800–814). Through a series of military conquests he established the Carolingian Empire, which encompassed all of Gaul and parts of Germany and Italy. Though illiterate himself, he sponsored a brief intellectual revival. (*p. 195*)

chartered companies Groups of private investors who paid an annual fee to a European government in exchange for a monopoly over trade in a foreign area. (*p. 397*)

Chavín The first major urban civilization in South America (900–250 B.C.E.). Its capital, Chavín de Huántar, was located high in the Andes Mountains of Peru. Chavín became dominant in a densely populated region that included the Peruvian coastal plain and the Andean foothills. (*p. 67*)

Chiang Kai-shek (Jiang Jieshi; 1887–1975) General and leader of Nationalist China after 1925. Although he succeeded **Sun Yat-sen** as head of the **Guomindang,** he became a military dictator and enemy of the communist movement led by **Mao Zedong.** (*p. 571*)

chiefdom Form of political organization with rule by a hereditary leader exercising power over a collection of villages and towns. Less powerful than a kingdom or empire, a chiefdom was based on gift giving and commercial links. (*p. 249*)

Chimú Powerful Peruvian civilization based on conquest. Located in the region earlier dominated by **Moche.** Conquered by **Inca** in 1465. (*p. 252*)

chinampas Raised fields constructed along lake shores in Mesoamerica to increase agricultural yields. (*p. 240*)

city-state A small independent state consisting of an urban center and the surrounding agricultural territory. A characteristic political form in early Mesopotamia, Archaic and Classical Greece, Phoenicia, and early Italy. (See also **polis.**) (*p. 15*)

civilization An ambiguous term often used to denote complex societies but sometimes used by anthropologists to describe a group of people sharing a set of cultural traits. (*p. 5*)

Cixi, Empress Dowager (1835–1908) Empress of China and mother of Emperor Guangxi. She put her son under house arrest, supported antiforeign movements, and resisted reforms of the government and armed forces. (*p. 553*)

clipper ship Large, fast, streamlined sailing vessel, often American built, of the mid-to-late nineteenth century. (*p. 493*)

Cold War (1945–1991) The ideological struggle between communism (Soviet Union) and capitalism (United States) for world influence. The Soviet Union and the United States came to the brink of actual war during the **Cuban missile crisis** but never attacked one another. The Cold War came to an end when the Soviet Union dissolved in 1991. (See also **North Atlantic Treaty Organization; Warsaw Pact.**) (*p. 604*)

Columbian Exchange The exchange of plants, animals, diseases, and technologies between the Americas and the rest of the world following Columbus's voyage. (*p. 401*)

Columbus, Christopher (1451–1506) Genoese mariner who in the service of Spain led expeditions across the Atlantic, establishing contact between the Americas and the Old World and initiating Spanish conquest and colonization. (*p. 351*)

Confucius Western name for the Chinese philosopher Kongzi (551–479 B.C.E.). His doctrine of duty and public service influenced subsequent Chinese thought and served as a code of conduct for government officials. (*p. 43*)

Congress of Vienna (1814–1815) Meeting of representatives of European monarchs called to reestablish the old order after the defeat of **Napoleon I.** (*p. 454*)

conquistadors Early-sixteenth-century Spanish adventurers who conquered Mexico, Central America, and Peru. See **Cortés, Hernán; Pizarro, Francisco.**) (*p. 356*)

Constantine (285–337 C.E.) Roman emperor (r. 312–337). After reuniting the Roman Empire, he moved the capital to Constantinople and made Christianity a favored religion. (*p. 135*)

Constitutional Convention Meeting in 1787 of the elected representatives of the thirteen original states to write the Constitution of the United States. (*p. 450*)

constitutionalism The theory developed in early modern England and spread elsewhere that royal power should be subject to legal and legislative checks. (*p. 371*)

Cortés, Hernán (1485–1547) Spanish explorer and conquistador who led the conquest of Aztec Mexico in 1519–1521. (*p. 356*)

Cossacks Peoples of the Russian Empire who lived outside the farming villages, often as herders, mercenaries, or outlaws. Cossacks led the conquest of Siberia in the sixteenth and seventeenth centuries. (*p. 430*)

cottage industries Weaving, sewing, carving, and other small-scale industries that can be done in the home. (*p. 286*)

cotton The plant that produces fibers from which cotton textiles are woven. Native to India, cotton spread throughout Asia and then to the New World. It has been a major cash crop in various places, including early Islamic Iran, Yi Korea, and nineteenth-century Egypt and the United States. A related species was exploited for fiber in pre-Columbian America. (*p. 296*)

Council of the Indies The institution responsible for supervising Spain's colonies in the Americas from 1524 to the early eighteenth century, when it lost all but judicial responsibilities. (*p. 383*)

creoles In colonial Spanish America, term used to describe someone of European descent born in the New World. Elsewhere in the Americas, the term is used to describe all non-native peoples. (*p. 386*)

Crimean War (1853–1856) Conflict between the Russian and Ottoman Empires fought primarily in the Crimean Peninsula. To prevent Russian expansion, Britain and France sent troops to support the Ottomans. (*p. 478*)

Crusades (1096–1291) Armed pilgrimages to the Holy Land by Christians determined to recover Jerusalem from Muslim rule. The Crusades brought an end to western Europe's centuries of intellectual and cultural isolation. (*p. 210*)

Cuban missile crisis (1962) Brink-of-war confrontation between the United States and the Soviet Union over the latter's placement of nuclear-armed missiles in Cuba. (*p. 616*)

cultural imperialism Domination of one culture over another by a deliberate policy or by economic or technological superiority. (*p. 654*)

Cultural Revolution (China) (1966–1969) Campaign in China ordered by **Mao Zedong** to purge the Communist Party of his opponents and instill revolutionary values in the younger generation. (*p. 619*)

culture Socially transmitted patterns of action and expression. *Material culture* refers to physical objects, such as dwellings, clothing, tools, and crafts. Culture also includes arts, beliefs, knowledge, and technology. (*p. 5*)

cuneiform A Mesopotamian system of writing in which wedge-shaped symbols represented words or syllables. It was used initially for Sumerian and Akkadian but later was adapted to other languages of western Asia. (*p. 20*)

Cyrus (600–530 B.C.E.) Founder of the Achaemenid Persian Empire. Between 550 and 530 B.C.E. he conquered Media, Lydia, and Babylon. He employed Persians and Medes in his administration and respected the institutions and beliefs of subject peoples. (*p. 90*)

czar See **tsar.**

Daoism Chinese school of thought, originating in the Warring States Period with Laozi (604–531 B.C.E.). Daoism offered an alternative to the Confucian emphasis on hierarchy and duty. Daoists believe that the world is always changing and is devoid of absolute morality or meaning. They accept the world as they find it, avoid futile struggles, and deviate as little as possible from the *Dao,* or "path" of nature. (See also **Confucius.**) (*p. 44*)

Darius I (ca. 558–486 B.C.E.) Third ruler of the Persian Empire (r. 521–486 B.C.E.). He established a system of provinces and tribute, began construction of Persepolis, and expanded Persian control in the east (Pakistan) and west (northern Greece). (*p. 90*)

Darwin, Charles (1809–1882) English naturalist. He studied the plants and animals of South America and the Pacific islands, and in his book *On the Origin of Species by Means of Natural Selection* (1859) set forth his theory of **evolution.** (*p. 513*)

Declaration of the Rights of Man (1789) Statement of fundamental political rights adopted by the French **National Assembly** at the beginning of the French Revolution. (*p. 451*)

deforestation The removal of trees faster than forests can replace themselves. (*p. 376*)

Delhi Sultanate (1206–1526) Centralized Indian empire of varying extent, created by Muslim invaders. (*p. 306*)

democracy A system of government in which all "citizens" (however defined) have equal political and legal rights, privileges, and protections, as in the Greek city-state of Athens in the fifth and fourth centuries B.C.E. (*p. 98*)

demographic transition A change in the rates of population growth. Before the transition, both birth and death rates are high, resulting in a slowly growing population; then the death rate drops but the birth rate remains high, causing a population explosion; finally the birth rate drops and the population growth slows down. This transition took place in Europe in the late nineteenth and early twentieth centuries, in North America and East Asia in the mid-twentieth,

and, most recently, in Latin America and South Asia. (*p. 635*)

Deng Xiaoping (1904–1997) Communist Party leader who forced Chinese economic reforms after the death of **Mao Zedong.** (*p. 630*)

dhow Ship of small to moderate size used in the western Indian Ocean, traditionally with a triangular sail and a sewn timber hull. (*p. 313*)

Dias, Bartolomeu (1450?–1500) Portuguese explorer who in 1488 led the first expedition to sail around the southern tip of Africa and sight the Indian Ocean. (*p. 349*)

Diaspora A Greek word meaning "dispersal," used to describe the communities of a given ethnic group living outside their homeland. Jews, for example, spread from Israel to western Asia and Mediterranean lands in antiquity and today can be found throughout the world. (*p. 78*)

Dirty War War waged by the Argentine military (1976–1982) against leftist groups. Characterized by the use of illegal imprisonment, torture, and executions. (*p. 626*)

divination Techniques for ascertaining the future or the will of the gods by interpreting natural phenomena such as, in early China, the cracks on oracle bones or, in ancient Greece, the flight of birds. (*p. 42*)

division of labor The breaking down of a manufacturing process into a series of steps. The pottery shop of Josiah Wedgwood and other eighteenth-century factories divided labor into many simple and repetitive tasks that could be performed by unskilled laborers. This greatly increased the productivity of labor and lowered the cost of goods. (See also **Wedgwood, Josiah.**) (*p. 466*)

driver A privileged male slave whose job was to ensure that a slave gang did its work on a plantation. (*p. 395*)

Druids The class of religious experts who conducted rituals and preserved sacred lore among some ancient Celtic peoples. They provided education and mediated disputes until suppressed by the Romans as a potential focus of opposition. (See also **Celts.**) (*p. 68*)

Dutch West India Company (1621–1794) Company chartered by the Dutch government to trade in the Americas and Africa. (*p. 397*)

economic sanctions Boycotts, embargoes, and other economic measures that one country uses to pressure another country into changing its policies. (*p. 650*)

Edison, Thomas (1847–1931) American inventor of the electric light bulb, acoustic recording on wax cylinders, and motion pictures. (*p. 505*)

Einstein, Albert (1879–1955) German physicist who developed the theory of relativity, which states that time, space, and mass are relative to each other and not fixed. (*p. 558*)

electricity A form of energy used in telegraphy from the 1840s on and for lighting, industrial motors, and railroads beginning in the 1880s. (*p. 505*)

electric telegraph A device for transmission of information over an electric wire. It was introduced in England and North America in the 1830s and 1840s and replaced systems of visual signals such as semaphores. (See also **submarine telegraph cables.**) (*p. 470*)

encomienda A grant of authority over a population of Amerindians in the Spanish colonies. It provided the grant holder a supply of cheap labor and periodic payments of goods by the Amerindians. It obliged the grant holder to spread Christianity. (*p. 386*)

Enlightenment A philosophical movement in eighteenth-century Europe that fostered the belief that one could reform society by discovering rational laws that governed social behavior. (*pp. 379, 445*)

equites In ancient Italy, prosperous landowners second in status to the senatorial aristocracy. The Roman emperors allied with this group to counterbalance the old aristocracy and used them to staff the imperial civil service. (*p. 129*)

Estates General France's traditional national assembly with representatives of the three estates, or classes, in French society: the clergy, nobility, and commoners. The calling of the Estates General in 1789 led to the French Revolution. (*p. 451*)

Ethiopia East African highland nation lying east of the Nile River. (See also **Menelik II; Selassie, Haile.**) (*p. 168*)

ethnic cleansing Effort to eradicate a people and its culture by means of mass killing and the destruction of historical buildings and cultural materials. Ethnic cleansing was used by both sides in the conflicts that accompanied the disintegration of Yugoslavia in the 1990s. (*p. 646*)

European Community (EC) An organization promoting economic unity in Europe formed in 1967 by consolidation of earlier, more limited, agreements. Replaced by the European Union (EU) in 1993. (*p. 613*)

Faisal I (1885–1933) Arab prince, leader of the Arab Revolt in World War I. The British made him king of Iraq in 1921, and he reigned under British protection until 1933. (*p. 548*)

Fascist Party Italian political party created by Benito Mussolini during World War I. It emphasized aggressive nationalism and was Mussolini's instrument for the creation of a dictatorship in Italy from 1922 to 1943. (See also **Mussolini, Benito.**) (*p. 568*)

fief In medieval Europe, land granted in return for a sworn oath to provide specified military service. (*p. 202*)

First Temple A sanctuary built in Jerusalem by King Solomon in the tenth century B.C.E. to be the religious center for the Israelite god Yahweh. The First Temple was destroyed by the Babylonians in 587 B.C.E., rebuilt on a modest scale in the late sixth century B.C.E., and replaced by King Herod's Second Temple in the late first century B.C.E. (destroyed by the Romans in 70 C.E.) (*p. 76*)

Five-Year Plans Plans that Joseph Stalin introduced to industrialize the Soviet Union rapidly, beginning in 1928. They set goals for the output of steel, electricity, machinery, and most other products. Many countries followed this example after World War II. (See also **Stalin, Joseph.**) (*p. 564*)

foragers People who support themselves by hunting wild animals and gathering wild edible plants and insects. (*p. 7*)

Forbidden City The walled section of Beijing where emperors lived between 1121 and 1924. A portion is now a residence for leaders of the People's Republic of China. (*p. 289*)

free-trade imperialism Economic dominance of a weaker country by a more powerful one, while maintaining the legal independence of the weaker state. In the late nineteenth century, free-trade imperialism characterized the relations between the Latin American republics, on the one hand, and Great Britain and the United States, on the other. (*p. 535*)

fresco A technique of painting on walls covered with moist plaster. It was used to decorate Minoan and Mycenaean palaces and Roman villas, and became an important medium during the Italian Renaissance. (*p. 52*)

Funan An early complex society in Southeast Asia between the first and sixth centuries C.E. It was centered in southern Vietnam and controlled the passage of trade across the Malaysian isthmus. (*p. 158*)

Gama, Vasco da (1460?–1524) Portuguese explorer. In 1497–1498 he led the first naval expedition from Europe to India, opening an important commercial sea route. (*p. 349*)

Gandhi, Mohandas K. (Mahatma) (1869–1948) Leader of the Indian independence movement and advocate of nonviolent resistance. Educated as a lawyer in England, he returned to India and became leader of the **Indian National Congress** in 1920. He appealed to the poor and led nonviolent demonstrations against colonial rule. Soon after independence he was assassinated for attempting to stop Hindu-Muslim rioting. (*p. 592*)

Genghis Khan (ca. 1167–1227) The title of Temüjin when he ruled the Mongols (1206–1227). It means the "oceanic" or "universal" leader. Genghis Khan was the founder of the Mongol Empire. (*p. 262*)

gens de couleur Free men and women of color in Haiti. They sought greater political rights and later supported the Haitian Revolution. (See also **L'Ouverture, François Dominique Toussaint.**) (*p. 457*)

gentry In China, the class of prosperous families, next in wealth below the rural aristocrats, from which the emperors drew their administrative personnel. Respected for their education and expertise, these officials became a privileged group and made the government more efficient and responsive. The term also denotes the class of landholding families in England below the aristocracy. *(p. 141)*

Ghana First known kingdom in sub-Saharan West Africa between the sixth and thirteenth centuries C.E. Also the modern West African country once known as the Gold Coast. *(p. 164)*

Gold Coast (Africa) Region of the Atlantic coast of West Africa occupied by modern Ghana; named for its gold exports to Europe from the 1470s onward. *(p. 349)*

Golden Horde Mongol khanate founded by Genghis Khan's grandson Batu in southern Russia. It adopted the Turkic language and Islam. Also known as the Kipchak Horde. *(p. 269)*

Gorbachev, Mikhail (b. 1931) Head of the Soviet Union from 1985 to 1991. His liberalization effort improved relations with the West, but he lost power after his reforms led to the collapse of Communist governments in eastern Europe. *(p. 631)*

Gothic cathedrals Large churches originating in twelfth-century France; built in an architectural style featuring pointed arches, tall vaults and spires, flying buttresses, and large stained-glass windows. *(p. 333)*

Grand Canal The 1,100-mile (1,700-kilometer) waterway linking the Yellow and the Yangzi Rivers. It was begun in the **Han** period and completed during the Sui Empire. *(p. 219)*

Great Circuit The network of Atlantic Ocean trade routes between Europe, Africa, and the Americas that underlay the **Atlantic system.** *(p. 398)*

"great tradition" Historians' term for a literate, well-institutionalized complex of religious and social beliefs and practices adhered to by diverse societies over a broad geographical area. (See also **"small tradition."**) *(p. 165)*

Great Western Schism A division of the Latin (Western) Christian Church between 1378 and 1417, when rival claimants to the papacy existed in Rome and Avignon. *(p. 339)*

Great Zimbabwe City, now in ruins (in the modern African country of Zimbabwe), whose many stone structures were built between about 1250 and 1450, when it was a trading center and the capital of a large state. *(p. 314)*

guild In medieval Europe, an association of men (rarely women), such as merchants, artisans, or professors, who worked in a particular trade and banded together to promote their economic and political interests. Guilds were also important in other societies, such as the Ottoman and Safavid empires. *(p. 331)*

Gujarat Region of western India famous for trade and manufacturing; the inhabitants are called Gujarati. *(p. 312)*

gunpowder A mixture of saltpeter, sulfur, and charcoal, in various proportions. The formula, brought to China in the 400s or 500s, was first used to make fumigators to keep away insect pests and evil spirits. In later centuries it was used to make explosives and fire projectiles. *(p. 229)*

Guomindang Nationalist political party founded on democratic principles by **Sun Yat-sen** in 1912. After 1925, the party was headed by **Chiang Kai-shek,** who turned it into an increasingly authoritarian movement. *(p. 554)*

Gupta Empire (320–550 C.E.) A powerful Indian state based, like its Mauryan predecessor, on a capital at Pataliputra in the Ganges Valley. It controlled most of the Indian subcontinent through military force and the prestige of its sophisticated culture. (See also **theater-state.**) *(p. 117)*

hadith A tradition relating the words or deeds of the Prophet Muhammad; next to the **Quran,** the most important basis for Islamic law. *(p. 187)*

Hammurabi Amorite ruler of **Babylon** (r. 1792–1750 B.C.E.). He conquered many city-states in southern and northern Mesopotamia and is best known for a code of laws. *(p. 17)*

Han A term used to designate (1) the ethnic Chinese people who originated in the Yellow River Valley and spread throughout regions of China suitable for agriculture and (2) the dynasty of emperors who ruled from 206 B.C.E. to 220 C.E. *(p. 140)*

Hanseatic League An economic and defensive alliance of the free towns in northern Germany, founded about 1241 and most powerful in the fourteenth century. *(p. 329)*

Harappa Site in modern Pakistan of one of the great cities of the Indus Valley civilization of the third millennium B.C.E. *(p. 29)*

Hatshepsut Queen of Egypt (r. 1473–1458 B.C.E.). She dispatched a naval expedition down the Red Sea to Punt (possibly Somalia), the faraway source of myrrh. After her death her name and image were frequently defaced. *(p. 47)*

Hebrew Bible A collection of sacred books containing diverse materials concerning the origins, experiences, beliefs, and practices of the Israelites. Most of the extant text was compiled by members of the priestly class in the fifth century B.C.E. and reflects the concerns and view of this group. *(p. 74)*

Hellenistic Age Historians' term for the era, usually dated 323–30 B.C.E., in which Greek culture spread across western Asia and northeastern Africa after the conquests of **Alexander** the Great. The period ended with the fall of the last major Hellenistic kingdom to Rome, but Greek cultural influence persisted. *(p. 106)*

Helsinki Accords (1975) Political and human rights agreement signed in Helsinki, Finland, by the Soviet Union and western European countries. (*p. 617*)

Henry the Navigator (1394–1460) Portuguese prince who promoted the study of navigation and directed voyages of exploration down the western coast of Africa. (*p. 348*)

Herodotus (ca. 485–425 B.C.E.) Heir to the technique of *historia*—"investigation"—developed by Greeks in the late Archaic period. From a Greek community in Anatolia, he traveled extensively, collecting information in western Asia and the Mediterranean lands. He chronicled the **Persian Wars** between the Greek city-states and the Persian Empire. (*p. 100*)

Hidalgo y Costilla, Miguel (1753–1811) Mexican priest who led the first stage of the Mexican independence war in 1810. He was captured and executed in 1811. (*p. 458*)

Hidden Imam Last in a series of twelve descendants of Muhammad's son-in-law Ali, whom **Shi'ites** consider divinely appointed leaders of the Muslim community. In occlusion since ca. 873, he is expected to return as a messiah at the end of time. (*p. 413*)

hieroglyphics A system of writing in which pictorial symbols represented sounds, syllables, or concepts. It was used for official and monumental inscriptions in ancient Egypt. Cursive symbol-forms were developed for rapid composition on other media, such as **papyrus.** (*p. 24*)

high culture Canons of artistic and literary masterworks recognized by dominant economic classes. (*p. 656*)

Hinduism A general term for a wide variety of beliefs and ritual practices that have developed in the Indian subcontinent since antiquity. Hinduism has roots in ancient Vedic, Buddhist, and south Indian religious concepts and practices. It spread along the trade routes to Southeast Asia. (*p. 113*)

Hiroshima City in Japan, the first to be destroyed by an atomic bomb, on August 6, 1945. The bombing hastened the end of World War II. (*p. 576*)

history The study of past events and changes in the development, transmission, and transformation of cultural practices. (*p. 5*)

Hitler, Adolph (1889–1945) Born in Austria, Hitler became a radical German nationalist during World War I. He led the National Socialist German Workers' Party—the **Nazi Party**—in the 1920s and became dictator of Germany in 1933. He led Europe into World War II. (*p. 568*)

Hittites A people who established an empire in central Anatolia and Syria in the Late Bronze Age. The Hittites vied with New Kingdom Egypt for control of Syria-Palestine before falling to unidentified attackers ca. 1200 B.C.E. (See also **Ramesses II.**) (*p. 46*)

Holocaust Nazis' program during World War II to kill people they considered undesirable. Some 6 million Jews perished during the Holocaust, along with millions of Poles, Gypsies, Communists, Socialists, and others. (*p. 579*)

Holocene The geological era since the end of the Great Ice Age about 11,000 years ago. (*p. 11*)

Holy Roman Empire Loose federation of mostly German states and principalities, headed by an emperor elected by the princes. It lasted from 962 to 1806. (*p. 205*)

hoplite A heavily armored Greek infantryman of the Archaic and Classical periods who fought in the close-packed phalanx formation. Hoplite armies—militias composed of middle- and upper-class citizens supplying their own equipment—excelled contemporary military forces. (*p. 96*)

horse collar Harnessing method that increased the efficiency of horses by shifting the point of traction from the animal's throat to the shoulders; its adoption favors the spread of horse-drawn plows and vehicles. (*p. 212*)

House of Burgesses Elected assembly in colonial Virginia, created in 1618. (*p. 389*)

humanists (Renaissance) European scholars, writers, and teachers associated with the study of the humanities (grammar, rhetoric, poetry, history, languages, and moral philosophy), influential in the fifteenth century and later. (*p. 335*)

Hundred Years War (1337–1453) Series of campaigns over control of the throne of France, involving English and French royal families and French noble families. (*p. 339*)

Husain, Saddam (b. 1937) President of Iraq since 1979. Waged war on Iran in 1980–1988. In 1990 he ordered an invasion of Kuwait but was defeated by United States and its allies in the Gulf War (1991). (*p. 628*)

Ibn Battuta (1304–1369) Moroccan Muslim scholar, the most widely traveled individual of his time. He wrote a detailed account of his visits to Islamic lands from China to Spain and the western Sudan. (*p. 302*)

Ibn Khaldun (1332–1406) Arab historian. He developed an influential theory on the rise and fall of states. Born in Tunis, he spent his later years in Cairo as a teacher and judge. In 1400 he was sent to Damascus to negotiate the surrender of the city, where he met and exchanged views with **Timur.** (*p. 272*)

Il-khan A "secondary" or "peripheral" khan based in Persia. The Il-khans' khanate, founded by Hülegü, a grandson of **Genghis Khan,** was based at Tabriz in northwest Iran. (*p. 269*)

import-substitution industrialization An economic system aimed at building a country's industry by restricting foreign trade, forcing consumers to buy local manufactures instead of imports. (*p. 598*)

Inca Largest and most powerful Andean empire. Controlled the Pacific coast of South America from Ecuador to Chile from its capital of Cuzco. (*p. 254*)

indentured servant A migrant to British colonies in the Americas who paid for passage by agreeing to work for a set term ranging from four to seven years. (*p. 389*)

Indian Civil Service The elite professional class of officials who administered the government of British India. Originally composed exclusively of well-educated British men, it gradually added qualified Indians. (*p. 491*)

Indian National Congress A movement and political party founded in 1885 to demand greater Indian participation in government. Led after 1920 by Mohandas K. Gandhi, it appealed increasingly to the poor and organized mass protests demanding self-government and independence. (See also **Gandhi, Mohandas K.**) (*pp. 492, 589*)

Indian Ocean Maritime System in premodern times, a network of seaports, trade routes, and maritime culture linking countries on the rim of the Indian Ocean from Africa to Indonesia. (*p. 155*)

indulgence The forgiveness of the punishment due for sins, granted by the Catholic Church as a reward for a pious act. Martin Luther's protest against the sale of indulgences is often seen as touching off the **Protestant Reformation.** (*p. 365*)

Industrial Revolution The transformation of the economy, environment, and living conditions, occurring first in England in the eighteenth century, that resulted from the use of steam engines, the mechanization of manufacturing, and innovations in transportation (*p. 463*)

investiture controversy Dispute between the popes and the Holy Roman Emperors over who held ultimate authority over bishops in imperial lands. (*p. 205*)

Iron Age Historians' term for the period during which iron became the primary metal for tools and weapons. Iron technology began at different times in different regions. (*p. 63*)

iron curtain Winston Churchill's term for the Cold War division between the Soviet-dominated East and the U.S.-dominated West. (*p. 604*)

Iroquois Confederacy An alliance of five northeastern Amerindian peoples (after 1722 six) that made decisions on military and diplomatic issues through a council of representatives. Allied first with the Dutch and later with the English, the Confederacy dominated the area from western New England to the Great Lakes. (*p. 390*)

Islam Religion expounded by the Prophet Muhammad (570–632 C.E.) on the basis of divine revelations, which were collected after his death into the **Quran.** In the tradition of Judaism and Christianity, Islam calls on people to recognize one creator god—Allah—who rewards or punishes believers after death according to how they led their lives. (See also **hadith.**) (*p. 178*)

Israel In antiquity, the land between the eastern shore of the Mediterranean and the Jordan River, occupied by the Israelites from the early second millennium B.C.E. The modern state of Israel was founded in 1948. (*p. 74*)

Janissaries Infantry, originally of slave origin, armed with firearms and constituting the elite of the Ottoman army from the fifteenth century until the corps was abolished in 1826. (*p. 409*)

Jesuits Members of the Society of Jesus, a Roman Catholic order founded by Ignatius Loyola in 1534. They played an important part in the **Catholic Reformation** and helped create conduits of trade and knowledge between Asia and Europe. (*p. 439*)

Jesus (ca. 5 B.C.E.–34 C.E.) A Jew from Galilee in northern Israel who sought to reform Jewish beliefs and practices. He was executed as a revolutionary by the Romans. Hailed as the Messiah and son of God by his followers, he became the central figure in Christianity, a belief system that developed in the centuries after his death. (*p. 133*)

Jinnah, Muhammad Ali (1876–1948) Indian Muslim politician who founded the state of Pakistan. A lawyer by training, he joined the **All-India Muslim League** in 1913. As leader of the League from the 1920s on, he negotiated with the British and the **Indian National Congress** for Muslim participation in Indian politics. From 1940 on, he led the movement for the independence of India's Muslims in a separate state of Pakistan, founded in 1947. (*p. 593*)

joint-stock company A business, often backed by a government charter, that sold shares to individuals to raise money for its trading enterprises and to spread the risks (and profits) among many investors. (*p. 375*)

junk A very large flatbottom sailing ship produced in the **Tang** and **Song Empires,** specially designed for long-distance commercial travel. (*p. 228*)

Kamakura Shogunate The first of Japan's decentralized military governments. (1185–1333). (*p. 235*)

Kamikaze The "divine wind," which the Japanese credited with blowing Mongol invaders away from their shores in 1281. Term later used for suicide dive bombers in World War II. (*p. 298*)

Kangxi (1654–1722) Qing emperor (r. 1662–1722). He oversaw the greatest expansion of the **Qing Empire.** (*p. 434*)

karma In Indian tradition, the residue of deeds performed in past and present lives that adheres to a "spirit" and determines what form it will assume in its next life cycle. (*p. 111*)

keiretsu Alliances of corporations and banks that dominate the Japanese economy. (*p. 629*)

khipu System of knotted colored cords used by preliterate Andean peoples to transmit information. (*p. 250*)

Khomeini, Ayatollah Ruhollah (1900?–1989) Shi'ite philosopher and cleric who led the overthrow of the shah of Iran in 1979 and created an Islamic republic. (*p. 627*)

Khubilai Khan (1215–1294) Last of the Mongol Great Khans (r. 1260–1294) and founder of the **Yuan Empire.** (*p. 284*)

Kievan Russia State established at Kiev in Ukraine ca. 879 by Scandinavian adventurers asserting authority over a mostly Slavic farming population. (*p. 196*)

Korean War (1950–1953) Conflict that began with North Korea's invasion of South Korea and came to involve the United Nations (primarily the United States) allying with South Korea and the People's Republic of China allying with North Korea. (*p. 614*)

Koryo Korean kingdom founded in 918 and destroyed by a Mongol invasion in 1259. (*p. 234*)

Kush An Egyptian name for Nubia, the region alongside the Nile River south of Egypt, where an indigenous kingdom arose beginning in the early second millennium B.C.E. (*p. 50*)

labor union An organization of workers in a particular industry or trade, created to defend the interests of members through strikes or negotiations with employers. (*p. 509*)

laissez faire The idea that government should refrain from interfering in economic affairs. The classic exposition of laissez-faire principles is Adam Smith's *Wealth of Nations* (1776). (*p. 475*)

lama In Tibetan Buddhism, a teacher. (*p. 284*)

Las Casas, Bartolomé de (1474–1566) First bishop of Chiapas, in southern Mexico. He devoted most of his life to protecting Amerindian peoples from exploitation. His major achievement was the New Laws of 1542, which limited the ability of Spanish settlers to compel Amerindians to labor for them. (See also **encomienda.**) (*p. 384*)

Latin West Historians' name for the territories of Europe that adhered to the Latin rite of Christianity and used the Latin language for intellectual exchange in the period ca. 1000–1500. (*p. 323*)

League of Nations International organization founded in 1919 to promote world peace and cooperation but greatly weakened by the refusal of the United States to join. It was superseded by the **United Nations** in 1945. (*p. 550*)

Legalism In China, a political philosophy that emphasized the unruliness of human nature and justified state coercion and control. The **Qin** ruling class invoked it to validate the authoritarian nature of their regime. It was superseded in the **Han** era by a more benevolent Confucian doctrine of moderation. (*p. 43*)

"legitimate" trade Exports from Africa in the nineteenth century that did not include the newly outlawed slave trade. (*p. 486*)

Lenin, Vladimir (1870–1924) Leader of the Bolshevik (later Communist) Party. He lived in exile in Switzerland until 1917, then returned to Russia to lead the Bolsheviks to victory during the Russian Revolution and the civil war that followed. (*p. 548*)

Leopold II (1835–1909) King of Belgium (r. 1865–1909). He was active in encouraging the exploration of Central Africa and became the ruler of the Congo Free State (to 1908). (*p. 528*)

Li Shimin (599–649) One of the founders of the **Tang Empire** and its second emperor (r. 626–649). He led the expansion of the empire into Central Asia. (*p. 219*)

liberalism A political ideology that emphasizes the civil rights of citizens, representative government, and the protection of private property. This ideology, derived from the **Enlightenment,** was especially popular among the property-owning middle classes of Europe and North America. (*p. 512*)

Library of Ashurbanipal A large collection of writings drawn from the ancient literary, religious, and scientific traditions of Mesopotamia. It was assembled by the sixth century B.C.E. Assyrian ruler Ashurbanipal. (*p. 74*)

Linear B A set of syllabic symbols, derived from Linear A, the undeciphered writing system of **Minoan** Crete, used in the Mycenaean palaces of the Late Bronze Age to write an early form of Greek. It was used primarily for palace records. (*p. 53*)

Little Ice Age A century-long period of cool climate that began in the 1590s. Its ill effects on agriculture in northern Europe were notable. (*p. 376*)

llama A hoofed animal indigenous to the Andes Mountains in South America. It was the only domesticated beast of burden in the Americas before the arrival of Europeans. It provided meat and wool. (*p. 67*)

loess A fine, light silt deposited by wind and water. It constitutes the fertile soil of the Yellow River Valley in northern China. Because loess soil is not compacted, it can be worked with a simple digging stick. (*p. 38*)

Long March (1934–1935) The 6,000-mile (9,600-kilometer) flight of Chinese Communists from southeastern to northwestern China. The Communists, led by **Mao Zedong,** were pursued by the Chinese army under orders from **Chiang Kai-shek.** The four thousand survivors of the march formed the nucleus of a revived Communist movement that defeated the **Guomindang** after World War II. (*p. 572*)

L'Ouverture, François Dominique Toussaint (1743–1803) Leader of the Haitian Revolution. He freed the slaves and gained effective independence for Haiti despite military interventions by the British and French. (*p. 457*)

ma'at Egyptian concept of divinely created and maintained order in the universe. Reflecting the ancient Egyptians' belief in an essentially beneficent world, the divine ruler was the earthly guarantor of this order. (See also **pyramid**.) (*p. 24*)

Macartney mission (1792–1793) The unsuccessful attempt by the British Empire to establish diplomatic relations with the **Qing Empire.** (*p. 436*)

Magellan, Ferdinand (1480?–1521) Portuguese navigator who led the Spanish expedition of 1519–1522 that was the first to sail around the world. (*p. 352*)

Mahabharata Indian epic chronicling the events leading up to a war between related kinship groups. It includes the *Bhagavad-Gita,* an important work of Indian sacred literature. (*p. 116*)

Mahayana Buddhism "Great Vehicle" branch of Buddhism followed in China, Japan, and Central Asia. The focus is on reverence for **Buddha** and for bodhisattvas, enlightened persons who have postponed nirvana to help others attain enlightenment. (*p. 113*)

Malacca Port city in the modern Southeast Asian country of Malaysia, founded about 1400 as a trading center on the Strait of Malacca. Also spelled Melaka. (*p. 317*)

Malay peoples Peoples originating in south China and Southeast Asia who settled the Malay Peninsula, Indonesia, and the Philippines, then spread eastward across the islands of the Pacific Ocean and west to Madagascar. (*p. 158*)

Mali Empire created by indigenous Muslims in West Africa from the thirteenth to fifteenth century. It was famous for its role in the trans-Saharan gold trade. (See also **Timbuktu.**) (*p. 307*)

Malthus, Thomas (1766–1834) Eighteenth-century English intellectual who warned that population growth threatened future generations because population growth would always outstrip increases in agricultural production. (*p. 634*)

mamluks Under this Islamic system of military slavery, Turkic military slaves predominated in the armed forces of the **Abbasid Caliphate** of the ninth and tenth centuries. Mamluks eventually founded their own state, ruling Egypt and Syria (1250–1517). (*pp. 182, 278*)

Manchuria Region of Northeast Asia bounded by the Yau River on the south and the Amur River on the east and north. (*p. 288*)

Manchus Federation of Northeast Asian peoples who founded the **Qing Empire.** (*p. 432*)

Mandate of Heaven Chinese religious and political ideology developed by the **Zhou,** according to which it was the prerogative of Heaven, the chief deity, to grant power to the ruler of China and to take away that power if the ruler failed to conduct himself justly. (*p. 42*)

mandate system Allocation of former German colonies and Ottoman possessions to the victorious powers after World War I, to be administered under **League of Nations** supervision. (*p. 556*)

manor In medieval Europe, a large, self-sufficient landholding consisting of the lord's residence (manor house), outbuildings, peasant village, and surrounding land. (*p. 200*)

mansabs In India, grants of land given in return for service by rulers of the **Mughal Empire.** (*p. 536*)

Mansa Kankan Musa Ruler of **Mali** (r. 1312–1337). His pilgrimage through Egypt to **Mecca** in 1324–1325 established the empire's reputation for wealth in the Mediterranean world. (*p. 308*)

Mao Zedong (1892–1976) Leader of the Chinese Communist Party (1927–1976). He led the Communists on the **Long March** (1934–1935) and rebuilt the Communist Party and Red Army during the Japanese occupation of China (1937–1945). After World War II, he led the Communists to victory over the **Guomindang.** He ordered the **Cultural Revolution** in 1966. (*p. 572*)

maroon A slave who ran away from his or her master. Often a member of a community of runaway slaves in the West Indies and South America. (*p. 396*)

Marshall Plan U.S. program to support the reconstruction of western Europe after World War II. By 1961 more than $20 billion in economic aid had been dispersed. (*p. 613*)

Marx, Karl (1818–1883) German journalist and philosopher, founder of the Marxist branch of **socialism.** He is best known for two books: *The Communist Manifesto* (1840) and *Das Kapital* (Vols. I–III, 1867–1894). (*p. 509*)

mass deportation The forcible removal and relocation of large numbers of people or entire populations. (*p. 71*)

mass production The manufacture of many identical products by the **division of labor** into many small repetitive tasks. This method was introduced into the manufacture of pottery by Josiah Wedgwood and into the spinning of cotton thread by Richard Arkwright. (See also **Industrial Revolution; Wedgwood, Josiah.**) (*p. 466*)

Mauryan Empire The first state to unify most of the Indian subcontinent. It was founded by Chandragupta Maurya in 324 B.C.E. and survived until 187 B.C.E. (See also **Ashoka.**) (*p. 115*)

Maya Mesoamerican civilization concentrated in Mexico's Yucatán Peninsula and in Guatemala and Honduras but never unified into a single empire. (*p. 242*)

Mecca City in western Arabia; birthplace of the Prophet **Muhammad,** and ritual center of the Islamic religion. (*p. 176*)

mechanization The application of machinery on a large scale to manufacturing and other activities. Early undertakings include the spinning of cotton thread and the weaving of cloth in late-eighteenth- and early-nineteenth-century England. (*p. 467*)

medieval Literally "middle age," a term that historians of Europe use for the period ca. 500 to ca. 1500, signifying its intermediate point between Greco-Roman antiquity and the Renaissance. (*p. 195*)

Medina City in western Arabia to which the Prophet Muhammad and his followers emigrated in 622 to escape persecution in Mecca. (*p. 178*)

megaliths Structures and complexes of very large stones constructed for ceremonial and religious purposes in **Neolithic** times. (*p. 12*)

Memphis The capital of Old Kingdom Egypt, near the head of the Nile Delta. Early rulers were interred in the nearby **pyramids.** (*p. 24*)

Menelik II (1844–1911). Emperor of Ethiopia (r. 1889–1911). He enlarged Ethiopia to its present dimensions and defeated an Italian invasion at Adowa (1896). (*p. 531*)

mercantilism European government policies of the sixteenth, seventeenth, and eighteenth centuries designed to promote overseas trade between a country and its colonies and accumulate precious metals by requiring colonies to trade only with their motherland country. (*p. 397*)

Meroë Capital of a kingdom in southern Nubia from the fourth century B.C.E. to the fourth century C.E. In this period Nubian culture shows more independence from Egypt and the influence of sub-Saharan Africa. (*p. 51*)

Middle Passage The part of the **Great Circuit** involving the transportation of enslaved Africans across the Atlantic to the Americas. (*p. 398*)

Ming Empire (1368–1644) Empire based in China that Zhu Yuanzhang established after the overthrow of the **Yuan Empire.** The Ming emperor **Yongle** sponsored the building of the **Forbidden City** and the voyages of **Zheng He.** (*pp. 289, 431*)

Minoan Civilization on the Aegean island of Crete in the second millennium B.C.E. The Minoans engaged in far-flung commerce around the Mediterranean and influenced the early Greeks. (*p. 52*)

mit'a Andean labor system based on shared obligations to help kinsmen and work on behalf of the ruler and religious organizations. (*p. 250*)

Moche Civilization of north coast of Peru (200–700 C.E.) that built extensive irrigation networks as well as impressive urban centers dominated by brick temples. (*p. 251*)

Moctezuma II (1466?–1520) Last Aztec emperor, overthrown by the Spanish conquistador Hernán Cortés. (*p. 357*)

modernization The process of reforming political, military, economic, social, and cultural traditions in imitation of the early success of Western societies. (*p. 485*)

Mohenjo-Daro Largest of the cities of the Indus Valley civilization. It was centrally located in the extensive floodplain of the Indus River in contemporary Pakistan. The large scale of construction at Mohenjo-Daro, the orderly grid of streets, and the standardization of building materials are evidence of central planning. (*p. 29*)

moksha The Hindu concept of the spirit's "liberation" from the endless cycle of rebirths. Physical discipline, meditation, and acts of devotion to the gods can help the spirit distance itself from desire for the things of this world and merge with the divine force that animates the universe. (*p. 111*)

monasticism Living in a religious community apart from secular society and adhering to a rule stipulating chastity, obedience, and poverty. It was a prominent element of medieval Christianity and Buddhism. Monasteries were the primary centers of learning and literacy in medieval Europe. (*p. 206*)

Mongols A people of this name is mentioned as early as the records of the **Tang Empire,** living as nomads in northern Eurasia. After 1206 they established an enormous empire under **Genghis Khan,** linking western and eastern Eurasia. (*p. 262*)

monotheism Belief in the existence of a single divine entity. Some scholars cite the devotion of the Egyptian pharaoh **Akhenaten** to the Aten (sun-disk) and his suppression of traditional gods as the earliest instance. The Israelite worship of Yahweh developed into an exclusive belief in one god, and this concept passed into Christianity and Islam. (*p. 78*)

monsoon Seasonal winds in the Indian Ocean caused by the differences in temperature between the rapidly heating and cooling landmasses of Africa and Asia and the slowly changing ocean waters. These strong and predictable winds enable sailors to cross the open sea and also bring large amounts of rainfall to parts of India, Southeast Asia, and China. (*pp. 109, 303*)

movable type Type in which each individual character is cast as a separate piece of metal. It replaced woodblock printing, allowing for the arrangement of individual letters and other characters on a page, rather than requiring the carving of entire pages at a time. It may have been invented in Korea in the thirteenth century. (See also **printing press.**) (*p. 234*)

Mughal Empire Muslim state (1526–1857) exercising dominion over most of India in the sixteenth and seventeenth centuries. (*p. 416*)

Muhammad (570–632 C.E.) Arab prophet; founder of religion of Islam. (*p. 177*)

Muhammad Ali (1769–1849) Leader of Egyptian modernization in the early nineteenth century. He ruled Egypt as an Ottoman governor, but had imperial ambitions. His descendants ruled Egypt until overthrown in 1952. (*p. 485*)

mummy A body preserved by chemical processes or special natural circumstances, often in the belief that the deceased will need it again in the afterlife. In ancient Egypt the bodies of people who could afford mummification underwent a complex process of removing organs, filling body cavities, dehydrating the corpse with natron, and then wrapping the body with linen bandages and enclosing it in a wooden sarcophagus. (*p. 27*)

Muscovy Russian principality that emerged gradually during the era of Mongol domination. The Muscovite dynasty ruled from 1276 to 1598. (*p. 427*)

Muslim An adherent of the Islamic religion; a person who "submits" (in Arabic, *Islam* means "submission") to the will of God. (*p. 178*)

Mussolini, Benito (1883–1945) Fascist dictator of Italy (1922–1943). He led Italy to conquer Ethiopia (1935), joined Germany in the Axis pact (1936), and allied Italy with Germany in World War II. He was overthrown in 1943 when the Allies invaded Italy. (*p. 568*)

Mycenae A fortified palace complex in southern Greece that controlled a Late Bronze Age kingdom. In Homer's epic poems Mycenae was the base of King Agamemnon, who commanded the Greek's besieging Troy. Archaeologists call Greek society of the second millennium B.C.E. "Mycenaean." (*p. 53*)

Napoleon I (1769–1832) Overthrew French Directory in 1799 and became emperor of the French in 1804. Failed to defeat Great Britain and abdicated in 1814. Returned to power briefly in 1815 but was defeated and died in exile. (*p. 453*)

Nasir al-Din Tusi (1201–1274) Persian mathematician and cosmologist whose academy near Tabriz provided the model for the movement of the planets that helped to inspire the Copernican model of the solar system. (*p. 272*)

National Assembly French Revolutionary assembly (1789–1791). Called first as the **Estates General,** the three estates came together and demanded radical change. It passed the **Declaration of the Rights of Man** in 1789. (*p. 451*)

nationalism A political ideology that stresses people's membership in a nation—a community defined by a common culture and history as well as by territory. In the late eighteenth and early nineteenth centuries, nationalism was a force for unity in western Europe. In the late nineteenth century it hastened the disintegration of the Austro-Hungarian and Ottoman Empires. In the twentieth century it provided the ideological foundation for scores of independent countries emerging from **colonialism.** (*p. 510*)

nawab A Muslim prince allied to British India; technically, a semi-autonomous deputy of the Mughal emperor. (*p. 488*)

Nazi Party German political party joined by Adolf Hitler, emphasizing nationalism, racism, and war. When Hitler became chancellor of Germany in 1933, the Nazi Party became the only legal party and an instrument of Hitler's absolute rule. Its formal name was National Socialist German Workers' Party. (See also **Hitler, Adolf.**) (*p. 568*)

Nehru, Jawaharlal (1889–1964) Indian statesman. He succeeded Mohandas K. Gandhi as leader of the **Indian National Congress.** He negotiated the end of British colonial rule in India and became India's first prime minister (1947–1964). (*p. 593*)

Neo-Assyrian Empire An empire extending from western Iran to Syria-Palestine, conquered by the Assyrians of northern Mesopotamia between the tenth and seventh centuries B.C.E. (*p. 70*)

Neo-Babylonian kingdom Under the Chaldaeans (nomadic kinship groups that settled in southern Mesopotamia in the early first millennium B.C.E.), **Babylon** again became a major political and cultural center in the seventh and sixth centuries B.C.E. After participating in the destruction of Assyrian power, the monarchs Nabopolassar and Nebuchadnezzar took over the southern portion of the Assyrian domains. By destroying the **First Temple** in Jerusalem and deporting part of the population, they initiated the **diaspora** of the Jews. (*p. 84*)

Neolithic The period of the Stone Age associated with the ancient **Agricultural Revolution(s).** (*p. 7*)

Nevskii, Alexander (1220–1263) Prince of Novgorod (r. 1236–1263). He submitted to the invading Mongols in 1240 and received recognition as the leader of the Russian princes under the Golden Horde. (*p. 275*)

New Economic Policy Policy proclaimed by Vladimir Lenin in 1924 to encourage the revival of the Soviet economy by allowing small private enterprises. Joseph Stalin ended the N.E.P. in 1928 and replaced it with a series of **Five-Year Plans.** (See also **Lenin, Vladimir.**) (*p. 552*)

New France French colony in North America, with a capital in Quebec, founded 1608. New France fell to the British in 1763. (*p. 390*)

New Imperialism Historians' term for the late-nineteenth- and early-twentieth-century wave of conquests by European powers, the United States, and Japan, which were followed by the development and exploitation of the newly conquered territories for the benefit of the colonial powers. (*p. 524*)

new monarchies Historians' term for the monarchies in France, England, and Spain from 1450 to 1600. The centralization of royal power was increasing within more or less fixed territorial limits. (*p. 339*)

nomadism A way of life, forced by a scarcity of resources, in which groups of people continually migrate to find pastures and water. (*p. 264*)

nonaligned nations Developing countries that announced their neutrality in the **Cold War.** (*p. 617*)

nongovernmental organizations (NGOs) Nonprofit international organizations devoted to investigating human rights abuses and providing humanitarian relief. (*p. 694*)

North Atlantic Treaty Organization (NATO) Organization formed in 1949 as a military alliance of western European and North American states against the Soviet Union and its east European allies. (See also **Warsaw Pact.**) (*p. 610*)

nuclear nonproliferation Goal of international efforts to prevent countries other than the five declared nuclear powers (United States, Russia, Britain, France, and China) from obtaining nuclear weapons. The first Nuclear Non-Proliferation Treaty was signed in 1968. (*p. 652*)

Olmec The first Mesoamerican civilization. Between ca. 1200 and 400 B.C.E., the Olmec people of central Mexico created a civilization that included intensive agriculture, wide-ranging trade, ceremonial centers, and monumental construction. The Olmec had great cultural influence on later Mesoamerican societies. (*p. 64*)

Oman Arab state based in Musqat, the main port in the southeast region of the Arabian peninsula. Oman succeeded Portugal as a power in the western Indian Ocean in the eighteenth century. (*p. 421*)

Opium War (1839–1842) War between Britain and the **Qing Empire** that was, in the British view, occasioned by the Qing government's refusal to permit the importation of opium into its territories. The victorious British imposed the one-sided **Treaty of Nanking** on China. (*p. 495*)

Organization of Petroleum Exporting Countries (OPEC) Organization formed in 1960 by oil-producing states to promote their collective interest in generating revenue from oil (*p. 620*)

Ottoman Empire Islamic state founded by Osman in north-western Anatolia ca. 1300. After the fall of the **Byzantine Empire,** the Ottoman Empire was based at Istanbul (formerly Constantinople) from 1453 to 1922. It encompassed lands in the Middle East, North Africa, the Caucasus, and eastern Europe. (*pp. 277, 406*)

Paleolithic The period of the Stone Age associated with the earliest human societies. It predates the **Neolithic** period. (*p. 7*)

Panama Canal Ship canal cut across the isthmus of Panama by United States Army engineers; it opened in 1915. It greatly shortened the sea voyage between the east and west coasts of North America. The United States turned the canal over to Panama on January 1, 2000. (*p. 537*)

papacy The central administration of the Roman Catholic Church, of which the pope is the head. (*p. 203*)

papyrus A reed that grows along the banks of the Nile River in Egypt. From it was produced a coarse, paper-like writing medium used by the Egyptians and many other peoples in the ancient Mediterranean and Middle East. (*p. 25*)

Parthians Iranian ruling dynasty between ca. 250 B.C.E. and 226 C.E. (*p. 151*)

patron/client relationship In ancient Rome, a fundamental social relationship in which the patron—a wealthy and powerful individual—provided legal and economic protection and assistance to clients, men of lesser status and means, and in return the clients supported the political careers and economic interests of their patron. (*pp. 125–127*)

Paul (ca. 5–65 C.E.) A Jew from the Greek city of Tarsus in Anatolia, he initially persecuted the followers of Jesus but, after receiving a revelation on the road to Damascus, became a Christian. He traveled throughout Syria-Palestine, Anatolia, and Greece, preaching the new religion and establishing churches. Finding his greatest success among pagans ("gentiles"), he began the process by which Christianity separated from Judaism. (*p. 133*)

pax romana Literally, "Roman peace," it connoted the stability and prosperity that Roman rule brought to the lands of the Roman Empire in the first two centuries C.E. (*p. 132*)

Pearl Harbor Naval base in Hawaii attacked by Japanese aircraft on December 7, 1941. The sinking of much of the U.S. Pacific Fleet brought the United States into World War II. (*p. 574*)

Peloponnesian War A protracted (431–404 B.C.E.) and costly conflict between the Athenian and Spartan alliance systems. Possession of a naval empire allowed Athens to fight a war of attrition. Ultimately, Sparta prevailed because of Athenian errors and Persian financial support. (*p. 104*)

perestroika Policy of "openness" that was the centerpiece of Mikhail Gorbachev's efforts to liberalize communism in the Soviet Union. (See also **Gorbachev, Mikhail.**) (*p. 631*)

Pericles (ca. 495–429 B.C.E.) Aristocratic leader who guided the Athenian state through the transition to full participatory democracy for all male citizens, supervised construction of the Acropolis, and pursued a policy of imperial expansion that led to the **Peloponnesian War.** (*p. 101*)

Perón, Eva Duarte (1919–1952) Wife of **Juan Perón** and champion of the poor in Argentina. She was a gifted speaker and popular political leader who campaigned to improve the life of the urban poor by founding schools and hospitals and providing other social benefits. (*p. 899*)

Perón, Juan (1895–1974) President of Argentina (1946–1955, 1973–1974). As a military officer, he championed the rights of labor. He built up Argentinean industry, became very popular among the urban poor, but harmed the economy. (*p. 599*)

Persepolis A complex of palaces, reception halls, and treasury buildings erected by the Persian kings **Darius I**

and Xerxes in the Persian homeland. It is believed that the New Year's festival was celebrated here, as well as the coronations, weddings, and funerals of the Persian kings, who were buried in cliff-tombs nearby. (*p. 92*)

Persian Wars Conflicts between Greek city-states and the Persian Empire, ranging from the Ionian Revolt (499–494 B.C.E.) through Darius's punitive expedition that failed at Marathon (490 B.C.E.) and the defeat of Xerxes' invasion of Greece by the Spartan-led Hellenic League (480–479 B.C.E.). **Herodotus** chronicled these events in the first "history" in the Western tradition. (*p. 101*)

Peter the Great (1672–1725) Russian tsar (r. 1689–1725). He introduced Western languages and technologies to the Russian elite, moving the capital from Moscow to the new city of St. Petersburg. (*p. 430*)

pharaoh The central figure in the ancient Egyptian state. Believed to be an earthly manifestation of the gods, he wielded absolute power. (*p. 24*)

Phoenicians Semitic-speaking Canaanites living on the coast of modern Lebanon and Syria in the first millennium B.C.E. From Tyre and Sidon, Phoenician sailors explored the Mediterranean, engaged in widespread commerce, and founded **Carthage** and other colonies in the western Mediterranean. (*p. 79*)

pilgrimage Journey to a sacred shrine by Christians seeking to show their piety, fulfill vows, or gain absolution for sins. Other pilgrimage traditions include the Muslim pilgrimage to **Mecca** and the pilgrimages made by early Chinese Buddhists to India in search of sacred Buddhist writings. (*p. 214*)

Pilgrims Group of English Protestant dissenters who established Plymouth Colony in Massachusetts in 1620 to seek religious freedom after having lived briefly in the Netherlands. (*p. 389*)

Pizarro, Francisco (1475?–1541) Spanish explorer who led the conquest of the **Inca** Empire of Peru in 1531–1533. (*p. 358*)

Planck, Max (1858–1947) German physicist who developed quantum theory and was awarded the Nobel Prize for physics in 1918. (*p. 558*)

polis The Greek term for a **city-state**, an urban center and the agricultural territory under its control. It was the characteristic form of political organization in southern and central Greece in the Archaic and Classical periods. Of the hundreds of city-states settled by Greeks, some were oligarchic, others democratic, depending on the powers delegated to the Council and the Assembly. (*p. 96*)

popular culture Entertainment spread by mass communications and enjoying wide appeal. (*p. 656*)

positivism A philosophy developed by the French count of Saint-Simon. Positivists believed that social and economic problems could be solved by the application of the scientific method, leading to continuous progress. Their ideas became popular in France and Latin America in the nineteenth century. (*p. 475*)

postmodernism Post-World War II intellectual movement and cultural attitude focusing on cultural pluralism and release from the confines and ideology of Western high culture. (*p. 658*)

Potosí Located in Bolivia, one of the richest silver mining centers and most populous cities in colonial Spanish America. (*p. 384*)

printing press A mechanical device for transferring text or graphics from a woodblock or type to paper using ink. Presses using movable type first appeared in Europe in about 1450. See also **movable type.** (*p. 336*)

Protestant Reformation Religious reform movement within the Latin Christian Church beginning in 1519. It resulted in the "protesters" forming several new Christian denominations, including the Lutheran and Reformed Churches and the Church of England. (*p. 366*)

proxy wars During the **Cold War,** local or regional wars in which the superpowers armed, trained, and financed the combatants. (*p. 624*)

Ptolemies The Macedonian dynasty, descended from one of Alexander the Great's officers, that ruled Egypt for three centuries (323–30 B.C.E.). From their capital at Alexandria, the Ptolemies took over the governing system created by Egyptian pharaohs. (*p. 106*)

Puritans English Protestant dissenters who believed that God predestined souls to heaven or hell before birth. They founded Massachusetts Bay Colony in 1629. (*p. 389*)

pyramid A large, triangular stone monument, used in Egypt and Nubia as a burial place for the king. The largest pyramids, erected during the Old Kingdom near Memphis, reflect the Egyptian belief that the proper burial of the divine ruler would guarantee the continued prosperity of the land. (See also **ma'at.**) (*p. 24*)

Qin A people and state in the Wei Valley of eastern China that conquered rival states and created the first Chinese empire (221–206 B.C.E.). The Qin ruler, **Shi Huangdi,** standardized many features of Chinese society and ruthlessly marshalled subjects for military and construction projects, engendering hostility that led to the fall of his dynasty shortly after his death. The Qin framework was largely taken over by the succeeding **Han** Empire. (*p. 140*)

Qing Empire Empire established in China by Manchus who overthrew the **Ming Empire** in 1644. At various times the Qing also controlled Manchuria, Mongolia, Turkestan, and Tibet. The last Qing emperor was overthrown in 1911. (*p. 433*)

Quran Book composed of divine revelations made to the Prophet Muhammad between ca. 610 and his death in 632; the sacred text of the religion of **Islam.** (*p. 179*)

railroads Networks of iron (later steel) rails on which steam (later electric or diesel) locomotives pulled long trains at high speeds. The first railroads were built in England in the 1830s. Their success caused a railroad-building boom throughout the world that lasted well into the twentieth century. (*p. 506*)

Rajputs Members of a mainly Hindu warrior caste from northwest India. The Mughal emperors drew most of their Hindu officials from this caste, and **Akbar I** married a Rajput princess. (*p. 417*)

Ramesses II A long-lived ruler of New Kingdom Egypt (r. 1290–1224 B.C.E.). He reached an accommodation with the **Hittites** of Anatolia after a standoff in battle at Kadesh in Syria. (*p. 48*)

Rashid al-Din (d. 1318) Adviser to the **Il-khan** ruler Ghazan, who converted to Islam on Rashid's advice. (*p. 270*)

recaptives Africans rescued by Britain's Royal Navy from the illegal slave trade of the nineteenth century and restored to free status. (*p. 487*)

reconquest of Iberia Beginning in the eleventh century, military campaigns by various Iberian Christian states to recapture territory taken by Muslims. In 1492 the last Muslim ruler was defeated, and Spain and Portugal emerged as united kingdoms. (*p. 340*)

Renaissance (European) A period of intense artistic and intellectual activity, said to be a "rebirth" of Greco-Roman culture. Usually divided into an Italian Renaissance, from roughly the mid-fourteenth to mid-fifteenth century, and a Northern (trans-Alpine) Renaissance, from roughly the early fifteenth to early seventeenth century. (*pp. 334, 365*)

Revolutions of 1848 Democratic and nationalist revolutions in Europe. The monarchy in France was overthrown. In Germany, Austria, Italy, and Hungary the revolutions failed. (*p. 454*)

Rhodes, Cecil (1853–1902) British entrepreneur and politician involved in the expansion of the British Empire from South Africa into Central Africa. The colonies of Southern Rhodesia (now Zimbabwe) and Northern Rhodesia (now Zambia) were named after him. (*p. 530*)

Roman Principate A term characterizing Roman government in the first three centuries C.E., based on the ambiguous title *princeps* ("first citizen") adopted by **Augustus** to conceal his military dictatorship. (*p. 129*)

Roman Republic The period from 507 to 31 B.C.E., during which Rome was largely governed by the aristocratic **Roman Senate.** (*p. 124*)

Roman Senate A council whose members were the heads of wealthy, landowning families. Originally an advisory body to the early kings, in the era of the **Roman Republic** the Senate effectively governed the Roman state. Under Senate leadership, Rome conquered an empire in the lands surrounding the Mediterranean Sea. In the first century B.C.E. quarrels among powerful and ambitious senators and failure to address social and economic problems led to civil wars and the emergence of the rule of the emperors. (*p. 124*)

Romanization The process by which the Latin language and Roman culture became dominant in the western provinces of the Roman Empire. The Roman government did not actively seek to Romanize the subject peoples, but indigenous peoples in the provinces often chose to Romanize for political and economic reasons. (*p. 133*)

Romanov, Mikhail (1590–1645) Russian tsar (r. 1613–1645). A member of the Russian aristocracy, he became tsar after the old line of Muscovite rulers was deposed. (*p. 428*)

Royal African Company A trading company chartered by the English government in 1672 to conduct its merchants' trade on the Atlantic coast of Africa. (*p. 397*)

sacrifice A gift given to a deity, often with the aim of creating a relationship, gaining favor, and obligating the god to provide some benefit to the sacrificer, sometimes in order to sustain the deity and thereby guarantee the continuing vitality of the natural world. The object devoted to the deity could be as simple as a cup of wine poured on the ground, a live animal slain on the altar, or, in the most extreme case, the ritual killing of a human being. (*p. 98*)

Safavid Empire Iranian kingdom (1502–1722) established by Ismail Safavi, who declared Iran a Shi'ite state. (*p. 413*)

Sahel Belt south of the Sahara; literally "coastland" in Arabic. (*p. 162*)

samurai Literally "those who serve," the hereditary military elite of the **Tokugawa Shogunate.** (*p. 437*)

Sandinistas Members of a leftist coalition that overthrew the Nicaraguan dictatorship of Anastasia Somoza in 1979 and attempted to install a socialist economy. The United States financed armed opposition by the Contras. The Sandinistas lost national elections in 1990. (*p. 626*)

Sasanid Empire Iranian empire, established ca. 226, with a capital in Ctesiphon, Mesopotamia. The Sasanid emperors established **Zoroastrianism** as the state religion. Muslim Arab armies overthrew the empire ca. 640. (*p. 173*)

satrap The governor of a province in the Achaemenid Persian Empire, often a relative of the king. (*p. 90*)

savanna Tropical or subtropical grassland, either treeless or with occasional clumps of trees. Most extensive in **sub-Saharan Africa** but also present in South America. (*p. 165*)

schism A formal split within a religious community. See **Great Western Schism.** (*p. 204*)

scholasticism A philosophical and theological system, associated with Thomas Aquinas, devised to reconcile Aristotelian philosophy and Roman Catholic theology in the thirteenth century. (*p. 334*)

Scientific Revolution The intellectual movement in Europe, initially associated with planetary motion and other aspects of physics, that by the seventeenth century had laid the groundwork for modern science. (*p. 378*)

"scramble" for Africa Sudden wave of conquests in Africa by European powers in the 1880s and 1890s. Britain obtained most of eastern Africa, France most of northwestern Africa. Other countries (Germany, Belgium, Portugal, Italy, and Spain) acquired lesser amounts. (*p. 528*)

scribe In many ancient societies, a professional position reserved for men who had undergone the lengthy training required to be able to read and write using **cuneiform, hieroglyphics,** or other early writing systems. (*p. 18*)

seasoning An often difficult period of adjustment to new climates, disease environments, and work routines, such as that experienced by slaves newly arrived in the Americas. (*p. 395*)

Selassie, Haile (1892–1975) Emperor of Ethiopia (r. 1930–1974) and symbol of African independence. He fought the Italian invasion of his country in 1935 and regained his throne during World War II, when British forces expelled the Italians. He ruled **Ethiopia** as a traditional **autocracy** until he was overthrown in 1974. (*p. 588*)

Semitic Family of related languages spoken across parts of western Asia and northern Africa. In antiquity these languages included Hebrew, Aramaic, and Phoenician. The most widespread modern language is Arabic. (*p. 15*)

"separate spheres" Nineteenth-century idea in Western societies that men and women, especially of the middle class, should have clearly differentiated roles in society: women as wives, mothers, and homemakers; men as breadwinners and participants in business and politics. (*p. 510*)

sepoy A soldier in South Asia, especially in the service of the British. (*p. 488*)

Sepoy Rebellion The revolt of Indian soldiers in 1857 against certain practices that violated religious customs; also known as the Sepoy Mutiny. (*p. 491*)

serf In medieval Europe, an agricultural laborer legally bound to a lord's property and obligated to perform set services for the lord. In Russia some serfs worked as artisans and in factories; serfdom was not abolished there until 1861. (*pp. 200, 431*)

shaft graves A term used for the burial sites of elite members of Mycenaean Greek society in the mid-second millennium B.C.E. At the bottom of deep shafts lined with stone slabs, the bodies were laid out along with gold and bronze jewelry, implements, weapons, and masks. (*p. 53*)

Shah Abbas I (1571–1629) Shah of Iran (r. 1587–1629). The most illustrious ruler of the **Safavid Empire,** he moved the imperial capital to Isfahan in 1598, where he erected many palaces, mosques, and public buildings. (*p. 414*)

Shamanism The practice of identifying special individuals (shamans) who will interact with spirits for the benefit of the community. Characteristic of the Korean kingdoms of the early medieval period and of early societies of Central Asia. (*p. 232*)

Shang The dominant people in the earliest Chinese dynasty for which we have written records (ca. 1750–1027 B.C.E.). Ancestor worship, divination by means of oracle bones, and the use of bronze vessels for ritual purposes were major elements of Shang culture. (*p. 40*)

Shi Huangdi Founder of the short-lived **Qin** dynasty and creator of the Chinese Empire (r. 221–210 B.C.E.). His tomb, with its army of life-size terracotta soldiers, has been partially excavated. (*p. 140*)

Shi'ites Muslims belonging to the branch of Islam believing that God vests leadership of the community in a descendant of Muhammad's son-in-law Ali. Shi'ism is the state religion of Iran. (See also **Sunnis.**) (*pp. 172, 413*)

Siberia The extreme northeastern sector of Asia, including the Kamchatka Peninsula and the present Russian coast of the Arctic Ocean, the Bering Strait, and the Sea of Okhotsk. (*p. 427*)

Silk Road Caravan routes connecting China and the Middle East across Central Asia and Iran. (*p. 151*)

"small tradition" Historians' term for a localized, usually non-literate, set of customs and beliefs adhered to by a single society, often in conjunction with a **"great tradition."** (*p. 165*)

socialism A political ideology that originated in Europe in the 1830s. Socialists advocated government protection of workers from exploitation by property owners and government ownership of industries. This ideology led to the founding of socialist or labor parties throughout Europe in the second half of the nineteenth century. (See also **Marx, Karl.**) (*p. 509*)

Socrates Athenian philosopher (ca. 470–399 B.C.E.) who shifted the emphasis of philosophical investigation from questions of natural science to ethics and human behavior. He attracted young disciples from elite families but made enemies by revealing the ignorance and pretensions of others, culminating in his trial and execution by the Athenian state. (*p. 103*)

Sokoto Caliphate A large Muslim state founded in 1809 in what is now northern Nigeria. (*p. 482*)

Solidarity Polish trade union created in 1980 to protest working conditions and political repression. It began the nationalist opposition to communist rule that led in 1989 to the fall of communism in eastern Europe. (*p. 631*)

Song Empire Empire in central and southern China (960–1126) while the Liao people controlled the north. Empire in southern China (1127–1279; the "Southern Song") while the Jin people controlled the north.

Distinguished for its advances in technology, medicine, astronomy, and mathematics. (*p. 226*)

Srivijaya A state based on the Indonesian island of Sumatra, between the seventh and eleventh centuries C.E. (See also **theater-state.**) (*p. 158*)

Stalin, Joseph (1879–1953) Bolshevik revolutionary, head of the Soviet Communist Party after 1924, and dictator of the Soviet Union from 1928 to 1953. Used **Five-Year Plans** to increase industrial production and terror to crush all opposition. (*p. 564*)

Stalingrad City in Russia, site of a Red Army victory over the German army in 1942–1943. The Battle of Stalingrad was the turning point in the war between Germany and the Soviet Union. Today Volgograd. (*p. 574*)

steam engine A machine that turns the energy released by burning fuel into motion. Thomas Newcomen built the first crude but workable steam engine in 1712. **James Watt** improved his device in the 1760s and 1770s. Steam power was later applied to moving machinery in factories and to powering ships and locomotives. (*p. 469*)

steel A form of iron that is both durable and flexible. It was first mass-produced in the 1860s and quickly became the most widely used metal in construction, machinery, and railroad equipment. (*p. 505*)

steppes Treeless plains, especially the high, flat expanses of northern Eurasia, which usually have little rain and are covered with coarse grass. Living on the steppes promoted the breeding of horses and the development of military skills that were essential to the rise of the Mongol Empire. (*pp. 165, 264*)

stirrup Device for securing a horseman's feet, enabling him to wield weapons more effectively. First evidence of the use of stirrups was among the Kushan people of northern Afghanistan in approximately the first century C.E. (*p. 155*)

stock exchange A place where shares in business enterprises are bought and sold. (*p. 375*)

Stone Age The historical period characterized by the production of tools from stone and other nonmetallic substances. It was followed in some places by the Bronze Age and more generally by the Iron Age. (*p. 7*)

submarine telegraph cables Insulated copper cables laid along the bottom of a sea or ocean for telegraphic communication. The first short cable was laid across the English Channel in 1851; the first successful transatlantic cable was laid in 1866. (See also **electric telegraph.**) (*p. 506*)

sub-Saharan Africa Portion of the African continent lying south of the Sahara. (*p. 164*)

Suez Canal Ship canal dug across the isthmus of Suez in Egypt, designed by Ferdinand de Lesseps. It opened to shipping in 1869 and shortened the sea voyage between Europe and Asia. Its strategic importance led to the British occupation of Egypt in 1882. (*p. 523*)

Suleiman the Magnificent (1494–1566) The most illustrious sultan of the **Ottoman Empire** (r. 1520–1566); also known as Suleiman Kanuni, "The Lawgiver." He significantly expanded the empire in the Balkans and eastern Mediterranean. (*p. 407*)

Sumerians The people who dominated southern Mesopotamia through the end of the third millennium B.C.E. They developed many fundamental elements of Mesopotamian culture—such as irrigation technology, **cuneiform,** and religious conceptions—taken over by their **Semitic** successors. (*p. 14*)

Sunnis Muslims belonging to branch of Islam believing that the community should select its own leadership. The majority religion in most Islamic countries. (See also **Shi'ites.**) (*p. 172*)

Sun Yat-sen (1867–1925) Chinese nationalist revolutionary, founder and leader of the **Guomindang** until his death. He attempted to create a liberal democratic political movement in China but was thwarted by military leaders. (*p. 554*)

Swahili Bantu language with Arabic loanwords spoken in coastal regions of East Africa. (*p. 421*)

Swahili Coast East African shores of the Indian Ocean between the Horn of Africa and the Zambezi River; from the Arabic *sawahil,* meaning "shores." (*p. 314*)

Taiping Rebellion (1853–1864) A Christian-inspired rural rebellion that threatened to topple the **Qing Empire.** (*p. 497*)

Tamil kingdoms The kingdoms of southern India, inhabited primarily by speakers of Dravidian languages, which developed in partial isolation, and somewhat differently, from the Aryan north. Elements of Tamil religious beliefs were merged into the Hindu synthesis. (*p. 117*)

Tang Empire Empire unifying China and part of Central Asia, founded 618 and ended 907. The Tang emperors ruled from their capital, Chang'an. (*p. 219*)

tax farming A government's use of private collectors to collect taxes. Individuals or corporations contract with the government to collect a fixed amount for the government and are permitted to keep as profit everything they collect over that amount. (*p. 271*)

technology transfer The communication of specific plans, designs, or educational programs necessary for the use of new technologies from one society or class to another. (*p. 293*)

Tenochtitlan Capital of the Aztec Empire, located on an island in Lake Texcoco. Its population was about 150,000 on the eve of Spanish conquest. Mexico City was constructed on its ruins. (*p. 245*)

Teotihuacan A powerful **city-state** in central Mexico (100–75 C.E.). Its population was about 150,000 at its peak in 600. (*p. 239*)

Terrorism Political belief that extreme and seemingly random violence will destabilize a government and permit the terrorists to gain political advantage. Though an old technique, terrorism gained prominence in the late twentieth century with the growth of worldwide mass media that, through their news coverage, amplified public fears of terrorist acts. (*p. 650*)

theater-state Historians' term for a state that acquires prestige and power by developing attractive cultural forms and staging elaborate public ceremonies (as well as redistributing valuable resources) to attract and bind subjects to the center. Examples include the **Gupta Empire** in India and **Srivijaya** in Southeast Asia. (*pp. 117, 160*)

Thebes Capital city of Egypt and home of the ruling dynasties during the Middle and New Kingdoms. Amon, patron deity of Thebes, became one of the chief gods of Egypt. Monarchs were buried across the river in the Valley of the Kings. (*p. 24*)

Theravada Buddhism "Way of the Elders" branch of Buddhism followed in Sri Lanka and much of Southeast Asia. Theravada remains close to the original principles set forth by the **Buddha;** it downplays the importance of gods and emphasizes austerity and the individual's search for enlightenment. (*p. 113*)

third-century crisis Historians' term for the political, military, and economic turmoil that beset the Roman Empire during much of the third century C.E.: frequent changes of ruler, civil wars, barbarian invasions, decline of urban centers, and near-destruction of long-distance commerce and the monetary economy. After 284 C.E. Diocletian restored order by making fundamental changes. (*p. 135*)

Third World Term applied to a group of developing countries who professed nonalignment during the **Cold War.** (*p. 617*)

three-field system A rotational system for agriculture in which one field grows grain, one grows legumes, and one lies fallow. It gradually replaced the two-field system in medieval Europe. (*p. 324*)

Tiananmen Square Site in Beijing where Chinese students and workers gathered to demand greater political openness in 1989. The demonstration was crushed by Chinese military with great loss of life. (*p. 630*)

Timbuktu City on the Niger River in the modern country of Mali. It was founded by the Tuareg as a seasonal camp sometime after 1000. As part of the **Mali** empire, Timbuktu became a major terminus of the trans-Saharan trade and a center of Islamic learning. (*p. 318*)

Timur (1336–1405) Member of a prominent family of the Mongols' Jagadai Khanate, Timur through conquest gained control over much of Central Asia and Iran. His descendants, the Timurids, maintained his empire for nearly a century and founded the **Mughal Empire** in India. (*p. 271*)

Tiwanaku Name of capital city and empire centered on the region near Lake Titicaca in modern Bolivia (375–1000 C.E.). (*p. 253*)

Tokugawa Shogunate (1600–1868) The last of the three shogunates of Japan. (*p. 437*)

Toltecs Powerful postclassic empire in central Mexico (900–1168 C.E.). It influenced much of Mesoamerica. Aztecs claimed ties to this earlier civilization. (*p. 244*)

tophet A cemetery containing burials of young children, possibly sacrificed to the gods in times of crisis, found at **Carthage** and other **Phoenician** settlements in the western Mediterranean. (*p. 83*)

trans-Saharan caravan routes Trading network linking North Africa with **sub-Saharan Africa** across the Sahara. (*p. 160*)

Treaty of Nanking (1842) The treaty that concluded the **Opium War**. It awarded Britain a large indemnity from the **Qing Empire,** denied the Qing government tariff control over some of its own borders, opened additional ports of residence to Britons, and ceded the island of Hong Kong to Britain. (*p. 497*)

Treaty of Versailles (1919) The treaty imposed on Germany by France, Great Britain, the United States, and other Allied Powers after World War I. It was resented by many Germans. (*p. 550*)

treaty ports Cities opened to foreign residents as a result of the forced treaties between the **Qing Empire** and foreign signatories. In the treaty ports, foreigners enjoyed extraterritoriality. (*p. 497*)

tributary system A system in which, from the time of the **Han** Empire, countries in East and Southeast Asia not under the direct control of empires based in China nevertheless enrolled as tributary states, acknowledging the superiority of the emperors in China in exchange for trading rights or strategic alliances. (*p. 222*)

tribute system A system in which defeated peoples were forced to pay a tax in the form of goods and labor. This forced transfer of food, cloth, and other goods subsidized the development of large cities. An important component of the Aztec and Inca economies. (*p. 246*)

trireme Greek and Phoenician warship of the fifth and fourth centuries B.C.E. It was sleek and light, powered by 170 oars arranged in three vertical tiers. Manned by skilled sailors, it was capable of short bursts of speed and complex maneuvers. (*p. 102*)

tropical rain forest High-precipitation forest zones of the Americas, Africa, and Asia lying between the Tropic of Cancer and the Tropic of Capricorn. (*p. 165*)

tropics Eguatorial region between the Tropic of Cancer and the Tropic of Capricorn. It is characterized by generally warm or hot temperatures year-round, though much variation exists due to altitude and other factors. Temperate zones north and south of the tropics generally have a winter season. (*p. 303*)

Troy Site in northwest Anatolia, overlooking the Hellespont strait, where archaeologists have excavated a series of Bronze Age cities. One of these may have been destroyed by Greeks ca. 1200 B.C.E., as reported in Homer's epic poems. (*p. 53*)

Truman Doctrine Foreign policy initiated by U.S. president Harry Truman in 1947. It offered military aid to help Turkey and Greece resist Soviet military pressure and subversion. (*p. 614*)

tsar (czar) From Latin *caesar,* this Russian title for a monarch was first used in reference to a Russian ruler by Ivan III (r. 1462–1505). (*pp. 276, 428*)

tyrant Greek term used for someone who seized and held power in violation of normal procedures. Tyrants appeared in many Greek **city-states** in the seventh and sixth centuries B.C.E. (*p. 98*)

Uigurs A Turkic-speaking people who controlled their own centralized empire from 744 to 840 in Mongolia and Central Asia. (*p. 225*)

ulama Muslim religious scholars. From the ninth century onward, the primary interpreters of Islamic law and the social core of Muslim urban societies. (*p. 185*)

Umayyad Caliphate First hereditary dynasty of Muslim caliphs (661 to 750). From their capital at Damascus, the Umayyads ruled an empire that extended from Spain to India. Overthrown by the **Abbasid Caliphate.** (*p. 180*)

umma The community of all Muslims. A major innovation against the background of seventh-century Arabia, where traditionally kinship rather than faith had determined membership in a community. (*p. 178*)

United Nations International organization founded in 1945 to promote world peace and cooperation. It replaced the **League of Nations.** (*p. 611*)

Universal Declaration of Human Rights A 1948 United Nations covenant binding signatory nations to the observance of specified rights. (*p. 652*)

universities Degree-granting institutions of higher learning. Those that appeared in Latin West from about 1200 onward became the model of all modern universities. (*p. 334*)

Urdu A Persian-influenced literary form of Hindi written in Arabic characters and used as a literary language since the 1300s. (*p. 318*)

utopian socialism A philosophy introduced by the Frenchman Charles Fourier in the early nineteenth century. Utopian socialists hoped to create humane alternatives to industrial capitalism by building self-sustaining communities whose inhabitants would work cooperatively. (See also **socialism.**) (*p. 475*)

Vargas, Getulio (1883–1954) Dictator of Brazil from 1930 to 1945 and from 1951 to 1954. Defeated in the presidential election of 1930, he overthrew the government and created Estado Novo ("New State"), a dictatorship that emphasized industrialization and helped the urban poor but did little to alleviate the problems of the peasants. (*p. 598*)

variolation The technique of enhancing immunity by exposing patients to dried mucous taken from those already infected. (*p. 434*)

varna/jati Two categories of social identity in Indian history. *Varnas* are the four major social divisions: the *Brahmin* priest class, the *Ksatriya* warrior/administrator class, the *Vaishya* merchant/farmer class, and the *Shudra* laborer class. Within each *varna* are many *jatis,* regional groups of people who have a common occupational sphere, and who marry, eat, and generally interact with other members of their group. (*pp. 110–111*)

vassal In medieval Europe, a sworn supporter of a king or lord committed to rendering specified military service to that king or lord. (*p. 200*)

Vedas Early Indian sacred "knowledge"—the literal meaning of the term—long preserved and communicated orally by Brahmin priests and eventually written down. These religious texts, including the thousand poetic hymns to various deities contained in the Rig Veda, are our main source of information about the Vedic period (ca. 1500–500 B.C.E.). (*p. 110*)

Victorian Age The reign of Queen Victoria of Great Britain (r. 1837–1901). The term is also used to describe late-nineteenth-century society, with its rigid moral standards and sharply differentiated roles for men and women and for middle-class and working-class people. (See also **"separate spheres."**) (*p. 510*)

Vietnam War (1954–1975) Conflict pitting North Vietnam and South Vietnamese communist guerrillas against the South Vietnamese government, aided after 1961 by the United States. (*p. 616*)

Villa, Francisco "Pancho" (1878–1923) A popular leader during the Mexican Revolution. An outlaw in his youth, when the revolution started, he formed a cavalry army in the north of Mexico and fought for the rights of the landless in collaboration with **Emiliano Zapata.** He was assassinated in 1923. (See also **Zapata, Emiliano.**) (*p. 595*)

Wari Andean civilization culturally linked to **Tiwanaku,** perhaps beginning as colony of Tiwanaku. (*p. 252*)

Warsaw Pact The 1955 treaty binding the Soviet Union and countries of eastern Europe in an alliance against the **North Atlantic Treaty Organization.** (*p. 614*)

Washington, George (1732–1799) Military commander of the American Revolution. He was the first elected president of the United States (1789–1799). (*p. 447*)

water wheel A mechanism that harnesses the energy in flowing water to grind grain or to power machinery. It was used in many parts of the world but was especially common in Europe from 1200 to 1900. (*p. 328*)

Watt, James (1736–1819) Scot who invented the condenser and other improvements that made the **steam**

engine a practical source of power for industry and transportation. The watt, an electrical measurement, is named after him. (*p. 469*)

Wedgwood, Josiah (1730–1795) English industrialist whose pottery works were the first to produce fine-quality pottery by industrial methods. (*p. 466*)

Western Front A line of trenches and fortifications in World War I that stretched without a break from Switzerland to the North Sea. Scene of most of the fighting between Germany, on the one hand, and France and Britain, on the other. (*p. 545*)

Wilson, Woodrow (1856–1924) President of the United States (1913–1921) and the leading figure at the Paris Peace Conference of 1919. He was unable to persuade the U.S. Congress to ratify the **Treaty of Versailles** or join the **League of Nations.** (*p. 549*)

witch-hunt The pursuit of people suspected of witchcraft. (*p. 378*)

Women's Rights Convention An 1848 gathering of women angered by their exclusion from an international antislavery meeting. They met at Seneca Falls, New York, to discuss women's rights. (*p. 461*)

World Bank A specialized agency of the United Nations that makes loans to countries for economic development, trade promotion, and debt consolidation. Its former name is the International Bank for Reconstruction and Development. (*p. 611*)

World Trade Organization (WTO) An international body established in 1995 to foster and bring order to international trade. (*p. 650*)

Xiongnu A confederation of nomadic peoples living beyond the northwest frontier of ancient China. Chinese rulers tried a variety of defenses and stratagems to ward off these "barbarians," as they called them, and succeeded in dispersing the Xiongnu in the first century C.E. (*p. 143*)

Yi kingdom (1392–1910) The Yi dynasty ruled Korea from the fall of the **Koryo** kingdom to the colonization of Korea by Japan. (*p. 295*)

yin/yang In Chinese belief, complementary factors that help to maintain the equilibrium of the world. Yin is associated with masculine, light, and active qualities; yang with feminine, dark, and passive qualities. (*p. 45*)

Yongle Reign period of Zhu Di (1360–1424), the third emperor of the **Ming Empire** (r. 1403–1424). He sponsored the building of the **Forbidden City,** a huge encyclopedia project, the expeditions of **Zheng He,** and the reopening of China's borders to trade and travel. (*p. 289*)

Yuan Empire (1271–1368) Empire created in China and Siberia by **Khubilai Khan.** (*p. 283*)

Yuan Shikai (1859–1916) Chinese general and first president of the Chinese Republic (1912–1916). He stood in the way of the democratic movement led by **Sun Yat-sen.** (*p. 554*)

Zapata, Emiliano (1879–1919) Revolutionary and leader of peasants in the Mexican Revolution. He mobilized landless peasants in south-central Mexico to seize and divide the lands of the wealthy. Though successful for a time, he was ultimately defeated and assassinated. (*p. 594*)

Zen The Japanese word for a branch of **Mahayana Buddhism** based on highly disciplined meditation. It is known in Sanskrit as *dhyana,* in Chinese as *chan,* and in Korean as *son.* (*p. 229*)

Zheng He (1371–1433) An imperial eunuch and Muslim, entrusted by the Ming emperor **Yongle** with a series of state voyages that took his gigantic ships through the Indian Ocean, from Southeast Asia to Africa. (*p. 290*)

Zhou The people and dynasty that took over the dominant position in north China from the **Shang** and created the concept of the **Mandate of Heaven** to justify their rule. The Zhou era, particularly the vigorous early period (1027–771 B.C.E.), was remembered in Chinese tradition as a time of benevolent rule. In the later Zhou period (771–221 B.C.E.), centralized control broke down, and warfare among many small states became frequent. (*p. 42*)

ziggurat A massive pyramidal stepped tower made of mud-bricks. It is associated with religious complexes in ancient Mesopotamian cities, but its function is unknown. (*p. 19*)

Zoroastrianism A religion originating in ancient Iran with the prophet Zoroaster. It centered on a single benevolent deity—Ahuramazda. Emphasizing truth-telling, purity, and reverence for nature, the religion demanded that humans choose sides in the struggle between good and evil. The religion of the Achaemenid and Sasanid Persians, Zoroastrianism may have influenced Judaism, Christianity, and other faiths. (*p. 93*)

Zulu A people of modern South Africa whom King Shaka united beginning in 1818. (*p. 482*)

INDEX

Abbas I, shah, 414, 415, 416

Abolitionists, 460–461, 486. *See also* Slave trade, African, end of

Absolutism, 371, 380

Acheh Sultanate, 419, 422

Adal, 354

Aden, 409

Administration: *See also* Bureaucracy; Civil service; Ottoman, 412; Mughal India, 416; colonial, 527–528; in British India, 591

Afghanistan: Soviet war in, 601, 628, 631; Taliban in, and bombing of, 650; rebuilding of, 651–652

Afghans, 418

Afonso I, 353

Africa, 399–401, 484 *(map)*. *See also* East Africa; Central Africa; North Africa; Sub-Saharan Africa; West Africa, *and specific countries;* Portuguese circumnavigation of, 348, 349; chronology (1500–1750), 362–363; and Atlantic trading system, 397; gold trade in, 348, 349, 400; Bight of Biafra and Angola, 400–401; European economic power in, 441; chronology (1750–1800), 442–443; European influence in, 481; new states in, 482; in nineteenth century, 482–488; chronology, 483; European penetration of, 485–487; modernization in Egypt and Ethiopia, 485; secondary empires, 487–488; chronology (1850–1950), 502–503; European colonies in (1914), 529 *(map)*; imperialism in, 525, 526, 531; gold trade in, 485, 530, 531, 539; mining boom in, 567; Christianity in, 587; chronology (1900–1920s), 587; self-government in, 589; chronology (1945–2001), 602–603; independence and decolonization of, 604, 605, 606 *(map)*, 608–609; population growth in, 635, 637

Africa, tropical: *See also* Sub-Saharan Africa; European colonization of, 528, 530; European exploration of, 485

African-Americans, 516; and World War I, 547; and jazz music, 657

African National Congress (ANC), 588, 609, 653

Africans: European contact with (1450–1550), 352–354; culture and beliefs of, 396; and Atlantic trading system, 400; and European trade, 499; Pan-African Congress and, 550; World War I and, 546–547; World War II and, 588; women, 654

African slave trade. *See* Slaves, African

Afrikaners, 530, 531

Agitator, The (Rivera), 597

Agrarian reform (Mexico), 595, 596

Agriculture: *See also* Cotton; Farmers; Irrigation; Landownership; Peasants; Sugar plantations; slave labor for, 388, 389; rice cultivation, 389, 401, 554; European crops to Americas, 401; Ottoman, 412; in Central Asia, 426; English enclosure movement, 464; in Qing China, 495; tropical (cash) crops, 528, 530, 533, 534, 538; mechanization of, 561; Soviet collectivization of, 564–566; green revolution in, 612; privatization of, in China, 630

Aguinaldo, Emilio, 533–534

Ahmed III, sultan, 412

AIDS (Acquired Immune Deficiency Syndrome), 580

Aircraft (aviation), 559; in World War II, 571 *(illus.)*, 573, 574, 579

Aircraft carriers, 573, 576

Air pollution, 472

Akbar, emperor, 355, 416, 417

Albania, 542

Aldrin, Edwin E. "Buzz," 617

Alexander II, tsar, 478, 514

Alexander III, tsar, 514

Algeria, 485, 585; independence of, 608 *and illus.,* 657

Algonkian people, 390

Allende, Salvador, 625–626

Alliances: before World War I, 542–543; Cold War, 604–605

All-India Muslim League, 591, 593

All Quiet on the Western Front (Remarque), 547

Alsace and Lorrain, 512, 550

Al-Umari, 344

Amazon rain forest, 599

Ambon, 422

American Anti-Slavery Society, 460

American Revolution, 445, 446–447; French support for, 451; and new republican institutions, 449–450

Americas (New World; Western Hemisphere): *See also* Caribbean region; Central America; Latin America; North America; South America, *and specific countries;* Spanish conquest of, 355–359; chronology (1500–1760), 362–363; demand for slaves in, 364; new food crops from, 376; Old World diseases in, 382,

401; Columbian exchange, 401–403; chronology (1750–1804), 442–443; chronology (1750–1875), 447; chronology (1850–1950), 502–503; Pan-Africanism in, 588; chronology (1945–2001), 602–603; chronology (1964–1990), 625

Amerindians (native peoples): Ocean exploration by, 343; colonization of West Indies by, 345–346; and Old World diseases by, 352, 382; women, 356 *(illus.)*, 357; allies to Spanish in Mexico, 356, 357, 359; forced labor of, 356, 359, 384, 386; Aztec, 356–358, 383, 387; Enlightenment thinkers and, 379–380; Latin American colonial, 383; rituals and beliefs of, 384; Maya, 384, 386; and creole elite, 386–387; and French fur trade, 390; Iroquois confederacy, 390–391; and Columbian exchange, 401–402; land claims of, 446, 458, 516; in Mexico, 594

Amnesty International, 654

Amsterdam, 374 *(illus.)*, 375

Amsterdam Exchange, 375

Amur River basin, 424, 431

Analytical engine, 468

Anatolia (modern Turkey), 406, 410. *See also* Turkey

Anglican Church, 370, 375

Angola, 400–401, 530, 609

Animals: *See also* Cattle; Horses; Hunting; Livestock; Sheep; Columbian exchange, 401–402

Antibiotics, 580

Apartheid, in South Africa, 609, 653

Appeasement of Nazi Germany, 570

Arabia (Arabian peninsula), 421. *See also* Saudi Arabia

Arabic language, 413

Arab-Israeli conflict, 619–620

Arabs: *See also* Islam; Middle East; Muslims; and Palestine question, 556, 558

Arafat, Yasir, 619

Arawak peoples, 345–346, 355–356 *and illus.*

Arbenz Guzmán, Jacobo, 610

Architecture: *See also specific types of buildings;* twentieth century, 560, 658

Argentina, 584; education for women in, 461; British investment in, 506, 536; immigration to, 507; industrialization in, 567, 598; economic independence of, 600; military rule in, 626

Aristocracy (nobility): European and taxes, 376; and French Revolution, 450; Russian boyars, 428, 430, 477, 514

Aristotle, 378

Armed forces: *See also* Military; Warfare; Spanish in Mexico and Peru, 356–358; and constitutional monarchy, 371; and European naval superiority, 371–373; Ottoman in Europe, 407; Ottoman Janissaries, 409–410, 412, 477; Safavid Iran, 415–416; British in colonial America, 446, 447; and French Revolution, 452, 454; British India sepoys, 488, 490–491; Chinese Bannermen, 496; colonial, 526; Ethiopian, 531; American in Philippines, 534; in World War I, 542–543, 545; Russian, 430, 548, 552; Chinese, 555, 573; Japanese, 570–571, 572; Nazi Wehrmacht, 569–570, 573–574, 576; Mexican revolutionary, 595; Soviet in Eastern Europe, 614; United States in Vietnam, 614, 616; Brazil military coup, 624–625

Armenia (Armenians), 548, 552

Armor, 359

Armstrong, Neil A., 617

Art and artists: of Safavid Iran, 413; Mexican Revolution and, 597 *(illus.)*; and popular culture, 656–657

Articles of Confederation (United States), 450

Artisans (craftspeople): Dutch, 373; in early modern Europe, 375; Ottoman glassmakers, 409 *(illus.)*

Aryans, 568

Asante people, 531

Asia, 637. *See also* Central Asia; East Asia; East Indies; Eurasia; Southeast Asia; chronology (1500–1760), 362–363; chronology (1750–1875), 442–443; chronology (1850–1950), 502–503; New Imperialism and, 525, 526; colonial powers in (1914), 532 *(map)*; chronology (1931–1949), 565; chronology (1945–2001), 602–603; decolonization of, 604; chronology (1975–1989), 625; industrial and commercial power in, 624, 628–631; population growth in, 635, 637; financial crisis in (1997), 649

Asians: European contact with (1450–1550), 352; immigration to Americas by, 476; and European trade, 499; immigration to United States, 517; in United States, 640

Asian Tigers, 630, 642

Assembly of Notables (France), 451

Astrakhan khanate, 428

Astrolabe, 348

Aswan Dam (Egypt), 528, 618

Atahualpa, 358

Atlantic Ocean, exploration before 1450, 344–346

Atlantic trading system (Atlantic economy), 352, 383, 392 *(map)*; chronology, 385; capitalism and mercantilism in, 397, 401, 403; Great Circuit and Middle Passage of, 398–399; Africa and, 399–401

Atomic bomb, 576, 578 *(illus.)*, 579, 616. *See also* Nuclear weapons

Aurangzeb, 417

Auschwitz (death camp), 579

Australia, 422, 441; immigration to, 507, 550

Austria-Hungary (1867–1918), 513; nationalism in, 512; conservatism in, 514; World War I and, 542, 543; post–World War I, 552, 561

Austria (to 1867 and 1918–present), 373, 613; French Revolution and, 452; Napoleon and, 454; and German unification, 512; war reparations from, 567; German annexation of, 570

Authoritarianism, 660. *See also* Dictatorship; Napoleon, in France, 453; in Japan, 518, 571; in Brazil, 598

Autocracy, 431, 514

Automobiles, 560

Aviation. *See* Aircraft (aviation)

Azerbaijan, 552

Azores (islands), 344, 348

Aztecs (Aztec civilization): Spanish conquest of, 356–358; elite families, 383, 387

Babbage, Charles, 468

Babur, 416

Baghdad, 413

Bahamas, the, 356

Balance of power, 373, 527, 570; and European democracy, 454; Superpowers (Cold War era), 601, 614, 642

Balboa, Vasco Núñez de, 352

Balfour, Arthur, 548

Balfour Declaration (1917), 548, 556

Balkans, 514, 542. *See also specific states*

Baltic republics, 574

Bananas, 401

Bangladesh, 605

Banking: in early modern Europe, 375

Bannermen (Chinese soldiery), 496

Bantu languages, 421

Barbados, 391

Bastille, storming of the (1789), 451

Batavia (Jakarta), 422

Batista, Fulgencio, 609

Battle of Britain (1940–1941), 574

Bay of Pigs invasion (1961), 610

Beans, 402

Beatles, 657

Beijing, 631; British and French invasion of, 497; Boxer Uprising and, 553; Forbidden City in, 555; Women's Conference (1995), 655 *(illus.)*

Belgium, 526, 574, 613; revolution of 1830 in, 456 *(illus.)*; industrialization in, 466; railroads in, 470; World War I and, 543, 545

Bengal, 589, 591

Benin, 353

Bentham, Jeremy, 475

Berlin, Soviet blockade of (1948–1949), 614

Berlin Conference (1885), 528

Berlin Wall, 614, 632

Biafra, Bight of, 400

Bible, and science, 379

Bill of Rights: English, 371; United States, 450, 652

Bin Laden, Usama, 650, 651–652

Birmingham Lunar Society, 467

Birth rates. *See* Fertility rates

Bismarck, Otto von, 504, 512, 513

"Black Hole of Calcutta," 488

Blacks, equal rights for, 461. *See also* African-Americans; Slaves, African

Blitzkrieg warfare, 573

Bolívar, Simón, 457–458

Bolivia: colonial mining in, 384; independence of, 457

Bolsheviks, 548–549, 552

Bombay, 488, 490

Bombs and bombing: *See also* Weapons and military technology; atomic, 576, 578 *(illus.)*, 579, 616; in World War II, 574, 576, 579, 581; of Serbia by NATO forces, 647; of Afghanistan by United States, 650

Bonner, Yelena, 631

Borlaug, Norman, 612

Borneo, 419, 533

Borsig Ironworks (Germany), 471 *(illus.)*

Bose, Pramatha Nath, 591

Bosnia-Herzogovina, 542, 646–647

Boston, colonial, 390

Boston Massacre (1770), 446

Botanical exchanges, 538–539

Boulton, Matthew, 467

Bourbon dynasty (France), 370 *(table)*, 372, 373

Bourgeoisie, 375, 376, 450. *See also* Middle class

Boxers Uprising (1900), 553

Brahmo Samaj (Divine Society), 492

Brazil, colonial, 383, 384, 403; Portuguese claims to, 349, 351; independence of, 457, 458; slavery in, 386, 388, 398, 399

Brazil, 567, 584, 597–599; abolition of slavery in, 460, 461; women's rights in, 461; slavery in, 474; demand for slaves in, 486; free blacks from, 487; coffee in, 474, 538; rubber in, 538; industrialization in, 598; Vargas regime and Depression in, 598–599; economic independence of, 600; military dictatorship in, 624–625, 626; rural-to-urban migration in, 640; foreign debt of, 649

Brazzaville Conference (1944), 609

Brest-Litovsk, Treaty of (1918), 549

Bretton Woods Conference (1944), 611

British. *See* England; Great Britain

Brezhnev, Leonid, 631

British East India Company (EIC), 427, 446, 481, 488, 489 *(map)*, 490–491, 493. *See also* India, under British rule

British Proclamation of 1763, 446

British South Africa Company, 531

Brunei Sultanate, 419

Buddhists, in Sri Lanka, 646

Buenos Aires, 458, 639
Buffalo, 517
Bulgaria, 632
Bureaucracy (bureaucrats): *See also* Administration; Civil service; colonial Latin American, 384; Meiji Japan, 518; Indian, 589; Soviet, 631
Burma (Myanmar), 533, 605
Burundi, 646
Bush, George, Sr., 633
Bush, George W., 652
Business: *See also* Capitalism; Corporations; joint stock companies, 375, 426; chartered trading companies, 397; Japanese alliances, 520, 554, 626; Great Depression and, 566
Byrd, Richard, 559

Cabral, Pedro Alvares, 349, 351
Cacao, 538, 597. *See also* Chocolate
Cakchiuquel, 382
Calculating machines, 468. *See also* Computers
Calcutta, 488
Calicut, 344, 354, 355
Calvin, John, 366
Calvinists, 370
Cambay, 419
Canada, 576; as French colony, 390–391, 403; women's rights in, 461, 553; immigration to, 507, 550
Canals, 375. *See also* Irrigation; in China, 436; and Industrial Revolution, 472
Canary Islands, 344, 349, 351
Cannon, 422; in naval warfare, 344, 349, 371, 372; Spanish, in Americas, 358, 359; English production of, 373; Ottoman, 406, 410; in Safavid Iran, 415; in Egypt, 486 *(illus.)*; chemical industry and, 505
Canoes, sailing, 343
Cape Colony, 493
Cape Verde Islands, 349
Capitalism: in Atlantic trading system, 397, 401, 403; in colonial Atlantic system, 397, 401, 403; laissez faire, 475; Marx and, 509; Cold War rivalry with Communism, 611, 613
Caramansa, 352
Caravan trade, 425
Caravel (ship), 348–349
Cárdenas, Lázaro, 596
Caribbean region. *See also* West Indies, *and specific countries*: Columbus in, 351; Spanish conquest of, 355–356, 359; abolition of slavery in, 461; Indian immigrants in, 476; American intervention in, 537
Caribs, 346, 357
Carter, James Earl "Jimmy," 626, 628
Casement, Roger, 530
Cassava, 355, 402–403, 402 *(illus.)*
Caste (jati) system, in India, 588
Castro, Fidel, 609, 624

Castro, Raoul, 609
Catholic Church: *See also* Christianity; Papacy. *See also* Jesuits; Papacy; African missions of, 353; reforms in, 366; Inquisition and, 370, 379; in colonial Latin America, 384; missionaries, 391; and French Revolution, 450, 453; in Africa, 487; in Mexico, 595, 596; in Poland, 631, 632
Catholic Reformation, 366
Cattle, 402, 565. *See also* Livestock; in Argentina, 597
Cavalry, 479; Ottoman, 410, 411
Ceausescu, Nicolae, 633
Central America, 626. *See also specific country*
Central Asia: *See also specific country*; Ottoman-Russian rivalry in, 405–406; power in, 425; land-based empires in, 426; chronology (1500–1800), 427; Chinese in, 431; and Qing China, 434; Russian control of, 531, 533, 552; agriculture in, 533, 539
Central Intelligence Agency (CIA), 610, 627
Centralization: *See also* Authoritarianism; Communist Party; Fascism; Monarchy; in Ottoman Empire, 477
Centro Internacional de Mejoramiento de Maiz y Trigo, 612
Cetshwayo, 530
Ceylon (Sri Lanka), 490, 534, 646
Chamberlain, Neville, 570
Chamorro, Violeta, 626
Champlain, Samuel de, 390
Charles I (England), 371
Charleston, 389
Charles V (Holy Roman Emperor), 366, 369 *(map)*, 373
Charles X (France), 454
Chartered trading companies, 397
Charter Oath (1868), 518
Chartist movement (Britain), 475–476
Chemical and biological weapons, 652
Chemical industry, 505
Chiang Kai-shek (Jiang Jieshi), 555, 571–572, 573; defeat of, 576
Chicago, 560
Child labor: Industrial Revolution and, 464, 467, 473–474, 476; banning of, 509
Children, 508; and industrialization, 501; in Victorian age, 510; abandoned, in Rio de Janeiro, 623
Children, education of. *See* Education; Schools
Chile, 461; independence of, 458; overthrow of Allende government in, 625–626
China, 567. *See also* China, People's Republic of; Qing Empire (China); Portuguese colony in, 355; maps of, 377; Jesuits in, 380, 426, 428 *(illus.)*, 439; Ming Empire, 344, 431–433; chronology, 483; chronology (1500–1800), 427; environmental stress in, 432, 436; and opium trade, 490, 492, 495, 499, 555; Great Britain and, 497–498, 499; women in, 497, 572; Japan

and, 518, 520, 541, 555, 561, 563; Boxer Uprising in, 553; Guomindang in, 554, 555, 570, 573, 576; warlord era (1920s), 555–556; Communists in, 555, 571–572, 573, 576; Sino-Japanese War in, 572–573; World War II losses of, 578; and United Nations, 611; population growth in, 637, 638; pollution in, 642
China, People's Republic of, 618–619. (*See also* Communist Party, in China); and Vietnam, 607; and Korean War, 614; and nonaligned nations, 618; industrialization in, 619; economic reform in, 630–631
Chinese immigrants: to Southeast Asia, 533; to United States, 476, 517
Chinese junks, 344, 348 *(illus.)*, 354
Chocolate, 402, *See also* Cocoa
Cholera, 472, 492, 580
Christianity (Christians): *See also* Bible, the; Christian missionaries; Clergy (priests), *and specific denominations and sects*; militancy of, 347; and Portuguese expeditions, 349, 353; in colonial Latin America, 384; and African slaves, 396; in Africa, 587
Christian missionaries: *See also* Jesuits; in Philippines, 419; in Africa, 487, 531; in India, 490; in China, 497; and imperialism, 526–527; in Southeast Asia, 533
Churchill, Winston, 574, 604
Church of England (Anglican church), 370, 375
Cinchona (tropical tree), 533, 534, 535 *(illus.)*, 538
Cities and towns: *See also* Urbanization, *and specific cities*; European (1500–1750), 374–376; in colonial Latin America, 384; in Safavid Iran, 414–415; Industrial Revolution and, 471–472; electrification of, 505–506, 508; in United States, 515–516; World War II destruction of, 579; African migration to, 586; Brazilian, 598; immigration to, 639–640
Citizenship, 476, 640; of Jews in Nazi Germany, 569, 579
City-states, in northern Italy, 347
Civil Code of 1804 (France), 453
Civil law, in Ottoman Empire, 478
Civil service: *See also* Administration; Bureaucracy; in India (ICS), 491, 492, 589
Civil war: in England (1642–1649), 371; in China (1850–1864), 497–498; Mexican. *See* Mexican Revolution; in United States (1861–1865), 461, 485; in Russia (1918–1921), 552; in Yugoslavia (1992–1995), 646–647
Cixi, Empress Dowager, 553
Class. *See* Social class *and specific class*
Clemenceau, Georges, 550
Clergy (priests): *See also* Religion; and Protestant Reformation, 366; as advisors to kings, 367, 370; and Amerindian Christianity, 384; and French Revolution, 450,

Clergy (priests) (*continued*)
452; at Suez Canal inauguration, 523;
Catholic in Poland, 632
Clermont (steamboat), 469
Cleveland, Grover, 533
Climate and weather, in Ming China, 431;
African drought, 400, 421, 482
Clinton, William J. "Bill," 650
Clipper ships, 493
Clothing: *See also* Textiles; Ottoman western-
ization, 478; for Muslim women, 628, 654
Clove plantations, 487, 488
CNN (Cable News Network), 655
Coal, and industrialization, 469, 473
Cochin, 355
Cocoa, 538, 597. *See also* Chocolate
Coffee, 412, 490, 533; in Brazil, 474, 538, 597
Coins (coinage), 349, 432; dies for, 411 *(il-
lus.)*; and inflation, 411, 416
Coke, for iron production, 469
Cold War era (1946–1991), 613–621. *See also*
Soviet Union, Cold War era; United States,
Cold War era; alliances of, 610–611; capitalism *vs.* communism in, 611, 613; Chinese
role in, 618–619; chronology, 607; confrontation of, 615 *(map)*; Cuban role in,
610, 624; and decolonization, 604–605; and
environmental crisis, 620–621; in Europe
and Korea, 613–614; Japan's role in, 618;
and Middle East, 619–620; nonaligned
nations in, 617–618; and nuclear arms
race, 616–617; superpowers' strategic interests in, 601, 614, 620, 642; and Third
World, 617–618; United Nations and, 611;
and Vietnam War, 614, 616; end of, 624
Colombia, 457, 537
Colonies (colonization): *See also* Decolonization; Expansion; French colonies; Great
Britain, colonial empire of; North America,
colonial; Latin America, colonial, *and specific colonies;* Europeans in Indian Ocean,
420 *(map);* empire and, 501–502, 504
Columbian Exchange, 401–403
Columbus, Christopher, 351, 352, 356
Comic magazines, Japanese, 656 *(illus.)*
Communication(s), 638. (*See also* Lan-
guage; Mass Media; Radio; Television);
telegraph, 470, 506; Latin American car-
tel, 598, 609; global expansion in, 630;
revolution in, 643; Internet revolution,
645, 656; innovation in, 655–656
Communism (Communist countries): Cold
War rivalry with capitalism, 611, 613; in
Cuba, 610; Eastern Europe, 632–633; in
Vietnam, 607
Communist Manifesto (Marx), 509
Communist Party (Communists): in China,
555, 573, 576, 630–631; Hitler's expulsion
of, 569; ideology of, 659; Soviet, 552, 564
Compass, 348
Computers, 641; and global culture, 659;
and media, 655–656

Concentration camps, 569
Concordat of 1801 (France), 453
Conference on Security and Cooperation in
Europe (CSCE), 617
Confucianism, in Japan, 438
Congo, 646
Congo Free State, 530
Congress of Vienna (1814–1815), 454
Congress Party (India), 637
Congress (United States), 460, 626
Conquistadors, 356. *See also* Latin
America, colonial
Conservatives, 454, 512; in Russia and
Austria-Hungary, 514
Constantinople, seige of, 406–407
Constitutional Convention (United States),
450
Constitutionalism, 371, 453
Constitutionalists (Mexico), 595
Constitutions: Haitian, 444; English, 449;
state, 449–450; United States, 450;
French, 452; Amendments to (United
States), 461, 553; Japanese (1889), 518;
Mexican (1917), 595; Japanese (1946), 618
Construction materials and techniques: *See
also* Architecture; Housing; bridge, 470
(illus.)
Consumer culture, 602, 641, 657
Consumer goods: and Atlantic trading sys-
tem, 401
Conté, Nicolas-Jacques, 448
Continental Congress (colonial United
States), 447
Contra War (Nicaragua), 626, 628
Cooke, William Fothergill, 470
Copernicus, Nicholas, 378–379
Copper, 506, 539
Copper coins, 411, 432
Cornwallis, Charles, 449
Corporations: *See also* Business; Industry,
506; Japanese, 520, 554, 628–629;
transnational, 641
Cortés, Hernán, 356, 357–358
Cosmopolitanism: Indian coastal cities,
355; in Istanbul, 415
Cossacks, 424, 430, 431
Cotton (cotton industry), 355. *See also* Tex-
tiles (textile industry); in Ottoman
Turkey, 412; British industrialization of,
466; in the United States, 460, 467, 469,
474; and soil depletion, 472; Egyptian,
485, 528; in Central Asia, 533
Council of the Indies, 383
Council of Trent (1563), 366
Crafts and craftspeople. *See* Artisans
(craftspeople), *and specific crafts*
Credit (loans): *See also* Foreign debt; in
Great Depression, 567; in Tokugawa
Japan, 437, 438
Creole elite, 386–387, 457
Crete, 542
Crimean War (1853–1856), 478–479, 514

Croatia, 646–647
Cromwell, Oliver, 371
Crossbows, 344
Crowther, Samuel Adjai, 487, 531
Cuba, 567, 626; abolition of slavery in, 460,
461; demand for slaves in, 486; free blacks
from, 487; United States interests in, 537
Cuban missile crisis (1962), 616
Cuba Revolution, 609, 624
Cueta (Morocco), 347
Cultural imperialism, 526–527, 654–655,
657. *See also* Westernization
Cultural relativism, 559
Cultural Revolution (1966, China), 619
Culture(s): African slave traditions, 396; in
colonial Middle Atlantic, 390; devalua-
tion of Mexican, 594; consumer, 602, 641,
657; and media, 655–656
Currency, 553. *See also* Coins (coinage)
Curzon, Lord, 589
Cuzco, 358
Czechoslovakia, 552, 570, 632; break up of,
633, 646; Soviet domination of, 613, 614
Czech Republic, 633, 646; life expectancy
in, 636

Da Gama, Christopher, 354
Da Gama, Vasco, 349, 353
Dams: Aswan (Egypt), 528, 618; hydroelec-
tric, 506, 555, 564, 618
D'Annunzio, Gabriele, 563
Darby, Abraham, 469
Darwin, Charles, 513
Das Kapital (Marx), 509
Death squads, in Brazil, 623, 625
Debt. *See* Credit (loans); Foreign debt
Declaration of Independence (United
States), 447, 451, 460
Declaration of the Rights of Man (French
Revolution), 451, 652–653
Decolonization, 605–610, 606 *(map)*, 617,
621; of Africa, 608–609; chronology
(1947–1971), 607; and Cold War alliances,
604–605; of Latin America, 609–610; in
Southern Asia, 605, 607; and United Na-
tions, 611
Deforestation, 469, 472; of Europe, 376;
sugar plantations, 394; in China, 436; in
United States, 517; in India, 588; and
need for cropland, 605; in Indonesia, 650
De Gaulle, Charles, 609
De Lesseps, Ferdinand, 537
Democracy: French Revolution and, 450; in
Great Britain, 514; Revolutions of 1848
and, 454; protest for, in China, 630
Demographic transition, 634–635. *See also*
Population (population growth)
Deng Xiaoping, 630
Denmark, 512, 574, 613
Depression: in French Revolution, 451;
United States (1873 and 1893), 517; great
(1930s), 563, 566–567, 581, 598

Developed nations. *See* Industrialized nations

Developing nations: and Great Depression, 567; Cold War alliances, 616–617; population growth in (1960s–1990s), 623, 624, 634, 635, 637, 643; urban growth in, 639–640; wealth inequality in, 639; environmental threats in, 641; and Western ideology, 659

Development. *See* Economic growth; Industrialization

De Witt Clinton (steam locomotive), 471 *(illus.)*

Dhows (Indian ships), 354

Diamond mining in South Africa, 530, 586 *(illus.)*

Dias, Bartolomeu, 349, 351

Díaz, Porfirio, 594

Dictatorship: *See also* Authoritarianism; military in Latin America, 567, 625, 626; populist, 453, 599

Diem, Ngo Dinh, 614

Dienbienphu, Battle of (1954), 607

Diplomacy: in early modern Europe, 373; Russian-Chinese, 431; Chinese, 436; of colonial governors, 526

Directory (France), 453

Dirty War (Argentina), 626

Discrimination: *See also* Racial discrimination; and immigrants, 476; against women, 510

Disease(s): *See also* Medicine (physicians); Sanitation (sewerage systems), *and specific diseases;* European colonization of New World and, 352, 356, 359, 361, 382, 401; and African slaves, 395, 399; dysentery, 395, 399, 472; influenza, 382, 549, 550, 580, 592; malaria, 382, 395, 399, 434, 527, 534; smallpox, 356, 359, 382, 399, 434, 472; cholera, 442, 492, 580; in China, 432, 434; yellow fever, 382, 457, 537; tuberculosis, 472, 580; and biomedical technology, 580; in Africa, 585–586

Diu, 354, 355

Divine kingship, in Mughal India, 417

Domestic servants, 509

Dominican Republic, 537

Dorabji, 591

Doss House, The (Makovsky), 515 *(illus.)*

Douglass, Frederick, 460

Driver, for slaves, 395

Drought, in Africa, 400, 421, 482

Du Bois, W. E. B., 608

Dupleix, Joseph François, 418

Durkheim, Emile, 559

Dutch. *See* Netherlands (Dutch)

Dutch East India Company (VOC), 397, 421–422, 426–427

Dutch East Indies, 533, 576, 607. *See also* Indonesia

Dutch schools, in Japan, 426, 438

Dutch West India Company, 397, 398

Dutch West Indies, 393, 396

Dyer, Reginald, 592

Dysentery, 395, 399, 472

Earhart, Amelia, 559

Earth Day (1970), 621

Earthquake, in Lisbon (1755), 378

East Africa: *See also specific countries;* Swahili Coast, 344, 354, 421; Portuguese trade with, 353–354, 421; Muslims in, 419; and Indian Ocean trade, 419, 421; secondary empires in, 487–488; World War II in, 574; British colonies in, 526; nationhood in, 646

East Asia: *See also* Southeast Asia *and specific countries;* resistance to European empires in, 441; chronology, 507, 543; (1931–1945), 570–573; industrialization of, 601

Eastern Eurasia (1500–1800), 424–439; land-based empires of, 425–426; global influences in, 426–427; Ming China, 431–433; Russian Empire, 427–431; Qing China, 433–437; Jesuits in, 434, 435–438, 439; Tokugawa Japan, 437–439

Eastern Europe: *See also* Warsaw Pact nations, *and specific countries;* industrialization in, 464; German warplane over, 571 *(illus.)*; and Nazi Holocaust, 579; Soviet domination of, 613, 624, 631–633, 632 *(map)*; chronology (1978–1990), 625; worker unrest in, 634 *(illus.)*; life expectancy in, 636–637; economies of, 650

East Germany, 614

East India Company, British (EIC), 427, 446, 481, 488, 489 *(map)*, 490–491, 493. *See also* India, under British rule

East India Company, Dutch (VOC), 397, 421–422, 426–427

East Indies (maritime Southeast Asia). *See also* Southeast Asia; Portuguese expedition to, 342; Malaysian exploration of, 343; spice trade in, 351; Dutch, 533, 576, 607

East Timor, 646

E-commerce, 656

Economic crisis: *See also* Depression; in Ottoman empire, 411–412; in Safavid Iran, 415–416; Ming China, 432; and French revolution, 450–451; in British empire, 514; United States (1873 and 1893), 517; in Soviet Union, 631

Economic domination (power): seventeenth century Dutch, 373–374; imperialism and, 526; of Europe and United States in Latin America, 609–610

Economic expansion (growth): in early modern Europe, 375; in North American colonies, 390; in Qing China, 434; and industrialization, 474; in British India, 491; in Africa, 585; post-war European recovery, 613; post-war Japan recovery, 618; and family planning in China, 638; and global inequality, 638–639; and technology, 642–643

Economic policy: reforms in British India, 490; in Bolshevik Russia, 552; in Communist China, 618; Japanese corporate, 628–629; People's Republic of China reform of, 630–631

Economic sanctions, 649

Economics (economic theories): *See also* Capitalism; Industrialization; Inflation; Taxation; Trade (trading); chronology (1991–2000), 647; laissez faire, 475; Malthusian, 643; Marxist-Leninist, 552

Economy: *See also* Global economy (world economy); Spanish decline, 373; chronology, 465; Tokugawa Japan, 437; world economy, 505–506, 537, 538–539; Soviet *vs.* capitalist models, 611, 613; and globalization, 602, 641, 645

Ecuador, 457

Edison, Thomas, 505, 518, 657

Education (educational institutions), 527. *See also* Literacy; Schools; Universities; Janissaries and, 409; for women, 461, 510; in Russia, 477; Ottoman reforms, 478; African mission schools, 487, 531; in India, 492; colonial Africa, 587; Asian investment in, 630; global, 657

Egypt, 355; Ottoman conquest of, 354, 406, 407; Mamluks in, 412; French invasion (1798–1801), 481; modernization in, 485; agriculture, 539; independence of, 556, 619; Cold War alliances of, 618; Israel and, 556, 620; and Suez Canal, 523, 618, 620

Einstein, Albert, 558, 645

Eisenhower, Dwight D., 614, 616

Electricity, 559; telegraph and, 470, 506; urbanization and, 505–506, 508; dams for, 506, 555, 564, 618; in Japan, 555, 618; in Russia, 564

Elite class: *See also* Aristocracy; Upper class; Latin American, 386–387; Chinese gentry, 436; Ottoman, 412, 478; Russian, 430; in British India, 490; colonial indigenous, 528; Latin American, 536; African colonial, 587; Mexican, 594, 609–610; Argentine, 597; and industrialization, 600; and popular culture, 656

Elizabeth I (England), 367, 372, 373

El Salvador, 626

Emancipation Proclamation (United States; 1863), 461

Enclosure movement (England), 464

Encomienda labor, 386

England: *See also* English colonies; Great Britain, *and individual monarchs;* church-state linkage in, 370; graphite from, 448; Irish immigrants in, 476; population increase in, 464; rivalry with France, 372–373; Royal Society and science in, 379; trade with India, 416

English colonies: *See also* Great Britain, colonial empire of; India, under British

English colonies (*continued*)
rule; and Atlantic trading system, 397; Jamaica sugar plantations, 394; in North America, 389–390, 403. *See also* American Revolution

English language, 597; as global second language, 657; in India, 588

Enlightenment, the, 379–380, 445–446

Entente (France, Great Britain and Russia), 532, 543

Environmental movement, 620

Environmental Protection Agency, 620

Environment (environmental stress), 640–642. *See also* Climate and weather; Deforestation; Drought; Natural disasters; and silver mining, 384; and plantation agriculture, 394; and African slave trade, 400; in China, 432, 436, 495; and pollution, 472, 509, 518, 641, 642; and electricity, 506; and world economy, 537, 538–539; and World War I, 550; and technology, 560–561; and World War II, 581; and Cold War, 605, 620; and technology, 640–641

Epidemics: *See also* Disease(s); and Amerindians, 359, 382, 458; and slave trade, 399; cholera, 472; influenza (1918–1919), 549, 550, 592

Equality (inequality), 638–639

Ericsson, Leif, 344

Eritrea, 646

Erosion, soil, 641

Estates General (France), 371, 451, 456

Estonia, 574, 633

Ethiopia, 531; Christian allies of, 354; modernization in, 485; Italian invasion of, 570; Haile Selassie regime in, 588; and Eritrean independence, 646

Ethnic cleansing, 646–647

Ethnic conflict, 624

Eugénie, Empress of France, 523

Eurasia. *See* Eastern Eurasia

Europe, encounters with (1450–1550), 352–359. *See also* Atlantic system; Eastern Europe; Western Europe, *and specific countries, empires and regions;* Americas, 355–359; Eastern Africa, 353–354; Indian Ocean states, 354–355; West Africa, 352–353

Europe, transformation of (1500–1750): chronology, 362–363, 367; monarchy and state power in, 366–367, 370–371; Ottoman attack on, 366, 407; geographical position of, 377; politics and economy of, 373–374; realm of ideas in, 376, 378–380; Reformation in, 365–366, 370; rural society, 376; urban society and technology in, 374–376; warfare and diplomacy in, 371–373

Europe (1750 to the present): and Indian Ocean colonization, 420 (*map*); and slave trade, 421; and Indian Ocean trade, 422; Industrial Revolution in, 441, 463; expansion of, 442; and telegraph communications, 470; chronology (1750–1875), 442–443, 447; government power in, 446; Napoleonic (1810), 455 (*map*); New World crops in, 464; and Qing China, 499; world trade domination by, 499; nationalism in, 501, 504, 512–513; chronology (1850–1950), 502–503, 507; great powers of (1871–1900), 513–514; power and arrogance of, 515; great powers of (1900–1913), 542–543; motion pictures in, 559, 560; radio in, 559; post WWII, 564; chronology (1931–1945), 565; domination of, 582; Latin American dependence on, 584; and Soviet-American arms race, 617; chronology (1945–2001), 602–603; population growth in, 637; wealth inequality in, 639; labor shortages and migration to, 640; industry in, 647; and developing countries, 659

European Community, 613, 629; environmental protection in, 642

European Economic Community (Common Market), 613

European empires, 359, 526, 659. *See also* Decolonization; New Imperialism, *and specific empires*

Europeans: exploration by (1420–1542), 350 (*map*). *See also* Exploration (expeditions); colonization and commerce of, 361; in Americas, 382–383; as indentured servants, 389, 393; and African slave trade, 400; in India, 418; in East Asia, 426–427; and Chinese imports, 434, 436; immigration to Americas by, 476; migration of (1850–1900), 507; and African colonialism, 585; and African independence, 608, 609; and popular culture, 656

European trading companies, 426–427. *See also specific companies*

Exchange, Colombian, 401–403. *See also* Trade (trading)

Exclusif (France;1698), 397

Expansion, 359. *See also* Colonies (colonization); Imperialism, *and specific empires;* of Ottoman Empire, 406–409, 410; Russian (1500–1800), 428, 429 (*illus.*); European, 442; of United States, 515–518

Exploration (expeditions), 342–359; Atlantic, before 1450, 344–346; European (1420–1542), 350 (*map*); Portuguese, 342, 347–349, 350 (*map*); Spanish, 347, 349–352, 350 (*map*); in Africa, 485

Explosives, 505. See also Bombs (bombing)

Exports. *See* Trade (trading)

Extermination camps, 579

Factory Act of 1833 (Britain), 476

Faisal, 548, 550, 556

Falkland Islands (Malvinas), 626

Family (family life): and industrialization, 473, 480; Victorian ideology of, 510; working class women and, 510; Turkish, 556; and African migration, 586; Third World promotion of, 635

Family planning, 637, 638

Famine: in China, 431, 573; in India, 491; in Ireland, 476, 507; in Soviet Union, 565–566

Farmers (farming): *See also* Agriculture; Peasants (peasantry); Rural society; cash crops for, 412; rebellion of, in China, 436; Japanese, 438, 555; colonial land claims of, 446; and automobile age, 561; in Argentina, 597

Farouk (Egypt), 556

Fascism, 567–570, 599

Feminism, 654. *See also* Women

Ferdinand of Aragon, 351

Ferdinand VII (Spain), 457

Fertility rates, 634, 635–636, 640

Fiji, 343

Film (motion pictures), 559–560, 655

Financial markets, 375. *See also* Banks; Coins (coinage); Currency; Economy; Foreign Debt; Inflation; Loans (credit)

Finland, 376, 574, 613

Finney, Ben, 343

Firearms (guns), 352, 415–416; and Amerindians, 391; mass production of, 469; muskets, 353, 359, 410, 491, 496; Ottoman use of, 409, 410; rifles, 479, 488, 491, 496, 505, 527; machine guns, 527, 531, 545, 547

First Estate (France), 450

First World War. *See* World War I

Fiscal crisis. *See* Depression; Economic crisis

Five Year Plans (Soviet Union), 564, 566

Fleming, Alexander, 580

Flooding, 436

Food (diet; nutrition): *See also* Agriculture; Farming, *and specific foods;* Amerindian, 355, 356 (*illus.*), 376, 402; European sugar consumption, 398; Old World to New World, 402; in World War I, 547

Food shortages: *See also* Famine; in Russia, 548; and green revolution, 612

Forced labor, 549. *See also* Slavery; Amerindians and, 356, 359, 384, 386; in Russia, 426, 431; in colonial Africa, 585

Ford, Henry, 560, 561, 599

Foreign corporations: in Mexico, 596

Foreign debt, 528, 647, 649

Foreign investment: in China, 630; in Latin America, 625, 626; in Mexico, 594

Forest products, 538. *See also* Deforestation; Paper

Fortifications, to withstand cannon, 371

Fourier, Charles, 475

France: *See also* French colonies; French Revolution; and Wars of Religion, 370, 372; monarchy in, 367, 370 (*table*), 371; and Atlantic trading system, 397; in Pondicherry (India), 418; and Haitian independence, 444, 456–457; pencil manufacture in, 448; industrialization in, 466; railroads in, 470; war with Russia (1854), 477; and Crimean War, 478; India and, 481, 488; rivalry with Britain, 481–482; and Algeria, 485, 608 *and illus.*; and Opium War treaty, 497–498; and World War I, 541, 545, 546, 550; colonial empire of, 501–502; liberalism in, 512, 513–514; and Suez Canal, 524, 618; imperialist moves of, 526; African claims of, 530, 585; in Indochina, 533, 574, 607; Entente with Britain and Russia, 542, 543; in Middle East, 556; motion pictures in, 559; German war reparations to, 567; and League of Nations, 569–570; Nazi invasion of, 574; and United Nations, 611; post-WW II nationalization in, 613; and NATO bombing of Serbia, 647

Franchise. *See* Voting rights

Franco-Prussian War (1870), 512

Franz Ferdinand, assassination of, 541, 542

Franz Josef (Austria), 523

Freedom, 659

Free-trade imperialism, 535. *See also* New Imperialism

French and Indian War (1756–1763), 391, 445

French colonies: *See also* Algeria; French Indochina; in North America, 382, 390–391, 403; fur trade in, 382, 390, 391; Atlantic system and, 397; Haiti, 394, 444, 456–457; Mexico, 460; independence of, 608, 609

French Equatorial Africa, 585

French Indochina, 533, 574, 607. *See also specific country*

French Revolution, 450–456, 462; society and fiscal crisis leading to, 450–451; protest turns to revolt, 451–452; reaction to and dictatorship, 453–454; Napoleon's Europe 1810, 455 *(map)*; retrenchment, reform and, 454, 456

Freud, Sigmund, 559

Fulton, Robert, 469

Fur trade: North American, 382, 390, 391; Siberian, 431

Galileo Galilei, 379, 379 *(illus.)*

Gandhi, Mohandas K. (Mahatma), 584, 592–593, 594, 645

Garvey, Marcus, 608

General Agreement on Tariffs and Trade (GATT), 649

Genoa, 347

Gens de couleur, 457. *See also* Creole elite

Gentry: Chinese, 436; English, 589

Georgia, 552

German language, 512

Germans: and Lutheranism, 366; in Pennsylvania, 390

Germany: industrialization in, 470, 471*(illus)*, 506; unification of, 504, 512; chemical industry in, 505; nationalism in, 510, 512–513; as model of centralization, 518, 564; imperialist ambitions of, 526; African colonies of, 530, 613; Chinese enclaves of, 541, 555; Ottoman alliance with, 548; and Lenin, 549; and World War I peace, 550, 552, 553; Nazi pact with Soviets, 553, 570; vote for women in, 553; war reparations from, 567; Great Depression in, 563, 567, 568, 569; rise of Hitler in, 568–570; in World War II, 573–574, 579; World War II losses of, 578, 579; and World War I, 502, 542–543; post-WW II occupation of, 613; reunification of (1990), 633; immigrant population in, 640; consumer culture in, 641

Ghana. *See* Gold Coast (Ghana)

Global culture, 602, 654–659, 660; cultural imperialism and, 654–655, 656, 657; elite culture and, 656, 657–658; mass media and, 654–655; spread of popular culture and, 656–657; diversity and, 658–659

Global economy (world economy): *See also* Globalization; environmental impact of, 537, 538–539; GNP per capita, 649 *(map)*; new technologies and, 505–506, 641; problems of, 647, 649–650

Global trade (globalization), 506, 602, 630, 645; European domination of, 499

Glorious Revolution (1688), 371

GNP (Gross National Product) per capita, 1990s, 650 *(map)*

Goa, 354, 409

Gods, African, 396. *See also* Religion

Gold Coast (Ghana), 349, 352; agricultural boom in, 585; self-government in, 589, 608; slave trade in, 399–400

Gold coins, 349, 411

Gold (gold trade): African, 348, 349; in Caribbean, 356; Aztec, 357; colonial Latin America, 358, 373, 384; in Atlantic system, 398; African, 400, 485, 530, 531, 539

Gomes, Fernão, 349

Gorbachev, Mikhail, 631, 633

Government: *See also* Administration; Bureaucracy; Constitutions; Monarchy; Political systems; Russian westernization, 364; absolutism *vs.* constitutionalism in Europe, 371; English colonial, 389; Ottoman, 410, 412–413, 478–479; Safavid Iran decline, 416; Central Asia centralization, 426; of Tokugawa Japan, 437, 438–439; Qing China, 436; Enlightenment critique of, 445–446; and laissez faire economics, 475; British colonial, 465, 490, 491; colonial, 526, 527–528; Soviet, under Stalin, 564–565, 566; and Great Depression, 566–567; fascist Italy, 568; European post-WW II, 613; ties to industry in Japan, 629; and population growth, 635

Grand Canal (China), 436

Grand National Consolidated Trade Union, 475

Graphite pencils, 448

Great Britain, 373. *See also* England; Great Britain, colonial empire of; monarchy in, 370 *(table)*; and Atlantic trading system, 397, 398; sugar consumption in, 398; Macartney mission to China, 436, 495; and Haitian independence, 444; and Seven Years War, 445; defeat of Napoleon by, 454, 455 *(map)*; end of slave trade by, 461; steam-powered warships of, 463; and industrial revolution, 465–466; railroads in, 469; war with Russia (1854), 477; and Crimean War, 478–479; rivalry with France, 481–482; abolitionist movement in, 486; in East Africa, 488; and Opium War treaty, 497–498; and Qing China, 499; power of, 499; chemical industry in, 505; nineteenth century dominance of, 506; women's rights in, 510, 553; liberalism in, 514; Suez Canal and, 524, 528, 618; and Latin America, 535–536, 594, 597, 598; Entente with France and Russia, 542; in World War I, 541, 545–546; peace of World War I and, 550; Middle East and, 556, 558; German war reparations to, 567; League of Nations and, 569–570; and Japanese atrocities in China, 573; World War II and, 574, 578, 579; Cold War and, 610; United Nations and, 611; post-WW II nationalization in, 613; and nuclear weapons test ban, 616; and Falklands dispute, 626; and NATO bombing of Serbia, 647

Great Britain, colonial empire of, 441, 501–502, 514, 526. *See also* English colonies; India, under British rule, *and specific colonies;* in Africa and Asia, 477; eastern, 482; Hong Kong, 497; Sierra Leone, 486–487; South Africa, 530–531; in Southeast Asia, 533; decolonization by, 605, 608–609

Great Circuit trade route, 398

Great depression, 563, 566–567; and World War II, 581; in Brazil, 598

Great Leap Forward (China), 618

Great Northern War (1700–1721), 430

Great Western (steamship), 469

Greco-Roman literature, 378

Greece, 613, 614; independence of, 454

Greenland, 344

Green Revolution, 612

Gropius, Walter, 560

Guam, 537

Guatemala, 382, 609

Guerrilla warfare: Chinese Communist, 572, 573; Cuban, 609; Vietnamese, 614, 616; Palestinian, 619; Afghan, 628

Guevara, Ernesto "Che," 609

Guilds, 414

Guinea, 609

Gujarat, 354, 355

Guns: *See also* Firearms; mass production of, 469; machine, 527, 531, 545, 547

Guomindang party (China), 554, 555, 570; defeat of, 576; and Sino-Japanese War, 573

Haile Selassie, 588
Haiti, 537; colonial sugar production in, 394; slave rebellion and independence of, 444, 456–457
Hakkas, 497
Hapsburg dynasty, 370 *(table)*
Harding, Warren, 563
Hart, Robert, 499
Havel, Vaclac, 633
Hawaiian Islands, 343, 533
Hayford, J. E. Casely, 589
Health and hygiene, 580, 634. *See also* Disease; Medicine (physicians); Sanitation; in Africa, 585–586
Heavenly Kingdom of Great Peace (Chinese religious movement), 497
Helena (Ethiopia), 354
Heliocentric theory, 378–379
Helsinki Accords, 617, 621
Henry of Navarre, 370
Henry the Navigator, 348, 349
Henry VIII (England), 367, 370, 373
Heyerdahl, Thor, 343
Hidalgo y Costilla, Miguel, 458
Hidden Imam, 413
High (elite) culture, 656
Hindi language, 418
Hinduism (Hindus), 492, 605. *See also* India; in Mughal India, 416, 417–418; in British India, 489 *(map)*, 491, 593; and Indian caste system, 588; in Bengal, 591; in Sri Lanka, 646
Hirohito (Japan), 576
Hiroshima, bombing of (1945), 576, 578 *(illus.)*, 616
Hispaniola, 355–356, 356, 394
Hitler, Adolf, 568–570, 574, 576, 659
Ho Chi Minh, 607, 616
Hollywood, 559, 560, 655
Holocaust, Nazi, 579, 581
Holy Roman Empire, 366, 369 *(map)*
Homosexuality, 415
Honduras, 537
Hong Kong, 497, 574; economic growth in, 630, 658
Hong Xiuquan, 497
Hormuz, 354, 409
Horses, 402, 509, 565; Amerindians and, 391; motorized transport and, 560, 561
Horton, James Africanus, 487
House of Burgesses, 389
Housing, urban, 508–509
Human rights, 617, 626, 645, 652–654. *See also* Rights
Hungary, 632, 636. *See also* Austria-Hungary; post–World War I, 552; Soviet domination of, 613, 614
Hunting: by Amerindians, 391; of Whales, 494
Huron people, 390

Husain, Saddam, 628, 633
Hussein ibn Ali, 548
Hutu-Tutsi rivalry (Rwanda), 646
Hyderabad, 418
Hydroelectric dams (plants), 506, 555, 564, 618
Hydrogen bomb, 616. *See also* Nuclear weapons
Hygiene, 634. *See also* Sewerage and sanitation

Iberian expansion, 346–352. *See also* Portuguese; Spanish expeditions
Iceland, 344
Ideas, 376, 378–380. *See also* Intellectuals; Political thought (ideology)
Imam Husayn, 413–414
Immigration (immigrants): *See also* Migration; to the Americas, 476; from Europe, 476, 515, 516 *(illus.)*; of Indians, 476, 530, 533; restrictions on, 550; to United States, 476, 507, 515, 516 *(illus.)*, 640; to industrialized countries, 624, 640; modern surge in, 638
Immunization, 580
Imperialism, 521. *See also* Colonies (colonialization); New Imperialism; *and specific empires;* and tropical ecology, 534–535; economic, in Latin America, 525, 526, 605, 609–610; cultural, 654–655, 657
Import-substitution industrialization, 598, 625
Inca (Inca empire): elite families, 383, 387; Spanish conquest of, 358
Indentured servants, 389, 393
Independence (independence movements): *See also* American Revolution; Decolonization; India, independence movement in; Latin American, 457–458, 594–599; Sub-Saharan Africa, 585–588
India, 567. *See also* India, under British rule; India, independence movement in; cotton textile manufacture in, 398, 416, 467, 490, 491, 538; Mughal Empire, 355, 407, 408 *(map)*, 411, 416–418, 488; Iran and, 413; and Southeast Asian culture, 419; railroads in, 538; cash crops in, 534, 538; chronology (1905–1947), 587; emigration from, 476, 530, 533; partition of, 590 *(map)*, 600; war with Pakistan, 605; population growth in, 637; religion and nationalism in, 646; nuclear weapons in, 652
India, under British rule, 441, 488–493, 514. *See also* British East India Company (EIC); (1707–1805), 489 *(map)*; chronology in, 483; commerce of, 492–493, 499; and Indian nationalism, 492, 588, 589, 591–592; political reform and industry in, 491–492; railroads in, 492, 493 *(illus.)*, 506; raj and rebellion in, 490–491; rise of nationalism in, 492; tropical cash crops in, 538

India, independence movement in (1905–1947), 502, 588–594; British rule and nationalism, 589, 591–592; Gandhi and militant nonviolence in, 584, 592; land and people, 588; Nehru's industrialization, 593; partition of, 590 *(map)*, 593–594
Indian Civil Service (ICS), 491, 492, 589
Indian National Congress, 492, 589, 592, 593
Indian Ocean exploration: before 1450, 343–344; before 1500, 346 *(map)*; chronology, 345; by Portuguese, 342, 349
Indian Ocean trade: Ming China and, 344; Swahili Coast, 344, 354, 421; Portuguese domination of, 354–355, 361, 409, 421, 426; and slave trade, 397; Dutch monopoly of, 397, 421–422, 426–427; Islam and, 418–419; East Africa, 419, 421; European colonization and, 420 *(map)*
Indigo plantations, 389
Indochina: *See also* Burma; Southeast Asia; Thailand; Vietnam; French, 533, 574, 607
Indonesia (Indonesians), 646; Indian Ocean exploration by, 343; cash crops in, 534, 538; Dutch decolonization of, 607; urban-to-rural relocation program in, 640; economy of, 650
Indulgences, 365
Industrialists, 474; Japanese, 437, 626
Industrialization, 501. *See also* Industrialized nations; Industrial Revolution; new technologies and, 505–506, 521, 524; in Russia, 514; in United States, 516; and imperialism, 526; in Japan, 518, 554–555, 628–629; in India, 591–592, 593; import-substitution, 598, 625; in Argentina, 599; colonial elites and, 600; Soviet, 563, 564, 566; in China, 619; and Asian Tigers, 629–630; and Western culture, 658–659
Industrialized nations: *See also specific nations;* and depression of 1930s, 567; migration, 624, 640; wealth of, 638–639
Industrial Revolution (1760–1851), 441, 463–480, 538; in Britain, 465–466, 466 *(illus.)*; changes in society, 474; child labor in, 464, 467, 473–474, 476; chronology of, 465; impact on cities and towns, 471–472; iron industry in, 469; mass production in, 466–467; mechanization in, 467, 469; railroads in, 469–470, 472; responses to, 474–476; rural environments, 472, 473 *(illus.)*; steam power in, 463, 467, 469–470, 471 *(illus.)*; and technological revolution, 466–471; telegraph in, 470; in the United States, 463, 467, 469, 472, 473 *(illus.)*, 474; working conditions, 473–474
Industry: *See also* Industrialization; Iron industry; Porcelain; Textile industry; Steel industry; Iranian silk, 412, 416; English pottery, 467–468; in British India, 491–492; chemical, 505; gender divisions in, 509; links to government in Japan, 626, 628–629

Inflation: and cheap silver, 411, 416, 432; in Germany, post–World War I, 553; in China, 576

Influenza, 382, 580; 1918–1919 epidemic, 549, 550, 592

Institutional Revolutionary Party (Mexico), 609

Intellectuals, 589; in tsarist Russia, 514. *See also* Enlightenment, the

Intermarriage, 465. *See also* Marriage

Internationalization. *See* Globalization

International Monetary Fund (IMF), 611, 650

International Rice Research Institute, 612

International Style, 560, 658

International Working Man's Association, 509

Internet, 645, 656

Iran, 405, 642. *See also* Safavid Empire (Iran); Islamic revolution in (1979), 627–628, 629 *(illus.)*; restriction on women in, 654

Iranian hostage crisis (1979), 628

Iraq, 556, 642; independence of, 619; and Gulf War, 633, 655; UN weapons inspection in, 652

Ireland, 373, 376, 613; famine and emigration from, 476, 507

Irigoyen, Hipólito, 598, 599

Iron curtain, 604, 610, 617, 621. *See also* Cold War

Iron production, 506, 539. *See also* Steel; English, 373; German, 471*(illus)*; Industrial Revolution and, 469; for warships, 463

Iroquois Confederacy, 390–391

Irrigation, 426, 491, 538–539, 588; in American West, 518; in Egypt, 618

Isabella of Castile, 351

Isfahan, 414–415

Islamic caliphates, 406

Islamic law (Shari'a), 410, 415, 417, 419

Islamic revolutions: in Iran and Afghanistan, 626–628

Islam (Islamic world): *See also* Muslim(s); and Indian Ocean trade, 344; expansion of, 361–362; reform in West Africa, 482; and literacy in Africa, 587; Shi'ite, 413–414, 627–628

Ismail, khedive of Egypt, 413, 485, 523

Israel, 618. *See also* Jews; Zionists; conflict with Egypt, 619, 620; and Palestinian nationhood, 619; United States' support of, 627; Bin Laden's jihad against, 651

Istanbul, 407, 414–415

Italy, 526, 613; northern city-states, 347; unification of, 512; in Triple Alliance (1882), 542; fascism in, 568; alliance with Nazi Germany, 570; invasion of Ethiopia by, 531, 570; in World War II, 576; aging of population in, 636

Iturbide, Agustín de, 458

Ivan IV, tsar, 428

Ivory, 353 *(illus.)*, 421; 485, 487, 488

Ivory Coast, 609

Izmir, 412

Jaja of Opobo, 487 *(illus.)*

Jamaica, colonial sugar production in, 394–395, 396

James II (England), 371

Jammu, 605

Jamshedpur steel works, 591–592

Janissaries, 409–410, 412, 477

Japan, 362, 425, 442; chronology (1500–1800), 427; Dutch schools in, 426, 438; closing of, 437–438; Tokugawa shogunate in, 437–439, 518; whaling in, 494 *(illus.)*; nationalism in, 501, 502, 570; expansion of, 519 *(map)*, 520; war with Russia (1904–1905), 514, 520, 542; Westernization and rise of (1850–1900), 518–520; industrialization in, 518, 554–555; German enclaves in China and, 541, 555; and World War I, 554–555, 561; militarism in, 563; Depression in, 567, 570; in World War II, 574, 576, 577 *(map)*, 578 *(illus.)*, 579; atomic bomb in, 576, 578 *(illus.)*, 616; post-WW II American occupation of, 613; Korean War and, 614, 618; industrial prosperity in, 618, 647, 658; economic growth in, 628–629; South Korea and, 630; fertility rates and aging of population in, 636; consumer culture in, 641; environmental protection in, 642; economic recession in, 649; comic magazines in, 656 *(illus.)*; digital television in, 656; and developing countries, 659

Java (Javanese), 422, 534; export crops of, 538; migrations of, 533

Jazz (music), 657

Jenkinson, Anthony, 405

Jerusalem, 619

Jesuits (Society of Jesus), 418; in India, 357; founding of, 366; in North America, 391; in China, 380, 426, 428 *(illus.)*, 434, 435–436, 439, 495; in Japan, 437–438

Jews: *See also* Israel; Zionism; Spanish expulsion of, 373; immigration of, to Israel (Palestine), 548, 556, 558, 619; in Nazi Germany, 569; World War II losses of, 578; Nazi Holocaust and, 579, 581; Russian, 631

Jiang Jieshi. *See* Chiang Kaishek

Jiang Qing, 619

Jiangxi (China), 572

Jihad (Muslim holy war), 482, 651

Jim Crow laws, 516

Jinnah, Muhammad Ali, 593

John IV (Portugal), 458

John Paul II, pope, 631

Johnson, Lyndon, 614

Joint-stock companies, 375, 426

Jordan, 619

Joseph Bonaparte (Spain), 457

Juárez, Benito, 460 *(illus.)*

Jubbadar, Ali-Quli, 414 *(illus.)*

Junks (Chinese boats), 344, 348 *(illus.)*, 354

Junta Central, 457

Kangxi (China), 432 *(illus.)*, 434, 439

Kashmir, 605

Katharine of Aragon, 370

Kazakhstan, 531, 533

Kazan Khanate, 428

Keiretsu (industrial alliances), 629

Kemal Atatürk, Mustafa, 556, 558 *(illus.)*

Kennedy, John F., 610, 614; and Cuban missile crisis, 616

Kenya, 421, 585, 650; independence of, 608–609

Kenyatta, Jomo, 608–609

Khanates of Kazan, 428

Khomeini, Ayatollah Ruhollah, 627–628, 629 *(illus.)*

Kiakhta, Treaty of (1727), 431

Kikuyu people, 608–609

Kilwa, 421

Knights, 349; Portuguese, 347

Knights of the Hospital of St. John (Hospitallers), 407

Kongo (kingdom), 353

Kon Tiki (raft), 343

Korea (Koreans), 613. *See also* North Korea; South Korea; chronology (1500–1800), 427; Japanese rule of, 520

Korean War (1950–1953), 601, 614

Kosovo, autonomy of, 647

Kosovo, Battle of (1389), 406

Kremer, Gerhard (Mercator), 377

Krushchev, Nikita, 616

Kuwait, 633

Kyoto (Heian), 437

Labor: *See also* Forced labor; Workers (working class); Andean mit'a, 386; indentured servants, 389, 393; division of, 466; Slave. *See* Slaves (slavery)

Labor movement, 475–476, 509

Labor unions, 475, 509; in United States, 517; Polish Solidarity, 631, 632

Labour Party (Britain), 593

Lagos, Nigeria, 586, 639

Laissez faire, 475

Land-grant system: in Ottoman Empire, 410, 411; in Mughal India, 418

Landowners (landownership): *See also* Gentry; European peasants and, 376; indentured servants and, 393; in Ottoman Empire, 412; French Revolution and, 450; English enclosure movement and, 464; in British India, 490; in China, 553; in India, 588; in Mexico, 594, 595, 596; in Argentina, 597, 599; in Brazil, 598

Language(s): *See also specific languages*; vernacular, 370–371; Osmanli, 410; Bantu, 412; Persian, 413; Swahili, 421; and German nationalism, 512; Spanish, 513; English, 588, 597, 657; and nation state, 646

Las Casas, Bartolomé de, 384

Latin America, colonial: *See also specific colonies;* 383–388; chronology, 385; economies of, 384, 386; revolutions in, 457–458, 459 *(map);* society in, 386–388; state and church in, 383–384; wealth of, and indigenous exploitation, 387

Latin America (Latin Americans), 584. *See also* Americas; South America, *and specific countries;* abolition of slavery in, 460, 461; women and racism in, 461; European migration to, 476; imperialism in, 525, 526; chronology (1876–1946), 587; Depression in, 567; 1900–1949, 594–599; Mexican revolution, 584, 594–596 *and map;* decolonization of, 604; United States' economic domination of, 605, 609–610; revolution, repression and democratic reform in, 624–626; population growth in, 635, 637; immigration to United States, 640; Cold War atrocities in, 642

Latvia, 633

Laws (legal codes): colonial Latin America, 384; mercantilist measures, 397; Napoleonic (1804), 453; British factory, 476; in Ottoman Empire, 478; women's property rights, 510; for environmental protection, 642

League of Nations, 553, 570, 572; mandate system of, 556; German withdrawal from, 569; Manchukuo and, 571

Lebanon, 556, 628; independence of, 619

Le Corbusier (Charles Jeanneret), 560

Legitimate trade, 486

Lenin, Vladimir, 548–549, 552

Leningrad, 574

Leopold II (Belgium), 528, 530

Leo X, pope, 365–366

Lepanto, Battle of (1571), 371–372, 410

Liaodong Peninsula, 520

Liberalism, 512, 513–514, 521

Liberia, 487

Libraries: Jesuit at Beijing, 428 *(illus.);* Chinese imperial, 498

Libya, 542, 574, 650

Life expectancy: for slaves, 395; in nineteenth-century Europe, 472; in Russia and former Soviet-bloc countries, 636–637

Liliuokalani (Hawaii), 533

Lima (Peru), 384, 403

Limits of Growth, The, 621

Lincoln, Abraham, 461

Lindbergh, Charles, 559

Linlithgow, Lord, 593

Lisbon earthquake (1755), 378

Literacy, 513, 587

Literature: *See also* Writing; Greco-Roman, 378; poets and poetry, 413, 434, 564; Mughal India, 417–418; twentieth century, 656, 658

Lithuania, 574, 633

Little Ice Age, 376

Live Aid (concert benefit; 1985), 654

Livestock, 401, 402; in Argentina, 597; and Soviet collectivization, 565

Livingstone, David, 485

Lloyd George, David, 550

Loans (credit): in Tokugawa Japan, 437, 439; in Great Depression, 567; foreign debt, 528, 647, 649

Locke, John, 380, 445, 449

London, 471–472, 507

Long March (China), 572 *and illus.*

Lorraine and Alsace, 512, 550

Los Angeles, 560, 561 *(illus.)*

Louisiana, colonial, 391

Louis Philippe (France), 454

Louis XIV (France), 371

Louis XVI (France), 450, 451, 452

Lovelace, Ada, 468

Lowell, Francis Cabot, 474

Ludendorff, Erich von, 549

Lusitania (ocean liner), 545

Luther, Martin, 365–366, 365 *(illus.)*

Lutheranism, 366

Luxembourg, 613

Macao, 355

Macartney, George, 436, 495

Macedonia, 542

Machine guns, 527, 531; in World War I, 545, 547

Madagascar, 657; Southeast Asian migration to, 343–344

Madeira islands, 344, 348

Magellan, Ferdinand, 342, 352

Mahan, Alfred T., 533

Mahmud II, sultan, 477

Maine (battleship), 537

Maize (corn), 355, 402, 403; introduction in Europe, 376, 464

Malabar Coast, 354, 355

Malacca, 354, 409, 421

Malaria, 382, 395, 399, 434, 527, 534

Malaya (Malay peninsula), 343, 421, 533, 576. *See also* Malaysia

Malay Federation, 605

Malaysia, 646, 649, 658

Mali, 344

Malindi, 353, 421

Malta, 410

Malthus, Thomas, 634

Malvinas (Falkland Islands), 626

Mamluks, in Egypt, 412

Manchuria, 424, 520; Japanese conquest of, 570–571

Manchus, 424, 432, 434, 495, 497. *See also* China, Qing Empire

Mandate system, 556

Mandela, Nelson, 609, 653

Mansabdars (officials), 416, 417

Mansa Kankan Musa, 344

Manuel (Portugal), 354

Manufactured goods (manufacturing): *See*

also Industrialization; Industrial Revolution, *and specific manufactures;* Dutch, 373–374; in Atlantic trading system, 398; African slave trade and, 400, 401; Iranian carpets, 415; mass production of, 466–467, 469; Japanese, 437, 518; pencils, 448; British to India, 491, 538; Brazilian import of, 598; computerization and, 641

Mao Zedong, 502, 618–619; Long March of, 572 *and illus.*

Mapmaking, 377 *and illus.,* 434

Marie Antoinette (France), 452

Marinetti, Filippo, 563

Maritime trade: *See also* Atlantic trading system; Indian Ocean trade; Dutch command of, 374, 375–376

Markets: women in, 393 *(illus.),* 585

Marley, Bob, 657

Marne, Battle of the (1914), 545

Maroons (runaway slaves), 388, 396

Marquesas Islands, 343

Marriage: and Protestant Reformation, 366; late age of, in early modern Europe, 375; in colonial Latin America, 383; intermarriage, 465

Married Women's Property Act (1882), 510

Marshall Plan, 613

Martí, José, 537

Marx, Karl, 509, 572

Marxist-Leninism, 610

Mary (mother of Jesus), 384

Massachusetts Bay Colony, 389–390

Mass media, 568. *See also* Communication(s); Film (motion pictures); Radio; Television; terrorism and, 651; global culture and, 655–656

Mass production, 466–467, 469

Mathematics: Pythagorean, 378; Babbage's analytical engine, 468

Mau Mau, 608–609

Maya people, 384, 646

May Fourth Movement (China), 555

Mazzini, Giuseppe, 512

McCormick Reaper, 473 *(illus.)*

McKinley, William, 533

Measles, 382

Mechanization, 467, 469

Media. *See* Mass media

Medicine (physicians): *See also* Disease; African traditional, 396; Chinese expertise, 434; women in, 461; Ottoman schools, 478; twentieth century technology for, 560; and biomedical technology, 580; and population growth, 634

Médicins Sans Frontières (Doctors Without Borders), 654

Mehmed II, sultan, 406

Meiji Restoration (Japan), 518

Mein Kampf (Hitler), 568

Melanesia, 343

Melville, Herman, 494

Men: European, and rape of Amerindian

women, 357; homosexuality of, in Iran, 415

Menabrea, L. F., 468

Menelik of Shoa, 485, 531

Mensheviks, 548, 549

Mercantilism, 397. *See also* Capitalism

Mercator, 377

Merchants (merchant class): of Italian city-states, 347; and trans-Saharan trade, 348; in Tokugawa Japan, 362, 437, 438–439; in early modern European cities, 375; colonial New England, 390, 446; in Safavid Iran, 414; and African ivory, 488; foreign, in China, 497; Chinese, 553

Mercury (metal), 384

Metals. *See* Mining *and specific metal*

Metternich, Klemens von, 454

Mexican Revolution, 584, 594–596 *and map*, 600; institutionalized, 595–596

Mexican Revolutionary Party, 596

Mexico, 646; Spanish conquest of, 356–358; Christianity in, 384; silver from, 411; independence of, 457, 458; culture of, 594; institutionalized revolution in, 595–596; economic dependence of, 599; industrial-financial elite in, 609–610; agricultural research in, 612; population control in, 635; fertility rate in, 640; financial crisis in, 649

Mexico City, 383, 403, 640

Middle Atlantic colonies, 390

Middle class: French bourgeoisie, 375, 376, 450; consumer goods for, 464; Indian, 492; women and family, 510; liberal ideology of, 512; Indian nationalism and, 588; Mexican, 594, 595; Argentine, 598, 599; Cuban exiles, 610

Middle East: *See also specific country;* chronology (1500–1750), 363–363; chronology (1750–1800), 442–443; Ottoman influence in, 478; African slaves in, 487; chronology (1850–1950), 502–503; and World War I, 541; after World War I, 556, 557 *(map),* 558, 561; chronology, 543; chronology (1945–2001), 602–603; Cold War and, 619–620; chronology (1979–1991), 625; Islamic revolutions in, 626–628; September 11 (2001) attacks and, 649

Middle Passage, 398–399

Midway, Battle of (1942), 576

Mies van der Rohe, Ludwig, 560

Migration (population movements): *See also* Immigration; in Kenya, 421; Ming Chinese, 432–433; of Europeans (1850–1900), 507; to industrialized nations, 640; rural-urban, 639–640; international, 643

Militant nonviolence, 592

Militarization: *See also* Armed forces; Navy; Warfare; German and Japanese, 563, 567

Military alliances: before World War I, 542–543; Cold War, 604–605

Military dictatorships: in Latin America, 567, 624–625, 626

Military technology. *See* Weapons and military technology

Millennium celebration in Australia, 660 *(illus.)*

Mills: cotton, 467, 469, 474; steel, 505, 598; sugar, 394, 395 *(illus.)*

Milverton, Lord, 589

Mining (minerals; metals), 473, 539. *See also* Coal; Copper; Gold; Silver *and specific metals and minerals;* in Central Asia, 426; in Africa, 567

Mines Act of 1842 (Britain), 476

Ming Empire (China): and Indian Ocean trade, 344; end of, 431–433

Minority populations, 513

Mit'a labor, 386

Mobutu, Joseph, 646

Moby Dick (Melville), 494

Moctezuma II, 357, 358 *(illus.)*

Modernism, 656

Modernization: *See also* Industrialization; Westernization; in Russia and Ottoman Empire, 477–478; in Egypt and Ethiopia, 485, 528; technologies of, 559–560

Moluccas, 351, 352

Mombasa, 421

Monarchy (emperors, kingship): *See also specific emperors; kings; queens;* and African trade monopoly, 353; and European state, 366–367; and absolutism, 371, 380; Ottoman sultan, 410; Safavid Iran, 414 *(illus.);* in Mughal India, 417; and Enlightenment, 445; and French Revolution, 451, 452, 454, 456; and Latin American independence, 457, 458; in Iran, 627

Money. *See* Banks; Coinage; Currency

Mongolia (Mongols), 425, 427, 431, 432; and Qing China, 434, 495

Monroe Doctrine (1823), 537

Morelos, José María, 458

Morocco, 347

Moro wars (Philippines), 419

Morse, Samuel, 470

Moscow, 427, 454

Motion pictures (film), 559–560, 655

Mountbatten, Lord, 593

Mozambique, 421, 530, 609

MTV (Music Television), 655

Mughal Empire (India), 355, 408 *(map),* 411, 416–418; chronology, 407; end of, 488

Muhammad, Mansa, 344

Muhammad Ali, 481, 485

Muir, John, 518

Multiculturalism, 658

Munich Conference (1938), 570

Muscovy, 427–428. *See also* Moscow

Muscovy Company, 405

Music, in twentieth century, 655, 657

Muskets, 353, 359, 410, 491, 496. *See also* Firearms (guns)

Muslims: *See also* Islam (Islamic world); Italian city-state alliances with, 347; Spanish expulsion of, 373; sixteenth and seventeenth century empires of, 408 *(map);* Shi'ite, 413–414, 628; Ottoman elite, 477; in British colonial (Indian) army, 491; in sub-Saharan Africa, 531; in India, 588, 591, 593; in Pakistan, 605; in Europe, 640; population growth in, 637; in Yugoslavia war, 647; Taliban in Afghanistan, 650; and war on terrorism, 652; and women's clothing, 654

Mussolini, Benito, 568, 576

Myanmar (Burma), 533, 605

Mysore, 481

Nadir Shah, 418

NAFTA (North American Free Trade Agreement), 650

Nagasaki, bombing of (1945), 616

Nana Sahib, 491

Nanjing (Nanking), 498 *(illus.),* 573; Treaty of (1842), 497, 498

Napoleon Bonaparte, 453–454, 457, 481; Europe of (1810), 455 *(map)*

Napoleon III (France), 454

Nasir, Gamal Abd al-, 617–618, 619

National Assembly (France), 451, 452

National Convention (France), 452–453, 457

Nationalism (nation-building), 477, 542, 600. *See also* Decolonization; Independence movements; in Europe, 501, 504, 512–513; in Germany, 510, 512–513; in Japan, 501, 502, 570; liberalism and, 512, 513–514; in Austria-Hungary, 514; Italian fascism and, 568; in China, 571; in India, 492, 588, 589, 591–592; in sub-Saharan Africa, 587–588; cold war alliances and, 601, 604–605; decolonization and, 605–610; in South Asia, 605, 607; in Vietnam, 607; in Africa, 608–609; Latin American economic dependence and, 609–610; religion in Eastern Europe and, 632

Nationalization: in Russia, 549; in Mexico, 596; in post-WW II Europe, 613; in Chile, 625–626; in Cuba, 624; of Iranian oil industry, 627

National liberation, 502

National parks, 518

National Revolutionary Party (PNR), 596

Nation state, 521. *See also* Nationalism; challenges to, 646–647

NATO (North Atlantic Treaty Organization), 610–611, 647

Natural disasters: Lisbon earthquake (1755), 378; in Ming China, 431

Natural selection, 513

Nature, power over, 479–480. *See also* Environment (environmental stress)

Navajo, 402

Navigation (navigational aids): astrolabe, 348; compass, 348; improvements in, 422

Navy (naval warfare): *See also* Warships; Ming Chinese, 344; early modern Europe, 371–372, 373; Portuguese innovation in, 353, 355; Ottoman, 355, 371–372, 410; British innovation and domination in, 372, 373, 465; British domination in, 465; in World War I, 545, 549; Japanese against China, 572–573; in World War II, 573, 576; submarine, 545, 549, 576; American in Pacific, World War II, 576; American in Persian Gulf, 628

Nawab, 418, 488

Nazi Germany, 568–570; and Holocaust, 579, 581

Ndebele people, 531

Nehru, Jawaharlal, 593, 605

Nemesis (warship), 463

Nerchinsk, Treaty of (1689), 431, 435

Netherlands (Dutch), 364, 574, 613. *See also* Dutch East India Company; rebellion in, 372; economic power of, 373–374; maritime trade domination by, 374, 375–376; banking in, 375; map making in, 377 *and illus.*; North American colony of, 390; and African slave trade, 393, 397; in West Indies, 393, 396, 397, 398; and colonial trade wars (1652–1678), 397; Indian Ocean trade domination by, 397, 421–422, 426–427; trade with India, 416, 488; Japan and, 426, 438; Cape Colony (South Africa), 493; decolonization by, 607; and oil embargo, 620

Newcomen, Thomas, 469

New Economic Policy (Soviet Union), 552

Newfoundland, 344

New France, 390–391

New Guinea, 343

New Imperialism (1869–1914), 523–539; Suez Canal and, 523–524 (*and illus.*), 539; economic and cultural factors in, 525–526; motives and methods for, 526–528; in Africa, 528–531; colonial powers in (1914), 532 *(map)*; Asian domination by West, 531–533; in Philippines, 533–534; and tropical ecology, 534–535; in Latin America, 535–537; and world economy, 537–538; and global environment, 537, 538–539

New Lanark, 475

New Laws of 1542 (colonial Latin America), 384

Newton, Isaac, 379

New Year's festival, 417 *(illus.)*

New York City, 390, 472, 507–508; electricity in, 505; skyscrapers in, 560; and World Trade Center attack, 650, 651 *(illus.)*

New Zealand, 343, 422, 441; immigration to, 507, 550

Nicaragua, 537; Sandinista revolution in, 626, 627 *(illus.)*, 628

Nicholas I, tsar, 477

Nicholas II, tsar, 514, 548

Niger, 609

Nigeria, 585, 586; independence of, 609

Niger River, 485, 487

Nixon, Richard, 619, 626

Nizam al-Mulk, 418

Nkrumah, Kwame, 608

NKVD (Stalin's secret police), 566

Nobel, Alfred, 505

Nobel Peace Prize, 647, 654

Nomads in Central Asia, 531

Nonaligned nations, 617–618

Nongovernmental organizations (NGOs), 654

Nonviolent protest, 592. *See also* Gandhi, Mohandas K.

North Africa: *See also specific countries;* East African slaves in, 487; chronology (1931–1945), 565; World War II in, 574, 582

North America: Russians in, 425; chronology, 543; radio in, 559; free trade in, 650

North America, colonial: chronology, 385; English, 389–390, 403; French, 382, 390–391, 403; Middle Atlantic, 390; New England, 389–390; the South, 389

North American Free Trade Agreement (NAFTA), 649

North Atlantic Treaty Organization (NATO), 610–611, 647

Northern Rhodesia (Zambia), 531

North German Confederation, 512

North Korea, 614, 652. *See also* Korea

North Vietnam, 607, 614, 616. *See also* Vietnam

Norway, 574

Novgorod, 428

Nuclear weapons: atomic bomb in World War II, 576, 578 *(illus.)*, 616; Cold War arms race and, 601, 616–617; safeguards against, 652

Oceania: *See also* Pacific Ocean; *and specific islands;* chronology (1945–2001), 602–603

Oil crisis (1974), 601, 620 *and illus.*

Oil industry, 601; in Mexico, 595, 596; nationalization of, 596, 627; in Iran, 627; in Middle East, 633

Oil palm production, 486, 533, 538

Oil-producing states, 620, 647. *See also* Iran, Iraq, Kuwait, Saudi Arabia; *and specific country*

Okinawa, 432

Oman, 421, 487

Opium trade, 490, 492, 495, 499, 555

Opium War (1839–1842), 495–497

Orange Free State, 531

Order of Christ, 349

Order of Knights Templar, 349

Organization of European Economic Cooperation (OEEC), 613

OPEC (Organization of Petroleum Exporting Countries), 620

Orthodox Christianity, 430

Osmanli language, 410

Ottoman Empire, 401, 406–413, 556. *See also* Turkey; and Ethiopia, 354; and Italian trade, 347; navy of, 355, 371–372, 410; threat to Europe from, 366, 407; and Battle of Lepanto, 371–372, 410; and Russia, 405–406, 427; expansion of, 406–407, 408 *(map)*, 409; chronology, 407; central institutions of, 409–410; crisis of (1585–1650), 410, 412; currency inflation in, 411; economic change in, 412–413; reform and westernization in, 442, 477–478; Greek independence from, 454; and Crimean War, 478–479; disintegration of, 479 *(illus.)*; collapse of, 502; in World War I, 541, 542, 561

Owen, Robert, 475

Ownership: *See also* Landowners (landownership); Property ownership; corporate, in Japan, 629

Pacific Ocean: exploration of, before 1450, 343; chronology, 345; exploration of, before 1500, 346 *(map)*; Magellan's crossing of, 342, 352

Pacific Ocean region: *See also* Oceania; chronology (1931–1949), 565

Pahlavi, Muhammad Reza, shah, 627

Painting: Iranian, 414 *(illus.)*; Mughal India, 417; Spanish colonial, 388 *(illus.)*

Pakistan, 593; and Afghanistan, 628; age distribution in, 637; and India partition, 590 *(map)*, 600; nuclear weapons in, 652; war with India, 605

Palestine Liberation Organization (PLO), 619

Palestine (Palestinians): anti-Israeli terrorism of, 651; and Balfour Declaration, 548, 556, 558; nationalism in, 619; 1947 United Nations resolution to divide, 611, 619

Palm oil, 486, 533, 538

Pan-African Congress, 550

Pan-Africanism, 588

Panama, 537, 626

Panama Canal, 537, 539, 626

Pankhurst, Emmeline, 511

Papacy: *See also specific pope;* and Treaty of Tordesillas (1494), 351; and Protestant Reformation, 365–366

Paris, 560; Parlement of, 450–451; French Revolution and, 453, 454; electrification and rebuilding of, 508; Peace Conference (1919), 550, 556

Parliament (England), 371, 446, 467, 476

Peace of Augsburg (1555), 366

Pearl Harbor attack (1941), 574

Peasants (peasantry): *See also* Farmers (farming); freedom of, 376; Ottoman rebellion of, 410; French Revolution and, 450, 451; Russian, 431, 477, 514, 549, 552; Egyptian, 485; Chinese Communism and, 553, 572, 573, 618; Soviet collectivization and, 564–566; Indian, 588; Mexican, 595, 596, 600, 610; Argentine, 598

Pedro I (Portugal), 458

Pencil manufacture, 448
Peng Yu, 638
Penn, William, 390
Pennsylvania, colonial, 390
People's Republic of China. *See* China, People's Republic of
Pepper trade, 355
Perestroika (Soviet restructuring), 631
Perón, Eva Duarte, 599
Perón, Juan, 599
Perry, Matthew, 520
Persian Gulf War (1991), 633; CNN coverage of, 655
Persian language, 413
Peru: colonial, 384; independence of, 457, 458
Peter I, tsar (the Great), 432 *(illus.)*; reforms of, 364, 430–431, 439
Petroski, Henry, 448
Philadelphia, colonial, 390
Philip II (Spain), 370, 371, 373
Philippine Islands, the, 342, 352; annexation by United States, 419, 518, 533–534, 537; in World War II, 576, 577*(map)*; independence of, 607; garbage pickers in, 639 *(illus.)*
Physics, revolution in, 558
Picasso, Pablo, 656
Pilgrims, 389
Pinochet, Augusto, 626
Pirates, 432
Pizarro, Francisco, 358
Planck, Max, 558
Plantations (plantation colonies): *See also* Sugar plantations; indigo, 389; slave labor on, 389, 460; tobacco, 389; clove, 487, 488
Poets and poetry: of Safavid Iran, 413; Chinese, 434; Italian futurist, 563
Poland, 428, 552; Nazi invasion of, 570, 574; World War II losses of, 578; Nazi Holocaust and, 579; Soviet domination of, 613, 631; Solidarity labor movement in, 631–632, 633; life expectancy in, 636
Political autonomy, 588. *See also* Independence (independence movements); Nationalism
Political reform. *See* Reform
Political rights. *See* Rights
Political systems and institutions: *See also* Administration; Democracy; Government; Monarchy, *and specific institutions;* in English colonies, 389–390; in China, 554
Political thought (ideology): the Enlightenment and, 445–446; positivism and utopian socialism, 475; socialism, 475, 509, 568; liberalism and nationalism, 512, 513–514; social Darwinism, 513, 527; and imperialism, 526; Ghandi's nonviolent protest, 592; socialism *vs.* capitalism, 621, 659
Politics, 465. *See also specific political parties and movements;* in early modern Europe, 373; chronology (1991–2000), 647

Pollution, 641. *See also* Environment (Environmental stress); and industrialization, 472; in United States, 518; urban, 509; controls for, in China, 642
Polygamy, 556, 587
Polynesian peoples, 343
Ponce de León, Juan, 356
Popes. *See* Papacy *and specific popes*
Popular culture, 656–657. *See also* Consumer culture
Popular dictatorship (authoritarianism), 453, 599
Population (population growth), 633–637; in Qing China, 362, 436, 495; in early modern European cities, 374; in colonial Latin America, 386; and laissez faire, 475; and nineteenth century European migration, 507–508; in industrialized European cities, 507–508; in United States, 515; in Southeast Asia, 533; in Japan, 554; post–World War II, 602; and fertility rates, 634, 635–636; in developing nations, 623, 624, 634, 637, 643; and demographic transition, 634–635; in industrialized nations, 634, 636–637; and poverty, 637–638; size and distribution of, 636 *(table)*; age structure comparison, 637 *(table)*; and environmental problems, 641
Porcelain: Chinese, 431, 434; Japanese, 437; English, 466–467
Portugal, 526, 613; and Spain compared, 355; expeditions of, 342, 346, 347–349; Indian Ocean exploration of, 342, 349; trade with Africa by, 352–354, 361; earthquake in (1755), 378; and Atlantic trading system, 397; Indian Ocean trade of, 361, 409, 421, 426; and African slave trade, 398–399, 400; Ottoman threat to, 409; East Indian colonies of, 421–422; African claims of, 530; and African independence, 609
Portugal and Brazil: initial claims to Brazil, 349, 351; and colonial Brazil, 383, 384, 386, 388; and Brazilian independence, 457
Positivism, 475
Postmodernism, 658
Potatoes, 376, 402, 464, 476, 547
Potosí silver mine (Bolivia), 384
Pottery, Wedgwood, 466–467. *See also* Porcelain
Poverty (the poor): *See also* Peasants (peasantry); in early modern European cities, 375; and indentured servitude in Americas, 389, 393; and French Revolution, 450, 452 *(illus.)*; and industrialization, 472–474; in India, 492, 588; and laissez faire, 475; and women, 510; literacy of, 513; and Ghandi, 592; in Mexico, 594, 609–610; in developing world, 623, 624, 643; and growing global inequality, 638–639; and population increase in, 637–638
Princip, Gavrilo, 541
Printing, in Netherlands, 374

Progress, 380, 467, 527, 559, 561
Propaganda, 568
Property ownership: *See also* Landowners (landownership); for women, 415, 510
Prostitution, 375, 510
Protestant Reformation, 365–366, 368 *(map)*; and witchcraft, 378
Protestants: *See also specific sect;* Spanish expulsion of, 373
Proxy wars, 590, 624, 628. *See also* Cold War era
Prussia, 373, 452, 454, 512. *See also* Germany; railroads in, 470
Psychoanalysis, 559
Publicity, 568
Puerto Rico, 356, 461, 537
Punjab, 560
Puritans, 370, 371, 389
Puyi (boy-emperor of China), 554
Pythagoras, 378

Qianlong, (China), 434
Qing Empire (China), 433–437, 433 *(map)*, 442, 445, 495–499. *See* China, Qing Empire; rivalry with Russia, 424–425, 431, 434; power and trade in, 433–434; conflicts in (1838–1870), 496 *(map)*; tea and diplomacy in, 434, 436; economic and social disorder in, 495; Jesuits in, 434, 435–436, 495; Macartney mission to, 436, 495; and Opium War (1839–1842), 495–497; population stress in, 362, 436–437, 495; White Lotus Rebellion in, 495; religious movement in, 497; and Taiping Rebellion (1850–1864), 497–498; decentralization and end of, 499
Quakers, 390, 396
Quebec Act of 1774 (Britain), 446
Quetzalcoatl, 356
"Quit India" campaign, 593

Racism (racial discrimination): in Haiti, 457; in Americas, 461–462; in United States, 516–517; Nazi, 568–569, 581; in Africa, 587; European colonial, 589; South African apartheid, 609, 653; and Third World population growth, 635; in United States, 654
Radar, 578–579
Radio, 559, 655
Radio cartel, 598
Railroads, 472, 571; in Britain, 469; in United States, 469–470, 506; in Russia, 477; in India, 492, 493 *(illus.)*, 506; in Latin America, 535–536 *(and illus.)*, 597; and world economy, 538; and environment, 539; in Africa, 585; Mexican, 596
Rain forest, 599
Rajputs, 417
Raw materials, 506. *See also* Metals; Mining, *and specific raw materials;* tropical, 506, 526; New imperialism and, 538; for World War II, 574, 576, 581

Reagan, Ronald, 626, 631, 639
Rebellions: *See also specific rebellions;* Dutch, 372; in Ottoman Empire, 410, 412; slave, 388, 396, 399, 444, 456–457; Sepoy (India), 491; in Qing China, 495, 497–498
Recaptive slaves, 487
Red Army (Soviet Union), 552
Red Guard (China), 619
Reformation: Catholic, 366; Protestant, 365–366, 368 *(map)*, 378
Reforms (reform movements): of Peter the Great (Russia), 364, 430–431, 439; in pre-revolutionary France, 451; municipal, 472; labor, 476; in Ottoman Empire, 477, 478, 542; and modernization in Egypt, 485; in India, under British rule, 490, 491–492; in colonial Africa, 587; in Mexican Revolution, 595–596; in Brazil, 599; economic in China, 630–631; *perestroika* in Soviet Union, 631
Refugees: and African slave trade, 400–401; from World War I, 550; from World War II, 564; Palestinian, 619
Reign of Terror (1793–1794), 452
Religion: *See also* Christianity; Clergy (priests); Hinduism; Islam; *and specific sect;* and European monarchy, 370; African slaves, 396; in Safavid Iran, 413–414; in Mughal India, 417; movement in Qing China, 497; and imperialism, 527 *(illus.)*; and cultural relativism, 559; and Eastern European nationalism, 632; and nation state, 646; in contemporary world *(map)*, 648
Remarque, Erich Maria, 547
Renaissance, 365
Republican institutions, in United States, 449–450
Revolution (1750–1850), 444–462; Enlightenment ideas and, 445–446; North American colonies, 446–447, 449–450; French, 450–456; Haitian independence, 444, 456–457; Latin American, 457–458, 459 *(map)*; and abolition of slavery, 460–461; and equal rights for women and blacks, 461–462
Revolutionaries, in Philippines, 533–534
Revolution of 1830 (Belgium), 456 *(illus.)*
Revolution of 1857 (India), 491
Revolution of 1905 (Russia), 514
Revolutions of 1848 (Europe), 454
Rhineland, 550
Rhodes, Cecil, 530–531
Rhodesia, 531, 609
Ricci, Matteo, 377, 426
Rice and rice cultivation: plantations in Americas, 389, 401; in China, 554 *(illus.)*; miracle strains of, 612 *and illus.*
Rifles, 505. *See also* Firearms (guns); and African ivory trade, 488; breech-loading, 479, 527; Enfield, 491; percussion-cap, 496

Rights: *See also* Citizenship; Human rights; Voting rights; constitutional, 450; French Revolution and, 451, 454; American Revolution and, 445, 446, 447; for women and blacks, 461–462; of Jews, in Nazi Germany, 569, 579
Rio de Janeiro: abandoned children in, 623; Market, 393 *(illus.)*
Ripa, Matteo, 435
Rivera, Diego, 597
Roads, Inca, 358
Romania, 633
Romanov, Mikhail, 428
Rome, Renaissance art of, 365
Roosevelt, Franklin D., 567, 579, 645
Roosevelt, Theodore, 518
Rousseau, Jean-Jacques, 445, 449
Roy, Rammohun, 492
Royal African Company (England), 397, 398, 399–400
Royal Society (England), 379
Rubber, 530, 533, 567, 597, 598, 599; Brazilian origins of, 538; synthetic, 578
Rural areas (rural society): early modern Europe, 376; and industrialization, 472, 473 *(illus.)*; modern suburban sprawl, 560
Russian Empire, 427–431, 513; rise of Romanovs, 427–428, 430; rivalry with Qing China, 424–425, 431, 434
Russian Orthodox Church, 431, 435
Russian Revolution (1905), 514
Russian Revolution (1917), 502, 548–549
Russia (Russians), 437. *See also* Russian Empire; Soviet Union; English trade with, 405; Ottoman rivalry with, 405–406; expansion of (1500–1800), 427, 429 *(illus.)*; war with Sweden, 428, 430; aristocracy (boyars) in, 428, 430, 477, 514; Napoleon's invasion of, 454; reform and westernization in, 477, 478; and Crimean War, 478; conservatism in, 514; war with Japan, 514, 520, 542; in Central Asia, 531, 533, 552; railroads in, 538; effect of World War I on, 545, 561; industrialization in, 464, 552; and Slavic peoples, 542; and World War I, 541; Entente with Britain and France, 542–543; vote for women in, 553; and demise of Soviet Union, 633; declining life expectancy in, 636, 637
Russo-Japanese War (1904–1905), 514, 520, 542
Rwanda, ethnic rivalry in, 646

Saarinen, Eero, 560
Sacrifices, Aztec, 357
Sadat, Anwar al-, 618
Safavid Empire (Iran), 408 *(map)*, 413–416; Ottoman wars with, 405, 410; chronology, 407; currency inflation in, 411, 416; society and religion in, 413–414; city life in, 414–415; crisis in, and collapse of, 415–416
Saint Domingue. *See* Haiti

St. Petersburg, 430, 439, 477, 515 *(illus.)*
Saint-Simon, Claude Henry de Rouvray, 475
Sakharov, Andrei, 631
Salvador, 384
Salvation, and Protestantism, 366
Samoa, 533
Samuri warriors, 437, 438
Sandinista revolution (Nicaragua), 626, 627 *(illus.)*, 628
Sanitation (sewerage systems), 492, 508, 560. *See also* Health and hygiene
San Martín, José de, 458
São Tomé, 349, 353
Satellite(s): Sputnik launch (1957), 617; communication transmission by, 655
Sati (widow burning), 492
Saudi Arabia, 650; and Afghanistan, 628; Gulf War role of, 633; restriction on women in, 654
Schools: *See also* Education; Literacy; Universities; colonial Latin America, 384; for Amerindians, 391; German, 505; African mission, 487, 531; in Japan, 518; Christian in Africa, 587; Mexican, 596
Science: *See also* Mathematics; Technology; industrialization and, 467; political domination and, 513; World War II and, 578–579
Scientific revolution, 378–379, 445, 558–559
Scotland, 371, 373
Seasoning, of slaves, 395
Second Estate (France), 450
Second World War. *See* World War II
Security Council (United Nations), 611, 619
Self-government (self-determination), 454, 589. *See also* Independence; Nationalism
Selim I, sultan, 407
Selim III, sultan, 477
Separate spheres, 510
Sepoy Rebellion (India), 491
Sepoys, 488, 490–491
September 11 (2001) attacks, 602, 650, 651 *(illus.)*
Serbia, 478, 543, 646; NATO bombing of, 647
Serfs (serfdom), 376; Russian, 431, 477, 514
Seven Years War (1756–1763), 391, 445, 488
Sewerage and sanitation, 492, 508, 560
Sexuality, 654; rape of Amerindian women by European men, 357; Male homosexuality, 415; Hollywood films and, 655
Shaka Zulu, 482
Sheep, 565, 597
Shi'ite Islam: in Safavid Iran, 413–414; and Iranian Revolution, 627–628
Ships (shipping), 422, 506. *See also* Navy; Warships; Chinese junks, 344, 348 *(illus.)*, 354; Portuguese caravels, 348–349; Indian dhows, 354; and colonial New England, 390; for slave trade, 398–399; steam-powered, 463, 469, 523, 538; clipper ships, 493; for whaling, 494; Suez Canal and, 523; ocean liners, 545; Japanese, 618
Shona people, 531

Shrines: Muslim in Jerusalem, 619
Siberia, 424, 427
Sibir khanate, 431
Sierra Leone, 349, 486–487
Silk production: Iranian, 412, 416
Silver coins, and inflation, 411, 416, 432
Silver mining: in colonial Latin America, 373, 384, 386; Incan, 358; and Atlantic trade system, 398
Singapore, 493, 574, 658; economic growth in, 630
Sino-Japanese War (1937–1945), 572–573
Sirius (steamship), 469
Skyscrapers, 560, 650, 651 *(illus.)*, 658
Slave Coast, 399–400
Slave labor camps (gulags), 565, 566
Slave rebellion: in Haiti, 444, 456–457; in Middle Passage, 399; West Indies, 388, 396
Slavery, 659. *See also* Forced labor; in Europe, 376; and United States Constitution, 450, 461; abolition of, 454, 457, 460–461, 533
Slaves, African, 421. *See also* Slave trade, African; in colonial sugar plantations, 386, 391, 393–396, 403, 474; cultural traditions and beliefs of, 396; and disease, 395, 399; European trade in, 361; and Middle Passage, 398–399; in North American colonies, 389; in Philadelphia, 390; punishment of, 395, 396 *(illus.)*; recaptive, 487; runaway communities, 388, 396; in Sokoto Caliphate, 482
Slave soldiery, 409–410, 416
Slave trade, African, 421; and Dutch, 397; in East Africa, 487; end of, 441, 461, 474, 485–486; and Latin American colonies, 383, 388; Middle Passage and, 398–399; Portuguese in, 349, 398–399, 400
Slavic speaking peoples, 514
Slovakia, 633, 646. *See also* Czechoslovakia
Slovenia, 646
Smallpox, 359, 382, 399, 434, 472; in New World, 356
Smith, Adam, 475
Snow, Charles, 580
Social classes (social stratification): *See also* Aristocracy; Castes; Elite class; Gentry; Peasants; Slaves; Workers; in colonial Latin America, 386–388; political roles of, 444–445; in French Revolution, 450; barriers in Britain, 465
Social Contract, The (Rousseau), 445
Social Darwinists, 513, 527
Socialism, 509, 568; utopian, 475
Social justice, 600, 653
Social reform. *See* Reform
Social science, 559
Social welfare: in Argentina, 599
Society of Jesus. *See* Jesuits
Society (societal conditions): chronology, 465; labor movements and socialism, 509; late nineteenth century changes,

506–510; population and migration, 507; and urbanization, 507–509; working class, 509–510; transformations of, 623–624; chronology (1991–2000), 647
Soil depletion, 394, 472
Sokoto Caliphate, 482
Solidarity (labor union), 631, 632, 633
South, United States: colonial, 389; cotton in, 469
South Africa, 585; Dutch Cape Colony, 493; nationalism in, 588; apartheid in, 609, 653
South African War (1899–1902), 531
South America, 534. *See also* Americas; Latin America; *and* specific country; Portuguese and Spanish claims to, 349, 351
South Asia: decolonization of, 606 *(map)*; European influence in, 481
South Carolina, colonial, 389
Southeast Asia, 422. *See also* East Asia; East Indies; Indian Ocean; Indochina; South Asia, *and specific countries;* Islam in, 419; Ming Chinese in, 433; British colonies in, 493, 526; European imperialism in, 533; cash crops in, 534, 538; Great Depression in, 567; World War II in, 574, 576, 582; rubber in, 598; 1990s economic boom in, 649
Southern Africa, 530–531. *See also specific country;* Zulu kingdom in, 482; independence of, 609
Southern Rhodesia, 531, 609. *See also* Zimbabwe
South Korea, 614, 658. *See also* Korea; age distribution in, 637; industrial prosperity in, 629–630, 647
South Vietnam, 607, 614, 616
Soviet Union (Union of Soviet Socialist Republics: USSR), *See also* Russia; 552; secret pact with Nazi Germany, 553, 570; collectivization of agriculture in, 564–566; environmental stress in, 564; industrialization in, 563, 564, 566; Great Depression in, 567; World War II and, 574, 576, 578, 581; post–World War II, 582
Soviet Union, Cold War era: rivalry with United States, 601, 604, 611, 612 *(map)*, 613, 616–617, 621; NATO threat to, 610–611; United Nations and, 611; economic policies of, 613; Cuba and, 610, 616, 624; Europe and, 613–614; nuclear arms race and, 616–617; China and, 618, 619; proxy wars of, 624; domination of Eastern Europe, 613, 624, 631–633, 632 *(map)*; and Islamic revolution, 627; and Afghanistan, 628; arms sales to Iraq from, 628; 1989 crisis in and collapse of, 602, 631–633; end of, 635 *(map)*; environmental stress in, 641, 642
Space exploration, 617
Spain, 613; Magellan's return to, 342; explorations and expeditions of, 347, 349–352, 350 *(map)*, 361; monarchy in, 367; eco-

nomic decline of, 373; Dutch independence from, 373, 374; and Philippines, 533
Spanish-American War, 534, 537
Spanish Armada, 372
Spanish colonies, 359. *See also* Latin America, colonial; Philippines, 419; in Taiwan, 426; Caribbean, 461; Mexican independence, 533
Spanish Inquisition, 370, 379
Spanish language, 513
Spear, Percival, 592
Spencer, Herbert, 513
Spice trade, 351; Portuguese monopoly on, 355; Dutch and, 421–422
Sputnik satellite (1957), 617
Squash, 402
Sri Lanka, 646. *See also* Ceylon
Stalin, Joseph, 552, 563, 564–566, 570
Stalingrad, Battle of, 574, 576
Stamp Act of 1765 (Britain), 446
Stanley, Henry Morton, 485
Steam engines, 467, 469
Steam locomotives, 471 *(illus)*
Steamships, 463, 469, 470 *(illus.)*, 493, 538
Steel (steel industry), 505, 506. *See also* Iron production; sword making, 359; in Japan, 437, 618; in India, 591–592; in Brazil, 598
Steppes, 430
Stock exchanges, 375
Stock market crash (1929), 566, 567
Student protests: of 1960s, 620; for democracy in China, 630–631
Submarine telegraph cable, 470, 506
Submarine warfare, 545, 549, 576
Sub-Saharan Africa, 584. *See also* Africa, tropical; *and specific countries;* and Atlantic trading system, 361, 401; Muslims in, 531; (1900–1945), 585–588; economic and social, changes in, 585–587; colonialism in, 599; religious and political changes in, 587–588; self-determination in, 600; independence movements in, 608–609; population growth in, 637; urban areas in, 640
Sudan, 421
Suez Canal, 506, 528, 570; and New Imperialism, 523–524 *(and illus.)*, 539; and Arab-Israeli conflict, 556, 620; crisis over (1958), 618
Suffragettes, 511. *See also* Voting rights, women and
Sufism, 417
Sugar mills, 394, 395 *(illus.)*
Sugar plantations: in West Africa, 349, 353; in colonial Latin America, 384, 386; in colonial West Indies, 391, 393–396, 403; in Cuba, 537; slavery in, 384, 391, 393–396, 403, 474
Sugar production, 401, 402, 533, 538; European consumption of, 398
Sukarno, 607, 617
Suleiman the Magnificent, 407
Sulu Empire, 419

Sumatra, 419, 422, 533
Sun gods, Inca, 358
Sun Yat-sen (Sun Zhongshan), 554, 555
Superpowers. *See also* Soviet Union, Cold
War era; United States, Cold War era:
strategic interests of, 601, 614, 620, 642
Surinam (Dutch Guiana), 396
Swahili Coast, 344, 354, 421
Swahili language, 421
Sweden, 613, 636; age distribution in, 637;
war with Russia, 428, 430
Sweet potatoes, 355, 402
Sydney (Australia) Millennium celebration
in, 660 *(illus.)*
Synthetic dyes, 505
Syria, 556; independence of, 619; Ottoman
conquest of, 406, 407

Tacky (Jamaican slave), 396
Tahiti, 343
Taiping Rebellion (1850–1864), 497–498
Taiwan, 426, 433, 520, 658; Pirates in, 432;
Chinese in, 576; industrial prosperity in,
630, 647
Taliban (Afghanistan), 650
Tanzania, 650
Tasman, Abel, 422
Tasmania, 422
Tata, Dorabji, 591
Tata, Jamsetji, 591
Taxation (taxes): and French monarchy,
371; in early modern Europe, 373, 376;
in Ottoman Empire, 410, 412, 422; in
Safavid Iran, 422; in colonial America,
446; and French Revolution, 450–451; of
African colonies, 528, 530; in China, 555,
573, 576
Tea and tea trade, 490, 491; in colonial
America, 446; with China, 436, 495; trans-
fer of, 533, 534
Teachers, women as, 510
Technology, 527. *See also* Computers; Manufacturing; Science; Ships (shipping);
Weapons and military technology; and
Industrial Revolution (1760–1851), 465,
466–471; of mass production, 466–467,
469; mechanization and, 467, 469; world
economy and, 439, 505–506; industrialization and, 521, 598; modernity and,
559–560; environmental effects of,
560–561, 640–641; biomedical, 580; cultural change and, 602, 658; Asian investment in, 630; economic expansion and,
642–643; Western culture and, 655; global
culture and, 659
Telegraph, 470, 506
Television, 655, 656
Tenochtitlan, 357, 358
Terrorism, 649–652; Stalinist, 566; Palestinian, 619; in Argentina, 626; and September 11 (2001) attacks, 602, 649, 651 *(illus.)*
Téwodros II (Ethiopia), 485, 486 *(illus.)*

Textiles (textile industry): *See also* Cotton
(cotton industry); Dutch, 373; and African
slave trade, 400; English wool, 467; Indian
cotton, 398, 416, 467, 490, 491, 538;
women and children in, 473–474
Thailand, 576, 658; economy in, 650
Thatcher, Margaret, 626
Theory of relativity, 558
Third Estate (France), 450, 451
Third Reich (Germany), 569
Third World, 601. *See also* Developing na-
tions; Cold World alliances of, 616–617;
population in, 635
Thirty Years War (1618–1648), 371
Tiananmen Square massacre (1989), 630–631
Time magazine, 645
Timor, 422
Tin, 539
Tipu Sultan, 481
Tobacco, 389, 391, 393, 401, 412, 537, 538
Tocqueville, Alexis de, 515
Tokugawa Ieyasu, 437
Tokugawa shogunate, 437–439, 518
Tokyo (Edo), 437; World War II bombing of,
576, 579
Tordesillas, Treaty of (1494), 351
Touissant L'Ouverture, François Do-
minique, 444, 457
Touré, Sékou, 609
Trade agreements, 412, 641
Trade routes, 359, 398
Trade (trading): *See also* Merchants; and
toleration, 364; Dutch dominance in, 374;
European with Latin American colonies,
386; European in Atlantic system, 398;
Mughal India, 416; in Central Asia, 425;
and industrial revolution, 464; British ad-
vantages for, 465; legitimate, 486; global-
ization of, 499, 506; in Great Depression,
567; globalization of, 602, 630, 645 (*See
also* Global economy); Japanese surplus,
629; US with China, 630; via Internet (e-
commerce), 656
Trade (trading), with Africa, 485–486. *See
also* Gold (gold trade); Slave trade, African
Trade unions, 475–476. *See also* Labor unions
Trading networks, 316. *See also* Atlantic
trading system
Traditions: folk, 378; in British India, 490
Transnational corporations, 641
Transportation, 638. *See also* Automobiles;
Canals; Railroads; Ships (shipping);
British waterways, 465; and industrializa-
tion, 472; and world economy, 538; in de-
veloped world, 641
Transvaal, 531, 586 *(illus.)*
Treaty ports, 497
Trench warfare, 545, 547
Trent, Council of (1563), 366
Tropical rain forest, 599
Tropics (tropical lands and peoples), 506.
See also Africa, tropical; *and specific*

countries and regions; ecology of, and im-
perialism, 534–535; botanical transfers
to, 538–539; rain forest in, 599
Trotsky, Leon, 552
Truman, Harry S, 604
Tuberculosis, 472, 580
Turkey, 614. *See also* Ottoman Empire; re-
form in, 542; post–World War I, 556; West-
ernization of, 556, 558 *(illus.)*; medical
knowledge in, 580; Cold War missiles in,
616
Turkic peoples: and Russians, 430
Twenty-One Demands (Japan), 555
Typhus, 382

Ukraine, 430, 552, 574
Union of South Africa, 531
Union of Soviet Socialist Republics (USSR).
See Soviet Union
Unions. *See* Labor unions
United Fruit Company, 610
United Nations, 659; founding of, 604, 611;
peacekeeping by, 611; and Korean War,
614; and China, 619; and 1947 partitioning of Palestine, 619; Security Council,
611, 619; and Gulf War, 633; weapons inspection by, 652; human rights declaration of, 652–654
United Provinces of the Río de la Plata, 458
United States, 601, 604, 642; American Revolution, 445, 446–447; new republican institutions in, 450–451; cotton industry in,
460, 467, 469, 474; abolition of slavery
in, 460–461; equal rights for women and
blacks in, 461–462; Industrial Revolution
in, 463, 469–470, 471 *and illus.*; railroads
in, 469–470, 517 (*map*); Civil War, 485;
and Qing China, 499; nationalism in, 501;
British investment in, 506; chronology,
507; immigration to, 476, 507, 515; as
emerging power (1865–1900), 515–518;
national parks in, 518; colonial empire of,
502, 518; imperialism of, 526, 539; Latin
American dependence on, 535–536,
584; and Japanese atrocities in China,
572–573; and Philippines, 533–534, 607;
World War I and, 541, 545, 547, 549; World
War I refugees in, 550; vote for women in,
553; post–World War I boom in, 553, 561;
automobile in, 560; motion pictures in,
559–560; pre–WW II isolationism of, 570;
World War II and, 576, 578; post–World
War II, 582; and Latin America, 594,
605, 609, 610; and Arab-Israeli conflict,
619–620, 626–627; environmental movement in, 620; proxy wars of, 624; and
Afghanistan, 628; and Islamic revolutions, 628; and Japanese markets, 629;
trade with China, 630; Persian Gulf War
and, 633; wealth inequality in, 639; Hispanic growth in, 640; consumer culture
in, 641, 657; Yugoslavian civil war and,

647; economic sanctions by, 649; Bin Laden's jihad against, 651; and war on terrorism, 652; feminism in, 654; cultural imperialism of, 655; and developing countries, 659

United States, Cold War era: Latin American domination by, 605, 609–610; and NATO alliance, 610–611; and nuclear arms race, 616–617; and Philippine independence, 607; rivalry with Soviet Union, 601, 604, 611, 612 (map), 613, 616–617, 621; and Third World, 617–618; and Vietnam War, 614, 616; and communist threat in Latin America, 624–626

Universal Declaration of Human Rights, 652–654

Universities: colonial Latin America, 384; in India, 492; women in, 510; in Japan, 518; purging of Iranian, 628; and English language, 658

Upper class: See also Aristocracy; Elites; in Mexico, 594

Urbanization: See also Cities and towns; and population boom, 464; and social structures, 507–509; in developing nations, 639–640

Urdu language, 418

Uruguay, 461

USS Cole (destroyer), 649

Usuman dan Fodio, 482

Utilitarianism, 475

Utopian socialism, 475

Uzbeks (Turks), 416

Vargas, Getulio, 598–599

Venezuela, independence of, 457

Venice, 347; Ottoman war with, 407, 409

Versailles, Treaty of (1919), 550, 552

Versailles Palace, 371, 372 (illus.)

Vespucci, Amerigo, 351

Victoria (England), 491

Victorian Age, 510

Vienna: Ottoman seige of, 407; Congress of, 454; growth of, 508 (illus.)

Vietnam War, 601, 607, 614, 616

Vikings, exploration by, 344

Villa, Francisco "Pancho," 595

Vinland, 344

Virginia Company, 389

Vivaldo brothers, 344

Volta, Alessandro, 470

Voltaire, 379, 434, 445

Voting rights (franchise), 509, 513; in Argentina and Brazil, 598; for women, 510, 511, 553

Wales, 464

Walesa, Lech, 633

Wallpaper, Chinese, 434

Warfare: See also Cold War; Military; Weapons and military technology; World Wars, and specific war; modernization of,

479; trench, 545, 547; aircraft in, 559, 571 (illus.). 573, 574, 579; German blitzkrieg, 573; guerilla, 572, 573, 609, 614, 616, 619, 628; Indian-Pakistani, 605; Islamic jihad, 482, 651; proxy, 590, 624, 628. See also Cold War

Warlord era, China (1920s), 555–556

War of the Spanish Succession (1701–1714), 373

War on Terrorism (2001–), 652

Warrior elite: European knights, 347, 349, 407; Japanese samurai, 437

Warsaw Pact nations, 617, 631, 632, 642. See also Eastern Europe

Warships: See also Navy; steam-powered, 463; British in Opium War, 495–496; Spanish-American War, 537; aircraft carriers, 573, 576

Wars of Religion (1562–1598), 370, 372

Washington, George, 447

Water pollution, 472, 580

Water transportation, in Britain, 465

Waterworks. See Canals; Dams; Irrigation

Watt, James, 469

Wealth, disparity in, 638–639; GNP per capita, 1990s, 649 (map)

Wealth of Nations (Smith), 475

Weapons and military technology: See also Cannon; Bombs (bombing); Firearms (guns); Portuguese navy, 354; Spanish superiority in, 357, 358, 359; in early modern Europe, 371; and African slave trade, 400; Ottoman, 410, 478; Russia under Peter I, 431; in Egypt, 485, 486 (illus.); for whaling, 494; and industrialization, 501; and imperialism, 527; World War II, 573, 578–579, 582; Cold War, 605; American sales of, 627; Soviet to Iraq, 628; American investment in, 631; in Persian Gulf War, 633; chemical and biological, 652

Weber, Max, 545

Wedgewood, Josiah, 434, 466–467

Weizman, Chaim, 548, 550

West Africa: Atlantic exploration from, 344; Portuguese trade in, 349, 352–353; English trade with, 397; Islamic reform in, 482; palm oil trade, 486; malaria in, 527; European colonies in, 529 (map), 530; decolonization of, 609; urban growth in, 640

Western Europe: See also Europe, and specific country; industrialization in, 466; Cold War alliances of, 610–611; post–World War II reconstruction of, 613; and end of Soviet-domination in Europe, 632

Westernization (western culture), 602. See also Cultural imperialism; of tsarist Russia, 364, 430; in Africa, 486–487; of British India, 490

West Germany, 613, 614

West Indies, 403. See also Caribbean region; West Indies, colonial, and specific islands; Amerindian colonization of, 345–346;

Dutch traders in, 393, 396, 397, 398; slavery in, 474

West Indies, colonial: See also specific colonies; empires; and Atlantic trading system, 397, 398; chronology, 385; slaves and sugar plantations in, 391, 393–396

Whaling, 494

Wheat: in Argentina, 597; new strains of, 612

Wheatstone, Charles, 470

White Lotus Rebellion (1794–1804), 495

Whitney, Eli, 467, 469

Wilhelm II (Germany), 513, 549

Wilhelm I (Prussia), 504, 512

Williams, Eric, 393

Willis, John, 534

Wilson, Woodrow, 549, 550, 556

Windmills, sugar plantation, 395 (illus.)

Witch-hunts: in early modern Europe, 378, 379

Women: Amerindian, 356 (illus.), 357; and European witch-hunts, 378; tsarist Russian, 364; and Protestant Reformation, 366; as prostitutes, 375, 510; in colonial markets, 393 (illus.); on sugar plantations, 395; and property ownership, 415, 510; in Safavid Iran, 414–415; as rulers in Aceh, 419; Russian, 430; and silk weaving, 438 (illus.); and American Revolution, 450; in French Revolution, 451–452, 453 (illus.), 454; in textile factories, 473; and cult of domesticity, 474; opposition to slavery by, 460; education of, 461, 510; equal rights for, 461; Ottoman, 478; in India, 492; in China, 497; industrialization and, 480, 501; as domestic servants, 509; working class, 509–510, 517, 650–651; Victorian Age, 510; voting rights for, 510, 511, 553; in United States, 517; and Turkish modernization, 556; wartime role of, 547, 581; Soviet, 566; in Nazi Germany, 569, 581; jobs for, in depression, 567; Chinese Communism and, 572; in African markets, 585; Argentine, 599; fertility of, 636; Islamic dress for, 628, 629 (illus.), 654; rights of, 654; Beijing Conference (1995), 655 (illus.)

Women's Rights Convention, 461

Wool industry, 467

Workers (working class): See also Labor; and French Revolution, 451, 452; and women's rights, 461; and industrial revolution, 473–474; living standards of, 474; and labor organizing, 475; voting rights for, 509; gender divisions in, 509–510; and United States prosperity, 517; and new technology, 559; sanitation and, 560; and automobile, 560; Argentine, 598, 599; Brazilian, 599; and revolution, 600; Eastern European unrest, 634 (illus.)

World Bank, 611, 612, 650

World Trade Center attack (2001), 649, 651 (illus.)

World Trade Organization (WTO), 649
World War I, 502, 541–553, 544 *(map)*, 561; stalemate (1914–1917), 545; homefront and economy, 546–547; Western front, 545, 547; battle experience, 547; Ottoman Empire in, 548; Russia and, 545, 548–549, 552; end of (1917–1918), 549; impact of, 550; peace treaties, 550, 552; territorial changes after, 551 *(map)*; aftermath, 552–553; Japan and, 554–555; Italian veterans of, 568; Indian support for Britain in, 592
World War II, 502, 573–582; in Asia and Pacific, 574, 576, 577 *(map)*; end of, 576; bombing in, 574, 576, 579; and Chinese civil war, 576, 578; in Europe and North Africa, 574, 575 *(map)*; death toll in, 578; refugees from, 564; role of aircraft in, 571*(illus.)*, 573, 574, 579; as war of move-ment, 573–574; as war of science, 578–579; antibiotics in, 580; holocaust in, 579, 581; homefront in, 581; environmental effects of, 581; Africans in, 588; Indians in, 593; Brazil and, 599; post-war reconstruction, 613
World Wide Web, 656
Wright, Frank Lloyd, 560
Wright, Orville and Wilbur, 559
Writing: *See also* Literature; in Southeast Asia, 419

Xhosa people, 530

Yakutsk, 424
Yangzi River delta, 426
Yellow fever, 382, 457, 537
Yellowstone national park, 518
Yeltsin, Boris, 633

Yemen, 422, 650
Yermak Timofeyovich, 431
Yohannes IV (Ethiopia), 485
Yorktown, Battle of (1781), 447, 449
Young Turks, 542
Yuan Shikai, 554
Yugoslavia, 552, 614, 633; civil war in, 646–647

Zaibatsu (Japanese corporations), 520, 554, 628–629
Zambia (Northern Rhodesia), 531
Zanzibar, 487, 488
Zapata, Emiliano, 584, 594, 595 *and illus.*
Zheng He, 344
Zimbabwe (Southern Rhodesia), 531, 609
Zionists, 550, 558, 619. *See also* Israel; Jews; and Balfour Declaration, 548, 556
Zulu kingdom, 482, 499, 530